A People & A Nation

A People & A Nation

A History of The United States

BRIEF NINTH EDITION

VOLUME I: TO 1877

MARY BETH NORTON
Cornell University

CAROL SHERIFF
College of William and Mary

DAVID W. BLIGHT
Yale University

HOWARD P. CHUDACOFF
Brown University

FREDRIK LOGEVALL
Cornell University

BETH BAILEY
Temple University

DEBRA MICHALS
Merrimack College

WADSWORTH
CENGAGE Learning™

Australia • Brazil • Japan • Korea • Mexico • Singapore • Spain • United Kingdom • United States

WADSWORTH
CENGAGE Learning

A People and A Nation, Volume I : To 1877,
Brief Ninth Edition

Mary Beth Norton, Carol Sheriff, David W. Blight,
Howard P. Chudacoff, Fredrik Logevall,
Beth Bailey, Debra Michals

Senior Publisher: Suzanne Jeans

Senior Sponsoring Editor: Ann West

Development Editor: Julia Giannotti

Assistant Editor: Megan Chrisman

Senior Marketing Manager: Katherine Bates

Marketing Coordinator: Lorreen Pelletier

Marketing Communications Manager:
  Caitlin Green

Senior Content Project Manager: Jane Lee

Senior Art Director: Cate Rickard Barr

Senior Print Buyer: Judy Inouye

Senior Rights Acquisition Specialist: Katie Huha

Production Service: Elm Street Publishing
  Services

Text Designer: Cia Boynton

Senior Photo Manager: Jennifer Meyer Dare

Cover Image: Catlin, George (1796–1872).
  Bod-a-sin, Chief of the Tribe, 1830. Oil on
  canvas 29 x 24 in. Credit: Smithsonian
  American Art Museum, Washington,
  DC/Art Resource, NY

Compositor: Integra Software Services Pvt. Ltd.

For product information and technology assistance, contact us at
Cengage Learning Customer & Sales Support, 1-800-354-9706

For permission to use material from this text or product,
submit all requests online at **www.cengage.com/permissions.**
Further permissions questions can be emailed to
permissionrequest@cengage.com.

Library of Congress Control Number: 2010934558

Student Edition:

ISBN-13: 978-0-495-91622-2

ISBN-10: 0-495-91622-6

Wadsworth
20 Channel Center Street
Boston, MA 02210
USA

Cengage Learning is a leading provider of customized learning solutions with office locations around the globe, including Singapore, the United Kingdom, Australia, Mexico, Brazil and Japan. Locate your local office at **international.cengage.com/region**

Cengage Learning products are represented in Canada by Nelson Education, Ltd.

For your course and learning solutions, visit **www.cengage.com.**

Purchase any of our products at your local college store or at our preferred online store **www.cengagebrain.com.**

Printed in Canada
1 2 3 4 5 6 7 14 13 12 11 10

Brief Contents

Contents

Features

Maps

Figures

Tables

Preface

In this ninth edition, *A People and A Nation, Brief,* has undergone significant revisions, while still retaining the narrative strength and focus that have made it so popular with students and teachers alike. Like other teachers and students, we are always re-creating our past, restructuring our memory, and rediscovering the personalities and events that have influenced us, injured us, and bedeviled us. This book represents our continuing rediscovery of America's history—its diverse people and the nation they created and have nurtured. As this book demonstrates, there are many different Americans and many different memories. We have sought to present as many of them as possible—in triumph and tragedy, in division and unity.

About *A People and A Nation, Brief*

A People and A Nation, first published in 1982, was the first major textbook in the United States to fully integrate social and political history. From the outset, the authors have been determined to tell the story of *all* the people of the United States. This book's hallmark has been its melding of social and political history—its movement beyond history's common focus on public figures and events to examine the daily life of America's people. All editions of the book have stressed the interaction of public policy and personal experience, the relationship between domestic concerns and foreign affairs, the various manifestations of popular culture, and the multiple origins of America and Americans. We have consistently built our narrative on a firm foundation in primary sources—on both well-known and obscure letters, diaries, public documents, oral histories, and artifacts of material culture. We have long challenged readers to think about the meaning of American history, not just to memorize facts. Both students and instructors have repeatedly told us how much they appreciate and enjoy our approach to the past.

This brief ninth edition, as with earlier brief editions, aims to preserve the integrity of the complete work—along with its unique approach—while condensing it. This edition reflects the scholarship, readability, and comprehensiveness of the full-length version. It also maintains the integration of social, cultural, political, economic, and foreign relations history that has been a hallmark of *A People and A Nation*.

Dr. Debra Michals has worked with us again, ensuring that the changes in content and organization incorporated in the full-length ninth edition were retained in the condensation. The authors attained reductions by paring down details rather than deleting entire sections. The brief ninth edition thus contains fewer statistics, fewer quotations, and fewer examples than the unabridged edition. The brief edition also includes more pedagogy than the unabridged edition: each main heading has a marginal question to give students a preview of the key topics covered. These questions are answered at the end of the chapter in the "Summary." Throughout the chapters, students get assistance from key terms that are boldfaced in the text and defined in the margins.

Themes in This Book

Several themes and questions stand out in our continuing effort to integrate political, social, and cultural history. We study the many ways Americans have defined themselves—gender, race, class, region, ethnicity, religion, sexual orientation—and the many subjects that have reflected their multidimensional experiences. We highlight the remarkably diverse everyday lives of the American people—in cities and on farms and ranches, in factories and in corporate headquarters, in neighborhoods and in legislatures, in love relationships and in hate groups, in recreation and in work, in the classroom and in military uniform, in secret national security conferences and in public foreign relations debates, in church and in voluntary associations, in polluted environments and in conservation areas. We pay particular attention to lifestyles, diet and dress, family life and structure, labor conditions, gender roles, migration and mobility, childbearing, and child rearing. We explore how Americans have entertained and informed themselves by discussing their music, sports, theater, print media, film, radio, television, graphic arts, and literature, in both "high" culture and popular culture. We study how technology has influenced Americans' lives, such as through the internal combustion engine and the computer.

Americans' personal lives have always interacted with the public realm of politics and government. To understand how Americans have sought to protect their different ways of life and to work out solutions to thorny problems, we emphasize their expectations of governments at the local, state, and federal levels; governments' role in providing answers; the lobbying of interest groups; the campaigns and outcomes of elections; and the hierarchy of power in any period. Because the United States has long been a major participant in world affairs, we explore America's participation in wars, interventions in other nations, empire-building, immigration patterns, images of foreign peoples, cross-national cultural ties, and international economic trends.

What's New in This Edition

This edition builds on its predecessors in continuing to enhance the global perspective on American history that has characterized the book since its first edition. From the "Atlantic world" context of European colonies in North and South America to the discussion of international terrorism, the authors have incorporated the most recent globally oriented scholarship throughout the volume. As in the eighth edition, we have worked to strengthen our treatment of the diversity of America's people by examining differences within the broad ethnic categories commonly employed and by paying attention to immigration, cultural and intellectual infusions from around the world, and America's growing religious diversity. We have also stressed the incorporation of different peoples into the United States through territorial acquisition as well as through immigration. At the same time, we have integrated the discussion of such diversity into our narrative so as not to artificially isolate any group from the mainstream. We have continued the practice of placing three probing questions at the end of each chapter's introduction to guide students' reading of the pages that follow.

Primary Sources

We believe students need lots of opportunities to engage in historical thinking around primary sources, and we have provided more opportunities for this type of work in the ninth edition. The new "Visualizing the Past" feature described below helps students engage with visual sources with guided captions and questions. In addition, the authors have identified for each chapter a set of primary sources that would add useful context for students; these are noted (with a feather icon) in the margins of the text. Students will be able to access each of these sources through links on the student CourseMate website. Instructors who want a fully integrated online primary source reader to use in conjunction with *A People and A Nation* will find it available as an "Editor's Choice" option inside the new CourseReader for U.S. History (described in the supplements section).

As always, the authors reexamined every sentence, interpretation, map, chart, illustration, and caption, refining the narrative, presenting new examples, and bringing to the text the latest findings of scholars in many areas of history, anthropology, sociology, and political science. Some chapter-opening vignettes are new to this edition. The maps have been completely redesigned and revised in this edition to be more dynamic, engaging, and relevant.

"Legacies," "Links to the World," and "Visualizing the Past"

Each chapter contains two brief feature essays: "Legacies for A People and A Nation" and "Links to the World." "Legacies" appears toward the end of each chapter and offers compelling and timely answers to students who question the relevance of historical study by exploring the historical roots of contemporary topics. New subjects of "Legacies" includes P.T. Barnum's publicity stunts, abstinence campaigns by moral reformers, Lincoln's second inaugural address, national parks, and mass-produced toys for children. Numerous other "Legacies" have been updated.

"Links to the World" examines both inward and outward ties between America (and Americans) and the rest of the world. "Links" appears at appropriate places in each chapter to explore specific topics at considerable length. Tightly constructed essays detail the often little-known connections between developments here and abroad. The topics range broadly over economic, political, social, technological, medical, and cultural history, vividly demonstrating that the geographical region that is now the United States has never lived in isolation from other peoples and countries. New to this edition are "Links" on turkeys, writing and stationery supplies, internal improvements, filibustering, the "back to Africa" movement, study abroad programs, Tokyo Rose, and swine flu. Each "Link" highlights global interconnections with unusual and lively examples that will both intrigue and inform students.

A brand new feature in this edition—"Visualizing the Past"—aims to give students the chance to examine primary source material and engage in critical thinking about them. For each chapter, the authors have selected one or two visual sources (including cartoons, photographic images, artwork, and magazine covers) that tell a story about the era with captions that help students understand how the careful examination of primary source content can reveal deeper insights into the period under discussion. We have chosen to focus on visual sources for this feature because these are often the hardest for instructors to find and prepare good pedagogy around—and because we have always given visual material a strong role in the text. An example from Chapter 25 includes a photograph of the women's "emergency brigade" demonstration during the 1937 sit-down strike by automobile workers in Flint, Michigan. The caption describes the scene and then asks questions that guide students in a deeper analysis of the image—and of its historical significance.

Section-by-Section Changes in This Edition

Mary Beth Norton, who had primary responsibility for Chapters 1 through 8 and served as coordinating author, augmented the treatment of early European explorations of the Americas (including the publicist Richard Hakluyt) and now explores the use of the calumet (the so-called peace pipe) by Indian nations and Europeans alike. She expanded the discussion of religious diversity in England and its colonies and the religious impulse for colonization and revised the section on the middle passage to give more attention to the experience of enslaved captives on shipboard. To clarify chronology, she moved some material on the French and Spanish colonies in North America from Chapter 3 to Chapter 4 and in the latter greatly increased coverage of the residents of the west in the eighteenth century—Native Americans, Spaniards, and French people alike. A new opening vignette is featured in Chapter 4 about Marie-Joseph Angélique, a slave convicted of starting a fire that destroyed the merchant quarter of Montreal. New scholarship on the Seven Years' War, the American Revolution, and the Constitutional Convention has been incorporated into Chapters 5 through 7. A table now conveniently summarizes state conventions' ratification votes. More information on women's political roles and aims has been added in conjunction with a considerably expanded treatment of partisanship in the early republic.

Carol Sheriff, responsible for Chapters 9 and 11 through 13, enhanced coverage of the nationalistic culture of the early republic and early New Orleans and revised the discussion of the War of 1812 and Aaron Burr. She has added discussions of the penny press, Henry David Thoreau, science and engineering, women's activities, and penitentiaries. The treatment of politics in general has been reworked, with special attention to political violence, and a new chart detailing the era's presidents has been included. Chapter 13 now contains considerably more information on the southwestern borderlands, includes more quotations from residents of the American West, and deals with anti-expansionism and the abuse of Indians in Catholic missions.

David W. Blight, who had primary responsibility for Chapter 10 and Chapters 14 through 16, has enhanced the discussion of the economic causes of secession and the Civil War and the economic history of the war itself, drawing on extensive new scholarship. Chapter 10 features a new chapter-opening vignette on the 1827 slave auction held at Monticello and Jefferson and Sally Hemings. He now considers the Union soldiers' ideology and has added material on the effects of the cultural impact of the large numbers of war dead in both North and South. Chapters 15 and 16 both include new treatments of judicial topics, and the latter also discusses scalawags and carpetbaggers at greater length than before.

Howard P. Chudacoff, responsible for Chapters 17 through 21 and Chapter 24, has extensively revised and updated the treatment of technological change in the late nineteenth century and of women's suffrage. He has added discussions of Native peoples in the Southwest, western folk heroes, government and water rights, labor violence in the West, female entertainers (and opposition to them from moralists like Anthony Comstock), Woodrow Wilson's racism, Marcus Garvey, and the Great Migration of African Americans to the North in the twenties. The new Chapter 20 opening vignette features the life of Frances Willard, the president of the Women's Christian Temperance Union. He has also consolidated the analysis of settlement houses in Chapter 21 to avoid repetition.

Fredrik Logevall, with primary responsibility for Chapters 22, 23, 26, and 28, updated the discussions of late nineteenth-century American imperialism and the origins of the Cold War and added new material on nurses and African American soldiers in WWI.

Beth Bailey, primarily responsible for Chapters 25, 27, and 29, incorporated new scholarship on popular culture, the institutional history of the New Deal, the ecological crisis of the thirties, the internment of Japanese citizens and Japanese Americans during WWII, the liberation of Europe, the GI Bill, and the return of veterans in the postwar period. She enhanced the discussion of wartime propaganda and censorship. The new Chapter 29 opening vignette on downwinders ties more closely to the cold war coverage through the chapter. Parts of Chapter 29 underwent extensive revision and reorganization as well.

Bailey and Logevall shared responsibility for Chapters 30 through 33. These chapters now include expanded consideration of the struggle for civil rights and social justice in the north and the opposition to that struggle in the form of protests against school busing. Chapter 31 has a new section on the freedom and responsibilities of youth and enhanced discussions of popular culture, women in the military, and religious cults. New material has been added on foreign policy and changes in American living patterns. As is always the case, Chapter 33, which covers the recent past, underwent thorough revision and reorganization. It covers the second term of George W. Bush, the election of Barack Obama, the Great Recession, and the Iraq and Afghanistan wars.

Teaching and Learning Aids

The supplements listed here accompany the ninth edition of *A People and A Nation*. They have been created with the diverse needs of today's students and instructors in mind.

For the Instructor

Aplia. Aplia™ is an online learning solution that helps students take responsibility for their learning by engaging them with course material, honing their critical thinking skills, and preparing them for class. Created by an instructor for other instructors, Aplia prompts history students to read carefully and think critically. For every chapter, text-specific exercises ask students to consider individual details that support larger historical concepts and draw conclusions rather than reciting historical facts. Every chapter includes at least one set of questions based on a map from the text. The assignments also give students experience reading and interpreting primary source documents, images, and other media. The automatically graded assignments include detailed, immediate explanations that ensure students put forth effort on a regular basis. Gradebook analytics help instructors monitor and address student performance on an individual or group basis. For more information, visit www.aplia.com/cengage.

Instructor Companion Site. Instructors will find here all the tools they need to teach a rich and successful U.S. History Survey course. The protected teaching materials include the *Instructor's Resource Manual* written by George C. Warren of Central Piedmont Community College, a set of customizable Microsoft® PowerPoint® lecture slides created by Barney Rickman of Valdosta State University, and a set of customizable Microsoft® PowerPoint® slides including all the images (photos, art, maps) from the text. The companion website also provides instructors with access to HistoryFinder and to the Wadsworth American History Resource Center (see descriptions below). Go to www.Cengage.com/history to access this site.

PowerLecture CD-ROM with ExamView® and JoinIn®. This dual-platform, all-in-one multimedia resource includes the *Instructor's Resource Manual*; Test Bank in Word® and PDF formats; customizable Microsoft® PowerPoint® slides of both lecture outlines and images from the text; and *JoinIn*® PowerPoint® slides with clicker content. Also included is ExamView®, an easy-to-use assessment and tutorial system that allows instructors to create, deliver, and customize tests in minutes. The test items, written by George C. Warren of Central Piedmont Community College, include multiple-choice, identification, geography, and essay questions.

HistoryFinder. This searchable online database allows instructors to quickly and easily search and download selections from among thousands of assets, including art, photographs, maps, primary sources, and audio/video clips. Each asset downloads directly into a Microsoft® PowerPoint® slide, allowing instructors to easily create exciting PowerPoint presentations for their classrooms.

eInstructor's Resource Manual. Written by George C. Warren of Central Piedmont Community College, this manual contains for each chapter a set of learning objectives, a comprehensive chapter outline, ideas for classroom activities, discussion questions, suggested paper topics, and a lecture supplement. It is available on the instructor's companion website and in the PowerLecture CD-Rom.

WebTutor™ *on Blackboard® and WebCT®.* With WebTutor's text-specific, pre-formatted content and total flexibility, instructors can easily create and manage their own custom course website. WebTutor's course management tool gives instructors the ability to provide virtual office hours, post syllabi, set up threaded discussions, track student progress with the quizzing material, and much more. For students, WebTutor offers real-time access to a full array of study tools, including audio chapter summaries, practice quizzes, glossary flashcards, and weblinks.

CourseMate. Cengage Learning's CourseMate brings course concepts to life with interactive learning, study, and exam preparation tools that support the printed textbook. Watch student comprehension soar as your class works with the printed textbook and the *A People and A Nation* CourseMate site, with interactive teaching and learning tools, and EngagementTracker, a first-of-its-kind tool that monitors student engagement in the course. Learn more at www.cengagebrain.com.

Student Resources

CourseMate. For students, CourseMate provides an online source of interactive learning, study, and exam preparation outside the classroom. Students will find outlines and objectives, focus questions, flashcards, quizzes, primary source links (including those noted in the text and marked with the feather icon), and video clips. CourseMate also includes an integrated **A People and A Nation eBook**. Students taking quizzes will be linked directly to relevant sections in the ebook for additional information. The ebook is fully searchable and students can even take notes and save them for later review. In addition, the ebook links to rich media assets such as video and MP3 chapter summaries, primary source documents with critical thinking questions, and interactive (zoomable) maps. Students can use the ebook as their primary text or as a companion multimedia support. It is available at www.cengagebrain.com.

Wadsworth American History Resource Center. Wadsworth's American History Resource Center gives your students access to a "virtual reader" with hundreds of primary sources, including speeches, letters, legal documents and transcripts, poems, maps, simulations, timelines, and additional images that bring history to life, along with interactive assignable exercises. A map feature, including Google Earth™ coordinates and exercises, will aid in student comprehension of geography and use of maps. Students can compare the traditional textbook map with an aerial view of the location today. It's an ideal resource for study, review, and research. In addition to this map feature, the resource center also provides blank maps for student review and testing. Ask your sales representative for more information on how to bundle access to the HRC with your text.

cengagebrain.com. Save your students time and money. Direct them to www. cengagebrain.com for choice in formats and savings and a better chance to succeed in class. Students have the freedom to purchase à la carte exactly what they need—when they need it. There, students can purchase a downloadable ebook or electronic access to the American History Resource Center, the premium study tools and interactive ebook in the *A People and A Nation* CourseMate, or eAudio modules from *The History Handbook.* Students can save 50 percent on the electronic textbook and can pay as little as $1.99 for an individual eChapter.

Reader Program. Cengage Learning publishes a number of readers, some containing exclusively primary sources, others a combination of primary and secondary sources, and many designed to guide students through the process of historical inquiry. Visit Cengage.com to browse the catalog of history offerings or ask your sales representative to recommend a reader that would work well for your specific needs.

Custom Options

Nobody knows your students like you, so why not give them a text tailored to their needs? Cengage Learning offers custom solutions for your course—whether it's making a small modification to *A People and A Nation* to match your syllabus or combining multiple sources to create something truly unique. You can pick and choose chapters, include your own material, and add supplementary map exercises along with the Rand McNally Atlas (including questions developed around the maps in the atlas) to create a text that fits the way you teach. Ensure that your students get the most out of their textbook dollar by giving them exactly what they need. Contact your Cengage Learning representative to explore custom solutions for your course.

Rand McNally Atlas of American History, 2e. This comprehensive atlas features more than 80 maps, with new content covering global perspectives, including events in the Middle East from 1945 to 2005, as well as population trends in the United States and around the world. Additional maps document voyages of discovery; the settling of the colonies; major U.S. military engagements, including the American Revolution and World Wars I and II; and sources of immigrations, ethnic populations, and patterns of economic change.

CourseReader. Cengage Learning's new CourseReader lets instructors create a customized electronic reader in minutes. Instructors can choose exactly what their students will be assigned by searching or browsing the extensive CourseReader database. Sources include hundreds of historical documents, images, and media, plus literary essays that can add interest and insight to a primary source assignment. Or instructors can start with the "Editor's Choice" collection created for *A People and A Nation* and then update it to suit their particular needs. Each source comes with all the pedagogical tools needed to provide a full learning experience—including headnotes and objective and essay questions, descriptive headnotes that put the reading into context, and both critical-thinking and multiple-choice questions designed to reinforce key points. Contact your local Cengage Learning sales representative for more information and packaging options.

Acknowledgments

The authors would like to thank the following persons for their assistance with the preparation of this edition: Philip Daileader, David Farber, Danyel Logevall, Jon Parmenter, Anna Daileader Sheriff, Benjamin Daileader Sheriff, and Selene Sheriff.

At each stage of this revision, a sizable panel of historian reviewers read drafts of our chapters. Their suggestions, corrections, and pleas helped guide us through this momentous revision. We could not include all of their recommendations, but the book is better for our having heeded most of their advice. We heartily thank:

Sara Alpern, Texas A&M University
Friederike Baer, Temple University
Troy Bickham, Texas A&M University
Robert Bionaz, Chicago State University
Victoria Bynum, Texas State University, San Marcos

Mario Fenyo, Bowie State University
Walter Hixson, University of Akron
Allison McNeese, Mount Mercy College
Steve O'Brien, Bridgewater State College
Paul O'Hara, Xavier University
John Putman, San Diego State University
Thomas Roy, University of Oklahoma
Manfred Silva, El Paso Community College
Michael Vollbach, Oakland Community College

The authors thank the helpful Cengage people who designed, edited, produced, and nourished this book. Many thanks to Ann West, senior sponsoring editor; Julia Giannotti, senior development editor; Jane Lee, content product manager; Debbie Meyer, project editor; Pembroke Herbert, photo researcher; and Charlotte Miller, art editor.

M. B. N.
C. S.
D. B.
H. C.
F. L.
B. B.

About the Authors

Mary Beth Norton

Born in Ann Arbor, Michigan, Mary Beth Norton received her B.A. from the University of Michigan (1964) and her Ph.D. from Harvard University (1969). She is the Mary Donlon Alger Professor of American History at Cornell University. Her dissertation won the Allan Nevins Prize. She has written *The British-Americans* (1972); *Liberty's Daughters* (1980, 1996); *Founding Mothers & Fathers* (1996), which was one of three finalists for the 1997 Pulitzer Prize in History; and *In the Devil's Snare* (2002), which was one of five finalists for the 2003 *LA Times* Book Prize in History and which won the English-Speaking Union's Ambassador Book Award in American Studies for 2003. She has co-edited three volumes on American women's history. She was also general editor of the *American Historical Association's Guide to Historical Literature* (1995). Her articles have appeared in such journals as the *American Historical Review, William and Mary Quarterly,* and *Journal of Women's History.* Mary Beth has served as president of the Berkshire Conference of Women Historians, as vice president for research of the American Historical Association, and as a presidential appointee to the National Council on the Humanities. She has appeared on Book TV, the History and Discovery Channels, PBS, and NBC and as a commentator on Early American history; and she lectures frequently to high school teachers through the Teaching American History program. She has received four honorary degrees and in 1999 was elected a fellow of the American Academy of Arts and Sciences. She has held fellowships from the National Endowment for the Humanities; the Guggenheim, Rockefeller, and Starr Foundations; and the Henry E. Huntington Library. In 2005–2006, she was the Pitt Professor of American History and Institutions at the University of Cambridge and Newnham College.

Carol Sheriff

Born in Washington, D.C., and raised in Bethesda, Maryland, Carol Sheriff received her B.A. from Wesleyan University (1985) and her Ph.D. from Yale University (1993). Since 1993, she has taught history at the College of William and Mary, where she has won the Thomas Jefferson Teaching Award, the Alumni Teaching Fellowship Award, and the University Professorship for Teaching Excellence. Her publications include *The Artificial River: The Erie Canal and the Paradox of Progress* (1996), which won the Dixon Ryan Fox Award from the New York State Historical Association and the Award for Excellence in Research from the New York State Archives, and *A People at War: Civilians and Soldiers in America's Civil War, 1854–1877* (with Scott Reynolds Nelson, 2007). Carol has written sections of a teaching manual for the New York State history curriculum, given presentations at Teaching American History grant projects, consulted on an exhibit for the Rochester Museum and Science Center, and appeared in the History Channel's *Modern Marvels* show on the Erie Canal, and she is engaged in several public-history projects marking the sesquicentennial of the Civil War. At William and Mary, she teaches the

U.S. history survey as well as upper-level classes on the Early Republic, the Civil War Era, and the American West. Most recently, Carol has been named Class of 2013 term distinguished professor in recognition of her teaching, scholarship, and service.

David W. Blight

Born in Flint, Michigan, David W. Blight received his B.A. from Michigan State University (1971) and his Ph.D. from the University of Wisconsin (1985). He is now Class of 1954 Professor of American History and director of the Gilder Lehrman Center for the Study of Slavery, Resistance, and Abolition at Yale University. For the first seven years of his career, David was a public high school teacher in Flint. He has written *Frederick Douglass's Civil War* (1989) and *Race and Reunion: The Civil War in American Memory, 1863–1915* (2001), which received eight awards, including the Bancroft Prize, the Frederick Douglass Prize, and the Abraham Lincoln Prize, as well as four prizes awarded by the Organization of American Historians. His most recent book is *A Slave No More: The Emancipation of John Washington and Wallace Turnage* (2007), which won three prizes. He has edited or co-edited six other books, including editions of W. E. B. DuBois, *The Souls of Black Folk* and *Narrative of the Life of Frederick Douglass*. David's essays have appeared in the *Journal of American History*, *Civil War History*, and Gabor Boritt, ed., *Why the Civil War Came* (1996), among others. In 1992–1993, he was senior Fulbright Professor in American Studies at the University of Munich, Germany; in 2006–2007, he held a fellowship at the Dorothy and Lewis B. Cullman Center, New York Public Library. A consultant to several documentary films, David appeared in the 1998 PBS series, *Africans in America*. He has served on the Council of the American Historical Association and teaches summer seminars for secondary school teachers as well as for park rangers and historians of the National Park Service.

Howard P. Chudacoff

Howard P. Chudacoff, the George L. Littlefield Professor of American History and Professor of Urban Studies at Brown University, was born in Omaha, Nebraska. He earned his A.B. (1965) and Ph.D. (1969) from the University of Chicago. He has written *Mobile Americans* (1972), *How Old Are You?* (1989), *The Age of the Bachelor* (1999), *The Evolution of American Urban Society* (with Judith Smith, 2004), and *Children at Play: An American History* (2007). He has also co-edited with Peter Baldwin *Major Problems in American Urban History* (2004). His articles have appeared in such journals as the *Journal of Family History*, *Reviews in American History*, and *Journal of American History*. At Brown University, Howard has co-chaired the American Civilization Program and chaired the Department of History, and serves as Brown's faculty representative to the NCAA. He has also served on the board of directors of the Urban History Association. The National Endowment for the Humanities, Ford Foundation, and Rockefeller Foundation have given him awards to advance his scholarship.

Fredrik Logevall

A native of Stockholm, Sweden, Fredrik Logevall is the John S. Knight Professor of International Studies and Professor of History at Cornell University, where he serves as director of the Mario Einaudi Center for International Studies. He received his B.A. from Simon Fraser University (1986) and his Ph.D. from Yale University (1993). His most recent book is *America's Cold War: The Politics of Insecurity* (with Campbell Craig, 2009). His other publications include *Choosing War* (1999), which won three prizes, including the Warren F. Kuehl Book Prize from the Society for Historians of American Foreign Relations (SHAFR); *The Origins of the Vietnam War* (2001); *Terrorism and 9/11: A Reader* (2002); as co-editor, *Encyclopedia of American Foreign Policy* (2002); and, as co-editor, *The First Vietnam War: Colonial Conflict and Cold War Crisis* (2007). Fred is a past recipient of the Stuart L. Bernath article, book, and lecture prizes from SHAFR and is a member of the SHAFR Council, the Cornell University Press faculty board, and the editorial advisory board of the Presidential Recordings Project at the Miller Center of Public Affairs at the University of Virginia. In 2006–2007, he was Leverhulme Visiting Professor at the University of Nottingham and Mellon Senior Fellow at the University of Cambridge.

Beth Bailey

Born in Atlanta, Georgia, Beth Bailey received her B.A. from Northwestern University (1979) and her Ph.D. from the University of Chicago (1986). She is now a professor of history at Temple University. Her research and teaching fields include war and society and the U.S. military, American cultural history (nineteenth and twentieth centuries), popular culture, and gender and sexuality. She is the author, most recently, of *America's Army: Making the All-Volunteer Force* (2009). Her other publications include *From Front Porch to Back Seat: Courtship in 20th Century America* (1988), *The First Strange Place: The Alchemy of Race and Sex in WWII Hawaii* (with David Farber, 1992), *Sex in the Heartland* (1999), and *The Columbia Companion to America in the 1960s* (with David Farber, 2001). She is co-editor of *A History of Our Time* (with William Chafe and Harvard Sitkoff, 7th ed., 2007). Beth has served as a consultant and/ or on-screen expert for numerous television documentaries developed for PBS and the History Channel. She has received grants or fellowships from the American Council of Learned Societies, the National Endowment for the Humanities, and the Woodrow Wilson International Center for Scholars; and she was named the Ann Whitney Olin scholar at Barnard College, Columbia University, where she was the director of the American Studies Program, and Regents Lecturer at the University of New Mexico. She has been a visiting scholar at Saitama University, Japan; at Trinity College at the University of Melbourne; and a senior Fulbright lecturer in Indonesia. She teaches courses on sexuality and gender and war and American culture.

Three Old Worlds Create a New

1

1492–1600

F ive years later, Alvar Nuñez Cabeza de Vaca still recalled the amazement he had encountered. "I reached four Christians on horseback who registered great surprise at seeing me so strangely dressed and in the company of Indians. They…neither spoke to me nor dared to ask anything."

Cabeza de Vaca and three other men, one an enslaved North African named Estevan, had just walked across North America. They, along with about six hundred others, had left Spain in June 1527 on an ill-fated expedition. After exploring the west coast of Florida, eighty men, including Cabeza de Vaca, were shipwrecked in late 1528 on the coast of modern Texas (probably near Galveston), at a place they named Isla de Malhado, or Island of Misfortune. Most of the survivors—alternately abused, aided, or enslaved by different Indian nations—gradually died. Cabeza de Vaca reached the mainland, where he survived as a traveling trader, exchanging seashells for hides and flint.

In January 1533, he stumbled on the other three. The Spaniards and Estevan plotted to leave but were unable to until September 1534. They walked south, then turned inland and headed north, exploring the upper reaches of the Rio Grande. They continued west, almost reaching the Pacific before turning south once more, guided from village to village by Indians. Vaca described the diets, living arrangements, and customs of many of the villages they saw, thus providing modern historians and anthropologists with an invaluable record of native cultures as they met Europeans.

For thousands of years before 1492, human societies in the Americas had developed in isolation from the rest of the world. That ended in the Christian fifteenth century, as Europeans sought treasure and trade, peoples from different cultures came into regular contact for the first time and were profoundly changed. Their interactions over the next 350 years involved cruelty and kindness, greed and deception, trade and theft, sickness and enslavement. The history of the colonies that would become the United States must be seen in this broad context of European exploration and exploitation.

1

Link to Cabeza de Vaca's original narrative in English.

The continents that European sailors reached in the late fifteenth century had their own histories, which the intruders largely ignored. The residents of the Americas were the world's most skillful plant breeders; they developed vegetable crops more nutritious and productive than in Europe, Asia, or Africa and invented systems of writing and mathematics. As in Europe, their societies rose and fell as leaders succeeded or failed. But the arrival of Europeans immeasurably altered the Americans' struggles with one another.

After 1400, European nations tried to acquire valuable colonies and trading posts worldwide. Initially interested in Asia and Africa, Europeans eventually focused mostly on the Americas. Even as Europeans slowly achieved dominance, their fates were shaped by Americans and Africans. In the Americas of the fifteenth and sixteenth centuries, three old worlds came together to produce a new.

As you read this chapter, keep the following questions in mind:

* **What were the key characteristics of the three worlds that met in the Americas?**

* **What impact did their encounter have on each of them?**

* **What were the crucial initial developments in that encounter?**

American Societies

What led to the development of major North American civilizations in the centuries before Europeans arrived?

Human beings originated on the continent of Africa, where human-like remains about 3 million years old have been found in what is now Ethiopia. Over many millennia, the growing population dispersed to other continents. Because the climate was far colder than it is now, much of the earth's water was concentrated in huge rivers of ice called glaciers. Sea levels were lower, and land masses covered a larger proportion of the earth's surface. Scholars long believed that the earliest inhabitants of the Americas crossed a land bridge known as Beringia (at the site of the Bering Strait) approximately 12,000–14,000 years ago. Yet new archaeological discoveries suggest that parts of the Americas may have been settled much earlier, possibly in three successive waves beginning roughly 30,000 years ago. When, about 12,500 years ago, the climate warmed and sea levels rose, Americans were separated from the connected continents of Asia, Africa, and Europe.

Paleo-Indians: The earliest peoples of the Americas.

Ancient America

The first Americans are called **Paleo-Indians**. Nomadic hunters of game and gatherers of wild plants, they spread throughout North and South America, probably as bands of extended families. By about 11,500 years ago, the Paleo-Indians were making fine stone projectile points, which they attached to wooden spears and used to kill bison (buffalo), woolly mammoths, and other large mammals. But as the Ice Age ended and the human population increased, all the large American mammals except the bison disappeared.

Chronology

12,000–10,000 B.C.E.	Paleo-Indians migrate from Asia to North America across the Beringia land bridge
7000 B.C.E.	Cultivation of food crops begins in America
ca. 2000 B.C.E.	Olmec civilization appears
ca. 300–600 C.E.	Height of influence of Teotihuacán
ca. 600–900 C.E.	Classic Mayan civilization
1000 C.E.	Ancient Pueblos build settlements in modern states of Arizona and New Mexico
1001	Norse establish settlement in "Vinland"
1050–1250	Height of influence of Cahokia Prevalence of Mississippian culture in modern midwestern and southeastern United States
14th century	Aztec rise to power
1450s–80s	Portuguese explore and colonize islands in the Mediterranean Atlantic
1477	Marco Polo's *Travels* describes China
1492	Columbus reaches Bahamas
1494	Treaty of Tordesillas divides land claims between Spain and Portugal in Africa, India, and South America
1496	Last Canary Island falls to Spain
1497	Cabot reaches North America
1513	Ponce de León explores Florida
1518–30	Smallpox epidemic devastates Indian population of West Indies and Central and South America
1519	Cortés invades Mexico
1521	Aztec Empire falls to Spaniards
1524	Verrazzano sails along Atlantic coast of United States
1534–35	Cartier explores St. Lawrence River
1534–36	Vaca, Estevan, and two companions walk across North America
1539–42	Soto explores southeastern United States
1540–42	Coronado explores southwestern United States
1587–90	Raleigh's Roanoke colony vanishes
1588	Harriot publishes *A Briefe and True Report of the New Found Land of Virginia*

Consequently, by approximately nine thousand years ago, the residents of what is now central Mexico began to cultivate food crops, especially maize (corn), squash, beans, avocados, and peppers. In the Andes Mountains of South America, people started to grow potatoes. As knowledge of agricultural techniques improved, vegetables proved a more reliable source of food than hunting and gathering. Most Americans started to adopt a more sedentary lifestyle that enabled them to tend fields regularly. Some established permanent settlements; others moved several times a year among fixed sites. They cleared forests through controlled burning, which created cultivable lands, by killing trees and fertilizing the soil with ashes and opened meadows to deer and other wildlife. Although they traded such items as shells, flint, salt, and copper, no society ever became dependent on another group.

Wherever agriculture dominated, complex civilizations flourished. With steady supplies of grains and vegetables, societies could broaden their focus from subsistence to trade, accumulating wealth, producing ornamental objects, and creating elaborate rituals and ceremonies. In North America, the successful cultivation of nutritious crops seems to have led to the growth and development of all the major civilizations: first the large city-states of Mesoamerica (modern Mexico and Guatemala) and then the urban clusters known collectively as the Mississippian culture (in the present-day United States). Each reached its peak influence after achieving success in agriculture. Each later collapsed after reaching the limits of its food supply.

Mesoamerican Civilizations

Scholars know little about the first major Mesoamerican civilization, the Olmecs, who about four thousand years ago lived in cities near the Gulf of Mexico. The Mayas and Teotihuacán, which developed approximately two thousand years later, are better recorded. Teotihuacán, founded in the Valley of Mexico about 300 B.C.E. (Before the Common Era), became one of the largest urban areas in the world, housing 100,000 people in the fifth century C.E. (Common Era). Teotihuacán's commercial network extended hundreds of miles, and Pilgrims traveled long distances to visit Teotihuacan's impressive pyramids and the great temple of Quetzalcoatl—the feathered serpent, primary god of central Mexico.

On the Yucatan Peninsula, in today's eastern Mexico, the Mayas built urban centers containing tall pyramids and temples, studied astronomy, and created an elaborate writing system. Their city-states engaged in near-constant warfare with one another—combined with inadequate food supplies, this caused the collapse of the most powerful cities by 900 C.E., thus ending the era of Mayan civilization.

Pueblos and Mississippians

Ancient native societies in what is now the United States learned to grow maize, squash, and beans from Mesoamericans. The Hohokam, Mogollon, and ancient Pueblo peoples of the modern states of Arizona and New Mexico subsisted by combining hunting and gathering with agriculture in an arid region of unpredictable rainfall. Hohokam villagers constructed extensive irrigation systems, but relocated when water supplies failed. Between 900 and 1150 C.E., Chaco Canyon, at the juncture of perhaps four hundred miles of roads, served as a major trading and processing center for turquoise. Yet the aridity caused the Chacoans to migrate to other sites.

Almost simultaneously, the unrelated Mississippian culture flourished in what is now the midwestern and southeastern United States. Relying largely on maize, squash, nuts, pumpkins, and venison, the Mississippians lived in hierarchically organized settlements. Their largest urban center was the **City of the Sun** (now called Cahokia), near modern St. Louis. Located on rich farmland near the confluence of the Illinois, Missouri, and Mississippi Rivers, Cahokia, like Teotihuacán and Chaco Canyon, served as a focal point for religion and trade. At its peak (in the eleventh and twelfth centuries C.E.), the City of the Sun covered more than 5 square miles and had a population of about twenty thousand—small by Mesoamerican standards but larger than London.

City of the Sun (Cahokia): Area located near modern St. Louis, Missouri, where about twenty thousand people inhabited a metropolitan area.

The sun-worshipping Cahokians developed an accurate calendar. The city's main pyramid (one of 120 of varying sizes), today called Monks Mound, remains the largest earthwork in the Americas. Yet following 1250 C.E., the city was abandoned. Archaeologists believe that climate change and the degradation of the environment, caused by overpopulation and the destruction of nearby forests, contributed to its collapse. Afterwards, warfare increased as large-scale population movements destabilized the region.

Aztecs

Far to the South, the Aztecs (also called Mexicas) migrated into the Valley of Mexico during the twelfth century. Their chronicles record that their primary deity, Huitzilopochtli—a war god represented by an eagle—directed them to establish their capital on an island where they saw an eagle eating a serpent. That island city became Tenochtitlán, the center of a

City of the Sun

Today the remains of the City of the Sun (Cahokia) are preserved in a state park in southern Illinois. The mounds are now either largely gone or greatly reduced in size, but archaeologists have been able to visualize the site. Few of their finds were more important than the two shown here: the woodhenge and the Birger figurine. Archaeologists discovered the post holes where the woodhenge once stood, showing how the sun-worshipping Cahokians monitored the sun's annual movements through shadows cast by poles they erected in a precise formation. The red clay Birger figurine, found near Cahokia, depicts a woman with a vine winding around her body sitting on a cat-faced serpent (symbol of the earth) and holding a hoe. Why would the woodhenge have been important for Cahokia's farmers? What is the significance of the squash vine and the other attributes of the Birger figurine?

Cahokia Mounds Historic Site

An artist's conception of the construction of Cahokia's woodhenge. Monks mound is in the background.

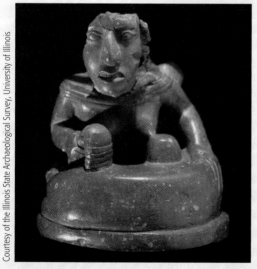

Courtesy of the Illinois State Archaeological Survey, University of Illinois

Front view of the Birger figurine.

Courtesy of the Illinois State Archaeological Survey, University of Illinois

Back view of the Birger figurine.

stratified society composed of hereditary classes of warriors, merchants, priests, common folk, and slaves.

The Aztecs conquered their neighbors, forcing them to pay tribute in textiles, gold, foodstuffs, and human sacrifices to Huitzilopochtli. They also engaged in ritual combat for further sacrificial victims to the war god. In the Aztec year Ten Rabbit (1502), at the coronation of Motecuhzoma II (the Spaniards mispronounced his name as Montezuma), thousands were sacrificed by having their hearts torn from their bodies.

North America in 1492

Over the centuries, the Americans who lived north of Mexico adapted their once similar ways of life to different climates and terrains, thus creating the diverse culture areas (ways of subsistence) that the Europeans encountered (see Map 1.1). Scholars often refer to such culture areas by language group (such as Algonquian or Iroquoian). Bands that lived in environments not suited to agriculture followed a nomadic lifestyle typified by the Paiutes and Shoshones, who inhabited the Great Basin (now Nevada and Utah). Because finding sufficient food was difficult, such hunter-gatherer bands were small, usually composed of one or more related families. The men hunted small animals, and women gathered seeds and berries.

In more favorable environments, larger groups, like the Chinooks of present-day Washington and Oregon, combined agriculture with gathering, hunting, and fishing. Residents of the interior (for example, the Arikaras of the Missouri River valley) hunted large animals while also cultivating maize, squash, and beans.

Trade routes linked distant peoples. For instance, hoe and spade blades manufactured from stone mined in modern southern Illinois have been found as far northeast as Lake Erie and as far west as the Plains. Commercial and other interactions among disparate groups speaking different languages were aided by the universal symbol of friendship—the calumet, a feathered tobacco pipe offered to strangers at initial encounters.

Gendered Division of Labor
Societies that relied on hunting large animals, such as deer and buffalo, assigned that task to men, allotting food preparation and clothing production to women. Before acquiring horses from the Spaniards, women carried the family's belongings whenever the band relocated. This sexual division of labor was universal among hunting peoples. Agricultural societies assigned work in divergent ways. The Pueblo defined agricultural labor as men's work. In the east, peoples speaking Algonquian, Iroquoian, and Muskogean languages allocated most agricultural chores to women, although men cleared the land. In all farming societies, women gathered wild foods and prepared food for consumption or storage, whereas men hunted.

Almost universally, women cared for young children, while older youths learned adult skills from their same-sex parent. Children had a lot of freedom. Young people commonly chose their own marital partners, and in most societies couples could easily divorce. Infants and toddlers were nursed until age two or older, and taboos prevented couples from having sexual intercourse during that period.

MAP 1.1

Native Cultures of North America

The Natives of the North American continent effectively used the resources of the regions in which they lived. As this map shows, coastal groups relied on fishing, residents of fertile areas engaged in agriculture, and other peoples employed hunting (often combined with gathering) as a primary mode of subsistence.

Source: Copyright © Cengage Learning

Social Organization   Southwestern and eastern agricultural peoples similarly lived in villages, sometimes with a thousand or more inhabitants. The Pueblos resided in multistory buildings constructed on terraces along the sides of cliffs or other easily defended sites. Northern Iroquois villages (in modern New York State) were composed of large, rectangular, bark-covered structures, or long houses; the name Haudenosaunee, which the Iroquois called themselves, means "People of the Long House." In the present-day southeastern United States, Muskogeans and southern Algonquians lived in large thatch houses. Most of the eastern villages were surrounded by wooden palisades and ditches to fend off attackers.

7

Jacques Le Moyne, an artist accompanying the French settlement in Florida in the 1560s (see page 30), produced some of the first European images of North American peoples. His depiction of native agricultural practices shows the gendered division of labor: men breaking up the ground with fishbone hoes before women drop seeds into the holes. But Le Moyne's version of the scene cannot be accepted uncritically: unable to abandon a European view of proper farming methods, he erroneously drew plowed furrows in the soil.

In all the agricultural societies, each dwelling housed an extended family defined matrilineally (through a female line of descent). Mothers, their married daughters, and their daughters' husbands and children all lived together. Matrilineal descent did not imply matriarchy, or the wielding of power by women, but denoted kinship and linked extended families into clans. The nomadic bands of the Prairies and Great Plains were most often related patrilineally (through the male line).

War and Politics   Long before Europeans arrived, residents fought one another for control of the best hunting and fishing territories, the most fertile agricultural lands, or the sources of essential items, such as salt (for preserving meat) and flint (for making knives and arrowheads). Bands of Americans protected by wooden armor engaged in face-to-face combat, since the clubs and throwing spears they used were effective only in close proximity. They began to shoot arrows from behind trees only when they confronted European guns. War captives were sometimes enslaved, but slavery was never an important labor source in pre-Columbian America.

Political structures varied considerably. Among Pueblos, the village council, composed of ten to thirty men, was the highest political authority; no government structure connected the villages. The Iroquois had an elaborate hierarchy incorporating villages into nations and nations into a confederation. A council comprising representatives from each nation made crucial decisions of war and peace. Women more often assumed leadership roles among agricultural peoples than among nomadic hunters. Female sachems (rulers) led Algonquian villages in what is now Massachusetts, but women never became heads of hunting bands. Iroquois women did not become chiefs, yet older women chose village chiefs and could both start wars (by calling for the capture of prisoners to replace dead relatives) and stop them (by refusing to supply warriors with foodstuffs).

Religion   All the American peoples were polytheistic, worshiping a multitude of gods. The major deities of agricultural peoples like the Pueblos and Muskogeans were associated with cultivation, and festivals centered on planting and harvest. The most important gods of hunters like those living on the Great Plains were associated with animals. Women held the most prominent positions in those agricultural societies where they were also the chief food producers; in hunting societies, men took the lead in religious and political affairs.

A variety of cultures, comprising more than 10 million people speaking over one thousand languages, inhabited America north of Mexico when Europeans arrived. The hierarchical kingdoms of Mesoamerica bore little resemblance to the nomadic hunting societies of the Great Plains or to the agriculturalists of the Northeast or Southwest. They did not consider themselves one people, nor did they consider uniting to repel the European invaders.

African Societies

Fifteenth-century Africa similarly housed a variety of cultures. In the north, along the Mediterranean Sea, lived the Berbers, who were Muslims, or followers of the Islamic religion. On the east coast of Africa, Muslim city-states engaged in extensive trade with India, the Moluccas (part of modern Indonesia), and China. Sustained contact and intermarriage among Arabs and Africans created the Swahili language and culture. Through the East African city-states passed the Spice Route, water-borne commerce between the eastern Mediterranean and East Asia; other trade traversed the Silk Road, the long land route across Central Asia.

South of the Mediterranean coast in the African interior lie the great Saharan and Libyan Deserts. The introduction of the camel in the fifth century C.E. made long-distance travel possible, and as Islam expanded after the ninth century, commerce controlled by Muslim merchants helped spread religious and cultural ideas. Below the deserts, the continent is divided between tropical rain forests (along the coasts) and grassy plains (in the interior). South of the Gulf of Guinea, the grassy landscape came to be dominated by Bantu-speaking peoples, who left their homeland in modern Nigeria about two thousand years ago.

> What were the chief characteristics of West African societies in the fifteenth century?

West Africa (Guinea)

West Africa was a land of tropical forests and savanna grasslands where fishing, cattle herding, and agriculture supported the inhabitants for ten thousand years before Europeans arrived in the fifteenth century. The northern region of West Africa, or Upper Guinea, was heavily influenced by Mediterranean Islamic culture. Trade via camel caravans between Upper Guinea and the Muslim Mediterranean was sub-Saharan Africa's major connection to Europe and West Asia. Africans sold ivory, gold, and slaves to northern merchants to obtain salt, dates, silk, and cotton cloth.

Upper Guinea runs northeast-southwest from Cape Verde to Cape Palmas. The people of its northernmost region—the so-called Rice Coast (present-day Gambia, Senegal, and Guinea)—fished and cultivated rice in coastal swamplands. The Grain Coast, to the south, was thinly populated and with only one good harbor (modern Freetown, Sierra Leone), not easily accessible from the sea. Its people farmed and raised livestock.

In Lower Guinea, south and east of Cape Palmas, most Africans were farmers who practiced traditional religions, rather than Islam. Like the agricultural Americans, they believed spirits inhabited particular places, and they developed rituals to ensure good harvests. Individual villages composed of kin groups were linked into hierarchical kingdoms, creating the decentralized political and social authority that existed when Europeans arrived.

Complementary Gender Roles

As in the Americas, West African societies assigned different tasks to men and women. The sexes generally shared agricultural duties. Men also hunted, managed livestock, and fished. Women were responsible for childcare, food preparation, manufacture, and trade. They managed local and regional networks through which families, villages, and small kingdoms exchanged goods.

Lower Guinea had similar social systems organized according to what anthropologists have called the dual-sex principle. Each sex handled its own affairs: male political and religious leaders governed men; females ruled women. Many West African societies practiced polygyny (one man's having several wives, each of whom lived separately with her children). Thus, few adults lived permanently in marital households, but the dual-sex system ensured that they were monitored by their own sex.

Throughout Guinea, religious beliefs stressed complementary male and female roles. Both women and men served as heads of the cults and secret societies that directed village spiritual life. Young women were initiated into the Sandé cult, young men into Poro. Although West African women rarely held formal power over men, female religious leaders governed women within the Sandé cult, enforcing conformity to behavioral norms.

Slavery in Guinea

West African law recognized individual and communal land ownership, but men seeking wealth needed labor—wives, children, or slaves—who could work the land. West Africans enslaved for life were vital to the economy. Africans could be enslaved for committing crimes, but usually slaves were enemy captives or people who enslaved themselves or their children to pay debts. An African slave owner had a right to the products of slaves' labor, although slave status did not always descend to the next generation. Some slaves were held as chattel; others could engage in trade, retaining a portion of their profits; and still others achieved prominent political or military positions. All, however, could be traded at any time.

Agricultural peoples, West African men and women enjoyed a relatively egalitarian relationship and worked communally in family groups or with members of their sex. Carried as captives to the Americas, they became essential laborers for European colonists.

European Societies

In the fifteenth century, Europeans, too, were agricultural peoples. In the hierarchical European societies, a few families wielded autocratic power over the majority. English society was organized as a series of interlocking hierarchies; that is, each person (except those at the top or bottom) was superior to some, inferior to others. Although Europeans were not subjected to perpetual slavery, Christian doctrine permitted the enslavement of "heathens" (non-Christians). Some Europeans, too, were held as serfs, which tied them to the land or to specific owners. In short, Europe's kingdoms resembled those of Africa or Mesoamerica but differed from the more egalitarian societies in America north of Mexico.

> What were the motives behind fifteenth- and sixteenth-century European explorations?

Gender, Work, Politics, and Religion

Most Europeans, like Africans and Americans, lived in small villages. European farmers, called peasants, owned or leased separate landholdings but worked the fields communally. Because fields had to lie fallow (unplanted) every second or third year to regain fertility, a family could only ensure its food supply if all villagers shared the work and the crops. Men did the fieldwork; women helped at planting and harvesting. In some regions, men concentrated on herding livestock. Women's duties consisted of childcare and household tasks, including preserving food, milking cows, and caring for poultry. If a husband was a city artisan or storekeeper, his wife might assist him in business. Because Europeans kept domesticated animals (pigs, goats, sheep, and cattle) for meat, hunting had little economic importance.

Men dominated European society. A few women—notably Queen Elizabeth I of England—achieved power by birthright, but most were excluded from political authority. They also held inferior social, religious, and economic positions, yet wielded power over children and servants.

Christianity was the dominant European religion. In the West, authority rested in the Catholic Church, based in Rome. Although Europeans were nominally Catholic, many adhered to local belief systems that the church deemed heretical. Still, Europe's Christian nations from the twelfth century on publicly united to drive nonbelievers (especially Muslims) from their domains and from the holy city of Jerusalem, triggering wars known as the Crusades. Nevertheless, in the fifteenth century, Muslims dominated the commerce and geography of the Mediterranean, especially after they conquered Constantinople (capital of the Christian Byzantine empire) in 1453. Few would have predicted that Christian Europeans would ever pose a challenge.

Effects of Plague and Warfare

When the fifteenth century began, European nations were recovering from the devastating Black Death epidemic, which traders seem to have brought from China in 1346. The disease recurred with severity in the 1360s and 1370s. The best estimate is that one-third of Europeans died. A precipitous economic decline followed—as did severe social, political, and religious disruption.

As plague ravaged the population, England and France waged the Hundred Years' War (1337–1453), initiated because English monarchs claimed the French throne. The war interrupted overland trade routes connecting England and Antwerp (in modern Belgium) to Venice, a Christian trading center, and thence to India and China. Needing a new way to their northern trading partners, eastern Mediterranean merchants forged a maritime route to Antwerp. Using a triangular, or lateen, sail (rather than square rigging) improved a ship's maneuverability, enabling vessels to sail from the Mediterranean and north around the European coast.

Political and Technological Change

After the Hundred Years' War, European monarchs consolidated their political power and raised revenues by taxing an already hard-pressed peasantry. The military struggle inspired new pride in national identity over former regional and dynastic loyalties. In England, Henry VII in 1485 founded the Tudor dynasty and united a previously divided land. In France, Charles VII's successors unified the kingdom. Most successful were Ferdinand of Aragón and Isabella of Castile; in 1492, they defeated the Muslims, who had lived in Spain and Portugal for centuries, thereafter establishing a strongly Catholic Spain by expelling Jews and Muslims.

movable type: Type in which each character is cast on a separate piece of metal.

printing press: A machine that transfers lettering or images by contact with various forms of inked surface onto paper or similar material fed into it in various ways.

The fifteenth century also brought technological change to Europe. **Movable type** and the **printing press**, invented in Germany in the 1450s, made information more accessible, including books about fabled lands across the seas. The most important books were Ptolemy's *Geography,* a description of the known world written in ancient times, first published in 1475; and Marco Polo's *Travels,* published in 1477. The *Travels* recounted a Venetian merchant's adventures in thirteenth-century China and described that nation as bordered on the east by an ocean. That book led Europeans to believe they could reach China by sea rather than via the Silk Road or the Spice Route. If it existed, a transoceanic route would allow northern Europeans to circumvent the Muslim and Venetian merchants who controlled their access to Asian goods.

Motives for Exploration

In the fifteenth and sixteenth centuries, European countries craved easy access to African and Asian goods—silk, dyes, perfumes, jewels, sugar, gold, and especially spices, which were desirable for seasoning food and as possible medicines. The allure of cinnamon or cloves stemmed from their rarity, extraordinary cost, and mysterious origins. They passed through so many hands en route to London or Seville that no European knew exactly where they came from. Acquiring products directly would improve a nation's income and its standing relative to other countries, thus providing a powerful incentive for exploration.

Spreading Christianity around the world supplemented the economic motive. Fifteenth-century Europeans saw no conflict between materialistic and spiritual goals. Explorers and colonizers—especially Roman Catholics—sought to convert "heathen" peoples and also hoped to increase their nation's wealth via direct trade with Africa, China, India, and the Moluccas.

Early European Explorations

To establish that trade, European mariners first had to explore the oceans. Seafarers needed not just maneuverable vessels and navigational aids but also knowledge of the sea, its currents, and winds. Wind would power their ships. But where would Atlantic breezes carry their square-rigged ships, which needed the wind directly behind the vessel?

What sailing innovation ultimately facilitated the widespread exploration of the Atlantic and Pacific?

Sailing the Mediterranean Atlantic

The answers would be found in the Mediterranean Atlantic, the expanse of ocean located south and west of Spain and bounded by the Azores (on the west) and the Canaries (on the south), with the Madeiras in their midst. Europeans reached all three sets of islands during the fourteenth century. Sailing to the Canaries from Europe was easy because strong Northeast trade winds blew southward along the Iberian and African coastlines. The voyage took about a week.

The Iberian sailor returning home, however, faced winds that blew directly at him. Rowing and tacking back and forth against the wind were tedious and ineffectual. Instead of waiting for the wind to change, mariners developed the new technique of sailing "around the wind"—literally sailing as directly against the wind as possible without changing course. In the Mediterranean Atlantic, a mariner would head northwest into the open ocean, until—weeks later—he reached the winds that would carry him home, the so-called Westerlies. This solution became the key to successful exploration of the Atlantic and the Pacific Oceans. Faced with a contrary wind, a sailor could simply sail around it until he found a wind to carry him on his way.

Islands of the Mediterranean Atlantic

During the fifteenth century, Iberian seamen regularly visited the three island groups. The uninhabited Azores were soon settled by Portuguese migrants who raised wheat for sale in Europe and sold livestock to passing sailors. By the 1450s, Portuguese colonists who settled the uninhabited Madeiras were employing slaves (probably Jews and Muslims brought from Iberia) to grow sugar for export. By the 1470s, Madeira had developed a colonial **plantation** economy. For the first time in history, a region was settled explicitly to cultivate a valuable crop—sugar—for sale elsewhere. Because the work was so backbreaking, only a supply of enslaved laborers (who could not quit) could ensure the system's success.

plantation: A large-scale agricultural enterprise growing commercial crops and usually employing coerced or slave labor.

The Canaries had indigenous residents—the Guanche people, who traded animal skins and dyes with Europeans. After 1402 the French, Portuguese, and Spanish sporadically attacked the islands. The Guanches resisted but were weakened by European diseases. The seven islands fell to Europeans, who carried off Guanches as slaves to the Madeiras or Iberia. Spain conquered the last island in 1496 and devoted it to sugar plantations.

Portuguese Trading Posts in Africa

Other Europeans saw the Mediterranean Atlantic islands as steppingstones to Africa. In 1415, Portugal seized control of Ceuta, a Muslim city in North Africa. Prince Henry the Navigator, son of King John I of Portugal, dispatched ships southward along the

African coast, attempting to discover an oceanic route to Asia. Not until after his death did Bartholomew Dias round the southern tip of Africa (1488) and Vasco da Gama finally reach India (1498), where at Malabar he located the richest source of peppercorns in the world.

Although West African states resisted European penetration of the interior, they let Portugal establish trading posts along their coasts. The African kingdoms charged traders rent and levied duties on imports. The Portuguese gained, too, profiting from transporting African gold, ivory, and slaves to Europe. By bargaining with African masters to purchase slaves and carrying those bondspeople to Iberia, the Portuguese introduced black slavery into Europe.

Lessons of Early Colonization

Portugal's success grew after it colonized São Tomé, located in the Gulf of Guinea, in the 1480s. With Madeira at its sugar-producing capacity, São Tomé proved an ideal new locale, and plantation agriculture there expanded rapidly. Planters imported slaves to work in the cane fields, creating the first economy based primarily on the bondage of black Africans.

By the 1490s, Europeans had learned three key colonization lessons in the Mediterranean Atlantic. First, they learned how to transplant crops and livestock to exotic locations. Second, they discovered that native peoples could be conquered (like the Guanches) or exploited (like the Africans). Third, they developed a model of plantation slavery and a system for supplying many such workers. The stage was set for a pivotal moment in world history.

Voyages of Columbus, Cabot, and Their Successors

What three themes in Columbus's log about his explorations would come to mark much of the future settlement of Europeans in the Americas?

Christopher Columbus: Italian explorer who claimed the island of San Salvador in the Bahamas for the king and queen of Spain.

Christopher Columbus understood the lessons of the Mediterranean Atlantic. Born in 1451 in the Italian city-state of Genoa, this self-educated son of a wool merchant was by the 1490s an experienced sailor and mapmaker. Drawn to Portugal and its islands, he voyaged to the Portuguese outpost on the Gold Coast, where he became obsessed with gold and witnessed the economic potential of the slave trade.

Like all accomplished seafarers, Columbus knew the world was round. But he thought that China lay only three thousand miles from the southern European coast. Thus, he argued, it would be easier to reach Asia by sailing west. Experts scoffed, accurately predicting that the two continents lay twelve thousand miles apart. When Columbus in 1484 asked the Portuguese rulers to back his plan, they rejected what appeared to be a crazy scheme.

Columbus's Voyage

Ferdinand and Isabella of Spain, jealous of Portugal's successes in Africa, agreed to finance Columbus's risky voyage. They hoped profits would finance a new expedition to conquer Muslim-held Jerusalem. On August 3, 1492, in command of three ships—the *Pinta,* the *Niña,* and the *Santa Maria*—Columbus set sail from the Spanish port of Palos.

On October 12, the vessels found land approximately where Columbus thought Cipangu (Japan) was located (see Map 1.2). He and his men landed on an island in

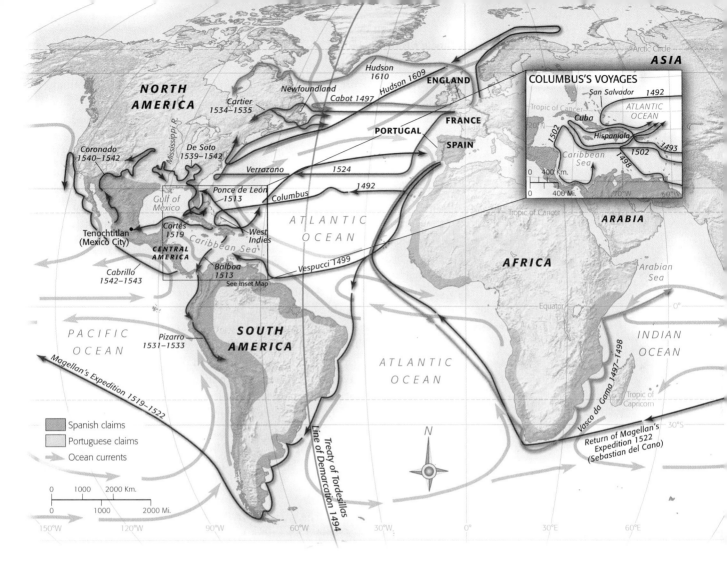

MAP 1.2

European Explorations in America

In the century following Columbus's voyages, European adventurers explored the coasts and parts of the interior of North and South America.

Source: Copyright © Cengage Learning

the Bahamas, which its inhabitants called Guanahaní but he renamed San Salvador. Later, he explored the islands now known as Cuba and Hispaniola, which their residents, the Taíno people, called Colba and Bohío. Because he thought he had reached the East Indies (the Spice Islands), Columbus referred to the inhabitants as "Indians." The Taínos thought the Europeans had come from the sky, and crowds gathered to meet and exchange gifts with Columbus.

Link to the logbook of Columbus's first voyage.

Columbus's Observations

Three themes predominate Columbus's log. First, he insistently asked the Taínos where he could find gold, pearls, and spices. They replied (via signs) that such products were on other islands or on the mainland. He came to mistrust such answers, noting, "They will tell me anything I want to hear."

Second, Columbus wrote about the strange and beautiful plants and animals. His interest was not only aesthetic. "There are many plants and trees here that could be worth a lot in Spain for use as dyes, spices, and medicines," he observed and planned to carry home "a sample of everything I can" for experts to examine.

Third, Columbus described the inhabitants, seizing some to take back to Spain. The Taínos were, he said, handsome, gentle, and friendly, though they told him of the fierce Caniba (today called Caribs) who lived on other islands, raided their villages, and ate some captives (hence today's word *cannibal*). Although Columbus distrusted the Caribs, he believed the Taínos to be likely converts to Catholicism as well as "good and skilled servants."

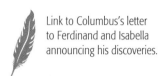

Link to Columbus's letter to Ferdinand and Isabella announcing his discoveries.

Thus, the records of the first encounter between Europeans and Americans revealed significant themes for centuries to come. Europeans wanted to extract profits by exploiting American resources, including plants, animals, and peoples alike, and like Columbus others later divided the native peoples into "good" (Taínos) and "bad" (Caribs). Columbus made three more voyages to the west, exploring most of the major Caribbean islands and sailing along the coasts of Central and South America. Until the day he died in 1506 at the age of fifty-five, he believed he had reached Asia. Even before his death, others knew better. Because the Florentine Amerigo Vespucci, who explored the South American coast in 1499, was the first to publish that a new continent had been discovered, Martin Waldseemüller in 1507 labeled the land "America." By then, Spain, Portugal, and Pope Alexander VI had signed the Treaty of Tordesillas (1494), confirming Portugal's dominance in Africa—and later Brazil—in exchange for Spanish preeminence in the rest of the Americas.

Norse: Also known as Vikings, they were a warrior culture from Scandinavia.

Vinland: The site of the first known attempt at European settlement in the Americas.

Norse and Other Northern Voyagers

About the year 1001, a **Norse** expedition under Leif Ericsson had sailed to North America across the Davis Strait, which separated their Greenland villages from Baffin Island (located northeast of Hudson Bay; see Map 1.1) by just 200 nautical miles, settling at a site they named **"Vinland."** Attacks by residents forced them out after a few years. In the 1960s, archaeologists determined that the Norse had established an outpost at what is now L'Anse aux Meadows, Newfoundland, but Vinland itself was probably farther south.

Some historians argue that during the fifteenth century Basque whalers and fishermen (from modern northern France and Spain) located rich fishing grounds off Newfoundland but kept the information secret. Fifteenth-century seafarers voyaged regularly between the European continent, England, Ireland, and Iceland. The mariners who explored the region that would become the United States and Canada built on their knowledge.

John Cabot: Italian explorer who established English claims to the New World

John Cabot's Explorations

The European generally credited with "discovering" North America is Zuan Cabboto, known today as **John Cabot**. More precisely, Cabot brought to Europe the first formal knowledge of the northern continental coastline and claimed the land for England. Like Columbus, Cabot was a master mariner from the Italian city-state of Genoa; the two men probably knew each other. Calculating that England—which traded with Asia only through intermediaries—would be eager to sponsor exploratory voyages, he gained financial backing from King Henry VII. He sailed from

In 1507, German mapmaker Martin Waldseemüller was the first person to designate the newly discovered southern continent as "America." He named the continent after Amerigo Vespucci, the Italian explorer who realized he had reached a "new world" rather than islands off the coast of Asia.

Bristol in late May 1497, reaching North America a month later. After exploring the coast of modern Newfoundland, Cabot rode the Westerlies back to England, arriving in fifteen days.

The voyages of Columbus, Cabot, and their successors linked the Eastern and Western Hemispheres. The Portuguese explorer Pedro Álvares Cabral reached Brazil in 1500; John Cabot's son Sebastian arrived in North America in 1507; France financed Giovanni da Verrazzano in 1524 and Jacques Cartier in 1534; and in 1609 and 1610, Henry Hudson explored the North American coast for the Dutch West India Company (see Map 1.2). All were searching for the legendary, nonexistent "Northwest Passage" through the Americas, an easy route to the riches of Asia. But, foreshadowing the future, Verrazzano observed that "the [American] countryside is, in fact, full of promise and deserves to be developed for itself."

Spanish Exploration and Conquest

What model of colonization did Spain establish that other nations would later attempt to follow?

Only Spain began colonization immediately. On his second voyage in 1493, Columbus brought to Hispaniola seventeen ships loaded with twelve hundred men, seeds, plants, livestock, chickens, and dogs—along with microbes, rats, and weeds. The settlement named Isabela (in the modern Dominican Republic) and its successors became the staging area for the Spanish invasion of America.

Cortés and Other Explorers

At first, Spanish explorers fanned out around the Caribbean basin. In 1513, Juan Ponce de León reached Florida, and Vasco Núñez de Balboa crossed the Isthmus

conquistadors: Spanish conquerors or adventurers in the Americas.

of Panama to the Pacific Ocean, followed by Pánfilo de Narváez and others who traced the coast of the Gulf of Mexico. In the 1530s and 1540s, **conquistadors** explored other regions claimed by Spain: Francisco Vásquez de Coronado journeyed through the southwestern portion of what is now the United States while Hernán de Soto explored the Southeast. Francisco Pizarro, who ventured into western South America, acquired the world's richest silver mines by conquering the Incas. But the most important conquistador was Hernán Cortés, who in 1521 seized the Aztec Empire.

Cortés landed a force on the Mexican mainland in 1519 to search for rumored wealthy cities. Local Mayas presented him with young enslaved women. One of them, Malinche (whom the Spaniards baptized as a Christian and renamed Doña Marina), became Cortés's translator, bore Cortés a son, Martín—one of the first *mestizos,* or mixed-blood children—and eventually married one of his officers.

Capture of Tenochtitlán

Traveling toward the Aztec capital, Cortés, with Malinche's help, recruited peoples whom the Aztecs had long subjugated. The Spaniards' strange beasts (horses, livestock) and noisy weapons (guns, cannon) awed their new allies. Yet the Spaniards, too, were awed. Years later, Bernal Díaz del Castillo recalled his first sight of Tenochtitlán: "We were amazed…on account of the great towers and cues [temples] and buildings rising from the water, and all built of masonry." Spaniards also brought smallpox to Tenochtitlán. The disease peaked in 1520, fatally weakening Tenochtitlán's defenders. Largely as a consequence, Tenochtitlán surrendered in 1521, and the Spaniards built Mexico City on its site. Cortes and his men seized a treasure of gold and silver. Thus, the Spanish monarchs controlled the richest, most extensive empire Europe had known since ancient Rome.

Spanish Colonization

Spain established the model of colonization based on three major elements that other countries would later imitate. First, the Crown sought tight control over the colonies, imposing a hierarchical government that allowed little autonomy to American jurisdictions. That included carefully vetting and limiting prospective emigrants and insisting that the colonies import all manufactured goods from Spain. Roman Catholic priests attempted to ensure colonists' conformity with orthodox religious views.

Second, men constituted most of the first colonists. Although some Spanish women later immigrated to America, the men took primarily Indian—and, later, African—women as wives or concubines, a development often encouraged by colonial administrators. They thereby began the racially mixed population that characterizes much of Latin America today.

Third, the colonies' wealth was based on the exploitation of the native population and slaves from Africa. Spaniards took over the autocratic rule once assumed by native leaders, who exacted labor and tribute from their subjects. Cortés established the **encomienda system**, which granted Indian villages to conquistadors in return for services, thus legalizing slavery in all but name.

encomienda **system:** Grants by the Spanish which awarded Indian labor to wealthy colonists.

In 1542, after criticism from colonial priest Bartolomé de las Casas, the monarch formulated new laws forbidding the conquerors from enslaving Indians yet allowing them to collect money and goods from tributary villages. That, combined with the declining Indian population, led the *encomenderos* to import Africans as their controlled labor force. They employed Indians and Africans primarily in gold and silver mines; on sugar plantations; and on horse, cattle, and sheep ranches. African slavery was more common on the larger Caribbean islands than on the mainland.

Many demoralized residents of Mesoamerica accepted the Christian religion brought to New Spain by Franciscan and Dominican friars—men who had joined religious orders bound by vows of poverty and celibacy. Spaniards leveled cities, constructing cathedrals and monasteries on the former sites of Aztec, Incan, and Mayan temples. Indians were exposed to European customs and religious rituals designed to assimilate Catholic and pagan beliefs. Friars juxtaposed the cult of the Virgin Mary with that of the corn goddess, and Indians melded aspects of their worldview with Christianity in a process called *syncretism*. Thousands of Indians embraced Catholicism, partly because it was the religion of their new rulers.

Gold, Silver, and Spain's Decline

The New World's gold and silver, initially a boon, ultimately brought about the decline of Spain as a major power. China gobbled up about half of the total output of New World silver mines. In the 1570s, the Spanish dispatched silver-laden galleons annually from Acapulco (on Mexico's west coast) to trade at their new settlement at Manila, in the Philippines, which netted them easy access to luxury Chinese goods, such as silk and Asian spices.

Such unprecedented wealth led to rapid inflation, which caused Spanish products to be overpriced in international markets and imported goods to become cheaper in Spain. The Spanish textile-manufacturing industry collapsed, as did many other businesses. The seemingly endless income from American colonies emboldened Spanish monarchs to spend lavishly on wars against the Dutch and the English. Late sixteenth- and early seventeenth-century monarchs repudiated the state debt, wreaking havoc on the nation's finances. When the South American gold and silver mines faltered in the mid-seventeenth century, Spain's economy crumbled, ending its international importance.

The Columbian Exchange

A mutual transfer of diseases, plants, and animals (called the **Columbian Exchange** by historian Alfred Crosby; see Map 1.3) resulted from the fifteenth and sixteenth century European voyages and from Spanish colonization. Many large mammals, such as cattle and horses, were native to the connected continents of Europe, Asia, and Africa, but not the Americas. The Americas' vegetable crops—particularly maize, beans, squash, cassava, and potatoes—were more nutritious and produced higher yields than those of Europe and Africa. In time, native peoples learned to raise and consume European livestock, and Europeans and Africans planted and ate American crops. The diets of all three peoples were enriched, helping the world's population to double over the next three hundred years. About three-fifths of all crops cultivated worldwide today were first grown in the Americas.

What were the results of contact between native populations and European settlers and explorers?

Columbian Exchange: The widespread exchange of animals, plants, germs, and peoples between Europe, Africa, and the Americas.

Smallpox and Other Diseases

Diseases carried from Europe and Africa, though, devastated the Americas. Indians fell victim to microbes that had long infested other continents, killing hundreds of thousands of Europeans but leaving survivors with some immunity. When Columbus landed on Hispaniola in 1492, approximately half a million people resided there. Fifty years later, there were fewer than two thousand native inhabitants.

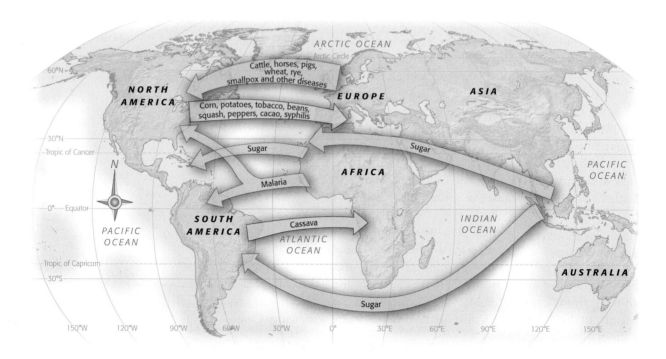

MAP 1.3

Major Items in the Columbian Exchange

As European adventurers traversed the world in the fifteenth and sixteenth centuries, they initiated the "Columbian Exchange" of plants, animals, and diseases. These events changed the lives of the peoples of the world forever, bringing new foods and new pestilence to both sides of the Atlantic.

Source: Copyright © Cengage Learning

Although measles, typhus, influenza, malaria, and other illnesses severely afflicted the native peoples, the greatest killer was smallpox. Historians estimate that over time, alien microorganisms could have reduced the precontact American population by as much as 90 percent. The epidemics recurred at twenty- to thirty-year intervals, appearing in tandem or in quick succession. Large numbers of deaths further strained native societies, rendering them more vulnerable to droughts, crop failures, or other challenges. A great epidemic, probably viral hepatitis, swept through coastal villages north of Cape Cod from 1616 to 1618, wiping out up to 90 percent of the inhabitants. Because of this dramatic depopulation, a few years later English colonists established settlements virtually unopposed.

The Americans, though, probably gave the Europeans syphilis, a virulent venereal disease. The first recorded European case occurred in Barcelona, Spain, in 1493, after Columbus's return from the Caribbean. Although less likely than smallpox to be fatal, syphilis was debilitating. Carried by soldiers, sailors, and prostitutes, it spread through Europe and Asia, reaching China by 1505.

Sugar, Horses, and Tobacco

The exchange of three commodities significantly altered Europe and the Americas. The European demand for sugar—a luxury foodstuff—led Columbus to take Canary Island sugar canes to Hispaniola in 1493. By the 1520s, Greater Antilles plantations worked by African slaves regularly shipped sugar to Spain. Half a century later,

Links to the World

Maize

Maize, to Mesoamericans, was a gift from Quetzalcoatl, the plumed serpent god. Cherokees told of an old woman whose blood produced the prized stalks after her grandson buried her body in a field. For the Abenakis, the crop began when a beautiful maiden ordered a youth to drag her by the hair through a burned-over field. The long hair turned into silk, the flower on corn stalks. Both tales' symbolic association of corn and women supports archaeologists' recent suggestion that—in eastern North America at least—female plant breeders were responsible for substantial improvements in the productivity of maize.

Sacred to the Indians who grew it, maize was a major dietary staple. They dried the kernels; ground into meal, maize was cooked as a mush or baked as flat cakes, the forerunners of modern tortillas. Although European invaders initially disdained maize, they soon learned it could be cultivated under many conditions—from sea level to twelve thousand feet, in abundant rainfall or in dry land. So Europeans, too, came to rely on corn, growing it in their American settlements and their homelands.

Maize cultivation spread to Asia and Africa. Today, China is second only to the United States in corn production, and corn is more widely grown in Africa than any other crop. Still, the United States produces 45 percent of the world's corn, and it is the nation's single largest crop.

More than half of American corn is consumed by livestock. Much of the rest is processed into syrup as a sweetener or into ethanol, a gasoline additive that reduces pollution and dependence on fossil fuels. Of the ten thousand products in a modern American grocery store, about one-fourth rely on corn. Today, this crop provides one-fifth of all the calories consumed by the earth's peoples. The gift of Quetzalcoatl has linked the globe.

The earliest known European drawing of maize, the American plant that was to have such an extraordinary impact on the entire world.

The LuEsther T. Mertz Library, NYBG/Art Resource, NY

21

Portugal's Brazil colony (founded 1532) produced sugar for the European market on a larger scale, and after 1640, sugar cultivation became the crucial component of English and French colonization in the Caribbean.

Through trade and theft, horses—which Columbus brought to America in 1493—spread among the peoples of the Great Plains by 1750. Lakotas, Comanches, and Crows, among others, used horses for transportation and hunting, calculated their wealth in number of horses owned, and waged war on horseback. After acquiring horses, their mode of subsistence shifted from hunting combined with gathering and agriculture, to almost entirely hunting buffalo.

In America, Europeans encountered tobacco, which at first they believed was medicinal. Smoking and chewing the "Indian weed" became a European fad after it was planted in Turkey in the sixteenth century. Despite the efforts of King James I of England, who in 1604 pronounced smoking "hatefull to the Nose, harmfull to the brain, [and] dangerous to the Lungs," tobacco's popularity climbed.

Europeans in North America

What were the reasons behind the failure of England's, Portugal's, and France's initial attempts at colonization?

Europeans were initially more interested in exploiting North America's natural resources than in establishing colonies. John Cabot reported that fish were plentiful near Newfoundland, so the French, Spanish, Basques, and Portuguese rushed to take advantage of abundant codfish. In the early 1570s, the English joined the Newfoundland fishery, selling salt cod to the Spanish in exchange for valuable Asian goods. The English became dominant in the region, which by century's end was the focal point of valuable European commerce.

Trade Among Indians and Europeans

Fishermen quickly realized they could increase profits by exchanging cloth and metal goods, such as pots and knives, for native trappers' beaver pelts, used to make fashionable hats in Europe. Initially, Europeans traded from ships along the coast, but later male adventurers set up outposts on the mainland.

Indians similarly desired European goods that could make their lives easier and establish their tribal superiority. Some bands concentrated completely on trapping for the European market and abandoned their traditional economies and became partially dependent on others for food. The intensive peltry trade also had serious ecological consequences. In some regions, beavers were wiped out. The disappearance of their dams led to soil erosion, which later increased when European settlers cleared forests for farmland.

Contest Between Spain and England

The English watched enviously as Spain was enriched by its American possessions. In the mid-sixteenth century, English "sea dogs" like John Hawkins and Sir Francis Drake raided Spanish treasure fleets from the Caribbean, helping to foment a war that in 1588 culminated in the defeat of the Spanish Armada off the English coast. English leaders started to consider planting colonies in the Western Hemisphere, thereby gaining better access to trade goods while preventing Spain from dominating the Americas.

Encouraging the queen and her courtiers in that aim was Richard Hakluyt, a clergyman who was fascinated by tales of exploratory voyages. He published English translations of numerous accounts of discoveries, insisting on England's preeminent claim to North America. In *Divers Voyages* (1582) and especially *Principall Navigations* (1589), he promoted the benefits of English colonization.

The first English colonial planners hoped to reproduce Spanish successes by dispatching to America men who would exploit the native peoples for their nation's benefit. A group that included Sir Walter Raleigh promoted a scheme to establish outposts for trade with the Indians and as bases for attacks on New Spain. Pleased, Queen Elizabeth I authorized Raleigh to colonize North America.

Roanoke

After two preliminary expeditions, in 1587 Raleigh sent 117 colonists to the territory he named Virginia, after Elizabeth, the "Virgin Queen." They established a settlement on Roanoke Island, in what is now North Carolina, but in 1590 a resupply ship found the colonists had vanished, leaving only the word *Croatoan* (the name of a nearby island) carved on a tree. Recent tree-ring studies have shown that the North Carolina coast experienced a severe drought between 1587 and 1589 that may have led colonists to abandon Roanoke.

Thus, England's first attempt to plant a permanent settlement on the North American coast failed, as had Portugal in Cape Breton Island (early 1520s), Spain in modern Georgia (mid-1520s), and France in South Carolina and northern Florida (1560s). All three enterprises collapsed because of the hostility of neighboring peoples and colonists' inability to be self-sustaining in foodstuffs.

Harriot's *Briefe and True Report*

Such failures are explained in Thomas Harriot's *A Briefe and True Report of the New Found Land of Virginia*, published in 1588. Harriot, a noted scientist sailing with the second voyage to Roanoke, revealed that, although the explorers depended on nearby villagers for food, they antagonized them by killing some of them for what Harriot admitted were unjustifiable reasons.

Harriot advised later colonizers to treat native peoples more humanely. But his book's description of America's economic potential illustrated why that advice would rarely be followed. Harriot stressed three points: the availability of familiar

A cheife Heroroans wyfe of Pomeoc. and her daughter of the age of. 8. or. 10. yeares.

A watercolor by John White, an artist with Raleigh's second preliminary expedition (and who later was governor of the ill-fated 1587 colony). He identified his subjects as the wife and daughter of the chief of Pomeioc, a village near Roanoke. Note the woman's elaborate tattoos and the fact that the daughter carries an Elizabethan doll, obviously given to her by one of the Englishmen.

Kennewick Man/ Ancient One

On July 28, 1996, Will Thomas, a college student wading in the Columbia River near Kennewick, Washington, felt a skull underfoot. Shocked, Thomas initially believed he had found a recent murder victim. Soon the skull was determined to be about 9200 years old. During the next decade, the skeleton dubbed "Kennewick Man" (by the press) or "Ancient One" (by local Indian tribes) was featured on television news and in magazines.

The oldest nearly complete skeleton found in the United States, the remains became the subject of a major federal court case. The issue was the interpretation of the Native American Graves Protection and Repatriation Act (NAGPRA), adopted by Congress in 1990 to prevent the desecration of Indian gravesites and to provide for the return of bones and sacred objects to native peoples. It defined the term *Native American* as "of, or relating to, a tribe, people, or culture that is indigenous to the United States." Led by the Umatillas, area tribes prepared to reclaim and rebury the remains. But eight anthropologists filed suit in federal court, contending that bones of such antiquity were unlikely to be linked to modern tribes and requesting access to them for scientific study.

Although the U.S. government supported the tribes' claims, in late August 2002 a federal judge ruled in favor of the anthropologists, a decision upheld on appeal two years later. He declared that the Interior Department had erred in concluding that all pre-1492 remains found in the United States should automatically be considered Native American. The Umatillas protested, contending that he clearly contradicted Congress's intent in enacting NAGPRA. In June 2006, Umatilla leaders visited the bones at a Seattle museum to honor and pray for them.

The debate over the skeleton reveals one facet of the continuing legacy of the often-contentious relationship between the nation's indigenous inhabitants and later immigrants.

Link to Harriot's text, illustrated by John White.

European commodities such as grapes, iron, copper, and fur-bearing animals; the potential profitability of exotic American products, such as maize and tobacco; and the relative ease of manipulating the native population. Harriot's *Briefe and True Report* depicted a bountiful land full of profitable opportunities. The people there would, he thought, "in a short time be brought to civilitie" through conversion to Christianity, admiration for European superiority, or conquest—if they did not die from disease. But European dominance of North America was never fully achieved as Harriot and others intended.

Summary

Initial contact among Europeans, Africans, and Americans that ended near the close of the sixteenth century, began approximately 250 years earlier when Portuguese sailors explored the Mediterranean Atlantic and the West African coast. Those seamen established commercial ties that brought African slaves first to Iberia and then to the islands Europeans conquered and settled. The Mediterranean Atlantic and its island sugar plantations nurtured the mariners. Except for the Spanish, early explorers regarded the Americas primarily as a barrier keeping them from an oceanic route to the riches of China and the Moluccas. European fishermen were the first to realize that the northern coasts had valuable products of fish and furs.

The Aztecs experienced hunger after Cortés's invasion, and their great temples were destroyed as Spaniards used their stones (and Indian laborers) to construct cathedrals. The conquerors employed, first Americans and later enslaved Africans to till the fields, mine the precious metals, and herd the livestock that generated immense profits.

The initial impact of Europeans on the Americas proved devastating in just decades. Europeans' diseases killed millions, and their livestock, along with other imported animals and plants, irrevocably modified the American environment. Europe, too, was changed: American foodstuffs like corn and potatoes improved nutrition, and American gold and silver first enriched, then ruined, the Spanish economy.

By the end of the sixteenth century, fewer people resided in North America than had lived there before Columbus's arrival. The Indians, Africans, and Europeans there inhabited a new world that combined foods, religions, economies, ways of life, and political systems that had developed separately for millennia. Understandably, conflict permeated that process.

Chapter Review

American Societies

What led to the development of major North American civilizations in the centuries before Europeans arrived?

Agricultural success facilitated the rise of North American civilizations in the era before Europeans arrived. After the Ice Age ended and the prevalence of large mammals decreased, many native peoples in what is now central Mexico about 9000 years ago shifted from hunting to cultivating food crops for survival, including maize (corn), squash, beans, avocados, and peppers. As agricultural methods improved, vegetables became a reliable and nutritious food source, and native people established more permanent settlements. Early Americans began developing trade, accumulating wealth, creating elaborate cultural ceremonies and rituals, and building urban centers. But food supply was so keenly linked to a civilization's success that the first large city-states of Mesoamerica and Mississippian culture ultimately collapsed when food sources became scarce.

North America in 1492

What were the gender dimensions of labor in native cultures?

Like Europeans, Native American societies assigned various tasks and responsibilities to members along gender lines. Native societies that were predominantly hunting assigned women to making food and clothing and carrying the family's possessions whenever they moved. Agricultural peoples had different patterns of the gendered division of labor; some, like the Pueblos, defined farming as men's work, while others, like the Algonquian, Iroquoian, and Muskogean, gave women most agricultural chores, and men hunted and cleared the land. Women just about everywhere raised children, gathered wild foods, and prepared all of what people ate. Agricultural families were defined matrilineally, through the female line of descent, and women assumed more leadership roles than in nomadic hunter peoples. They rarely became chiefs, but older women chose chiefs and could start or stop wars.

African Societies

What were the chief characteristics of West African societies in the fifteenth century?

People in West Africa made their living fishing, cattle herding, or farming, depending on where they lived. Those in Upper Guinea fished and grew rice; those in Lower Guinea farmed. Upper Guinea was also the region's trade link to Europe and Asia. Islamic culture influenced life in Upper Guinea, while people in the lower region practiced more traditional religions. Like other cultures around the world, West Africans designated tasks according to gender, although their roles were seen as complementary. Both sexes farmed; men hunted and managed livestock and fished, while women cared for children, prepared the food, and managed trade networks. In Lower Guinea, male political and religious leaders ruled men, while women ruled women. Polygyny was common throughout West Africa. So was slavery. In West Africa, a person could be enslaved for committing a crime, to repay debts, or as an enemy's captive, but slave status did not automatically transfer to the next generation, and some slaves could engage in trade and keep some of the profits or rise to important military or political positions.

European Societies

What were the motives behind fifteenth- and sixteenth-century European explorations?

The driving force behind early European explorations was the quest for a transoceanic trade route—the Northwest Passage—that would provide direct access to desirable African and Asian goods such as silks, dyes, jewels, sugar, gold, and spices. If such a route existed, it would allow northern Europeans to bypass the Muslim and Venetian merchants who served as middle men for these items. Rulers also believed that the more they controlled access to these much-desired products, the better their nation's standing would be relative to other countries. Another, secondary motivation was to spread Christianity and convert those they considered to be heathen peoples.

Early European Explorations

What sailing innovation ultimately facilitated the widespread exploration of the Atlantic and Pacific?

The new technique of "sailing around the wind" made travel faster and less arduous for explorers, which ultimately made them increasingly inclined to take on such expeditions. While sailors would travel with the wind in one direction, returning home had previously meant rowing against the wind or waiting for the wind to change on their journeys home, so return trips were difficult and took weeks longer. But sailing around the wind sped up the journey; when mariners met with a difficult wind, they would now literally sail around it until they could find a wind that would easily and quickly carry them on their way. Consequently, more and more mariners set out to explore the Atlantic and Pacific.

Voyages of Columbus, Cabot, and Their Successors

What three themes in Columbus's log about his explorations would come to mark much of the future settlement of Europeans in the Americas?

First, Columbus's log notes his quest for gold and other riches and his mixed attitudes toward the native peoples he encountered. Second, he wrote that the region's resources (plants, animals, and people) could be exploited to generate profits for his host country of Spain. In particular, he described the vast potential value of the dyes, spices, and medicines that could be made from plants found in the Americas. Third, Columbus wrote that the inhabitants could be easily converted to Catholicism and remade into servants. His and other explorers' discoveries inspired further exploration by European nations, though for most, colonization would lag for generations.

Spanish Exploration and Conquest

What model of colonization did Spain establish that other nations would later attempt to follow?

Spain developed a model of colonization in the Americas based on three key concepts. First, Spain's monarchy maintained firm control over its colonies with virtually no autonomy granted to American colonies. Second, men made up the majority of early colonists, taking first Indian, and later African, women as wives or concubines. Third, the development of the colonies and the exploitation of their resources was based on exploiting native people and African slaves as labor.

The Columbian Exchange

What were the results of contact between native populations and European settlers and explorers?

Native Americans and Europeans exchanged diseases, plants, and animals when they came into contact in North and South America in the fifteenth and sixteenth centuries. Native American vegetable crops were more nutritious than those in Europe and Africa, while Europeans brought livestock that helped enrich Indians' diets, too. The Spanish also brought horses to their American territories, which aided the shift in native society of the Great Plains from hunting combined with some farming and gathering, to almost exclusively hunting buffalo as their main form of subsistence. Europeans brought many diseases from typhus to malaria to hepatitis, all of which devastated tribal populations, but none as much as smallpox. Europeans, meanwhile, acquired syphilis from Native Americans, which was debilitating, but not usually fatal.

Europeans in North America

 What were the reasons behind the failure of England's, Portugal's, and France's initial attempts at colonization?

In a nutshell, all three failed because colonists were unable to be self-sustaining and at the same time, did little to diminish hostilities between them and native peoples. In fact, while many colonists relied on Indians for food, they also antagonized them by, as one British scientist wrote, unjustly killing some. Ironically, the solution this scientist, Thomas Harriot, proposed was on the one hand to treat native people with greater humanity, but on the other hand, to take advantage of the fact that they are easily manipulated toward whatever ends Europeans sought.

Suggestions for Further Reading

David Abulafia, *The Discovery of Mankind: Atlantic Encounters in the Age of Columbus* (2008)

Alfred W. Crosby, *The Columbian Exchange: Biological and Cultural Consequences of 1492* (1972)

John H. Elliott, *Empires of the Atlantic World: Britain and Spain in America, 1492–1830* (2006)

Alvin Josephy, Jr., ed., *America in 1492* (1992)

Peter C. Mancall, *Hakluyt's Promise: An Elizabethan's Obsession for an English America* (2007)

Charles C. Mann, *1491: New Revelations of the Americas Before Columbus* (2005)

D. W. Meinig, *Atlantic America, 1492–1800* (1986)

Samuel Eliot Morison, *The European Discovery of America: The Southern Voyages*, A.D. 1492–1616 (1974); *The Northern Voyages*, A.D. 1500–1600 (1971)

John K. Thornton, *Africa and Africans in the Making of the Atlantic World, 1400–1680* (1992)

Go to the CourseMate website for primary source links, study tools, and review materials for this chapter. www.cengagebrain.com

Europeans Colonize North America

1600–1650

2

C aptain William Rudyerd seemed like the sort of man Puritan colonists in the Americas would prize, so when his older brother urged the planners of the new settlement to appoint him muster master general, they agreed. Rudyerd followed the dissenting English faith, and as a soldier, he vigorously trained the settlers to defend themselves from attack. He also vigorously defended his status, wreaking havoc in the fragile community. He beat to death a servant suffering from scurvy (whom he mistook as lazy) and quarreled with settlers, whom he believed failed to show him the respect due to a gentleman of noble birth.

One of Rudyerd's antagonists was the Reverend Lewis Morgan, with whom the captain argued about religious books and church services. The disagreements escalated into insults. "Your foul mouthed answer deserves rather sharp retribution than any equal respect from a gentleman," the captain once haughtily told the clergyman.

Similar conflicts occurred throughout the Anglo-American settlements, as gentlemen accustomed to unquestioning deference learned that in the colonies, their social standing could be challenged. But Rudyerd and Morgan's disputes were especially dangerous because they lived on Providence Island, an isolated Puritan outpost off the coast of modern Nicaragua.

Providence Island, founded by Puritans in 1630—the same year as Massachusetts Bay—sought to establish an English beach-head in the tropics as an entrée to colonizing Central America. Yet its perilous location amid Spanish settlements, its failure to establish a local economy, and, ultimately, its desperate attempts to stay afloat financially by serving as a base for English priva-teers caused its downfall. That decision angered the Spaniards, who attacked in 1635 and 1640. In May 1641, a Spanish fleet of seven ships carrying two thousand soldiers and sailors captured the island. The survivors scattered to other Caribbean settle-ments, to English mainland colonies, or back to England.

Spain no longer predominated in the Americas. By the 1640s, France, the Netherlands, and England had colonies in

North America. Like Spanish outposts, French and Dutch colonies were settled largely by European men who interacted with indigenous peoples, using their labor or seeking to convert them to Christianity. As with conquistadors, French and Dutch merchants (on the mainland) and planters (in the Caribbean) hoped to make a quick profit and return home. The English were also interested in profiting from North America, but along different lines.

Unlike other Europeans, most English settlers came to stay. In the area that became New England, they arrived in family groups and re-created the European agricultural economy and family life to an extent impossible in colonies where single men predominated. English colonies in the Chesapeake and Caribbean islands were based on large-scale agricultural production, relying on servants and slaves for labor.

Setters prospered only after adapting to the environment, something the Providence Islanders never achieved. The first permanent English colonies survived because Indians helped them learn to grow such unfamiliar American crops as maize and squash. They also developed trading relationships with native peoples and other European colonies. Needing field laborers, they first used English indentured servants, then African slaves. Thus, the early history of what became the United States and the English Caribbean is best understood as a series of complex interactions among European, African, and American peoples and environments.

As you read this chapter, keep the following questions in mind:

* Why did different groups of Europeans choose to migrate to the Americas?

* How did different native peoples react to their presence?

* In what ways did the English colonies in the Chesapeake and New England differ, and in what ways were they alike?

Chronology

1558	Elizabeth I becomes queen
1565	Founding of St. Augustine (Florida), oldest permanent European settlement in present-day United States
1598	Oñate conquers Pueblos in New Mexico for Spain
1603	James I becomes king
1607	Jamestown founded, first permanent English settlement in North America
1608	Quebec founded by the French
1610	Founding of Santa Fe, New Mexico
1614	Fort Orange (Albany) founded by the Dutch
1619	Virginia House of Burgesses established, first representative assembly in the English colonies
1620	Plymouth colony founded, first permanent English settlement in New England
1622	Powhatan Confederacy attacks Virginia

1624	Dutch settle on Manhattan Island (New Amsterdam) English colonize St. Kitts, first island in Lesser Antilles settled by Europeans James I revokes Virginia Company's charter
1625	Charles I becomes king
1630	Massachusetts Bay colony founded
1634	Maryland founded
1636	Williams expelled from Massachusetts Bay, founds Providence, Rhode Island Connecticut founded
1637	Pequot War in New England
1638	Hutchinson expelled from Massachusetts Bay, goes to Rhode Island
1642	Montreal founded by the French
1646	Treaty ends hostilities between Virginia and Powhatan Confederacy

Spanish, French, and Dutch North America

How did the Jesuits' treatment of
Native Americans differ from that
of explorers and other settlers?

Spaniards established the first permanent European settlement within the modern United States, but others had tried previously. Twice in the 1560s, Huguenots (French Protestants) escaping persecution planted colonies on the south Atlantic coast. A passing ship rescued the starving survivors of the first, located in present-day South Carolina. The second, near modern Jacksonville, Florida, was destroyed in 1565 by a Spanish expedition commanded by Pedro Menéndez de Avilés, who sought Spanish domination of the strategically important region. Menéndez set up a small fortified outpost named St. Augustine—now the oldest continuously inhabited European settlement in the United States.

The local Guale and Timucua nations initially allied themselves with the powerful newcomers and welcomed Franciscan friars. The relationship ruptured quickly as natives resisted Spanish authority. Still, the Franciscans offered the Indians spiritual solace for the diseases and troubles besetting them after the Europeans' invasion. Eventually, they gained numerous converts across Florida and the islands along the Atlantic coast.

New Mexico

In 1598, roughly thirty years after the founding of St. Augustine, Juan de Oñate, a Mexican-born adventurer whose wife descended from Cortés and Moctezuma, led about five hundred soldiers and settlers to New Mexico seeking riches. The Pueblo peoples greeted them cordially. But when the Spaniards used torture, murder, and rape to extort food and clothing from the villagers, the residents of Acoma killed several soldiers, including Oñate's nephew. The invaders responded ferociously, killing more than eight hundred people and capturing the remainder. All the captives above age twelve were enslaved for twenty years, and men older than twenty-five had one foot amputated. Horrified, other Pueblo villages surrendered.

Oñate's bloody victory proved illusory. New Mexico held little wealth and was too far from the Pacific coast to help protect Spanish sea-lanes. Many Spaniards returned to Mexico, and officials considered abandoning the isolated colony, which lay 800 miles north of the nearest Spanish settlement. Instead, they maintained a small military outpost and a few Christian missions, with the capital at Santa Fe (founded 1610) (see Map 4.1). As in southern regions, Spanish leaders were granted *encomiendas* guaranteeing them control over Pueblo villagers' labor. But in the absence of mines or fertile agricultural lands, such grants yielded small profit.

Quebec and Montreal

On the Atlantic coast, the French focused on the area that Jacques Cartier had explored in the 1530s. They tried to establish permanent bases along the Canadian coast but failed until 1605, when they founded Port Royal. In 1608, Samuel de Champlain set up a trading post at an interior site that he renamed Quebec (the Iroquois called it Stadacona). It was the most defensible spot in the St. Lawrence River valley and controlled access to the continent's heartland. In 1642, the French established a second post, Montreal, at the falls of the St. Lawrence.

Prior to these settlements, fishermen were the major transporters of North American beaver pelts to France, but the new posts quickly took over (see Table 2.1). Only a few Europeans resided in New France; most were men; some married Indian women. The colony's leaders gave land grants along the river to wealthy seigneurs (nobles), who imported tenants to work their farms. A few Frenchmen brought their

Acoma Pueblo

Today, as in the late sixteenth century when it was besieged and eventually captured by the Spanish conquistador Juan de Oñate, the Acoma Pueblo sits high atop an isolated mesa. Long before the Spaniards arrived in modern New Mexico, the location was selected because it was easily defensible; some structures that date back to the eleventh century are still standing in the middle of the village. Building on a mesa 365 feet high was safer than living on the plains below, but it caused other problems—most notably, with the water supply. To this day there is no source of water in the village. Acoma's residents had to carry water up a steep set of stairs cut into the mesa's side (today there is an almost equally steep road). The women of Acoma were and are accomplished potters. Some pots, like the one shown here, were designed with a low center of gravity. How would that design help women to reach the top of the mesa with much needed water? How would they carry such pots?

© Kevin Fleming/CORBIS

Field Museum of Natural History FMNH Neg # A109998c

Acoma Pueblo today. The village is now used primarily for ritual purposes; few people reside there permanently because all water must be trucked in.

A pot designed for carrying water to the top of the mesa.

TABLE 2.1   The Founding of Permanent European Colonies in North America, 1565–1640

Colony	Founder(s)	Date	Basis of Economy
Florida	Pedro Menéndez de Avilés	1565	Farming
New Mexico	Juan de Oñate	1598	Livestock
Virginia	Virginia Co.	1607	Tobacco
New France	France	1608	Fur trading
New Netherland	Dutch West India Co.	1614	Fur trading
Plymouth	Separatists	1620	Farming, fishing
Maine	Sir Ferdinando Gorges	1622	Fishing
St. Kitts, Barbados, et al.	European immigrants	1624	Sugar
Massachusetts Bay	Massachusetts Bay Co.	1630	Farming, fishing, fur trading
Maryland	Cecilius Calvert	1634	Tobacco
Rhode Island	Roger Williams	1636	Farming
Connecticut	Thomas Hooker	1636	Farming, fur trading
New Haven	Massachusetts migrants	1638	Farming
New Hampshire	Massachusetts migrants	1638	Farming, fishing

wives and took up agriculture; still, twenty-five years after Quebec's founding, there were just sixty-four resident families, along with traders and soldiers. Northern New France never grew much beyond the river valley between Quebec and Montreal (see Map 2.1). Thus, it differed from New Spain, characterized by scattered cities and direct supervision of Indian laborers.

Jesuit Missions in New France

French missionaries of the Society of Jesus (Jesuits), a Roman Catholic order dedicated to converting nonbelievers to Christianity, first arrived in Quebec in 1625. The Jesuits, whom the Indians called Black Robes, tried to persuade indigenous peoples to live near French settlements and adopt European agricultural methods. Failing that, they tried to introduce Catholicism without insisting that Indians fundamentally alter their traditions. The Black Robes learned Indian languages and traveled to remote regions, where they lived among hundreds of potential converts.

Link to excerpts about Indian and Jesuit relations.

Jesuits sought to gain the confidence of influential men and to undermine the authority of village shamans, the traditional religious leaders. Immune to smallpox (having survived it already), they explained epidemics as God's punishment for sin. It helped that shamans' traditional remedies proved ineffective against the new pestilence. Jesuits predicted eclipses and amazed the villagers by communicating with each other over long distances through marks on paper (letters). The Indians' desire to harness the power of literacy made them receptive to the missionaries' spiritual message.

Over time, the Jesuits gained thousands of converts. Catholicism offered women the inspiring role model of the Virgin Mary, personified in Montreal and Quebec by communities of nuns who taught and ministered to Indian women and children. Many converts altered native customs allowing premarital sexual relationships

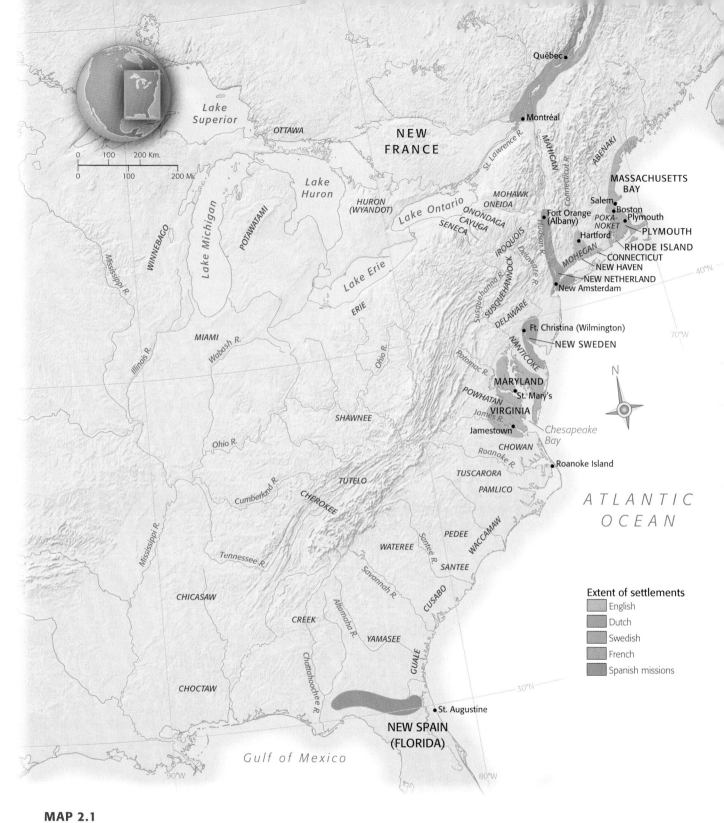

Lake Superior

OTTAWA

NEW FRANCE

Québec

Montréal

St. Lawrence R.

Lake Huron

Lake Michigan

POTAWATAMI

WINNEBAGO

HURON
(WYANDOT)

Lake Ontario

MOHAWK
ONEIDA
ONONDAGA
CAYUGA
SENECA

IROQUOIS

Lake Erie

ERIE

MIAMI

Wabash R.

Illinois R.

Mississippi R.

Ohio R.

Ohio R.

SHAWNEE

TUTELO

CHEROKEE

Cumberland R.

Tennessee R.

CHICASAW

CREEK

Altamaha R.

YAMASEE

CHOCTAW

Chattahoochee R.

GUALE

Mississippi R.

MAHICAN

ABENAKI

Connecticut R.

Hudson R.

MASSACHUSETTS
BAY

Salem
Boston
Fort Orange
(Albany)   POKA-   Plymouth
NOKET
Hartford   PLYMOUTH
MOHEGAN   RHODE ISLAND
CONNECTICUT
NEW HAVEN
NEW NETHERLAND
New Amsterdam

40°N

70°W

Delaware R.

Susquehanna R.

Susquehanna R.

DELAWARE

NANTICOKE

Ft. Christina (Wilmington)
NEW SWEDEN

Potomac R.

MARYLAND
St. Mary's

POWHATAN

VIRGINIA
James R.
Jamestown

Chesapeake
Bay

CHOWAN

Roanoke R.

Roanoke Island

TUSCARORA

PAMLICO

N

ATLANTIC
OCEAN

PEDEE

WATEREE

Santee R.

WACCAMAW

SANTEE

CUSABO

Savannah R.

Extent of settlements

English
Dutch
Swedish
French
Spanish missions

30°N

St. Augustine

NEW SPAIN
(FLORIDA)

Gulf of Mexico

90°W

80°W

0   100   200 Km.
0   100   200 Mi.

MAP 2.1

European Settlements and Indian Tribes in Eastern North America, 1650

The few European settlements established in the East before 1650 were widely scattered, hugging the shores of the Atlantic Ocean and the banks of its major rivers. By contrast, America's native inhabitants controlled the vast interior expanse of the continent, and Spaniards had begun to move into the West.

Source: Copyright © Cengage Learning

33

and easy divorce because Catholic doctrine prohibited both. Yet they resisted strict European child-rearing methods. Jesuits recognized that aspects of native culture could be compatible with Christianity. Their conversion efforts were further aided by their lack of interest in labor tribute or land.

New Netherland

New Netherland: Dutch colony in America.

New Amsterdam: Dutch colony that would become New York.

Jesuit missionaries faced little competition from other Europeans, but not so for French fur traders. In 1614, five years after Henry Hudson explored the river that now bears his name, his sponsor, the Dutch West India Company, established an outpost (Fort Orange) at present-day Albany, New York. The Dutch sought beaver pelts, and their presence so close to Quebec threatened French regional domination. The Netherlands, at the time the world's dominant commercial power, sought trade rather than colonization. Thus, **New Netherland** remained small. The colony's southern anchor was **New Amsterdam**, founded in 1624 on Manhattan Island.

New Netherland was a small outpost of the Dutch West India Company's vast commercial empire extending to Africa, Brazil, the Caribbean, and modern-day Indonesia. Autocratic directors-general ruled the colony. Few migrants arrived despite an offer in 1629 of large land grants, or patroonships, to anyone bringing fifty settlers to the province. (Only one such tract—Rensselaerswyck, near Albany—was ever developed.) As late as the mid-1660s, New Netherland had only about five thousand inhabitants. Some were Swedes and Finns in the former colony of New Sweden (founded in 1638 on the Delaware River; see Map 2.1), which the Dutch seized in 1655.

Indian allies of New France and New Netherland clashed partly because of fur-trade rivalries. In the 1640s, the Iroquois, who traded chiefly with the Dutch and lived in modern upstate New York, warred with the Hurons, who traded primarily with the French and lived in present-day Ontario. The Iroquois wanted to become the major peltry supplier to Europeans and protect their hunting territories. With guns from the Dutch, they virtually exterminated the Hurons, whose population was already decimated by a smallpox epidemic. The Iroquois thus established themselves as a major force in the region.

The Caribbean

What made the Caribbean islands initially desirable for colonization?

In the first half of the seventeenth century, the Spanish concentrated on colonizating the Greater Antilles—Cuba, Hispaniola, Jamaica, and Puerto Rico. They ignored smaller islands, partly because of resistance by their Carib inhabitants, partly because the mainland offered greater wealth for less effort. But the tiny islands attracted other European powers as bases from which to attack Spanish vessels loaded with American gold and silver and as sources of valuable tropical products such as dyes and fruits.

Warfare and Hurricanes

England was the first northern European nation to establish a permanent foothold in the smaller Caribbean islands (the Lesser Antilles), settling on St. Christopher (St. Kitts) in 1624, then other islands, such as Barbados (1627) and Providence (1630). France colonized Guadeloupe and Martinique by defeating the Caribs, whereas the Dutch easily gained control of St. Eustatius (strategically located near St. Christopher). Along with indigenous inhabitants, Europeans worried about conflicts with Spaniards and each other. Like Providence Island, many colonies changed hands during the seventeenth century. For example, the English drove the Spanish out of Jamaica in 1655, and the French soon assumed half of Hispaniola, creating St. Domingue (modern Haiti).

Great windstorms called *hurakán* by the Taíno (hurricanes in English) also posed a threat. Almost annually in late summer, one or two islands suffered significant hurricane damage. Survivors expressed awe at the destructive storms, which repeatedly forced them to rebuild and replant.

Sugar Cultivation

Sugar was the primary reason Europeans wanted these imperiled islands. Europeans loved sugar with its sweet taste and quick energy boost. Sugar entered Europe at approximately the same time as coffee and tea—the stimulating, addictive, and bitter Asian drinks improved by sweetening.

After experimenting with tobacco, cotton, and indigo, English residents of Barbados discovered in the 1640s that the island's soil and climate were ideal for sugar cane. At the time, sugar came primarily from the Madeiras, the Canaries, São Tomé, and Brazil. Barbadians initially copied the Brazilians' machinery and small-scale production methods, which used servants and slaves. By the mid-1650s, substantial planters increased the size of their landholdings, built sugar mills, and purchased more laborers—first English and Irish servants, then African slaves.

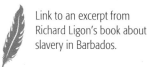

Link to an excerpt from Richard Ligon's book about slavery in Barbados.

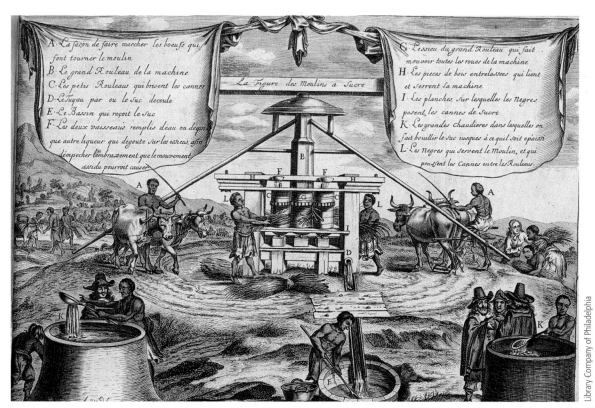

In the 1660s, a French book illustrated the various phases of sugar processing for curious European readers. Teams of oxen (A) turned the mill, the rollers of which crushed the canes (C), producing the sap (D), which was collected in a vat (E), then boiled down into molasses (K). African slaves, with minimal supervision by a few Europeans (foreground), managed all phases of the process.

Sugar remained the most valuable American commodity for more than a century. In the 1700s, sugar grown by slaves in British Jamaica and French St. Domingue dominated the world market. Yet the future economic importance of the Europeans' American colonies lay on the mainland.

English Interest in Colonization

What two developments prompted England to consider North American colonization in the early seventeenth century?

After Raleigh's Roanoke colony failed, two decades passed before the English attempted to settle North America again. When they tried in 1606, they were successful using a model unlike those of other European powers. England sent large numbers of men and women to establish agriculturally based colonies on the mainland. Two major developments prompted approximately 200,000 English people to move to North America in the seventeenth century.

Social and Economic Change

The first was dramatic social and economic change. In the 150 years after 1530, largely due to importation of nutritious American crops, England's population doubled. More people competed for food, clothing, and other goods; this led to inflation. Wages also fell as the number of workers increased. Some English people—especially those with sizable landholdings that could produce food and clothing fibers for the growing population—substantially profited. Others, particularly landless laborers and those with small landholdings, fell into poverty. When landowners raised rents, seized lands that peasants had long used in common (enclosure), or combined small holdings into large units, they forced tenants out. Consequently, the population of the cities swelled. London more than tripled in size to 375,000 by 1650.

Homeless people filled the streets. Fearing overcrowding, officials concluded that colonies established in North America could siphon off England's "surplus population." Similarly, many English people hoped they could improve their circumstances by migrating to a land-rich, apparently empty continent and its islands. Emigration proved attractive to younger sons of gentlemen as William Rudyerd, who were excluded from inheriting land by wealthy families' practice of primogeniture, which reserved all real estate for the eldest son.

English Reformation

The sixteenth century also witnessed a religious transformation that eventually led many English dissenters to leave. In 1533, Henry VIII, wanting a male heir and infatuated with Anne Boleyn, asked the pope to annul his twenty-year marriage to Spanish-born queen Catherine of Aragón, despite the birth of a daughter. When the pope refused, Henry founded the Church of England and—with Parliament's concurrence—proclaimed himself its head. Initially, the reformed Church of England differed little from Catholicism. Under Henry's daughter Elizabeth I (child of his later marriage to Anne Boleyn), though, new currents of religious belief dramatically affected the established church, so termed because it had the official imprimatur of the government and was supported by tax revenues.

Protestant Reformation: Split of reformers from Roman Catholic church; triggered by Martin Luther.

John Calvin: Early Protestant theologian who believed in "predestination."

These currents constituted the **Protestant Reformation**, led by Martin Luther, a German monk, and **John Calvin**, a French cleric and lawyer. Challenging the Catholic doctrine that priests were intermediaries between laypeople and God, Luther and Calvin insisted that people could interpret the Bible for themselves. Both rejected Catholic rituals and the elaborate church hierarchy. They also asserted that the key to salvation was faith in God, rather than the Catholic combination of faith and good works. Calvin went further, stressing the need for total submission to God's will.

Puritans, Separatists, and Presbyterians   Elizabeth I tolerated diverse forms of Christianity as long as she was acknowledged as head of the Church of England. During her long reign (1558–1603), Calvin's ideas gained influence in England, Wales, and especially Scotland. (In Ireland, also part of her realm, Catholicism remained dominant.) The Scottish church eventually adopted Presbyterianism, which eliminated bishops and placed religious authority in clerics and laymen called presbyteries. By the late sixteenth century, though, many Calvinists—including those who came to be called Puritans, because they wanted to purify the church, or Separatists, because they wanted to leave it—believed that English and Scottish reformers had not gone far enough. Henry had simplified the church hierarchy and the Scots had altered it; they wanted to abolish it. Henry and the Scots had subordinated the church to the state; they wanted a church free from political interference. The established churches of England and Scotland, like similar entities throughout Europe, continued to nominally encompass all residents of the realm. Calvinists in England and Scotland wanted to confine church membership to the "saved"—those they believed God had selected for salvation before birth.

Paradoxically, a key article of their faith insisted that people could not know if they were "saved" because mortals could not comprehend or affect their predestination to heaven or hell. Thus, pious Calvinists daily confronted serious dilemmas: If one was predestined and could not alter one's fate, why attend church or do good works? Calvinists admitted that their judgments as to eligibility for church membership only approximated God's unknowable decisions. And they reasoned that God gave the elect the ability to accept salvation and lead a good life. Therefore, piety and good works could indicate one as saved.

Stuart Monarchs   Elizabeth I's Stuart successors—her cousin James I (1603–1625) and his son Charles I (1625–1649)—exhibited less tolerance for Calvinists. As Scots, they also had little respect for the representative government that developed in England under the Tudors and (see Table 2.2). The wealthy landowners in Parliament had grown accustomed to having considerable influence on government policies. But James I publicly declared the divine right of kings, the notion that a monarch's power came from God and that his subjects had a duty to obey him.

TABLE 2.2   Tudor and Stuart Monarchs of England, 1509–1649

Monarch	Reign	Relation to Predecessor
Henry VIII	1509–1547	Son
Edward VI	1547–1553	Son
Mary I	1553–1558	Half-sister
Elizabeth I	1558–1603	Half-sister
James I	1603–1625	Cousin
Charles I	1625–1649	Son

Both James I and Charles I wanted to enforce religious conformity. Because Calvinists—and remaining Catholics in England and Scotland—challenged many important precepts of the established churches, the Stuart monarchs authorized the removal of dissenting clergymen. In the 1620s and 1630s, some Puritans, Separatists, Presbyterians, and Catholics decided to move to America, where they hoped to practice their beliefs freely. Some fled to avoid arrest and imprisonment.

The Founding of Virginia

How did English cultural traditions clash with those of Native Americans in Virginia?

The impetus for England's first permanent colony in the Western Hemisphere was religious and economic. The newly militant English Protestants wanted to combat "popery" at home and in the Americas. Accordingly, in 1606 a group of merchants and wealthy gentry, some of them aligned with religious reformers, obtained a royal charter for the Virginia Company as a **joint-stock company**. Such forerunners of modern corporations pooled the resources of many small investors through stock sales. Yet colonies required ongoing capital investments. The lack of immediate returns thus generated tension between stockholders and colonists. Although Virginia Company investors anticipated great profits, neither the Maine nor **Jamestown** settlement earned much.

joint-stock companies: Business corporations that amassed capital through sales of stock to investors.

Jamestown: First successful English colony, established in 1607.

Jamestown and Tsenacommacah

In 1607, the Virginia Company dispatched 104 men and boys to a region near Chesapeake Bay called Tsenacommacah by its native inhabitants. In May, they established a settlement called Jamestown on a swampy peninsula in a river. Ill-equipped for survival, the colonists fell victim to dissension and disease. The gentlemen and soldiers at Jamestown expected to rely on local Indians for food and tribute, but they refused. Moreover, the settlers arrived in the midst of a severe drought (now known to be the worst for 1,700 years), which persisted until 1612.

The weroance (chief) of Tsenacommacah, Powhatan, had inherited rule over six Algonquian villages and later controlled twenty-five others (see Map 2.1). In late 1607 negotiations with colonial leader Captain **John Smith**, the weroance tentatively agreed to an alliance with the Englishmen. In exchange for foodstuffs, Powhatan wanted guns, hatchets, and swords, which would give him a technological advantage over his people's enemies.

John Smith: Colonial leader of Jamestown who established order, good relations with Indians.

Link to John Rolfe's letter explaining why he wants to marry Pocahontas.

The fragile relationship soon foundered on mutual mistrust. The weroance relocated his primary village in early 1609 to a place the newcomers could not access easily. Without Powhatan's assistance, the settlement experienced a "starving time" (winter 1609–1610). Many died and at least one colonist resorted to cannibalism. In spring 1610, the survivors left on a newly arrived ship but en route encountered a new governor, more settlers, and supplies, so they returned to Jamestown. To gain the upper hand with Indians, settlers in 1613 kidnapped Powhatan's daughter, Pocahontas. In captivity, she converted to Christianity and married colonist John Rolfe. He had fallen in love, but she probably married him for diplomatic reasons; their union initiated peace between the English and Powhatans. Funded by the Virginia Company, she and Rolfe sailed to England to promote the colony. She died at Gravesend in 1616, leaving an infant son who returned to Virginia as a young adult.

Algonquian and English Cultural Differences In Tsenacommacah and elsewhere on the North American coast, English settlers and local Algonquians focused on their cultural differences, although both groups held deep religious beliefs, subsisted primarily through agriculture, accepted social and political hierarchy, and observed well-defined gender roles. English men regarded Indian men as lazy because they did not cultivate crops and spent their time hunting (a sport, not work, in English eyes). Indian men thought English men effeminate because they did the "woman's work" of cultivation.

Among Algonquians like the Powhatans, political power and social status did not necessarily pass through the male line, instead flowing through sisters' sons. English gentlemen inherited their position from their father. English political and military leaders ruled autocratically, whereas Algonquian leaders (even Powhatan) had limited authority over their people. Accustomed to the powerful kings, the English overestimated the chief's ability to make treaties that would bind their people.

Furthermore, Algonquian and English concepts of property differed. Most Algonquian villages held their land communally. Land could not be bought or sold absolutely, although certain rights to use it (for example, for hunting or fishing) could be transferred. Once, English villagers, too, had used land in common, but in the previous century had become accustomed to individual farms. The English also refused to accept Indians' claims to traditional hunting territories, insisting that only cultivated land could be owned or occupied. Ownership of such "unclaimed" property, the English believed, lay with the English monarchy, in whose name **John Cabot** had claimed North America in 1497.

John Cabot: Italian explorer who established English claims to North America.

The English believed in the superiority of their civilization. Although they often anticipated living peacefully alongside indigenous peoples, they expected native peoples to adopt English customs and convert to Christianity. They showed little respect for the Indians when English interests were at stake, as was demonstrated in Virginia once the settlers found a salable commodity.

Tobacco Cultivation That commodity was tobacco. In 1611, John Rolfe planted seeds of a variety from the Spanish Caribbean, which was superior to the strain Indians grew. Nine years later, Virginians exported 40,000 pounds of cured leaves, and by the late 1620s shipments jumped to 1.5 million pounds. The great tobacco boom had begun, fueled by high prices and profits. The price later fell sharply and fluctuated annually depending on supply and international competition.

Tobacco cultivation made Virginia prosper and altered life for everyone. It required abundant land, because a field could produce only three satisfactory crops before it had to lie fallow for several years to regain its fertility. Thus, applicants asked the Virginia Company for land grants on both sides of the James River. Virginians established farms far from apart along the riverbanks—which was convenient for tobacco cultivation but dangerous for defense.

Indian Assaults Opechancanough, Powhatan's brother and successor, watched the English colonists' expansion and attempts to convert natives to Christianity. Recognizing the danger, he attacked along the James River on March 22, 1622. By day's end, 347 colonists (about one-quarter) lay dead. Only a warning from two Christian converts saved Jamestown from destruction.

Reinforced by shipments of men and arms from England, the settlers repeatedly attacked Opechancanough's villages. A peace treaty was signed in 1632, but in April 1644 the elderly Opechancanough assaulted the invaders one last time; then, in 1646, survivors formally subordinated themselves to England.

End of Virginia Company

The 1622 assault killed the Virginia Company, which remained unprofitable due to internal corruption and the heavy cost of settlement. Before its demise, the company developed two precedent-setting policies. First, to attract settlers, in 1617 it established the "headright" system, giving each arrival who paid his or her own way a land grant of 50 acres; those who financed the passage of others received similar headrights. To English farmers who owned little or no land, the headright system offered a powerful incentive to move to Virginia. To wealthy gentry, it promised the possibility of vast agricultural enterprises. Two years later, the company authorized landowning men of major Virginia settlements to elect representatives to an assembly called the **House of Burgesses**. Just as they had at home, English landholders expected to elect members of Parliament and control local governments.

House of Burgesses: First elected representative legislature in North America that first met in 1619.

When James I revoked the charter in 1624, transforming Virginia into a royal colony, he continued the company's headright policy but abolished the assembly. Virginians protested, and by 1629 the House of Burgesses was functioning again. Two decades after the first permanent English settlement in North America, the colonists successfully insisted on governing themselves. Thus, England's American possessions differed from the autocratic rule in the Spanish, Dutch, and French colonies.

Life in the Chesapeake

What were the myths and realities of indentured servitude in the Chesapeake?

By the 1630s, tobacco was the chief source of revenue in Virginia and in the second English Chesapeake colony: Maryland. Given by Charles I to George Calvert, first Lord Baltimore, as a personal possession (proprietorship), it was settled in 1634. (Virginia and Maryland border Chesapeake Bay—see Map 2.1—and are referred to collectively as "the Chesapeake.") The Calvert family intended the colony as a haven for persecuted fellow Catholics. Cecilius Calvert, second Lord Baltimore, became the first colonizer to offer freedom of religion to all Christian settlers codified in Maryland's Act of Religious Toleration (1649).

Except for religion, the two Chesapeake colonies were similar. Tobacco planters spread out along riverbanks because rivers offered dependable transportation and established isolated farms instead of towns. Each farm or group of farms had its own wharf, where oceangoing vessels could load or discharge cargo.

Demand for Laborers

Planting, cultivation, harvesting, and curing tobacco were repetitious, time-consuming, and labor-intensive tasks. Successful Chesapeake farms required workers, but with their populations reduced by war and disease, Indians could not supply such needs. Nor were enslaved Africans available: traders could more easily and profitably sell slaves to Caribbean sugar planters. By 1650, only three hundred blacks lived in Virginia.

Chesapeake tobacco farmers thus looked primarily to England for labor. Because of the headright system, a tobacco farmer could obtain land and labor by importing Enlish workers. He could use his profits to pay for the passage of more workers and thereby gain more land. Success could even bring him into the region's new planter gentry.

Male laborers and a few women immigrated to America as **indentured servants**— that is, in return for their passage they contracted to work from four to seven years. Indentured servants accounted for 75 to 85 percent of the approximately 130,000 English immigrants to Virginia and Maryland during the seventeenth century. The rest were young couples with one or two children.

Roughly three-quarters of servants were males ages fifteen to twenty-four; only one in five or six was female. Most young men came from farming or laboring families, often from regions experiencing severe social disruption. Some had moved several times within England before relocating to America. Typically, they came from the middling ranks—what contemporaries called the "common sort."

indentured servants: Young men and women, usually unemployed and poor, who were given free passage to America, plus basic needs such as food, shelter, and clothing, in exchange for labor, usually for four to seven years.

Conditions of Servitude

Servants who fulfilled their indenture earned "freedom dues" of clothes, tools, livestock, corn, tobacco, and sometimes land. From a distance at least, America seemed to offer chances for advancement unavailable in England. Yet servants typically worked six days a week, ten to fourteen hours a day, in sweltering climates. Masters could discipline or sell them, and they faced severe penalties for running away. Laws required masters to supply servants with sufficient food, clothing, and shelter and prohibited beating them excessively. Cruelly treated servants could seek court assistance, sometimes winning verdicts directing their transfer to more humane masters or release from indenture.

All Chesapeake residents first had to survive "seasoning," a bout with disease (probably malaria) that usually occurred during their first Chesapeake summer. They often endured recurrences of malaria, along with dysentery, typhoid fever, and other illnesses. About 40 percent of male servants did not survive to become freedmen. Even men of twenty-two who weathered seasoning could expect to live only another twenty years.

For those who survived, though, opportunities were real. Until the late seventeenth century, former servants often became independent farmers ("freeholders"). But in the 1670s, tobacco prices entered a fifty-year period of stagnation and decline, while land grew scarce and expensive. In 1681, Maryland dropped its requirement that servants receive land with their freedom dues, forcing many freed servants to live as wage laborers or tenant farmers. By 1700, the Chesapeake was no longer a land of opportunity.

Standard of Living

Life in the early Chesapeake was hard. Farmers (and sometimes their wives) toiled in the fields alongside servants. Because hogs needed little tending, Chesapeake households subsisted mainly on pork and corn, a filling diet but not sufficiently nutritious. Families supplemented with fish, shellfish, wildfowl, and vegetables they grew such as lettuce and peas. The difficulty of preserving food for winter consumption magnified the health problems caused by epidemic disease.

Few households had more than farm implements, bedding, and basic cooking and eating utensils. Chairs, tables, candles, and knives and forks were luxury items. The ramshackle houses commonly had just one or two rooms. Colonists devoted their income to their farms, purchasing livestock and laborers instead of improving their standard of living. Rather than making clothing or tools, families imported them from England.

Chesapeake Families   The predominance of males (see Figure 2.1), the incidence of servitude, and the high mortality rates produced unusual patterns of family life. Female servants could not marry while indentured because masters feared pregnancies would deprive them of workers. Many male ex-servants could not marry at all because of the scarcity of women. In contrast, nearly every free Chesapeake woman married, and widows usually remarried within months of a husband's death. Because of high infant mortality and marriages delayed by servitude or broken by death, Chesapeake women commonly reared only one to three healthy children, where English women had at least five.

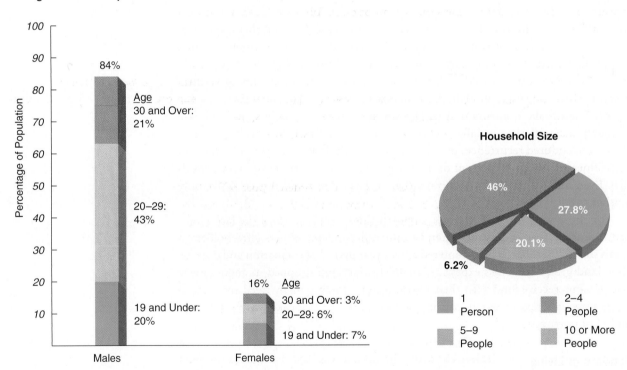

FIGURE 2.1
Population of Virginia, 1625

The only detailed census taken in the English mainland North American colonies during the seventeenth century was prepared in Virginia in 1625. It listed a total of 1,218 people, constituting 309 "households" and living in 278 dwellings—so some houses contained more than one family. The chart shows, on the left, the proportionate age and gender distribution of the 765 individuals for whom full information was recorded, and, on the right, the percentage variation in the sizes of the 309 households. The approximately 42 percent of the residents of the colony who were servants were concentrated in 30 percent of the households. Nearly 70 percent of the households had no servants at all.

Source of data: Robert S. Wells, *The Population of the British Colonies in America Before 1776.* © 1975 Princeton University Press, 2003 renewed PUP. Reprinted by permission of Princeton University Press.

Thus, Chesapeake families were few, small, and short-lived. In one Virginia county, more than three-quarters of the children had lost at least one parent by age twenty-one. Children were put to work as soon as possible on the farms of parents, stepparents, or guardians. Their schooling, if any, was haphazard; whether Chesapeake-born children learned to read or write depended on whether their parents were literate and taught them.

Chesapeake Politics   Throughout the seventeenth century, immigrants composed a majority of the Chesapeake population. Most members of Virginia's House of Burgesses and Maryland's House of Delegates (established in 1635) were immigrants; they also dominated the governor's council, which simultaneously served as the highest court, part of the legislature, and executive adviser to the governor. A cohesive, native-born ruling elite emerged only in the early eighteenth century.

In seventeenth-century Chesapeake, most property-owning white males could vote and chose as their legislators (burgesses) local elites who seemed to be the natural leaders. But because most such men were immigrants lacking strong ties to one another or to the colonies, the assemblies did not create political stability and were contentious.

The Founding of New England

Economic and religious motives drew people to New England. Environmental factors and the Puritans' organization of the New England colonies meant that northern settlements developed very differently from their southern counterparts.

What were John Winthrop's expectations for the Massachusetts Bay Company colony?

Contrasting Regional Demographic Patterns   Royal bureaucrats in late 1634 ordered port officials in London to collect information on travelers departing for the colonies. The records for 1635 document the departure of 53 vessels—20 to Virginia, 17 to New England, 8 to Barbados, 5 to St. Christopher, 2 to Bermuda, and 1 to Providence Island. Almost 5,000 people set sail, 2,000 for Virginia, about 1,200 for New England, and the rest for island destinations. Nearly three-fifths were between the ages of 15 and 24.

But among those bound for New England, such youths constituted less than one-third of the total; nearly 40 percent were older, and another third were younger. Whereas women made up 14 percent of those going to Virginia, they composed almost 40 percent of New England-bound passengers. New England migrants often traveled in family groups, brought more goods and livestock, and traveled with people from the same region. Their lives in North America must have been less lonely than their southern counterparts.

Contrasting Regional Religious Patterns   Puritan congregations became key institutions in colonial New England, whereas no church had much impact on the early development of the Chesapeake colonies. Spread-out Chesapeake settlement patterns made it difficult to organize a church. Catholic and Anglican bishops in England ignored their coreligionists in America, and Chesapeake congregations languished. Not until the 1690s did the Church of England take firmer root in Virginia; by then, it also replaced Catholicism as the Maryland's established church, and Calvinists were in the minority in both colonies.

In New England and the Chesapeake, religion affected the lives of pious Calvinists, who were expected to reassess the state of their souls regularly. Many devoted themselves to self-examination and Bible study, and families prayed together daily. Yet because even the most pious could never be certain that they were among the elect, anxiety troubled them. It lent an intensity to Calvinists' beliefs and concern with proper behavior—theirs and others'.

Separatists

Separatists who thought the Church of England too corrupt to be salvaged became the first religious dissenters to move to New England. In 1609, a Separatist congregation relocated to Leiden, in the Netherlands, where they found religious freedom—and tolerance for religions and behaviors they abhorred. Hoping to isolate their children from corrupting influences, these people, known today as Pilgrims, received permission from the Virginia Company to colonize its northern territory.

In September 1620, more than one hundred people, only thirty of them Separatists, sailed from England on the crowded *Mayflower*. In November, they landed on Cape Cod, farther north than intended. They moved across Massachusetts Bay to a fine harbor (named **Plymouth** by John Smith in 1614) and into the empty dwellings of a Pautuxet village whose inhabitants had died in the epidemic of 1616–1618.

Plymouth: Colony established by Pilgrims in Massachusetts.

J. D. Bangs, Courtesy of Leiden American Pilgrim Museum, The Netherlands

Some scholars now believe that this 1638 painting by Dutch artist Adam Willaerts depicts the Plymouth colony about fifteen years after its founding. The shape of the harbor, the wooden gate, and the houses straggling up the hill all coincide with contemporary accounts of the settlement. No one believes that Willaerts himself visited Plymouth, but people returning from the colony to the Netherlands, where the Pilgrims had lived for years before emigrating, could well have described Plymouth to him.

Pilgrims and Pokanokets

Because they landed outside the jurisdiction of the Virginia Company, some non-Separatists questioned the authority of the colony's leaders. In response, the **Mayflower Compact**, signed shipboard in November 1620, established a temporary "Civil Body Politic." Male settlers elected a governor and made decisions at town meetings. Later, Plymouth created an assembly to which landowning male settlers elected representatives.

The residents of Plymouth were poorly prepared to subsist in the new environment. Only half of the *Mayflower*'s passengers lived until spring. Survivors owed much to the Pokanokets (a branch of the Wampanoags), who controlled the area. Pokanoket villages had suffered terrible losses in the recent epidemic, so to protect themselves from the powerful Narragansetts of the southern New England coast, the Pokanokets allied themselves with the newcomers. In spring 1621, their leader, Massasoit, agreed to a treaty, and during the colony's first difficult years the Pokanokets supplied the settlers with foodstuffs. The colonists also relied on Squanto, a Pautuxet who served as a conduit between native peoples and Europeans. Captured by fishermen in the early 1610s and taken to Europe, Squanto learned to speak English. After returning, he became the settlers' interpreter and taught them about the environment.

Massachusetts Bay Company

Before the 1620s ended, another group of Puritans (Congregationalists, who hoped to reform the Church of England from within) launched the colonial enterprise that would dominate New England. Charles I, who became king in 1625, attempted to suppress Puritan practices. Some Congregationalist merchants, concerned about their prospects in England, sent colonists to Cape Ann (north of Cape Cod) in 1628. The following year the merchants obtained a royal charter, constituting themselves as the Massachusetts Bay Company.

The new joint-stock company quickly attracted Puritans who feared they would lose the ability to practice their religion freely in their homeland. Committed to reforming the Church of England, they decided to do so from New England. Congregationalist merchants transfered the Massachusetts Bay Company's headquarters there, so they could handle their affairs, secular and religious, as they pleased. Like the Plymouth settlers, they expected to profit from the codfishery and timber exports.

Governor John Winthrop

In October 1629, the Massachusetts Bay Company elected **John Winthrop**, a member of the lesser English gentry, as its governor. Until his death twenty years later, he served continuously in various leadership positions. Winthrop organized the initial segment of the great Puritan migration. In 1630, more than one thousand English men and women moved to Massachusetts—most to Boston. By 1643, nearly twenty thousand more had followed.

On board the *Arbella*, en route to New England in 1630, John Winthrop preached a sermon, "A Model of Christian Charity," outlining his expectations for the colony. He stressed the communal nature of the endeavor, where differences in status or wealth—though retained—would not imply worth. Instead, he explained that, God had planned the world so that "every man might have need of other, and from hence they might be all knit more nearly together." In America, Winthrop asserted, "we shall be as a city upon a hill, the eyes of all people are upon us."

Link to Mayflower Compact.

Mayflower Compact: Agreement signed by *Mayflower* passengers to establish order in their new settlement.

John Winthrop: Governor of Massachusetts Bay colony who wrote "A Model of Christian Charity."

Link to John Winthrop's "A Model of Christian Charity" speech.

Links to the World

Turkeys

Near the end of their first year in North America, Plymouth colonists held a traditional English feast celebrating the harvest. Famously, they invited Massasoit's Pokanokets, and they probably consumed turkey. But why was this bird, originally from America and enjoyed at Thanksgiving today, named for a region of the then-Ottoman Empire? The native peoples of the Americas had their own words for the fowl; Aztecs, for example, called a male bird *huexoloti* and a female *totolin*.

When Columbus carried the birds back to Spain after his first voyage, the Iberian peninsula was a major focal point for Mediterranean commerce, and Spanish mariners sailed frequently to the Middle East. One Spanish vessel took some *huexoloti* and *totolin* to the Ottoman Empire. There, farmers familiar with distant Asian relatives of the bird improved the breed, ultimately producing a plumper, tamer version. By the end of the 1500s, "turkeys" were widely consumed throughout the British Isles.

When Thomas Harriot in his 1588 *Briefe and True Report* mentioned the wild North American version of the birds, he termed them "Turkie cockes and Turkie hennes." He did not use the names native people used because these birds were not new to his audience.

Jamestown and Plymouth settlers also recognized the birds in the colonies as relatives of the fowls they enjoyed in England. But they regarded the North American birds as inferior since they seemingly could not be tamed and ravaged crops. Instead, settlers imported English turkeys to raise for meat.

Were the "turkeys" consumed at the so-called First Thanksgiving the wild American birds, or the tame Ottoman-English variety? It remains a mystery. But that they were termed "turkeys" linked them to the Mediterranean, Europe, and the Middle East as animals in the Columbian Exchange.

Victoria & Albert Museum, London; UK/The Bridgeman Art Library

Turkeys from the Americas quickly traveled around the world, as is illustrated by this Mughal painting from the Islamic empire in India. The local artist Ustad Mansur painted a "turkey-cock" brought to the emperor Jahangir in 1612 from Goa—a Portuguese enclave on the west coast of the Indian subcontinent. Presumably the turkey had been transported from the Iberian peninsula to that European outpost, whence the fowl made its way to Jahangir's court—where it was immortalized by an artist to whom it was an unusual sight.

Winthrop foresaw in Puritan America a true commonwealth in which each person put the good of the whole ahead of him- or herself. Although that society would be characterized by hierarchies of status and power, Winthrop hoped its members would live by the precepts of Christian love. Early Massachusetts and its Caribbean counterpart, Providence Island, had some bitter quarrels and un-Christian behavior, though remarkably, in New England Winthrop's ideal persisted for generations.

Covenant Ideal

Puritans' communal ideal was embodied in the doctrine of the covenant, the notion that God made a contract with them when they were chosen for their special mission to America. They also covenanted with one another to work together. Founders of churches, towns, and colonies in Anglo-America often drafted documents outlining the principles on which their institutions would be based. The Pilgrims' Mayflower Compact was a covenant as was the Fundamental Orders of Connecticut (1639), which defined the basic law for the settlements along the Connecticut River valley beginning in 1636.

The leaders of Massachusetts Bay likewise transformed their company charter into the basis for a covenanted community based on mutual consent. Under pressure from landowning male settlers, they gradually changed the General Court—officially the company's small governing body—into a colonial legislature. They also granted the status of freeman, or voting member, to property-owning adult male church members. Less than two decades after the Puritans arrived in Massachusetts Bay, the colony had a functioning system of self-government composed of a governor and a two-house legislature as well as a judicial system modeled on England's.

New England Towns

The colony's land distribution system furthered the communal ideal. In Massachusetts, groups of men—often from the same English village—applied together for land grants on which to establish towns (novel governance units that did not exist in England). Receiving a grant, these men then determined how the land would be distributed. Understandably, they copied their home villages, first laying out house and church lots. Then they gave each family parcels of land around the town center and reserved the best and largest plots for the most distinguished residents, including the minister. People with low status in England received smaller, less desirable allotments. Still, every man and even a few single women obtained land.

Town centers developed quickly, evolving in three distinctly different ways. Some, chiefly isolated agricultural settlements in the interior, tried to sustain Winthrop's vision of community based on diversified family farms. A second group, the coastal towns like Boston and Salem, became bustling seaports, focal points for trade and places of entry for immigrants. The third category, commercialized agricultural towns, grew up in the Connecticut River valley, where easy water transportation enabled farmers to sell surplus goods.

Pequot War and Its Aftermath

Migration into the Connecticut valley ended the Puritans' relative freedom from clashes with nearby Indians. Relocating under the direction of their minister, Thomas Hooker, their new settlements were remote from other English towns, although the river promised access to the ocean. The site, however, fell within the territory of the powerful Pequots.

Pequot War: Clash in 1637 that resulted as English colonists moved to settle in the Connecticut Valley on land inhabited by the Pequot Indians. The colonists were victorious and took over the Indians' land.

The Pequots' dominance stemmed from their role as primary intermediaries in the trade between New England Algonquians and the Dutch in New Netherland. With the arrival of English settlers, previously subordinate bands could now trade directly with Europeans. Clashes between Pequots and English colonists began earlier, but the establishment of settlements in the Connecticut valley moved them toward war. After two English traders were killed (not by Pequots), the English raided a Pequot village. Pequots then attacked Wethersfield, Connecticut, in April 1637, killing nine and capturing two. To retaliate, an expedition burned the main Pequot town on the Mystic River. The Englishmen and their Narragansett allies slaughtered at least four hundred Pequots, mostly women and children, capturing and enslaving the survivors.

For the next four decades, New England Indians accommodated themselves to the European invasion. They traded with newcomers and sometimes worked for them, but they resisted incorporation into English society. Native Americans persisted in using traditional farming methods, which did not employ plows or fences, and women continued as chief cultivators. When Indian men learned "European" trades, they chose those—like broom making and basket weaving—that most resembled their customary occupations and ensured independence. The one European practice they adopted was keeping livestock, for domesticated animals provided sources of meat once hunting territories became English farms and wild game vanished.

Missionary Activities   Most colonists showed little interest in converting the Algonquians to Christianity. Only a few Massachusetts clerics, notably John Eliot and Thomas Mayhew, seriously undertook missionary work. Eliot insisted that converts reside in towns, farm the land in English fashion, assume English names, wear European-style clothing and shoes, cut their hair, and stop observing their own customs. He met with little success. Only eleven hundred Indians (out of many thousands) lived in the fourteen "Praying Towns" Eliot established, and just 10 percent were baptized.

The missions in New France, however, were more successful. Puritan services lacked Catholicism's beautiful ceremonies and special appeal for women, and the Calvinist Puritans could not offer assurances of a heavenly afterlife. Yet, on the island of Martha's Vineyard, Thomas Mayhew converted many Indians to Calvinist Christianity partly by allowing Wampanoag Christians to lead traditional lives and by training their men as ministers.

While conversion often alienated new Christians from their relatives and traditions, many Indians hoped to use the Europeans' religion to cope with the dramatic changes the intruders had wrought. The combination of disease, alcohol, new trading patterns, and loss of territory disrupted customary ways of life. Shamans had little success in restoring tradition. Many Indians must have concluded that the Europeans' ideas could help them survive.

John Winthrop's description of a great smallpox epidemic that swept through southern New England in the early 1630s reveals the relationship among smallpox, conversion to Christianity, and English land claims. "Divers of them, in their sickness, confessed that the Englishmen's God was a good God; and that if they recovered, they would serve him," he noted in his diary in 1633. But by July, Winthrop observed that most Indians within a 300-mile radius of Boston had died of smallpox. He concluded, "the Lord hath cleared our title to what we possess."

Life in New England

New England's colonizers lived differently than their Algonquian neighbors and Chesapeake counterparts. Algonquian bands usually moved four or five times yearly to maximize their environment. In spring, women planted the fields, but once crops were established, they gathered wild foods while men hunted and fished. Villagers returned for harvest, separated again for fall hunting, and wintered together in a sheltered spot. Women probably determined the timing of these moves, because their activities used the environment more intensively than did men's.

What was the impact of religion on colonial life in New England?

English people lived year-round in the same location. Household furnishings and house sizes resembled those in the Chesapeake, but New Englanders' diets were somewhat more varied. They replowed fields, finding it less arduous to fertilize with manure than to clear new fields every few years. They fenced croplands to keep out cattle, sheep, and hogs that were their chief meat sources. Animal crowding more than human crowding caused New Englanders to spread out across the countryside.

New England Families Because Puritans commonly moved to America as families, the age range in early New England was wide; and because many more women migrated to New England than to the tobacco colonies, the population could immediately reproduce itself. Lacking tropical diseases, New England was, after the initial difficult years, healthier than the Chesapeake and Britain. Adult male migrants to the Chesapeake lost about a decade from their English life expectancy of fifty to fifty-five years; their Massachusetts counterparts gained five or more years.

Consequently, whereas Chesapeake had few, mostly small families, New England families were numerous, large, and long-lived. Most New England men married; immigrant women married young (at age twenty, on the average); and marriages lasted longer and produced more children likely to live to maturity. Seventeenth-century Chesapeake women raised one to three healthy children; New England women reared five to seven.

The presence of many children combined with Puritans' stress on reading the Bible led to concern for education. Living in towns, colonists could establish small schools; girls and boys were taught basic reading by their parents or a school "dame," and boys could learn writing, arithmetic, and Latin. Whereas early Chesapeake parents commonly died before their children married, New England parents exercised much control over their adult offspring.

Wadsworth Atheneum Museum of Art, Hartford, CT. Gift of Mrs. Walter H. Clark. Endowed by her daughter, Mrs. Thomas L. Archibald/Art Resource, NY

In 1664, an eight-year-old girl, Elizabeth Eggington, became the subject of the earliest known dated New England painting. Her mother died shortly after her birth, perhaps because of childbirth complications; the girl's rich clothing, elaborate jewelry, and feather fan not only reveal her family's wealth but also suggest that she was much loved by her father, a merchant and ship captain. Unfortunately, Elizabeth died about the time this portrait was painted; perhaps it—like some other colonial portraits of young children—was actually painted after her death to memorialize her.

Young men could not marry without acreage and depended on their fathers for that land. Daughters, too, needed a dowry of household goods from parents. Parents relied on children's labor and often seemed reluctant to see them marry. These needs sometimes led to generational conflicts, but generally, children obeyed their parents' wishes.

Impact of Religion

Puritans controlled the governments of Massachusetts Bay, Plymouth, Connecticut, and other early northern colonies. Congregationalism was the only officially recognized religion; except in Rhode Island, other sects had no freedom of worship. In Massachusetts Bay and New Haven, church membership was a prerequisite for voting. Early colonies taxed residents to build churches and pay ministers' salaries, but only New England based criminal codes on the Old Testament. New Englanders were required to attend religious services, and people who expressed contempt for ministers could be punished with fines or whippings.

Strict codes of conduct meant colonists could be tried for drunkenness, card playing, dancing, or idleness—although frequent prosecutions suggest that New Englanders often enjoyed such activities. Couples who had sex during their engagement (as revealed by the birth of a baby less than nine months after their wedding) were fined and publicly humiliated. Men, and a handful of women, who engaged in behaviors that today would be called homosexual were seen as sinful, and some were executed.

In New England, church and state were thus intertwined. Puritans objected to secular interference in religious affairs yet expected the church to influence politics and society. They also believed that the state was obliged to support and protect the one true church—theirs. Although they came to America seeking religious freedom, they saw no contradiction in refusing that freedom to those with different beliefs.

Roger Williams

Roger Williams: A minister who advocated complete separation of church and state and religious toleration.

Roger Williams, a Separatist who migrated to Massachusetts Bay in 1631, quickly ran afoul of Puritan orthodoxy. He told fellow settlers that the king of England had no right to grant them land already occupied by Indians, that church and state should be separate, and that Puritans should not impose their ideas on others. In October 1635, Massachusetts tried Williams for challenging the validity of the colony's charter and for maintaining that New England Congregationalists had not separated sufficiently from England's corrupt institutions and practices.

Convicted and banished, Williams journeyed in early 1636 to the head of Narragansett Bay, where he founded the town of Providence on land he obtained from the Narragansetts and Wampanoags. Providence and other towns in what became Rhode Island tolerated all religions, including Judaism. Along with Maryland, Williams's colony founded presaged the religious freedom that eventually became a hallmark of the United States.

Anne Hutchinson

Anne Hutchinson: Dissenter feared not only for her theology but also because she challenged gender roles; banished from Massachusetts.

Anne Hutchinson presented a more sustained challenge to Massachusetts' leaders. A skilled medical practitioner popular with Boston women, she admired John Cotton, a minister who stressed the covenant of grace, or God's free gift of salvation. Most Massachusetts clerics emphasized the need for good works, study, and reflection for receiving God's grace. (In its extreme form, this doctrine could verge on the covenant of works, meaning that

Blue Laws

Seventeenth-century New England colonies enacted statutes, now called *blue laws*, preventing residents from working or engaging in recreation on Sundays, when they were supposed to attend church. Colonists were fined for plowing fields, pursuing wandering livestock, drinking in taverns, or playing games on the Sabbath. Harsher punishments met thieves who took advantage of church attendance to break into homes.

The term appears to have been coined by the Reverend Samuel Peters, a loyalist, in his *General History of Connecticut*, published in London in 1781. Peters used *blue laws* to refer to Connecticut's early legal code in general, defining it as "bloody Laws; for they were all sanctified with whippings, cutting off the ears, burning the tongue, and death." Eventually, *blue laws* acquired its current meaning of legislation regulating behavior on Sundays. States continued to enact such statutes through the nineteenth century, but as in the colonial period, enforcement varied.

Still, they remained on the books. A 1961 Supreme Court decision, *McGowan v. Maryland*, upheld that state's law restricting what could be sold on Sundays. Whereas colonial legislators were attempting to prevent Sunday work, modern Americans seem more concerned about halting Sunday shopping. Not until 1991 did the last state (North Dakota) repeal a law requiring all stores to be closed on Sundays, and only in 2003 did New York State remove its ban on Sunday liquor sales. During the recession beginning in 2008, remaining blue laws have been challenged by people hoping to stimulate local commercial activity, and the internet campaign—"Keep Sunday Special"—collapsed. Still, persistent pleas to "restore the observance of the Lord's Day in our nation" show the continuing legacy of the seventeenth century.

people could earn their salvation.) Hutchinson began holding women's meetings in her home. Stressing the covenant of grace, she asserted that the elect could be assured of salvation and communicate directly with God, which lessened the importance of the institutional church.

Thus, Hutchinson threatened Puritan orthodoxy. In November 1637, officials charged her with maligning the colony's ministers by accusing them of preaching the covenant of works. For two days, she defended herself, matching scriptural references with John Winthrop. But then Hutchinson boldly declared that God had spoken to her and would curse the Puritans if they harmed her. Excommunicated, she was exiled to Rhode Island in 1638, along with her family and some followers. Years later, after moving to New Netherland, she and most of her children were killed by Indians.

Authorities in Massachusetts perceived Anne Hutchinson as a threat to religious orthodoxy and traditional gender roles. Puritans believed in equality before God, but they considered actual women inferior to men. The magistrates' comments during her trial reveal that they were almost as outraged by her "masculine" behavior as by her religious beliefs. A clergyman told her, "You have stepped out of your place, you have rather been a Husband than a Wife and a preacher than a Hearer."

To New England authorities, an orderly society required the obedience of wives to husbands, subjects to rulers, and ordinary folk to gentry. English people intended to make many changes by colonizing North America, but not the gendered division of labor, the assumption of male superiority, or the maintenance of social hierarchies.

Summary

By the mid-seventeenth century, Europeans had come to North America and the Caribbean to stay, indelibly altering their lives and those of native peoples. Europeans killed Indians with weapons and diseases and had varying success converting them to Christianity. Contacts with indigenous peoples taught Europeans to eat new foods and recognize—however reluctantly—other cultures. The prosperity and survival of many European colonies depended heavily on the cultivation of American crops (maize and tobacco) and an Asian crop (sugar), thus attesting to the importance of post-Columbian ecological exchange.

To a greater extent than their European counterparts, the English transferred the society and politics of their homeland to a new environment. Their sheer numbers, coupled with their need for vast quantities of land for crops and livestock, inevitably produced conflict with Indian neighbors. New England and the Chesapeake differed in the sex ratio and age range of their immigrant populations, their diverse economies, their settlement patterns, and the impact of religion. Yet their expansions engendered similar internal and external tension. Both regions would become embroiled in increasingly fierce rivalries besetting the European powers that would affect Americans of all races until after the mid-eighteenth century, when the Anglo-American colonies won their independence.

Chapter Review

Spanish, French, and Dutch North America

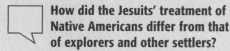
How did the Jesuits' treatment of Native Americans differ from that of explorers and other settlers?

Spanish and other settlers typically sought to dominate the native populations, controlling their labor and often enslaving them, sometimes through the use of violence. The French Jesuits who settled New France (Montreal and Quebec) initially tried to convert Indians to Christianity and convince them to farm in the European style. When that failed, missionaries introduced Catholicism without insisting that Indians abandon their traditions. Missionaries learned Indian languages and lived among potential converts, and while they tried to undermine the authority of shamans, Jesuits also recognized the compatibility of some aspects of native culture with Christianity. This somewhat flexible approach, combined with their lack of interest in land or tribute, made at least some Indians receptive to conversion.

The Caribbean

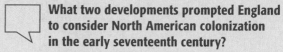
What made the Caribbean Islands initially desirable for colonization?

European colonizers had different reasons for being drawn to the Caribbean Islands. Spain, which focused on larger islands, saw them as offering the potential for greater wealth with less effort than smaller islands might. Other countries saw the smaller islands as a base to attack Spanish vessels transporting gold, silver, and other valuable commodities from the Americas. The second reason for settling on the smaller islands was sugar cultivation. Sugar was in high demand in Europe, particularly since the sweetener improved the taste of coffee and tea and provided a sweet, yet quick, energy boost.

English Interest in Colonization

What two developments prompted England to consider North American colonization in the early seventeenth century?

First, dramatic population growth in England, partly as a result of more nutritious foods of American origin, increased competition for food, clothing, shelter, and jobs. That, in turn, spurred inflation; wages also fell. Some profited, but those at the lower end of the socioeconomic spectrum—those with little or no land—lapsed into poverty and homelessness. Cities became overcrowded, leading officials to see colonizing North America as a way to reduce England's "surplus" population and related woes. Others hoped to improve their lot in the land-rich colonies. Second, the Protestant Reformation sparked new forms of Christianity that diverged from the Church of England, and while Elizabeth I tolerated such dissent, her successors, the Stuart monarchs, did not. Ultimately, seeking to practice freely their religious beliefs (and avoid imprisonment), some English Puritans, Separatists, and Catholics fled to America.

The Founding of Virginia

How did English cultural traditions clash with those of Native Americans in Virginia?

While both were religious, Englishmen considered Indian men lazy because they let women cultivate crops while they hunted, which the British regarded as a sport and not work. Native Americans thought Englishmen were effeminate because they farmed, which Indians considered women's work. Political power in Algonquian culture passed through sisters' sons rather through the father, as was the custom in England. Because the British were used to powerful kings, they assumed Indian chiefs held the same autocratic control and ability to make treaties, when in reality, they had limited authority. Most importantly, where the English believed in individual farms and private land ownership, the Algonquians held land communally as a village.

Life in the Chesapeake

What were the myths and realities of indentured servitude in the Chesapeake?

Chesapeake tobacco farmers filled their extensive demand for labor with indentured servants from England—typically young men who worked for four to seven years in exchange for their passage. Indentured servitude for these young men represented a chance at upward mobility. Most gained "freedom dues" at the completion of their contract, including clothes, tools, livestock, casks of corn and tobacco, and sometimes land. But they worked long hours, six or seven days a week, doing intense physical labor in hot climates. Masters could discipline or sell them, and if indentured servants fled, they faced extreme penalties, although some did win verdicts against cruel masters calling for their transfer or release from indenture. Exposure to disease combined with intense labor so that only 60 percent of indentured men lived to become freedmen, and many who did, lived only another twenty years.

The Founding of New England

What were John Winthrop's expectations for the Massachusetts Bay Company colony?

First elected governor in 1629, John Winthrop was instrumental in organizing the first Puritan migration from England to the colony. While in transit, he delivered his famous sermon, calling for the new colony to serve as a moral and spiritual example for the rest of the world, a "city upon a hill." He urged colonists of varying ranks to work together, to mediate status differences and to unite around their communal interests. He envisioned a true commonwealth, where people put the common good ahead of their own and were governed by Christian brotherhood.

Life in New England

What was the impact of religion on colonial life in New England?

Although Puritans fled England to practice their faith freely in New England, they offered no such freedom of worship to those who dissented from their beliefs. Puritans controlled the government in many early northern colonies and made Congregationalism the only recognized religion, with church membership and voting rights linked. Colonists were punished with fines or whippings for missing religious services. In addition, strict behavioral codes meant colonists were tried for drunkenness, card playing, dancing, or idleness. Couples who had sex during their engagement were fined and publicly humiliated. People who behaved in ways that today would be called homosexual were sometimes executed. Dissenters such as Roger Williams or Anne Hutchinson, who challenged Puritan orthodoxy, were tried and banished—Williams founded Providence, Rhode Island, based on religious tolerance and was subsequently joined by Hutchinson. Beyond challenging church authority, Hutchinson violated gender norms by preaching.

Suggestions for Further Reading

Virginia DeJohn Anderson, *Creatures of Empire: How Domestic Animals Transformed Early America* (2004)

Richard S. Dunn, *Sugar and Slaves: The Rise of the Planter Class in the English West Indies, 1624–1713* (1972)

David Hackett Fischer, *Champlain's Dream: The European Founding of North America* (2008)

Alison Games, *Migration and the Origins of the English Atlantic World* (1999)

David D. Hall, *Worlds of Wonder, Days of Judgment: Popular Religious Belief in Early New England* (1989)

Karen O. Kupperman, *The Jamestown Project* (2007)

Mary Beth Norton, *Founding Mothers & Fathers: Gendered Power and the Forming of American Society* (1996)

Carla Gardina Pestana, *Protestant Empire: Religion and the Making of the British Atlantic World* (2009)

Helen C. Rountree, *Pocahontas, Powhatan, Opechancanough: Three Indian Lives Changed by Jamestown* (2005)

David J. Weber, *The Spanish Frontier in North America* (1992)

 **CourseMate**

Go to the CourseMate website for primary source links, study tools, and review materials for this chapter. www.cengagebrain.com

North America in the Atlantic World

3

1650–1720

She was starving. Offered a piece of boiled horse's foot by a compassionate neighbor, the slave gulped it down and grabbed another piece from a child. Later, she recalled that "savoury it was to my taste. . . . Thus the Lord made that pleasant refreshing, which another time would have been an abomination." But Mary Rowlandson's mistress then threatened to kill her, saying that she had "disgraced" the household by begging for food.

What had brought the wife of the Reverend Joseph Rowlandson of Lancaster, Massachusetts, to such distress? On February 10, 1676, a force of Wampanoags, Narragansetts, and Nipmucks had killed fourteen townspeople (including her daughter) and captured twenty-three others in the conflict that New Englanders called King Philip's War. Carried away, she endured their hardships in the wintry countryside of western Massachusetts and southern New Hampshire. She became the slave of Quinnapin, a Narragansett sachem, and his three wives, one of whom, Weetamoo, herself a Wampanoag sachem, was her mistress. Both were eventually killed by the colonists after the death of their leader, the Wampanoag known as King Philip, in August 1676. But months earlier, in May, Mary Rowlandson had been ransomed from her captors for £20—roughly equivalent to $500 today.

Mary Rowlandson's famous 1682 narrative, *The Sovereignty and Goodness of God,* exposes the sufferings she shared with her captors and her inability to sympathize with or understand them. When Weetamoo's baby died, Mary remarked coldly that "there was one benefit in it, that there was more room" in the wigwam. Her narrative illustrates the contentious relationships of Anglo New Englanders and their native neighbors.

Much tension was related to the mainland colonies' involvement in a growing international network. North America, like England, was becoming embedded in a worldwide matrix of trade and warfare. Oceangoing vessels now crisscrossed the globe, carrying European goods to America and Africa, Caribbean sugar to New England and Europe, Africans to the Americas, and New England fish and wood products—and occasionally Indian slaves—to the Caribbean. North American colonies expanded their territorial claims and diversified their economies after the mid-seventeenth century.

Three developments shaped mainland English colonial life between 1640 and 1720: escalating conflicts with Indians and other European colonies; the expansion of slavery; and changes in the colonies' political and economic relationships with England.

The explosive growth of the slave trade significantly altered the Anglo-American economy. Mariners and ship owners profited handsomely from their human cargoes, as did planters who could afford slaves. Initially, the slave trade involved Indians and already enslaved Africans from the Caribbean, but it soon focused on cargoes from Africa. The large influx of West African slaves expanded agricultural productivity, fueled the international trading system, and dramatically reshaped colonial society.

The burgeoning North American economy attracted new attention from colonial administrators. After the Stuarts were restored to the throne in 1660 (having lost it briefly during the English Civil War), London bureaucrats attempted to supervise American settlements so England benefited from their economic growth.

As English settlements expanded, they came into violent conflict with powerful Indian nations, the Dutch, the Spanish, and the French. All European colonies confronted significant crises during the 1670s. By 1720, war—between Europeans and Indians, among Europeans, and among Indians allied with colonial powers—had become a familiar feature of American life. No longer isolated, the people and products of North American colonies had become integral to the world trading system and enmeshed in its conflicts.

As you read this chapter, keep the following questions in mind:

* **What were the consequences of the transatlantic slave trade in North America and Africa?**

* **How did English policy toward the colonies change from 1650 to 1720?**

* **What were the causes and results of new friction between Europeans and native peoples?**

The Growth of Anglo-American Settlements

Why did New York's development lag behind that of other British colonies in the seventeenth century?

Between 1642 and 1646, civil war between supporters of King Charles I and the Puritan-dominated Parliament engulfed England. Parliament triumphed, leading to the execution of the king in 1649 and interim rule by the parliamentary army's leader, Oliver Cromwell, during the so-called Commonwealth period. But after Cromwell's death, Parliament restored the monarchy with Charles I's son and heir agreeing to restrictions on his authority. Assuming the throne in 1660 (see Table 3.1), Charles II rewarded nobles and other supporters with huge tracts of land on the North American mainland, thereby establishing six of the thirteen polities that would form the American nation: New York, New Jersey, Pennsylvania (including Delaware), and North and South Carolina (see Map 3.1). Known as the Restoration colonies, they were proprietorships, where one man or several men owned the soil and controlled the government.

Chronology

1642–46	English Civil War
1649	Charles I executed
1651	First Navigation Act passed to regulate colonial trade
1660	Stuarts (Charles II) restored to throne
1663	Carolina chartered
1664	English conquer New Netherland New York founded New Jersey established
1670s	Marquette, Jolliet, and La Salle explore the Great Lakes and Mississippi valley for France
1675–76	Bacon's Rebellion disrupts Virginia government; Jamestown destroyed
1675–78	King Philip's War devastates New England
1680–1700	Pueblo revolt temporarily drives Spaniards from New Mexico
1681	Pennsylvania chartered
1685	James II becomes king
1686–88	Dominion of New England established, superseding all charters of colonies from Maine to New Jersey
1688–89	James II deposed in Glorious Revolution William and Mary ascend throne
1689	Glorious Revolution in America; Massachusetts, New York, and Maryland overthrow colonial governors
1688–99	King William's War fought on northern New England frontier
1691	New Massachusetts charter issued
1692	Witchcraft crisis in Salem; nineteen people hanged
1696	Board of Trade and Plantations established to coordinate English colonial administration Vice-admiralty courts established in America
1701	Iroquois adopt neutrality policy toward France and England
1702–13	Queen Anne's War fought by French and English
1711–13	Tuscarora War (North Carolina) leads to capture or migration of most Tuscaroras
1715	Yamasee War nearly destroys South Carolina

New York

In 1664, Charles II gave his brother James the region between the Connecticut and Delaware Rivers, including the Hudson valley and Long Island. That the Dutch had settled there mattered little; the English and Dutch were engaged in sporadic warfare. In August, James's warships anchored off Manhattan Island, demanding New Netherland's surrender. Although in 1672 the Netherlands briefly retook the colony, the Dutch permanently ceded it in 1674.

In 1664, a significant minority of English people (mostly Puritan New Englanders on Long Island) already lived in the territory James renamed New York, along with the Dutch, Indians, Africans, Germans, Scandinavians, and other Europeans (see Table 3.2). The Dutch West India Company had imported slaves, intending some for resale in the Chesapeake although many remained in New Netherland as laborers. At the time of the English conquest, almost one-fifth of Manhattan's approximately fifteen hundred inhabitants were of African descent.

TABLE 3.1   Restored Stuart Monarchs of England, 1660–1714

Monarch	Reign	Relation to Predecessor
Charles II	1660–1685	Son
James II	1685–1688	Brother
Mary	1688–1694	Daughter
William	1688–1702	Son-in-law
Anne	1702–1714	Sister, sister-in-law

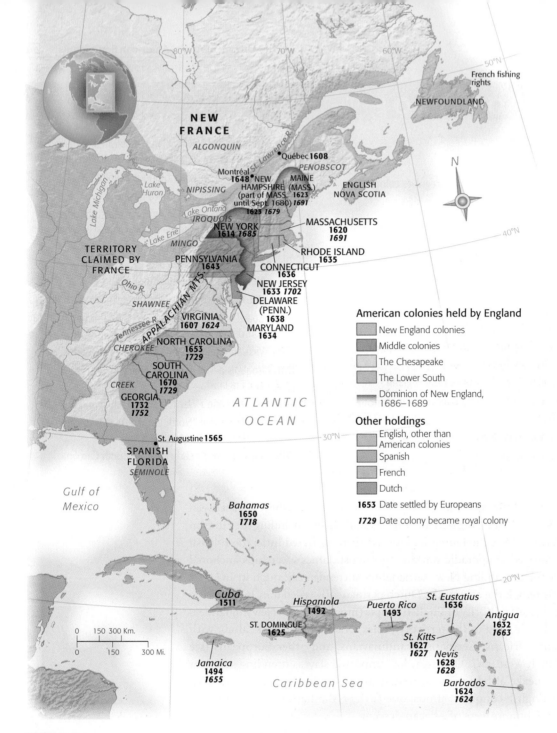

MAP 3.1

The Anglo-American Colonies in the Early Eighteenth Century

By the early eighteenth century, the English colonies nominally dominated the Atlantic coastline of North America. But the colonies' formal boundary lines are deceiving because the western reaches of each colony were still largely unfamiliar to Europeans and because much of the land was still inhabited by Native Americans.

Source: Copyright © Cengage Learning

Recognizing the population's diversity, James's representatives moved cautiously in establishing English authority. The Duke's Laws, a 1665 legal code, applied solely to the English settlements on Long Island, only later extended to the entire colony. James initially maintained Dutch local government, confirmed Dutch land titles, and allowed Dutch residents to maintain customary legal practices. Each

TABLE 3.2   The Founding of English Colonies in North America, 1664–1681

Colony	Founder(s)	Date	Basis of Economy
New York (formerly New Netherland)	James, duke of York	1664	Farming, fur trading
New Jersey	Sir George Carteret, John Lord Berkeley	1664	Farming
North Carolina	Carolina proprietors	1665	Tobacco, forest products
South Carolina	Carolina proprietors	1670	Rice, indigo
Pennsylvania (incl. Delaware)	William Penn	1681	Farming

town could choose which church—Dutch Reformed, Congregational, or Church of England—to support with its taxes. Much to the dismay of English residents, there was no provision for a representative assembly. James distrusted legislative bodies, and not until 1683 did he agree to an elected legislature. The English takeover thus had little immediate effect. The duke did not promote migration, so its population grew slowly, barely reaching eighteen thousand by 1698. Until the 1720s, Manhattan remained a commercial backwater to Boston.

New Jersey   In 1664, the duke of York regranted the land between the Hudson and Delaware Rivers—East and West Jersey—to his friends Sir George Carteret and John Lord Berkeley. That left the duke's own colony hemmed in between Connecticut and the Jerseys, hindering its economic growth. Meanwhile, the Jersey proprietors quickly attracted settlers, promising generous land

The Dutch artist Johannes Vingboons painted this view of New Amersterdam/New York in 1665, shortly after the English takeover. Note the windmill, the tall government buildings, and the small row houses—which made the settlement resemble European villages of its day. The contrast to Plymouth (page 44) is striking.

grants, limited religious freedom, and—without the Crown's authorization—a representative assembly. Many Puritan New Englanders migrated to the Jerseys, along with Barbadians, Dutch New Yorkers, and eventually Scots. By 1726, New Jersey had 32,500 inhabitants, only 8,000 fewer than New York.

Quakers: Members of a religious sect that embraced egalitarianism and rejected traditional religious hierarchies. They believed that the Holy Spirit or the "inner light" could inspire every soul.

Within twenty years, the Society of Friends, also called **Quakers**, purchased Carteret's share (West Jersey) and some of Berkeley's (East Jersey). Rejecting religious hierarchies, Quakers believed that anyone could directly receive God's "inner light" and that all people were equal in God's sight. With no formally trained clergy, Quakers allowed men and women to speak in meetings and become "public Friends" who traveled to spread God's word. Quakers proselytized throughout the Atlantic world in the 1650s. Authorities rejected Quakers' radical egalitarianism, and they encountered persecution everywhere.

Pennsylvania

William Penn: The proprietor of the last unallocated tract of American territory at the king's disposal, which would become Pennsylvania.

In 1681, Charles II granted the region between Maryland and New York to his friend **William Penn**, a prominent Quaker. Penn held the colony as a personal proprietorship, one that earned profits for his descendants until the American Revolution. Penn saw his province as a haven for persecuted coreligionists. Penn offered land to settlers on liberal terms, promising religious toleration, although only Christian men could vote; guaranteeing English liberties, and pledging to establish a representative assembly. He also publicized the availability of land in Pennsylvania through promotional tracts in German, French, and Dutch.

By mid-1683, more than three thousand people—among them Welsh, Irish, Dutch, and Germans—had moved to Pennsylvania, and within five years the population reached twelve thousand. Philadelphia, sited on the easily navigable Delaware River, drew merchants and artisans from throughout the English-speaking world. From mainland and Caribbean colonies alike came Quakers who brought experience on American soil and trading connections. Pennsylvania's fertile lands enabled residents to export surplus flour and other foodstuffs to the West Indies. Philadelphia rapidly acquired more than two thousand citizens and challenged Boston's commercial dominance.

Penn attempted to treat native peoples fairly. He learned to speak the language of the Delawares (or Lenapes), from whom he purchased land to sell to European settlers. Penn also established strict trade regulations and forbade the sale of alcohol to Indians. His policies attracted native peoples who moved to Pennsylvania in the late seventeenth century to escape clashes with English colonists in Maryland, Virginia, and North Carolina. Ironically, however, the same toleration that attracted Native Americans also brought non-Quaker Europeans—Scots-Irish, Germans, and Swiss—who showed little respect for Indian land claims and would clash repeatedly with them.

Carolina

The southernmost proprietary colony, granted by Charles II in 1663, stretched from the southern boundary of Virginia to Spanish Florida. Strategically, a successful English settlement there would prevent Spaniards from pushing farther north. The fertile, semitropical land also promised to yield such exotic and valuable commodities as figs, olives, wines, and silk. The proprietors named their new province Carolina in honor of Charles. The "Fundamental Constitutions of Carolina," which they asked the political philosopher John Locke to draft, outlined a colony governed by landholding aristocrats and characterized by a structured distribution of political and economic power.

But Carolina failed to follow this plan. Instead, it quickly developed two distinct population centers, which in 1729 split into separate colonies under royal rule. Virginia planters settled the Albemarle region that became North Carolina. They established a society like their own, based on cultivating tobacco and exporting forest products. The other population center, which eventually formed South Carolina, developed at Charles Town, founded in 1670. Many of its early residents were sugar planters from overcrowded Barbados who expected to reestablish plantation agriculture and escape hurricanes. They were disappointed: sugar would not grow in Carolina, and a destructive hurricane struck in 1686.

The settlers raised corn and cattle, which they sold to Caribbean planters. They also depended on trade with nearby Indians for commodities they could sell elsewhere, mostly deerskins, sent to Europe, and enslaved Indians, who were shipped to Caribbean islands and northern colonies. During the first decade of the eighteenth century, South Carolina exported an average of 54,000 skins annually, which peaked at 160,000. Before 1715, Carolinians exported 30,000 to 50,000 Indian slaves.

Chesapeake

The English Civil War retarded the development of the earlier English settlements. Struggles between supporters of the king and Parliament caused military clashes in Maryland and political upheavals in Virginia. Once the war ended and immigration resumed, the colonies expanded again. Some settlers, especially those on Virginia's eastern shore and southern border, raised grain, livestock, and flax, to be sold to English and Dutch merchants. Tobacco growers began importing increasing numbers of English indentured servants as farms developed into plantations. Less concerned about Indian attack after the 1646 defeat of the Powhatan Confederacy, colonists sought to enlarge their landholdings.

Chesapeake tobacco planters also started to acquire enslaved workers. Most came from a population that historian Ira Berlin has termed "Atlantic creoles"—people (perhaps of mixed race) who came from other European settlements in the Atlantic world, primarily Iberian outposts. Not all Atlantic creoles arriving in the Chesapeake were bondspeople; some were free or indentured. With them, the Chesapeake became a "society with slaves," where slavery coexisted with various labor systems.

New England

In New England, migration ceased after the Civil War began in 1642. While Puritans were challenging the king and then governing England as a commonwealth, they had little incentive to leave their homeland. Yet the Puritan colonies' population grew dramatically by natural increase. By the 1670s, New England's population more than tripled to approximately seventy thousand, creating pressure on available land. Colonial settlement spread into the Massachusetts and Connecticut interior, and many later generations migrated—north to New Hampshire or Maine, southwest to New York or New Jersey—seeking available farmland. Others learned such skills as blacksmithing or carpentry to support themselves in the growing towns.

Those who remained in the small, densely populated older New England communities experienced witchcraft accusations and trials after 1650. The accused allies of the Devil were thought to harness spirits for good or evil. A witch might engage in fortunetelling, prepare healing potions, or cause the death of a child or animal. Only New England witnessed many witch trials witches (about one hundred in all before 1690). Most of the accused were middle-aged women who had angered their neighbors. Historians have concluded that daily interactions in close-knit communities fostered quarrels that led some colonists to believe others had diabolically caused certain misfortunes. Even so, judges and juries were skeptical: only a few of the accused were convicted, and fewer were executed.

Colonial Political Structures

By the last quarter of the seventeenth century, almost all the Anglo-American colonies had well-established political and judicial structures. In New England, property-holding men or the legislature elected the governors; in other regions, the king or proprietor appointed them. A council, elected or appointed, advised the governor and served as the upper house of the legislature. Each colony had a judiciary with local justices of the peace and county courts, and most had local governing bodies.

A Decade of Imperial Crises: The 1670s

How did settlers' interests collide with those of Native Americans?

Between 1670 and 1680, New France, New Mexico, New England, and Virginia experienced bitter conflicts as their interests collided with those of America's original inhabitants.

New France and the Iroquois

In the mid-1670s, Louis de Buade de Frontenac, the governor-general of Canada, decided to expand New France south and westward to establish a trade route to Mexico and gain control of the valuable fur trade. Accordingly, he encouraged the explorations of Father Jacques Marquette, Louis Jolliet, and René-Robert Cavelier de La Salle in the Great Lakes and Mississippi valley regions. His goal led to conflict with the powerful Iroquois Confederacy, composed of five Indian nations—the Mohawks, Oneidas, Onondagas, Cayugas, and Senecas. (In 1722, the Tuscaroras became the sixth.)

Link to Marquette's account of his exploration of the Mississippi.

Under the terms of a unique defensive alliance forged in the sixteenth century, a representative council made war decisions for the entire Iroquois Confederacy. Before the arrival of Europeans, the Iroquois waged wars primarily for captives to replenish their population. Foreigners brought ravaging disease by 1633, intensifying the need for captives. Simultaneously, Europeans created an economic motive for warfare: the desire to dominate the fur trade and gain unimpeded access to European goods. The 1640s war with the Hurons initiated several conflicts with other Indians known as the **Beaver Wars**, in which the Iroquois fought to control the lucrative peltry trade. Iroquois did not trap beaver; instead, they raided other villages for pelts or attacked Indians carrying furs to European outposts. Then the Iroquois traded that booty for European-made blankets, knives, guns, alcohol, and other items.

Beaver Wars: Series of conflicts between the Hurons (and other Indians) and Iroquois in a quest for pelts.

As Iroquois dominance grew, in the mid-1670s to 1690s, the French repeatedly attacked, seeing the Iroquois as a threat to France's plans to trade with western Indians. Although in 1677 New Yorkers and the Iroquois established a formal alliance known as the Covenant Chain, the English only offered weapons to aid their trading partners. The confederacy held its own and even expanded its reach, enabling it in 1701 to negotiate neutrality treaties with France and other Indians. For the next half-century, the Iroquois maintained their power through trade and diplomacy rather than warfare.

Pueblo Peoples and Spaniards

In New Mexico, too, 1670s events led to a crisis with long-term consequences. Under Spanish domination, Pueblo peoples had added Christianity to their beliefs while retaining traditional rituals. But as decades passed, Franciscans adopted violent tactics to eliminate the native religion. Priests and secular colonists who held *encomiendas* placed heavy labor demands on the people, who were also suffering from Apache raids and food shortages caused by a drought. In 1680, the Pueblos revolted under the leadership of **Popé**, a respected shaman, driving the Spaniards out of New Mexico. Although Spain restored its authority by 1700, Spanish governors now stressed cooperation with the Pueblos, relying on their labor but no longer violating their cultural integrity. The **Pueblo Revolt of 1680** constituted the most successful and longest-sustained Indian resistance movement in colonial North America.

Spanish military outposts (*presidios*) and Franciscan missions offered some protection to Pueblos, but other Indians' desire to obtain horses and guns led to violence throughout the region. Navajos, Apaches, and Utes attacked each other and the Pueblos for captives and hides to trade to the Spanish. Spaniards often kept female and child captives as domestic laborers and sent men to Mexican silver mines. When Comanches migrated west from the Great Plains in the late seventeenth century, Utes allied with them, and after the Pueblo revolt that alliance dominated New Mexico's northern borderlands for several decades.

In the more densely settled English colonies, hostilities developed in the 1670s over land. In New England and Virginia, tensions erupted as settlers increasingly encroached on Native American territories.

Popé: Leader of the Pueblo Revolt against Spanish in 1680.

Pueblo Revolt of 1680: The most successful Indian uprising in American history. Pueblo Indians rebelled against Spanish authority and drove the Spanish from their New Mexico settlements.

King Philip's War

By the early 1670s, the growing settlements in southern New England surrounded Wampanoag ancestral lands on Narragansett Bay. The local chief, Metacom, or King Philip, was troubled by territorial loss and the impact of European culture and Christianity on his people. Philip led attacks on nearby communities in June 1675. Other Algonquian peoples, among them Nipmucks and Narragansetts, joined King Philip's forces. In the fall, they attacked settlements in the northern Connecticut River valley, and the war spread to Maine when the Abenakis entered the conflict. In early 1676, the Indian allies devastated villages like Lancaster, where they captured Mary Rowlandson and others and attacked Plymouth and Providence; later Abenaki assaults forced the abandonment of most Maine settlements. Altogether, the alliance wholly or partially destroyed twenty-seven of ninety-two towns and attacked forty others, pushing the line of English settlement back toward the east and south.

In summer 1676, the Indian coalition ran short of food and ammunition. On June 12, the Mohawks—ancient Iroquois enemies of New England Algonquians—devastated a major Wampanoag encampment while most of the warriors were attacking an English town. After King Philip was killed that August, the southern alliance crumbled. Fighting continued on the Maine frontier for another two years until the English and Abenakis agreed to end the conflict in 1678.

In addition to the Wampanoags, Nipmucks, Narragansetts, and Abenakis who were captured and sold into slavery, still more died of starvation and disease. New Englanders had broken the power of the southern coastal tribes. Thereafter, the southern Indians lived in small clusters, subordinated to the colonists and often working as servants or sailors. Only on Martha's Vineyard did Christian Wampanoags (who had not participated in the war) preserve their cultural identity.

King Philip's War: Major war between Indians and New England settlers.

The settlers paid a terrible price for their victory: an estimated one-tenth of the adult male population was killed or wounded. Proportional to population, it was the most costly conflict in American history. The heavy losses also caused Puritan colonists to question whether God had turned against them. New Englanders did not fully rebuild abandoned interior towns for thirty years, and not until the American Revolution did per capita income reach pre-1675 levels.

Bacon's Rebellion: Uprising that resulted from many conflicts, among them mounting land shortage and settlers' desires for Indian lands.

Bacon's Rebellion

In the early 1670s, conflict wracked Virginia when ex-servants, unable to acquire land, eyed territory reserved by treaty for Virginia's Indians. Governor William Berkeley resisted starting a war, and dissatisfied colonists rallied behind a recent immigrant, the gentleman Nathaniel Bacon, who shared their frustration that desirable land had been claimed. Using as a pretext the July 1675 killing of an indentured servant by Doeg Indians, settlers attacked the Doegs and Susquehannocks, a more powerful nation. In retaliation, Susquehannocks raided outlying farms early in 1676.

The governor outlawed Bacon and his men; the rebels then held Berkeley hostage, forcing him to authorize them to attack the Indians. During the chaotic summer of 1676, Bacon alternately pursued Indians and battled the governor. In September, Bacon's forces burned Jamestown to the ground. But after Bacon died of dysentery the following month, the rebellion collapsed. Even so, a new treaty in 1677 opened much of the disputed territory to settlement. The end of Bacon's Rebellion pushed most of Virginia's Indians west beyond the Appalachians.

Link to Nathaniel Bacon's Manifesto.

The Atlantic Trading System

How was slavery at the center of the expanding trade network between Europe and the colonies?

In the 1670s and 1680s, the Chesapeake's prosperity rested on tobacco, which depended on an ample labor supply. But fewer English men and women proved willing to indenture themselves. Population pressures had eased in England, and the Restoration colonies gave migrants other settlement options. Furthermore, fluctuating tobacco prices and land scarcity made the Chesapeake less appealing. Wealthy Chesapeake tobacco growers found the answer to their labor problem in the Caribbean sugar islands, where Dutch, French, English, and Spanish planters purchased African slaves.

Why African Slavery?

Slavery was practiced in Europe and Islamic lands for centuries. European Christians justified enslaving heathen peoples, especially those of exotic origin, in religious terms, arguing that it might lead to their conversion. Muslims, too, enslaved infidels and imported tens of thousands of black African bondspeople into North Africa and the Middle East. Others believed that wartime prisoners could be enslaved. Consequently, when Portuguese mariners encountered African societies holding slaves, they purchased bondspeople. Indeed, they initially bought slaves in one African nation and sold them in another. From the 1440s on, Portugal imported large numbers of slaves into the Iberian Peninsula; by 1500, enslaved Africans composed one-tenth of the population of Lisbon, Portugal, and Seville, Spain. In 1555, some were taken to England.

Iberians exported African slavery to New Spain and Brazil. Because the Catholic Church prevented the formal enslavement of Indians in those domains and free laborers refused to work in mines or on sugar plantations, African bondspeople became mainstays of the Caribbean and Brazilian economies. The first enslaved Africans in the Americas were imported from Angola, Portugal's early trading partner, and the Portuguese word *Negro* came into use as a descriptor.

English people had few moral qualms about enslaving other humans. Slavery was sanctioned in the Bible and widely practiced by contemporaries. Yet English colonists initially lacked clear categories for "race" and "slave." For example, the 1670 Virginia law that first tried to define the enslaveable declared that "all servants not being christians imported into this colony by shipping shal be slaves for their lives." Such nonracial phrasing reveals that Anglo-American settlers had not yet fully developed the meaning of *race* and *slave* that would come over time.

Atlantic Slave Trade   North American mainland planters could not have obtained bondspeople without the rapid development of an Atlantic trading system. Although this elaborate Atlantic economic system has been called the triangular trade, people and products did not move across the ocean in easily diagrammed patterns. Instead, a complicated web of exchange tied the peoples of the Atlantic world together (see Map 3.2).

The expanding trade network between Europe and its colonies was fueled by the sale and transport of slaves, the exchange of commodities produced by slave labor, and the need to feed and clothe bound laborers. By the late seventeenth century, the basis of the European economic system shifted from the Mediterranean and Asia to the Atlantic, with commerce in slaves and the products of slave labor, as its core.

Chesapeake tobacco and Caribbean and Brazilian sugar were shipped to Europe, where they were in demand. The profits paid for African laborers and European manufactured goods. The African coastal rulers received their payment for slaves in European manufactures and East Indian textiles. Europeans purchased slaves from Africa for resale in their colonies, acquired sugar and tobacco from America, and dispatched their manufactures everywhere.

Europeans fought bitterly to control the lucrative trade. The Portuguese, who at first dominated it, were supplanted by the Dutch in the 1630s. In the Anglo-Dutch wars, the Dutch lost to the English, who controlled the trade through the Royal African Company. Holding a monopoly on English trade with sub-Saharan Africa, the company maintained seventeen forts and trading posts, dispatched to West Africa hundreds of ships carrying English goods, and transported about 100,000 slaves to England's Caribbean colonies. After the company's monopoly expired in 1712, independent traders carried most of the Africans imported into the colonies.

By the middle of the eighteenth century, American tobacco had become closely associated with African slavery. An English woodcut advertising tobacco from the York River in Virginia accordingly depicted not a Chesapeake planter but rather an African, shown with a hoe in one hand and a pipe in the other. Usually, of course, slaves would not have smoked the high-quality tobacco produced for export, although they were allowed to cultivate small crops for their own use.

West Africa and the Slave Trade   Most of the enslaved people carried to North America originated in West Africa, some from the Rice and Grain Coasts, many others from the Gold and Slave Coasts and the Bight of Biafra (modern Nigeria) and Angola. Certain coastal rulers served as intermediaries, facilitating permanent slave-trading posts and supplying resident Europeans with slaves. Such rulers simultaneously controlled Europeans' access to bound laborers and desirable trade goods, such as textiles, iron bars, alcohol, tobacco, guns, and cowry shells from the Maldive Islands (in the Indian Ocean), used as currency. At least 10 percent of all slaves exported to the Americas passed through Whydah, Dahomey's major slave-trading port. Portugal, England, and France established forts there, and Europeans had to pay fees to Whydah's rulers before they could begin to acquire cargoes.

The slave trade affected African regions unevenly. It helped to create such powerful eighteenth-century kingdoms as Dahomey and Asante (formed from the Akan States), while rulers in parts of Upper Guinea, especially modern Gambia and Senegal, largely resisted involvement. Traffic in slaves destroyed smaller polities and disrupted traditional economic patterns. Agricultural production intensified, especially in rice-growing areas, to supply slave ships with foodstuffs. Because prisoners of war constituted most of the exported slaves, active traders were also successful warriors. Some nations even initiated conflicts to acquire captives.

MAP 3.2

Atlantic Trade Routes

By the late seventeenth century, an elaborate trade network linked the countries and colonies bordering the Atlantic Ocean. The most valuable commodities exchanged were enslaved people and the products of slave labor.

Source: Copyright © Cengage Learning

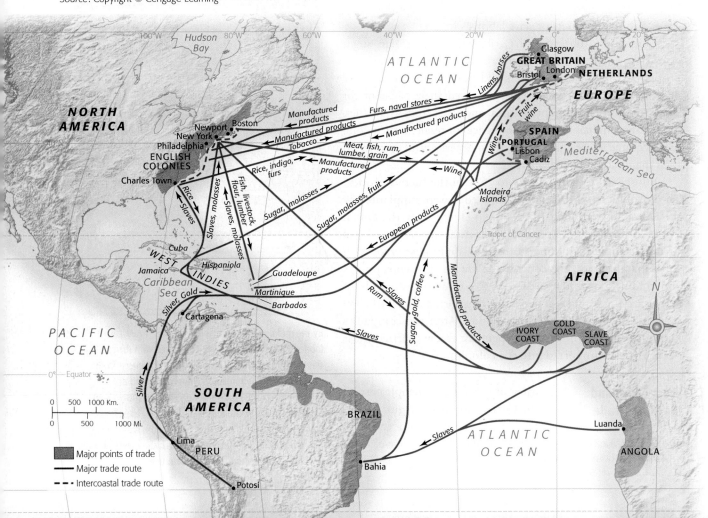

Links to the World

Exotic Beverages

Seventeenth-century colonists developed a taste for tea (from China), coffee (from Arabia), chocolate (from Mesoamerica), and rum. Demand for these once-exotic beverages helped reshape the world economy after the mid-seventeenth century. Approximately two-thirds of the people who migrated across the Atlantic before 1776 were involved, primarily as slaves, in the production of tobacco, calico, and these four drinks. The exotic beverages profoundly affected culture, too, as they moved from luxury to necessity.

Each beverage had its own consumption pattern. Chocolate, brought to Spain from Mexico and consumed hot at intimate gatherings, became the drink of aristocrats. Coffee became the morning beverage of English and colonial businessmen, who praised its caffeine for keeping them focused. Coffee was served in new public coffeehouses, patronized by men, which opened first in London in the late 1660s and in Boston by the 1690s. By the mid-eighteenth century, though, tea—consumed at home in the afternoon at tea tables

presided over by women—supplanted coffee in England and America. Tea was genteel; rum was the drink of the masses, made possible by new technology and the increasing production of sugar.

American colonies played a vital role in the production, distribution, and consumption of these beverages. Cacao plantations in South America multiplied to meet the rising chocolate demand. Rum involved Americans in every phase of its production and consumption. The sugar grown on Caribbean plantations was transported to the mainland in barrels and ships made from North American wood. There the syrup was turned into rum at 140 distilleries. Americans drank an estimated four gallons per person annually, but exported much of the rum to Africa, where it could purchase more slaves to produce more sugar to make more rum.

Thus, these beverages linked the colonies to the world and altered their economic and social development.

The frontispiece of Peter Muguet, Tractatus De Poto Caphe, Chinesium The et de Chocolata, *1685. Muguet's treatise visually linked the three hot, exotic beverages recently introduced to Europeans. The drinks are consumed by representatives of the cultures in which they originated: a turbaned Turk (with coffeepot in the foreground), a Chinese man (with teapot on the table), and an Indian drinking from a hollowed, handled gourd (with a chocolate pot and ladle on the floor in front of him).*

Library of Congress

New England and the Caribbean

New England had the most complex relationship to the trading system. It produced only one item England wanted: tall trees for masts for sailing vessels. To buy English manufactures, New Englanders needed profits earned elsewhere, especially in the Caribbean. By the late 1640s, decades before the Chesapeake became dependent on *production* by slaves, New England relied on *consumption* by slaves and owners. New England farmers and merchants profited by selling foodstuffs (primarily corn and salt fish) and wood for barrels to Caribbean sugar planters.

Shopkeepers in the interior of New England and middle colonies bartered with local farmers for grains, livestock, and barrel staves, then traded those items to merchants located in port towns. Such merchants dispatched ships to the Caribbean, where they exchanged their cargoes for molasses, sugar, fruit, dyestuffs, and slaves. Fully reloaded, the ships returned to Boston, Newport, New York, or Philadelphia. Americans distilled molasses into rum, the only part of the trade that could be termed triangular. Rhode Islanders took rum to Africa and traded it for slaves, whom they carried to Caribbean islands to exchange for more molasses to produce more rum.

Slaving Voyages

middle passage: The brutal and often fatal journey of slaves from Africa to America.

Tying the system together was the voyage (commonly called the **middle passage**) that brought Africans to the Americas. On shipboard, men were shackled in pairs in the hold except for some exercise on deck, whereas women and children could usually move freely in their daytime work of food preparation and cleaning. Many resisted enslavement by refusing to eat, jumping overboard, or joining in revolts, which rarely succeeded. Their communal singing and drumming, reported by numerous observers, must have lifted their spirits and forged solidarity. Conditions were hellish, as captains often packed people into holds that were hot, crowded, and reeking of vomit.

The traumatic voyage brought heavy fatalities of captives and crew. Roughly 10 to 20 percent of the newly enslaved died en route; on long or disease-ridden voyages, mortality rates were higher. Another 20 percent died before the ships left Africa or shortly after arriving in the Americas. One in every four or five sailors died on voyages, chiefly through exposure to such diseases as yellow fever and malaria.

Sailors signed on to slaving voyages reluctantly. Slave merchants were notoriously greedy and captains brutal—to sailors and captives. Unfortunately, the sailors, often the subject of abuse, in turn abused bondspeople. Yet through intimate contact with the enslaved, they learned the value of freedom, and sailors became known for their fierce attachment to independence.

Slavery in North America and the Caribbean

What skills did African slaves bring to America that proved vital to the development of colonial South Carolina?

Barbados, America's first "slave society" (an economy wholly dependent on enslavement), spawned others. As the island's population expanded, about 40 percent of the early English residents dispersed to other colonies. They carried their laws, commercial contacts, and slaveholding practices with them. A large proportion of the first Africans imported into North America came via Barbados. In addition to the many Barbadians who settled in Carolina, others moved to southern Virginia, New Jersey, and New England.

African Enslavement in the Chesapeake

Newly arrived Africans in the Chesapeake were often assigned to outlying parts of plantations (called quarters) until they learned some English and the routines of American tobacco cultivation. The crop that originated in the Americas was also being grown in various locations in West Africa, so Chesapeake planters, who in the late seventeenth century were still experimenting with curing and processing techniques, could well have drawn on their laborers' expertise Such Africans—mostly men—lived with ten to fifteen workers housed together in one or two buildings, supervised by an Anglo-American overseer. Each man was to cultivate two acres of tobacco a year. Their lives must have been filled with toil and loneliness, for few spoke the same language, and all worked six days a week. Many used their Sunday off to cultivate gardens or to hunt or fish to supplement their meager diet. Only rarely could they form families, because of the scarcity of women.

Slaves usually cost about two and a half times as much as indentured servants, but they could supply a lifetime of service, assuming they survived—which large numbers did not, having been weakened by the voyage and sickened by new diseases. Those with enough money could acquire slaves, accumulate greater wealth, and establish large plantations worked by tens, if not hundreds, of bondspeople, whereas the less affluent could not even afford indentured servants. Anglo-American society in the Chesapeake thus became increasingly stratified as the gap between rich and poor planters widened.

So many Africans were imported into Virginia and Maryland that by 1710 people of African descent composed one-fifth of the population. Even so, a decade later American-born slaves outnumbered their African-born counterparts in the Chesapeake, a trend that continued thereafter.

 Link to Colonial Virginia and Maryland slave laws.

African Enslavement in South Carolina

Africans who came with their masters to South Carolina from Barbados in 1670, composing one-quarter to one-third of the early population. The Barbadian slaveowners quickly discovered that African-born slaves' skills were well suited to South Carolina's semitropical environment. African-style dugout canoes became the chief means of transportation in the colony, which was crossed by rivers with large islands. Fishing nets copied from African models proved more efficient. Baskets that enslaved laborers wove and gourds that they hollowed out came into general use as food and drink containers. Finally, Africans adapted their cattle herding techniques in America. Because meat and hides were an early export, Africans contributed to South Carolina's prosperity.

In 1693, as slavery was taking root in South Carolina, Spanish Florida officials began offering freedom to runaways who convert to Catholicism. Hundreds of South Carolina fugitives fled there, although not all gained freedom. Many settled in a town founded for them near St. Augustine, Gracia Real de Santa Teresa de Mose, headed by former slave Francisco Menendez.

After 1700, South Carolinians started importing slaves directly from Africa. In 1710, the African-born constituted a majority of the enslaved population in the colony and, by 1750, bondspeople composed a majority of its residents. The similarity of the South Carolinian and West African environments, coupled with the substantial African-born population, ensured the survival of more aspects of West African culture than elsewhere. Only in South Carolina did enslaved parents give their children African names and develop a dialect that combined English and African terms. (Known as Gullah, it has survived to the present in isolated areas.) In South Carolina, as in Guinea, African women became the primary petty traders, dominating Charles Town markets.

Rice and Indigo

Slave importation coincided with the successful introduction of rice in South Carolina. English people knew nothing about producing rice, but people from Africa's Rice Coast had long worked with the crop. Rice-growing techniques from West Africa, especially cultivation in inland swamps and tidal rivers, were widely adopted. South Carolinians preferred slaves from the Rice Coast, and they preferred women, possibly due to women's crucial role in cultivating rice in West Africa. There, they sowed and weeded the crop, pounded harvested rice with a mortar and pestle to remove the hulls and bran, and then winnowed to separate the grains from the chaff. South Carolinians utilized the West African system of pounding rice by hand until the late eighteenth century.

Every field worker on rice plantations had to cultivate three to four acres a year. Most were female, because enslaved men were assigned to jobs like blacksmithing or carpentry. Planters also expected slaves to grow part of their own food. Under the "task" system of predefined work assignments, experienced slaves could complete their tasks by early afternoon; after that and on Sundays, they were free to work their own gardens or on other projects. One scholar has suggested this unique **task system** used in South Carolina by the early eighteenth century resulted from negotiations between slaves familiar with rice cultivation and masters who desperately needed their expertise.

task system: Each slave had a daily or weekly quota of tasks to complete.

Developers of South Carolina's second cash crop—indigo—also used the task system and drew on slaves' specialized skills. Indigo, the only source of blue dye for the growing English textile industry, was much prized. Eliza Lucas, who managed her father's plantations, experimented with indigo cultivation during the early 1740s. Drawing on the knowledge of slaves and overseers from the Caribbean, she developed the planting and processing techniques later adopted colony-wide. South Carolina indigo never matched the quality of the Caribbean's, but indigo plantations flourished because Parliament offered Carolinians a bounty on every pound exported to Great Britain.

Indian Enslavement in North and South Carolina

In 1708, enslaved Indians composed roughly 14 percent of South Carolina's population. The lucrative traffic in Indian slaves significantly affected South Carolina's relationship with its indigenous neighbors. Native Americans knew they could find a ready market for captive enemies in Charles Town and used it to rid themselves of rivals. Yet as settlers and traders shifted their priorities, first one set of former allies, then another, were enslaved.

The trade in Indian slaves began when the Westos (originally known as the Eries), migrated south from the Great Lakes in the mid-1650s, fleeing their Iroquois enemies after the Beaver Wars. The Westos raided Spain's lightly defended Florida missions and sold Indian captives to Virginians. With the establishment of Carolina, the proprietors monopolized of trade with the Westos, which infuriated settlers shut out of commerce in slaves and deerskins. The planters secretly financed attacks on the Westos, wiping them out by 1682. Southeastern Indians protected themselves from such slave raids by subordination to the English or Spanish, or by coalescing into larger political units, such as those known later as Creeks, Chickasaws, or Cherokees.

At first, the Carolinians did not conflict with neighboring Indians. But in 1711, the Tuscaroras, an Iroquoian people, attacked a Swiss-German settlement at New Bern, North Carolina, which had expropriated their lands, which ignited the **Tuscarora War**. South Carolinians and their Indian allies combined to defeat the Tuscaroras. Afterward, more than a thousand Tuscaroras were enslaved, and the remainder drifted northward, where they joined the Iroquois Confederacy.

Tuscarora War: War in the Carolinas from 1711 through 1713 that pitted Tuscarora Indians against colonists and their Indian allies.

Four years later, the Yamasees, who aided the Carolinians against the Tuscaroras, turned on their English allies. In what seems a long-planned retaliation for abuses by traders and threats to their lands, the Yamasees enlisted the Creeks and other Muskogean peoples to attack outlying English settlements. In spring and summer 1715, English and African refugees by the hundreds streamed into Charles Town. The Yamasee-Creek offensive was thwarted when reinforcements arrived from the north, colonists hastily armed their African slaves, and Cherokees joined the fight. Afterward, Carolinian involvement in the Indian slave trade ceased, because their native neighbors moved away for self-protection. The native peoples of the Carolinas regrouped and rebuilt, for they were no longer subjected to slavers' raids.

Enslavement in the North

Atlantic creoles from the Caribbean and native peoples from the Carolinas and Florida, along with Indians enslaved for crime or debt, composed the bound laborers in the northern mainland colonies. The intricate involvement of northerners in the commerce surrounding the slave trade ensured that many people of African descent lived in America north of Virginia and that "Spanish Indians" became part of the New England population. Some bondspeople resided in urban areas, especially New York, which in 1700 had a larger black population than any other mainland city. Women worked as domestic servants, men as unskilled laborers on the docks.

Yet even in the North, most bondspeople worked in the countryside doing agricultural tasks. Dutch farmers in the Hudson valley and northern New Jersey were likely to rely on enslaved Africans, as were the owners of large landholdings in Rhode Island's Narragansett region. Some toiled in new enterprises, such as ironworks, alongside hired laborers and indentured servants. Although few northern colonists owned slaves, those who did relied heavily on their labor and wanted to preserve the institution of slavery.

The Granger Collection, New York

An advertisement for a sale of slaves of African descent that appeared in the *New York Journal* in 1768. The expertise of two would have appealed to urban buyers: a cooper would have been useful to a barrelmaker or shipper, and the seamstress might have attracted attention from dressmakers. The other bondspeople mentioned could have been purchased by people who wanted house servants or laborers.

Slave Resistance As slavery grew, so did slaves' resistance. Usually, resistance meant malingering or running away, but occasionally bondspeople planned rebellions. Seven times before 1713, the English Caribbean experienced major revolts. The first mainland slave revolt occurred in New York in 1712. The rebels set a fire and ambushed those who tried to put it out, killing eight and wounding twelve. Of those caught and tried, eighteen were executed. Their decapitated bodies were left rotting outdoors as a warning.

Imperial Reorganization and the Witchcraft Crisis

How did mercantilism benefit some colonies economically and hurt others?

English officials seeking new sources of revenue focused on the expanding Atlantic trade in slaves and the products of slave labor. Parliament and the Stuart monarchs drafted laws to harness the profits of the trade for the mother country.

Mercantilism and Navigation Acts Like other European nations, England based its commercial policy on mercantilism, the theory that viewed the economic world as a collection of national states, whose governments competed for shares of a finite amount of wealth. What one nation gained, another nation lost. Each nation sought economic self-sufficiency and a favorable balance of trade by exporting more than it imported. Colonies played an important role, supplying the mother country with valuable raw materials and a market for the mother country's manufactured goods.

Parliament's Navigation Acts—passed between 1651 and 1673—established three principles of mercantilist theory. First, only English or colonial merchants could legally trade in the colonies. Second, certain valuable American products could be sold only in the mother country or other English colonies. Initially, these "enumerated" goods included wool, sugar, tobacco, indigo, ginger, and dyes; and later rice, naval stores (masts, pitch, tar, and turpentine), copper, and furs. Third, foreign goods for sale in the colonies had to be shipped through England, paying English import duties. Years later, new laws established a fourth principle: the colonies could not export items (such as wool clothing, hats, or iron) that competed with English products.

These laws adversely affected Chesapeake planters who could not seek foreign markets for their staple crops. The statutes initially helped English Caribbean sugar producers by driving Brazilian sugar from the home market, but later prevented English planters from selling sugar elsewhere. Others benefited: the laws stimulated a lucrative colonial shipbuilding industry, especially in New England. And the northern and middle colonies produced many unenumerated goods—fish, flour, meat and livestock, and barrel staves—that could be traded directly to the French, Spanish, or Dutch Caribbean islands if transported in English or American ships.

English authorities soon learned that enforcing mercantilist laws would be difficult. The American coast's many harbors were havens for smugglers, and colonial officials often looked the other way when illegally imported goods were sold. Because American juries tended to favor local smugglers, Parliament in 1696 established American vice-admiralty courts, which operated without juries and adjudicated violations of the Navigation Acts.

Colonial Autonomy Challenged

By the early 1680s, mainland colonies had become accustomed to a considerable degree of political autonomy. Massachusetts, Plymouth, Connecticut, and Rhode Island operated independently, subject neither to the king nor a proprietor. Whereas Virginia was a royal colony and New Hampshire (1679) and New York (1685) gained that status, all other mainland settlements were proprietorships, over which England exercised little control. In the English colonies, free adult men who owned some property expected to have a voice in their governments, especially about taxation.

After James II became king in 1685, he and his successors sought to tighten the reins of colonial government and reduce the colonies' political autonomy. English officials saw New England as a hotbed of smuggling. Moreover, Puritans denied religious freedom to non-Congregationalists and maintained laws incompatible with English practice. The charters of all colonies from New Jersey to Maine were revoked, and the Crown established a Dominion of New England in 1686. (For the boundaries of the Dominion, see Map 3.1.) Sir Edmund Andros, the governor, had immense power: Parliament dissolved the assemblies, and Andros needed only the consent of an appointed council to make laws and levy taxes.

Glorious Revolution in America

New Englanders endured Andros's **autocratic** rule for more than two years. Then James II's power crumbled when he angered his subjects by levying taxes without parliamentary approval and by converting to Catholicism. In April 1689, Boston's leaders jailed Andros and his associates. The following month they received news of the bloodless coup known as the Glorious Revolution, in which James was replaced in late 1688 by his daughter Mary and her husband, the Dutch prince William of Orange. With Protestants William and Mary in power, the Glorious Revolution affirmed the supremacy of Parliament and Protestantism.

autocratic: Absolute or dictatorial rule.

In other colonies, the Glorious Revolution inspired revolt. In Maryland the Protestant Association overturned the government of the Catholic proprietor, and in New York a militia officer of German origin, Jacob Leisler, assumed control of the government. Bostonians, Marylanders, and New Yorkers saw themselves as carrying out the colonial phase of the English revolt.

But William and Mary also believed that England should exercise tighter control over its unruly American possessions. Consequently, only the Maryland rebellion received royal sanction, primarily because of its anti-Catholic thrust. In New York, Leisler was hanged for treason, and Massachusetts became a royal colony with an appointed governor. The province retained its town meeting system and continued to elect its council, but the 1691 charter eliminated the religious test for voting and office holding. A parish of the Church of England appeared in Boston. The **"city upon a hill,"** as John Winthrop had envisioned it, had ended.

city upon a hill: John Winthrop's vision of the Puritan settlement in New England as a model for the world.

King William's War

A war with the French and their Algonquian allies compounded New England's difficulties. King Louis XIV of France allied himself with the deposed James II, and England declared war on France in 1689—Known today as the Nine Years' War, it was called King William's War by the colonists. Even before war broke out in Europe, Anglo-Americans and Abenakis clashed over English settlements in Maine that had been reoccupied after the 1678 truce and were expanding. Attacks wholly or partially destroyed several towns, and colonial expeditions against Montreal and Quebec in 1690 failed. Even the Peace of Ryswick (1697), which ended the war in Europe, did not bring peace to the northern frontiers. Maine could not be resettled for several decades because of the continuing conflict.

The 1692 Witchcraft Crisis

New Englanders feared a repetition of the devastation of King Philip's War. For eight months in 1692, witchcraft accusations spread through Essex County, Massachusetts—a heavily populated area directly threatened by the Indian attacks in neighboring southern Maine and New Hampshire. Before the crisis ended, fourteen women and five men were hanged, one man was pressed to death with heavy stones, fifty-four people confessed to being witches, and more than 140 people were jailed.

The crisis began in late February when several children and young women in Salem Village charged older female neighbors with torturing them in spectral form. Other accusers and confessors chimed in, among them female domestic servants orphaned in the Maine war. These young women offered fellow New Englanders a compelling explanation for the troubles afflicting them: their province was under direct assault not only by Indians and the French but also by the Devil and his allied witches.

The so-called afflicted girls accused not just the older women commonly suspected of such offenses but also prominent men from the Maine frontier who had traded with or failed to defeat the Indians. Their leader, accusers declared, was the Reverend George Burroughs, a Harvard graduate who had ministered in Maine and Salem Village and was charged with bewitching soldiers sent to combat the Abenakis. The colony's magistrates, who were also its political and military leaders, were willing to believe such accusations, because it freed them from responsibility for losses on the frontier.

In October, the worst phase of the crisis ended when the governor dissolved the special court established to try the suspects. He and prominent clergymen regarded the descriptions of spectral torturers as "the Devil's testimony," and therefore untrustworthy. Most critics did not think the afflicted were faking, that witches did not exist or that confessions were false. Rather, they questioned whether guilt could be legally established by the evidence presented in court. During the final trials in 1693, almost all the defendants were acquitted, and the governor reprieved the few found guilty.

Link to excerpts from the Salem Witchcraft papers.

New Imperial Measures

In 1696, England created the fifteen-member Board of Trade and Plantations, the chief government organ concerned with the American colonies. The board gathered information, reviewed Crown appointments in America, scrutinized colonial legislation, supervised trade policies, and advised ministries on colonial issues. It had no enforcement powers and shared jurisdiction with the customs service, the navy, and a member of the ministry. Although this reform improved colonial administration, supervision of the American provinces remained decentralized and haphazard.

Debating the Witchcraft Trials

By late September 1692, disagreements over the Salem witchcraft trials (which had begun in June) sharply divided the intellectual leaders of Massachusetts Bay. Key among them were the colony's ministers, and especially a father and son: the Reverend Increase Mather and his son Cotton. Both were prolific authors, and both chose to present their views in print. The twenty-nine-year-old Cotton Mather strongly supported the trials and, at the request of the governor, wrote *The Wonders of the Invisible World* to defend the procedures and verdicts. Through its typeface, the title page of his book revealed its subject: DEVILS. On the title page of the related book by his father, *Cases of Conscience*, the less-prominent words were instead "evil Spirits," and rather than language affirming the "Grievous Molestations by Daemons and Witchcrafts" it included the caution that "infallible proofs" would be required to find the accused guilty. Even though Increase inserted an addendum at the end of his text insisting that he agreed with his son, anyone simply comparing the title pages could recognize that he was attempting to conceal competing opinions about the trials within his own family. What other contrasts between the two books are evident in the contents of the title pages?

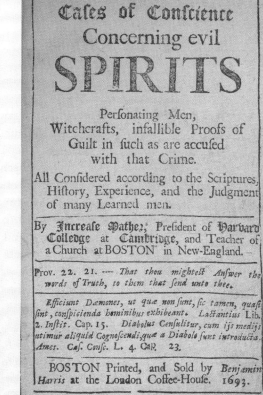

Americans of African Descent

After the 1670s, the rise of southern economies based on the enslavement of Africans, coupled with employment of enslaved Africans in northern colonies, dramatically altered the American population. By 1775, more than a quarter-million Africans had been imported into the territory that later became the United States; they and their descendants constituted about 20 percent of the population at that time.

According to the 2000 census, 12.5 percent of the Americans now claim descent from African ancestors. Because the legal importation of African slaves ended in 1808 and because the United States attracted relatively few voluntary migrants of African descent until the late twentieth century, most of today's native-born African Americans have colonial ancestors. Conversely, most European Americans are descended in part from the massive European migrations of the nineteenth and early twentieth centuries.

The modern African American population includes people with various skin colors, reflecting past interracial sexual relationships (coerced and voluntary). African Americans, free and enslaved, have had children with Europeans and Indians since the colonial period; more recently, they have intermarried with Asian immigrants. State laws, enacted from the early years of the American republic until 1967—when they were struck down by the Supreme Court—forbade legal marriages between people of European descent and those of other races. Thus, if people of color wanted to wed legally, they had to marry other people of color.

Recently, increasing numbers of interracial unions have produced multiracial children. The 2000 census for the first time allowed Americans to define themselves as members of more than one race. Previous laws defined people with any African ancestry as "black"; on census forms today, people of African descent seem less willing to define themselves as multiracial. Their racial self-definition thus continues to be influenced by a legacy of discrimination.

Most colonists resented alien officials who arrived to implement the policies of king and Parliament, but they adjusted to them and to the Navigation Act's trade restrictions. They fought another of Europe's wars—the War of the Spanish Succession, called Queen Anne's War in the colonies—from 1702 to 1713, without enduring the stresses of the first, despite the heavy economic burdens the conflict imposed. Colonists who allied with the royal government received offices and land grants, and composed "court parties" that supported English officials. Others, who lacked well-placed friends or who defended colonial autonomy, made up the opposition, or "country" interest. By the end of the 1725, most men in both groups were American born. They were from elite families whose wealth derived in the South from staple-crop production and in the North from commerce.

Summary

The years from 1650 to 1720 established the basic economic and political patterns in mainland colonial society. In 1650, two isolated centers of English population, New England and the Chesapeake, existed along the seaboard, along with the Dutch New Netherland. In 1720, nearly the entire North American east coast was in English hands, and Indian control east of the Appalachian Mountains had been broken by King Philip's War, Bacon's Rebellion, the Yamasee and Tuscarora wars, and Queen

Anne's War. West of the mountains, the Iroquois reigned. Most of the population was American-born, except for the African-born people in South Carolina and the Chesapeake. Economies originally based on the fur trade had become more complex and closely linked with the mother country, and political structures had become more uniform. The adoption of large-scale slavery and production of tobacco, rice, and indigo in the Chesapeake and Carolinas distinguished them from northern colonies as true slave societies.

The northern colonies, too, rested on profits from the Atlantic trading system, the key element of which was traffic in slaves. New England sold corn, salt fish, and wood products to the West Indies, where slaves consumed the foodstuffs and whence planters shipped sugar and molasses in barrels. Pennsylvania and New York also found the Caribbean islands a ready market for their livestock, grains, and wheat flour.

Meanwhile, north of Mexico Spanish settlements remained centered on Florida missions and on New Mexican presidios and missions. The French had explored the Mississippi valley but had not yet planted many settlements in the Great Lakes or the west. Both nations' colonists depended on indigenous people's labor and goodwill. Yet the Spanish and French presence to the south and west of English settlements ensured future conflicts among European powers in North America.

By 1720, key elements of the imperial administrative structure that would govern the English colonies until 1775 were in place. Anglo-Americans' commitment to autonomous local government would later lead them into conflict with Parliament and the king.

Chapter Review

The Growth of Anglo-American Settlements

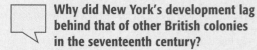 **Why did New York's development lag behind that of other British colonies in the seventeenth century?**

Granted to James the Duke of York in 1664, New York remained a shadow of Boston until well into the 1720s largely because James, unlike William Penn of Pennsylvania and other proprietors, did not encourage migration with offers of land grants and religious freedom to would-be colonists. Instead, his colony remained hemmed in by Connecticut and New Jersey, which each made successful overtures to draw populations helpful to development. English citizens who might have considered migrating to New York were turned off by James's decision to retain the Dutch local government, land title, and legal practices that had been in place when he assumed control of the former Dutch colony. He also allowed towns to decide which church to support with its taxes and refused a legislative assembly—which many English colonists wanted—until 1683.

A Decade of Imperial Crises: The 1670s

How did settlers' interests collide with those of Native Americans?

Settlers' and Native Americans' interests clashed in two pivotal areas: control of trade and desire for more land. New France and the Iroquois Confederacy clashed over control of the valuable fur trade, which the Iroquois had fought hard to attain. Bitter battles and attacks lasted for twenty years, before culminating in a neutrality treaty. Similarly, in the densely settled New England colonies in the 1670s, hostilities developed as Wampanoags led by King Phillip felt threatened by the Anglo-American communities that surrounded their territory. And in Virginia Nathaniel Bacon and his followers also focused on seizing desirable interior land from Indians, ultimately attacking them and pushing them further west.

The Atlantic Trading System

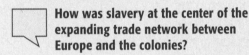

How was slavery at the center of the expanding trade network between Europe and the colonies?

First, the Chesapeake developed around tobacco farming, which required a vast supply of workers. Fewer English workers were available as population pressures in England eased and Restoration colonies offered land and other opportunities to would-be settlers. Tobacco growers instead turned to slave labor, as did other plantation colonies, thereby expanding the sale and transport of slaves. In addition, commodities produced by slave labor helped boost exports and trade networks, while the need to feed and clothe slaves stimulated new business opportunities for other colonies. New England, for example, profited by selling foodstuffs to feed slaves. The slave trade itself created a global economic network and tensions among European nations seeking to control the lucrative trade.

Slavery in North America and the Caribbean

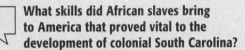

What skills did African slaves bring to America that proved vital to the development of colonial South Carolina?

African-born slaves had several skills that were crucial to the economic development of South Carolina. From a similarly semi-tropical climate, these slaves adapted dugout canoes from their homeland that became a key means of transportation in the many rivers of the Carolinas. Their fishing nets also proved more efficient. African cattle herding techniques aided in producing the meat and hides that were an early export from the region. Some slaves, particularly women, also knew how to cultivate rice, which was rapidly becoming a staple crop in South Carolina. The area's other crash crop—indigo (the only source of blue dye for the growing English textile industry)—similarly drew on the knowledge of slaves transported to South Carolina from the Caribbean, where indigo plantations flourished.

Imperial Reorganization and the Witchcraft Crisis

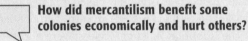

How did mercantilism benefit some colonies economically and hurt others?

Mercantilism was grounded in the notion that the world contained a finite amount of wealth, and that if one nation gained, another had to lose. For England, that meant controlling colonial trade and development in ways that benefited the mother country. England passed the Navigation Acts between 1651 and 1673, which allowed only English merchants to trade in the colonies, permitted certain American products to be sold only to England or other English colonies, and required foreign goods bound for the colonies to ship through England and pay related duties. Later, it additionally prevented colonists from exporting anything that competed with English goods. For Chesapeake planters, these policies had a negative effect, preventing them from selling staple crops in foreign markets. English sugar producers in the Caribbean were initially helped, as their Brazilian competitors were driven from the market, but later suffered when they were prevented from selling their sugar elsewhere. New England benefitted from the emergence of a lucrative shipbuilding industry, while the northern and middle colonies gained from trading goods not included the Navigation Acts such as fish, flour, meat, livestock, and barrels.

Suggestions for Further Reading

Ned Blackhawk, *Violence over the Land: Indians and Empires in the Early American West* (2006)

David Eltis, *The Rise of African Slavery in the Americas* (1998)

Alan Gallay, *The Indian Slave Trade: The Rise of the English Empire in the American South, 1670–1717* (2002)

Andrew Knaut, *The Pueblo Revolt of 1680* (1995)

Jill Lepore, *The Name of War: King Philip's War and the Origins of American Identity* (1998)

Edmund S. Morgan, *American Slavery, American Freedom: The Ordeal of Colonial Virginia* (1975)

Jennifer L. Morgan, *Laboring Women: Reproduction and Gender in New World Slavery* (2004)

Mary Beth Norton, *In the Devil's Snare: The Salem Witchcraft Crisis of 1692* (2002)

Marcus Rediker, *The Slave Ship: A Human History* (2007)

Betty Wood, *The Origins of American Slavery* (1997)

Go to the CourseMate website for primary source links, study tools, and review materials for this chapter. www.cengagebrain.com

American Society Transformed

4

1720–1770

The crime was devastating, the punishment terrible. Marie-Joseph Angélique, a Portuguese-born slave of African descent, was hanged in Montréal on June 21, 1734. Judges had convicted Angélique of setting a fire that destroyed the merchant quarter of the town, the Hotel-Dieu, a convent, and a hospital. Under torture, she confessed, insisting she had acted alone. Afterward, her body was left hanging for hours, then it was burned and her ashes scattered.

Angelique had been a slave in an English colony—probably New York—before being purchased nine years earlier by a Montreal wealthy merchant, Sieur de Francheville, and his wife. She worked in their large household with several free laborers and an enslaved Indian boy. She was one of 150 or so bondspeople living among the 3,000 Montreal residents.

Angélique was the immediate suspect. After her master's death in late 1733, she asked her mistress for her freedom, presumably so she could leave Montréal with her lover, Claude Thibault, a former French soldier who was also a Francheville servant. Denied, she threatened to "roast" her mistress, who retaliated by preparing to sell her to a French Caribbean island. She and Claude set fire to another house in January, before attempting unsuccessfully to flee together. Witnesses testified that Angelique had earlier hinted at plans to burn down the Francheville house. Yet until she was tortured, Angelique proclaimed her innocence. She never implicated Claude Thibault, who vanished from New France.

Angélique's tragic story as a woman of African descent who had spent time in the English colonies points up the movement of peoples around the Atlantic world that after 1720 brought new groups to the British colonies. A massive eighteenth-century migration of European and African peoples changed the nature of the North American population. Ethnic diversity was especially pronounced in the small cities of Anglo America, although the colonies south of New England drew the largest number of newcomers, many to the fertile countryside. They swelled the

Chapter Outline

population, altered political balances, and introduced new religious sects. Unwilling immigrants (slaves and transported convicts), too, clustered primarily in the middle and southern colonies.

Several key themes marked the development of Europe's North American colonies in the mid-eighteenth century: population growth (through natural increase and immigration), new ethnic diversity, the increasing importance of urban centers, the creation of a prosperous urban elite including merchant families like the Franchevilles, rising consumption, and the new significance of internal markets. In the French and British mainland colonies, exports dominated the economy. Settlers along the Atlantic and Gulf coasts were tied to an international commercial system that fluctuated wildly. Yet expanding local populations demanded greater quantities and types of goods, and Europe could not keep up. Therefore, colonists increasingly depended on their own resources. Intermarried networks of wealthy families developed in Europe's American possessions by the 1760s. These well-off, educated colonists participated in transatlantic intellectual life, such as the Enlightenment, whereas some colonists of the "lesser sort" could neither read nor write. Most colonists worked with their hands from dawn to dark. Divisions were most pronounced in British America, the largest and most prosperous settlements. By the last half of the century, social and economic distance among different ranks of Anglo-Americans had widened and produced new conflicts.

In 1720, much of North America was under Indian control. Fifty years later, indigenous peoples still dominated the interior, yet their lives were altered as European settlements expanded. As France moved from the St. Lawrence to the Gulf of Mexico and Spanish outposts expanded east and west from a New Mexican heartland, and as British colonies filled the territory between the Appalachian Mountains and the Atlantic, North America was transformed.

As you read this chapter, keep the following questions in mind:

* **What were the effects of demographic, geographic, and economic changes on Europeans, Africans, and Indian nations alike?**

* **What were the key elements of eighteenth-century colonial cultures?**

* **What developments at midcentury began the process of political and religious change in British North America?**

Geographic Expansion and Ethnic Diversity

What spurred population growth in the British colonies in the thirty years before 1775?

In the mid-eighteenth century, dramatic population growth, along with geographic expansion, characterized British mainland colonies. About 250,000 European-Americans and African Americans resided in the colonies in 1700. Thirty years later, that number had more than doubled, reaching 2.5 million by 1775.

Although migration from Africa, Scotland, Ireland, England, and Germany contributed to population growth, most came from natural increase. Once the difficult early decades of settlement had passed, the American population doubled

Chronology

1690	Locke's *Essay Concerning Human Understanding* published, a key example of Enlightenment thought
1718	New Orleans founded in French Louisiana
1721–22	Smallpox epidemic in Boston leads to first widespread adoption of inoculation in America
1732	Founding of Georgia
1733	John Peter Zenger is tried for and acquitted of "seditious libel" in New York
1739	Stono Rebellion (South Carolina) leads to increased white fears of slave revolts
	George Whitefield arrives in America; Great Awakening broadens
1739–48	King George's War affects American economies
1740s	Black population of the Chesapeake begins to grow by natural increase, contributing to rise of large plantations
1741	New York City "conspiracy" reflects whites' continuing fears of slave revolts
1751	Franklin's *Experiments and Observations on Electricity* published, important American contribution to Enlightenment science
1760–75	Peak of eighteenth-century European and African migration to English colonies
1765–66	Hudson River land riots pit tenants and squatters against large landlords
1767–69	Regulator movement (South Carolina) tries to establish order in backcountry
1771	North Carolina Regulators defeated by eastern militia at Battle of Alamance

approximately every twenty-five years. Women were young when they began child-bearing (early twenties for European-Americans, late teens for African Americans), and married women became pregnant every two or three years, having five to ten children. With the colonies' healthy environment, a large proportion of children reached maturity. About half of the population of Anglo America was under sixteen years old in 1775. (Less than one-quarter of the United States population is currently under sixteen.)

Spanish and French Territorial Expansion
British North America's growing population was sandwiched between the Appalachian Mountains (on the west) and the Atlantic coast (on the east). By contrast, Spanish and French territories expanded across North America with modest population increases. At the end of the eighteenth century, Texas had only about three thousand Spanish residents and California fewer than one thousand; the largest Spanish colony, New Mexico, included twenty thousand or so. Mainland French colonies' population increased from approximately fifteen thousand in 1700 to about seventy thousand in the 1760s, clustered in a few scattered locations. Still, French and Spanish geographic expansion dramatically affected native peoples.

Venturing into the Mississippi Valley in the early eighteenth century, the French and Spanish encountered powerful Indian nations like the Quapaws, Osages, and Caddos. A few Europeans—priests, soldiers, farmers, traders, ranchers—met native peoples who wanted access to manufactured goods, and who accordingly sought friendly relations. The Spanish and French invaders had to adapt to Indian diplomatic and cultural practices. French officials, for example, often complained of being forced to endure lengthy calumet ceremonies; and Spaniards, unaccustomed to involving women in diplomacy, had to accede to Texas Indians' use of female representatives. The European nations established neighboring outposts

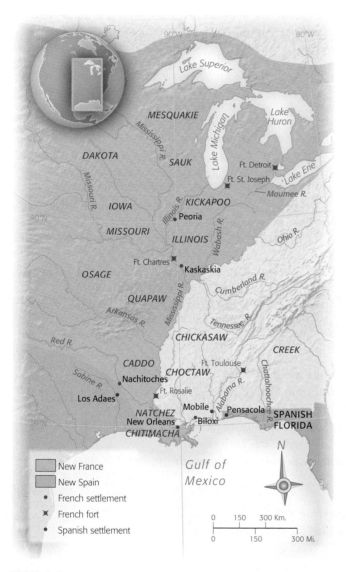

MAP 4.1

Louisiana, ca. 1720

By 1720, French forts and settlements dotted the Mississippi River and its tributaries in the interior of North America. Two isolated Spanish outposts were situated near the Gulf of Mexico.

Source: Copyright © Cengage Learning

 Link to Eulalia Perez's account of her work in a California Spanish mission.

in the lower Mississippi region in 1716—the French at Natchitoches (west of the Mississippi), the Spaniards at Los Adaes (see Map 4.1). France had settled Biloxi Bay (in the modern state of Mississippi) in 1699, and strengthened its presence near the Gulf of Mexico by establishing New Orleans in 1718.

Spaniards focused first on Texas (establishing San Antonio in 1718), then the region they called Alta (upper) California. After learning that Russians who hunted sea otters along the northwest coast wanted to colonize the region, they sent expeditions north from their missions in Baja California. From a base at San Diego, where the Franciscan Junipero Serra set up the first mission in Alta California in July 1769, they traveled by land and sea to Monterey Bay, where in April 1770 they claimed Alta California for Spain. Over the next decades, they established presidios and missions along the coast from modern San Francisco to San Diego. There, Spanish Franciscan friars and a few settlers from Mexico lived amid thousands of Indians who had converted to Christianity.

France and the Mississippi

Along the Mississippi, French posts north of New Orleans became the glue of empire. *Coureurs de bois* (literally, "forest runners") used the American interior's waterways to carry goods between Quebec and the new Louisiana territory. Indians traded furs and hides for guns, ammunition, and other items. The Osages were so eager to acquire firearms that they became, in effect, commercial hunters; their women were sometimes so fully occupied processing hides that older men prepared the communities' meals. The largest French settlements, known collectively as *le pays de Illinois* ("the Illinois country"), never totaled much above three thousand people The shortage of European women led to interracial unions between French men and Indian women, creating mixed-race people known as *metís*. French expansion helped reshape native alliances elsewhere. For example, the equestrian Comanches of the Plains, who could now trade with the French, no longer needed Spanish goods or their previous allies, the Utes. Deprived of powerful partners, the Utes negotiated peace with New Mexico in 1752. Once enslaved by Spaniards, Utes enslaved Paiutes and other nonequestrian peoples. They exchanged hides and slaves—mostly young women—for horses and metal goods until the end of Spanish rule in the region.

To French officials, Louisiana's chief function was protection of the valuable Caribbean islands and prevention of Spanish and British expansion. Profit-seeking farmers and Indian traders from Canada demanded slaves from the French government. Officials dispatched more than six thousand Africans, mostly from Senegal, in the decade after 1719. But residents never developed a successful plantation economy. Skins and hides from the Indians, along with tobacco and indigo, composed Louisiana's major eighteenth-century exports. Enslaved Africans were carried north to the Illinois country, where as farm laborers and domestic servants they made up nearly 40 percent of the population in the 1730s.

Louisiana's expansion claimed lands belonging to Natchez Indians. In 1729, the Natchez and newly arrived slaves attacked the colony's northern reaches, killing more than 10 percent of Europeans. The French retaliated, slaughtering the Natchez and their allies, but under French rule, Louisiana remained a fragile colony.

Involuntary Migrants from Africa

Elsewhere in the Americas, slavery took firm hold during the eighteenth century. In all, more Africans than Europeans came to the Americas—the majority as slaves— with half arriving between 1700 and 1800. Most were transported to Brazil or the Caribbean, primarily in British or Portuguese vessels. Of at least 11 million enslaved people brought to the Americas during slavery, only 260,000 were imported by 1775 into the region that became the United States. In South America and the Caribbean, a surplus of enslaved males over females and high mortality rates meant that only a continuing influx of slaves could maintain a consistent work force. On the North American mainland, South Carolina, where rice cultivation was difficult and unhealthful (because malaria-carrying mosquitoes bred in rice swamps), similarly required an inflow of slaves.

Slaves came from various ethnic groups and regions of Africa (see Map 4.2). More than 40 percent embarked from West Central Africa (modern Congo and Angola), nearly 20 percent from the Bight of Benin (modern Togo, Benin, and southwestern Nigeria), about 13 percent from the Bight of Biafra (today's Cameroon, Gabon, and southeastern Nigeria), and approximately 9 percent from the Gold Coast (modern Ghana and neighboring countries). Smaller proportions came from East Africa and the Windward and Rice Coasts (modern Senegal, Gambia, and Sierra Leone).

Standard slave-trading practice—of loading an entire cargo at one port and selling them in another—meant that people from the same area were typically taken to the Americas together. That was heightened by planter partiality for particular ethnic groups. Virginians favored Igbos from the Bight of Biafra, whereas South Carolinians and Georgians selected Senegambians and people from West Central Africa. Rice planters' desire for Senegambians, who were experienced rice cultivators, makes sense, but historians disagree about the reasons behind other preferences.

Possibly tens of thousands of enslaved Africans were Muslims, some of whom were literate in Arabic and came from aristocratic families. The discovery of noble birth could lead to slaves' being returned home. Job Ben Solomon, for example, a slave trader from Senegal, had been captured by raiders while selling bondspeople in Gambia and sent to Maryland in 1732. A letter he wrote in Arabic so impressed his owners that he was liberated the next year. Despite the approximately 260,000 slaves brought to the mainland, after 1740 American-born people of African descent came to dominate the enslaved population because of natural increase.

MAP 4.2

Major Origins and Destinations of Africans Enslaved in the Americas

As this schematic map shows, enslaved Africans were drawn from many regions of western Africa (with some coming from the interior of the continent) and were shipped to areas throughout the Americas.

Source: Copyright © Cengage Learning

Although about 40 percent of the Africans were male, women and children composed a majority of slave imports; females were valued for their reproductive and productive capacities. A planter who owned adult female slaves could watch his labor force expand steadily—through the births of their children, designated as slaves in every colony.

In the Chesapeake, the number of bondspeople grew rapidly because imports were added to an enslaved population that also expanded through natural increase. Work routines for cultivating tobacco, coupled with a roughly equal sex ratio, reduced slave mortality and increased fertility. Even in unhealthful South Carolina, American-born slaves outnumbered the African-born by 1750.

Newcomers from Europe

About 500,000 Europeans moved to British North America during the eighteenth century, most after 1730. Influenced by mercantilist thought, British authorities regarded a large, industrious population at home as an asset. They deported "undesirables"—vagabonds and Jacobite rebels (supporters of the deposed Stuart monarchs)—but otherwise discouraged emigration. Instead, they recruited German and French Protestants to the colonies by promising free land and religious

Slaves' Symbolic Resistance

Although revolts and running away have been the focus of many studies of enslaved Africans' resistance to bondage in North America, archaeological finds from the mid-eighteenth-century such as those illustrated here have revealed important aspects of slaves' personal lives and other forms of resistance. The set of objects found in Annapolis constitutes a *minkisi*, or West African spiritual bundle. Africans and African Americans placed such bundles of objects, each with a symbolic meaning (for example, bent nails reflected the power of fire), under hearths or sills to direct the spirits, who entered and left houses through doors or chimneys. Their primary purpose was to protect bondspeople from the power of their masters—for example, by preventing the breakup of a family. The statue of a man was uncovered in an enslaved blacksmith's quarters. It too reflects resistance, but of a different sort: the quiet rebellion of a talented craftsman who used his master's iron and his own time and skill to secretly create a remarkable object. Can students today derive insights about enslaved people's lives from such artifacts as these, even though the illiterate bondspeople left no written records? If so, what?

Artifact found in an excavation in Alexandria, Virginia.

A minkisi *from the eighteenth century found under the floor of the Charles Carroll house in Annapolis, Maryland.*

Link to Benjamin Franklin's "Observations Concerning the Increase of Mankind, 1751."

toleration. After 1740, they relaxed citizenship requirements to a small fee, seven years' residence, Protestantism, and an oath of allegiance to the king.

The most successful migrants came well prepared, having learned from earlier migrants that land and resources were abundant and that they would need capital. People who arrived penniless did less well; approximately 40 percent of the newcomers fell into that category, immigrating as bound laborers. Worst off were the 50,000 or so migrants who came as criminals convicted of such offenses as theft and murder. Many unskilled and perhaps one-third female, they were typically dispatched to Maryland to work in tobacco fields, as ironworkers, or as household servants.

Scots-Irish, Scots, and Germans

One of the largest groups of immigrants—over 150,000— were families from Ireland or Scotland. About 70,000 Scots-Irish descendants of Presbyterian Scots who had settled in Northern Ireland during the seventeenth century joined 35,000 who came to America from Scotland (see Table 4.1). Another 45,000 Protestants and Catholics migrated from southern Ireland (often as individuals). High rents, poor harvests, and religious discrimination (in Ireland) pushed people from their homeland. Such immigrants usually landed in Philadelphia or New Castle, Delaware. They moved into the western Pennsylvania backcountry. Later migrants moved to the backcountry of Maryland, Virginia, and the Carolinas. Frequently unable to afford land, they lived illegally on acreage belonging to Indians, land speculators, or colonial governments. They gained a reputation for lawlessness, drinking, and fighting.

Migrants from Germany and German-speaking areas of Switzerland numbered about 85,000 between 1730 and 1755. They, too, usually came in family groups and landed in Philadelphia. Many, like earlier English migrants, contracted to work as servants for several years to pay for their passage. When free, Germans settled together. Many moved west into Pennsylvania and south into the Maryland and Virginia backcountry as well as Charles Town and the southern interior. Germans belonged to various Protestant sects, adding to Pennsylvania's religious diversity. By century's end, Germans were one-third of Pennsylvania's residents. Benjamin Franklin predicted inaccurately in 1751 that they would "Germanize" Pennsylvania.

The most concentrated period of colonial immigration fell between 1760 and 1775, when more than 220,000 free and enslaved people arrived—nearly 10 percent of British North America's population. Tough economic times led many to seek a better life in America; simultaneously, the slave trade burgeoned. Late-arriving free immigrants had little choice but to remain in the cities or move to the edges of settlement; land elsewhere was fully occupied. In the peripheries, they rented or bought property from land speculators.

Maintaining Ethnic and Religious Identities

Half of the colonial population south of New England had non-English origins by 1775. Assimilation into Anglo-American culture depended on settlement patterns, group size, and migrants' cultural ties. The French Protestants (**Huguenots**) who migrated to Charles Town or New York City were unable to sustain their language or religious practices for more than two generations, whereas Huguenots settling in the Hudson Valley remained recognizably French and Calvinist for a

Huguenots: French Calvinist dissenters from that country's dominant Catholicism.

TABLE 4.1   Who Moved to America from England and Scotland in the Early 1770s, and Why?

	English Emigrants	Scottish Emigrants	Free American Population
Destination			
13 British colonies	81.1%	92.7%	—
Canada	12.1	4.2	—
West Indies	6.8	3.1	—
Age Distribution			
Under 21	26.8	45.3	56.8%
21–25	37.1	19.9	9.7
26–44	33.3	29.5	20.4
45 and over	2.7	5.3	13.1
Sex Distribution			
Male	83.8	59.9	—
Female	16.2	40.1	—
Unknown	4.2	13.5	—
Traveling Alone or with Families			
In families	20.0	48.0	—
Alone	80.0	52.0	—
Known Occupation or Status			
Gentry	2.5	1.2	—
Merchandising	5.2	5.2	—
Agriculture	17.8	24.0	—
Artisanry	54.2	37.7	—
Laborer	20.3	31.9	—
Why They Left			
Positive reasons (e.g., desire to better one's position)	90.0	36.0	—
Negative reasons (e.g., poverty, unemployment)	10.0	64.0	—

Note: Between December 1773 and March 1776, the British government questioned individuals and families leaving ports in Scotland and England for the American colonies to learn who they were, where they were going, and why they were leaving. This table summarizes just a few of the findings of the official inquiries, which revealed a number of significant differences between the Scottish and English emigrants.

Source of data: Bernard Bailyn, *Voyagers to the West* (New York: Knopf, 1986), Tables 4.1, 5.2, 5.4, 5.7, 5.23, and 6.1.

century. The equally small group of colonial Jews maintained a distinct identity wherever they settled. In places like New York and Newport, Rhode Island, they established synagogues and preserved their religion.

Members of larger migrant groups (Germans, Irish, and Scots) found it easier to sustain European ways. Some ethnicities dominated certain localities. Where migrants from different countries settled the same region, ethnic antagonisms surfaced. One German clergyman in Pennsylvania, for example, claimed that Scots-Irish migrants were "lazy, dissipated and poor." Anglo-American elites fostered antagonisms to maintain their power and frequently subverted naturalization laws to depriving even long-resident immigrants a voice in government.

Ultimately, elites would need the support of non-English Americans. When they moved toward revolution in the 1770s, they deliberately began speaking of "the rights of man," rather than "English liberties," to attract recruits.

Economic Growth and Development in British America

How were the colonies' economic fates increasingly linked to world markets?

The dramatic population increase of Anglo America caused colonial economies to grow, despite the vagaries of international markets. By contrast, the population and economy of New Spain's northern Borderlands stagnated, for the isolated settlements produced few items for export. French Canada exported large quantities of furs and fish, but the government's trade monopoly ensured that profits primarily ended up in the home country. The Louisiana colony required substantial government subsidies to survive. Of France's American possessions, only the Caribbean islands flourished.

Commerce and Manufacturing in the British Colonies

In British North America, the rising population demanded more goods and services, fueling the development of small-scale colonial manufacturing and a complex internal trade network. Roads, bridges, mills, and stores were built to serve new settlements. A lively coastal trade developed; by the late 1760s, more than half of the vessels leaving Boston sailed to other mainland colonies, collecting goods for export and distributing imports and American-made items. Colonies no longer depended wholly on European goods, and the American population generated sufficient demand to support local manufacturing.

Iron making became the largest industry, surpassing England's by 1775. Ironworks in the Chesapeake and middle colonies required sizable investments and substantial workforces—usually indentured servants, convicts, and slaves—who dug the ore, chopped trees for charcoal production, and smelted and refined the ore. Because the work was dirty, dangerous, and difficult, convicts and servants often fled, but enslaved men could learn valuable skills and accumulate property when paid for doing extra assigned tasks.

Colonial prosperity nevertheless depended heavily on overseas demand for tobacco, rice, indigo, fish, and timber products. By selling such items, colonists earned credit to purchase English and European imports. If demand for American exports slowed, the colonists' income and purchasing power dropped, producing economic downswings.

Wealth and Poverty   Despite fluctuations, the American economy grew during the eighteenth century, partly from higher earnings from exports. That produced better living standards for property-owning Americans. Early in the century, as the price of British manufactures fell, households acquired amenities such as chairs and earthenware dishes. Diet also improved as trade brought more varied foodstuffs. After 1750, luxury items could be found in the wealthy's homes, and the "middling sort" imported English ceramics and teapots. Even the poorest property owners had better household goods.

New arrivals did not have the advancement opportunities of their predecessors. Still, at least two-thirds of rural householders owned their own land by 1750. But in the cities, laborers' families lived close to destitution. By the 1760s, applicants for assistance overwhelmed public urban poor-relief systems, and some cities built workhouses or almshouses to shelter growing numbers of elderly and infirm people along with widows and their children.

Regional Economies   Within this overall picture, varying regional patterns emerged, in part because of **King George's War**, also called the War of the Austrian Succession (1739–1748).

New England's export economy rested on trade with the Caribbean: northern forests supplied the timber to build ships that carried salt fish to feed slaves on sugar plantations. The war increased demand for New England's ships and sailors, thus invigorating the economy; but New Englanders suffered major losses of men and materiel in Caribbean battles and in their successful attack on the fortress of Louisbourg (in modern Nova Scotia), which guarded the sea-lanes leading to New France. When the shipbuilding boom ended with the war, the economy stagnated, and widows and orphans crowded relief rolls. Britain even returned Louisbourg to France in the Treaty of Aix-la-Chapelle (1748).

By contrast, King George's War and its aftermath brought prosperity to the middle colonies and the Chesapeake, because the fertile soil and longer growing season in both regions readily produced an abundance of grain. After 1748, when several poor harvests in Europe caused flour prices to skyrocket, Philadelphia and New York took the lead in the foodstuffs trade. Some Chesapeake planters began to convert tobacco fields to wheat and corn. Tobacco remained the largest single export from the mainland colonies, yet grain cultivation significantly changed Chesapeake settlement by encouraging the development of port towns (like Baltimore), where merchants and shipbuilders would handle the new trade.

That South Carolina's staple crop was rice determined its distinctive economic pattern, as did its vulnerability to Atlantic hurricanes. Storms periodically devastated its rice and indigo crops, causing hardship and bankruptcies. Yet after Parliament in 1730 removed rice from the list of enumerated products, South Carolinians prospered by trading directly with Europe. The outbreak of war disrupted that trade, and the colony entered a depression that ended in the 1760s. Overall, though, South Carolina grew faster than other British colonies and had the highest average wealth per freeholder in mainland Anglo America by the American Revolution.

The newest British settlement, Georgia, was chartered in 1732 as a haven for imprisoned English debtors. Its founder, **James Oglethorpe**, envisioned Georgia as a garrison where farmers who would defend the southern flank of English settlement against Spanish Florida. Accordingly, its charter prohibited slavery, but neighboring

King George's War: Also known as the War of Austrian Succession, started out as a conflict between Britain and Spain, but then escalated when France sided with Spain.

James Oglethorpe: Founder of Georgia colony.

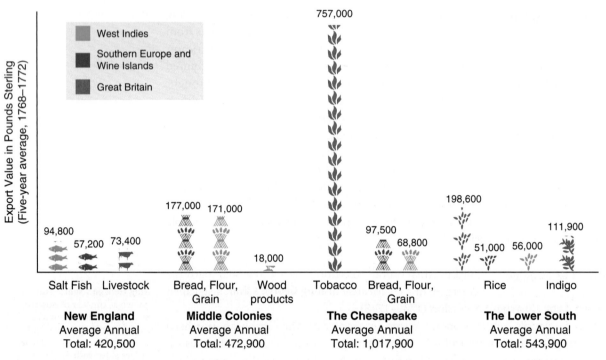

FIGURE 4.1
Regional Trading Patterns

As this figure shows, the different regions of the British mainland colonies had distinct trading patterns: they exported diverse products to different markets. By far the most valuable export was the tobacco grown by Chesapeake slaves.

Source: Adapted from James F. Shepard and Gary M. Walton, *Shipping, Maritime Trade, and the Economic Development of Colonial North America* [Cambridge: University Press, 1972].

Carolina rice planters had the restriction removed in 1751. Thereafter, Georgia developed into a rice-planting slave society resembling South Carolina.

Regional variations highlight the British mainland colonies' disparate experiences within the empire. Despite increasing coastal trade, the colonies' economic fortunes depended on the shifting markets of Europe and the Caribbean. Without an unprecedented crisis in the British imperial system (discussed in Chapter 5), it seems unlikely they could have been persuaded to join in a common endeavor. Even with that impetus, unity proved difficult to maintain.

Colonial Cultures

How did rituals function in colonial America?

By 1750, British America was denser and more diverse than a half-century earlier with new extremes of wealth and poverty, especially in the growing cities. Native-born colonial elites sought to distinguish themselves from ordinary folk as they consolidated their hold on local power.

Genteel Culture   Colonists who acquired wealth through trade, agriculture, or manufacturing spent their money ostentatiously, dressing fashionably, traveling in horse-drawn carriages, and hosting lavish parties. They built large houses containing rooms for dancing, cardplaying, or drinking tea. Sufficiently well-off to enjoy "leisure" time (a first for North America), they attended concerts and the theater, gambled at horse races, and played billiards and other games. They also cultivated polite manners. Although the effects of accumulated wealth were most pronounced in Anglo America, elite families in New Mexico, Louisiana, and Quebec set themselves off from the "lesser sort." Together, these wealthy families deliberately constructed a genteel culture different from that of ordinary colonists.

Men from such families prided themselves on their possessions, their positions in the political and economic hierarchy, their education, and their intellectual connections to Europe. Many had been tutored by private teachers; some attended college. (Harvard, the first colonial college, founded in 1636, was joined by William and Mary in 1693 and Yale in 1701.) In the seventeenth century, only aspiring clergymen attended college, but by the mid-eighteenth century, as colleges broadened their curricula to include mathematics, science, law, and medicine, young men from elite or upwardly mobile families slowly enrolled. American women were mostly excluded from advanced education, except those who joined nunneries in Canada or Louisiana.

The Enlightenment

The intellectual current known as the **Enlightenment** deeply affected the clergymen who headed colonial colleges and their students. Around 1650, some European thinkers analyzed nature to determine the laws governing the universe. They employed experimentation and abstract reasoning to discover general principles behind phenomena like the motions of planets. Enlightenment philosophers emphasized acquiring knowledge through reason, challenging previously unquestioned assumptions. **John Locke**'s *Essay Concerning Human Understanding* (1690) disputed the notion that human beings are born imprinted with innate ideas. All knowledge, Locke asserted, derived from observations. Belief in witchcraft and astrology and similar phenomena thus were attacked.

The Enlightenment supplied educated, well-to-do people in Europe and America with a common vocabulary and a unified world-view, one that insisted the enlightened eighteenth century was better and wiser than previous ages. It joined them in the common endeavor to make sense of God's creation. Thus American naturalists like John and William Bartram supplied European scientists with information about New World plants and animals for newly formulated classification systems. A prime example of America's participation in the Enlightenment was **Benjamin Franklin**, who retired from a successful printing business in 1748 at age forty-two, devoting himself to scientific experimentation and public service. His *Experiments and Observations on Electricity* (1751) established the basic theory of electricity still used today.

Gift of Joseph W. R. Rogers and Mary C. Rogers. Museum of Fine Arts, Boston. Reproduced with permission. Museum of Fine Arts, Boston

Elizabeth Murray, the subject of this 1769 painting by John Singleton Copley, was the wife of James Smith, a wealthy rum distiller. Her fashionable dress and pose would seem to mark her as a lady of leisure, yet both before and during her marriage this Scottish immigrant ran a successful dry goods shop in Boston. She thus simultaneously catered to and participated in the new culture of consumption.

Enlightenment: Intellectual revolution that elevated reason, science, and logic.

John Locke: British philosopher and major Enlightenment thinker; known for his emphasis on the power of human reasoning.

Benjamin Franklin: American who embodied Enlightenment ideas.

Smallpox Inoculation

Smallpox, the world's greatest killer of human beings, repeatedly ravaged North American colonists and Indians. Thus, when the vessel *Seahorse* arrived in Boston from the Caribbean in April 1721 with smallpox-infected people on board, New Englanders feared the worst and quarantined the ship. It was too late: smallpox escaped into the city, and by June several dozen people were afflicted.

But the Reverend Cotton Mather, a member of London's Royal Society (an Enlightenment organization), had read years earlier of a medical technique previously unknown to Europeans but widely employed in North Africa and the Middle East. Called inoculation, it involved taking pus from the pustules (or poxes) of an infected person and inserting it into a small cut on the arm of a healthy individual. With luck, that person would experience a mild case and gain lifetime immunity. Mather's interest was further piqued by his slave Onesimus, a North African who had been inoculated as a youth and who described the procedure in detail.

With the disease coursing through the city, Mather promoted inoculation to the local medical community. But the city's doctors ridiculed his ideas, except for Zabdiel Boylston, a physician and apothecary. The two men inoculated their children and about two hundred others. After the epidemic ended, Bostonians could see the results: of those inoculated, just 3 percent had died; among the thousands who contracted the disease naturally, mortality was 15 percent. Even Mather's most vocal opponents supported inoculation thereafter.

Thus, through transatlantic links forged by the Enlightenment and enslavement, American colonists learned how to combat the deadliest disease. Today, thanks to a successful campaign by the World Health Organization, smallpox has been eradicated.

An Hiſtorical

ACCOUNT

OF THE

SMALL-POX

INOCULATED

IN

NEW ENGLAND,

Upon all Sorts of Perſons, *Whites, Blacks,* and of all Ages and Conſtitutions.

With ſome Account of the Nature of the Infection in the NATURAL and INOCULATED Way, and their different Effects on HUMAN BODIES.

With ſome ſhort DIRECTIONS to the UNEXPERIENCED in this Method of Practice.

Humbly dedicated to her Royal Highneſs the Princeſs of WALES, by *Zabdiel Boylſton,* Phyſician.

LONDON:

Printed for S. CHANDLER, *at the* Croſs-Keys *in the* Poultry. M.DCC.XXVI.

Private Collection/Picture Research Consultants & Archives

Several years after he and Cotton Mather combated a Boston smallpox epidemic by employing inoculation, Zabdiel Boylston published this pamphlet in London to spread the news of their success. The dedication to the Princess of Wales was designed to indicate the royal family's support of the procedure.

Enlightenment rationalism affected politics, too. Locke's *Two Treatises of Government* (1691) and works by French and Scottish philosophers challenged a divinely sanctioned, hierarchical political order originating in the power of fathers over families. Men created governments and could alter them, Locke declared. A ruler who broke the social contract and failed to protect people's rights could legitimately be ousted from power peacefully or violently. Enlightenment theorists proclaimed God's natural laws governed even monarchs.

Oral Cultures

The world in which such ideas were discussed was select. Most residents of North America were illiterate. Those who could read often could not write. Books were scarce until the 1750s, and colonial newspapers did not appear until the 1720s. Parents, older siblings, or local widows who needed extra income taught youngsters to read. More fortunate boys (and genteel girls after the 1750s) might learn to write in private schools. Few Americans other than some Church of England missionaries in the South tried to instruct enslaved children. And only the most zealous Indian converts learned Europeans' literacy skills.

Thus, the cultures of colonial North America were primarily oral, communal, and local. Face-to-face conversation was the major means of communication. Different locales developed divergent cultural traditions. Through public rituals colonists forged their cultural identities.

Religious and Civic Rituals

Church attendance was perhaps the most important ritual. In early New England, men and women sat on opposite sides of a central aisle, arranged by age, wealth, and church membership. By the mid-eighteenth century, wealthy husbands and wives sat in privately owned pews; their children, servants, slaves, and the less fortunate sat in sex-segregated fashion at the rear, sides, or balcony of the church. In eighteenth-century Virginia, planter families purchased pews, and in some parishes landed gentlemen strode in as a group before the service, deliberately drawing attention to their exalted position. In Quebec City, formal processions celebrated Catholic feast days; each participant's rank determined his place in the procession. By contrast, Quaker meeting houses in Pennsylvania and elsewhere used an egalitarian but sex-segregated seating system. The various seating and entrance rituals symbolized social rank and local values.

Communal culture also centered on civic involvement. In New England, governments proclaimed official days of thanksgiving (for good harvests, military victories, etc.) and days of fasting and prayer (during difficulties such as droughts or epidemics). Everyone was expected to participate. Because able-bodied men between ages sixteen and sixty were required to serve in local militias, monthly musters also brought the community together.

In the Chesapeake, important rituals occurred on court and election days. When the county court met, men came to file lawsuits, appear as witnesses, or serve as jurors. Court attendance provided civic education; from the proceedings men learned what behavior was expected. Elections served the same purpose, for property-holding men voted in public. An election official, often flanked by the candidates for office, would call each man forward to declare his preference. Voters would then be thanked politely by the gentleman selected, often treated later to rum at nearby taverns.

This trade card (advertisement) issued by a Philadelphia tobacco dealer in 1770 shows a convivial group of wealthy men at a tavern. Both the leisurely activity depicted here and the advertisement itself were signs of the new rituals of consumption. Merchants began to advertise only when their customers could choose among different ways of spending money.

Throughout colonial North America, the public punishment of criminals served to humiliate the offender and remind the community of proper behavioral standards. Public hangings, whippings, and sitting in the stocks expressed community outrage and restored harmony. Judges often assigned penalties that shamed miscreants. When a New Mexico man assaulted his father-in-law, he was directed to pay medical expenses and kneel before him publicly to beg his forgiveness. Even after pardoned of capital offenses, New Englanders were frequently ordered to wear nooses around their necks for years, as a reminder to all of their violation of community norms.

Rituals of Consumption By 1770, Anglo-American households allocated one-quarter of their spending to consumer goods, which fostered new rituals centered on consumption and created what historians have termed "an empire of goods." In the seventeenth century, settlers acquired necessities by bartering with neighbors or ordering from a home-country merchant. By the middle of the eighteenth century, specialized shops selling nonessentials proliferated in cities like Philadelphia and New Orleans. In 1770, Boston had more than five hundred stores, offering millinery, sewing supplies, tobacco, gloves, tableware, and the like. Even small towns had one or two retail establishments. Colonists would set aside time to "go shopping," a novel and pleasurable leisure activity that initiated consumption rituals.

Colonists took pleasure in owning and displaying lovely objects for neighbors and kin to see: a mirror, a ceramic bowl, or clothing made from special fabric. A rich man might hire an artist to paint his family using the objects, thereby creating a record to be admired.

Poor, rural people similarly took pleasure in inexpensive purchases. One Virginia woman traded hens and chickens for a pewter dish. Local slaves exchanged cotton they had grown in their free time for colorful ribbons and hats they must have worn proudly.

Tea and Madeira Tea drinking, a consumption ritual dominated by women, played an important role throughout Anglo America. Households with aspirations to genteel status sought the necessary items for proper tea consumption: pots, cups, strainers, sugar tongs, bowls, and special tables. Tea provided a focal point for socializing and, because of its cost, served as a status symbol. Wealthy women regularly entertained friends at afternoon tea parties. Tea also appeared healthful; thus even poor households consumed it, although without the fancy equipment of their wealthier neighbors. Another genteel drink was Madeira wine from the Portuguese islands. By 1770, Madeira had become the elite's favored drink, expensive to purchase. Opening the bottle, letting it breathe, decanting and serving it with appropriate glassware were accomplished with elaborate ceremony. After the 1750s, urban dwellers could buy Madeira at specialized stores.

Rituals on the "Middle Ground" Other rituals allowed the disparate cultures of colonial North America to interact. Particularly important rituals developed on what the historian Richard White has termed the "middle ground"—the psychological and geographical space in which Indians and Europeans encountered each other, primarily via trade or warfare.

When Europeans sought to trade with Indians, they encountered an indigenous exchange system that stressed gift giving over buying and selling. Successful bargaining required French and English traders to present Indians with gifts (cloth, rum, gunpowder, and other items) before negotiating for pelts and skins. Only after those gifts were reciprocated could formal trading begin. For example, Indians in northeastern North America wanted heavy cloths called strouds. Because British manufacturers produced such material in response to natives' demands, British traders acquired an important advantage over their French competitors. Rum became a crucial component, as traders concluded that drunken Indians would sell their furs more cheaply, and some Indians refused to hunt or trade unless they first received rum. Alcohol abuse hastened the deterioration of villages already devastated by disease and dislocation.

Intercultural rituals also developed to deal with murders. Where Europeans sought primarily to punish the murderer, Indians regarded such "eye for an eye" revenge as just one possible response. Compensation could also be accomplished by capturing another Indian or a colonist to take the dead person's place, or by "covering the dead"—providing the deceased's family with goods. Eventually, the French and the Algonquians evolved an elaborate ritual from both societies' traditions: murderers were identified but deaths were usually "covered" by trade goods rather than blood revenge.

Colonial Families

Families constituted the basic units of colonial society, constituting the chief mechanism for production and consumption. Never-married adults were rare. Yet family forms and structures varied widely, and not all were headed by couples.

> How did European American families differ from those of Indians or African Americans?

Indian and Mixed-Race Families

As Europeans consolidated their hold on North America, Indians had to adapt. Bands reduced by disease and warfare recombined into new units; for example, the Catawbas emerged in the 1730s in the western Carolinas by merging several earlier peoples, including Yamasees and Guales. Likewise, European authorities reshaped Indian family forms. Whereas many Indian societies had permitted easy divorce, European missionaries frowned on it; societies that had allowed polygynous marriages (including New England Algonquians) redefined them, designating one wife as "legitimate" and others as "concubines."

With continued high mortality, extended kin became increasingly important, with other relatives—sometimes nonkin—assuming child-rearing responsibilities when parents died. Once Europeans established dominance in any region, Indians were unable to pursue traditional modes of subsistence, driving them to unusual family structures and new economic strategies. In New England, for instance, Algonquian husbands and wives survived by working, and sometimes living, separately (perhaps wives as domestic servants, husbands as sailors). Some native women married African American men due to sexual imbalances in both populations. In New Mexico, detribalized Navajos, Pueblos, Paiutes, and Apaches employed as servants by Spanish settlers clustered in the small Borderlands towns. Known as *genizaros,* they lost contact with Indian cultures, instead living on the fringes of Latino society.

Wherever the population contained relatively few European women, sexual liaisons occurred between European men and Indian women. The resulting mixed-race population of *mestizos* and *métis* worked as a familial "middle ground" to ease other cultural interactions. In New France and the Anglo-American backcountry, such families resided in Indian villages and their children sometimes became prominent Native American leaders. By contrast, in the Spanish Borderlands the offspring of Europeans and *genizaros* were shunned. Largely denied legal marriage, they bore generations of "illegitimate" children of various racial mixtures, giving rise in Latino society to multiple labels describing precise degrees of skin color.

European American Families

To eighteenth-century Anglo-Americans, the word *family* meant everyone in one household (including servants or slaves). In 1790, the average home in the United States contained 5.7 free people; few included extended kin, such as grandparents. Family members worked together to produce goods for consumption or sale. The head of the household represented it to the outside world, voting in elections, managing the finances, and holding legal authority over the rest of the family—his wife, children, and servants or slaves.

In English, French, and Spanish America, the vast majority of European families supported themselves by cultivating crops and raising livestock. While the work differed by region or crop, tasks were allocated by sex. The mistress oversaw her female helpers in what Anglo-Americans called "indoor affairs"—preparing food, cleaning the house, doing laundry, and making clothes. Along with cooking, food preparation involved cultivating a garden, harvesting and preserving vegetables, salting and smoking meat, drying apples and pressing cider, milking cows and making butter and cheese. The husband and his male helpers managed "outdoor affairs," cultivating fields, building fences, chopping wood, harvesting and marketing crops, tending livestock, and butchering cattle and hogs. Farm work was so extensive that a married couple could not do it alone; if childless, they needed servants or slaves.

African American Families

Most African American families lived as components of European American households. More than 95 percent of colonial African Americans were held in perpetual bondage. In South Carolina, a majority of the population was of African origin; in Georgia, about half; and in the Chesapeake, 40 percent. Portions of the Carolina low country were nearly 90 percent African American by 1790.

Where African Americans lived determined the shape of their families. In the North, the scarcity of other blacks often made it difficult for bondspeople to form stable households. In the Chesapeake, men and women who regarded themselves as married (slaves could not legally wed) frequently lived on different quarters or different plantations. Children generally resided with mothers. On large Carolina and Georgia rice plantations, enslaved couples usually lived together and accumulated property by working for themselves completing daily "tasks." Some Georgia slaves sold surplus produce, earning money for clothing or such luxuries as tobacco, but rarely enough for their freedom.

Forms of Resistance

Because all British colonies legally permitted slavery, bondspeople had few options for escaping servitude other than fleeing to Florida, where the Spanish offered protection. Some recently arrived Africans stole boats or ran off to join the Indians or establish independent communities on the frontier. Among American-born slaves, family ties strongly affected such decisions. As one South Carolina planter wrote, slaves "love their families dearly and none runs away from the other." Consequently, many owners sought to keep families together. In the Chesapeake, where family members often lived separately, affectionate ties could cause slaves to run away, especially if family members were sold.

Although colonial slaves rarely rebelled collectively, they resisted in other ways. Bondspeople rejected owners' attempts to commandeer their labor on Sundays without compensation. Extended-kin groups protested excessive punishment of relatives and sought to live near one another. If parents and children were separated by sale, other relatives helped with child rearing. Just as among Indians, the extended family served a more important function for African Americans than for European-Americans.

Most slave families carved out some autonomy, especially in their working and spiritual lives, particularly in the Lower South. Some African Americans preserved traditional beliefs or Islamic faith; others converted to Christianity, comforted by its assurances that everyone would be free and equal in heaven. South Carolina and Georgia slaves jealously guarded their ability to control their time after completing their "tasks." Even on Chesapeake tobacco plantations, slaves planted gardens, trapped, or fished to supplement their meager diets. Late in the century, some Chesapeake planters began to hire slaves out, often allowing the workers to keep some of their earnings.

City Life

In cities, African Americans and European Americans resided in neighborhoods together. (In 1760s Philadelphia, one-fifth of the work force was enslaved, and by 1775 blacks composed nearly 15 percent of New York City's population.) Such cities were medium-sized towns by today's standards. In 1750, the largest, Boston and Philadelphia, had just seventeen thousand and thirteen thousand inhabitants, respectively. Unlike their rural

Fire posed a major hazard to colonial cities; several suffered considerable damage in the seventeenth and eighteenth centuries from fires that raged out of control for hours. In the mid-eighteenth-century, cities like New York organized volunteer companies, such as the Hand-in-Hand company pictured here on an unidentified city street about 1750. The firemen are passing buckets of water from the well on the left to the engine on the right, where men on each side operate the pump that directs a stream of water on the fire. The chief is shouting orders through his trumpet at the right of the engine, and the people on the far right are carrying items from the burning building.

counterparts, city dwellers purchased food and wood, and men's jobs frequently took them away from home, giving them more contact with the broader world.

By the 1750s, most major cities had at least one weekly newspaper. Anglo-American newspapers combined local reports with the latest "advices from London" (usually two to three months old). People who could not afford newspapers could either read them (or listen to them read aloud) at taverns and coffeehouses. Contact with the outside world, however, meant sailors sometimes brought deadly diseases into port. Boston, New York, Philadelphia, and New Orleans endured smallpox and yellow fever epidemics, which Europeans and Africans in the countryside largely escaped.

Politics: Stability and Crisis in British America

What were the myths and realities of colonial assemblies?

Early in the eighteenth century, Anglo-American political life exhibited new stability. Despite substantial migration, most mainland residents were born in America. Men from genteel families dominated the political structures, for voters (free male property holders) typically deferred to their well-educated "betters" in election.

Colonial Assemblies

Throughout the Anglo-American colonies, political leaders sought to increase the powers of elected assemblies relative to that of governors and other appointed officials. Assemblies began to claim privileges associated with the British House of Commons, such as initiating tax legislation and controlling the militia. Assemblies also influenced British appointees by threatening to withhold their salaries. In some colonies (Virginia and South Carolina, for example), elite assemblymen presented a united front to royal officials, but in others (such as New York), they fought among themselves bitterly. To win hotly contested elections, New York's genteel leaders began competing for votes. Yet in 1735 the New York government imprisoned newspaper editor **John Peter Zenger**, who vigorously criticized it on the charge of "seditious libel." Arguing that the truth could not be defamatory, his lawyer helped establish a free-press principle in American law.

John Peter Zenger: Central figure in a trial that opened the way for freedom of the press.

Assemblymen saw themselves as acting to prevent encroachments on colonists' liberties—for example, by preventing governors from imposing oppressive taxes. By midcentury, they were comparing the structure of their governments to Britain's balanced polity, equating their governors with the monarch, their councils with the aristocracy, and their assemblies with the House of Commons. All three were believed essential to good government, but Anglo-Americans viewed governors and appointed councils as Britain's representatives and potential threats to colonial ways of life. Many colonists saw the assemblies, however, as the people's protectors. And the assemblies regarded themselves as the people's representatives.

In reality, the assemblies, controlled by dominant families whose members were reelected year after year, rarely responded to poorer constituents' concerns. They also failed to reapportion themselves to provide representation for new settlements; this led to grievances among backcountry dwellers, especially non-English ethnic groups. The colonial ideal of the assembly as the defender of liberty was a myth. In truth, the most ably represented were wealthy male colonists, particularly the assembly members themselves.

At midcentury, the political structures that had stabilized in a period of relative calm confronted a series of crises—ethnic, racial, economic, regional—that exposed internal tensions and foreshadowed the disorder of the revolutionary era. Significantly, they demonstrated that the political accommodations arrived at after the **Glorious Revolution** could no longer adequately govern Britain's American empire.

Glorious Revolution: Overthrow of James II in favor of William and Mary.

Slave Rebellions in South Carolina and New York

Early on Sunday, September 9, 1739, about twenty enslaved men, most likely Catholics from Kongo, gathered near the Stono River south of Charles Town. September fell in the midst of the rice harvest (and thus a stressful time for male Africans, less accustomed than women to rice cultivation), and September 8 was, to Catholics, the birthday of the Virgin Mary. Seizing guns and ammunition, the slaves killed storekeepers and nearby planter families. Then, joined by other bondsmen, they headed toward Florida in hopes of finding refuge. By midday, however, the militia attacked the nearly one hundred fugitives, killing some and dispersing the rest. A week later, most of the remaining conspirators were captured and executed. But for two years, rumors about escaped renegades haunted the colony.

After the **Stono Rebellion**, laws governing African Americans were stiffened throughout British America. In New York City, the site of the first mainland slave revolt in 1712, the Stono news, coupled with fears of Spain generated by the outbreak of King George's War, set off a reign of terror in the summer of 1741. Colonial authorities suspected a biracial gang of thieves and arsonists of fomenting a slave uprising under the guidance of a European thought to be a Spanish priest. By summer's end, thirty-one blacks and four whites had been executed for participating in the alleged plot. The Stono Rebellion and the New York "conspiracy" confirmed Anglo-Americans' deepest fears about the dangers of slaveholding and revealed the assemblies' inability to prevent internal disorder.

Stono Rebellion: A slave uprising in 1739 in South Carolina.

Rioters and Regulators

By midcentury, with most fertile land east of the Appalachians purchased or occupied, conflicts over land titles and conditions of landholding escalated. In 1746, for example, some New Jersey farmers clashed violently with agents of the East Jersey proprietors, who claimed the farmers' land and demanded annual payments, called quit-rents. The most serious land riots occurred along the Hudson River in 1765–1766. Late in the seventeenth century, the governor of New York had granted huge tracts in the lower Hudson Valley to prominent families. They then divided these estates into small farms, which they rented to poor Dutch and German migrants who regarded tenancy as a step toward independence.

After 1740, though, New Englanders and Europeans increasingly migrated to the region, resisting tenancy and often squatting. In the mid-1760s, the Philipse family sued farmers who had lived on Philipse land for two decades. New York courts ordered squatters to make way for tenants with valid leases. Instead, farmers rebelled, terrorizing proprietors and tenants, and on one occasion battling a county sheriff and his posse. The rebellion lasted nearly a year, ending only when British troops captured its leaders.

Violent conflicts erupted in the Carolinas as well. The Regulator movements of the late 1760s (South Carolina) and early 1770s (North Carolina) pitted backcountry farmers against wealthy eastern planters who controlled colonial governments. In South Carolina, Scots-Irish settlers protested their lack of an adequate voice in political affairs. For months, they policed the countryside in vigilante bands known as Regulators, complaining of lax and biased law enforcement. North Carolina Regulators, who objected to heavy taxation, lost a battle with eastern militiamen at Alamance in 1771.

A Crisis in Anglo-American Religion

What was the social and political impact of the Great Awakening?

The most widespread crisis was religious. From the mid-1730s through the 1760s, waves of religious revivalism—today known as the First **Great Awakening**—swept over various colonies, primarily New England (1735–1745) and Virginia (1750s–1760s). Orthodox Calvinists sought to combat Enlightenment rationalism, which denied innate human depravity.

The economic and political uncertainty accompanying King George's War made colonists receptive to **evangelists'** messages. With no prior religious affiliation, many recent immigrants and backcountry residents became potential converts.

The Great Awakening began in New England, where descendants of the Puritan founding generation composed Congregational church memberships. While church members were predominantly female, men and women responded with equal fervor to the Awakening. In the mid-1730s, the Northampton, Massachusetts, preacher and theologian Reverend Jonathan Edwards, gained new youthful followers with Calvinist-based message that individuals could attain salvation only by acknowledging their depraved nature and surrendering completely to God's will.

George Whitefield

The effects of such conversions remained isolated until 1739, when **George Whitefield**, a Church of England clergyman already celebrated for leading revivals in England, arrived in America. A gripping orator, Whitefield toured the British colonies for fifteen months, effectively generating the Great Awakening. One historian has termed him "the first modern celebrity" because of his skillful self-promotion and clever manipulation of his listeners and the newspapers. Everywhere he traveled, his fame preceded him. Readers snapped up books by and about him, the first colonial bestsellers. Thousands of free and enslaved folk from Boston to Savannah heard him speak and experienced conversion. Whitefield's journey created new interconnections among the previously distinct colonies.

Regular clerics initially welcomed Whitefield and his American-born imitators, but many soon concluded that the "revived" religion ran counter to their doctrines. They disliked the emotional style of the revivalists, who took churchgoers away from their usual church services. Particularly troublesome to the orthodox were the female exhorters who publically proclaimed their right to expound God's word.

Impact of the Awakening

Opposition to the Awakening heightened rapidly, further splintering the already fragmented American Protestantism. Congregationalists and Presbyterians split into "Old Lights"—traditional clerics and their followers—and "New Light" evangelicals. New sects such as Methodists and Baptists gained adherents. Paradoxically, the angry fights and the rapid rise in the number of distinct denominations eventually created an American willingness to tolerate religious diversity. Since no single sect could make an unequivocal claim to orthodoxy, they had to coexist if they were to survive.

Most significantly, the Awakening challenged traditional social patterns, particularly the colonial tradition of deference. Itinerant preachers, only a few of whom were ordained, claimed they understood the will of God better than elite college-educated clerics. They and their followers divided the world into the saved and the damned without respect to gender, age, or status. New Lights also defended the rights of people to dissent from a community consensus, thereby challenging the fundamental tenets of colonial political life. The Awakening's egalitarian themes simultaneously attracted ordinary folk and repelled the elite.

Virginia Baptists

By the 1760s, Baptists had gained a secure foothold in Virginia; inevitably, their beliefs clashed with genteel lifestyles. They dressed plainly, in contrast to the gentry's opulence. They addressed one another as "Brother" and "Sister" regardless of social status, and they elected their

Great Awakening: Protestant revival movement that emphasized each person's urgent need for salvation by God.

evangelist: A preacher or minister who enthusiastically promotes the Christian gospels.

George Whitefield: English preacher who toured the colonies and played a major role in the Great Awakening.

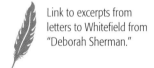

Link to excerpts from letters to Whitefield from "Deborah Sherman."

This painting by John Collet shows the charismatic evangelist George Whitefield preaching out of doors in Britain, but the same scene would have been repeated many times in the colonies, especially after the clergy of established churches denied him access to their pulpits, deeming him too radical for their liking. Note the swooning woman in the foreground; women were reputed to be especially susceptible to Whitefield's message. Is the worker offering him a mug of ale derisively or devotedly? The answer is not clear, except that the gesture underscores the diversity of Whitefield's audience—not all were genteel or middling folk.

congregations' leaders. Their monthly meetings, which attracted hundreds of people, introduced new public rituals that rivaled weekly Anglican services.

Strikingly, almost all the Virginia Baptist congregations included free and enslaved members, and some had African American majorities. Church rules applied equally to all members; interracial sexual relationships, divorce, and adultery were forbidden. Congregations forbade masters from breaking up slave couples through sale. Biracial committees investigated complaints about members' misbehavior. Churches excommunicated slaves for stealing from their masters and masters for physically abusing their slaves.

By injecting an egalitarian strain into Anglo-American life at midcentury, the Great Awakening had important social and political consequences, calling into question habitual modes of behavior in the **secular** as well as the religious realm.

secular: Not specifically relating to religion or to a religious body.

"Self-Made Men"

Americans universally celebrate the "self-made man" (always someone explicitly *male*) of humble origins who gains prominence through extraordinary efforts. Most commonly cited examples are Andrew Carnegie (a poor immigrant from Scotland) and John D. Rockefeller (born on a hardscrabble farm in upstate New York).

The initial exemplars of this tradition, though, lived in the eighteenth century. Benjamin Franklin's *Autobiography* chronicled his method for achieving success after beginning life as the seventeenth child of a Boston candle maker. From such humble origins Franklin became a wealthy, influential man active in science, politics, education, and diplomacy. Yet Franklin's tale is rivaled by that of a man apparently born a slave in South Carolina. He acquired literacy, worked as a sailor, purchased his freedom, became an influential abolitionist, married a wealthy Englishwoman, and published a popular autobiography that predated Franklin's. His first master called him Gustavus Vassa, but when publishing his *Interesting Narrative* in 1789, he called himself Olaudah Equiano.

In that *Narrative*, Equiano said he was born in Africa in 1745, kidnapped at age eleven, and transported to Barbados and then to Virginia, where a British naval officer purchased him. For years, scholars have relied on that account for its insights into the middle passage. But evidence recently uncovered by Vincent Carretta, although confirming much of Equiano's autobiography, shows that Equiano twice identified his birthplace as Carolina and was three to five years younger than he claimed. Carretta speculates that the *Narrative* gained its credibility from Equiano's African birth and that admitting his real age would have raised questions about his early life.

Equiano, or Vassa, thus truly "made himself," just as Benjamin Franklin and many others have done. (Franklin typically omitted, rather than altered, inconvenient parts of his history—for example, having an illegitimate son.) Equiano used information undoubtedly gleaned from acquaintances who *had* experienced the middle passage to craft an accurate depiction of its horrors. In the process, he became one of the first Americans to explicitly reinvent himself.

Summary

Over the half-century before 1770, North America was transformed, partly by the dramatic geographic expansion of French and Spanish settlements and partly by newcomers from Germany, Scotland, Ireland, and Africa who brought their languages, customs, and religions. Such transformations affected America's Native residents as well as the newcomers. European immigrants were concentrated in the growing cities and backcountry of British North America. By contrast, slaves from Africa lived and worked within 100 miles of the Atlantic coast. In many colonial South regions, 50 to 90 percent of the population was of African origin.

The economic life of Europe's North American colonies proceeded simultaneously on two levels. On the farms, plantations, and ranches where most colonists resided, arduous labor alike dominated people's lives while providing goods for consumption or sale. Simultaneously, an intricate international trade network affected the economies of the British, French, and Spanish colonies and their Native trading partners and allies. The bitter wars fought by European nations during the eighteenth century inevitably created new opportunities for overseas sales or disrupted traditional markets. The few who reaped the profits of international commerce were the wealthy class of merchants and landowners who dominated colonial life.

A century and a half after European first settled in North America, the colonies mixed diverse European, American, and African traditions into a novel cultural blend. Europeans who interacted regularly with peoples of African and American origin—and with Europeans from other nations—developed new methods of accommodating intercultural differences while also creating ties within their own potentially fragmenting communities. Initially, many colonists continued to identify themselves as French, Spanish, or British rather than as Americans, but in the 1760s some Anglo-Americans began to realize that their interests did not necessarily coincide with Great Britain's and challenged British authority.

Chapter Review

Geographic Expansion and Ethnic Diversity

What spurred population growth in the British colonies in the thirty years before 1775?

Immigration—particularly Scots-Irish and Germans—contributed to some of the population growth among European Americans, but the largest single factor was natural increase (live births). Once the difficult years of early settlement passed and the sex ratio evened out in the South, the population doubled every twenty-five years. Natural increase also boosted the African American enslaved population after 1740, and in some regions the slave population was further augmented by new imports of enslaved people.

Commerce and Manufacturing in British North America

How were the colonies' economic fates increasingly linked to world markets?

As colonies became more entwined in overseas trade, their fortunes were increasingly tied to the ups and downs of those economies. Although colonists developed small-scale manufacturing and broader trade networks to meet increased local demand for goods and services, they nonetheless required external markets for their products—tobacco, rice, indigo, fish, and timber. They used the money made from these items to purchase European and English imports. If demand for American goods fell, so did colonists' income, causing economic downturns. The outbreak of King George's War, for example, increased overseas demand for grain grown in the Chesapeake and led tobacco farmers to convert more of their acreage to the crop, while New England suffered when the shipbuilding boom of the war years ended.

Colonial Cultures

How did rituals function in colonial America?

Cultural rituals played a central role in colonial life, both to create community and to reinforce social status. Church rituals were among the most important, but also the most revealing, with seating arrangements organized by sex, class, age, or wealth. Civic rituals likewise generated community involvement and revealed the behavior communities expected of their members. In New England, everyone was required to participate in official holidays or local militia musters; in the Chesapeake, rituals centered on court or election days; and public punishment of criminals throughout North America was designed to reinforce behavioral standards. Even simple rituals, such as tea-drinking, reinforced gender norms and distinctions of wealth and status. Finally, colonists adapted rituals to facilitate trade with Indians, who had vastly different customs. Europeans seeking to trade with Indians engaged in the gift-giving system typical of native cultures before trade could begin.

Colonial Families

How did European American families differ from those of Indians or African Americans?

Anglo Americans used the word "family" to describe everyone in a household: parents, children, extended kin, and slaves. Families typically supported themselves by farming, with each member assigned a task according to gender norms. (Women did indoor work and related tasks; men did outdoor work.) Indian families were more fluid; before contact with Europeans, they permitted divorce, for example. After contact, extended kin became more important, particularly as families were decimated by disease. Shortages of European women in some colonies led to increased intermarriages, with children raised in Indian villages rather than among settlers. Most African Americans were enslaved, and their families subsumed under European American households. In the Chesapeake, slaves couples who considered themselves married (despite laws prohibiting slave marriage) often lived apart, in different quarters or plantations, with children residing with mothers (and potentially sold off at any time.)

Politics: Stability and Crisis in British America

What were the myths and realities of colonial assemblies?

Anglo-American assemblymen believed they safeguarded colonists' liberties from encroachments by the British government, such as oppressive taxation. Regarding Britain's appointed councils and governors as potential threats, colonists looked to assemblies as their protectors. In truth, elite, wealthy families dominated the assemblies and paid little regard to poorer constituents' concerns, nor did they reapportion themselves so that new settlements would gain representatives, which angered backcountry residents and non-English immigrants.

A Crisis in Anglo-American Religion

What was the social and political impact of the Great Awakening?

Socially, the Great Awakening challenged traditional norms and patterns. Women, for example, began to claim an equal right to preach, and Protestant denominations further split into the "Old Lights"—who followed traditional teachings and ministers—and the "New Light" evangelicals. While initially sparking animosity, ultimately the rise of new denominations promoted greater tolerance for religious diversity. The Great Awakening's egalitarianism also challenged the colonial tradition of deference, in which people knew their place and respected their so-called "betters." New Lights attracted ordinary people as followers and preachers and argued that the world was divided into the saved and the damned without respect to gender, age or status.

Suggestions for Further Reading

Marilyn Baseler, "Asylum for Mankind": America 1607–1800 (1998)

Richard R. Beeman, The Varieties of Political Experience in Eighteenth-Century America (2004)

James F. Brooks, Captives and Cousins: Slavery, Kinship, and Community in the Southwest Borderlands (2002)

William E. Burns, Science and Technology in Colonial America (2005)

Richard Bushman, The Refinement of America: Persons, Houses, Cities (1992)

Kathleen DuVal, The Native Ground: Indians and Colonists in the Heart of the Continent (2006)

Rhys Isaac, The Transformation of Virginia, 1740–1790 (1982)

Jill Lepore, New York Burning: Liberty, Slavery, and Conspiracy in Eighteenth-Century Manhattan (2005)

Harry S. Stout, The Divine Dramatist: George Whitefield and the Rise of Modern Evangelicalism (1991)

Stephanie G. Wolf, As Various as Their Land: The Everyday Lives of 18th Century Americans (1992)

Go to the CourseMate website for primary source links, study tools, and review materials for this chapter.
www.cengagebrain.com

Severing the Bonds of Empire

1754–1774

The well-born Scotswoman Janet Schaw chose an inopportune time to visit her older brother in North America. Sailing from Edinburgh in October 1774, she arrived in the West Indies in January 1775, where she visited planter families, some whom were also Scots, and did some shopping before sailing on to meet her brother in North Carolina. There she encountered "rusticks" who had, in her opinion, a "rooted hatred" for the mother country and were forming "schemes" detrimental to Britain and America.

Janet Schaw soon learned that an American congress had forbidden "every kind of diversion, even card-playing." When Wilmington residents held a ball before the ban took effect, she found the event "laughable," like seventeenth-century Dutch paintings of comic, carousing peasants. She also reported that "the Ladies have burnt their tea in a solemn procession," but sniffed, "the sacrifice was not very considerable, as I do not think any one offered above a quarter of a pound." All the "genteel" merchants, she observed, "disapprove of the present proceedings" and were planning to leave. She concluded that the trouble in the colonies had been caused by "mistaken notions of moderation" in parliamentary policy. Schaw returned to Scotland within the year. Her brother's property was later confiscated by the state for his refusing to take an oath of allegiance, but he remained in his new homeland until his death.

In retrospect, John Adams identified the period between 1760 and 1775 as the era of the true American Revolution. The Revolution, Adams declared, ended before the fighting started, for it was "in the Minds of the people," involving not the actual winning of independence but a shift of allegiance from Britain to America. Today, not all historians would concur. But none would deny the importance of the events of those crucial years, in which mainland colonies united against British policies.

During the 1760s and early 1770s, an ever-widening split occurred between Great Britain and Anglo America. In the long history of British settlement in the Western Hemisphere, tension had occasionally marred the relationship between individual provinces and the mother country. Still, it rarely lasted long or was widespread, except during the crisis following the Glorious Revolution in 1689. In the 1750s, however, a series of events beginning with the Seven Years' War drew the colonists' attention toward their relations with Great Britain.

Britain's overwhelming victory in that war, confirmed by treaty in 1763, forever altered the balance of power in North America. France was ousted from the continent and Spain from Florida, with major consequences for interior indigenous peoples and British colonists. Indians, who were experts at playing European powers against one another, lost a major diplomatic tool. Anglo-Americans no longer feared the French on their northern and western borders or the Spanish in the Southeast. The coastal British colonies would never have risked breaking with their mother country, some historians contend, had France controlled the Mississippi River and the Great Lakes in 1776.

The British victory in 1763 left Great Britain with a massive war-related debt. Consequently, Parliament for the first time imposed revenue-raising taxes on the colonies in addition to the customs duties that had long regulated trade. That exposed differences in the political thinking of Americans and Britons that had previously been obscured by a shared political vocabulary.

During the 1760s and early 1770s, Anglo American men and women resisted new tax levies and Britain's attempts to tighten controls over provincial governments. The colonies' elected leaders became increasingly suspicious of Britain's motives. They laid aside old antagonisms to coordinate their responses to the new measures. As late as the summer of 1774, though, most were seeking a solution within the empire; few harbored thoughts of independence.

As you read this chapter, keep the following questions in mind:

* **What were the causes and consequences of the Seven Years' War?**

* **What British policies did Americans protest, and what theories and strategies did they develop to support those protests?**

* **Why did the Tea Act of 1773 cause such a major escalation in tensions between the mainland colonies and Great Britain?**

Renewed Warfare Among Europeans and Indians

What was at stake in the Seven Years' War?

In the mid-eighteenth century, the British colonies along the Atlantic seaboard were surrounded by potentially hostile neighbors: Indians, the Spanish in Florida and the Gulf of Mexico, and the French along the rivers and lakes stretching from the St. Lawrence to the Mississippi. Spanish outposts posed little threat, for Spain was no longer a major power. However, France's forts and settlements dominated the North American interior. In all three Anglo-French wars between 1689 and 1748, Britain could not shake France's hold on the American frontier. Under the Peace of Utrecht, which ended Queen Anne's War in 1713, England won control of such peripheral northern areas as Newfoundland, Hudson's Bay, and Acadia (Nova Scotia)

Chronology

1754	Albany Congress meets to try to forge colonial unity		1766	Stamp Act repealed
	Washington defeated at Fort Necessity, Great Meadows, Pennsylvania			Declaratory Act insists that Parliament can tax the colonies
1755	Braddock's army defeated in Pennsylvania		1767	Townshend Acts lay duties on trade within the empire, send new officials to America
1756	Britain declares war on France; Seven Years' War officially begins		1768	Fort Stanwix treaty opens Kentucky to Anglo-American settlement
1759	British forces take Quebec		1768–70	Townshend duties resisted; boycotts and public demonstrations divide merchants and urban artisans
1760	American phase of war ends with fall of Montreal to British troops			
	George III becomes king		1770	Lord North becomes prime minister
1763	Treaty of Paris ends Seven Years' War			Townshend duties repealed, except for tea tax
	Pontiac's allies attack forts and settlements in West			Boston Massacre kills five colonial rioters
	Proclamation of 1763 attempts to close land west of Appalachians to settlement		1772	Boston Committee of Correspondence formed
1764	Sugar Act lays new duties on molasses, tightens customs regulations		1773	Tea Act aids East India Company
				Bostonians protest the Tea Act
	Currency Act outlaws paper money issued by the colonies		1774	Coercive Acts punish Boston and Massachusetts as a whole
1765	Stamp Act requires stamps on all printed materials in colonies			Quebec Act reforms government of Quebec
	Sons of Liberty formed			First Continental Congress called

and gained access to the Great Lakes region previously dominated by France. But Britain made no territorial gains in King George's War (see Table 5.1.)

Iroquois Neutrality   During Queen Anne's War and King George's War, the Iroquois Confederacy maintained a neutrality policy first developed in 1701. While British and French forces vied for nominal control of North America, the confederacy skillfully manipulated the Europeans, refusing to commit warriors to either side despite gifts from both. The Iroquois continued a long-standing conflict with Cherokees and Catawbas in the South, thus giving their young warriors combat experience and replacing population losses with new captives. They also cultivated peaceful relationships with Pennsylvania and Virginia, partly to obtain the colonists' imprimatur for their domination of the Shawnees and Delawares. And they forged ties with Algonquians of the Great Lakes region, thereby making themselves indispensable go-betweens for commerce between the Atlantic coast and the West. Thus, the Iroquois consolidated their control over the interior north of Virginia and south of the Great Lakes.

But the region inhabited by the Shawnees and Delawares (now western Pennsylvania and Virginia and eastern Ohio) provided the spark that set off a major war. In a significant reversal of previous patterns, that conflict spread from America to Europe, decisively resolving the contest for North America.

As early as the late 1730s, trouble began as British traders pushed west from the Carolinas and Virginia, challenging French power beyond the Appalachians.

TABLE 5.1 The Colonial Wars, 1689–1763

American Name	European Name	Dates	Participants	American Sites	Dispute
King William's War	Nine Years' War	1689–97	England, Holland versus France, Spain	New England, New York, Canada	French power
Queen Anne's War	War of Spanish Succession	1702–13	England, Holland, Austria versus France, Spain	Florida, New England	Throne of Spain
King George's War	War of Austrian Succession	1739–48	England, Holland, Austria versus France, Spain, Prussia	West Indies, New England, Canada	Throne of Austria
French and Indian War	Seven Years' War	1756–63	England versus France, Spain	Ohio country, Canada	Possession of Ohio country

The French had difficulty supplying their settlements during a successful British naval blockade of the St. Lawrence during King George's War. This heightened French colonial officials' fear of British incursions, especially when in the 1740s Iroquois negotiators, claiming to speak for the Delawares and Shawnees, ceded large land tracts to Pennsylvania officials. Squatters (mainly Scots-Irish and Germans) had negotiated agreements with the Delawares for settlement rights. But the agreements reached by the Penn family's agents and the Iroquois ignored local Indians and squatters, all of whom were told to move. Disgruntled Delawares and Shawnees migrated west, where they joined other displaced eastern Indians.

The region to which they moved, claimed by both Virginia and Pennsylvania, was coveted by wealthy Virginians, who, organized as the Ohio Company, received a huge land grant in 1749. The company's agents established trading posts that aimed to dominate the crucial area where the Allegheny and Monongahela Rivers join to form the Ohio (see Map 5.1). But France relied on the Ohio River for access to its posts on the Mississippi. Thus, in the early 1750s, Pennsylvania fur traders, Ohio Company representatives, the French military, squatters, Iroquois, Delawares, and Shawnees jostled for position in the region. A 1752 raid by the French and their native allies on a trading outpost sited at modern Cleveland rid the region of Pennsylvanians, but the Virginians posed a serious challenge. Accordingly, in 1753, the French pushed southward, building fortified outposts at strategic points.

Albany Congress In response to the French threat, delegates from seven northern and middle colonies gathered in Albany, New York, in June 1754. They sought to persuade the Iroquois to abandon their neutrality and to coordinate plans for colonial defense. The Iroquois saw no reason to change a policy that served them well for half a century. And although the Albany Congress delegates adopted a Plan of Union (which would have established an elected intercolonial legislature with the power to tax), their provincial governments uniformly rejected the plan, fearing a loss of autonomy.

While the Albany Congress delegates deliberated, the war began. Virginia Governor Robert Dinwiddie sent a small militia troop to build a palisade at the forks of the Ohio. When a substantial French force arrived, the Virginia militia surrendered. The French then constructed Fort Duquesne. Learning of the confrontation, the inexperienced young officer who commanded the Virginia reinforcements

MAP 5.1

European Settlements and Indians, 1754

By 1754, Europeans had expanded the limits of the English colonies to the eastern slopes of the Appalachian Mountains. Few independent Indian nations still existed in the East, but beyond the mountains they controlled the countryside. Only a few widely scattered English and French forts maintained the Europeans' presence there.

Source: Copyright © Cengage Learning

pressed on. He encountered a French detachment, and Tanaghrisson, the leader of his Ohio Indian scouts, killed the French commander. Tanaghrisson started a war to force the British to defend the Ohio Country against the French. The Virginians were trapped by pursuing French troops in a crudely built Fort Necessity at Great Meadows, Pennsylvania. After a day-long battle (on July 3, 1754), during which more than one-third of his men were killed or wounded, twenty-two-year-old George Washington surrendered.

Seven Years' War

Washington's blunder and Tanaghrisson's aggression helped ignite a war that eventually encompassed nearly the entire world. In July 1755, a few miles south of Fort Duquesne, the French and Indians attacked British and colonial troops. In the devastating defeat, General Edward Braddock was killed. The Pennsylvania frontier was repeatedly attacked by Delawares for two more years; over a thousand residents were killed. Settlers felt betrayed because the Indians attacking them had once been (an observer noted) "allmost dayly familiars at their houses."

Seven Years' War: Major French-English conflict that was the first worldwide war.

Britain declared war on France in 1756, thus formally beginning the Seven Years' War. Even before then, Britons and New Englanders feared that France would try to retake Nova Scotia, where most of the population descended from seventeenth-century French settlers who had intermarried with local M'ikmaqs. Afraid that the approximately twelve thousand French Nova Scotians would abandon their neutrality policy, British commanders in 1755 forced about seven thousand from their homeland—the first large-scale modern deportation, now called ethnic cleansing. Ships crammed with Acadians sailed to each mainland colony. Many families were separated, some forever. After 1763, the survivors relocated: some returned to Canada, others to France or its Caribbean islands. Many settled in Louisiana, where they became known as Cajuns (derived from *Acadian*).

British officers tried unsuccessfully to coerce the colonies into supplying men and materiel to the army. When William Pitt, the civilian official heading the war effort in 1757, agreed to reimburse the colonies' wartime expenditures and placed recruitment in local hands, he gained greater American support. (Even so, Virginia burgesses appropriated more funds to defend against possible slave insurrections than to fight the French and Indians.) Many colonial militiamen served alongside red-coated regulars from Britain; the two groups maintained an antagonistic relationship, however.

Adding to the tensions were the actions of Anglo-American merchants in Boston, Philadelphia, and New York, who continued trading with the French West Indies. They bribed customs officers to look the other way while cargoes of fish, flour, timber, and other products bound for such neutral ports as Dutch St. Eustatius or Spanish Monte Cristi (on Hispaniola) actually ended up in the French Caribbean, and they acquired valuable French sugar in return. British officials failed to stop the illicit commerce. North America also supplied France with vital materiel during the war.

Nevertheless, in July 1758, British forces recaptured the fortress at Louisbourg, winning control of the entrance to the St. Lawrence River. In the fall, Delawares and Shawnees accepted British peace overtures, and the French abandoned Fort Duquesne. Then, in September 1759, General James Wolfe's regulars defeated the French and

The First Worldwide War

Today, we call two twentieth-century conflicts world wars, but the contest that historians term the "Great War for the Empire" was actually the first worldwide war. It began in spring 1754 in southwestern Pennsylvania, over whether Britain or France would build a fort at the forks of the Ohio. That it eventually involved combatants around the world attests to the growing importance of European nations' overseas empires and the increasing centrality of North America to their struggles for dominance.

The contest at the forks of the Ohio helped to reinvigorate a conflict between Austria and Prussia that sent European nations scrambling for allies. Eventually England, Hanover, and Prussia lined up against France, Austria, Russia, Sweden, and Saxony, and, later, Spain. The war in Europe would last seven years. In 1763, these nations signed a peace treaty that returned the continent to the prewar status, but in the rest of the world Britain had vanquished France and Spain.

In the Caribbean, Britain seized the French islands of Guadeloupe and Martinique, and took Havana from Spain. In North America, the British recaptured the French fortress of Louisbourg and conquered Quebec. In Africa, Britain overwhelmed France's slave-trading posts in Senegambia. In India, British forces won control of Bengal. Late in the war, a British expedition took Manila in the Philippines from Spain.

Thus, the war that started in the American backcountry revealed the steadily growing links between North America and the rest of the world. Winners and losers had to pay for this first worldwide war. Financial struggles in Britain and France produced revolutions abroad (for Britain, in America) and at home (for France).

National Maritime Museum, London

In 1771, artist Dominic Serres, the Elder, depicted British naval vessels attacking the French fortress at Chandernagore in India in 1757 (at left in background). Cannon fire from the warships was critical to the British victory, one of the keys to the conquest of India during the Seven Years' War.

took Quebec. Sensing a British victory, the Iroquois abandoned neutrality, hoping to gain a postwar advantage by allying with Britain. A year later, the British captured Montreal, the last French stronghold, and the American phase of the war ended.

In the **Treaty of Paris** (1763), France ceded its major North American holdings to Britain. Spain, an ally of France toward war's end, gave Florida to the victors. France ceded Louisiana west of the Mississippi to Spain, in partial compensation for its ally's losses elsewhere. The British thus gained control of the continent's fur trade. No longer would the English seacoast colonies have to worry about the threat posed by France's extensive North American territories.

The British triumph stimulated some Americans like Benjamin Franklin to predict a glorious future for British North America. Such men, who would lead the resistance to British measures after 1763, opposed laws that would retard America's growth and supported steps to increase Americans' control over their own destiny.

Treaty of Paris: Treaty by which France ceded most of its holdings to Great Britain and some smaller amounts to Spain.

Link to Benjamin Franklin's "Join or Die" cartoon.

1763: A Turning Point

Indigenous peoples of the interior first felt the impact of Britain's victory. After Britain gained the upper hand in the American war in 1758, Creeks and Cherokees lost their ability to force concessions by threatening to turn instead to France or Spain. In desperation and retaliation for British atrocities, Cherokees attacked the Carolina and Virginia frontiers in 1760. Though initially victorious, the Indians were defeated the following year. Late in 1761, a treaty allowed the construction of British forts in Cherokee territories and opened a large tract to European settlement.

How did colonists' ideas about government differ from those of the British in the 1760s?

Neolin and Pontiac

In the Ohio country, the Ottawas, Chippewas, and Potawatomis reacted angrily when Great Britain, no longer facing French competition, raised prices on trade goods and ended traditional gift-giving practices. As settlers moved into the Monongahela and Susquehanna valleys, a shaman named Neolin urged Indians to oppose European settlement and influence on their culture. Contending that Indian peoples were destroying themselves by dependence on European goods (especially alcohol), Neolin advocated peaceful and armed resistance. If all Indians west of the mountains united to reject the invaders, Neolin declared, the Master of Life would replenish the depleted deer herds and look kindly upon his people.

Heeding Neolin's call, in spring 1763, Ottawa war chief Pontiac forged an unprecedented alliance among Hurons, Chippewas, Potawatomis, Delawares, Shawnees, and Mingoes (Pennsylvania Iroquois). Pontiac besieged Fort Detroit while war parties attacked other British outposts in the Great Lakes. Detroit withstood the siege, but by late June the other forts west of Niagara and north of Fort Pitt had fallen. Indians then raided the Virginia and Pennsylvania frontiers, slaying at least two thousand settlers. They carried off many enslaved African Americans, frightening planters, who feared an Indian-black alliance. In early August, colonial militiamen defeated an Indian force at Bushy Run, Pennsylvania. Pontiac ended the Detroit siege in late October; a treaty ending the war was negotiated three years later.

For nearly eighty years, European settlers and Indians in "Penn's Woods" avoided major conflicts. But the Indian attacks and settlers' response—especially the massacre of several families of defenseless Conestoga Indians in December 1763 by fifty Scots-Irish men known as the Paxton Boys—revealed that violence in the region would become endemic.

Proclamation of 1763

Proclamation of 1763: England's attempt to end Indian problems by preventing westward movement by colonists.

London officials had no experience managing an area as vast as the territory it acquired from France, which included French settlers along the St. Lawrence and many Indian communities. In October, the ministry issued the **Proclamation of 1763,** designating the headwaters of rivers flowing into the Atlantic from the Appalachians as the temporary western boundary for colonial settlement (see Map 5.1). Its promulgators expected to prevent clashes by forbidding colonists to move onto Indian lands. But it infuriated colonists who had squatted west of the line and land speculation companies from Pennsylvania and Virginia.

After 1763, the latter groups (which included such men as George Washington, Thomas Jefferson, Patrick Henry, and Benjamin Franklin) lobbied vigorously to have their claims validated by colonial governments and London administrators. At a treaty conference at Fort Stanwix, New York, in 1768, they negotiated with Iroquois representatives to push the boundary line farther west and south. The Iroquois, still claiming to speak for the Delawares and the Shawnees agreed to the deal, which yielded valuable trade goods and did not affect their own territories. Although the Virginia land companies eventually gained the support of the House of Burgesses, they never made headway in London because administrators worried that western expansion would require funds they did not have.

Benjamin West, the first well-known American artist, engraved this picture of a prisoner exchange at the end of Pontiac's Uprising, with Colonel Henry Bouquet supervising the return of settlers abducted during the war. In the foreground, a child resists leaving the Indian parents he had grown to love. Many colonists were fascinated by the phenomenon West depicted—the reluctance of captives to abandon their adoptive Indian families.

Ohio Historical Society

George III

Financing Britain's debt from the Seven Years' War—and defending newly acquired territories—bedeviled King George III, who in 1760 succeeded his grandfather, George II. During the crucial years between 1763 and 1770, when the rift with the colonies widened and various political crises beset England, the twenty-two-year-old king replaced ministries rapidly. Although determined to assert the power of the monarchy, George III stubbornly regarded adherence to the status quo as the hallmark of patriotism.

Selected as prime minister in 1763, George Grenville confronted a financial crisis: England's indebtedness had nearly doubled since 1754, from £73 million to £137 million. Prewar annual expenditures amounted to no more than £8 million; now the yearly interest on the debt reached £5 million. Grenville's ministry needed funds, but the British were already heavily taxed. Because the colonists benefited from wartime expenditures, Grenville concluded that Anglo-Americans should pay a larger share of the empire's costs.

Theories of Representation

Americans believed they could be represented only by men who lived nearby and for whom they or their property-holding neighbors actually voted. Grenville and his English contemporaries, however, believed that Parliament—king, lords, and commons acting together—represented all British subjects (even overseas) and whether or not they could vote. In Parliament, the particular constituency that chose a member of the House of Commons had no special claim on that member's vote, nor did the member have to live near his constituents. According to this theory, called virtual representation, all Britons—including colonists—were represented in Parliament. Thus, their consent to acts of Parliament could be presumed. In the colonies, by contrast, members of the assemblies' lower houses were viewed as specifically representing the regions that elected them. Before Grenville proposed to tax the colonists, the two notions coexisted. But events of the 1760s revealed their incompatibility.

Real Whigs

Colonists had become accustomed to a central government with limited authority. They believed that a good government was one that largely left them alone, a view matching the theories of British writers known as the Real Whigs. Drawing on a tradition of dissenting thought reaching back to John Locke, Real Whigs stressed the dangers inherent in a powerful government, particularly a monarchy. Some favored republicanism, which proposed to eliminate monarchs and rest power more directly on the people. Real Whigs warned the people to guard constantly against government's attempted encroachments on their liberty and property.

As Britain tightened the reins in the 1760s and early 1770s, many Americans saw parallels in their circumstances and Real Whig ideology. Excessive and unjust taxation, they believed, could destroy their freedoms, and they saw oppressive designs behind the actions of Grenville and his successors. In the mid-1760s, however, colonial leaders merely questioned the wisdom of Grenville's proposed laws.

Sugar and Currency Acts

In 1764, Parliament passed the Sugar and Currency Acts. The **Sugar Act** (also known as the Revenue Act) revised existing customs regulations and laid new duties on some foreign imports into the colonies. Its key provisions, advocated in London by influential Caribbean sugar planters, aimed at discouraging American rum distillers from smuggling French West Indian molasses. Although the Sugar Act resembled the Navigation Acts, it broke with tradition by deliberately seeking to raise revenue rather than channel American trade through Britain. The Currency Act outlawed most colonial paper money, because British merchants had complained that Americans paid debts in inflated local currencies.

Sugar Act: Act passed by British Parliament that sought to raise revenues by taxing colonial imports, notably the sugar trade.

The Sugar and Currency Acts were imposed on an already depressed economy. A business boom accompanied the Seven Years' War, but prosperity ended in 1760 when the war shifted overseas. Urban merchants found few buyers for imported goods, and the loss of military demand for foodstuffs hurt American farmers. The bottom dropped out of the European tobacco market, threatening the livelihood of Chesapeake planters. Sailors and artisans had little work. Thus, the prospect of increased import duties and inadequate currency aroused merchants' hostility.

Without precedent for a united campaign against acts of Parliament, Americans in 1764 took uncoordinated steps. Eight colonial legislatures sent petitions to

Parliament requesting the Sugar Act's repeal. They argued that its commercial restrictions would hurt Britain as well as the colonies and that they had not consented to its passage. Their protests had no effect.

The Stamp Act Crisis

How did the Stamp Act raise issues that would lead to the American Revolution?

Stamp Act: Obliged colonists to purchase and use special stamped (watermarked) paper for newspapers, customs documents, various licenses, college diplomas, and legal forms used for recovering debts, buying land, and making wills.

The **Stamp Act** (1765), Grenville's most important proposal, required tax stamps on most printed materials, placing the heaviest burden on merchants and the colonial elite, who used printed matter more than ordinary folk. Anyone who purchased a newspaper, made a will, transferred land, accepted a government appointment, or borrowed money would have to pay the tax. Never before had a revenue measure of such scope been proposed for the colonies. The act also required that tax stamps be purchased with scarce sterling coin. Violators would be tried by vice-admiralty courts, where judges rendered decisions, leading Americans to fear the loss of their right to trial by jury. Finally, such a law broke with the colonial tradition of self-imposed taxation.

James Otis's *Rights of the British Colonies*

The young Massachusetts attorney James Otis Jr., penned the most important colonial pamphlet protesting the Sugar Act and the proposed Stamp Act: *The Rights of the British Colonies Asserted and Proved*. Otis exposed the dilemma that confounded colonists for the next decade. How could they oppose certain acts of Parliament without questioning Parliament's authority over them? On the one hand, Otis asserted, Americans were "entitled to all the natural, essential, inherent, and inseparable rights" of Britons, including the right not to be taxed without their consent. On the other, Otis admitted that, under the British system since the Glorious Revolution, "the power of parliament is uncontrollable but by themselves, and we must obey . . . till they will be pleased to relieve us."

Link to the Virginia Stamp Act resolutions.

Otis's first contention implied that Parliament could not constitutionally tax the colonies because Americans were not represented in its ranks. Yet his second point accepted the prevailing theory of British government: that Parliament was the sole, supreme authority in the empire. To resolve the dilemma, Otis proposed colonial representation in Parliament, but the British believed that colonists were already virtually represented in Parliament, and Anglo-Americans knew that a handful of colonial delegates to London would easily be outvoted. When Americans learned of the act's adoption in the spring of 1765, they reacted indecisively. Few colonists publicly favored the law, but colonial petitions failed to prevent its adoption. Perhaps Otis was correct: the only course was to pay the stamp tax, reluctantly but loyally.

Patrick Henry and the Virginia Stamp Act Resolves

A twenty-nine-year-old lawyer serving his first term in the Virginia House of Burgesses, Patrick Henry was appalled by his fellow legislators' complacency. "Alone, unadvised, and unassisted, on a blank leaf of an old law book," he wrote the Virginia Stamp Act Resolves.

Little in Henry's earlier life foreshadowed his political success. The son of a prosperous Scots immigrant to western Virginia, Henry had little formal education.

After marrying at eighteen, he failed at farming and storekeeping before turning to the law to support his wife and six children. Henry lacked legal training, but his oratorical skills made him an effective advocate, first for his clients and later for his political beliefs.

Patrick Henry introduced his seven proposals near the end of the legislative session, when many burgesses had already departed. The few burgesses remaining in Williamsburg adopted five of Henry's resolutions by a bare majority. But some colonial newspapers printed Henry's seven original resolutions as if they had been uniformly passed by the House. One was rescinded and two others were never voted on.

The four propositions adopted by the burgesses repeated Otis's arguments, asserting that colonists had never forfeited their rights as British subjects, which included consent to taxation. The other three resolutions went further. The repealed resolution claimed the burgesses had the "exclusive right" to tax Virginians, and the two never considered asserted that Virginians need not obey tax laws passed by other legislative bodies (namely, Parliament).

Continuing Loyalty to Britain

Though contending for their rights, the colonists did not seek independence. Maryland lawyer Daniel Dulany, who's *Considerations on the Propriety of Imposing Taxes on the British Colonies* was the most widely read pamphlet of 1765, expressed the consensus: "The colonies are dependent upon Great Britain, and the supreme authority vested in the king, lords, and commons, may justly be exercised to secure, or preserve their dependence." But, warned Dulany, there was a distinction between a condition of "dependence and inferiority" and one of "absolute vassalage and slavery."

Over the next ten years, America's political leaders searched for a way to control their internal affairs, especially taxation, but remain under British rule. The notion that Parliament could exercise absolute authority over colonial possessions inhered in the British theory of government. Even Britain's harshest critics in the 1760s and 1770s questioned only the wisdom of specific policies, not the principles on which they rested. In effect, the Americans wanted British leaders to revise their fundamental understanding of government.

Anti-Stamp Act Demonstrations

In August, the Loyal Nine, a Boston artisans' social club, organized an anti-Stamp Act demonstration. Hoping to show that people of all ranks opposed the act, they approached leaders of the city's rival laborers' associations, based in Boston's North End and South End neighborhoods. The two groups, composed of unskilled workers and poor tradesmen, often battled each other, but the Loyal Nine convinced them to lay aside their differences for the demonstration.

On August 14, the demonstrators hung an effigy of Andrew Oliver, the province's stamp distributor, from a tree on Boston Common. That night a large crowd led by

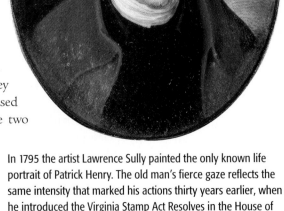

In 1795 the artist Lawrence Sully painted the only known life portrait of Patrick Henry. The old man's fierce gaze reflects the same intensity that marked his actions thirty years earlier, when he introduced the Virginia Stamp Act Resolves in the House of Burgesses.

fifty well-dressed tradesmen paraded the effigy around the city. The crowd built a bonfire near Oliver's house and added the effigy to the flames. Demonstrators broke most of Oliver's windows and threw stones at officials. During the melee, the North End and South End leaders toasted their union. Oliver publicly promised not to fulfill the duties of his office.

But another crowd action twelve days later, aimed at Oliver's brother-in-law, Lieutenant Governor Thomas Hutchinson, drew no praise from respectable Bostonians. On August 26, a mob attacked the homes of several customs officers and destroyed Hutchinson's elaborately furnished townhouse. But Hutchinson took some comfort in the fact that "the encouragers of the first mob never intended matters should go this length and the people in general express the utmost detestation of this unparalleled outrage."

Link to Hutchinson's account of the destruction of his house.

Americans' Divergent Interests

Few colonists sided with Britain during the 1760s, but groups had divergent goals. The skilled craftsmen who composed the Loyal Nine and merchants, lawyers, and other educated elites preferred orderly demonstrations. For the city's laborers, economic grievances may have been paramount. Certainly, their "hellish Fury" as they wrecked Hutchinson's house suggests resentment against his display of wealth.

Colonists, like Britons, had a long tradition in which disfranchised people took to the streets to redress grievances. But the Stamp Act controversy for the first time drew ordinary urban folk into transatlantic politics, including recent non-English-speaking immigrants targeted by the double taxation of foreign-language newspapers. Matters that previously concerned only the gentry or colonial legislatures were now discussed everywhere.

The entry of unskilled workers, slaves, and women into imperial politics threatened and aided elite men who wanted to oppose British measures. Anti-Stamp Act demonstrations occurred in cities and towns stretching from Halifax in the north to the Caribbean island of Antigua in the south. They were so successful that, by November 1, when the law was to take effect, not one stamp distributor would carry out his duties. But wealthy men recognized that mobs composed of the formerly powerless could endanger their dominance of society.

Sons of Liberty

They therefore attempted to channel resistance into acceptable forms by creating an intercolonial association, the **Sons of Liberty**. Composed of merchants, lawyers, and prosperous tradesmen, the Sons of Liberty by early 1766 linked protest leaders from New York to those in Charleston, South Carolina, and those in Portsmouth, New Hampshire. With taverns as settings for the exchange of news and opinions, many members were tavern owners.

Sons of Liberty: Groups formed to resist the Stamp Act.

In Charleston (formerly Charles Town) in October 1765, a crowd shouting, "Liberty Liberty and stamp'd paper" forced the resignation of the South Carolina stamp distributor. But the Charleston chapter of the Sons of Liberty was horrified when in January 1766 local slaves paraded through the streets similarly crying, "Liberty!" Freedom from slavery was not what elite slaveowners had in mind.

In Philadelphia, resistance leaders were dismayed when an angry mob threatened to attack Benjamin Franklin's house. Laborers believed Franklin to be partly responsible for the Stamp Act because he had obtained the post of stamp distributor for a friend. But Philadelphia's artisans—the backbone of the opposition movement there and elsewhere—were loyal to Franklin, one of their own who had made good and protected his home. The resulting split between Philadelphia's better-off tradesmen and common laborers prevented an alliance as successful as Boston's.

Opposition and Repeal   During fall and winter 1765–1766, Stamp Act opponents pursued various strategies. Colonial legislatures petitioned Parliament to repeal the law, and courts closed because they could not obtain the stamps now required for legal documents. In October, nine colonies sent delegates to a general congress—the first since 1754—in New York to draft a protest stressing the law's adverse economic effects. Meanwhile, the Sons of Liberty held mass meetings to rally public support. Finally, American merchants organized nonimportation associations to pressure British exporters, expecting that since one-quarter of all exports went to the colonies by the 1760s, London merchants whose sales suffered would lobby for repeal.

In March 1766, Parliament repealed the Stamp Act. The nonimportation agreements had created allies for the colonies among wealthy London merchants. But the main factor in winning repeal then was the appointment of a new prime minister. Lord Rockingham, who replaced Grenville in summer 1765, opposed the Stamp Acts an unwise and divisive law. Thus, Rockingham linked repeal to passage of a **Declaratory Act**, which asserted Parliament's authority to tax and legislate Britain's American possessions.

News of the repeal arrived in Newport, Rhode Island, in May, and the Sons of Liberty dispatched messengers throughout the colonies. They organized celebrations commemorating the event and Americans' loyalty to Britain. Their goal achieved, the Sons of Liberty dissolved.

Declaratory Act: Affirmed parliamentary power to legislate its colonies "in all cases whatsoever."

Resistance to the Townshend Acts

In summer 1766, another change in the ministry in London revealed how fragile the colonists' victory had been. The new prime minister, William Pitt, fostered cooperation between the colonies and Britain during the Seven Years' War. But Pitt fell ill, and Charles Townshend became the dominant force in the ministry. An ally of Grenville, Townshend renewed efforts to obtain funds from Britain's American possessions (see Table 5.2).

How did the Sons of Liberty politicize ordinary Americans during resistance to the Townshend Acts?

The duties Townshend proposed in 1767 seemed to extend the Navigation Acts by focusing on trade goods like paper, glass, and tea. But they differed first by applying to British imports, not to those from foreign countries. Second, the revenues would pay some colonial officials, thereby eliminating assemblies' ability to threaten to withhold salaries from uncooperative officials. Additionally, Townshend's scheme established an American Board of Customs Commissioners and vice-admiralty courts at Boston, Philadelphia, and Charleston. This angered merchants, whose profits would be threatened.

TABLE 5.2   British Ministries and Their American Policies

Head of Ministry	Major Acts
George Grenville	Sugar Act (1764)
	Currency Act (1764)
	Stamp Act (1765)
Lord Rockingham	Stamp Act repealed (1766)
	Declaratory Act (1766)
William Pitt/ Charles Townshend	Townshend Acts (1767)
Lord North	Townshend duties (except for the tea tax) repealed (1770)
	Tea Act (1773)
	Coercive Acts (1774)
	Quebec Act (1774)

John Dickinson's Farmer's Letters

Passage of the Townshend Acts drew quick response from the colonies. One series widely-published essays, *Letters from a Farmer in Pennsylvania*, by prominent lawyer John Dickinson, expressed a broad consensus. Dickinson contended that Parliament could regulate colonial trade but could not raise revenue. By distinguishing between trade regulation and taxation, Dickinson avoided the sticky issues of consent and the colonies' relationship to Parliament. But his argument obligated the colonies to assess Parliament's motives in passing trade laws before deciding whether to obey them.

The Massachusetts assembly responded to the Townshend Acts by drafting a letter to the other colonial legislatures, suggesting a joint protest petition. When Lord Hillsborough, recently named to secretary of state for America, learned of the Massachusetts circular, he ordered that colony's Governor Francis Bernard to insist that the assembly recall it. He also directed other governors to prevent their assemblies from discussing it. Hillsborough's order motivated colonial assemblies to unite against this new threat to their prerogatives. In late 1768, the Massachusetts legislature resoundingly rejected recall by a vote of 92 to 17. Bernard immediately dissolved the assembly, and other governors similarly responded.

Rituals of Resistance

John Wilkes: British opponent of King George III who became a hero to American colonists.

The number of votes cast against recalling the circular letter—92—assumed ritual significance for the resistance. The number 45 was already symbolic because **John Wilkes**, a radical Londoner sympathetic to the American cause, had been jailed for publishing an essay entitled *The North Briton*, No. 45. In Boston, the silversmith Paul Revere made a punchbowl weighing 45 ounces that held 45 gills (half-cups). Charleston's tradesmen decorated a tree with 45 lights, set off 45 rockets, and carrying 45 candles, adjourned to a tavern where 45 tables were set with 45 bowls of wine, 45 bowls of punch, and 92 glasses.

Such public rituals taught illiterate Americans about the reasons for resistance. When Boston's revived Sons of Liberty invited hundreds of residents to dine with them each August 14 to commemorate the first Stamp Act demonstration, crowds gathered. Likewise, the public singing of songs supporting the American cause helped spread the word.

The Revolutionary Symbolism of Female Spinners

By the 1760s, middling and well-to-do urban colonists purchased fabric and ordered clothing from tailors and dressmakers. Only the poorer residents of rural America continued to spin wool or flax into yarn, then wove that yarn into cloth and made their own wearing apparel. Urban dwellers, accustomed for decades to following the latest English fashions, had long looked down on rustics who wore homespun—and yet the ability to spin was still seen as a quintessentially feminine occupation, with many young girls being taught that skill. One wealthy Philadelphia poet wrote that working at her wheel reminded her of "a train of Female Hands/ Chearful uniting in Industrious Bands." And so when colonists joined to boycott British goods, one of the key ways in which women could publicize their support for American resistance was to bring their wheels to a public location. What message does the poem convey about the spinners' aims and impact? What was the importance of women undertaking in public a task usually performed in their own homes, if at all?

A

VERSE,

Occasioned by feeing the North-Spinning, in *BOSTON*.

BOSTON, behold the pretty Spinners here,
    And fee how gay the pretty Sparks appear :
See Rich and Poor all turn the Spinning Wheel,
All who Compaffion for their Country feel,
All who do love to fee Induftry live,
And fee Frugality in *Bofton* thrive.

Britain, behold thy Trade ftole from thy Hand,
And carried on in *Bofton*'s diftant Land :
See now thy Trade and Trades men, all expire,
And fee them all cut fhort of their Defire,
Th' Defire they had that *Bofton*'s Trade fhould fpoil,
That they might reap the Fruit of all our Toil ;
And they might take what we'he been flaving for,
And rule us by the Parlimental Law :
But thanks to GOD, their ill Defigns are cropt,
And their Tirannical Defigns are ftopt.

Now they have run their Chain's extended Length,
And exhaufted all their once encourag'd Strength :
Now have their ill Defigns, all found an end,
Now they have made a Foe of every Friend :
Now let them ftarve and die the Death of thofe,
Who do the Intereft of their King oppofe.

BOSTON: Printed and Sold 1769.

A Boston poet in 1769 produced this broadside verse to praise spinners who had gathered in the North End of the City

An eighteenth-century American flax wheel of the sort that would have been used in a public spinning demonstration. Wheels for spinning wool were too large to move easily.

The Sons of Liberty and other American leaders made a deliberate effort to involve ordinary folk in the campaign against the Townshend duties. Most important, they urged colonists of all ranks and both sexes to sign agreements not to purchase or consume British products. The new consumerism that had linked colonists economically now supplied them with a ready method of displaying their allegiance.

Daughters of Liberty

As the primary purchasers of textiles and household goods, women played a central role in the nonconsumption movement. More than three hundred Boston matrons publicly promised not to buy or drink tea, "Sickness excepted." As Janet Schaw later noted, the women of Wilmington, North Carolina, burned their tea after walking through town in a solemn procession. Women exchanged recipes for tea substitutes or drank coffee instead. The best known of the protests, the so-called Edenton Ladies Tea Party, was actually a meeting of prominent North Carolina women who pledged to work for the public good and support resistance to British measures.

In many towns, young women calling themselves Daughters of Liberty met to spin in public squares to persuade other women to make homespun and wear homespun clothing, thereby ending the colonies' dependence on British cloth. These patriotic displays served the same purpose as male rituals involving the numbers 45 and 92. When young ladies from well-to-do families sat outdoors at spinning wheels all day, eating only American food, drinking local herbal tea, and listening to patriotic sermons, they served as political instructors, a role they proudly accepted.

Divided Opinion over Boycotts

Colonists were by no means united in support of nonimportation and nonconsumption. Resistance to the Townshend Acts exposed new splits in American ranks. The most significant rifts divided urban artisans and merchants, allies in 1765.

The Stamp Act boycotts had helped revive a depressed economy by creating demand for local products and reducing merchants' inventories. But in 1768 and 1769, merchants enjoyed boom times and had no incentive to support boycotts. Artisans supported nonimportation enthusiastically, recognizing that the absence of British goods would create a market for their manufactures. Thus tradesmen formed the core of the crowds that coerced importers and their customers by picketing stores, publicizing offenders' names, and sometimes destroying property.

Such tactics were effective: colonial imports from England dropped dramatically in 1769, especially in New York, New England, and Pennsylvania. But the tactics also aroused heated opposition. Some Americans who supported resistance questioned the use of violence to force others to join the boycott. The threat to private property inherent in the campaign frightened wealthier and more conservative men and women. Political activism by ordinary colonists challenged the ruling elite's domination, as many had feared in 1765.

Disclosures that leading merchants had violated the nonimportation agreement caused dissension in the ranks of the boycotters, so Americans were relieved when news arrived in April 1770 that the Townshend duties had been repealed, except for the tea tax. A new prime minister, Lord North, persuaded Parliament that duties on trade within the empire were ill-advised. The other Townshend Acts remained in force, but provisions for paying officials' salaries and tightening customs enforcement appeared less objectionable.

Confrontations in Boston

On the day Lord North proposed repeal of the Townshend duties, a confrontation between civilians and soldiers in Boston led to five Americans' deaths. The decision to base the American Board of Customs Commissioners in Boston ultimately caused the confrontation.

Mobs targeted the customs commissioners from their arrival in November 1767. In June 1768, their seizure of patriot leader John Hancock's sloop *Liberty* on suspicion of smuggling caused a riot in which customs officers' property was destroyed. The ministry brought in troops to maintain order. The assignment of two regiments to their city confirmed Bostonians' worst fears about the oppressive potential of British power. Guards on Boston Neck, the entrance to the city, checked travelers and their goods. Redcoat patrols roamed the city, questioning and

> How did Samuel Adams's Committees of Correspondence mark a turning point in Americans' political thinking?

Courtesy of the John Carter Brown Library at Brown University

Shortly after the Boston Massacre, Paul Revere printed this illustration of the confrontation near the customs house on March 5, 1770. Offering visual support for the patriots' version of events, it showed the British soldiers firing on an unresisting crowd (instead of the aggressive mob described at the soldiers' trial) and—even worse—a gun firing from the building itself, which has been labeled "Butchers Hall."

sometimes harassing passersby. Parents feared for the safety of daughters, who were subjected to soldiers' coarse sexual insults. Additionally, many redcoats sought off-duty employment, competing for unskilled jobs with the city's workingmen. The two groups brawled repeatedly in taverns and on the streets.

Boston Massacre:
Confrontation between colonists and British troops in which five colonists where shot and killed.

Link to accounts from the Boston Massacre trial.

Boston Massacre

On the evening of March 5, 1770, a crowd of laborers threw snowballs at soldiers guarding the Customs House. Against orders, the sentries fired on the crowd, killing four and wounding eight, one of whom died a few days later. Reportedly the first to die was Crispus Attucks, a sailor of mixed Nipmuck and African origins. Resistance leaders idealized Attucks and the other dead rioters as martyrs for liberty, holding a solemn funeral and later commemorating March 5 annually.

Despite the political benefits patriots derived from the massacre, they probably did not approve the crowd action that provoked it. Since the destruction of Hutchinson's house in August 1765, men allied with the Sons of Liberty had supported orderly demonstrations. Thus, when the soldiers were tried in November, John Adams and Josiah Quincy Jr., both unwavering patriots, acted as their defense attorneys. Almost all were acquitted, and the two men convicted were released after being branded on the thumb. Undoubtedly, this favorable outcome persuaded London officials not to retaliate against the city.

A British Plot?

For more than two years after the Boston Massacre, a superficial calm emerged. In June 1772, Rhode Islanders, angry with overzealous customs enforcement by the British naval schooner *Gaspée*, attacked and burned it in Narragansett Bay near Providence. Because the perpetrators were never identified, there were no adverse consequences for colonists. The most outspoken newspapers, such as the *Boston Gazette*, the *Pennsylvania Journal*, and the *South Carolina Gazette*, published essays drawing on Real Whig ideology and accusing Great Britain of scheming to oppress the colonies. After the Stamp Act's repeal, the protest leaders praised Parliament; following repeal of the Townshend duties, they warned of impending tyranny. The single ill-chosen stamp tax now seemed part of a plot against American liberties. Essayists pointed to the stationing of troops in Boston and the growing number of vice-admiralty courts as evidence of plans to enslave the colonists. Indeed, patriot writers repeatedly used the word *enslavement*. Most free colonists had direct knowledge of slavery, and the threat of enslavement by Britain must have had peculiar force.

Although some colonists were increasingly convinced that they should seek freedom from parliamentary authority, they continued to acknowledge their British identity and allegiance to George III. They began to envision a system that would enable them to be ruled by their own elected legislatures while remaining subordinate to the king. But any such scheme violated Britons' conception of their government, which posited that Parliament—which they believed encompassed the king as well as lords and commons—wielded sole, undivided sovereignty over the empire. Then, in fall 1772, the North ministry began to implement the Townshend Act that would pay governors and judges from customs revenues. In early November, voters at a Boston town meeting established a **Committee of Correspondence** to publicize the decision by exchanging letters with other Massachusetts towns. Heading the committee was Samuel Adams.

Committees of Correspondence: Local committees established throughout colonies to coordinate anti-British actions.

Samuel Adams and Committees of Correspondence

Fifty-one in 1772, Samuel Adams was about a decade older than the other American resistance leaders. He had been a Boston tax collector, a member and clerk of the Massachusetts assembly, an ally of the Loyal Nine, and one of the Sons of Liberty. Adams drew a sharp contrast between a corrupt, vice-ridden Britain and the colonies, peopled by simple, liberty-loving folk. An experienced political organizer, Adams's Committee of Correspondence sought to create an informed consensus among the residents of Massachusetts.

Until 1772, the protest movement was confined largely to the seacoast and major cities and towns. Adams wanted to widen the movement's geographic scope. Accordingly, the Boston town meeting directed the Committee of Correspondence "to state the Rights of the Colonists and of this Province in particular;" to list "the Infringements and Violations thereof that have been, or from time to time may be made;" and to send copies to other towns.

The statement of colonial rights declared that Americans had absolute rights to life, liberty, and property. The idea that "a British house of commons, should have a right, at pleasure, to give and grant the property of the colonists" was "irreconcileable" with "the first principles of natural law and Justice . . . and of the British Constitution." They complained of taxation without representation, the presence of unnecessary troops and customs officers on American soil, the use of imperial revenues to pay colonial officials, and the expanded jurisdiction of vice-admiralty courts.

The document, which was printed as a pamphlet for distribution to the towns, exhibited none of the hesitation of 1760s' claims against Parliament. No longer were resistance leaders—at least in Boston—preoccupied with defining the limits of parliamentary authority, nor did they mention the necessity of obedience to Parliament. They placed American rights first, loyalty to Great Britain a distant second.

The towns' response to the pamphlet must have thrilled Samuel Adams. While some towns disagreed with Boston's assessment, most aligned with the city. The town of Holden declared that "the People of New England have never given the People of Britain any Right of Jurisdiction over us." The citizens of Petersham commented that resistance to tyranny was "the first and highest social Duty of this people." Beliefs like these made the next crisis in Anglo-American affairs the last.

Tea and Turmoil

> How did the Tea Act push the country to the brink of revolution?

The tea tax was the only Townshend duty still in effect by 1773. After 1770, some Americans continued to boycott English tea; others resumed drinking it. Tea figured prominently in the colonists' diet and social lives, so the boycott meant forgoing a favorite beverage and altering habitual forms of socializing.

Reactions to the Tea Act

In May 1773, Parliament passed the **Tea Act** to save the East India Company from bankruptcy. The company, which held a monopoly on British trade with the East Indies, was important to the British economy and to the prominent British politicians who invested in its stock. Under the act, only the East India Company's agents

Tea Act: England's attempt to bail out East India Company that heightened tensions between the British and the colonies.

could legally sell tea in America. That enabled the company to avoid intermediaries and to price its tea competitively with that of smugglers. Resistance leaders, however, interpreted the measure as designed to make them admit Parliament's right to tax them, for the less expensive tea would still be taxed under the Townshend law. Others saw the Tea Act as the first step in an East India Company monopoly on all colonial trade. Residents of the four cities to receive the first tea shipments prepared to meet this perceived threat to their freedom.

In New York City, tea ships never arrived. In Philadelphia, Pennsylvania's governor persuaded the captain to return to Britain. In Charleston, the tea was unloaded; some was destroyed, the rest sold in 1776 by the new state government. The only confrontation occurred in Boston, where both sides—the town meeting and Governor Thomas Hutchinson, two of whose sons were tea agents—rejected compromise.

The first of three tea ships, the *Dartmouth,* entered Boston harbor on November 28. Customs laws required cargo to be landed and the duty paid within twenty days of a ship's arrival; otherwise, the cargo would be seized and sold at auction. After several mass meetings, Bostonians voted to post guards on the wharf to prevent the tea from being unloaded. Hutchinson refused to permit the vessels to leave the harbor.

On December 16, one day before the cargo would have been confiscated, more than five thousand people (nearly a third of the city's population) crowded into Old South Church. Chaired by Samuel Adams, the meeting hoped to convince Hutchinson to send the tea back. But he refused. In the early evening, Adams reportedly announced "that he could think of nothing further to be done—that they had now done all they could for the Salvation of their Country." Cries then rang out from the crowd: "Boston harbor a tea-pot tonight!" Within minutes, about sixty men crudely disguised as Indians assembled at the wharf, boarded the ships, and dumped the cargo into the harbor. By 9 P.M., 342 chests of tea worth approximately £10,000 floated on the water.

Among the "Indians" were many Boston artisans, including the silversmith Paul Revere. Five masons, eleven carpenters and builders, three leatherworkers, a blacksmith, two barbers, a coachmaker, a shoemaker, and twelve apprentices have been identified as participants. That their ranks also included four farmers from outside Boston, ten merchants, two doctors, a teacher, and a bookseller illustrated the resistance movement's widespread support.

Coercive and Quebec Acts

Coercive (Intolerable) Acts: A series of restrictive laws comprised of the Boston Port Bill, the Massachusetts Government Act, the Justice Act, the Quartering Act, plus the unrelated Quebec Act. Intended by the British Parliament to primarily punish Massachusetts, the acts instead pushed most colonies to the brink of rebellion.

Responding to the tea party, in March 1774, Parliament adopted the first of four laws that became known as the **Coercive, or Intolerable, Acts**. Parliament ordered Boston's port closed until the tea was paid for, prohibiting all but coastal trade in food and firewood. Later in the spring, Parliament passed three other punitive measures. The Massachusetts Government Act altered the province's charter, substituting an appointed council for the elected one, increasing the governor's powers, and forbidding most town meetings. The Justice Act provided that a person accused of committing murder while suppressing a riot or enforcing the laws could be tried outside the colony. Finally, the Quartering Act allowed military officers to commandeer privately owned buildings to house their troops.

Women's Political Activism

In the twenty-first century, female citizens of the United States participate at every level of American public life. Nancy Pelosi was elected Speaker of the House, third in line for the presidency, in January 2007; Hillary Rodham Clinton ran for president in 2008 and became Secretary of State in 2009; and Sonia Sotomayor and Elena Kagan joined the Supreme Court as its second and third current female members in 2009 and 2010, respectively. Nearly one hundred women sit in the House and Senate; many serve in state offices. But before the 1760s, American women were seen as having no appropriate public role. A male essayist expressed the consensus in the mid-1730s: "the Governing Kingdoms and Ruling Provinces are Things too difficult and knotty for the fair Sex, it will render them grave and serious, and take off those agreeable Smiles that should always accompany them."

That changed when colonists resisted new British taxes and laws in the 1760s. Because women made household purchasing decisions, and because with spinning and cloth manufacture their labor could replace imported clothing, their participation was vital. For the first time in American history, women took political stands, deciding whether to boycott British goods. The groups they established to promote home manufactures—dubbed "Daughters of Liberty"—constituted the first American women's political organizations.

Since then, American women have taken part in many political movements, among them antislavery societies, pro- and anti-woman suffrage organizations, the Women's Christian Temperance Union, and the civil rights movement. The legacy of revolutionary-era women continues today. Contemporary Americans would find it impossible to imagine their country without female activists of all affiliations.

Parliament then turned to reforming Quebec's government. Intended to ease strains emerging since the British conquest of the formerly French colony, the Quebec Act granted greater religious freedom to Catholics—alarming Protestant colonists, who equated Roman Catholicism with despotism. It also reinstated French civil law, which had been replaced by British procedures in 1763, and it established an appointed council (rather than an elected legislature). Finally, to protect northern Indians against Anglo-American settlement, the act annexed to Quebec the area west of the Appalachians, east of the Mississippi River, and north of the Ohio River—thereby removing the region from the jurisdiction of seacoast colonies. Wealthy colonists who hoped to develop the Ohio country now faced the prospect of dealing with officials in Quebec.

Members of Parliament who voted for the punitive legislation believed they had solved the problem posed by the troublesome Americans. But to resistance leaders, the Coercive Acts and the Quebec Act proved what they had feared since 1768: that Britain had planned to oppress them.

The Boston Committee of Correspondence urged all colonies to join an immediate boycott of British goods. But Rhode Island, Virginia, and Pennsylvania suggested convening another intercolonial congress to consider an appropriate response, and in mid-June 1774 Massachusetts acquiesced. Even the most ardent patriots hoped for reconciliation. Americans were approaching confrontation but had yet to reach an irrevocable break. So the colonies agreed to send delegates to Philadelphia in September to a Continental Congress.

127

Summary

At the outbreak of the Seven Years' War in western Pennsylvania, no one could have predicted such dramatic change in Britain's mainland colonies. Yet that conflict simultaneously removed France from North America and created a huge debt that Britain had to repay, developments with major implications for the imperial relationship.

After the war ended in 1763, the number of colonists who defined themselves as political actors increased substantially. Once linked unquestioningly to Great Britain, they began to develop an American identity. Their concept of the political process differed from that of the mother country, and they held a different definition of what constituted representation and consent to government actions. They also came to understand that their economic interests did not necessarily coincide with those of Great Britain. Parliamentary acts such as the Stamp Act and the Townshend Acts elicited colonial responses that produced further responses from Britain. Tensions escalated and climaxed when Bostonians destroyed the East India Company's tea.

In late summer 1774, Americans were committed to resistance but not independence. During the next decade, they would forge a new American nationality.

Chapter Review

Renewed Warfare Among Europeans and Indians

What was at stake in the Seven Years' War?

The Seven Years' War was ultimately a contest over land between the British, French, Native Americans, and some settlers. All parties vied for control of large tracts of western land. The Iroquois, believing themselves the voice of the Delawares and Shawnees, negotiated to cede the land to Pennsylvania; the two tribes then moved west onto land claimed by Virginia and Pennsylvania, while France sought to hold and expand its possessions along the Ohio River, which it relied on for trade. After battling with Indians, France continued to push southward in its land grabbing, and Anglo-American colonists gathered in Albany, New York, to address the French threat. England declared war in 1756 and, after winning the protracted battle, the issue of land between European nations was settled when France ceded most of its North American territories to Britain.

1763: A Turning Point

How did colonists' ideas about government differ from those of the British in the 1760s?

British authorities believed that Parliament—which included the king, lords, and Commons—represented *all* British subjects regardless of where they lived. In this system of virtual representation, the people's consent to Parliament's actions was assumed. Americans, on the other hand, increasingly believed in direct representation, that they could only be represented by men who lived nearby and whom they elected. Moreover, they understood the lower houses as representing the regions that elected them. Living on the other side of the ocean, colonists were also accustomed to a central government with limited authority and embraced the Real Whig notion that good government was one that left them alone to manage their affairs. As England imposed taxes and greater control over the colonies beginning in 1763, many Americans felt their freedom was endangered and questioned whether authority should lie with the monarchy or the people.

The Stamp Act Crisis

How did the Stamp Act raise issues that would lead to the American Revolution?

Angry about the heavy taxes and questioning Britain's right to impose them, colonists began to wonder how they might resist Parliament yet remain British subjects. At issue for essayists such as James Otis was that as British subjects, they possessed the right to consent to taxation—which had not been granted under the Stamp Act. On the other hand, Parliament was a supreme authority to which they must yield. Other leaders, such as Patrick Henry and the Virginia House of Burgesses, were unwilling to relinquish the right to consent to taxation. For ten years, Americans struggled with how to control their internal affairs yet remain under British rule. Protests led to the act's repeal in 1766, but questions about government nonetheless remained.

Resistance to the Townshend Acts

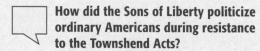

How did the Sons of Liberty politicize ordinary Americans during resistance to the Townshend Acts?

Ordinary Americans were not accustomed to being involved in political affairs, which they understood as handled by elites. But the Sons of Liberty made a conscious effort to draw people from all ranks into their anti-Townshend campaign, partly because they needed widespread participation for their boycott of British products designed in protest to the act. To rally a wider populace, they created rituals that would teach illiterate Americans about the reasons for resistance, including celebrations commemorating previous demonstrations and political songs. Women helped, too, by spinning yarn outdoors in public, symbolically displaying their patriotism for all to see.

Confrontations in Boston

How did Samuel Adams's Committees of Correspondence mark a turning point in Americans' political thinking?

An original member of the Sons of Liberty, Adams wanted to widen the movement's scope beyond its stronghold in New England cities and seacoast towns and create consensus among Massachusetts residents for the cause of liberty. The pamphlet he produced for the Boston Committee of Correspondence in 1772 was widely distributed. It stated the rights of colonists to life, liberty, and property, and it outlined complaints against England for taxation without representation, unnecessary troops and customs officers on American soil, the use of imperial revenues to pay colonial officials, and the expanded jurisdiction of vice-admiralty courts. Far more radical than earlier documents, this one did not seek to define the limits of Parliamentary authority but instead declared colonists' allegiance to America first and England a distant second.

Tea and Turmoil

How did the Tea Act push the country to the brink of revolution?

When Parliament imposed the Tea Act on the colonies in May 1773, it was attempting to save the East India Company from bankruptcy, but colonists thought it was designed to make them admit Parliament's right to tax them. Citizens in several cities wanted to prevent the tea from being unloaded from ships; in Boston, that led to a protest in which the tea was dumped in the harbor by men dressed as Indians. Parliament responded with punitive laws, known as the Coercive or Intolerable Acts, ordering the city to pay for the tea and closing the port until it did. Other acts reorganized the state's government, banned town meetings, and allowed officers to commandeer private buildings to house troops. Colonists saw such measures as proof that Britain would oppress them and sent delegates to a Continental Congress in Philadelphia in 1774 to decide how to respond.

Suggestions for Further Reading

Fred Anderson, *The War That Made America: A Short History of the French and Indian War* (2005)

Bernard Bailyn, *The Ideological Origins of the American Revolution* (1967)

T. H. Breen, *The Marketplace of Revolution: How Consumer Politics Shaped American Independence* (2004)

Benjamin L. Carp, *Rebels Rising: Cities and the American Revolution* (2007)

Gregory Dowd, *War Under Heaven: Pontiac, the Indian Nations, and the British Empire* (2002)

Marc Egnal, *A Mighty Empire: The Origins of the American Revolution* (1988)

Merrill Jensen, *The Founding of a Nation: A History of the American Revolution, 1763–1776* (1968)

Pauline R. Maier, *From Resistance to Revolution: Colonial Radicals and the Development of American Opposition to Britain, 1765–1776* (1972)

Gary B. Nash, *The Unknown American Revolution: The Unruly Birth of Democracy and the Struggle to Create America* (2005)

Peter Silver, *Our Savage Neighbors: How Indian War Transformed Early America* (2008)

Go to the History CourseMate website for primary source links, study tools, and review materials for this chapter. www.cengagebrain.com

A Revolution, Indeed

6

1774–1783

The Shawnee chief Blackfish named his new captive Sheltowee, or Big Turtle, and adopted him as his son. In February 1778, Blackfish's warriors had caught the lone hunter, Daniel Boone, who then persuaded his fellow frontiersmen to surrender to the Shawnees (British allies). Boone had moved his family from North Carolina to Kentucky three years before as the Revolutionary War began. His contemporaries and some historians have questioned Boone's allegiances during the Revolution. His encounter with the Shawnees highlights ambiguities of revolutionary-era loyalties.

The Shawnees sought captives to cover the death of their chief, Cornstalk, killed months earlier while a prisoner of American militiamen in the Ohio country. Half of the twenty-six men taken were adopted into Shawnee families; those less willing to conform to Indian ways were dispatched as prisoners to the British fort at Detroit. Boone, who assured Blackfish that in the spring he would negotiate the surrender of women and children remaining at his Boonesborough settlement, watched and waited. In June 1778 he escaped, hurrying home to warn the Kentuckians of an impending attack.

When Shawnees and their British allies appeared outside the Boonesborough stockade in mid-September, Boone agreed to negotiate. Although the settlers refused to move back across the mountains, fragmentary evidence suggests that they promised allegiance to the British to avert a battle. But discussions dissolved into a melee, with Indians futilely besieging the fort for a week before withdrawing. That threat gone, Boone was charged with treason and court-martialed by the Kentucky militia. Although he was cleared, questions about the incident and its aftermath haunted him for the rest of his life.

Where did Daniel Boone's loyalties lie? To the British, the Americans, or other Kentuckians? His actions made all three seem possible. Had he betrayed the settlers to Shawnees, seeking to establish British authority in Kentucky? Had he—as he later claimed—twice deceived the Shawnees? Or was the survival of the fragile settlements his highest priority? Kentucky was a borderland where British, Indians, and American settlers vied for control. Boone and other Appalachian backcountry residents did not always face clear-cut choices as they struggled under precarious circumstances.

The American Revolution uprooted thousands of families, disrupted the economy, reshaped society by forcing many colonists into permanent exile, and created a nation from thirteen separate colonies. The struggle for independence required revolutionary leaders to accomplish three separate but related tasks. First, they had to transform a consensus favoring loyal resistance into a coalition supporting independence. They pursued various measures (from persuasion to coercion) to enlist European-Americans in the patriot cause, while seeking neutrality from Indians and slaves.

Second, to win independence, patriot leaders needed international recognition and aid, particularly from France. Thus they dispatched to Paris the most experienced American diplomat, Benjamin Franklin, who skillfully negotiated the Franco-American alliance of 1778, crucial to winning independence.

Only the third task directly involved the British. George Washington, commander-in-chief of the American army, soon recognized that his goal should be not to win battles, but to survive to fight another day. The British concentrated on winning and did not consider the difficulties of their main goal, retaining the colonies' allegiance. Americans' triumph owed less to their military powers than to endurance and Britain's mistakes.

As you read this chapter, keep the following questions in mind:

* **What choices of allegiance confronted residents of North America after 1774? Why did people of various descriptions make the choices they did?**

* **What military strategies did the British and American forces adopt?**

* **How did the new nation win independence?**

Government by Congress and Committee

Where did backcountry Indians' loyalties lie at the onset of the Revolution?

Continental Congress: Group of representatives appointed by conventions in most of the North American colonies of Great Britain.

When the fifty-five delegates to the First **Continental Congress** convened in Philadelphia in September 1774, they knew that any measures they adopted would likely enjoy widespread support. That summer, participants at well-publicized open meetings throughout the colonies promised (like some North Carolina men) to "strictly adhere to, and abide by, such Regulations and Restrictions as the Members of the said General Congress shall agree to." Most congressional delegates were selected by extralegal provincial conventions whose members were chosen at local gatherings, because governors had forbidden regular assemblies to conduct formal elections. By designating delegates to Congress, Americans openly defied British authority.

First Continental Congress

The colonies' leading political figures—mostly lawyers, merchants, and planters representing every colony but Georgia—attended the Philadelphia Congress. The

Chronology

1774	First Continental Congress meets in Philadelphia, adopts Declaration of Rights and Grievances
	Continental Association implements economic boycott of Britain; committees of observation established to oversee boycott
1774–75	Provincial conventions replace collapsing colonial governments
1775	Battles of Lexington and Concord; first shots of war fired
	Second Continental Congress begins
	Washington named commander-in-chief
	Dunmore's proclamation offers freedom to patriots' slaves who join British forces
1776	Paine publishes *Common Sense*, advocating independence

	British evacuate Boston
	Declaration of Independence adopted
	New York City falls to British
1777	British take Philadelphia
	Burgoyne surrenders at Saratoga
1778	French alliance brings vital assistance to America
	British evacuate Philadelphia
1779	Sullivan expedition destroys Iroquois villages
1780	British take Charleston
1781	Cornwallis surrenders at Yorktown
1782	Peace negotiations begin
1783	Treaty of Paris signed, granting independence to the United States

Massachusetts delegation included Samuel Adams, the Boston resistance organizer, and his younger cousin John, an ambitious lawyer. New York sent John Jay, a talented young attorney. Virginia elected Richard Henry Lee and Patrick Henry, and George Washington. These men became the chief architects of the new nation.

Congressmen faced three tasks when they convened at Carpenters' Hall on September 5: defining American grievances, developing a resistance plan, and articulating their constitutional relationship with Great Britain. Radical congressmen, like Lee of Virginia, argued that colonists owed allegiance only to George III and that Parliament had no legitimate authority over them. Conservatives, like Pennsylvania's Joseph Galloway and his allies, proposed a union requiring Parliament and a new American legislature to consent jointly to all laws affecting the colonies. Delegates narrowly rejected Galloway's proposal, but they did not embrace the radicals' position either.

Finally, they accepted wording proposed by John Adams. The crucial clauses in the Congress's Declaration of Rights and Grievances declared that Americans would obey Parliament, but only voluntarily, and would resist all taxes in disguise, like the Townshend duties. Remarkably, this position—which would have seemed radical years earlier—represented a compromise in the fall of 1774.

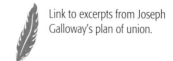 Link to excerpts from Joseph Galloway's plan of union.

Continental Association The delegates agreed on the laws they wanted repealed (notably the Coercive Acts) and implemented an economic boycott while petitioning the king for relief. They adopted the Continental Association, which called for nonimportation of British goods, effective December 1, 1774; nonconsumption of British products, effective March 1, 1775; and nonexportation of American goods to Britain and the British West Indies, effective September 10, 1775.

More comprehensive than previous economic measures, the Association's provisions appealed to different groups and regions. The nonimportation agreement banned commerce in slaves and manufactures, which accorded with the

Virginia gentry's desire to halt or slow the arrival of enslaved Africans. (Leading Virginians believed slave importations discouraged free Europeans with useful skills from immigrating.) Delaying nonconsumption until three months after implementing nonimportation allowed northern urban merchants time to sell items they acquired before December 1. In 1773, many Virginians had vowed to stop exporting tobacco, to raise prices in a then-glutted market. So they enthusiastically welcomed an Association that banned exportation while permitting them to profit from higher prices for their 1774 crop. It also benefited northern exporters of wood and foodstuffs to the Caribbean with a final selling season before the embargo.

Committees of Observation

To enforce the Continental Association, Congress recommended the election of committees of observation and inspection in every American locality. By specifying that committee members be chosen by all men qualified to vote, Congress guaranteed them a broad popular base. The seven to eight thousand committeemen became local leaders of American resistance.

Initially charged with overseeing implementation of the boycott, within six months these committees became de facto governments. They examined merchants' records, publicizing those who continued to import British goods. They promoted home manufactures, encouraging simple modes of dress and behavior that symbolized Americans' commitment to liberty. Because expensive leisure-time activities were believed to reflect vice and corruption, Congress urged Americans to forgo dancing, gambling, horseracing, and cardplaying.

The committees gradually extended their authority. They attempted to identify opponents of American resistance, developing elaborate spy networks, circulating copies of the Continental Association for signatures, and investigating questionable remarks and activities. Suspected dissenters were urged to support the colonial cause publicly; if they refused, the committees had them watched, restricted their movements, or tried to force them into exile. People engaging in casual political exchanges one day could find themselves charged with "treasonable conversation" the next.

Provincial Conventions

Meanwhile, during the winter and early spring of 1775, colonial governments were collapsing. Only a few legislatures met without challenges to their authority. In most colonies, popularly elected provincial conventions took over the government, sometimes replacing the legislatures or holding concurrent sessions. In late 1774 and early 1775, these conventions approved the Continental Association, elected delegates to the Second Continental Congress (scheduled for May), organized militias, and gathered arms.

Royal officials suffered continuous humiliation. Courts were prevented from meeting; taxes were paid to the conventions' agents rather than to provincial tax collectors; and militiamen would muster only when committees ordered. During the six months preceding the battles at Lexington and Concord, independence was being won at the local level. Still, most Americans proclaimed loyalty to Great Britain.

Contest in the Backcountry

While the committees of observation consolidated their authority in the East, some colonists headed west. Ignoring the Proclamation of 1763, pronouncements by colonial governors, and the threat of Indian attacks, land-hungry folk—many of them recent immigrants from Ireland and soldiers who demobilized in North America after the Seven Years War—swarmed onto lands along the Ohio River and its tributaries after the mid-1760s. Sometimes they purchased property from opportunists with grants of dubious origin; often, they claimed land as squatters. Britain's 1771 decision to abandon (and raze) Fort Pitt removed final restraints on settlement there and rendered the Proclamation of 1763 unenforceable. By late 1775, thousands of new homesteads dotted the backcountry from western Pennsylvania south through Virginia and eastern Kentucky into western North Carolina.

Distrust and Warfare   Few of the backcountry folk viewed the region's native peoples positively. Frontier dwellers had little interest in the small-scale trade that had sustained an uneasy peace; they wanted land for crops and livestock.

In 1774 Virginia, headed by a new governor, **Lord Dunmore**, asserted its title to the developing backcountry. During spring and early summer, tensions mounted as Virginians surveyed Kentucky land on the south side of the Ohio River—territory claimed by the Shawnees. **"Lord Dunmore's War"** consisted of one large-scale confrontation between Virginia militia and some Shawnee warriors. Neither side won, but in the immediate aftermath thousands of settlers—including Boone and his associates—flooded across the mountains.

When war began, the loyalties of Indians and settlers in the backcountry remained, like Boone's, fluid. Hostile to each other, the side each would take in the struggle might depend on which could better serve their interests. Understanding that, the Continental Congress moved to reoccupy Fort Pitt and establish other garrisons in the Ohio country. With this protection, up to twenty thousand settlers poured into Kentucky and western Pennsylvania by 1780.

Native Americans' grievances against European American newcomers predisposed many to ally with Great Britain. Yet some chiefs urged caution: the British abandonment of Fort Pitt (and them) suggested that Britain might not protect them in the future. Furthermore, Britain hesitated to use its potential native allies and initially sought from Indians only neutrality.

Patriots also wanted Indians' neutrality. In 1775, the Second Continental Congress sent a message to Indian communities, describing the war as "a family quarrel between us and Old England" and requesting that they "not join on either side." The Iroquois pledged neutrality. But some Cherokees led by Chief Dragging Canoe hoped to use the "family quarrel" to regain land. In summer 1776, they attacked western Virginia and Carolina settlements. After a militia campaign destroyed many Cherokee towns, Dragging Canoe and his followers fled west, establishing new villages. Other Cherokees agreed to a treaty that ceded more of their land.

Frontier Hostilities   Shawnees and Cherokees continued to attack backcountry settlements, but dissent within their ranks crippled their efforts. The British victory over France in 1763 had destroyed the Indians'

Lord Dunmore: Royal governor of Virginia who promised freedom to slaves who fought to restore royal authority.

Lord Dunmore's War: Confrontation between Virginians and the Shawnee Indians in 1774. During the peace conference that followed, Virginia gained uncontested rights to lands south of the Ohio country in exchange for its claims on the northern side.

Frontier Refugees

As a result of its victory in the Seven Years' War, Great Britain in 1763 took command of Fort Detroit, located on the river that connected Lakes Huron and Erie, shown here in an eighteenth-century watercolor. The strategic site controlled water access to the three western-most Great Lakes; such water travel was crucial in an era with few and poor frontier roads. The American revolutionaries tried twice to capture Detroit, from which Indian raiding parties attacked frontier settlements, but both times the colonial forces were defeated by Britain's Native allies. Thus throughout the war Detroit served as a magnet for loyalist refugees, among them Marie-Therese Berthelet Lasselle, who fled with her family to the fort in 1780 from their trading post at what is now Fort Wayne,

Indiana. Depicted here is her self-portrait in watercolor on silk, with additional silk embroidery. What can we learn about frontier female refugees from such sources? What does this tell us about her priorities, as well as her skills?

Only genteel women learned to produce such works as these, combining embroidery and watercolor. Great artistic skill contributed to this remarkable self-portrait by Marie-Therese Lasselle.

Monroe County Historical Commissions, Monroe, Michigan

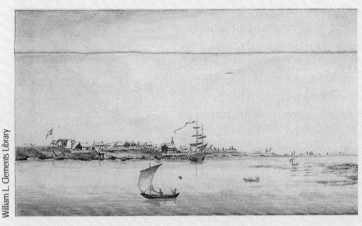

The artist who painted this watercolor of early Detroit is unknown. The view shows both the village and the fort that protected the residents.

William L. Clements Library

ability to maintain their independence: playing European powers against one another. Only a few communities (the Stockbridge Indians of New England and the Oneidas in New York) unwaveringly supported the American revolt; most others either remained neutral or sporadically aligned with the British. In 1778 and early 1779, a frontier militia force under George Rogers Clark captured British posts in modern Illinois (Kaskaskia) and Indiana (Vincennes). Still, the revolutionaries could never overtake the redcoats' stronghold at Detroit.

Backcountry warfare between settlers and Indians persisted long after the Revolution ended. Indeed, the Revolutionary War constituted a brief chapter in the ongoing struggle for control of the region west of the Appalachians, which began in 1763 and continued into the next century.

Choosing Sides

In 1765, Stamp Act protests were supported by most colonists in the Caribbean, Nova Scotia, and the future United States. Demonstrations occurred in Halifax, Nova Scotia, St. Christopher, and Nevis, as well as in Boston, New York, Charleston, and other mainland towns. When the Stamp Act took effect, though, Caribbean islanders loyally paid the duties. In Nova Scotia and the Caribbean, many colonists came to question the aims and tactics of the resistance movement.

> How did colonists choose sides in the conflict with England?

Nova Scotia and The Caribbean

Despite the British victory in the Seven Years War, northern mainland and southern island colonies felt vulnerable to French counterattack. Additionally, sugar planters—on some islands outnumbered by their bondspeople twenty-five to one—feared potential slave revolts. Neither region had a large population of European descent or strong local political structures. Fewer people lived in Halifax in 1775 than in the late 1750s, and with successful men heading to England, the sugar islands had only a few resident planters to provide leadership.

Nova Scotians and West Indians had economic reasons for supporting the mother country. In the mid-1770s, the northerners finally broke into the Caribbean market with their dried, salted fish. They reduced New England's domination of the northern coastal trade, and they benefited from Britain's wartime retaliatory measures against the rebels' commerce. British sugar producers relied on their trade monopoly within the empire, for more efficient French planters could sell their sugar for one-third less. Further, the British planters' lobbyists in London won the islands' exclusion from some of the Townshend Act provisions.

Patriots

Many residents of the thirteen colonies supported resistance, then independence. Active revolutionaries accounted for about two-fifths of the European American population and included small and middling farmers, members of dominant Protestant sects, Chesapeake gentry, merchants, city artisans, elected officeholders, and people of English descent. Wives usually, but not always, adopted their husbands' political stance. Although patriots supported the Revolution, they pursued divergent goals within the broader coalition. Some sought limited political reform; others, extensive political change; and still others, social and economic reforms. (The ways their concerns interacted are discussed in Chapter 7.)

Loyalists

About one-fifth of the European American population remained loyal to Great Britain, firmly rejecting independence. Most **loyalists** had long opposed the men who became patriot leaders for varying reasons. British-appointed government officials; Anglican clergy and lay Anglicans in the North; tenant farmers; members of persecuted religious sects; back-country southerners who had rebelled against eastern rule in the late 1760s and early 1770s; and non-English ethnic minorities, especially Scots—all feared the power of those who controlled the colonial assemblies and who had previously shown little concern for their welfare. Joined by merchants whose trade depended on imperial connections and by former British military men who had settled in America after 1763, they formed a loyalist core.

loyalists: Colonists who retained a profound reverence for the British crown and believed that if they failed to defend their king, they would sacrifice their personal honor.

During the war, loyalists congregated in cities held by the British army. When those posts were evacuated at war's end, loyalists scattered throughout the British Empire—Britain, the Bahamas, and especially Canada. In Nova Scotia, New Brunswick, and Ontario, roughly seventy thousand former Americans laid the foundations of British Canada.

Neutrals

Between patriots and loyalists, there remained in the middle perhaps two-fifths of the European American population. Some, like the Quakers, were sincere pacifists. Others opportunistically shifted their allegiance to whatever side happened to be winning. Still others cared little about politics and obeyed whoever was in power. Such colonists resisted British and Americans alike when their demands seemed too heavy—when taxes became too high or when calls for militia service came too often. They made up a large proportion of the backcountry population (including Boone's Kentucky), where Scots-Irish settlers had little love for either the patriot gentry or the English authorities.

To patriots, apathy or neutrality was as heinous as loyalism. By winter 1775–1776, the Second Continental Congress recommended that "disaffected" persons be disarmed and arrested. State legislatures passed laws prescribing severe penalties for suspected loyalists or neutrals. Many began to require voters (or, in some cases, all free adult men) to take oaths of allegiance; refusal usually meant banishment to England or extra taxes. After 1777, many states confiscated the property of banished persons, using it to fund the war. The patriots' policies ensured that their scattered and persecuted opponents could not band together against the revolutionary cause.

African Americans

In New England, with few resident bondspeople, revolutionary fervor was widespread, and free African Americans enlisted in patriot militias. The middle colonies, where bondspeople constituted a small but substantial proportion of the population, were more divided but largely revolutionary. In Virginia and Maryland, where free people constituted a slender majority, the potential for slave revolts raised occasional but not disabling fears. By contrast, South Carolina and Georgia, where slaves composed more than half of the population, were less enthusiastic about resistance. Georgia sent no delegates to the First Continental Congress and reminded its representatives at the second to consider its circumstances, "with our blacks and tories [loyalists] within us," when voting on independence.

Bondspeople faced a dilemma during the Revolution. Their goal was *personal* independence, but how best could they escape from slavery? To most slaves, supporting the British held promise. In late 1774 and early 1775, bondsmen offered to assist the British army in return for freedom.

Slaveowners' worst fears were realized in November 1775, when Virginia's royal governor, Lord Dunmore, offered to free any slaves and indentured servants willing to join the British forces. About one thousand African Americans rallied to the British; although many perished in a smallpox epidemic, three hundred reached occupied New York City under British protection. Because other commanders renewed Dunmore's proclamation, tens of thousands of runaways eventually joined the British. At war's end, at least nine thousand left with the redcoats.

Links to the World

New Nations

The American Revolution created the United States and led to the formation of three other nations: English-dominated Canada, Sierra Leone, and Australia.

In modern Canada before the Revolution, only Nova Scotia had many English-speaking settlers. Largely New Englanders, they were recruited after 1758 to repopulate the region forcibly taken from the exiled Acadians. During and after the Revolution, loyalist families moved to the region that is now Canada, which remained under British rule. Some exiles settled in Quebec as well. In a few years, the loyalist refugees transformed the former French colony, laying the foundation of the modern bilingual (but majority English-speaking) Canadian nation.

Sierra Leone, too, was founded by colonial exiles—African Americans who had fled to the British army during the war, many of whom ended up in London. Seeing the refugees' poverty, charitable merchants—calling themselves the Committee for Relief of the Black Poor—developed a plan to resettle the African Americans elsewhere. The refugees rejected the Bahamas, fearing reenslavement there. They accepted a return to their ancestors' homeland. In early 1787, vessels carrying about four hundred settlers reached Sierra Leone in West Africa, where representatives of the Black Poor Committee acquired land. The first years were difficult, and many died of disease and deprivation. But in 1792, they were joined by several thousand other loyalist African Americans who had originally moved to Nova Scotia. The influx ensured the colony's survival; it remained a part of the British Empire until its independence in 1961.

At the Paris peace negotiations in 1782, American diplomats rejected British suggestions that the United States continue to serve as a dumping ground for convicts. Britain thus needed another destination for people sentenced for crimes such as theft, assault, and manslaughter. It sent them to Australia, claimed for Britain in 1770. Britain continued this practice until 1868, but voluntary migrants also came. The modern nation was created from a federation of separate colonial governments on January 1, 1901.

Thus, the founding event in the history of the United States links the nation to the formation of its northern neighbor and to new nations in West Africa and the Asian Pacific.

Thomas Rowlandson, an English artist, sketched the boatloads of male and female convicts as they were being ferried to the ships that would take them to their new lives in the prison colony of Australia. Note the gibbet on the shore with two hanging bodies—symbolizing the fate these people were escaping.

An early view of the settlement of black loyalists in West Africa, the foundation of the modern nation of Sierra Leone.

Although bondspeople did not pose a serious threat early on, patriots turned rumors of slave uprisings to their advantage. In South Carolina, resistance leaders argued that the Continental Association would protect masters from their slaves. Undoubtedly, many wavering Carolinians were drawn into the revolutionary camp by fear that divisiveness among free people would encourage rebellion by bondspeople.

Patriots could never completely ignore the threats posed by loyalists, neutrals, slaves, and Indians. Occasionally backcountry militiamen refused to turn out for duty on the seacoast because they feared Indian attacks in their absence. Sometimes southern troops refused to serve in the North because they would not leave their regions unprotected against a slave insurrection. But the impossibility of a large-scale slave revolt, coupled with dissension in Indian communities and the patriots' successful campaign to disarm and neutralize loyalists, ensured that the revolutionaries control the countryside.

War and Independence

How did Thomas Paine's *Common Sense* help reshape the war's purpose?

On January 27, 1775, Lord Dartmouth, secretary of state for America, wrote to General Thomas Gage in Boston, urging decisive action. Opposition could not be "very formidable," Dartmouth wrote.

Battles of Lexington and Concord

In response, on April 14 Gage sent an expedition to confiscate colonial military stockpiles at Concord. Bostonians dispatched two messengers, William Dawes and Paul Revere (later joined by Dr. Samuel Prescott), to rouse the countryside. When the British vanguard of several hundred men approached Lexington at dawn on April 19, they found just seventy militiamen—about half of the town's adult male population—mustered on the common. Realizing they could not halt the redcoats' advance, the Americans' commander ordered his men to withdraw. But as they dispersed, a shot rang out; British soldiers then fired. When they stopped, eight Americans lay dead, and another ten wounded. The British moved on to nearby Concord.

There, the militia contingents were larger. At the North Bridge, three British men were killed and nine wounded. Thousands fired from houses and from behind trees as British forces retreated to Boston. By day's end, the redcoats had suffered 272 casualties, including 70 deaths. The arrival of reinforcements and the American militia's lack of coordination prevented heavier British losses. The patriots suffered just 93 casualties.

First Year of War

By the evening of April 20, thousands of American militiamen had gathered around Boston, summoned by local committees. Many stayed only until spring planting, but those who remained were organized into formal units. Officers under the command of General Artemas Ward of the Massachusetts militia ordered that latrines be dug, water supply protected, supplies purchased, military discipline enforced, and defensive fortifications constructed.

For nearly a year, the two armies sat and stared at each other across siege lines. The redcoats attacked only once, on June 17, when they drove the Americans from trenches atop Breed's Hill in Charlestown. In that misnamed Battle of Bunker Hill,

In 1775, an unknown artist painted the redcoats entering Concord. The fighting at North Bridge, which occurred just a few hours after this triumphal entry, signaled the start of open warfare between Britain and the colonies.

the British incurred their greatest wartime losses: over 800 wounded and 228 killed. The Americans lost less than half that number.

During the same eleven-month period, patriots captured the British Fort Ticonderoga on Lake Champlain, acquiring much-needed cannon. Trying to bring Canada into the war, patriots also mounted a northern campaign that ended in disaster at Quebec in early 1776 when troops were ravaged by smallpox. But the long lull in fighting between the main armies at Boston during the war's first year gave both sides time to regroup and strategize.

British Strategy

Lord North and his new American secretary, Lord George Germain, made three central assumptions about the war. First, they concluded that patriot forces could not withstand the assaults by trained British regulars. Convinced that the 1776 campaign would decide the war, they dispatched Great Britain's largest force ever: 370 transport ships carrying 32,000 troops and tons of supplies, accompanied by 73 naval vessels and 13,000 sailors. Among them were thousands of professional German soldiers, who had been hired out to Britain.

Second, British officials and army officers adopted a conventional strategy of capturing major American cities and defeating the rebel army with minimal casualties. Third, they assumed that military victory would achieve the colonies' allegiance.

All three assumptions proved false. London officials also missed the significance of the American population's dispersal over an area 1,500 miles long and more than 100 miles wide. Although Britain would control each of America's largest ports at some time during the war, less than 5 percent of the population lived in those cities. Furthermore, with a vast coastline, commerce was easily rerouted. Hence, the loss of cities did little to damage the American cause.

Most of all, London officials did not initially understand that military triumph would not necessarily bring political victory. Securing the colonies would require Americans to return to their original allegiance. After 1778, the ministry strategized to achieve that through the expanded use of loyalist forces and the restoration of civilian authority in occupied areas. But the policy came too late.

Second Continental Congress

Britain had a bureaucracy to supervise the war; Americans had only the Second Continental Congress. The delegates who convened in Philadelphia on May 10, 1775, had to assume the mantle of intercolonial government. As the summer passed, Congress organized the colonies for war. It authorized the printing of money, established a committee to supervise foreign relations, strengthened the militia, and ordered that thirteen frigates be built for a new Continental Navy (eventually, it comprised forty-seven vessels). Most important, it created the Continental Army.

Until Congress met, the Massachusetts provincial congress supervised Ward and the militiamen encamped at Boston. But that army, composed of men from all over New England, heavily drained local resources. Consequently, Massachusetts asked the Continental Congress to direct the army. Initially, Congress had to choose a commander-in-chief. John Adams proposed the appointment of a Virginian "whose Skill and Experience as an Officer, whose independent fortune, great Talents and excellent universal Character, would command the Approbation of all America": **George Washington**. The Congress unanimously concurred.

George Washington: American military leader and the first President of the United States (1789–1797).

George Washington

Washington had not participated prominently in the prerevolutionary agitation. Devoted to the American cause, he was dignified, conservative, and a man of integrity. The younger son of a Virginia planter, Washington did not expect to inherit substantial property and planned to work as a surveyor. But the early death of his older brother and his marriage to the wealthy widow Martha Custis made George Washington one of Virginia's largest slaveholders. After his mistakes early in the Seven Years War, he had repaired his reputation by rallying the troops and maintaining calm during Braddock's defeat in 1755.

Washington had remarkable stamina and leadership ability. More than six feet tall when most men were five inches shorter, he displayed a commanding presence. Even a loyalist admitted that Washington could "atone for many demerits by the extraordinary coolness and caution which distinguish his character."

British Evacuate Boston

Washington took command of the army surrounding Boston in July 1775. By March 1776, when the arrival of cannon from Ticonderoga enabled him to pressure the redcoats, the army was prepared. Yet an assault on Boston proved unnecessary. Sir William Howe, the new commander, wanted to transfer his men to New York City. The patriots' cannon decided the matter. On March 17, the British and many loyalist allies abandoned Boston forever.

At war for months, American leaders denied seeking a break with Great Britain until a pamphlet published in January 1776 advocated that move.

Common Sense

Thomas Paine's **Common Sense** immediately sold tens of thousands of copies. The author, a radical English printer who had lived in America only since 1774, called for independence and challenged many common American assumptions about government and the colonies' relationship to Britain. He advocated the establishment of a republic, a government by the people with no king or nobility. Paine insisted that Britain had exploited the colonies. And for the frequent assertion that an independent America would be weak and divided, he substituted an unlimited confidence in America's strength once freed from European control.

By late spring, independence had become inevitable. On May 10, the Second Continental Congress recommended that individual colonies form new governments, replacing colonial charters with state constitutions. On June 7, Richard Henry Lee of Virginia, seconded by John Adams, introduced the crucial resolution: "that these United Colonies are, and of right ought to be, free and independent States … that all political connection between them and the State of Great Britain is, and ought to be, totally dissolved." Congress did not immediately adopt Lee's resolution, postponing a vote until early July. Meanwhile, a five-man committee—including Thomas Jefferson, John Adams, and Benjamin Franklin—was directed to draft a declaration of independence.

Jefferson and the Declaration of Independence

The committee assigned primary responsibility for writing the declaration to thirty-four-year-old Thomas Jefferson, who was known for his eloquence. A Virginia lawyer and member of the House of Burgesses, Jefferson was educated at the College of William and Mary and in the law offices of a prominent attorney. His knowledge of history and political theory was evident in the declaration and his draft of the Virginia state constitution. While Jefferson wrote and debated in Philadelphia, his beloved wife Martha suffered a miscarriage at their home, Monticello. Not until after her 1782 death from complications following the birth of their sixth (but only third surviving) child, did Jefferson fully commit himself to public service.

Common Sense: A pamphlet written by Thomas Paine that advocated freedom from British rule.

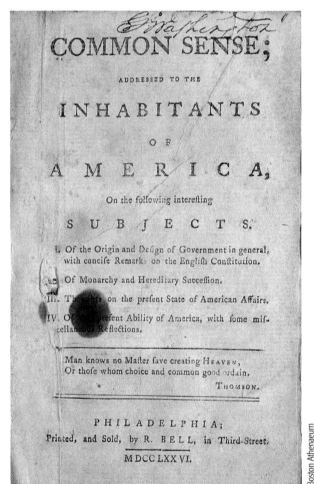

That America's patriot leaders read Thomas Paine's inflammatory *Common Sense* soon after it was published in early 1776 is indicated by this first edition, owned by George Washington himself.

Declaration of Independence: Proposed by the Second Continental Congress, this document proclaimed independence of the Thirteen Colonies from British rule.

The draft of the declaration reached Congress on June 28, 1776. The delegates voted for independence four days later, then debated the wording of the declaration for two more days, adopting it with changes on July 4. The **Declaration of Independence** (see Appendix) concentrated on George III, accusing the king of attempting to destroy representative government in the colonies and of oppressing Americans.

The declaration's chief long-term importance lay in the statements of principle that have since as the American ideal: "We hold these truths to be self-evident: That all men are created equal; that they are endowed by their Creator with certain unalienable rights; that among these are life, liberty and the pursuit of happiness; that, to secure these rights, governments are instituted among men, deriving their just powers from the consent of the governed; that whenever any form of government becomes destructive of these ends, it is the right of the people to alter or to abolish it, and to institute new government."

When the delegates in Philadelphia voted to accept the Declaration of Independence, they were committing treason. Therefore, when they concluded with the assertion that they "mutually pledge[d] to each other our lives, our fortunes, and our sacred honor," they spoke the truth.

The Struggle in the North

What was France's role in the American Revolution?

In late June 1776, the first ships carrying Sir William Howe's troops from Halifax appeared off the New York coast (see Map 6.1). On July 2, redcoats landed on Staten Island, but Howe waited for more troops from England before attacking, giving Washington time to march his army of seventeen thousand from Boston to defend Manhattan.

New York and New Jersey

Still inexperienced, Washington and his men made major mistakes, losing battles at Brooklyn Heights and on Manhattan Island. The city fell to the British, who captured nearly three thousand American soldiers. Washington retreated into Pennsylvania, and British forces took most of New Jersey. Occupying troops met little opposition; the revolutionary cause appeared in disarray. "These are the times that try men's souls," wrote Thomas Paine in his pamphlet *The Crisis*.

The British then forfeited their advantage as redcoats in New Jersey went on a rampage of rape and plunder. In retaliation, Washington crossed the Delaware River at night to attack a Hessian encampment at **Trenton** early on December 26. The patriots captured more than nine hundred Hessians and killed another thirty; only three Americans were wounded. Days later, Washington attacked at Princeton. Having gained command of the field, Washington set up winter quarters at Morristown, New Jersey.

Trenton: New Jersey battle where Washington took almost a thousand Hessian prisoners on December 26. It significantly boosted the flailing morale of Washington's troops to fight on.

Campaign of 1777

British strategy for 1777 aimed to isolate New England from the other colonies. General John Burgoyne would lead redcoat and Indian invaders down the Hudson River from Canada to rendezvous near Albany with a similar force moving east. The combined forces would then link up with Howe's troops in New York City. But Howe was planning to capture Philadelphia. In 1777, this independent operation of British armies in America ultimately resulted in disaster.

Howe took Philadelphia, but he delayed before beginning the campaign, took six weeks to transport his troops by sea, and ended up only 40 miles closer to Philadelphia than when he started. This gave Washington time to prepare a defense. At Brandywine Creek and Germantown, the two armies clashed. Although the British won both engagements, the Americans handled themselves well. The redcoats captured Philadelphia in late September, but to little effect. The campaign season was nearly over; the revolutionary army had gained confidence in itself and its leaders; and, far north, Burgoyne was being defeated.

MAP 6.1

The War in the North, 1775–1778

The early phase of the Revolutionary War was dominated by British troop movements in the Boston area, the redcoats' evacuation to Nova Scotia in the spring of 1776, and the subsequent British invasion of New York and New Jersey.

Source: Copyright © Cengage Learning

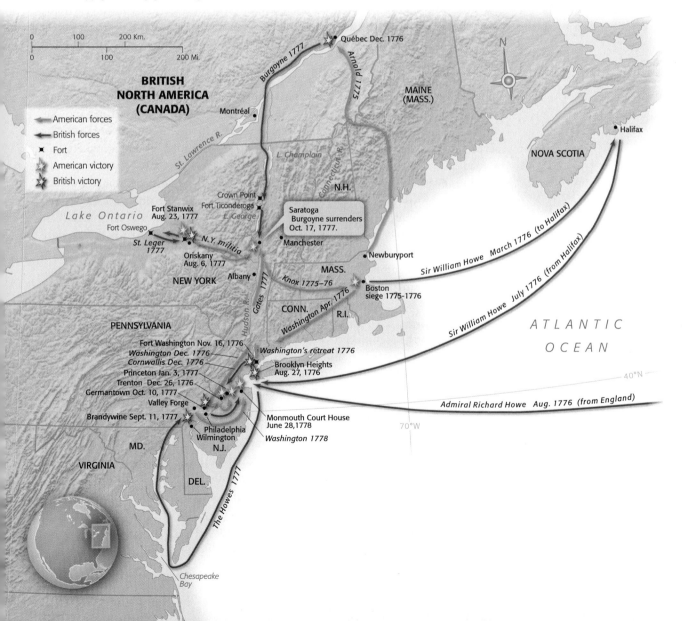

Burgoyne and his men had set out from Montreal in mid-June. An easy triumph at Fort Ticonderoga in July was followed in August by two setbacks—the redcoats and Indians marching east along the Mohawk River turned back after a battle at Oriskany, New York; and in a clash near Bennington, Vermont, American militiamen nearly wiped out eight hundred of Burgoyne's German mercenaries. After several skirmishes, Burgoyne was surrounded near **Saratoga**, New York. On October 17, 1777, he surrendered his force of more than six thousand men.

Saratoga: A turning point in the American Revolution. The American victory in this battle convinced France that Americans could win the war, leading France to ally with the colonists.

Mary and Joseph Brant: Mohawk leaders who supported the British.

Iroquois Confederacy Splinters

The August 1777 battle at Oriskany divided the Iroquois Confederacy. Although the Six Nations had pledged neutrality, two influential Mohawk leaders, the siblings **Mary and Joseph Brant**, believed the Iroquois should ally with the British to protect their territory from land-hungry colonists. The Brants won over the Senecas, Cayugas, and Mohawks, but the Oneidas preferred the American side and brought the Tuscaroras with them. The Onondagas split into three factions, one on each side and one supporting neutrality. At Oriskany, some Oneidas and Tuscaroras joined patriot militiamen in fighting their Iroquois brethren, shattering three hundred years of friendship.

The collapse of Iroquois unity had significant consequences. In 1778, British-allied warriors raided frontier villages in Pennsylvania and New York. The Americans the following summer dispatched an expedition to burn Iroquois crops and settlements. The devastation led many bands to seek food and shelter north of the Great Lakes during the winter of 1779–1780. Many Iroquois settled permanently in Canada.

Burgoyne's surrender at Saratoga overjoyed patriots and discouraged loyalists and Britons. Most important, the American victory at Saratoga drew France into the conflict. The American Revolution gave the French an opportunity to avenge their defeat in the Seven Years' War. Even before Benjamin Franklin arrived in Paris in late 1776, France covertly supplied the revolutionaries with military necessities. Indeed, 90 percent of the gunpowder Americans used during the war's first two years came from France, transported via the French Caribbean island of Martinique.

Franco-American Alliance of 1778

Benjamin Franklin worked tirelessly to strengthen ties between the two nations. Adopting a plain style of dress, Franklin played on the French image of Americans as virtuous farmers. In 1778, the countries signed two treaties. In the Treaty of Amity and Commerce, France recognized American independence and established trade ties. In the Treaty of Alliance, France and the United States promised—assuming that France would declare war on Britain, which it soon did—that neither would negotiate peace without consulting the other. France also abandoned claims to Canada and to North American territory east of the Mississippi River. The most visible symbol of Franco-American cooperation was the Marquis de Lafayette, a young nobleman who volunteered for service with George Washington in 1777 and fought with American forces.

With the alliance, France aided Americans openly, sending troops, naval vessels, arms, ammunition, clothing, and blankets. Second, Britain now had to fight France in the Caribbean and elsewhere. Spain's entry into the war in 1779 as an ally of France (but not of the United States) transformed the Revolution into a global war. The French aided the Americans throughout the conflict, but in its last years that assistance proved vital.

Life in the Army and on the Home Front

How was the Continental Army staffed?

Only in the first months of the war was the revolutionaries' army manned primarily by the semi-mythical "citizen-soldier," who exchanged his plow for a gun. After a few months, early arrivals went home. They reenlisted only briefly when the contending armies neared their farms and towns. In such militia units, elected officers and the soldiers who chose them reflected social hierarchies in their regions of origin, yet also retained a flexibility absent from the Continental Army, composed of men in statewide units led by appointed officers.

Continental Army   Continental soldiers, unlike militiamen, were primarily young, single, or propertyless men who enlisted for long periods or for the war's duration, partly for monetary bonuses or land. They saw in military service an opportunity to assert their masculinity and claim postwar citizenship and property-owning rights. As the fighting dragged on, bonuses grew larger. To meet their quotas, towns and states recruited, including recent immigrants; about 45 percent of Pennsylvania soldiers were of Irish origin, and about 13 percent were German.

Dunmore's proclamation led Congress in January 1776 to modify an earlier policy prohibiting African Americans in the regular army. Recruiters in northern states turned increasingly to bondsmen, who were often promised freedom after the war. Southern states initially resisted, but later all except Georgia and South Carolina enlisted black soldiers. Approximately five thousand African Americans served in the Continental Army, typically in racially integrated units where they were assigned tasks that others shunned, such as burying the dead or foraging for food. Overall, they composed about 10 percent of the regular army, but they seldom served in militia units.

American wives and widows of poor soldiers came to the army with their menfolk because they were too impoverished to survive alone. Such camp followers—roughly 3 percent of the total number of troops—worked as cooks, nurses, and launderers for rations and low wages. The women, along with civilian commissaries and militiamen who floated in and out at irregular intervals, were difficult to manage, especially because they were not subject to military discipline.

Officer Corps   The officers of the Continental Army developed intense pride and commitment to the revolutionary cause. The realities of warfare were often dirty and corrupt, but officers drew strength from a developing image of themselves as professionals who sacrificed for the nation. When Benedict Arnold, an officer who fought heroically for the patriot cause early in the war, defected to the British, they made his name a metaphor for villainy.

Unlike poor women, officers' wives did not travel with the army but made extended visits while the troops were in camp (usually during the winters). They

Courtesy of Mae Theresa Bonitto

Barzillai Lew, a free African American born in Groton, Massachusetts, in 1743, served in the Seven Years' War before enlisting with patriot troops in the American Revolution. An accomplished fifer, Lew fought at the Battle of Bunker Hill. Like other freemen in the north, he cast his lot with the revolutionaries, in contrast to southern bondspeople, who tended to favor the British.

Lord Cornwallis: British general whose surrender at Yorktown in 1781 effectively ended the Revolutionary War.

Link to excerpts from the journal of J. P. Martin, a revolutionary soldier.

brought food, clothing, and household furnishings to make their stay more comfortable, and they entertained each other and their menfolk at teas, dinners, and dances. Socializing created friendships later renewed when some of their husbands became the new nation's leaders.

Hardship and Disease   Ordinary soldiers endured more hardships than officers. Wages were low, and often the army could not meet the payroll. Rations (a daily standard allotment of bread, meat, vegetables, milk, and beer) did not always appear, and men had to forage for food. Clothing and shoes were often of poor quality. When conditions deteriorated, troops threatened mutiny (though only a few followed through) or, more often, deserted. Punishments for desertion or offenses such as theft and assault were harsh; convicted soldiers were sentenced to hundreds of lashes, whereas officers were publicly humiliated, deprived of their commission, and discharged in disgrace.

Endemic disease in the camps—dysentery, fevers, and, early in the war, smallpox—made matters worse. Most native-born colonists had neither been exposed to smallpox nor inoculated and were vulnerable when smallpox spread through the northern countryside in early 1774. The disease ravaged Bostonians during the British occupation, troops attacking Quebec in 1775–1776, and the African Americans who fled to join Lord Dunmore (1775) or **Lord Cornwallis** (1781). Most British soldiers had already survived smallpox (which was endemic in Europe), so it posed little threat to redcoats.

Recognizing smallpox's potential to decimate the revolutionaries' ranks, Washington ordered that the regular army be inoculated in 1777. Some would die from the risky procedure and survivors would be incapacitated for weeks. Yet inoculation, coupled with the increasing numbers of foreign-born (and mostly immune) enlistees, helped to protect Continental soldiers later in the war, contributing significantly to the eventual American victory.

American soldiers and sailors captured by the British endured great suffering, especially those held in makeshift prisons or on prison ships near Manhattan. Because Britain refused to recognize the legitimacy of the American government, Redcoat officers regarded the patriots as rebellious traitors rather than as prisoners of war with a right to decent treatment. The meager rations and crowded, unsanitary conditions meant that half to two-thirds of the prisoners fell victim to disease, especially dysentery. Particularly notorious was the hulk *Jersey*; survivors reported fighting over scraps of disgusting food, being covered with "bloody and loathesome filth," and each day having to remove the bodies of five to ten of their dead comrades.

Home Front

Men who enlisted in the army, served in Congress, or were captured were absent for long periods of time. Their womenfolk, who previously had handled only the "indoor affairs" of the household, thus shouldered the "outdoor affairs" as well. John and Abigail Adams took great pride in Abigail's developing skills as a "farmeress." She stopped calling the farm "yours" in letters to her husband and began referring to it as "ours." Most women, like Abigail, did not work in the fields but supervised field workers and managed their families' finances.

Wartime disruptions affected all Americans. People suffered from shortages of necessities like salt, soap, and flour. Severe inflation added to the country's woes. Soldiers on both sides plundered farms and houses, looking for food or salable items; they burned fence rails and took horses and oxen to transport their wagons. Moreover, they carried smallpox and other diseases wherever they went. Women had to decide whether to deliberately risk their children's lives by inoculating them with smallpox or to chance youngsters' contracting the disease "in the natural way." Many, including Abigail Adams, chose the former were relieved when their children survived.

Victory in the South

In early 1778, in the wake of the Saratoga disaster, British military leaders reassessed their strategy. Loyalist exiles in London persuaded them to shift the field of battle southward, contending that loyal southerners would welcome the redcoat army as liberators. Southern colonies that had returned to friendly civilian control could serve as bases for attacking the middle and northern states.

> What risky—but ultimately wise—move did American diplomats make in negotiating peace with England after the American Revolution?

South Carolina and the Caribbean

Sir Henry Clinton, who replaced Howe, oversaw the regrouping of British forces. He ordered the evacuation of Philadelphia in June 1778 and sent a convoy that captured the French Caribbean island of St. Lucia, thereafter a key British base. He also dispatched a small expedition to Georgia. When Savannah and then Augusta fell into British hands, Clinton became convinced that a southern strategy would succeed. In late 1779, he sailed from New York to besiege Charleston, the most important Southern city (see Map 6.2). Although afflicted by smallpox, Americans trapped there held out for months. On May 12, 1780, General Benjamin Lincoln surrendered the entire southern army—fifty-five thousand men. The redcoats then spread through South Carolina, establishing garrisons at key points. Hundreds of South Carolinians proclaimed renewed loyalty to the Crown.

Success of the southern campaign depended on controlling the seas, for the British armies were widely dispersed and travel by land was difficult. The Royal Navy safely dominated the American coastline, but French naval power posed a threat. American privateers infested Caribbean waters, seizing cargoes to and from the British islands. Furthermore, after late 1778 France picked off those islands one by

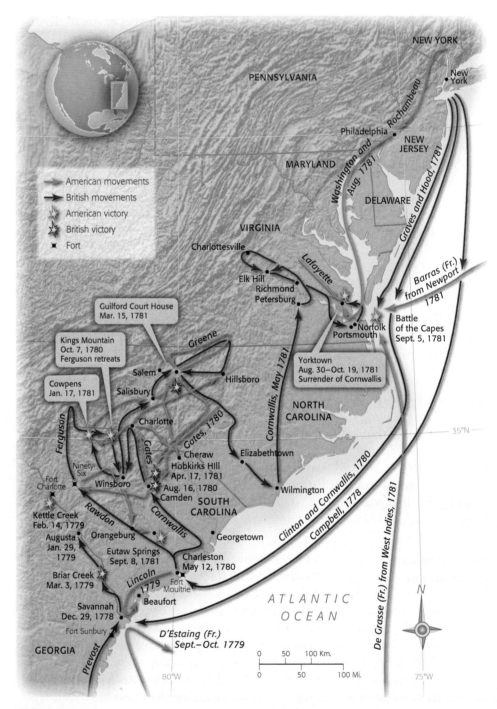

MAP 6.2

The War in the South

The southern war—after the British invasion of Georgia in late 1778—was characterized by a series of British thrusts into the interior, leading to battles with American defenders in both North and South Carolina. Finally, after promising beginnings, Cornwallis's foray into Virginia ended with disaster at Yorktown in October 1781.

Source: Copyright © Cengage Learning

one, including Grenada—second only to Jamaica in sugar production. In early 1781, the British captured St. Eustatius (the Dutch island that was the main conduit for moving military supplies from Europe to America). But the victory might have cost them the war, for Admiral Sir George Rodney failed to pursue the French fleet under Admiral François de Grasse when it sailed from the Caribbean to Virginia, where it played a major role in the **battle at Yorktown**.

The redcoats never established control of the areas they seized in South Carolina or Georgia. Patriot bands operated freely, and the fall of Charleston spurred them to greater exertions. Patriot women in four states formed the Ladies Association, raising money to buy shirts for needy soldiers. Recruiting efforts were stepped up.

Nevertheless, the war in South Carolina went badly for the patriots throughout 1780. At Camden in August, forces under Lord Cornwallis, the new British commander, defeated a reorganized southern army led by Horatio Gates. Thousands of enslaved African Americans joined the redcoats. Running away from their patriot masters individually and as families, they disrupted farming in the Carolinas and Georgia in 1780 and 1781. Tens of thousands of slaves were lost to their owners. Not all of them joined the British or won their freedom. Many served the redcoats as scouts or laborers in camps or occupied cities like New York.

battle of Yorktown: The battle at Yorktown, Virginia, which resulted in the defeat of British military leader Lord Cornwallis and his surrender to George Washington.

Greene and the Southern Campaign

After the Camden defeat, Washington (who had to remain in the North to contain the British army occupying New York) appointed General Nathanael Greene to command the southern campaign. Greene was appalled by conditions in South Carolina. His troops needed clothing, blankets, and food. He told a friend that incessant guerrilla warfare had "so corrupted the principles of the people that they think of nothing but plundering one another."

Greene moved cautiously. He adopted a conciliatory policy toward the many Americans who had switched sides, an advantageous move in a region where people changed their allegiance up to seven times in less than two years. He ordered his troops to treat captives fairly and not loot loyalist property. He helped the shattered provincial congresses of Georgia and South Carolina reestablish civilian authority in the interior—a goal the British were never able to accomplish. With only sixteen hundred regulars, Greene could not afford to have frontier militia companies occupied in defending their homes from Indian attack. He accordingly pursued diplomacy to keep Indians out of the war. Although royal officials initially won some Indian allies, by war's end only the Creeks remained allied with Great Britain.

Even before Greene took command of the southern army in December 1780, the tide was turning. In October, at King's Mountain, a backcountry force defeated redcoats and loyalists. Then in January 1781, Greene's aide Daniel Morgan routed the British regiment Tarleton's Legion at Cowpens. Greene confronted British troops under Lord Cornwallis at Guilford Court House, North Carolina, in March. Although Cornwallis controlled the field at day's end, most of his army was destroyed. Greene returned to South Carolina, where he forced the redcoats to retire to Charleston.

Surrender at Yorktown

Cornwallis headed north into Virginia, where he joined forces with redcoats commanded by the American traitor Benedict Arnold. He then withdrew to the peninsula between the York and James Rivers, where he fortified Yorktown. Washington moved more than seven

Revolutionary Origins

Many historians today would contend that the American Revolution was not truly "revolutionary," if revolution means overturning an earlier power structure. The nation won its independence and established a republic, both radical events in the eighteenth century, but essentially the same men who led the colonies also led the new country (with the exception of British officials and appointees). In contrast, the nearly contemporary French Revolution witnessed the execution of the monarch and many aristocrats and a significant redistribution of authority. So the legacy of the American Revolution appears at once radical and conservative.

Throughout the more than two hundred years since the "Revolution," varying groups have claimed to represent the spirit of the Revolution. People protesting discriminatory policies against women and minorities (usually "liberals") invoke the "created equal" language of the Declaration of Independence. Left-wing organizations rail against concentrations of wealth and power. Those protesting higher taxes (usually "conservatives" wanting a reduced role for government) often adopt the symbolism of the Boston Tea Party, as in the "tea-party" movement opposing Obama administration policies. Right-wing militias arm themselves, preparing to defend their homes and families against a malevolent government, just as they believe the minutemen did in 1775. Indeed, so-called minutemen have formed vigilante groups to guard the United States–Mexico border against illegal aliens. The message of the Revolution can be invoked to support extralegal demonstrations of any description, from invasions of military bases by antiwar protesters to demonstrations outside abortion clinics. But the Revolution can also be invoked to oppose such street protests, because—some would argue—in a republic, change should come peacefully, via the ballot box.

Just as Americans in the eighteenth century disagreed over the meaning of their struggle, so the legacy of revolution remains contested early in the twenty-first century both for the nation.

---

thousand French and American troops south from New York City. When De Grasse's fleet arrived in time to defeat the Royal Navy vessels sent to relieve Cornwallis, the British general was trapped (see Map 6.2). On October 19, 1781, Cornwallis surrendered.

When news of the defeat reached London, Parliament voted to cease offensive operations in America, authorizing peace negotiations. Washington returned with the main army to the environs of New York, where in March 1783, his underpaid—and, they thought, underappreciated—officers threatened to mutiny unless Congress guaranteed them adequate compensation. Washington, warned in advance of the so-called Newburgh Conspiracy, defused the crisis with a well-reasoned and patriotic speech. At the end of the year, he resigned as commander-in-chief. Still, Washington established an enduring precedent: civilian control of the American military.

The war had been won, but at terrible cost. More than thirty-five thousand American men died, about one-quarter of them from battle and one-half while prisoners of the British. In the South, years of guerrilla warfare and the loss of thousands of runaway slaves shattered the economy. Indebtedness soared, and local governments were crippled, as few people could pay taxes. Some formerly wealthy planters descended into insolvency.

Treaty of Paris   Yet Americans rejoiced when they learned of the signing of the preliminary peace **treaty of Paris** in November 1782. American diplomats—Benjamin Franklin, John Jay, and John Adams—ignored their instructions from Congress to be guided by France and negotiated directly with Great Britain. Their instincts were sound: the French government was more an enemy to Britain than a friend to the United States. French ministers worked secretly to prevent the establishment of a strong, unified government in America. Spain's desire to lay claim to the region between the Appalachian Mountains and the Mississippi River further complicated the negotiations. But the American delegates proved adept at power politics, achieving their main goal: independence as a united nation. Weary of war, the new British ministry made so many concessions that Parliament ousted it shortly after peace terms were approved.

The treaty, signed on September 3, 1783, granted independence to a nation named "the United States of America." Generous boundaries delineated that new nation: to the north, approximately the present-day boundary with Canada; to the south, the 31st parallel (about the modern northern border of Florida); to the west, the Mississippi River. Florida, which Britain had acquired in 1763, reverted to Spain (see Map 7.2). The Americans also gained unlimited fishing rights off Newfoundland. In ceding so much land, Britain ignored the territorial rights of its Indian allies. British diplomats also poorly served loyalists and British merchants. The treaty's ambiguously worded clauses regarding prewar debts and the postwar treatment of loyalists proved impossible to enforce.

treaty of Paris: A treaty signed in 1783 when the British recognized American independence and agreed to withdraw all royal troops from the colonies.

 Link to the petition of Connecticut slaves for freedom.

Summary

Having unified the disparate mainland colonies, the victorious Americans had claimed their place in the family of nations and forged a successful alliance with France. With an inexperienced army, they had defeated the world's greatest military power. They won only a few actual victories—most notably, at Trenton, Saratoga, and Yorktown—but their army survived to fight again. Ultimately, the Americans wore their enemy down.

In winning the war, the Americans abandoned their British identity, excluding from their new nation loyalist neighbors unwilling to break with the mother country. They established republican governments at state and national levels and created new national loyalties. They also claimed most of the territory east of the Mississippi River and south of the Great Lakes, thereby greatly expanding land open to settlement and threatening traditional Indian dominance of the interior.

In the future, Americans would face new challenges: ensuring the survival of their republic in a world dominated by the bitter rivalries among Britain, France, and Spain.

Chapter Review

Government by Congress and Committee

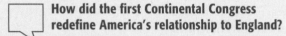

How did the first Continental Congress redefine America's relationship to England?

Congressmen meeting at the First Continental Congress in September 1774 were not ready for a complete break from England, but they did outline America's grievances, develop a resistance plan, and define America's relationship to Great Britain. Debate covered the spectrum of opinion from the radical call to obey only the king and not Parliament to the more conservative view that would have Parliament and a new American legislature jointly enacting colonial laws. In the end, the group compromised and agreed in the Declaration of Rights and Grievances to obey Parliament on a voluntary basis (rather than as subjects) and resist all taxes.

Contest in the Backcountry

Where did backcountry Indians' loyalties lie at the onset of the Revolution?

Initially, Indians were inclined to ally with Great Britain, given the hostility they experienced from European American settlers in the backcountry. But other chiefs had their doubts: England had abandoned them in vacating Fort Pitt years earlier. Both the Americans and the British sought a pledge of neutrality, and while some, such as the Iroquois, agreed, others, such as the Cherokees and Shawnees, attacked backcountry settlements in western Virginia and the Carolinas, hoping to use the conflict to regain lost land. A few Indian communities supported the Americans, but most others remained neutral or sporadically sided with the British.

Choosing Sides

How did colonists choose sides in the conflict with England?

Not everyone supported independence from Great Britain. In fact, only two-fifths of the European American population of the thirteen colonies were Patriots seeking to separate from England—among them small and middling farmers, Chesapeake gentry, merchants, city artisans, elected officeholders—and even then, their specific goals varied. Loyalists who opposed the break with England represented one-fifth of the population and included Anglican clergy; parishioners in the North; tenant farmers; members of persecuted religious sects; backcountry southerners; ethnic minorities, especially Scots; and merchants who relied on British trade. Two-fifths of the population remained neutral, including pacifist groups such as the Quakers. Finally, free blacks in the North in the middle colonies took the Patriots' side, while southern bondspeople thought they'd have a better chance at personal freedom by allying with the British, who made such promises to runaway slaves.

War and Independence

How did Thomas Paine's *Common Sense* help reshape the war's purpose?

While Americans had been at war with Great Britain for months, most leaders denied seeking a complete break from England and focused on achieving some autonomy and a redress for various grievances. In January 1776, Paine's widely popular pamphlet called for independence and the establishment of a republic (a government by the people with no king or nobility). He argued that once America broke from European control, it would become strong and prosperous. Within months of its publication, the Second Continental Congress passed a resolution that the colonies should be free and all ties to Great Britain dissolved and charged five men, among them Thomas Jefferson, to write a Declaration of Independence.

The Struggle in the North

What was France's role in the American Revolution?

Initially, France secretly sent military supplies to the Americans and regarded the revolution as a chance to avenge its defeat to Britain in the Seven Years' War. Once Americans won the Battle of Saratoga, the French openly supported them, sending naval vessels, ammunition, and troops. France's assistance proved vital to American victory in the final years of the war. Americans and the French signed two treaties in 1778, the Treaty of Amity and Commerce, which recognized American independence and set up trade relations; and the Treaty of Alliance, which promised neither side would negotiate peace (in conflicts with Britain) without consulting the other. France also abandoned claims to Canada and to North American territory east of the Mississippi River.

Life in the Army and on the Home Front

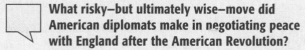

How was the Continental Army staffed?

Only in the war's earliest months were battlefields filled by militia men, who left their fields to fight. After that, American leaders organized an army comprising young, single, often propertyless men who enlisted for a period of time for money or land. Towns were required to send their quota of soldiers and did so by enlisting everyone, including recent immigrants. Initially, African Americans were banned from the army, but by 1776, that prohibition was lifted, as northern recruiters promised slaves their freedom after the war. About five thousand enlisted, composing 10 percent of the army, though they were typically in segregated units and often given tasks others rejected, such as burying the dead. Wives and widows of poor soldiers often followed the camps, too, working as cooks, nurses, and launderers for rations or low wages.

Victory in the South

What risky—but ultimately wise—move did American diplomats make in negotiating peace with England after the American Revolution?

During the signing of a preliminary peace treaty in Paris in 1782 ending the American Revolution, diplomats Benjamin Franklin, John Jay, and John Adams ignored Congress's instructions to let Paris lead the way.

Congress wanted them to follow the terms of the 1778 Treaty of Alliance, in which Americans promised not to make peace with England without consulting France first (and vice versa). Instead, the diplomats trusted their instincts and negotiated on their own. Turns out they were right: French ministers had secretly tried to prevent a strong government from taking hold in America. War-weary Britain not only gave America its independence, but also ceded vast tracts of land and unlimited fishing rights off Newfoundland.

Suggestions for Further Reading

Edwin G. Burrows, *Forgotten Patriots: The Untold Story of American Prisoners during the Revolutionary War* (2008).

Robert McCluer Calhoon, *The Loyalists in Revolutionary America, 1760–1781* (1973)

Colin Calloway, *The American Revolution in Indian Country* (1995)

Stephen Conway, *The War of American Independence, 1775–1783* (1995)

Sylvia Frey, *Water from the Rock: Black Resistance in a Revolutionary Age* (1991)

Pauline Maier, *American Scripture: Making the Declaration of Independence* (1997)

Charles Niemeyer, *America Goes to War: A Social History of the Continental Army* (1997)

Mary Beth Norton, *Liberty's Daughters: The Revolutionary Experience of American Women, 1750–1800* (2nd ed., 1996)

Cassandra Pybus, *Epic Journeys of Freedom: Runaway Slaves of the American Revolution and their Global Quest for Liberty* (2006)

Charles Royster, *A Revolutionary People at War: The Continental Army and American Character, 1775–1783* (1980)

Forging a National Republic

7

1776–1789

On December 26, 1787, a group of Federalists—supporters of the proposed Constitution—gathered in Carlisle, a Pennsylvania frontier town. The men planned to fire a cannon to celebrate their state convention's ratification vote two weeks earlier, but a large crowd of Antifederalists stopped them. First, the Antis blocked the cannon. Then, they attacked the Federalists, who fled as the angry Antis burned a copy of the Constitution.

The next day, Federalists fired their cannon and read the ratification proclamation. Antifederalists paraded and burned effigies of two Federalists. When Federalist officials arrested demonstrators for rioting, the Antifederalist-dominated militia broke them out of jail.

For weeks, participants argued in the Carlisle newspaper about what the demonstrations meant. Federalist proclaimed that the respectable celebrants acted with "good order" and called Antifederalist opponents "worthless ragamuffins." Replying, Antifederalists pronounced the Federalists "an unhallowed riotous mob." Constitution supporters called themselves "friends of government," but through their advocacy of government that aimed to suppress the people's liberties, they revealed they were secretly aristocrats.

The Carlisle riots presaged violent disputes over the new Constitution in Albany (New York), Providence (Rhode Island), and other cities. In a struggle that began in 1775 and persisted until century's end, Americans argued over how to implement republican principles and who best represented the people.

Republicanism—the idea that governments should be based on the consent of the people—originated with theorists in ancient Greece and Rome. Republics, they declared, were desirable yet fragile government forms. Unless citizens were virtuous—sober, moral, and industrious—and agreed on key issues, republics would fail. When Americans left Britain, they abandoned the idea that the best governments balanced participation by a king, the nobility, and the people. Instead, they embraced republicanism, in which the people were sovereign. During and after the war,

Americans wondered how to ensure political stability, foster consensus, and create and sustain a virtuous republic.

America's leaders attempted to inculcate virtue in their countrymen and countrywomen. After 1776, literature, theater, art, architecture, and education pursued moral goals. Women's education became important, for the mothers of the republic's children would ensure the nation's future. Almost all white men assumed that women, African Americans, and Indians should have no role in politics; men saw the first two groups as household dependents, the last as outside the polity. Still, they disagreed on how many of their number should be included in the political process and how their new governments should be structured.

Then there were Thomas Jefferson's words in the Declaration of Independence: "all men are created equal." Given that statement of principle, how could white republicans justify holding African Americans in perpetual bondage? Some freed their slaves or voted for state laws abolishing slavery. Others denied that blacks were "men" in the same sense as whites.

The most important task facing Americans was constructing a unified national government. Before 1765, many circumstances divided the British mainland colonies: diverse economies, varying religious traditions and ethnic compositions, competing western land claims, and different polities. But the Revolutionary War brought them together, creating a new nationalistic spirit that replaced loyalties to state and region.

Still, America's first national government under the Articles of Confederation proved too weak and decentralized. Political leaders tried another approach in drafting the Constitution in 1787. Some historians have argued that the Articles of Confederation and the Constitution reflect opposing philosophies, the Constitution representing an "aristocratic" counterrevolution against the "democratic" Articles. The two documents are more accurately viewed as successive attempts to solve the same problems—the relationship of states and nation and the extent to which authority should be centralized. Both applied theories of republicanism to problems of governance; neither was entirely successful in resolving those difficulties.

As you read this chapter, keep the following questions in mind:

* **What were the elements of the new national identity? How did women, Indians, and African Americans fit into that identity?**

* **What problems confronted the new nation's leaders as they attempted to establish the first modern republic?**

* **How and why were those problems resolved differently at different times?**

Creating a Virtuous Republic

When the colonies declared independence, John Dickinson recalled years later, "We knew that the people of this country must unite themselves under some form of Government and that this could be no other than the republican form"—in short, self-government by the people. But how should that goal be implemented?

> How were notions of republican virtue gendered in post-revolutionary America?

Chronology

1776	Second Continental Congress directs states to draft constitutions	1786	Annapolis Convention meets, discusses reforming government
	Abigail Adams advises her husband to "Remember the Ladies"	1786–87	Shays's Rebellion in western Massachusetts raises questions about future of the republic
1777	Articles of Confederation sent to states for ratification	1787	Royall Tyler's *The Contrast*, first successful American play, performed
	Vermont becomes first jurisdiction to abolish slavery		Northwest Ordinance organizes territory north of Ohio River and east of Mississippi River
1781	Articles of Confederation ratified		Constitutional Convention drafts new form of government
1783	Treaty of Paris signed, formalizing American independence	1788	Hamilton, Jay, and Madison write *The Federalist* to urge ratification of the Constitution by New York
1784	Diplomats sign treaty with Iroquois at Fort Stanwix, but Iroquois repudiate it two years later		Constitution ratified
1785	Land Ordinance of 1785 provides for surveying and sale of national lands in Northwest Territory	1789	William Hill Brown publishes *The Power of Sympathy*, first American novel
1785–86	United States negotiates treaties at Hopewell, South Carolina, with Choctaws, Chickasaws, and Cherokees		Massachusetts orders towns to support public schools
		1800	Weems publishes his *Life of Washington*

Varieties of Republicanism

Three definitions of republicanism emerged in the new United States. Ancient history and political theory informed the first, held by the educated elite (such as the Adamses of Massachusetts). The histories of popular governments in Greece and Rome suggested that republics could succeed only if they were small and homogeneous. According to classical republican theory, unless a republic's citizens were virtuous men willing to sacrifice private interests for the common good, the government would collapse. In return for sacrifices, a republic offered equality of opportunity. Rank would be based on merit rather than inherited status. Society would be governed by members of a "natural aristocracy," men whose talent elevated them from possibly humble beginnings to positions of power.

A second definition, advanced by other elites and some skilled craftsmen, drew on economic theory. This version of republicanism followed Scottish theorist Adam Smith in emphasizing individuals' pursuit of rational self-interest. When republican men sought to improve their own economic and social circumstances, the nation would benefit. Republican virtue would be achieved through the pursuit of private interests, rather than through subordination to communal ideals.

The third notion of republicanism was less influential but more egalitarian than the others. Men who advanced this version, among them Thomas Paine, called for widening men's political participation. They wanted government to respond directly to the needs of ordinary folk, rejecting that the "lesser sort" should defer to their "betters." They were democrats in the modern sense. For them, the untutored wisdom of the people embodied republican virtue.

Depicting Virtue

In the 1780s, American printers began publishing magazines that became important vehicles for promoting their notions of virtue. For monthly or bi-monthly magazines filled with locally written poems and essays publishers needed illustrations—something not required by weekly newspapers. One of the most important and longest lasting of these publications was the *Columbian Magazine*, published in Philadelphia from 1786 to 1792. Seen here are two of the many illustrations its printer commissioned from local artists. *Venerate the Plow* celebrated American agriculture, with the female figure symbolizing America (note the 13 stars in a circle over her head) holding a sheaf of grain. In the other, Columbia presents a girl and a boy (the "rising race") to Minerva (goddess of wisdom), who leans on a pedestal lauding independence as "the reward of wisdom, fortitude, and perseverance." In the background, a farmer plows his field and ships ply the ocean. What future did Americans see for themselves, as represented in these pictures?

Columbian Magazine, 1786

Columbian Magazine, 1787

All three strands of republicanism contrasted America's industrious virtue with the corruption of Britain and Europe. In the first version, that virtue manifested itself in frugality and self-sacrifice; in the second, it would prevent self-interest from becoming vice; in the third, it was the justification for including propertyless free men as voters. Most agreed that a virtuous country would be composed of hard-working citizens who would dress simply, elect wise leaders, and forgo conspicuous consumption of luxury goods.

Virtue and the Arts

As citizens of the United States constructed their republic, they expected to replace the vices of monarchical Europe—immorality, selfishness, and lack of public spirit—with the virtues of republican America. They sought to embody republican principles in their governments and in their culture, expecting painting, literature, drama, and architecture to convey nationalism and virtue.

Americans faced a contradiction, however. To some republicans, fine arts were manifestations of vice, signaling luxury and corruption. Why did a frugal farmer need a painting or a novel? Why should anyone spend hard-earned wages to see a play in a lavish theater? The first American artists and authors wanted to produce works embodying virtue, but many viewed those works as corrupting, regardless of their content.

Still, authors and artists tried. In Royall Tyler's *The Contrast* (1787), the first successful American play, Colonel Manly's virtuous conduct was contrasted with Billy Dimple's reprehensible behavior. The era's most popular book, Mason Locke Weems's *Life of Washington*, published in 1800 after George Washington's death, was intended to "hold up his great Virtues ... to the imitation of Our Youth." The famous tale Weems invented—six-year-old George bravely admitting cutting down his father's favorite cherry tree—ended with George's father exclaiming, "Such an act of heroism in my son, is worth more than a thousand trees."

Painting and architecture, too, were to exemplify high moral standards. Prominent artists Gilbert Stuart and Charles Willson Peale painted portraits of upstanding republican citizens. John Trumbull's canvases sought to inspire patriotism with scenes of historical milestones such as the Battle of Bunker Hill and Cornwallis's surrender at Yorktown. When the Virginia government asked Thomas Jefferson, then minister to France, for advice on designing the state capitol in Richmond, Jefferson recommended copying a simple but noble Roman building, the Maison Carrée at Nîmes. Jefferson's ideals that would guide American architecture for a generation: simplicity of line, harmonious proportions, a feeling of grandeur.

Despite the artists' efforts (or perhaps because of them), some Americans detected signs of luxury and corruption by the mid-1780s. The resumption of European trade after the war brought imported fashions. Elite families again attended balls and concerts. Parties no longer seemed complete without gambling and cardplaying. Social clubs for young people multiplied. Especially alarming was the establishment in 1783 of the Society of the Cincinnati, a hereditary association for Revolutionary War officers and their firstborn sons. Although organizers hoped to advance the citizen-soldier, opponents feared that the group would become the nucleus of a native-born aristocracy. These developments challenged the United States' self-image as a virtuous republic.

Educational Reform

Americans' concern for the infant republic's future focused their attention on children. Education was previously seen as the concern of individual families. Now schooling would serve a public purpose. If young people were to resist vice and become useful citizens, they would need education. The 1780s and 1790s thus witnessed two major changes in educational practice.

Link to Royall Tyler's *The Contrast*.

Writing and Stationery Supplies

In the seventeenth century, colonists stressed teaching children to read the Bible; writing was less necessary, and many people could read but not write. Yet as the eighteenth century progressed, writing skills acquired new significance as family members parted by the Revolutionary War needed to communicate with each other and new opportunities arose for merchants who could handle distant correspondents. After the war, Americans placed greater emphasis on teaching youngsters to write.

Writing drew on materials from around the world. Sheets of paper came from Britain or, increasingly, from American paper mills; more than thirty were built between 1750 and 1780. Quill pens (goose feathers) often originated in Germany or Holland. Penknives to sharpen blunt quills and inkpots (made of brass, glass, or pewter) also came from Britain. But the Americans could not write without additional items from international trade.

For example, to absorb ink properly, paper needed to be treated with pounce, a powder made from gum sandarac (a tree resin from North Africa) and pumice (powdered volcanic glass). Lacking envelopes, eighteenth-century writers folded papers, addressed them on the outside, and sealed them with wax made in Holland or Britain from lac (a resinous secretion of insects, still used today for shellac) from India and cinnabar, a red quartz-like crystal, from Spain. Ink was manufactured from various ingredients: oak galls from Aleppo (in Syria), gum arabic (sap from acacia trees) from Sudan, and alum and copperas (derived from stones) from Britain. Most likely ink was shipped from Britain in powdered form; in America, another key ingredient, urine, would be added so the alum would blend with the other substances.

Therefore, children learning to write in one of the new academies used implements that involved Americans in a commercial chain that linked them to Great Britain, the European continent, North Africa, and the Middle East.

Historic Odessa Foundation

This writing desk, made in Pennsylvania in the mid-to-late eighteenth century, would have been owned by a well-to-do family from the mid-Atlantic states. The pigeon holes would hold incoming and outgoing letters; the many drawers could store paper, ink, seals and sealing wax, and other supplies. The new importance of writing thus produced a perceived need for novel types of furniture.

Terra Foundation for American Art, Chicago/Art Resource, NY

Judith Sargent Stevens (later Murray), by John Singleton Copley, ca. 1770–1772. The eventual author of tracts advocating improvements in women's education sat for this portrait two decades earlier, during her first marriage. Her clear-eyed gaze suggests both her intelligence and her seriousness of purpose.

Link to Judith Sargent Murray's "On the Equality of the Sexes."

Abigail Adams: Wife of Revolutionary figure John Adams (and second U.S. President). Influenced by the ideology of the Revolution, her letter to her husband is considered an early effort for greater rights for women.

First, some northern states began using tax money to support public elementary schools. In 1789, Massachusetts became one of the first states requiring towns to offer free public elementary education. Second, since mothers would have to be educated if they were to instruct their children adequately, Massachusetts insisted that elementary schools teach girls as well as boys. Throughout the United States, private academies were founded to provide advanced schooling for teenage girls from well-to-do families. Colleges remained closed to women, but a few fortunate girls could study history, geography, rhetoric, and mathematics.

Judith Sargent Murray   Judith Sargent Murray of Gloucester, Massachusetts, became the chief theorist of women's education in the early republic. Murray argued that women and men had equal intellectual capacities, although inadequate education might make women seem less intelligent. Therefore, concluded Murray, boys and girls should be offered equivalent schooling. She further contended that girls should be taught to support themselves: "Independence should be placed within their grasp."

Murray's ideas were part of a general rethinking of women's position that resulted from the Revolution. Men and women realized that female patriots had made important contributions to independence. Consequently, Americans developed new ideas about women's in republican society.

Women and the Republic

The best-known expression of those new ideas appeared in a letter **Abigail Adams** addressed to her husband in March 1776. "In the new Code of Laws which I suppose it will be necessary for you to make I desire you would Remember the Ladies," she wrote. "Remember all Men would be tyrants if they could. … If perticuliar care and attention is not paid to the Laidies [sic] we are determined to foment a Rebelion, and will not hold ourselves bound by any Laws in which we have no voice, or Representation." With these words, Abigail Adams applied the ideology developed to combat parliamentary supremacy. She argued that, because men were "Naturally Tyrannical," the United States should reform marriage laws, which subordinated wives to their husbands, giving men control of family property and denying wives the right to independent legal action.

Abigail Adams did not ask for woman suffrage, but others claimed that right, and some authors began to define the "rights of women" in general terms. The New Jersey state constitution in 1776 defined voters carelessly as "all free inhabitants" who met property qualifications. They thereby unintentionally gave the vote to property-holding white spinsters and widows and free black landowners. Qualified women and African Americans regularly voted in New Jersey's local and congressional elections until 1807, when they were disfranchised by the state legislature. That women chose to vote was evidence of how the Revolution altered their perception of their place in the nation's political life.

Even after the war, most European-Americans viewed women in traditional terms, affirming their primary function as wives, mothers, and mistresses of households. Because wives could not own property or participate directly in economic life, women came to be seen as the embodiment of self-sacrificing, republicanism. Through new female-run charitable associations, better-off women assumed public responsibilities among them caring for poor widows and orphans. Thus, men were freed to pursue their economic self-interests, while wives and daughters fulfilled the family's obligation to the common good. The ideal republican man, therefore, was an individualist, seeking advancement for himself and his family. The ideal republican woman put the well-being of others first.

The First Emancipation and the Growth of Racism

> What contributed to the growing number of free blacks in America after the revolution?

Revolutionary ideology exposed one of the primary contradictions in American society. There were 700,000 African Americans—roughly 20 percent of the population—residing in the new republic. European-Americans and African Americans saw the irony in slaveholders' claims that they sought to prevent Britain from "enslaving" them. In 1773, Dr. Benjamin Rush called slavery "a vice which degrades human nature," warning ominously that "the plant of liberty is of so tender a nature that it cannot thrive long in the neighborhood of slavery."

African Americans used revolutionary ideology to their advantage. In 1779, a group of slaves from Portsmouth, New Hampshire, addressed the state legislature, pleading "that the name of slave may not more be heard in a land gloriously contending for the sweets of freedom." The same year, several bondsmen in Fairfield, Connecticut, petitioned the legislature for their freedom, characterizing slavery as a "flagrant Injustice." How could men who were "nobly contending in the Cause of Liberty," they asked, continue "this detestable Practice"?

Emancipation and Manumission

Both legislatures responded negatively, but the postwar years witnessed the gradual abolition of slavery in the North. Responding to lawsuits filed by enslaved men and women, Massachusetts courts decided in 1783 that the state constitution prohibited slavery. Other states adopted gradual emancipation laws between 1780 (Pennsylvania) and 1804 (New Jersey). New Hampshire did not formally abolish slavery, but only eight slaves were reported on the 1800 census and none in 1810. Although no southern state adopted emancipation laws, the legislatures of Virginia (1782), Delaware (1787), and Maryland (1790 and 1796) loosened earlier laws restricting slaveowners' ability to free their bondspeople. South Carolina and Georgia never considered such

Private collection, photograph courtesy of Hirschl & Adler Galleries, New York

A sailor of African descent posed proudly for this portrait around 1790. Unfortunately, neither the name of the sailor nor the name of the artist is known today.

acts, and North Carolina insisted that manumissions (emancipations of individual slaves) be approved by county courts.

Revolutionary ideology thus had limited impact on the economic interests of large slaveholders. Only in the northern states—societies with slaves, not slave societies—could state legislatures abolish slavery. Even there, legislators' concern for the *property* rights of slave owners led them to favor gradual over immediate emancipation. For example, New York's law freed children born into slavery after July 4, 1799, but only after they reached their mid-twenties. Laws failed to emancipate the existing slave population. Although emancipation laws forbade the sale of slaves to jurisdictions where slavery remained legal, slaveowners regularly circumvented such provisions. The 1840 census recorded the presence of slaves in several northern states.

Growth of Free Black Population   The number of free people of African descent in the United States grew dramatically in the initial post-Revolution years. Most slaves emancipated before the war were mulattos, born of unions between bondswomen and their masters, who manumitted the children. Wartime escapees from plantations, slaves who served in the American army, and those emancipated by their owners or by state laws, contributed to the nearly 60,000 free people of color in the United States by 1790. Ten years later, they numbered more than 108,000—nearly 11 percent of the total African American population.

In the Chesapeake, manumissions were speeded by economic changes, such as declining soil fertility and the shift from tobacco to grain production. Because grain cultivation was less labor-intensive than tobacco growing, planters had "excess" slaves. They occasionally solved that problem by freeing less productive or more favored bondspeople. The enslaved also negotiated agreements with owners allowing them to live and work independently until they could purchase themselves. Virginia's free black population more than doubled between 1790 and 1810; also by 1810, nearly one-quarter of Maryland's African American population was no longer in bondage.

Freedpeople's Lives   In the 1780s, rural freedpeople headed to northern port cities such as Boston and Philadelphia. With better employment opportunities, especially in domestic service, women outnumbered male migrants by three to two. Some freedmen also worked in domestic service, but larger numbers were unskilled laborers and sailors. A few women and many men (nearly one-third of those in Philadelphia in 1795) were skilled workers or retailers. They exchanged the surnames of former masters for names like Newman or Brown and established independent two-parent families. They also began to occupy distinct neighborhoods, probably due to discrimination.

Even whites who recognized African Americans' right to freedom were unwilling to accept them as equals. Laws discriminated against freedpeople as they had against slaves. Several states—among them Delaware, Maryland, and South Carolina—adopted laws denying property-owning black men the vote. South Carolina forbade free blacks from testifying against whites in court. New Englanders used indenture contracts to control freed youths, who were often denied public education. Freedmen found it difficult to purchase property and find good jobs.

Gradually, freedpeople developed their own institutions. In Charleston, mulattos formed the Brown Fellowship Society, which provided insurance coverage, financed a school, and helped to support orphans. In 1794, former slaves in Philadelphia and Baltimore, led by Reverend Richard Allen, founded societies that eventually formed the **African Methodist Episcopal (AME) church**. AME churches sponsored schools and—along with African Baptist, African Episcopal, and African Presbyterian churches—became cultural centers for free blacks.

African Methodist Episcopal (AME) church: The first black-run Protestant denomination.

Development of Racist Theory

Their endeavors were especially important because the postrevolutionary years witnessed the development of formal racist theory in the United States. Before the Revolution, European-Americans regarded slaves as inferior. Influential writers argued that African slaves' seemingly debased character derived from their enslavement, rather

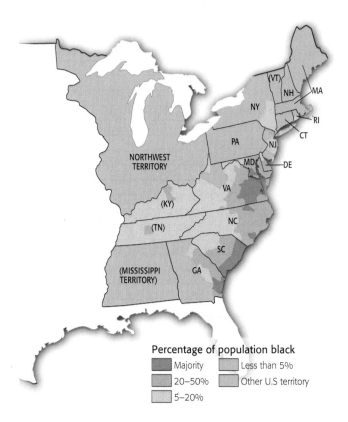

MAP 7.1

African American Population, 1790: Proportion of Total Population

The first census clearly indicated that the African American population was heavily concentrated in just a few areas of the United States, most notably in coastal regions of South Carolina, Georgia, and Virginia. Although there were growing numbers of blacks in the backcountry—presumably taken there by migrating slaveowners—most parts of the North and East, with the exception of the immediate vicinity of New York City, had few African American residents.

Source: From Lester J. Cappon et al., eds., *Atlas of Early American History: The Revolutionary Era, 1760–1790.* Copyright © 1976 by Princeton University Press.

Percentage of population black

- Majority
- 20–50%
- 5–20%
- Less than 5%
- Other U.S territory

than enslavement's being the consequence of inherited inferiority. After the Revolution, slaveowners needed to defend holding other human beings in bondage against the proposition that "all men are created equal." Consequently, they argued that people of African descent were less than fully human and that the principles of republican equality applied only to European-Americans.

Egalitarian thinking among European-Americans downplayed status distinctions within their own group and differentiated all "whites" from people of color—Indians and African Americans. Decades earlier, Indians began to refer to themselves as "red." Experience as slaves on American soil forged the identity "African" or "black" from the various ethnic and national affiliations of people who survived the transatlantic crossing. Thus, in the revolutionary era "whiteness," "redness," and "blackness"—along with the superiority of the first, the inferiority of the latter two—developed in tandem.

With racism came the assertion that, as Thomas Jefferson insisted in 1781, blacks were "inferior to the whites in the endowments both of body and mind." There followed the belief that blacks were congenitally lazy, even though owners often argued that slaves were "natural" workers. Third was the notion that blacks were sexually promiscuous and that African American men lusted after European American women. The specter of interracial sexual intercourse involving black men and white women haunted early American racist thought. Significantly, the more common sexual exploitation of enslaved women by their masters aroused little concern.

African Americans challenged these racist notions. Benjamin Banneker, a free black mathematical genius, in 1791 sent Thomas Jefferson a copy of his latest almanac (including astronomical calculations) to show blacks' mental powers. Jefferson admitted Banneker's intelligence but said Banneker was exceptional; Jefferson required more evidence if he were to rethink his position on people of African descent generally.

A White Men's Republic

At its birth, leaders defined the republic as a white male enterprise, as laws from the 1770s on linked "whiteness" and male citizenship rights. Some historians have argued that the subjugation of blacks, Indians, and women was a necessary precondition for theoretical equality among white men. Identifying common racial antagonists helped create white solidarity and lessened the threat to gentry power posed by the enfranchisement of poorer men. Moreover, excluding women from politics reserved power for men. After the Revolution, the division of American society between slave and free became a division between blacks—some of whom were free—and whites.

Designing Republican Governments

How did Americans' former experience as British subjects influence the state governments they established?

In May 1776, the Second Continental Congress directed states to devise new republican governments to replace provincial conventions and committees that had met since colonial governments collapsed in 1774 and 1775. Thus American men concentrated on drafting state constitutions and devoted little attention to national government.

State Constitutions

First, state political leaders struggled to define a "constitution" and eventually concluded that legislative bodies should not draft their constitutions. Following Vermont in 1777 and Massachusetts in 1780, they elected conventions exclusively to draft constitutions. Thus, states sought authorization from the people—the theoretical sovereigns in a republic—before establishing new governments. After preparing new constitutions, delegates submitted them to voters for ratification.

Framers of state constitutions concerned themselves primarily with outlining the distribution of and limitations on government power. If authority was not confined within reasonable limits, the states might become tyrannical, as Britain had.

Under colonial charters, Americans learned to fear the power of the governor—usually the appointed agent of the king or proprietor—and to see the legislature as their defender. Accordingly, the first state constitutions typically provided for the governor to be elected annually (commonly by the legislature), limited the number of terms he could serve, and gave him little independent authority. Simultaneously, they expanded the legislature's powers. Every state except Pennsylvania and Vermont retained a two-house structure, with members of the upper house having longer terms and meeting higher property-holding standards than the lower house. They also redrew electoral districts to reflect population patterns. Finally, most states lowered property qualifications for voting. Thus, the revolutionary era witnessed the first deliberate attempt to broaden the base of American government.

Limiting State Governments

But the state constitutions' authors wanted to prevent tyrants from holding office. They consequently included explicit limitations on government authority to protect the inalienable rights of individual citizens. Seven constitutions contained bills of rights, and others had similar clauses. Most guaranteed freedom of the press, rights to fair trials, and protection against general search warrants. An independent judiciary was charged with upholding such rights. Most states also guaranteed freedom of religion, but with restrictions. For example, seven states required that officeholders be Christians, and some supported churches with tax money.

Constitution makers put greater emphasis on preventing state governments from becoming tyrannical than on making them effective wielders of political authority. Establishing such weak political units, especially in wartime, practically ensured that the constitutions would need revision.

Revising State Constitutions

By the mid-1780s, some political leaders concluded that the best way to limit government power was to balance legislative, executive, and judicial powers, a design called checks and balances. The national Constitution drafted in 1787 also embodied that principle.

Yet the constitutional theories applied at the state level did not immediately influence Americans' conception of national government. Because American officials initially focused on the war, the Continental Congress evolved by default. Not until late 1777 did Congress send the **Articles of Confederation**—which outlined the national government—to the states for ratification, and those Articles simply made law the unplanned arrangements of the Continental Congress.

Articles of Confederation: The first document that sought to create the terms of a national government. It reserved substantial powers for the states, granting to each state its "sovereignty, freedom and independence."

Articles of Confederation

The chief organ of national government was a unicameral (one-house) legislature in which each state had one vote. Its powers included conducting foreign relations, mediating interstate disputes, controlling maritime affairs, regulating Indian trade, and valuing state and national coinage. The United States of America was described as "a firm league of friendship" in which each state "retains its sovereignty, freedom and independence, and every Power, Jurisdiction and right, which is not by this confederation expressly delegated to the United States, in Congress assembled."

The Articles required unanimous consent of state legislatures for ratification or amendment, and a clause concerning western lands proved troublesome.

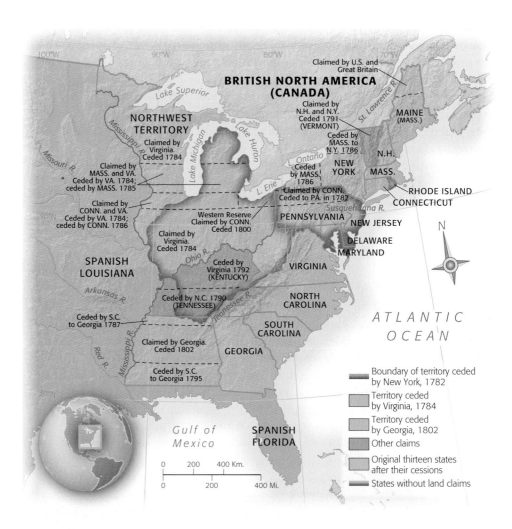

MAP 7.2

Western Land Claims and Cessions, 1782–1802

After the United States achieved independence, states competed with one another for control of valuable lands to which they had possible claims under their original charters. That competition led to a series of compromises among the states or between individual states and the new nation, indicated on this map.

Source: Copyright © Cengage Learning

The draft accepted by Congress allowed states to retain land claims from their original charters. But states with definite western boundaries (such as Maryland and New Jersey) wanted other states to cede to the national government their land-holdings west of the Appalachian Mountains. They feared states with large claims could expand and overpower their smaller neighbors. Maryland refused to accept the Articles until 1781, when Virginia surrendered its western holdings to national jurisdiction (see Map 7.2). Other states followed, establishing the principle that unorganized lands would be held by the nation.

The unicameral legislature, whether it was called the Second Continental Congress (until 1781) or the Confederation Congress (thereafter), was too inefficient to govern effectively. The Articles' authors had not given adequate thought to the distribution of power within the national government or to the relationship between the Confederation and the states. Their Congress was a legislative body and a collective executive (there was no judiciary), but it had no independent income and no authority to compel states to accept its rulings. Under the Articles, national government lurched from crisis to crisis. (See the appendix for the text of the Articles of Confederation.)

Trials of the Confederation

> How did fears of a strong central government ultimately tie the hands of the Confederation Congress?

Finance posed the most persistent problem. Because legislators levied taxes reluctantly, Congress and the states first tried to finance the war by printing currency. Although the money was backed only by good faith, it circulated freely and without excessive depreciation during 1775 and most of 1776. Demand for military supplies and civilian goods was high, stimulating trade and local production.

Financial Affairs   But in late 1776, as the American army suffered reverses in New York and New Jersey, prices rose and inflation set in. State governments fought inflation by controlling wages and prices and requiring acceptance of paper currency equally with specie (coins). States also borrowed funds, established lotteries, and levied taxes. Their efforts were futile, as was Congress's attempt to stop printing currency and rely on state contributions. By early 1780, it took forty paper dollars to purchase one silver dollar. Soon Continental currency was worthless (see Figure 7.1).

In 1781, faced with total collapse of the monetary system, Congress undertook reforms. After establishing a department of finance under the wealthy Philadelphia merchant Robert Morris, it asked states to amend the Articles of Confederation to allow a national duty of 5 percent on imported goods. Morris put national finances on a solid footing, but the customs duty was never adopted. The states' resistance reflected fear of a too-powerful central government.

Foreign Affairs   Because the Articles denied Congress the power to establish a national commercial policy, foreign trade exposed the new government's weaknesses. After the war, Britain, France, and Spain restricted American trade with their colonies. Congress watched helplessly as British goods flooded the United States while American produce could no longer be sold in the British West Indies, once its prime market. Although Americans reopened commerce

FIGURE 7.1
Depreciation of Continental Currency, 1777–1780

The depreciation of Continental currency accelerated in 1778, as is shown in this graph measuring its value against one hundred silver dollars. Thereafter, its value dropped almost daily. (Source: Data from John J. McCusker, "How Much Is That in Real Money? A Historical Price Index for Use as a Deflator of Money Values in the Economy of the United States," *Proceedings of the American Antiquarian Society*, Vol.101, Pt. 2 [1991], Table C-1.)

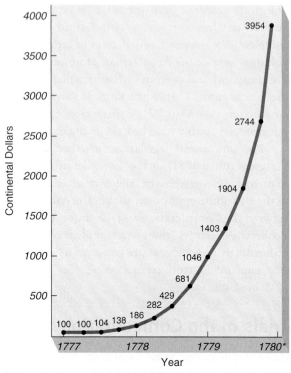

* Currency abandoned in April 1780

with other European countries and started a profitable trade with China in 1784, neither substituted for access to closer and larger markets.

Congress furthermore had difficulty dealing with the Spanish on the nation's southern and western borders. Spain in 1784 closed the Mississippi River to American navigation. Congress, through its Department of Foreign Affairs, opened negotiations with Spain in 1785, but talks collapsed the following year after Congress divided sharply: southerners and westerners insisted on navigation rights, whereas northerners were willing to abandon that claim for commercial concessions in the West Indies.

Peace Treaty Provisions

Provisions of the 1783 Treaty of Paris, too, caused serious problems. Article Four, which promised payment of pre-war debts (most owed by Americans to British merchants), and Article Five, which recommended that states allow loyalists to recover their confiscated property, aroused opposition. States passed laws denying British subjects the right to sue for recovery of debts or property in American courts. Another reason for state opposition was that sales of loyalists' property and possessions had helped finance the war. Because many purchasers were prominent patriots, states hesitated to question the legitimacy of their property titles.

The refusal of state and local governments to comply with Articles Four and Five gave Britain an excuse to maintain military posts on the Great Lakes. Furthermore, Congress's inability to convince states to implement the treaty disclosed its lack of power, even in an area—foreign affairs—in which it had authority under the Articles and undermined the republic's credibility.

Order and Disorder in the West

What was the significance of the Northwest Ordinance?

The United States assumed that the Treaty of Paris cleared its title to all land east of the Mississippi except that held by Spain. Recognizing that land cessions should be obtained from the most powerful tribes, Congress initiated negotiations with northern and southern Indians.

Indian Relations   At Fort Stanwix, New York, in 1784, American diplomats negotiated a treaty with chiefs who claimed to represent the Iroquois; and at Hopewell, South Carolina, in late 1785 and early 1786, they negotiated with emissaries from the Choctaw, Chickasaw, and Cherokee nations. In 1786, the Iroquois repudiated the Fort Stanwix treaty, denying that the negotiators were authorized to speak for the Six Nations. The confederacy threatened new attacks on frontier settlements, but the flawed treaty stood. By 1790, the once-dominant confederacy was confined to a few scattered reservations. In the South, too, the United States took the treaties as confirmation of its sovereignty. European-Americans poured over the southern Appalachians, provoking the Creeks to declare war. In 1790, they came to terms with the United States.

Western nations, such as the Shawnees, Chippewas, Ottawas, and Potawatomis, rejected Iroquois hegemony as early as the 1750s. After Iroquois power collapsed, they formed a confederacy and demanded negotiations with the United States. As a united front, they hoped to avoid the piecemeal surrender of land by individual bands and villages. But in the postwar world, Indian nations could no longer play European and American powers against one another. France was gone; Spanish territory lay far to the west and south; and British power was confined to Canada. Only the United States remained.

Ordinance of 1785   Shortly after state land cessions were completed, Congress organized the Northwest Territory, bounded by the Mississippi River, the Great Lakes, and the Ohio River (see Map 7.2). Ordinances passed in 1784, 1785, and 1787 outlined the process through which the land could be sold and governments organized.

Congress in 1785 wanted the land surveyed into townships 6 miles square, each divided into 36 sections of 640 acres (1 square mile). Revenue from the sale of the sixteenth section of each township would support public schools—the first federal aid to education in American history. One dollar was the minimum price per acre; the minimum sale was one section. The resulting minimum outlay, $640, was unaffordable for ordinary Americans, except veterans who received part of their army pay in land warrants. Proceeds from western land sales constituted the first independent revenues available to the national government.

Northwest Ordinance   The most important of the three land policies—the Northwest Ordinance of 1787—contained a bill of rights guaranteeing settlers freedom of religion and the right to a jury trial, forbidding cruel and unusual punishments, and nominally prohibiting slavery. Eventually, that prohibition became an important symbol for antislavery northerners, but at the time it had little effect. Some residents already held slaves, and Congress would not deprive them of their property. The ordinance also allowed slaveowners to "lawfully reclaim" runaways who took refuge in the territory—the first national fugitive slave law. It prevented slavery from taking deep root by discouraging slaveholders from moving into the territory, but enslavement was not abolished in the Old Northwest until 1848.

The ordinance of 1787 also specified how territorial residents could organize state governments and seek admission to the Union. Early in the nation's history, therefore, Congress established a policy of admitting new states on the same basis as the old. Having suffered under the rule of a colonial power, congressmen understood the importance of preparing the new nation's first "colony" for eventual self-government. In 1787, the ordinance was purely theoretical. Miamis, Shawnees, and Delawares refused to acknowledge American sovereignty and attacked pioneers who ventured too far north of the Ohio River. In 1788, the Ohio Company, to which Congress had sold a large tract of land, established the town of Marietta at the juncture of the Ohio and Muskingum Rivers. But Indians prevented the company from extending settlement into the interior.

Not until after the Articles of Confederation were replaced with a new constitution could the United States muster sufficient force to implement the Northwest Ordinance. Thus, although the ordinance is often viewed as one of the few lasting accomplishments of the Confederation Congress, it existed within a context of political impotence.

From Crisis to the Constitution

How did the question of slavery become linked to the new U.S. Constitution?

Under the Articles of Confederation, Congress could not levy taxes, force states to establish a uniform commercial policy, or enforce treaties. Partly as a result, the American economy slid into a depression within a year after war's end. Exporters of staple crops (especially tobacco and rice) and importers of manufactured goods suffered from the postwar restrictions that European powers imposed on American commerce. Although recovery began by 1786, some estimates suggest that between 1775 and 1790 America's per capita gross national product declined by nearly 50 percent.

Taxation and the Economy

The near-total cessation of foreign commerce in non-military items during the war stimulated domestic manufacturing. Despite the influx of European goods after 1783, the postwar period witnessed stirrings of American industrial development. Because of continuing population growth, the domestic market assumed greater importance. Moreover, foreign trade patterns shifted from Europe and toward the West Indies. Foodstuffs shipped to the French and Dutch Caribbean islands became America's largest export, replacing tobacco (and thus accelerating the Chesapeake's conversion to grain). South Carolina resumed large-scale slave importation, as planters sought to replace workers lost to wartime disruptions. Yet without British subsidies American indigo could not compete with Caribbean indigo, and rice planters struggled to find new markets.

Representatives of Virginia and Maryland met at Mount Vernon (George Washington's plantation) in March 1785 to negotiate a trade agreement on the Potomac River, which divided the two states. The successful meeting led to an invitation to other states to discuss trade policy at a convention in Annapolis, Maryland. Nine states named representatives to the meeting in September 1786, only five delegations attended. Consequently, they issued a call for another convention in Philadelphia nine months later, "to devise such further provisions as shall … appear necessary to render the constitution of the federal government adequate to the exigencies of the Union."

Initially, few other states responded. But states had huge war debts, issuing securities to soldiers instead of pay and to others for supplies and loans. During the hard times of the early 1780s, many veterans and other creditors sold those securities to speculators, who stood to gain when states taxed the citizenry to pay them off. In 1785, Congress requisitioned more taxes from the states to cover national war bonds. Most states tried to comply, but popular protests led the legislatures to adopt laws relieving taxpayers of some obligations. In Massachusetts, when the state levied heavy taxes at full price in specie, farmers who feared having to sell their land to pay the tax, responded furiously. The actions of men from the state's western counties, many of them veterans from leading families, proved that reform was needed.

Shays's Rebellion

Daniel Shays, a former Continental Army officer, led the disgruntled westerners. On January 25, 1787, about fifteen hundred troops assaulted the Springfield federal armory. The militiamen defending the armory fired on their former comrades-in-arms, who withdrew after suffering twenty-four casualties. Some (including Shays) fled the state; two were hanged; and most escaped punishment by paying small fines and taking oaths of allegiance to Massachusetts. The state legislature reduced the burden on landowners with new import duties and by easing tax collections.

Terming Massachusetts "tyrannical" and styling themselves "Regulators," Shaysites insisted that "whenever any encroachments are made either upon the liberties or properties of the people, if redress cannot be had without, it is virtue in them to disturb government." Thus, they linked their rebellion to the earlier independence struggle.

Constitutional Convention

To political leaders, the rebellion confirmed the need for a stronger federal government. After most states appointed delegates, the Confederation Congress belatedly endorsed the convention, "for the sole and express purpose of revising the Articles of Confederation." In mid-May 1787, fifty-five men, representing every state but Rhode Island, assembled in Philadelphia.

Most delegates to the Constitutional Convention were substantial men of property. They wanted to give the national government new authority over taxation and foreign commerce, but also sought to advance their states' interests. Many had been state legislators, and some helped to draft state constitutions. Most were born in America; more than half had attended college. The youngest delegate was twenty-six, the oldest—Benjamin Franklin—eighty-one. George Washington was elected presiding officer. A dozen men did the bulk of the convention's work; among them Virginia's **James Madison** deserves the title "Father of the Constitution."

Madison and the Constitution

The shy James Madison was thirty-six years old in 1787. A Princeton graduate raised in western Virginia, he served on the local Committee of Safety and was elected to the provincial convention, the state's lower and upper houses, and the Continental

James Madison: Known as the "Father of the Constitution" and was elected President of the United States in 1808.

Library of Congress

James Madison (1751–1836), the youthful scholar and skilled politician who earned the title "Father of the Constitution."

Virginia Plan: A proposal calling for the establishment of a strong central government rather than a confederation of states. It gave Congress virtually unrestricted rights of legislation and taxation, power to veto any state law, and authority to use military force against the states.

New Jersey Plan: A proposal calling for a single-chamber congress in which each state had an equal vote, just as the Articles, but strengthened the taxing and commercial powers of Congress.

Congress (1780–1783). Although Madison returned to serve in the Virginia legislature in 1784, he kept up with national politics, partly through correspondence with his friend Thomas Jefferson.

To prepare for the Philadelphia meeting, Madison bought more than two hundred books on history and government, analyzing their accounts of past confederacies and republics. He summed up his research in a paper entitled "Vices of the Political System of the United States." After listing the flaws he perceived in the current government (among them "encroachments by the states on the federal authority" and lack of unity), Madison revealed his belief that the government had to be constructed so it could not become tyrannical or fall under the influence of a particular faction. Rejecting the common assertion that republics had to be small, Madison asserted that a large, diverse republic was preferable. Because the nation would include many factions, no one of them could control the government. Political stability would result from compromises among the contending parties.

Virginia and New Jersey Plans

The so-called **Virginia Plan**, introduced on May 29 by Edmund Randolph, embodied Madison's conception of national government. The plan provided for a two-house legislature, the lower house elected directly by the people and the upper house selected by the lower; representation in both houses proportional to property or population; an executive elected by Congress; a national judiciary; and congressional veto over state laws. Had it been adopted intact, it would have created a government in which national authority reigned unchallenged and state power was diminished. Proportional representation in both houses would also have given large states a dominant voice in the national government.

Many delegates believed the Virginia Plan went too far toward national consolidation. After two weeks of debate, disaffected delegates—particularly those from small states—united under William Paterson of New Jersey. On June 15, Paterson presented an alternative, the **New Jersey Plan**, calling for strengthening the Articles rather than overhauling the government. Paterson proposed retaining a unicameral Congress in which each state had an equal vote, but giving Congress new powers of taxation and regulation. Although the convention initially rejected Paterson's position, he and his allies won several victories in subsequent months.

Debates over Congress

The delegates agreed that the new national government should have a two-house (bicameral) legislature. Further, they concurred that "the people" should be directly represented in at least one house. But they differed on three key questions: Should representation in both houses of Congress be proportional to population? How was representation to be apportioned among the states? How were the members of the two houses to be elected?

The last issue proved the easiest to resolve. Delegates thought it "essential" that the lower branch of Congress be elected directly by the people and "expedient" that members of the upper house be chosen by state legislatures. If the convention had not agreed to allow state legislatures to elect senators, the Constitution would have run into opposition among state leaders. The plan also placed the election of one house of Congress one step removed from the "lesser sort," whose judgment wealthy convention delegates did not trust.

The delegates accepted the principle of proportional representation in the House of Representatives. But small states wanted equal representation in the Senate, which would give them relatively more power at the national level. Large states supported a proportional plan that would give them more votes in the upper house. For weeks, the convention deadlocked. A committee appointed to devise a compromise recommended equal representation in the Senate, with a proviso that all appropriation bills originate in the lower house. But only the absence of several opponents of the compromise during the vote averted a breakdown.

Slavery and the Constitution

The remaining question of how to apportion representation in the lower house divided the nation along sectional lines. Delegates concurred that a census should be conducted every decade to determine the nation's population and that Indians who paid no taxes should be excluded. Delegates from states with large slave populations wanted African and European inhabitants counted equally; delegates from states with few slaves wanted only free people counted. Slavery thus became linked to the new government. Delegates resolved the dispute with a formula developed by the Confederation Congress in 1783 to allocate financial assessments among states: three-fifths of slaves would be included in population totals. (The formula reflected delegates' judgment that slaves were less efficient producers of wealth than free people, not that they were 60 percent human and 40 percent property.) Although the words slave and slavery do not appear in the Constitution, the document contained direct and indirect protections for slavery. The **three-fifths clause**, for example, assured white southern male voters congressional representation out of proportion to their numbers and a disproportionate influence on the selection of the president, because the number of each state's votes in the electoral college was determined by the size of its congressional delegation. In return for southerners' agreement that commercial regulations could be adopted by a simple majority vote (rather than two-thirds), New Englanders agreed that Congress could not end the importation of slaves for twenty years. The fugitive slave clause required states to return runaways to their masters. By guaranteeing national assistance to states threatened with "domestic violence," the Constitution promised aid in putting down future slave revolts and incidents like Shays's Rebellion.

three-fifths clause: Allowed three-fifths of all slaves to be counted for congressional representation and, thereby, in the electoral college that selected the president.

Congressional and Presidential Powers

With issues of slavery and representation resolved, delegates concurred that the national government needed the authority to tax and to regulate foreign and interstate commerce. But instead of giving Congress the wide latitude of the Virginia Plan, delegates enumerated congressional powers and then granting Congress the "necessary and proper" authority to carry them out. Discarding the Virginia Plan's congressional veto, the convention implied but did not explicitly authorize a national judicial veto of state laws. The Constitution plus national laws and treaties would constitute "the supreme law of the land; and the judges in every state shall be bound thereby," Article VI declared ambiguously. Delegates drafted a long list of actions forbidden to states, including impairing contractual obligations—that is, preventing the relief of debtors. And they provided that religious tests could never be required of U.S. officeholders.

The convention placed primary responsibility for foreign affairs with a new official, the president, who was also designated commander-in-chief of the armed forces. That raised the question, unspecified in the Constitution's text, of whether the president or Congress acquired special powers in wartime. With the Senate's consent, the president could appoint judges and other federal officers. To select the president, delegates established the electoral college, whose members would be chosen in each state by legislatures or voters. If a majority of electors failed to unite behind one candidate, the House of Representatives (voting as states, not as individuals) would choose the president. The chief executive would serve for four years but be eligible for reelection.

separation of powers: The establishment of three distinct branches of government each with varying political powers.

federalism: System in which states and central governments have distinctive roles and powers.

checks and balances: A separation of powers between the various branches of government, designed to prevent one branch from dominating the others.

The key to the Constitution was the distribution of political authority—its **separation of powers** among executive, legislative, and judicial branches of the national government, and division of powers between states and nation (called **federalism**). Two-thirds of Congress and three-fourths of the states had to concur on amendments. The branches balanced one another, their powers entwined to prevent each from acting independently. The president could veto congressional legislation, but that veto could be overridden by two-thirds majorities in both houses, and his treaties and major appointments required the Senate's consent. Congress could impeach the president and federal judges, but courts would have the final say on interpreting the Constitution. These **checks and balances** would keep the government from becoming tyrannical, but at times, they prevented the government from acting quickly and decisively. Furthermore, the Constitution drew such a vague line between state and national powers that the United States fought a civil war in the next century over that issue.

The convention held its last session on September 17, 1787. Of the forty-two delegates present, only three refused to sign the Constitution, two partly because it lacked a bill of rights. Benjamin Franklin encouraged unity, admitting, "I confess that there are several parts of this constitution which I do not at present approve." Yet he urged its acceptance "because I expect no better, and because I am not sure, that it is not the best." Only then was the Constitution made public. (See the appendix for the full text of the Constitution.)

Opposition and Ratification

What were the differences between Federalists and Antifederalists in the Constitution debate?

Later the same month, the Confederation Congress submitted the Constitution to the states. The ratification clause provided for the new system to take after approval by special conventions in at least nine states. Thus the national Constitution, unlike the Articles of Confederation, would rest directly on popular authority.

As states elected delegates to the special conventions, newspaper essays and pamphlets defended or attacked the Philadelphia convention's decisions. Every newspaper in the country printed the Constitution, and most supported its adoption. Although most citizens concurred that the national government should have more power over taxation and foreign and interstate commerce, some believed the proposed government held the potential for tyranny. As happened in Carlisle, Pennsylvania, the debate frequently spilled out into the streets.

Federalists and Antifederalists

Supporters of the proposed Constitution called themselves **Federalists**. Building on classical republicanism, they envisioned a virtuous, collectivist, self-sacrificing republic led by a manly aristocracy of talent. They argued that putting good, elite men in charge of a carefully structured government would eliminate the possibility of tyranny. A republic could be large if the government's design prevented any one group from controlling it. The separation of powers among legislative, executive, and judicial branches, and the division of powers between states and nation, would accomplish that.

Federalists: The name supporters of new Constitution gave themselves during the ratification struggle.

The Federalists termed those who opposed the Constitution **Antifederalists**, thus casting them negatively. While recognizing the need for a national source of revenue, Antifederalists feared a too-powerful central government. To them, states were the protectors of individual rights; consequently, weakening the states could bring arbitrary power. Antifederalist arguments often listed potential abuses of government authority.

Antifederalists: So dubbed by the Federalists, the Antifederalists were opposed to the Constitution because they feared it gave too much power to the central government and it did not contain a bill of rights.

Heirs of the Real Whig ideology of the late 1760s and early 1770s, Antifederalists stressed the need for constant vigilance to avert oppression. Indeed, some of the Antifederalists had originally promulgated those ideas—Samuel Adams, Patrick Henry, and Richard Henry Lee led the opposition to the Constitution. Joining them were small farmers preoccupied with guarding their property against excessive taxation, backcountry Baptists and Presbyterians, and upwardly mobile men who would benefit from an economic and political system less tightly controlled than that the Constitution envisioned.

 Link to "The Federalist Papers."

Bill of Rights

Antifederalists focused on the Constitution's lack of a bill of rights. Even if the new system weakened the states, people could be protected from tyranny by specific guarantees of rights. The Constitution did contain some prohibitions on congressional power. For example, the writ of habeas corpus, which prevented arbitrary imprisonment, could not be suspended except in "cases of rebellion or invasion." But Antifederalists found such constitutional provisions to be few and inadequate. They wanted a bill of rights.

Letters of a Federal Farmer, perhaps the most widely read Antifederalist pamphlet, listed the rights that should be protected: freedom of the press and religion, trial by jury, and guarantees against unreasonable searches. From Paris, Thomas Jefferson declared, "A bill of rights is what the people are entitled to against every government on earth."

 Link to *Letters of a Federal Farmer*.

Ratification

Many states were persuaded when Federalists argued that a national government with the power to tax foreign commerce would lessen the financial burdens that had prompted Shays's Rebellion and similar protests elsewhere. Four of the first five states to ratify did so unanimously, but disagreements then surfaced. Massachusetts, where Antifederalist forces were bolstered by a backlash against the state's heavy-handed treatment of the Shays rebels, ratified by a majority of only 19 of 355 votes cast and recommended amendments

TABLE 7.1   Ratification of the Constitution by State Conventions

State	Date	Vote
Delaware	December 7, 1787	30-0
Pennsylvania	December 12, 1787	46-23
New Jersey	December 18, 1787	38-0
Georgia	January 2, 1788	26-0
Connecticut	January 9, 1788	128-40
Massachusetts	February 6, 1788	187-168
Maryland	April 28, 1788	63-11
South Carolina	May 23, 1788	149-73
New Hampshire	June 21, 1788	57-47
Virginia	June 25, 1788	89-79
New York	July 26, 1788	30-27
North Carolina	November 21, 1789	194-77
Rhode Island	May 29, 1790	34-32

identifying rights. In June 1788, when New Hampshire ratified, the requirement of nine states was satisfied. But New York and Virginia had not yet voted, and the new Constitution could not succeed without those key states.

Pro-Constitution forces won by 10 votes in the Virginia convention, which recommended adding rights specifications. In New York, James Madison, John Jay, and Alexander Hamilton, writing collectively as "Publius," published *The Federalist*, eighty-five essays explaining the theory behind the Constitution and answering critics. Their arguments, coupled with Federalists' promise to add a bill of rights, helped win the battle. On July 26, 1788, New York ratified the Constitution by just 3 votes. Although the last states—North Carolina and Rhode Island—did not join the Union until November 1789 and May 1790, respectively, the new government was a reality. (See Table 7.1 for the details of ratifying convention votes.)

Celebrating Ratification   Americans in many cities celebrated ratification with parades on July 4, 1788, linking the acceptance of the Constitution to the adoption of the Declaration of Independence. The processions dramatized the history and unity of the new nation, seeking to counteract the dissent that had engulfed such towns as Carlisle, Pennsylvania. The processions aimed to educate people about the Constitution's significance and political leaders' hopes for industry and frugality by the American public.

About five thousand people participated in the Philadelphia parade. Floats portraying such themes as "The Grand Federal Edifice" stretched for a mile and a half. More than forty groups of tradesmen sponsored floats, followed by lawyers, doctors, clergymen, and congressmen. Symbolizing the nation's future, students from the University of Pennsylvania and other schools bore a flag labeled "The Rising Generation."

The Township and Range System

Anyone flying over the American countryside west of the Appalachians today can see the township and range system inscribed on the landscape. Roads cross the land in straight lines, meeting at 90-degree angles, carving the terrain into a checkerboard. Originated in the Land Ordinance of 1785, that system organized land sales in the Northwest Territory.

English and native peoples traditionally bounded their lands by natural landmarks such as hills, streams, trees, and rock outcroppings. That system was known as *metes and bounds*. Some early settlers employed surveyors, who created lots of varying sizes divided by lines laid out abstractly on the soil. Sometimes those lines related to natural features, such as the long, narrow lots in French Canada that fronted on the St. Lawrence River.

But because North America was settled piecemeal, no one system dominated until the Land Ordinance of 1785. Thereafter, the ordinance's system became the template for the U.S. government's land distribution.

After a surveyor established an east-west baseline and a north-south meridian on a particular tract, he laid out rectangular townships composed of thirty-six numbered square-mile sections. He ignored natural features; potential buyers would learn for themselves which sections had rivers, hills, or assets like salt licks. The initial policy of selling equally priced sections gave way by 1832 to allow individuals to purchase as few as 40 acres and, after 1854, to price variations. As the United States expanded westward, the township and range system followed, democratizing access to land and opening land for settlement.

The legacy of the Land Ordinance of 1785 for the American people and nation still marks the landscape west of the Ohio River.

Summary

During the 1770s and 1780s, the nation developed an economy independent of the British and attempted to protect the national interest, defend its borders, and promote trade. Some Americans outlined artistic and educational goals for a properly virtuous people. The formulation of American racist thought was also part of the developing Union. Emphasizing race (rather than status as slave or free) as a determinant of African Americans' status allowed men who now termed themselves "white" to define republicanism to exclude most men but themselves. White women, viewed as household dependents, had a limited role in the republic, as mothers of the next generation and as selfless contributors to the nation's welfare.

In 1775, most Americans believed that "that government which governs best governs least," but by the late 1780s many changed their minds. Drafters and supporters of the Constitution concluded that a more powerful central government was needed. During ratification debates, they contended that their proposals were just as "republican" as the Articles of Confederation.

Both sides adhered to republican principles, but Federalists embraced classical republicanism, stressing the community over the individual. Antifederalists wanted a weak central government, formal protection of individual rights, and a loosely regulated economy. The Federalists won when the Constitution was adopted, however narrowly. The 1790s, the first decade under the Constitution, would witness hesitant steps toward creating a true nation, the United States of America.

Chapter Review

Creating a Virtuous Republic

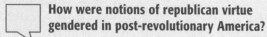

How were notions of republican virtue gendered in post-revolutionary America?

Leaders wanted the new United States to be a republican form of government, and while they debated the specifics, they agreed that in a republic, citizens were virtuous men willing to forgo personal profit for the best interests of the nation. The notion of virtue—the absence of vice or corruption—became increasingly important and inspired educational reform to help children become useful citizens. Some argued that since childrearing was women's role, they, too, would need education to help raise virtuous future citizens. Since women could not own property or participate in politics, their role was as the embodiment of self-sacrificing republicanism, using their nurturing skills to run charitable associations aiding the poor and others. This, in turn, conveyed virtue on their families and freed men to pursue their economic self-interests. The ideal republican male sought upward mobility for himself and his family, while the ideal republican woman put the needs of others first.

The First Emancipation and the Growth of Racism

What contributed to the growing number of free blacks in America after the revolution?

Slaves who escaped plantations during the war, those who served in the military, or those who had been freed by their owners or state laws accounted for many of the 60,000 free people of color in the U.S. by 1790 and 108,000 by 1800. Northern states, which were less reliant on slave labor, increasingly freed slaves and were more likely to adopt laws abolishing slavery. But even there, many states respected owners' "property rights" and preferred gradual manumission over outright abolition. In the courts, too, blacks challenged the contradictions between forced bondage and the ideology of the Revolution, and while often unsuccessful, their actions forced policymakers to grapple with this issue. Postwar economic changes also spurred manumissions, particularly in the Chesapeake, where the shift from tobacco to grain production meant far fewer slaves were required, doubling the free black population in Virginia between 1790 and 1810, for example.

Designing Republican Governments

How did Americans' former experience as British subjects influence the state governments they established?

Coming from their experience under Great Britain, Americans feared the prospect of tyranny developing in the new nation, and as such, early state constitutions sought to limit governors' power through annual elections and term limitations. They further provided little independent authority for governors while expanding that granted to legislatures, typically in a two-house structure. And states put more power in the hands of the people by redrawing election districts to reflect the population and reducing property requirements for voting. To protect citizens' rights, several states included a bill of rights guaranteeing freedom of the press, rights to fair trials, and sometimes freedom of religion even if officeholders had to be Christians. Ultimately, the emphasis on preventing tyranny made states weak politically. Subsequent revisions to state constitutions in the mid-1780s increased the power of the governor and reduced that of the legislature via a system of checks and balances.

Trials of the Confederation

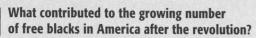

How did fears of a strong central government ultimately tie the hands of the Confederation Congress?

The Articles of Confederation limited congressional power in a number of areas that, in turn, led to financial and policy problems for the new nation. First, because of state resistance to a large central government, a much-needed customs duty was never adopted. Second, Congress's limited ability to establish a national commercial policy left it unable to take action when Britain, France, and Spain restricted American trade. Third, Congress had little power to enforce the 1783 Treaty of Paris's promises that prewar debts (owed by Americans to British merchants) would be repaid and that loyalists would be able to recover confiscated property. States passed various laws prohibiting both, which gave the British an excuse to maintain military posts on the Great Lakes. Worse, the inability to enforce the treaty hurt the republic's credibility in foreign affairs.

Order and Disorder in the West

What was the significance of the Northwest Ordinance?

One of the lasting accomplishments of the Confederation Congress, the Northwest Ordinance of 1787 effectively outlined how territory gained in the Treaty of Paris would be organized, how land could be divided and sold, how new states would be admitted to the Union, as well as the rights of people living there. It included a bill of rights guaranteeing freedom of religion and the right to a jury trial, and it forbade cruel and unusual punishments and nominally prohibited slavery. But its ban on slavery was more symbolic than actual because it did not deny slaveholders living in the territory to the right of their property and included the first fugitive slave law. Still, it discouraged slaveholders from moving into the territory and prevented slavery from taking hold on a large scale.

From Crisis to the Constitution

How did the question of slavery become linked to the new U.S. Constitution?

Slavery came into play at the Constitutional Convention as states debated how their populations should be counted in determining the number of representatives each would get in the lower house of Congress. Slave states wanted their bondspeople fully counted, while those from states with few slaves wanted only free people counted. The dispute was resolved by a formula known as the three-fifths compromise, noting that three-fifths of slaves would be included in population totals used to determine congressional districts. While the words *slave* and *slavery* are not used in the Constitution, it nonetheless included direct and indirect protections for slavery, among them assistance in putting down revolts, returning fugitive slaves to masters, and agreeing not to end the importation of bondspeople for twenty years.

Opposition and Ratification

What were the differences between Federalists and Antifederalists in the Constitution debate?

Federalists supported ratification of the Constitution and believed a strong national government led by a talented elite. Moreover, they argued that dividing power between the legislative, executive, and judicial branches, as well as between states and the nation, would prevent one faction from controlling the government or a tyrant from seizing power. Antifederalists, so dubbed by their opponents, feared a too-powerful central government and saw states as protectors of individual rights. As such, they supported state sovereignty, and while they agreed on the need for central currency and taxation, Antifederalists were concerned that the Constitution did not include a bill of rights to safeguard people's individual rights.

Suggestions for Further Reading

Richard Beeman, *Plain, Honest Men: The Making of the American Constitution* (2009)

Ira Berlin and Ronald Hoffman, eds., *Slavery and Freedom in the Age of the American Revolution* (1983)

Cathy N. Davidson, *Revolution and the Word: The Rise of the Novel in America* (1987)

Edith Gelles, *Portia: The World of Abigail Adams* (1992)

Woody Holton, *Unruly Americans and the Origins of the Constitution* (2007)

Peter S. Onuf, *Statehood and Union: A History of the Northwest Ordinance* (1987)

Jack N. Rakove, *Original Meanings: Politics and Ideas in the Making of the Constitution* (1996)

Leonard L. Richards, *Shays's Rebellion: The American Revolution's Final Battle* (2002)

David Waldstreicher, *In the Midst of Perpetual Fetes: The Making of American Nationalism, 1776–1820* (1997)

Gordon S. Wood, *The Creation of the American Republic, 1776–1787* (1969)

 Go to the CourseMate website for primary source links, study tools, and review materials for this chapter. www.cengagebrain.com

8

The Early Republic: Conflicts at Home and Abroad

1789–1800

In late 1798, wealthy Philadelphia matron Deborah Norris Logan became the target of widespread criticism. Her husband, Jefferson supporter Dr. George Logan, had undertaken a personal peace mission to France, fearing war between the United States and its former ally. When Logan's wife defended his actions, she endured a campaign unlike any experienced by an American woman. That episode suggests the political symbolism now embodied by women, the growing division between the Federalist and Republican factions, and the significance of foreign affairs in the early republic.

First to attack was the Federalist newspaper editor William Cobbett, who observed with sly sexual innuendo in his *Porcupine's Gazette* in July that "it is said that JEFFERSON went to his friend Doctor Logan's farm and spent three days there, soon after the Doctor's departure for France. *Query*: What did he do there?" Later Cobbett suggested that George and Deborah Logan should be publicly shamed—him, presumably, for treason and her, Cobbett implied, for adultery. Republican newspapers leaped to Deborah's defense, attacking the vulgarity of the suggestions about her and Vice President Jefferson.

Although initially Deborah Logan secluded herself at her country estate, on Jefferson's advice she returned to Philadelphia to prove she was "not afraid nor ashamed to meet the public eye." As reports emerged that her husband had had some success in quelling hostilities, she reveled in the praise showered on him. George Logan was enthusiastically welcomed home by Jeffersonian partisans. However, in January 1799, Congress, controlled by Federalists, adopted the so-called Logan Act—still in effect—which forbids private citizens from undertaking unauthorized diplomatic missions.

The Logan controversy was one of many battles in the 1790s. The fight over ratifying the Constitution presaged wide divisions over the major political, economic, and diplomatic questions confronting the republic: the extent to which authority should be centralized; the relationship between national power and states'

Chapter Outline

Building a Workable Government
First Congress | Bill of Rights | Executive and Judiciary | Debate over Slavery

Domestic Policy Under Washington and Hamilton
Washington's First Steps | Alexander Hamilton | National and State Debts | Hamilton's Financial Plan | First Bank of the United States | Interpreting the Constitution | Report on Manufactures | Whiskey Rebellion

The French Revolution and the Development of Partisan Politics
Republicans and Federalists | French Revolution | Edmond Genêt | Democratic Societies

Partisan Politics and Relations with Great Britain
Jay Treaty Debate | Bases of Partisanship | Washington's Farewell Address | Election of 1796

John Adams and Political Dissent
XYZ Affair | Quasi-War with France | Alien and Sedition Acts | Virginia and Kentucky Resolutions | Convention of 1800

VISUALIZING THE PAST *Newspapers of the Early Republic*

The West in the New Nation
War in the Northwest Territory | "Civilizing" the Indians | Iroquois and Cherokees

"Revolutions" at the End of the Century
Fries' Rebellion | Gabriel's Rebellion | Election of 1800

LINKS TO THE WORLD *Haitian Refugees*

LEGACY FOR A PEOPLE AND A NATION *Dissent During Wartime*

SUMMARY

rights; the formulation of foreign policy in an era of continual warfare in Europe; and the limits of dissent. Americans had not anticipated the acrimonious disagreements that rocked the 1790s or the difficulties that would develop as the United States attempted to deal with Indian nations within its borders.

Most important, Americans could not understand the division of citizens into two competing factions. In republics, they believed, the rise of such factions signified decay and corruption. Yet on numerous occasions, as with Deborah and George Logan, Federalist and Republican leaders sought to mobilize their supporters, thereby reworking the nation's political practice if not its theory. As the decade closed, Americans were still grappling with the implications of partisan politics, as evidenced by the hotly contested 1800 election.

As you read this chapter, keep the following questions in mind:

* **What major challenges confronted the new republic?**

* **What disputes divided the nation's citizens?**

* **How did Americans react to those disputes?**

Building a Workable Government

At first, consensus appeared possible. Only a few Antifederalists ran for office in 1788, and even fewer were elected. Thus, most members of the First Congress supported a strong national government. The drafters of the Constitution had deliberately left key issues undecided, so the nationalists' domination of Congress meant that their views prevailed.

> What was the purpose of the Bill of Rights?

First Congress

Congress faced four immediate tasks when it convened in April 1789: raising revenue, responding to states' calls for a bill of rights, setting up executive departments, and organizing the federal judiciary. James Madison, representing Virginia in the House of Representatives, became influential in Congress. He persuaded Congress to adopt the Revenue Act of 1789, imposing a 5 percent tariff on certain imports. Therefore, the First Congress achieved an effective national tax law.

Bill of Rights

Madison opposed additional restrictions on the national government, believing that its limited powers made a **Bill of Rights** unnecessary. But Madison subsequently changed his mind, observing to a friend that "in every Gov[ernmen]t power may oppress." When introducing nineteen proposed amendments in June, he urged fellow congressmen to respond to the people's will, noting in particular that North Carolina refused to ratify the Constitution without a Bill of Rights. After heated debates, Congress approved twelve amendments. The states ratified ten, which became part of the Constitution on December 15, 1791 (see the appendix for the Constitution and all amendments). Their adoption defused Antifederalist opposition.

The First Amendment prohibited Congress from passing any law restricting the right to freedom of religion, speech, press, peaceable assembly, or petition. The

Bill of Rights: The first ten amendments of the Constitution that guaranteed personal liberties.

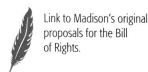

Link to Madison's original proposals for the Bill of Rights.

Chronology

1789	Washington inaugurated as first president
	Judiciary Act organizes federal court system
	French Revolution begins
1790	Hamilton's *Report on Public Credit* proposes assumption of state debts
1791	First ten amendments (Bill of Rights) ratified
	First national bank chartered
1793	France declares war on Britain, Spain, and the Netherlands
	Washington's neutrality proclamation keeps the United States out of war
	Democratic societies founded, the first grassroots political organizations
1794	Whiskey Rebellion in western Pennsylvania protests taxation
1795	Jay Treaty with England resolves issues remaining from the Revolution

	Pinckney's Treaty with Spain establishes southern boundary of the United States
	Treaty of Greenville with Miami Confederacy opens Ohio to settlement
1796	First contested presidential election: Adams elected president, Jefferson vice president
1798	XYZ affair arouses American opinion against France
	Sedition Act penalizes dissent
	Virginia and Kentucky Resolutions protest suppression of dissent
1798–99	Quasi-War with France
	Fries's Rebellion in Pennsylvania protests taxation
1800	Franco-American Convention ends Quasi-War
	Gabriel's Rebellion threatens Virginia slaveowners
1801	Thomas Jefferson elected president by the House of Representatives after stalemate in electoral college

Second Amendment guaranteed the right "to keep and bear arms," because of the need for a "well-regulated Militia." The Third Amendment limited the conditions under which troops could be quartered in private homes. The next five pertained to judicial procedures. The Fourth Amendment prohibited "unreasonable searches and seizures"; the Fifth and Sixth established the rights of accused persons; the Seventh specified the conditions for jury trials in civil (as opposed to criminal) cases; and the Eighth forbade "cruel and unusual punishments." The Ninth and Tenth Amendments reserved to the people and the states other unspecified rights and powers.

Executive and Judiciary   Congress also considered the organization of the executive branch. It agreed to continue the three administrative departments established under the Articles of Confederation: War, Foreign Affairs (renamed State), and Treasury. Congress instituted two lesser posts: the attorney general—the nation's official lawyer—and the postmaster general. Controversy arose over whether the president alone could dismiss officials whom he appointed with the Senate's consent. Ultimately, the House and Senate agreed that he had such authority. That established the principle that heads of executive departments are accountable solely to the president.

Judiciary Act of 1789:
Outlined the federal judiciary's jurisdiction and established the Supreme Court, as well as district and appellate courts.

The most far-reaching law, the **Judiciary Act of 1789**, defined the federal judiciary's jurisdiction and established a six-member Supreme Court, thirteen district courts, and three appellate courts. Its most important provision, Section 25, allowed appeals from state to federal courts when cases raised certain types of constitutional questions. It presumed that Article VI of the Constitution, which stated that federal statutes and treaties were "the supreme Law of the Land," implied the right of appeal from state to federal courts, yet the Constitution did not explicitly permit such actions. In the nineteenth century, judges and legislators committed to states' rights would challenge Section 25's constitutionality.

During its first decade, the Supreme Court handled few cases of any importance, and several members resigned. But in a 1796 decision, *Ware v. Hylton*, the Court for the first time declared a state law unconstitutional. It also reviewed the constitutionality of an act of Congress, upholding its validity in the case of *Hylton v. U.S.* The most important case of the decade, *Chisholm v. Georgia* (1793), established that states could be sued in federal courts by citizens of other states. Five years later, the Eleventh Amendment to the Constitution overturned that decision.

Debate over Slavery

Constitutional provisions forbade Congress from prohibiting the importation of slaves for twenty years, but in 1790 three Quaker groups petitioned Congress to end slavery. Legislators insisted, as they would for the next seven decades, that slavery was integral to the Union and that abolition would cause bigger problems, primarily how to deal with a sizable population of freed people.

Some northern congressmen—and Benjamin Franklin—contested the southerners' position. But Congress accepted a committee report denying it the power to halt slave importations before 1808 or emancipate slaves at any time, that authority "remaining with the several States alone."

Domestic Policy Under Washington and Hamilton

> How did the chartering of the Bank of the United States provoke an early constitutional debate?

George Washington did not seek the presidency. In 1783, he returned to Mount Vernon as a Virginia planter. But his fellow countrymen never regarded Washington as just another private citizen. Americans concurred that only George Washington had sufficient stature to serve as the republic's first president, an office designed with him in mind. The unanimous vote of the electoral college formalized that consensus. Washington could not ignore his country's call and headed to New York City, the nation's capital.

Washington's First Steps

Washington acted cautiously during his first months in office in 1789, knowing he would set precedents. When the title by which he should be addressed aroused controversy (Vice President John Adams favored "His Highness, the President of the United States of America, and Protector of their Liberties"), Washington said nothing. The accepted title soon became simply "Mr. President." By using the heads of executive departments as chief advisers, he created the cabinet. Washington also exercised his veto power over congressional legislation sparingly—only if he thought a bill was unconstitutional.

Washington's first major task was to choose the heads of the executive departments. For the War Department, he selected Henry Knox of Massachusetts, who was his artillery general during the war. For the State Department, he selected fellow

Alexander Hamilton: Secretary of Treasury under President George Washington.

Virginian Thomas Jefferson, who had been minister to France. For secretary of the treasury, the president chose the brilliant, ambitious **Alexander Hamilton**.

Alexander Hamilton

The illegitimate son of a Scottish aristocrat and a woman whose husband had divorced her for adultery and desertion, Hamilton was born in the British West Indies in 1757. His early years were spent in poverty, working as a mercantile clerk after his mother's death when he was eleven. In 1773, with financial support from friends, Hamilton enrolled at King's College (later Columbia University). Eighteen months later the seventeen-year-old contributed a pamphlet to the prerevolutionary publication wars. A devoted patriot, Hamilton volunteered for the American army, where in 1777 Washington appointed him as an aide, and they developed great mutual affection.

At twenty-three, Hamilton wed Elizabeth Schuyler, daughter of a wealthy New York family. After the war, he practiced law in New York City and served as a delegate to the Annapolis Convention and the Constitutional Convention. His contributions to *The Federalist* in 1788 revealed him as one of the republic's chief political thinkers.

As treasury secretary and presidential adviser, Hamilton's primary loyalty lay with the nation. Caribbean-born, Hamilton had no natal ties to any state; he neither sympathized with nor fully understood demands for local autonomy. His fiscal policies aimed at consolidating national power, and he favored close ties with Britain.

Second, Hamilton cynically believed people to be motivated by economic self-interest. This set him apart from those Americans who believed public-spirited citizens would pursue the common good rather than private advantage. Hamilton's beliefs influenced the way he tackled the new nation's tangled finances.

National and State Debts

Congress ordered the new treasury secretary to assess the public debt. The country's war debts fell into three categories: those owed by the nation to foreign governments and investors, mostly to France (about $11 million); those owed by the national government to merchants, soldiers, revolutionary bondholders (about $27 million); and, finally, debts owed by state governments (roughly $25 million). On the national debt, Americans recognized that, if their new government was to succeed, it would have to repay financial obligations incurred while winning independence.

State debts were another matter. Some states—notably, Virginia, Maryland, North Carolina, and Georgia—had already paid off most war debts by levying taxes and handing out land grants in lieu of money. They opposed taxing their citizens so the national government could assume other states' debts. Massachusetts, Connecticut, and South Carolina still had sizable unpaid debts and welcomed national assumption. Consolidating state debt in the hands of the national government would help concentrate power at the national level.

National Portrait Gallery, Smithsonian Institution

Alexander Hamilton, by James Sharpless, about 1796. This profile of Hamilton, painted near the end of Washington's presidency, shows the secretary of the treasury as he looked during the years of his first heated partisan battles with Thomas Jefferson and James Madison.

Hamilton's Financial Plan

In his first **Report on Public Credit** in January 1790, Hamilton proposed that Congress assume outstanding state debts, combine them with national obligations, and issue new securities covering principal and accumulated unpaid interest. Hamilton hoped to ensure that holders of the public debt—many of them wealthy merchants and speculators—had a financial stake in the new government's survival. Opposition coalesced around James Madison, whose state of Virginia had mostly eliminated its war debt and who wanted to avoid rewarding wealthy speculators who purchased debt certificates at a small fraction of their value from needy veterans and farmers.

The House initially rejected the assumption of state debts, but the Senate adopted Hamilton's plan largely intact. Compromises followed, linking the assumption bill to another controversial issue: location of the permanent national capital. Deals were struck. A southern site on the Potomac River became the capital, and the first part of Hamilton's program became law in August 1790.

Report on Public Credit: Hamilton's plan to ensure that wealthy merchants, who held the public debt, would be linked to the government's financial survival.

First Bank of the United States

Four months later, Hamilton submitted to Congress a second report on public credit, recommending the chartering of a national bank modeled on the Bank of England. The Bank of the United States, to be chartered for twenty years, was to be capitalized at $10 million. Just $2 million would come from public funds; private investors supplied the rest. The bank would act as collecting and disbursing agent for the Treasury, and its notes would become the nation's currency. But another issue loomed: did the Constitution give Congress the power to establish such a bank?

Interpreting the Constitution

James Madison thought not. He pointed out that Constitutional Convention delegates rejected a clause authorizing Congress to issue corporate charters. President Washington sought other opinions. Attorney General Edmund Randolph and Secretary of State Thomas Jefferson agreed with Madison. Jefferson referred to Article I, Section 8, of the Constitution, which gave Congress the power "to make all Laws which shall be necessary and proper." The key word, Jefferson argued, was *necessary*: Congress could do what was needed, but not what was merely desirable. Thus, Jefferson formulated the strict-constructionist interpretation of the Constitution.

Hamilton's *Defense of the Constitutionality of the Bank*, presented in February 1791, expounded a broad-constructionist view of the Constitution. Hamilton argued that Congress could choose any means not specifically prohibited by the Constitution to achieve a constitutional end. He reasoned if the end was constitutional and the means was not *un*constitutional, then the means was constitutional.

Washington concurred, and the bill became law. The bank proved successful, as did the debt program. The new nation's securities became desirable investments for citizens and wealthy foreigners, especially those in the Netherlands. The influx of capital, coupled with the high prices that American grain now commanded in European markets, eased farmers' debt burdens and contributed to a new prosperity.

Report on Manufactures

In December 1791, Hamilton presented to Congress his *Report on Manufactures*, his third and final prescription for the American economy. Hamilton argued that the nation could never be truly independent as long as it relied heavily on Europe for manufactured goods. He urged Congress to promote the immigration of technicians and laborers and to support industrial development through limited use of protective tariffs. Many of Hamilton's ideas were implemented in later decades, but congressmen in 1791 believed that America's future lay in agriculture and the carrying trade. Congress rejected the report.

That year, Congress tried another of Hamilton's suggestions—an excise tax on whiskey distilled within the United States. Although proceeds from the Revenue Act of 1789 covered the interest on the national debt, the national government required additional income to fund state debts. A tax on whiskey affected few westerners—farmers who grew corn and large distillers who turned it into whiskey—and might also reduce whiskey consumption of whiskey. (Eighteenth-century Americans, notorious for their heavy drinking, consumed about twice as much alcohol per capita as today's rate.) Moreover, western farmers and distillers were Jefferson's supporters, and Hamilton saw the benefits of taxing them rather his merchant supporters.

Whiskey Rebellion

News of the tax sparked protests in the west, where residents were upset that the government that protected them inadequately from Indian attacks was now proposing to tax them disproportionately. Unrest continued for two years on the frontiers of Pennsylvania, Maryland, and Virginia. Large groups drafted petitions protesting the tax, deliberately imitated 1760s' crowd actions, and occasionally harassed tax collectors.

President Washington maintained restraint until violence erupted in July 1794, when western Pennsylvania farmers resisted two excise tax collectors. When about seven thousand rebels convened on August 1 to plot the destruction of Pittsburgh, Washington acted to prevent a repeat of Shays's Rebellion. On August 7, he told insurgents to disperse and summoned nearly thirteen thousand militiamen. By the time federal forces marched westward in October and November, the disturbances ceased. Troops met no resistance and arrested only twenty suspects. Two men were convicted of treason, but Washington pardoned both. The importance of the **Whiskey Rebellion** lay in the forceful message it conveyed. The national government, Washington had demonstrated, would not allow violent resistance to its laws. In the republic, people dissatisfied with laws should try to peacefully amend or repeal them.

Whiskey Rebellion: Tax protest by western farmers that turned violent. Washington's response, sending in troops, demonstrated that only peaceful protests would be tolerated in a republic.

The French Revolution and the Development of Partisan Politics

Why did U.S. leaders find the rise of political factions disturbing?

By 1794, some Americans were beginning to seek change through electoral politics. In a monarchy, formal opposition groups called factions were expected. In a government of the people, however, sustained factional disagreement was considered a sign of corruption. Still, that did not halt partisanship.

Republicans and Federalists

Jefferson and Madison became convinced as early as 1792 that Hamilton's policies favoring wealthy commercial interests at the expense of agriculture would eventually impose a corrupt government on the United States. Characterizing themselves as the true heirs of the Revolution, they charged Hamilton with plotting to subvert republican principles and called themselves and their followers Republicans. Hamilton likewise accused

Jefferson and Madison of attempting to destroy the republic. Hamilton and his supporters called themselves Federalists to link themselves with the Constitution. Newspapers aligned with the two sides published attacks on political opponents.

Washington tried to remain aloof from the political dispute dividing his chief advisers. The growing controversy persuaded him to promote political unity by seeking office again in 1792. But beginning in 1793, developments in foreign affairs magnified the disagreements, for France (America's wartime ally) and Great Britain (America's most important trading partner) resumed the periodic hostilities that originated a century earlier.

French Revolution   In 1789, many Americans welcomed the news of the French Revolution. The French people's success in overthrowing an oppressive monarchy enabled Americans to see themselves as the vanguard of an inevitable trend that would reshape the world in republican terms. By 1793, violence in France continued, and political leaders rapidly succeeded each other. Executions mounted; the king was beheaded early that year. Although many Americans, including Jefferson and Madison, retained sympathy for the revolution, others—among them Alexander Hamilton—cited France as a prime example of the perversion of republicanism.

Debates within the United States intensified when the newly republican France became enmeshed in conflict with other European nations. Seeking to keep neighboring monarchies from intervening and hoping to spread republicanism, French

Erich Lessing/Art Resource, NY

The violence of the French Revolution, especially the guillotining of King Louis XVI, shocked Americans, causing many to question whether the United States should remain that nation's ally.

leaders declared war on Austria and then, in 1793, on Britain, Spain, and Holland. That confronted the Americans with a dilemma. The 1778 Treaty of Alliance with France bound them as allies "forever." Yet the United States was connected to Great Britain through a shared history, language, and renewed economic ties. Americans still purchased most of their manufactured goods from Great Britain and, because U.S. revenues depended heavily on import tariffs, the nation's economic health required uninterrupted trade with England.

Edmond Genêt

Edmond Genêt: French minister to the United States.

The situation intensified in April 1793, when **Edmond Genêt**, a representative of the French government, arrived in Charleston, South Carolina. Genêt's arrival made President Washington wonder. Should he receive Genêt, thus officially recognizing the French revolutionary government? Or should he proclaim neutrality?

Washington resolved his dilemma by receiving Genêt but also issuing a proclamation that the United States would adopt "a conduct friendly and impartial toward the belligerent powers." Federalist newspapers defended the proclamation, while Republicans only reluctantly accepted the enormously popular neutrality policy.

Genêt's faction fell from power in Paris, and he sought political asylum in the United States. But the domestic divisions Genêt helped to widen were perpetuated by clubs called Democratic societies, formed by Americans sympathetic to the French Revolution and worried about the Washington administration.

Democratic Societies

More than forty Democratic societies organized between 1793 and 1800. Members saw themselves as seeking the same goal as the 1760s resistance movement: protecting people's liberties against encroachments by corrupt and self-serving rulers. They protested government fiscal and foreign policy, repeatedly proclaiming their belief in "the equal rights of man," particularly free speech, free press, and free assembly. Like the Sons of Liberty, the Democratic societies comprised chiefly artisans and craftsmen, although professionals, farmers, and merchants also joined. They allied with congressional Republicans.

The rapid spread of citizens' groups outspokenly critical of the administration disturbed Hamilton and Washington. Calling them dangerously subversive, the groups' "real design," a Federalist newspaper asserted, was "to involve the country in war, to assume the reins of government and tyrannize over the people." The counterattack climaxed in the fall of 1794, when Washington accused the societies of fomenting the Whiskey Rebellion. As the first organized political dissenters in the United States, Democratic societies alarmed officials, who had not yet accepted the idea that one component of a free government was organized loyal opposition.

Partisan Politics and Relations with Great Britain

What fueled the growing partisanship in the new republic at the end of the eighteenth century?

In 1794, George Washington dispatched Chief Justice John Jay to London to negotiate unresolved questions in Anglo-American relations. The United States wanted to establish freedom of the seas and to assert its right, as a neutral nation, to trade freely with both combatants. Further, Great Britain still held posts in the American Northwest, thus violating the 1783 peace treaty. Settlers there believed the British were responsible for renewed warfare with neighboring Indians. Americans also wanted a commercial treaty and sought compensation for the slaves who left with the British army after the war.

Jay Treaty Debate   The negotiations proved difficult. Britain agreed to evacuate the western forts and ease restrictions on American trade to England and the Caribbean. The treaty established two arbitration commissions—one to deal with prewar debts Americans owed to British creditors and the other to hear claims for captured American merchant ships—but Britain refused slaveowners compensation for lost bondspeople. Most Americans, including the president, expressed dissatisfaction with some treaty clauses.

The Senate debated the **Jay Treaty** in secret, and the public only learned of its provisions after ratification in late June 1795. Protests followed; newspaper essays and popular gatherings urged Washington to reject the treaty. Southern planters criticized the lack of compensation for runaway slaves and objected to the commission on prewar debts, which might make them pay obligations dating back to the 1760s. Federalists countered with their own meetings and essays, contending that the Jay Treaty would prove preferable to no treaty at all. The president signed the pact in mid-August. One opportunity remained to prevent it from taking effect: Congress had to appropriate funds and, according to the Constitution, appropriation bills had to originate in the House of Representatives.

Washington delayed submitting the treaty to the House until March 1796, futilely hoping the opposition would have dissipated. During the debate, Republicans argued against the appropriations, and they asked Washington to give the House all negotiations documents. In resisting the request, Washington established a power still used today—executive privilege, in which the president may withhold information from Congress if he deems it necessary.

The treaty's opponents initially commanded a congressional majority, but soon pressure mounted for appropriating the necessary funds, fostered by a Federalist campaign targeting middle-state congressmen whose districts would benefit from approval. Petitions contended that failure to fund the treaty would lead to war with Britain, thus endangering Pennsylvania frontier settlements and New York and New Jersey commercial interests. Further, Federalists linked the Jay Treaty with the more popular **Pinckney's Treaty**. In 1795, Thomas Pinckney of South Carolina negotiated a treaty with Spain giving the United States navigation privileges on the Mississippi River and the right to land and store goods at New Orleans tax free. The overwhelming support for Pinckney's Treaty helped to overcome opposition to the Jay Treaty. In late April, the House appropriated the money by 51 to 48. The vote divided along partisan and regional lines: all but two southerners opposed the treaty; all but three congressional Federalists supported it; and a majority of middle-state representatives voted yes.

The Federalists' campaign to sway public opinion ironically violated their fundamental philosophy of government—that ordinary people should defer to the judgment of elected leaders. The Federalists had won the battle, but in the long run they lost the war, for Republicans proved more effective in appealing to the citizenry.

Jay Treaty: Pact that sought to resolve mounting tensions between Britain and the United States in the years after the Revolution. Britain agreed to relinquish control of its western U.S. posts, establish commissions to receive claims for ships damaged by British seizures, and broaden U.S. access to trade with the West and British.

Pinckney's Treaty: Also called the Treaty of San Lorenzo, it won westerners the right of duty-free access to New Orleans and the use of the Mississippi River for commerce.

Bases of Partisanship

The terms used by Jefferson and Madison (the people versus aristocrats) or by Hamilton and Washington (true patriots versus subversive rabble) do not adequately explain growing divisions in the electorate. Differences between agrarian and commercial interests do not cover it either, as more than 90 percent of Americans lived in rural areas. Nor did the divisions in the 1790s simply repeat the Federalist-Antifederalist debate of 1787–1788. Although most Antifederalists became Republicans, the party's leaders, Madison and Jefferson, had supported the Constitution.

Republicans, especially prominent in the southern and middle states, were confident and optimistic about politics and the economy. Southern planters foresaw a prosperous future based partly on westward expansion, which they expected to dominate. Republicans employed democratic rhetoric to win over small farmers south of New England and ethnic groups—especially Irish, Scots, and Germans. Artisans also joined the coalition. Republicans emphasized developing America's resources and remained sympathetic to France.

Federalists, concentrated among the commercial interests of New England, came mostly from English stock. They stressed the need for order, hierarchy, and obedience to authority. Wealthy New England merchants aligned with the Federalists, as did the region's farmers who, prevented from expanding production because of New England's poor soil, gravitated toward the more conservative party. To Federalist eyes, potential enemies—internal and external—threatened the nation, necessitating a protective alliance with Great Britain. Given the dangers posed by European warfare, Federalists' vision of international affairs may have been accurate. But because Federalists offered little hope of a better future, Republicans ultimately prevailed.

Washington's Farewell Address

After the treaty debate, wearied by criticism, George Washington decided to retire. In September, Washington published his Farewell Address, most of which Hamilton wrote. In it Washington outlined two principles that guided American foreign policy until the late 1940s: to maintain commercial but not political ties to other nations and to enter no permanent alliances. He also stressed America's uniqueness—its exceptionalism—and the need for independent action in foreign affairs, today called unilateralism.

Some interpret Washington's desire to end partisan strife as a call for politicians to consider the good of the whole nation. But given the impending presidential election, the Farewell Address appears as an attack on the Republican opposition. Washington advocated unity behind the Federalist banner. Both Federalists and Republicans saw themselves as the true heirs of the Revolution and perceived their opponents as misguided, unpatriotic troublemakers.

election of 1796: Federalist John Adams won by three votes and, as the second-highest vote-getter in the electoral college, Thomas Jefferson became vice president.

Election of 1796

The presidential **election of 1796** saw the first serious contest for the position. Federalists in Congress put forward Vice President John Adams, with the diplomat Thomas Pinckney as his running mate. Congressional Republicans chose Thomas Jefferson as their presidential candidate; the lawyer, Revolutionary War veteran, and politician Aaron Burr of New York ran for vice president.

Most state legislatures appointed electors, and the method of voting in the electoral college did not account for the possibility of party slates. The Constitution's drafters had not foreseen the development of competing political organizations, so there was no way to support one person for president and another for vice president. The electors voted for two people. The man with the highest total became president; the second highest, vice president.

That procedure was the Federalists' undoing. Adams won the presidency with 71 votes, but Jefferson won 68 votes, 9 more than Pinckney, to become vice president. The incoming administration was thus politically divided. The president and vice president, once allies, became bitter enemies.

John Adams and Political Dissent

As president, John Adams never abandoned an outdated notion that the president should be above politics and factionalism. Thus, Adams kept Washington's cabinet intact, despite its key members' allegiance to his chief Federalist rival, Alexander Hamilton. Adams was often passive, letting others (usually Hamilton) lead when he should have. But Adams's detachment did enable him to weather the greatest international crisis yet: the Quasi-War with France.

> What was the underlying purpose of the Alien and Sedition Acts of 1798?

XYZ Affair

The Jay Treaty improved America's relationship with Great Britain, but it provoked France to retaliate by ordering its ships to seize American vessels carrying British goods. In response, Congress authorized ship building and stockpiling weapons and ammunition. President Adams also sent three commissioners to Paris to negotiate a settlement. For months, the commissioners sought talks with Talleyrand, the French foreign minister, but Talleyrand's agents demanded a bribe of $250,000 first. The Americans refused. Adams informed Congress of the impasse and recommended increases in defense appropriations.

Convinced that Adams deliberately sabotaged negotiations, congressional Republicans insisted that the dispatches be turned over to Congress. Adams complied, aware that releasing the reports would work to his advantage. He withheld only the names of the French agents, referring to them as X, Y, and Z. The revelation that the Americans were treated with contempt stimulated anti-French sentiment in the United States and became known as the **XYZ Affair**. Cries for war resounded. Congress abrogated the Treaty of Alliance and authorized American ships to seize French vessels.

XYZ Affair: French demand for bribes from American negotiators that triggered great anger.

Quasi-War with France

Thus began an undeclared war with France fought in Caribbean waters between warships of the U.S. Navy and French privateers. Although Americans initially suffered heavy merchant shipping losses, by early 1799 the U.S. Navy established its superiority. Its ships captured eight French privateers and naval vessels, easing the threat to America's vital Caribbean trade.

Republicans, who opposed war and sympathized with France, could not quell anti-French feelings. Because Agent Y boasted of a "French party in America," Federalists accused Republicans of traitorous designs. A New York newspaper declared that anyone who remained "lukewarm" after reading the XYZ dispatches "must have a soul black enough to be fit for treason Strategems and spoils."

Alien and Sedition Acts

Now that the country seemed to see the truth of what Federalists argued since the Whiskey Rebellion in 1794—that Republicans were subversive foreign agents—Federalists sought to codify that belief into law. In 1798, the Federalist-controlled Congress adopted four laws known as the **Alien and Sedition Acts**, intended to suppress dissent and to prevent further growth of the Republican faction.

Three of the acts targeted recently arrived immigrants, whom Federalists accurately suspected of sympathizing with Republicans. The Naturalization Act lengthened the residency period required for citizenship and ordered resident aliens to register with the federal government. The two Alien Acts provided for the detention of enemy aliens in wartime and gave the president authority to deport any alien he deemed dangerous to national security.

The fourth statute, the Sedition Act, outlawed conspiracies to prevent enforcement of federal laws, punishable by five years in prison and a $5,000 fine. And writing, printing, or uttering "false, scandalous and malicious" statements against the government or the president "with intent to defame…or to bring them or either of them, into contempt or disrepute" became a crime punishable by up to two years' imprisonment and a fine of $2,000. Today, a law punishing speech alone would be unconstitutional. But in the eighteenth century, when organized political opposition was suspect, many Americans supported the Sedition Act's free speech restrictions.

The Sedition Act led to fifteen indictments and ten guilty verdicts. Among those convicted were a congressman and former newspaper editor, Matthew Lyon of Vermont; and James Callender, a Scots immigrant and scandalmonger, whose exposés forced Alexander Hamilton to acknowledge an extramarital affair. After turning his attention to President Adams, Callender was convicted, fined, and jailed for nine months. Republican newspaper editors nevertheless continued their criticisms of Federalists, energized rather than quashed by the persecution.

Virginia and Kentucky Resolutions

Jefferson and Madison combated the acts in another way. Petitioning the Federalist-controlled Congress to repeal the laws would fail, and Federalist judges refused to allow accused individuals to question the Sedition Act's constitutionality. Accordingly, the Republican leaders turned to the state legislatures. Concealing their role to avoid being indicted for sedition, Jefferson and Madison drafted resolutions that were introduced into the Kentucky and Virginia legislatures in the fall of 1798. Because a compact among the states created the Constitution, the resolutions contended, people speaking through their states had a right to judge the constitutionality of federal measures. Both pronounced the Alien and Sedition Acts unconstitutional, and thus advanced the doctrine later known as nullification.

Although they stood alone, the **Virginia and Kentucky Resolutions** had considerable influence. First, they placed the opposition party in the revolutionary tradition of resistance to tyrannical authority. Second, their theory of union inspired the Hartford Convention of 1814 and southern states' rights advocates in the 1830s and thereafter. Jefferson and Madison identified a key constitutional issue: How far could states go in opposing the national government? The question would not be definitively answered until the Civil War.

Alien and Sedition Acts: A series of laws passed in 1789 under the label of national security but that were intended to suppress dissent and block the rise of the Republican faction.

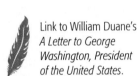

Link to William Duane's *A Letter to George Washington, President of the United States*.

Link to the Virginia and Kentucky Resolutions.

Virginia and Kentucky Resolutions: Jefferson's and Madison's response to the Alien and Sedition Acts. The Resolution stressed states' rights and the power of nullification in response to Alien and Sedition Acts.

Newspapers of the Early Republic

In the 1790s newspaper editors and publishers, unlike today, did not attempt to present news objectively, and indeed, none of their readers expected them to do so. Instead, newspapers were linked to the rapidly expanding political factions of the new nation—the partisan groupings (not yet political parties in the modern sense) terming themselves *Federalists* and *Republicans*. The "official" paper of the Federalists was *The Gazette of the United States* (colonial papers supported by individual governments too had been called *gazettes*—just as the London Gazette was tied to the English government). Among the Republicans' many allied newspapers was *The New-York Journal, and Patriotic Register*. A reader comparing the front pages of two randomly selected issues could see at a glance the differences between the two. *The Gazette of the United States* filled its first page with sober news articles, whereas the face *The New-York Journal* presented to the world was consumed entirely with advertisements, some headed by intriguing design elements. Which would appeal more directly to America's artisans and forward-thinking agriculturalists: the dull newsprint of the Federalists, or the eye-catching ads of the Republicans?

Convention of 1800   Federalists split over France. Hamilton and his supporters called for a declaration legitimizing the undeclared naval war. Adams, though, received private signals—among them George Logan's report—that the French government regretted its treatment of the American commissioners.

Adams dispatched William Vans Murray to Paris to negotiate with Napoleon Bonaparte, France's new leader. The United States sought compensation for ships France had seized since 1793 and abrogation of the treaty of 1778. The Convention of 1800, which ended the Quasi-War, provided the latter but not the former. Still, it freed the United States to follow the independent diplomatic course George Washington urged in his Farewell Address.

The West in the New Nation

How did the new nation begin to expand its boundaries westward?

By the end of the eighteenth century, the nation added three states (Vermont, Kentucky, and Tennessee) and more than 1 million people to the nearly 4 million in the 1790 census. It also nominally controlled the land east of the Mississippi River and north of Spanish Florida. Control of the land north of the Ohio River was achieved only after considerable bloodshed, for the land was dominated by a powerful western confederacy of eight Indian nations led by the Miamis.

War in the Northwest Territory   General Arthur St. Clair, first governor of the Northwest Territory, futilely tried to open more land to settlement through failed treaty negotiations with the western confederacy in early 1789. Subsequently, Little Turtle, the confederacy's war chief, defeated forces led by General Josiah Harmar (1790) and by St. Clair (1791) in battles near the present Indiana and Ohio border. More than six hundred of St. Clair's men died, and more were wounded, in the United States' worst defeat in frontier history.

In 1793, the Miami Confederacy declared that peace would come only if the United States recognized the Ohio River as its northwestern boundary. But the national government refused. A reorganized army under the Revolutionary War hero General Anthony Wayne defeated the confederacy in August 1794 at the Battle of Fallen Timbers (near present-day Toledo, Ohio). Negotiating successfully with the confederacy was crucial for the new nation, because otherwise warfare would continue as American settlers continued west. The United States lacked the resources for a prolonged frontier conflict, so Wayne reached an agreement with the confederacy in August 1795.

The resulting Treaty of Greenville gave the United States the right to settle much of what was to become Ohio. Indians received the acknowledgment they had long sought: American recognition of their rights to the soil. At Greenville, the United States formally accepted the principle of Indian sovereignty, by virtue of residence, over lands native peoples had not ceded. Never again would the U.S. government claim that it acquired Indian territory solely through negotiation with a European or North American country.

Pinckney's Treaty with Spain that year established the 31st parallel as the boundary between the United States and Florida. Spanish influence in the Old Southwest raised questions about the loyalty of American settlers in the region, much of it still unceded and occupied by Creeks, Cherokees, and other Indians. A Southwest Ordinance (1790) attempted to organize the territory; by permitting slavery, it made the region attractive to slaveholders.

"Civilizing" the Indians

Even Indian peoples who lived independent of federal authority came within the orbit of U.S. influence. The nation's stated goal was to "civilize" them. Henry Knox, secretary of war, contended in 1789 that the government should "impart our knowledge of cultivation and the arts to the aboriginals of the country." The first step, Knox suggested, should be to introduce to Indian peoples "a love for exclusive property" by giving livestock to individual Indians. The **Indian Trade and Intercourse Act of 1793** codified Knox's plan, promising that the federal government would supply Indians with animals and agricultural implements, and instructors.

The plan incorrectly posited that Indians' traditional commitment to communal landowning could be overcome, and it ignored their centuries-long agricultural experience. Policymakers focused on Indian men: because they hunted, male Indians were "savages" who should be "civilized" by learning to farm. That women tradi-

Indian Trade and Intercourse Act of 1793: Series of U.S. laws that attempted to "civilize" Indians according to European American standards.

In 1805, an unidentified artist painted Benjamin Hawkins, a trader and U.S. agent to the Indians of the Southeast, at the Creek agency near Macon, Georgia. Hawkins introduced European-style agriculture to the Creeks, who are shown here with vegetables from their fields. Throughout the eastern United States, Indian nations had to make similar adaptations of their traditional lifestyles in order to maintain their group identity.

Greenville County Museum of Art

tionally farmed was irrelevant because, to officials, Indian women—like those of European descent—should confine themselves to child rearing, household chores, and home manufacturing.

Iroquois and Cherokees The Iroquois Confederacy was devastated by the war. Restricted to small reservations increasingly surrounded by Anglo-American farmlands, men could no longer hunt and often spent their days in idle carousing. Quaker missionaries started a demonstration farm among the Senecas to teach men to plow, but women showed greater interest. The same was true among the Cherokees of Georgia. As their southern hunting territories were reduced, Cherokee men did begin to raise cattle and hogs, but they startled reformers by treating livestock like wild game, allowing the animals to run free and shooting them when needed. Men also started to plow the fields, although Cherokee women continued to handle cultivation and harvest.

Iroquois men became more receptive to the Quakers' lessons after the spring of 1799, when a Seneca named Handsome Lake experienced some remarkable visions. Like earlier prophets, Handsome Lake preached that Indian peoples should renounce alcohol, gambling, and other destructive European customs. He directed followers to reorient men's and women's work assignments as the Quakers advocated, as he recognized that only by adopting the European sexual division of labor could the Iroquois retain an autonomous existence.

"Revolutions" at the End of the Century

What gave rise to new potential revolutions in America at the end of the eighteenth century?

Three events at the end of the eighteenth century were real or potential revolutions: Fries's Rebellion, Gabriel's Rebellion, and the election of Thomas Jefferson. Each mirrored the tensions and uncertainties of the young republic. The Fries rebels resisted national authority to tax. Gabriel and his followers challenged the slave system crucial to the Chesapeake economy. And the venomous presidential election of 1800 exposed a structural flaw in the Constitution that had to be corrected.

Fries's Rebellion The tax resistance named for Revolutionary War veteran John Fries arose among German American farmers in Pennsylvania's Lehigh Valley in 1798–1799. To finance the Quasi-War, Congress enacted taxes on land, houses, and legal documents. German Americans, imbued with revolutionary ideals (at least two-fifths were veterans), regarded the taxes as a threat to their liberties and livelihoods. Asserting a right of resistance to unconstitutional laws, they raised liberty poles, signed petitions to Congress, and nonviolently prevented assessors from evaluating their homes. A federal judge ordered the arrest of twenty resisters. In response, in March 1799 Fries led 120 militiamen to Bethlehem, where they surrounded a tavern temporarily housing the prisoners. Fearing a violent confrontation, a federal marshal let the men go. Fries and many of his neighbors were tried; he and two others were convicted of treason; thirty-two more, of violating the Sedition Act. Although Fries and the other "traitors" were sentenced to hang, Adams pardoned them two days before their scheduled execution. Still, the region's residents remained, Republican partisans.

Gabriel's Rebellion

Like their white compatriots, African Americans became familiar with concepts of liberty and equality during the Revolution. They, too, witnessed the benefits of fighting collectively for freedom. Buoyed by news of the successful slave revolt in St. Domingue in 1793, Gabriel, an enslaved Virginia blacksmith, planned the second end-of-the-century revolution.

For months, Gabriel visited Sunday services at black Baptist and Methodist congregations, where bondspeople gathered free of their owners. Gabriel first recruited other skilled African Americans who like himself lived in semi-freedom under minimal supervision. Next, he enlisted rural slaves. The rebels planned to attack Richmond on the night of August 30, 1800; set fire to the city; seize the state capitol; and capture the governor, James Monroe. At that point, Gabriel believed, other slaves and poor whites would join in.

Heavy rain forced a postponement. Several planters then learned of the plot. Gabriel avoided arrest for weeks, but militia troops apprehended and interrogated other rebel leaders. Twenty-six rebels, including Gabriel, were hanged. Ironically, only slaves who betrayed their fellows won freedom as a result of the rebellion.

At his trial, one of Gabriel's followers told his judges that, like George Washington, "I have adventured my life in endeavouring to obtain the liberty of my countrymen, and am a willing sacrifice in their cause." Southern state legislatures responded by increasing the severity of slave laws. Talk of emancipation ceased in the South, and slavery became more firmly entrenched.

Election of 1800

The third end-of-the-century revolution was a Republican "takeover"—the election of Thomas Jefferson as president and a Congress dominated by Republicans. Prior to November 1800, Federalists and Republicans campaigned for congressional seats and maneuvered to control the electoral college. Both sides wanted to avoid reproducing the divided results of 1796. Republicans again nominated Thomas Jefferson and Aaron Burr; Federalists named John Adams, with Charles Cotesworth Pinckney of South Carolina as vice president. The network of Republican newspapers forged in the fires of Sedition Act prosecutions vigorously promoted the Jeffersonian cause. Jefferson and Burr had tied with 73, while Adams had 64 and Pinckney 63. Under the Constitution, the election had to be decided in the existing House of Representatives.

Balloting lasted six days; in the end, a deal was struck that gave Jefferson the presidency on the thirty-sixth ballot. A crucial consequence of the election was the adoption of the Twelfth Amendment, which provided that electors would henceforth cast separate ballots for president and vice president.

The defeated Federalists turned to strengthening their hold on the judiciary. President Adams named his secretary of state, John Marshall, chief justice; his thirty-four years of service left a lasting imprint on constitutional interpretation. Adams spent his last hours in office on March 3, 1801, appointing so-called midnight justices to positions created in the hastily adopted Judiciary Act of 1801. Federalists thus hoped to prevent Jefferson from exerting immediate influence on the judicial branch.

Links to the World

Haitian Refugees

Less than a decade after winning independence, the United States confronted its first immigration crisis. Among the approximately 600,000 residents of St. Domingue in the early 1790s, about 100,000 were free people, almost all of them slaveowners; half were whites, the rest mulattos. When after the French Revolution those free mulattos sought greater social and political equality, slaves seized the opportunity to revolt. By 1793, they triumphed, led by former slave, Toussaint L'Ouverture. In 1804, they ousted the French, establishing the republic of Haiti. Thousands of whites and mulattos, accompanied by as many slaves as they could transport, sought asylum in the United States.

American political leaders nonetheless feared the consequences of their arrival. Southern plantation owners worried that slaves so familiar with ideas of freedom and equality would mingle with their bondspeople. Many were uncomfortable with the immigration of numerous free people of color. Most southern states adopted laws forbidding the entry of Haitian slaves and free mulattos, but they were difficult to enforce, as was a similar congressional act. More than fifteen thousand refugees—white, black, and mixed-race—flooded into the United States and Spanish Louisiana. Many ended up in Virginia or Charleston, Savannah, and New Orleans.

In New Orleans and Charleston, the influx of mulattos aroused a heightened color consciousness that placed light-skinned people at the top of a hierarchy of people of color. After the United States purchased Louisiana in 1803, the number of free people of color there almost doubled in three years, largely because of a final surge of immigration from Haiti. In Virginia, the Haitian revolt inspired slaves in 1800 to plan the incident now known as Gabriel's Rebellion.

The Haitian refugees thus linked European-Americans and African Americans to events in the West Indies.

Louisiana State Museum

A free woman of color in Louisiana early in the nineteenth century, possibly one of the refugees from Haiti. Esteban Rodriguez Mir, named governor of Spanish Louisiana in 1782, ordered all slave and free black women to wear head wraps rather than hats—which were reserved for whites—but this woman and many others subverted his order by nominally complying, but nevertheless creating elaborate headdresses.

Dissent During Wartime

The Quasi-War with France in 1798 and 1799 brought the first attempt to suppress dissent. By criminalizing dissenting speech, the Sedition Act of 1798 tried to quiet the Republicans' criticism of the war and President John Adams. Fifteen men were indicted and ten fined and jailed (including a congressman) after being convicted under the statute.

Although Americans might assume that their right to free speech under the First Amendment—now more fully accepted than two centuries ago—protects dissenters during wartime, history suggests otherwise. Every conflict has stimulated efforts by government and individuals to suppress dissenters. During the Civil War, the Union jailed civilian Confederate sympathizers; during the First World War, the government deported immigrant aliens who too vocally criticized the war effort. World War II brought the silencing of isolationists' voices, denying those who opposed American entry into the war public outlets for their ideas.

Americans remain divided over whether the proper course of action in the 1960s and 1970s was dissent from, or acquiescence to, government policy. The USA PATRIOT Act, adopted after the September 11, 2001 attacks, removed long-standing restrictions on federal government surveillance of citizens, controversially granting access to library records. Criticism of the wars in Iraq and Afghanistan has raised questions: Do newspapers that publish classified information or pictures of abused prisoners overstep their bounds? Can political figures censure the conduct of the wars without seeming unpatriotic?

Freedom of speech is never easy to maintain, and wartime conditions make it tougher. When the nation comes under attack, many patriotic Americans argue that dissent should cease. Others contend that people must always have the right to speak freely. Events in the United States since the 9/11 attacks suggest that this legacy remains contentious for the American people.

Summary

As the nineteenth century began, inhabitants of the United States faced changes. Indians east of the Mississippi River surrendered some traditions to preserve others. Some African Americans struggled unsuccessfully to free themselves from slavery, then confronted more constraints under increasingly restrictive laws.

For European-Americans, the first eleven years under the Constitution established enduring precedents for congressional, presidential, and judicial action— among them establishment of the cabinet, interpretations of key clauses of the Constitution, and stirrings of judicial review of state and federal legislation. Building on successful negotiations with Spain (Pinckney's Treaty), Britain (the Jay Treaty), and France (the Convention of 1800), the United States developed its diplomatic independence.

Yet the 1790s spawned debates over foreign and domestic policy and saw the beginnings of organized factionalism and grassroots politicking, if not yet formal parties. The Whiskey and Fries Rebellions showed that regional conflicts persisted. The waging of an undeclared war against France proved contentious. In 1801, the Jeffersonian ideal of agrarian, decentralized republicanism prevailed over Alexander Hamilton's vision of a powerful centralized economy and strong national government.

Chapter Review

Building a Workable Government

What was the purpose of the Bill of Rights?

Several states threatened not to ratify the Constitution because they feared it would create a too powerful national government. Leaders from states such as North Carolina thought that a bill of rights would expressly state key liberties of the people that should be protected, among them freedom of the press, freedom of speech, freedom of religion, and the right to peaceable assembly. At first, James Madison thought the Bill of Rights was unnecessary, but he changed his mind and submitted nineteen amendments—ten of which the states ratified—that were added to the Constitution on December 15, 1791 and later known as the Bill of Rights.

Domestic Policy Under Washington and Hamilton

How did the chartering of the Bank of the United States provoke an early constitutional debate?

Treasury Secretary Alexander Hamilton asked Congress to charter a national bank, modeled on England's, which would act as a collecting and disbursing agent for the treasury and the source for national currency. Some political leaders were unsure if the Constitution gave it the power to establish a bank. Some, like James Madison and Thomas Jefferson, took a strict-constructionist interpretation of the Constitution, arguing that it allowed Congress only to make laws deemed "necessary"—not merely what was desirable. Hamilton took a broad-constructionist view, stating that Congress could use any means not prohibited by the Constitution to achieve a constitutional end. President Washington agreed, and the bill establishing the Bank of the United States became law.

The French Revolution and the Development of Partisan Politics

Why did U.S. leaders find the rise of political factions disturbing?

In the new republic, leaders had not yet come to understand or embrace dissent as a natural part of democratic government. Factions were seen as linked to monarchies and deemed a sign of corruption in republics. Washington tried to smooth over discord when Jefferson and Madison critiqued treasury secretary Alexander Hamilton's policies as favoring commercial interests over agriculture. Both sides accused the other of trying to subvert republican principles or destroy the new republic. Similarly, when dozens of Democratic societies sprang up in the 1790s, Washington and Hamilton feared their rapid growth as subversive and dangerous to the unity they believed necessary for the republic's survival.

Partisan Politics and Relations with Great Britain

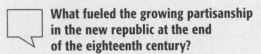

What fueled the growing partisanship in the new republic at the end of the eighteenth century?

Several different factors divided people and leaders. Debates over who the true patriots were fueled some discord, as did growing differences between agrarian and commercial interests. Republicans optimistically put their faith in the nation's future prosperity, enticing southerners, small farmers, and artisans to ally with them. Federalists, on the other hand, were often New England merchants who sought order and organized authority. Foreign affairs also divided the Republicans and Federalists. As tensions mounted between France and Great Britain in 1793, Americans, too, took sides. Federalists supported an ongoing alliance with Great Britain, which they thought would protect their interests from internal and external enemies, while many others wanted to support France's new revolutionary government.

John Adams and Political Dissent

What was the underlying purpose of the Alien and Sedition Acts of 1798?

Adopted by the Federalist-controlled Congress, these acts were designed to suppress dissent—still seen as dangerous and subversive rather than a natural part of a republic—and weaken the competing Republican faction. Hence, the acts targeted recent immigrants, typically Republican supporters, by lengthening the residency requirement for citizenship among other rules, as well as allowing the president to detain or deport any alien considered dangerous to national security. The Sedition Act outlawed antigovernment conspiracies and curbed free speech by making the writing or uttering of false, malicious or scandalous statements against the government illegal. Although the Federalists expected the acts to weaken their critics, the laws only increased dissent.

The West in the New Nation

How did the new nation begin to expand its boundaries westward?

The United States nominally controlled the land east of the Mississippi and north of Spanish Florida, and later, through warfare and treaty, managed to extend its northernmost boundary to the Ohio River. Initially, leaders attempted to negotiate with Indians living there for the land; when that failed, war with eight Indian nations ensued, culminating in 1795 with the Treaty of Greenville. This agreement allowed the United States to settle most of what would become Ohio in exchange for acknowledging the principle of Indian sovereignty—by virtue of residence—over lands that had not been ceded.

"Revolutions" at the End of the Century

What gave rise to new potential revolutions in America at the end of the eighteenth century?

Three events revealed unresolved issues—and growing tensions—in the new republic. First, Fries's Rebellion questioned the power of the central government to tax, seeing it—much as early revolutionaries had—as a threat to personal liberties and livelihoods. Second, Gabriel's Rebellion of semifree blacks sought to challenge the slave system in the Chesapeake (but ended up inspiring stricter slave laws in the South). And finally the hotly contested 1800 presidential election revealed a structural flaw in the Constitution, which required that presidential electors vote for two men without designating one as president and the other as vice president, thus creating the tie between Jefferson and Burr. It led to the Twelfth Amendment, which provided that electors cast separate ballots for presidential and vice presidential candidates.

Suggestions for Further Reading

Joyce Appleby, *Capitalism and a New Social Order: The Republican Vision of the 1790s* (1984)

Susan Branson, *These Fiery Frenchified Dames: Women and Political Culture in Early National Philadelphia* (2001)

Douglas Egerton, *Gabriel's Rebellion: The Virginia Slave Conspiracies of 1800 and 1802* (1993)

Stanley Elkins and Eric McKitrick, *The Age of Federalism, 1788–1800* (1993)

Joseph J. Ellis, *Founding Brothers: The Revolutionary Generation* (2000)

James Horn, Jan Ellen Lewis, and Peter S. Onuf, eds., *The Revolution of 1800: Democracy, Race, and the New Republic* (2002)

Richard Labunski, *James Madison and the Struggle for the Bill of Rights* (2006)

David Andrew Nichols, *Red Gentlemen & White Savages: Indians, Federalists, and the Search for Order on the American Frontier* (2008)

Jeffrey L. Pasley, *"The Tyranny of Printers": Newspaper Politics in the Early American Republic* (2001)

Thomas P. Slaughter, *The Whiskey Rebellion* (1986)

Defining the Nation

9

1801–1823

Eager to stand apart from the allegedly aristocratic ways of his Federalist predecessors, President Thomas Jefferson displayed impatience for ceremony. But on his first New Year's Day in office, he awaited the ceremonial presentation of a much-heralded tribute to his commitment, as one gift bearer put it, to "defend Republicanism and baffle all the arts of Aristocracy." Crafted in Massachusetts, the belated inaugural gift weighed more than twelve hundred pounds and measured four feet in diameter, bearing the inscription "THE GREATEST CHEESE IN AMERICA—FOR THE GREATEST MAN IN AMERICA."

The "mammoth cheese" was conceived the previous July and made by the "Ladies" of Cheshire, a Massachusetts farming community as resolutely Jeffersonian-Republican as it was Baptist. As a religious minority in largely Congregationalist New England, the Cheshire Baptists celebrated a president whose vision featured agrarianism and separation of church and state.

Federalist editors joked that the mammoth cheese's maggot-infested condition upon delivery symbolized the nation under Republican rule. Its size represented the excesses of democracy, in which even women and backwoods preachers could play leading roles. Federalists' derision of the mammoth cheese only inspired additional showy expressions of democratic pride. In the following months, a Philadelphia baker sold "Mammoth Bread," while two years later in 1804, a "mammoth loaf" was served in the Capitol to Republicans, including President Jefferson. Behind such symbolism lay serious political ideologies. Jeffersonians believed virtue derived from agricultural endeavors. They thus celebrated the acquisition of the Louisiana Territory, but efforts to expand their agriculturally based "empire of liberty" westward were resisted by Native Americans and their European allies, and sometimes by Federalists. The War of 1812 largely removed such resistance, and the United States began its expansion west. Although that war ended with few issues resolved, it had profound consequences for American development. It secured the United States' sovereignty, opened much of the West to European-Americans and their African American slaves, and helped spur revolutions in transportation and industry.

Contemporary observers hailed postwar nationalism as an "Era of Good Feelings," but when economic boom turned to bust, nationalistic unity faded. No issue proved more divisive than slavery's future in the West, as Missouri's petition for statehood revealed.

As you read this chapter, keep the following questions in mind:

* **What characterized the two main competing visions for national development?**

* **How did America's relationship with Europe influence political and economic developments?**

* **In what ways did nonvoting Americans—most blacks, women, and Native Americans— take part in defining the new nation?**

Political Visions

Was Jefferson's election and political vision truly "the revolution of 1800"?

In his inaugural address, Jefferson addressed the electorate as citizens with common beliefs: "We are all republicans, we are all federalists.... A wise and frugal government, which shall restrain men from injuring one another, which shall leave them free to regulate their pursuits of industry and improvement, and shall not take from the mouth of labor the bread it had earned. This is the sum of good government."

But outgoing president John Adams did not hear Jefferson's call for unity, having left Washington before dawn. Former friends, the two men now disliked each other. Democratic-Republicans—as the Republicans of the 1790s now called themselves—and Federalists bitterly disagreed on how society and government should be organized. Federalists advocated a strong national government to promote economic development. Democratic-Republicans believed that limited government would foster republican virtue. Nearly two decades later, Jefferson would call his election "the revolution of 1800."

Separation of Church and State

The mammoth cheese symbolized the Cheshire farmers' gratitude for Jefferson's commitment to the separation of church and state. Jefferson believed that "religion is a matter which lies solely between Man & his God." New England Baptists hailed Jefferson as a hero, but New England Federalists thought their worst fears were confirmed. During the 1800 election, Federalists had waged a venomous campaign, incorrectly labeling Jefferson an atheist. Their rhetoric proved so effective that, after Jefferson's election, some New England women hid their Bibles in their gardens and wells to foil Democratic-Republicans allegedly bent on confiscating them.

Jefferson became president during a period of religious revivalism, particularly among Methodists and Baptists, whose democratic preaching—all humans, they said, were equal in God's eyes—encouraged a growing democratic political culture. Thus, the Cheshire Baptists informed the president that their cheese had been made "without a single slave to assist."

Link to Jefferson's letter to Danbury Baptists.

Chronology

1801	Marshall becomes chief justice		1812	Madison reelected president
	Jefferson inaugurated as president		1812–15	War of 1812
1801–05	United States defeats Barbary pirates		1813	Tecumseh's death
1803	*Marbury v. Madison*			Boston Manufacturing Company starts textile mill in Waltham, Massachusetts
	Louisiana Purchase			
1804	Jefferson reelected president, Clinton vice President		1814	Treaty of Ghent
			1814–15	Hartford Convention
1804–06	Lewis and Clark expedition		1815	Battle of New Orleans
1805	Tenskwatawa emerges as Shawnee leader		1817	Regular steamboat travel begins on Mississippi
1807	*Chesapeake* affair			
	Embargo Act		1817–1825	Erie Canal constructed
1808	Congress bans slave importation		1819	*McCulloch v. Maryland*
	Madison elected president			Adams-Onis Treaty
1808–13	Tenskwatawa and Tecumseh organize Indian resistance		1819–early 1820s	First major depression
			1820–1821	Missouri Compromise
1811	National Road begun		1823	Monroe Doctrine

Political Mobilization The revolution of 1800, which gave the Democratic-Republicans majorities in both houses of Congress along with the presidency, resulted from an electorate limited largely to property-holding men. Under the Constitution, states regulated voting. Nowhere but New Jersey could women vote; that right was granted inadvertently and revoked in 1807. In 1800, free black men meeting property qualifications could vote everywhere but Delaware, Georgia, South Carolina, and Virginia, though local custom often kept them from exercising that right. Partisan politics nonetheless captured Americans' imaginations. Political mobilization took place locally, as candidates rallied popular support on militia training grounds, in taverns and churches, at court gatherings, and during holiday celebrations. Voters and nonvoters expressed their views through parades, petitions, songs and debates. Importantly, they devoured a growing print culture of pamphlets, broadsides (posters), almanacs, and newspapers.

The Partisan Press Read aloud in taverns, artisans' workshops, and homes, newspapers gave national importance to local events. In 1800, the nation had 260 newspapers; by 1810, it had 396, virtually all of them partisan.

The parties adopted official organs. After his election, Jefferson persuaded the *National Intelligencer* to move from Philadelphia to Washington, where it became the Democratic-Republicans' voice. In 1801, Alexander Hamilton launched the *New York Evening Post* as the Federalist vehicle. Published six or seven times a week, party papers helped feed the growing obsession with partisan politics.

Limited Government To bring into his administration men sharing his vision of individual liberty, an agrarian republic, and limited government, Jefferson rejected appointments that Adams made in his presidency's last

Courtesy, The Henry Francis du Pont Winterthur Museum

Although most places limited the vote to property-owning white men, elections, such as this one in Philadelphia, drew multi-racial crowds of men, women, and children.

days and dismissed Federalist customs collectors. He awarded treasury and judicial offices to Republicans. Jeffersonians worked to make the government leaner. If Alexander Hamilton had viewed the national debt as the engine of economic growth, Jefferson deemed it the source of government corruption. Secretary of the Treasury Albert Gallatin halved the army budget and reduced the 1802 navy budget by two-thirds. He moved to reduce the national debt from $83 million to $57 million, hoping to retire it altogether by 1817. Jefferson closed two of five diplomatic missions abroad, at The Hague and in Berlin. And the Democratic-Republican–controlled Congress oversaw the repeal of all internal taxes, including the despised whiskey tax of 1791.

Ideas of liberty also distinguished Democratic-Republicans from Federalists. Opposition to the Alien and Sedition Acts of 1798 had united Republicans. Jefferson now declined to use the acts against his opponents, instead pardoning those convicted of violating them.

Congress let the Sedition Act expire in 1801 and the Alien Act in 1802, and repealed the Naturalization Act of 1798, which required fourteen years of residency for citizenship. The 1802 act that replaced it required five years of residency, loyalty to the Constitution, and the forsaking of foreign allegiances and titles. It remained the basis of naturalized American citizenship into the twentieth century.

Judicial Politics   To many Democratic-Republicans, the judiciary represented a centralizing and undemocratic force, since judges were appointed, not elected, and served for life. At Jefferson's prompting, the House impeached (indicted) and the Senate convicted Federal District Judge John Pickering of New Hampshire, whose alleged alcoholism made him an easy mark. The House also impeached Supreme Court Justice Samuel Chase for judicial misconduct. A staunch Federalist, Chase had pushed for prosecutions under the Sedition Act, campaigned for Adams in 1800, and denounced Jefferson's administration. But Democratic-Republicans failed to muster the two-thirds Senate majority necessary for conviction. The failure to remove Chase preserved the Court's independence and established the precedent that criminal actions, not political disagreements, justified removal from office.

The Marshall Court

Although Jefferson appointed three new Supreme Court justices, the Court remained a Federalist stronghold under John Marshall. Even after the Democratic-Republicans achieved a majority of Court seats in 1811, Marshall remained influential as chief justice. Under the Marshall Court (1801–1835), the Supreme Court upheld federal supremacy over the states while protecting commercial interests.

Marshall made the Court an equal branch of government. Marshall strengthened the Court by having it speak with a unified voice; rather than issuing individual concurring judgments, justices now issued joint majority opinions. From 1801 through 1805, Marshall wrote twenty-four of the Court's twenty-six decisions; through 1810 he wrote 85 percent of the opinions.

Judicial Review

In his last hours in office, Adams named Federalist William Marbury a justice of the peace in the District of Columbia. Jefferson's secretary of state, James Madison, declined to certify the appointment, allowing the new president to appoint a Democratic-Republican. Marbury sued, requesting a writ of mandamus (a court order forcing the president to appoint him). If the Supreme Court ruled in Marbury's favor in **Marbury v. Madison**, the president probably would not comply, and the Court could not force him to do so. Yet, by refusing to issue the writ, the Federalist-dominated bench would hand the Democratic-Republicans a victory.

Marbury v. Madison: Case in which the Supreme Court's power to determine the constitutionality of laws was established.

To avoid both pitfalls, Marshall recast the issue. He ruled that Marbury had a right to his appointment but that the Supreme Court could not compel Madison to honor it because the Constitution did not grant the Court power to issue a writ of mandamus. Without specific mention in the Constitution, Marshall wrote, the section of the Judiciary Act of 1789 authorizing the Court to issue writs was unconstitutional. Thus, the Supreme Court denied itself the power to issue writs of mandamus but established its far greater power to judge the constitutionality of laws. In doing so, Marshall fashioned the theory of judicial review. Because the Constitution was "the supreme law of the land," Marshall wrote, any federal or state act contrary to the Constitution must be null and void. This power of the Supreme Court to determine the constitutionality of legislation and presidential acts enhanced the independence of the judiciary and breathed life into the Constitution.

Election of 1804

In the first election after the Twelfth Amendment's ratification, Jefferson dropped Burr as his running mate and, to have a North-South balance, chose George Clinton of New York. They swamped their opponents—South Carolinian Charles Cotesworth Pinckney and New Yorker Rufus King—in the electoral college by 162 votes to 14, carrying fifteen of the seventeen states. That 1804 election escalated the animosity between Burr and Hamilton, who supported Burr's rival in the New York gubernatorial election. When Hamilton called Burr a liar, Burr challenged Hamilton to a duel. Because New York had outlawed dueling, the encounter happened in New Jersey. Details of the duel remain hazy but the outcome was clear: Hamilton died after being shot by Burr. New York and New Jersey prosecutors indicted Burr for murder.

Burr fled to the West. While historians disagree about his motives, the "Burr Conspiracy" was understood at the time to involve a scheme with Brigadier General James Wilkinson to create a new empire by militarily taking what is now Texas and

Link to a Federalist handbill attacking Aarron Burr.

by persuading existing western territories to leave the United States. Tried for treason in 1807, Burr faced a prosecution aided by President Jefferson but overseen by Jefferson's rival Chief Justice Marshall. Prompted by Marshall to interpret treason narrowly, the jury acquitted Burr, who fled to Europe.

Nationalism and Culture

As statesmen bickered, other Americans conveyed their nationalist visions artistically. Nearly three decades after the Constitution's ratification, painters continued to memorialize great birth scenes of American nationhood, such as the Declaration of Independence's signing, Revolutionary War battles, and the Constitutional Convention. Four of John Trumbull's revolutionary scenes, commissioned in 1817, still hang on the Capitol building rotunda in Washington.

Architecturally, Americans self-consciously constructed an independent nation. Designed by Major Pierre Charles L'Enfant, the city of Washington was meant to embody a "reciprocity of sight": Each of the government's three branches—the legislative, judicial, and executive—should keep an eye on one another. Across America, wealthier people commissioned "federal" style homes, which imitated the simplicity of classical architecture.

The era's best-selling book was Noah Webster's spelling book, which proposed making English more "republican." It sold an estimated 100 million copies by the end of the nineteenth century. Webster advocated a national language that, unlike "King's English," would not require elite training. Words should be spelled as they sound—for example, "honor" should replace "honour." A shared language would unite an increasingly far-flung population.

National Expansion Westward

By 1800, hundreds of thousands of white Americans had settled in the rich Ohio River and Mississippi River valleys, intruding on Indian lands. In the Northwest, they raised foodstuffs, primarily wheat; in the Southwest, they cultivated cotton. During the American Revolution, cotton production was profitable only for the Sea Island planters in South Carolina and Georgia, who grew the long-staple variety. Short-staple cotton, which grew in the interior, was unmarketable because its sticky seeds required removal by hand. After New England inventor **Eli Whitney** designed a cotton gin in 1793, allowing one person to remove the same number of seeds that previously required fifty people, cultivation of short-staple cotton spread rapidly into Louisiana, Mississippi, Alabama, Arkansas, and Tennessee. The cotton gin greatly increased the demand for slaves, who seeded, tended, and harvested cotton fields.

American settlers depended on free access to the Mississippi River and its Gulf port, New Orleans. Whoever controlled the port of New Orleans had a hand on the American economy's throat.

New Orleans

Spain, which acquired France's territory west of the Mississippi after the Seven Years' War (1763), secretly transferred it back to France in 1800 and 1801. American officials discovered the transfer in 1802, when Napoleon seemed poised to rebuild a French empire in the New World.

> Why was the Louisiana Purchase among Jefferson's most popular decisions as president?

Eli Whitney: Invented the cotton gin that made cleaning of southern cotton fast and cheap.

At the time of the Louisiana Purchase in 1803, New Orleans was already a bustling port, though boosters predicted an even brighter future under American "wings."

American concerns intensified when Spanish officials, on the eve of ceding control to the French, violated Pinckney's treaty by denying Americans the privilege of storing their products at New Orleans prior to transshipment to foreign markets. Western farmers and eastern merchants thought Napoleon had closed the port; they talked war.

To relieve the pressure for war and win western farmers' support, Jefferson urged Congress to authorize the call-up of eighty thousand militiamen. He also sent Virginia Governor James Monroe to join Robert Livingston in France to buy the port of New Orleans and as much of the Mississippi valley as possible. Arriving in Paris in April 1803, Monroe learned that France had already offered to sell Louisiana to the United States for a mere $15 million. With St. Domingue torn from French control by revolution and slave revolt, Napoleon abandoned dreams of a New World empire and no longer needed Louisiana as its breadbasket. He urgently needed money to wage war against Britain. On April 30, Monroe and Livingston signed a treaty buying the 827,000-square-mile territory (see Map 9.1).

Louisiana Purchase: The United States bought the Louisiana Territory (the area from the Mississippi River to the Rocky Mountains) from France in 1803 for $15 million. The purchase virtually doubled the area of the United States.

Louisiana Purchase

The **Louisiana Purchase** ensured that the United States would control the Mississippi's mouth, pleasing western settlers who relied on the river to market their goods. It also inspired those who imagined the United States as the nexus of international trade networks reaching between Europe and Asia. Louisiana promised to fulfill easterners' dreams of cheap, fertile lands. Its vast expanse meant, too, that land could be reserved for Indians displaced by white settlers and their black slaves. But some doubted its constitutionality; others worried that it belied the Democratic-Republicans' commitment to debt reduction; and some New England Federalists complained that it undermined their commercial interests and threatened the republic by spreading the population beyond where it could be controlled. Overall, though, the Louisiana Purchase was the most popular achievement of Jefferson's presidency.

When the United States acquired Louisiana, hundreds of thousands of people there became American subjects, including Native Americans from various nations, as well as people of European and African descent—or, often, a complex mixture of the two. Around New Orleans, Louisiana's colonial heritage was reflected in its people: creoles of French and Spanish descent, slaves of African descent, free people of color, and Acadians, or Cajuns (descendants of French settlers in eastern Canada), and some Germans, Irish, and English. The 1810 census reported that 97,000 non-Indians lived in the area. Although Jefferson imagined the West as an "empire of liberty," free people of color and slaves soon discovered they were excluded from the Louisiana Purchase treaty's provision that "the inhabitants of the ceded territory" would gain American citizenship. Denied the right to vote and serve on juries, New Orleans' people of color fought to retain their rights to form families and to bequeath as they pleased, and some succeeded.

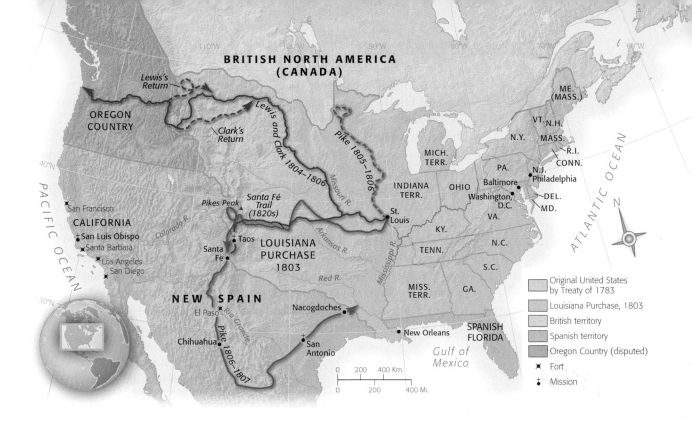

MAP 9.1

Louisiana Purchase

The Louisiana Purchase (1803) doubled the area of the United States and opened the trans-Mississippi West for American settlement.

Source: Copyright © Cengage Learning.

Lewis and Clark Expedition

Jefferson had a long-standing interest in the trans-Mississippi West, fearing that, if Americans did not claim it, the British, who still controlled present-day Canada and parts of the Pacific Northwest, would. He launched a military-style mission to chart the region's commercial possibilities—its water passages to the Pacific and trading opportunities with Indians—while cataloguing its geography, peoples, flora, and fauna.

The expedition, headed by Meriwether Lewis and William Clark, began in May 1804 and lasted for more than two years; it traveled up the Missouri River, across the Rockies, and down the Columbia to the Pacific Ocean—and back. The **Lewis and Clark Expedition** members "discovered" (as they saw it) dozens of previously unknown Indian tribes. Although the Corps of Discovery, as the expedition came to be called, was prepared for possible conflict, its goal was peaceable: to foster trade relations, win political allies, and tap into Indians' knowledge of the landscape. Lewis and Clark brought twenty-one bags of gifts for Native American leaders to establish goodwill and to stimulate interest in trade. Most interactions were cordial, but when Indians were unimpressed by the gifts, tensions arose.

The Corps of Discovery proved democratic in seating enlisted men on courtsmartial and allowing Clark's black slave York and the expedition's female guide **Sacagawea** to vote on where to locate winter quarters in 1805. But, unlike other

Lewis and Clark Expedition: Expedition led by Meriwether Lewis and William Clark to explore the Louisiana Territory.

Sacagawea: Female guide who aided Lewis and Clark in exploring the Louisiana Territory.

211

expedition members, neither York nor Sacagawea drew wages, and when York later demanded his freedom, Clark repaid him with "a severe trouncing."

Lewis and Clark failed to discover a Northwest Passage to the Pacific, and the route they mapped across the Rockies proved perilous, but their explorations contributed to nationalist visions of American expansion. Fossils and Native American artifacts they collected were displayed in Charles Willson Peale's "American Museum," an institution emphasizing the uniqueness of America's geography and its republican experiment. Nationalists overlooked Indians' land claims. Although Jefferson had more sympathy for Indians than did many contemporaries—he took interest in their cultures and believed Indians to be intellectually equal to whites—he lobbied, unsuccessfully, for a constitutional amendment that would transport them west of the Mississippi into Louisiana Territory. He became involved in efforts to pressure the Chickasaws to sell their land, and if legal methods failed, he advocated trickery. Traders, he suggested, might run them into debt, which they would have to repay "by a cessation of lands."

Divisions Among Indian Peoples

Some Indian nations adopted white customs as a means of survival and often agreed to sell their lands and move west. These "accommodationists" (or "progressives") were opposed by "traditionalists," who urged adherence to native ways and refused to relinquish their lands. Distinctions between accommodationists and traditionalists were not always so clear-cut, however.

In the early 1800s, two Shawnee brothers, Tenskwatawa (1775–1837) and **Tecumseh** (1768–1813), led a traditionalist revolt against American encroachment by fostering a pan-Indian federation centered in the Old Northwest and reaching into parts of the South. By the 1800s, the Shawnees lost most of their Ohio land, occupying scattered sites there and in the Michigan and Louisiana territories. Despondent, Lalawethika—Tenskwatawa's name as a youth—turned to a combination of European remedies (particularly whiskey) and Native American ones, becoming a shaman in 1804. But when European diseases ravaged his village, he despaired.

Tecumseh: The Shawnee leader who sought to unite several tribes from Canada to Georgia against encroachment on their lands by American settlers; allied with the British in the War of 1812.

Tenskwatawa and Tecumseh

Lalawethika emerged from an illness in 1805 as a new man, renamed Tenskwatawa ("the Open Door") or—by whites—"the Prophet." Claiming to have died and been resurrected, he traveled in the Ohio River valley as a religious leader, attacking the decline of moral values among Native Americans, warning against whiskey and condemning intertribal battles. He urged Indians to return to the old ways: to hunt with bows and arrows, not guns; to stop wearing hats; and to give up bread for corn and beans.

By 1808, Tenskwatawa and his older brother Tecumseh focused on resisting American aggression. They invited all Indians to settle in pan-Indian towns in Indiana, first at Greenville (1806–1808) and then at Prophetstown (1808–1812). This challenged the treaty-making process by denying the claims of Indians who were given the same land under the Treaty of Greenville of 1795. Younger Indians flocked to Tecumseh, the more political of the two brothers.

Convinced that only an Indian federation could stop white settlement, Tecumseh sought to unify northern and southern Indians from Canada to Georgia. Among southern Indians, only one Creek faction welcomed him, but his efforts alarmed white settlers and government officials. In November 1811, while Tecumseh was in the South, Indiana governor William Henry Harrison moved against Tenskwatawa's followers. During the battle of Tippecanoe, the army burned their town; as they fled, the Indians exacted revenge on white settlers. When Harrison avowed reprisals, Tecumseh allied with the British. This alliance in the West, combined with American neutrality rights on the high seas, was propelling the United States toward war with Britain.

The Nation in the Orbit of Europe

The republic's economy relied heavily on fishing and the carrying trade, with the American merchant marine transporting commodities between nations. Merchants in Boston, Salem, and Philadelphia traded with China, sending cloth and metal to swap for furs with Chinook Indians on the Oregon coast, and then sailing to China to trade for porcelain, tea, and silk. The slave trade lured American ships to Africa. Not long after Jefferson's first inaugural address, the United States was at war with Tripoli—a state along North Africa's Barbary Coast—over a principle that would long be a cornerstone of American foreign policy: freedom of the seas. That is, outside of national territorial waters, the high seas should be open for free transit.

> What led to the War of 1812?

First Barbary War   In 1801, the bashaw (pasha) of Tripoli declared war on the United States for its refusal to pay tribute for safe passage of its ships through the Mediterranean. After two years of stalemate, Jefferson declared a blockade of Tripoli, but when the American frigate *Philadelphia* ran aground in the harbor, its three hundred officers and sailors were imprisoned. Jefferson refused to ransom them, and a small American force accompanied by Arab, Greek, and African mercenaries marched from Egypt to the "shores of Tripoli" to seize the port of Derne. A treaty ended the war in 1805, but the United States continued to pay tribute to the three other Barbary states—Algiers, Morocco, and Tunis—until 1815. In the intervening years, the United States became embroiled in European conflicts.

At first, Jefferson distanced the nation from European turmoil in the wake of the French Revolution. After the Senate ratified the Jay Treaty in 1795, the United States and Great Britain reconciled. Britain withdrew from its western forts on American soil and interfered less in American trade with France. Then, in May 1803, two weeks after Napoleon sold Louisiana to the United States, France was at war against Britain and, later, Britain's allies, Prussia, Austria, and Russia. Initially, the United States benefited, as merchants gained control of most of the West Indian trade. After 1805, when Britain defeated the French and Spanish fleets at Trafalgar, Britain's Royal Navy tightened its control of the oceans. Two months later, Napoleon crushed the Russian and Austrian armies at Austerlitz. Stalemated, France and Britain launched a commercial war, blockading trade and costing the United States dearly.

Threats to American Sovereignty   To replenish their supply of sailors, British vessels stopped American ships and impressed (forcibly recruited) British deserters, British-born naturalized American seamen, and other sailors suspected of being British. Perhaps six to eight thousand Americans were impressed between 1803 and 1812. Alleged deserters—many of them American citizens—faced British courts-martial. Americans saw the principle of "once a British subject, always a British subject" as a mockery of U.S. citizenship and their national sovereignty. Americans also resented the British interfering with their West Indian trade and seizing American vessels within U.S. territorial waters.

In April 1806, Congress responded with the Non Importation Act, barring British manufactured goods from American ports. Because the act exempted most cloth and metal articles, it had little impact on British trade; instead, it warned the British what to expect if they continued to violate American neutral rights. In November, Jefferson suspended the act while Baltimore lawyer William Pinkney joined James Monroe in London to negotiate a settlement. The treaty they carried home did not mention impressments; hence, the president never submitted it for ratification.

Tense Anglo-American relations came to a head in June 1807 when the USS *Chesapeake,* sailing from Norfolk for the Mediterranean, was stopped by the British frigate *Leopard,* whose officers demanded to search the ship for British deserters. Refused, the *Leopard* opened fire, killing three Americans and wounding eighteen others. The British seized four deserters, three of whom held American citizenship; one was hanged. The incident outraged Americans and exposed American military weakness.

The Embargo of 1807

Jefferson responded with what he called "peaceable coercion." In July, the president closed American waters to British warships and increased military and naval expenditures. In December 1807, Jefferson put economic pressure on Great Britain by invoking the Non-Importation Act, followed by the **Embargo Act**. The embargo, which forbade exports from the United States to any country, was a short-term measure to avoid war by pressuring Britain and France to respect American rights and by preventing confrontation between American merchant vessels and European warships.

Embargo Act of 1807: Forbade exports from the United States to any country.

The embargo's biggest economic impact, however, fell on the United States. Exports declined by 80 percent in 1808, squeezing New England shippers and their workers. Manufacturers fared well, as the domestic market became theirs exclusively. Merchants began to shift from shipping to manufacturing. In 1807, there were twenty cotton and woolen mills in New England; by 1813, there were more than two hundred.

International Slave Trade

They had only to look at the vibrant slave trade to see how scarcity bred demand. With Jefferson's encouragement, Congress voted in 1807 to abolish the international slave trade as of January 1, 1808—the earliest date permissible under the Constitution. South Carolina still allowed the legal importation of slaves, but most of the state's planters favored a ban, nervous about adding to the black population of a state where whites were outnumbered. The final bill provided that smuggled slaves would be sold according to the laws of the state or territory in which they arrived, underscoring that even illegal slaves were property. Had the bill not done so, threatened one Georgia congressman, the result might have been "resistance to the authority of the Government," even civil war. During the last four months of 1807, sixteen thousand African slaves arrived at Gadsden Wharf in Charleston, where they were detained by merchants eager to wait out the January 1 deadline. Although many slaves—hundreds, if not thousands—died in the disease-ridden holding pens before they could be sold, merchants calculated the increased value of those who survived until the ban took effect would outweigh the losses. After January 1, 1808, a brisk—and profitable—illegal slave trade took over. In 1819, Congress authorized the president to use force to intercept slave ships along the African coast, but the small American navy could not halt the illicit trade.

Election of 1808

As the 1808 presidential election approached, Democratic Republicans suffered from factional dissent and dissatisfaction in seaboard states hobbled by the trade restrictions. Although nine state legislatures passed resolutions urging Jefferson to run again, the president declined a third term. He supported James Madison, his secretary of state, as the Democratic-Republican standard-bearer. Madison won the endorsement of the party's congressional caucus, and Madison and Vice President George Clinton headed the ticket. Charles Cotesworth Pinckney and Rufus King again ran on the Federalist ticket.

Boarding and Taking of the American Ship Chesapeake *(1816) portrays crew from the British frigate* Leopard *fighting to search the USS* Chesapeake *for British navy deserters. The sailors of the* Chesapeake *resisted, but the British overpowered them and seized four deserters, three of them American citizens. Americans were humiliated and angered by the British violation of American rights.*

William L. Clements Library

The younger Federalists played up the widespread disaffection with Democratic-Republican policy, especially the embargo. Pinckney received only 47 electoral votes to Madison's 122, but he carried all of New England except Vermont, and won Delaware. Federalists also gained seats in Congress and captured the New York State legislature. Still, the transition from one Democratic-Republican administration to the next went smoothly.

Women and Politics

Wives eased the transition of elected and appointed officials by encouraging political and diplomatic negotiation. Such negotiations often occurred in social settings, even private homes. Women played crucial roles in bridging ideological divides by fostering conversation, providing an ear or a voice for unofficial messages, and—in international affairs—standing as surrogates for their nation. Wives' interactions among themselves served political purposes, too: when First Lady Dolley Madison visited congressmen's wives, she cultivated goodwill for her husband while collecting recipes so she could serve regionally diverse cuisine at White House functions.

Jeffersonians wanted women's support of the embargo. Sympathetic women responded by spurning imported fabric and making (or directing their slaves to make) homespun clothing. Federalists, however, encouraged women to "keep commerce alive," and sympathetic women bought smuggled goods.

Failed Policies

Under domestic opposition, the embargo collapsed. Instead, the Non-Intercourse Act of 1809 reopened trade with all nations except Britain and France, and authorized the president to resume trade with those two nations once they respected American neutral rights. In June

1809, President Madison reopened trade with Britain after its minister to the United States offered assurances that Britain would repeal restrictions on American trade. But his Majesty's government in London repudiated the minister's assurances, leading Madison to revert to nonintercourse.

When the Non-Intercourse Act expired in 1810, Congress substituted Macon's Bill Number 2, reopening trade with Great Britain and France but providing that, when either nation stopped violating American commercial rights, the president would suspend American commerce with the other. When Napoleon accepted, Madison declared nonintercourse on Great Britain in 1811. Although the French continued to seize American ships, Britain became the focus of American hostility because it dominated the seas.

In spring 1812, the British admiralty ordered its ships not to stop, search, or seize American warships, and in June Britain reopened the seas to American shipping. But before word of this policy change reached America, Congress declared war.

Link to President Madison's "War Message" to Congress.

War Hawks: Militant Republicans who demanded more aggressive policies and who wanted war with Britain.

Mr. Madison's War

The House voted 79 to 49 for war; the Senate, 19 to 13. Democratic-Republicans favored war by 98 to 23; Federalists opposed it 39 to 0. Those who favored war, including President Madison, pointed to assaults on American sovereignty and honor: impressment, violation of neutral trading rights, and British alliances with western Indians. Others saw an opportunity to conquer and annex British Canada. Most militant were land-hungry southerners and westerners—the "**War Hawks**"—led by John C. Calhoun of South Carolina and first-term congressman and House Speaker Henry Clay of Kentucky. Most representatives from the coastal states, especially the Northeast, feared trade disruption and opposed "Mr. Madison's War."

Initially, Federalists benefited from antiwar sentiment. They joined renegade Democratic-Republicans in supporting New York City mayor DeWitt Clinton for president in 1812. Clinton lost to Madison by 128 to 89 electoral votes, but Federalists gained some congressional seats and carried many local elections. The pro-war South and the West remained solidly Democratic-Republican.

The War of 1812

What were the consequences of the War of 1812?

Lasting from 1812 to 1815, the war unfolded in skirmishes, for which the U.S. armed forces were ill prepared. The U.S. Military Academy at West Point, founded in 1802, produced only eighty-nine regular officers, and campaigns were executed poorly. Although the U.S. Navy had a corps of experienced officers, it proved no match for the Royal Navy.

The government's efforts to lure recruits—with sign-up bonuses, and promises of three months' pay and rights to purchase 160 acres of western land—met with mixed success. At first, recruitment went well among westerners, motivated by civic spirit, desire for land, anti-Indian sentiment, and fears of Tecumseh's pan-Indian organization. But with pay delays and inadequate supplies, recruitment dwindled. In New England, Federalists discouraged enlistments. Militias in New England and New York often refused to fight outside their states. Desperate, New York offered freedom to slaves who enlisted, and compensation to their owners, and the U.S. Army made the same offer to slaves in the Old Northwest and in Canada. But in the Deep South, fear of arming slaves kept them out of the military except in New Orleans, where a free black militia dated back to Spanish control of Louisiana.

The British recruited slaves by promising freedom in exchange for service. In the end, British forces outnumbered the Americans.

Invasion of Canada

Despite recruitment problems, Americans expected to take Canada easily. Canada's population was sparse, its army small, and the Great Lakes inaccessible to the Royal Navy in the Atlantic. Americans hoped, too, that French Canadians might welcome U.S. forces.

Americans aimed to split Canadian forces and isolate pro-British Indians, especially Tecumseh, whom the British had promised an Indian nation in the Great Lakes region. In July 1812, U.S. general William Hull, territorial governor of Michigan, marched his troops, who outnumbered those of the British, into Upper Canada (modern Ontario), hoping to conquer Montreal. But by abandoning Mackinac Island and Fort Dearborn, and by surrendering Fort Detroit, he left the Midwest exposed. Captain Zachary Taylor provided the only bright spot, giving the Americans a land victory with his September 1812 defense of Fort Harrison in Indiana Territory. By the winter of 1812–1813, the British controlled about half of the Old Northwest.

Naval Battles

Despite victories on the Atlantic by the USS *Constitution* (nicknamed "Old Ironsides"), the USS *Wasp,* and the USS *United States,* the American navy—which began the war with just seventeen ships— could not match the powerful Royal Navy. By 1814, the Royal Navy blockaded nearly all American ports along the Atlantic and Gulf coasts. After 1811, American trade overseas declined by nearly 90 percent, and the lost customs duties threatened to bankrupt the federal government and prostrate New England.

The contest for control of the Great Lakes, the key to the war in the Northwest, evolved as a shipbuilding race. Under Master Commandant Oliver Hazard Perry and shipbuilder Noah Brown, the United States outbuilt the British on Lake Erie and defeated them at the bloody Battle of Put-in-Bay on September 10, 1813, gaining control of Lake Erie.

Burning Capitals

A ragged group of Kentucky militia volunteers, armed with swords and knives, marched 20 to 30 miles a day to join General William Henry Harrison's forces in Ohio. Now 4,500 strong, Harrison's forces took Detroit before crossing into Canada, where at the Battle of the Thames they defeated British, Shawnee, and Chippewa forces in October 1813. Among the dead was Tecumseh. The Americans then razed the Canadian capital of York (now Toronto).

After defeating Napoleon in Europe in April 1814, the British launched a land counteroffensive against the United States, concentrating on the Chesapeake Bay. Royal troops occupied Washington, D.C., in August and set it ablaze. The presidential mansion and parts of the city burned all night. The president and cabinet fled. Dolley Madison stayed to oversee the removal of cabinet documents and to save a Gilbert Stuart portrait of George Washington.

The British intended the attack on Washington as a diversion. The major battle occurred in September 1814 at Baltimore, where the Americans held firm. Francis Scott Key, detained on a British ship, watched the bombardment of Fort McHenry and wrote "The Star-Spangled Banner" (which became the national anthem in 1931). The British inflicted heavy damage but achieved little militarily; their offensive on Lake Champlain also failed. The war reached a stalemate.

Selling War

The War of 1812 was not always a popular war, but in its aftermath many Americans trumpeted the war's successes. To the left, we see a recruitment poster from 1812, in which General William Henry Harrison seeks additional cavalrymen. Hampered in part by transportation difficulties, Harrison is unable to offer much—soldiers are even requested to supply their own bacon as well as their own horses—but he does promise that the expedition will be short, undoubtedly a concern to men eager to return to the fall harvest. To the right, we see a handkerchief made in 1815, after the Treaty of Ghent and the Battle of New Orleans; it features the United States' victories against the world's greatest naval power, Great Britain. Made with a decorative border, the kerchief may have been for display. What similar values do we see promoted in the two images, and what factors—such as their intended audiences, their purposes, and when they were created—might account for any differences between them?

With a tiny regular army, the United States often had to rely on short-term recruits to wage war on the British.

Chicago History Museum

Made in 1815 from cotton textiles—whose domestic production soared during the War of 1812, with trade cut off from Britain—this handkerchief helps promote American "liberty and independence."

© Collection of the New-York Historical Society, USA/Bridgeman Art Library Ltd.

War in the South

To the south, two wars were happening simultaneously. In the Patriots War, a private army of Americans, secretly supported by the Madison administration, tried to seize East Florida from Spain. What started as a settlers' rebellion along the Georgia-Florida border—to grab more land, strike at the Spaniards' Indian allies, and later to protest the Spaniards' arming of black soldiers—turned into a war, with the Patriots backed by U.S. forces and Georgia militia. Federalists condemned the invasion of a neutral territory, and the Senate refused twice (in 1812 and 1813) to support a military seizure of Florida. Embarrassed, Madison withdrew his support, and the movement collapsed in May 1814.

In the war with Britain, the southern theater proved more successful. The final campaign began with an American attack on the Red Stick Creeks along the Gulf of Mexico and the British around New Orleans and ended with Americans gaining new territory. Responding to Tecumseh's call to resist U.S. expansion, in 1813 the Red Sticks attacked Fort Mims, about 40 miles from Mobile, killing hundreds of white men, women, and children. Seeking revenge, General Andrew Jackson of Tennessee rallied his militiamen and Indian opponents of the Red Sticks and crushed the Red Sticks at Horseshoe Bend (in present-day Alabama) in March 1814. This led to the Treaty of Fort Jackson, in which the Creeks ceded 23 million acres, or about half of their holdings, and withdrew to southern and western Mississippi Territory.

Jackson became a major general and continued south toward the Gulf of Mexico. After seizing Pensacola (in Spanish Florida) and then securing Mobile, Jackson's forces marched to New Orleans. Three weeks later, on January 8, 1815, Jackson's poorly trained army held its ground against two British frontal assaults. At day's end, more than two thousand British soldiers lay dead or wounded, while the Americans suffered only twenty-one casualties.

The Battle of New Orleans occurred two weeks after the war's conclusion: word had not yet reached America that British and United States diplomats had signed the **Treaty of Ghent** on December 24, 1814. Still, the Battle of New Orleans catapulted General Andrew Jackson to national political prominence.

Treaty of Ghent: Treaty that ended the War of 1812, restoring the prewar status quo.

Treaty of Ghent

The Treaty of Ghent essentially restored the prewar status quo. It provided for an end to hostilities, release of prisoners, restoration of conquered territory, and arbitration of boundary disputes. But the United States received no satisfaction on impressment, blockades, or other maritime rights for neutrals, and British demands for territorial cessions from Maine to Minnesota went unmet. The British dropped their promise of an independent Indian nation.

Napoleon's defeat allowed the United States to discard its prewar demands, because peace in Europe made impressment and interference with American commerce moot issues. Similarly, war-weary Britain—its treasury nearly depleted—stopped pressing for military victory.

American Sovereignty Reasserted

The War of 1812 affirmed the independence of the American republic and ensured Canada's independence from the United States. Trade and territorial disputes with Great Britain continued, but they never again led to war. The return of peace allowed the United States to again focus on the Barbary Coast, where the dey (governor) of Algiers declared war on the United States. In the Second Barbary War, U.S. forces held hundreds of Algerians while negotiating a treaty in the summer of 1815 that forever freed the United States from paying tributes for passage in the Mediterranean. The Second Barbary War reaffirmed America's commitment to freedom of the seas.

Hartford Convention: Federalist meeting that was perceived as disloyalty during time of war and began the downfall of the party.

Domestic Consequences

The War of 1812 had profound domestic consequences. The Federalists' hopes of returning to national prominence diminished with the **Hartford Convention.** New England delegates—frustrated by the stalemated war and the shattered New England economy—met in Hartford, Connecticut, for three weeks in the winter of 1814–1815 to discuss revising the national compact or pulling out of the republic. Although moderates prevented a resolution of secession—withdrawal from the Union—delegates condemned the war and the embargo while endorsing constitutional changes that would weaken the South's power and make it harder to declare war. When news arrived of Jackson's victory in New Orleans and the Treaty of Ghent, the Hartford Convention made the Federalists look wrong-headed, even treasonous. By the 1820s, the party faded from the national scene.

With Tecumseh's death, midwestern Indians lost their powerful leader; with the British withdrawal, they lost their strongest ally. Some accommodationists, such as the Cherokees, temporarily flourished, but the war effectively disarmed traditionalists bent on resisting American expansion. Although the Treaty of Ghent pledged the United States to end hostilities with Indians and to restore their prewar "possessions, rights, and privileges," Indians could not make the United States honor the agreement.

For American farmers, the war opened formerly Indian land for cultivating cotton in the Old Southwest and wheat in the Old Northwest. It stimulated industry, as Americans could no longer rely on overseas imports, particularly textiles. The War of 1812 thus fueled demand for raw cotton, and the newly acquired lands in the Southwest beckoned southerners who migrated there with slaves, or with expectations of someday owning slaves. The war's conclusion accelerated three trends that would dominate U.S. history for upcoming decades: westward expansion, industrial takeoff, and slavery's entrenchment.

The Nationalist Program

How did the American System mark the triumph of Federalist economic policy?

In his final year as president, James Madison and the Democratic-Republicans absorbed the Federalist idea that the federal government should encourage economic growth. His agenda, which Henry Clay later called the American System, included a national bank, improved transportation, and a protective tariff—a tax on imported goods to protect American manufacturers from foreign competition. Yet true to his Jeffersonian roots, Madison argued that only a constitutional amendment could authorize the federal government to build local roads and canals.

American System

Clay and other congressional leaders, such as Calhoun of South Carolina, believed the American System would ease sectional tension. The tariff would stimulate New England industry, whose goods would find markets in the South and West. The South's and West's agricultural products—cotton and foodstuffs—would feed New England mills and workers. Manufactured and agricultural products would move along roads and canals that tariff revenues would fund. A national bank would handle the transactions.

In 1816, Congress chartered the Second Bank of the United States (the bank's first charter expired in 1811) to serve as a depository for federal funds and to issue currency, collect taxes, and pay the government's debts. The Second Bank of the United States would also oversee state and local banks, ensuring that their paper money had backing in specie (precious metals). Like its predecessor, the bank mixed public and private ownership; the government provided one-fifth of the bank's capital and appointed one-fifth of its directors.

Congress also passed the Tariff of 1816, which taxed imported woolens and cottons, iron, leather, hats, paper, and sugar. The tariff divided the nation. New England and the western and Middle Atlantic states would benefit from it and thus applauded it, whereas many southerners objected that it raised prices on consumer goods and could prompt Britain to retaliate with a tariff on cotton.

Southerners such as Calhoun promoted roads and canals to "bind the republic together." However, on March 3, 1817, the day before leaving office, President Madison, citing constitutional scruples, vetoed Calhoun's "Bonus Bill," which would have authorized federal funding for such public works.

Early Internal Improvements

Federalists and Democratic-Republicans agreed that improved transportation would promote national prosperity. For Federalists, roads and canals were necessary for commercial development; for Jeffersonians, they would spur western expansion and agrarian growth. In 1806, Congress passed (and Jefferson had signed) a bill authorizing funding for the Cumberland Road (later, the National Road), running 130 miles between Cumberland, Maryland, and Wheeling, Virginia (now West Virginia). In 1820, Congress authorized a survey of the National Road to Columbus, Ohio, a project completed in 1833.

Most transportation initiatives received funding from states, private investors, or both. Between 1817 and 1825, New York constructed the **Erie Canal**, linking the Great Lakes to the Atlantic seaboard. Although southern states constructed modest canals, the South's trade depended on river going steamboats after 1817, when steamboats began traveling regularly upriver on the Mississippi. With canals and steamboats, western agricultural products could travel to market faster and less expensively, fueling westward expansion. Canals expanded commercial networks into regions without natural waterways and reoriented midwestern commerce through the North.

Erie Canal: Major canal that linked the Great Lakes to the Atlantic seaboard, opening the upper Midwest to wider development.

The Era of Good Feelings

James Monroe, Madison's successor, was the third Virginian elected president since 1801. A former senator and twice governor of Virginia, he served under Madison as secretary of state and of war and used his association with Jefferson and Madison to attain the presidency. In 1816, he and his running mate, Daniel Tompkins, trounced the last Federalist presidential nominee, Rufus King, garnering all the electoral votes except those of the Federalist strongholds of Massachusetts, Connecticut, and Delaware. A Boston newspaper dubbed this one-party period the **"Era of Good Feelings."**

Led by Federalist chief justice John Marshall, the Supreme Court became the bulwark of the nationalist agenda. In ***McCulloch v. Maryland*** (1819), the Court struck down a Maryland law taxing banks that were not chartered by its legislature—a law aimed at hindering the Baltimore branch of the Second Bank of the United States. At issue was state versus federal jurisdiction. Writing for a unanimous Court, Marshall asserted the supremacy of the federal government over the states. The Court ruled, too, that

Era of Good Feelings: Period of one-party politics during administration of James Monroe.

McCulloch v. Maryland: Supreme Court decision that restated national supremacy over states.

Congress had the power to charter banks. The Marshall Court thus supported the Federalist view that the federal government could promote interstate commerce.

Government Promotion of Market Expansion

Later Supreme Court cases validated government promotion of economic development and encouraged business enterprise. In *Gibbons v. Ogden* (1824), the Supreme Court overturned the New York law granting Robert Fulton and Robert Livingston a monopoly on the New York–New Jersey steamboat trade. Chief Justice Marshall ruled that the federal power to license new enterprises took precedence over New York's grant of monopoly rights and declared that Congress's power under the commerce clause of the Constitution extended to "every species of commercial intercourse." Within two years, the number of steamboats in New York increased from six to forty-three. A later ruling under Chief Justice Roger Taney, *Charles River Bridge v. Warren Bridge* (1837), encouraged new enterprises and technologies by favoring competition over monopoly.

Federal and state courts, in conjunction with state legislatures, encouraged the proliferation of corporations—organizations holding property and transacting business as if they were individuals. Corporation owners, called shareholders, were granted limited liability, or freedom from personal responsibility for the company's debts beyond their original investment.

The government assisted commercial development, too, by expanding the number of U.S. post offices from three thousand in 1815 to fourteen thousand in 1845 and by protecting inventions through patent laws and domestic industries through tariffs on foreign imports.

Boundary Settlements

Monroe's secretary of state, John Quincy Adams, son of John and Abigail Adams, managed the nation's foreign policy from 1817 to 1825. He pushed for expansion of American fishing rights in Atlantic waters, political distance from Europe, and peace. Under Adams's leadership, in 1817 the United States and Great Britain signed the Rush-Bagot Treaty limiting them to one ship each on Lake Champlain and Lake Ontario and to two ships each on the remaining Great Lakes. This first modern disarmament treaty demilitarized the U.S.-Canadian border. Adams then pushed for the Convention of 1818, which fixed the U.S.-Canadian boundary from Lake of the Woods in Minnesota westward to the Rockies along the 49th parallel. They disagreed on the boundary west of the Rockies, so Britain and the U.S. settled on joint occupation of Oregon for ten years (renewed indefinitely in 1827).

Adams's negotiations resulted in the Adams-Onís Treaty, in which the United States gained Florida. Although the Louisiana Purchase omitted reference to Spanish-ruled West Florida, the United States claimed the territory as far east as the Perdido River (the present-day Florida-Alabama border). During the War of 1812, the United States seized Mobile and the remainder of West Florida; after the war, Adams claimed East Florida. In 1819, Don Luís de Onís, the

Travelers, merchants, and livestock clogged portions of the National Road, shown here alongside Milestone 3 in Baltimore in 1829.

Courtesy of the Maryland Historical Society

Spanish minister to the United States, agreed to cede Florida without payment if the United States renounced its dubious claims to northern Mexico (Texas) and assumed $5 million of claims by American citizens against Spain. The Treaty also defined the southwestern boundary of the Louisiana Purchase and divided Spanish Mexico and Oregon Country at the 42nd parallel.

Monroe Doctrine

Adams's desire to insulate the United States and the Western Hemisphere from European conflict brought about his greatest achievement: the **Monroe Doctrine**. Between 1808 and 1822, the United Provinces of Río de la Plata (present-day northern Argentina, Paraguay, and Uruguay), Chile, Peru, Colombia, and Mexico broke from Spain. In 1822, the United States became the first nation outside Latin America to recognize the new states. But with reactionary regimes ascending in Europe and France now occupying Spain, the United States feared that continental powers would attempt to return the new Latin American states to colonial rule.

Monroe Doctrine: Foreign policy statement that proclaimed that American continents are not to be subjected to European colonization and demanded nonintervention by Europe into the New World nations.

Monroe's message to Congress in December 1823 became known as the Monroe Doctrine. He announced that the American continents "are henceforth not to be considered subjects for future colonization by any European power." This addressed American anxiety about Latin America and Russian expansion beyond Alaska and its settlements in California. Monroe demanded nonintervention by Europe in the affairs of independent New World nations, and he pledged U.S. noninterference in European affairs, including Europe's existing New World colonies. European nations stayed out of New World affairs because they feared the British Royal Navy, not the United States' proclamations.

Sectionalism Exposed

The embargo, the War of 1812, and postwar internal improvements encouraged the southern and northern economies to develop in different but interrelated ways. While the South became dependent on cotton, the North underwent an accelerated industrial development. With their commitment to an agrarian nation, Jeffersonians did not promote industry, but some entrepreneurs did.

How did the admission of new states after the War of 1812 ultimately divide the nation?

Early Industrial Development

Despite their separatism, Americans relied on British technology to combine the many steps of textile manufacturing—carding (or disentangling) fibers, spinning yarn, and weaving cloth—under one factory. The first American water-powered spinning mill was established in 1790 by Samuel Slater, a British immigrant who reconstructed from memory the complex machines he had used in England. But Slater's mill only carded and spun yarn; hand-weaving it into cloth was often done by farm women seeking to earn cash. In 1810, Bostonian Francis Cabot Lowell visited the British textile center of Manchester, touring factories and later sketching from memory what he had seen. In 1813, he and his business associates founded the Boston Manufacturing Company, uniting all phases of textile manufacturing under one roof in Waltham, Massachusetts. A decade later, the Boston Manufacturing Company established a model industrial village—named for its now-deceased founder—along the banks of the Merrimack River. At Lowell, Massachusetts, there were boarding houses for workers, a healthy alternative to Manchester's tenements and slums.

When the British flooded the American market with cheap textiles after the War of 1812, Lowell realized the domestic market required protection. He lobbied hard to include cotton textiles in the Tariff of 1816, persuading reluctant South Carolinians to support it.

Northern industrialization was linked to slavery. Much of the capital came from merchants who partly made their fortunes through the trade. Two of the most prominent industries—textiles and shoes—expanded with a growing southern cotton economy. Southern cotton fed northern textile mills, and northern shoe factories sold "Negro brogans" (work shoes) to southern planters.

Panic of 1819

Immediately after the war, the international demand for (and price of) American commodities reached new heights. Poor weather in Europe led to crop failures, increasing demand for northern foodstuffs and Southern cotton, which, in turn, touched off western land speculation. Speculators raced to buy large tracts of land at modest, government-established prices and then to resell them at a hefty profit to would-be settlers.

Prosperity proved short-lived. By the late 1810s, Europeans could grow their own food again, and Britain's new Corn Laws established high tariffs on imports. Cotton prices fell in England. Wars in Latin America interfered with mining and reduced the supply of precious metals, leading European nations to hoard specie. American banks furiously printed paper money and expanded credit even further. Fearful of inflation, the Second Bank of the United States demanded in 1819 that state banks repay loans in specie. State banks then called in the loans and mortgages they had made. Falling commodity prices meant that farmers could not pay their mortgages, and plummeting land values—from 50 to 75 percent in portions of the West—meant they could not meet their debts even by selling their farms. The nation's banking system collapsed, triggering a financial panic.

Foreclosures soared. Unemployment skyrocketed, reaching 75 percent in Philadelphia. Workers and their families could not make it through the winter without charity for food, clothing, and firewood.

Americans everywhere contemplated the virtues and hazards of rapid market expansion, disagreeing on where to place the blame for its shortcomings. Even as the nation's economy rebounded in the early 1820s, amid a flurry of internal improvement projects, no one could predict in what region or sector the nation's fortunes would lie.

Missouri Compromise

America also faced a political crisis in 1819 about slavery's westward expansion. Residents of the Missouri Territory petitioned Congress for admission to the Union with a constitution permitting slavery. Missouri's admission would give slaveholding states a two-vote majority in the Senate and set a precedent for new western states created from the vast Louisiana Purchase.

Following the Louisiana Purchase and especially after the end of the War of 1812, the American population surged westward, leading five new states to join the Union: Louisiana (1812), Indiana (1816), Mississippi (1817), Illinois (1818), and Alabama (1819). Of these, Louisiana, Mississippi, and Alabama permitted slavery. Because Missouri was on the same latitude as free Illinois, Indiana, and Ohio, its admission as a slave state would thrust slavery farther westward and northward.

For two and a half years, the issue dominated Congress. When Representative James Tallmadge Jr. of New York proposed gradual emancipation in Missouri, some

Industrial Piracy

Great Britain, which in the late eighteenth century pioneered mechanical weaving and power looms, knew the value of its head start in the industrial revolution and prohibited the export of textile technology. British-born brothers Samuel and John Slater, their Scottish-born power-loom-builder William Gilmore, and Bostonians Francis Cabot Lowell and Nathan Appleton evaded British restrictions to establish America's first textile factories.

As a supervisor in a British cotton-spinning factory, Samuel Slater had mastered the machinery and the process. To get around British technology laws, Slater emigrated to the United States disguised as a farmer. In 1790 in Pawtucket, Rhode Island, he opened the first water-powered spinning mill in America, rebuilding the complex machines from memory. With his brother John and their Rhode Island partners, Moses and Obadiah Brown and William Almy, Slater later built mills in Rhode Island and Massachusetts. In 1815, he hired a recent immigrant, William Gilmore, to build a water-powered loom like those in Britain. In the 1820s, the Slaters introduced steam-powered looms.

In 1810, while vacationing in Edinburgh, Scotland, Francis Cabot Lowell met fellow Bostonian Nathan Appleton. Impressed by the British textile mills, they planned to introduce water-powered mechanical weaving into the United States. Lowell went to Britain's textile center in Manchester, visiting and observing the factories by day; at night, he sketched the power looms and processes he had seen. Back in the United States, he and others formed the Boston Associates, which created the Waltham-Lowell Mills based on Lowell's industrial piracy. Within a few years, textiles would be a major American industry, and the Boston Associates would dominate it.

Thus, the modern American industrial revolution began with international links, not homegrown American inventions.

This contemporary painting shows the Boston Manufacturing Company's 1814 textile factory at Waltham, Massachusetts. All manufacturing processes were brought together under one roof, and the company built its first factories in rural New England to tap roaring rivers as a power source.

Courtesy of Gore Place Society, Waltham, Massachusetts

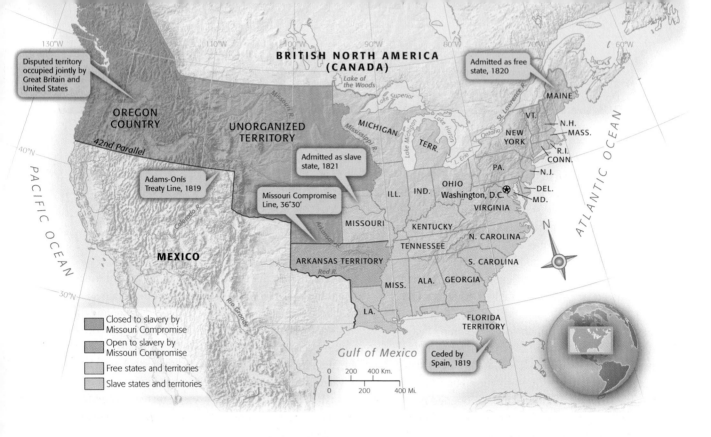

MAP 9.2

Missouri Compromise and the State of the Union, 1820

The compromise worked out by House Speaker Henry Clay established a formula that avoided debate over whether new states would allow or prohibit slavery. In the process, it divided the United States into northern and southern regions.

Source: Copyright © Cengage Learning

southerners accused the North of threatening to destroy the Union. The House, which had a northern majority, passed the Tallmadge Amendment, but the Senate rejected it.

House Speaker Henry Clay—himself a western slaveholder—suggested a compromise in 1820. Maine, carved out of Massachusetts, would enter as a free state, followed by Missouri as a slave state, maintaining the balance between slave and free states. In the rest of the Louisiana Territory north of Missouri's southern border of 36°30', slavery would be prohibited forever (see Map 9.2).

The compromise carried but almost unraveled when Missouri submitted a constitution barring free blacks from entering the state. Opponents contended that it violated the federal constitutional provision that citizens of each state were "entitled to all privileges and immunities of citizens in the several States." Proponents countered that many states already barred free blacks. In 1821, Clay proposed a second compromise: Missouri would guarantee that its laws would not discriminate against citizens of other states. (Once admitted to the Union, Missouri twice adopted laws barring free blacks.) For more than three decades, the **Missouri Compromise** would govern congressional policy toward admitting new slave states. But the compromise masked rather than suppressed the simmering political conflict over slavery's westward expansion.

Missouri Compromise:
Sought to end the debate over the number of slave and free states admitted to the Union by admitting Missouri as a slave state and Maine as a free state and banned slavery in the Louisiana Territory north of the 36°30' latitude line.

States' Rights and Nullification

Under the Constitution, the exact nature of the relationship between the states and the federal government was initially ambiguous, because Constitutional Convention delegates disagreed on whether states or nation should prevail in an irreconcilable conflict. The Tenth Amendment offered a slight clarification: powers not delegated to the central government, it said, were reserved to the states or to the people.

When New England Federalists met in Hartford at the end of 1814 to prepare a list of grievances against "Mr. Madison's War," they drew on the doctrine of nullification, first announced sixteen years earlier in the Kentucky and Virginia Resolutions, written by Thomas Jefferson and James Madison, respectively. Opposing the Alien and Sedition Acts, these founding fathers asserted that, if the national government assumed powers not delegated to it by the Constitution, states could nullify federal actions—that is, declare them inoperative within state borders. Some New England Federalists discussed taking nullification further by seceding. Their formulation of states' rights to nullify federal authority left a legacy for dissent that was reinvoked in crises up to the present.

In the following decade, South Carolina nullified federal tariffs, and in 1861 southern states threatened by Abraham Lincoln's election as president claimed the right of secession. Although the Civil War supposedly settled the issue—states could neither nullify federal law nor secede—southern states opposing the Supreme Court's 1954 ruling in favor of school integration again claimed the right to nullify "unauthorized" federal policy within their borders. In the early twenty-first century, as the U.S. Congress failed to muster a two-thirds majority to propose a constitutional amendment banning gay marriage, dozens of states ratified their own such constitutional amendments. Symbolically, the threat of secession remains potent. Decrying the 2009 federal stimulus package to aid the ailing national economy, Texas Governor Rick Perry declared that his state might secede rather than face unwanted spending, taxation, and debt. The Hartford Convention's legacy provides Americans who dissent from national policy with a model for using state governments, and threats of secession, as vehicles for their protests.

Summary

The partisanship of the 1790s made the early republic a period of vigorous political engagement. With a vision of an agrarian nation that protected individual liberty, Jeffersonians promoted a limited national government—one that stayed out of religious affairs and spent little on military forces, diplomatic missions, and economic initiatives. The rival Federalists, who exerted their influence through the judiciary, declared federal supremacy over the states even as the judiciary affirmed its own supremacy over other government branches. Federalists hoped a strengthened federal government would promote commerce and industry.

Despite his belief in limited government, Jefferson considered the acquisition of the Louisiana Territory and the Corps of Discovery his greatest presidential accomplishments. Americans soon streamed into the Louisiana Territory. More would have gone if not for Indians (and their British allies) and poorly developed transportation routes.

With its economy focused on international shipping, the greatest threats to the United States came from abroad. In its wars with the Barbary states, the United States sought to guard its commerce and ships on the high seas. Although the War of 1812 was a military stalemate, it inspired a new sense of nationalism and launched an era of American development.

The Treaty of Ghent reaffirmed American independence; thereafter, the nation settled disputes with Great Britain by negotiation. The war also dealt a blow to Indian resistance in the Midwest and Southwest, while accelerating American industrial growth. Federalists' opposition to the war undermined their credibility, and their party faded from the national political scene by 1820. The absence of partisan conflict created what contemporaries called an Era of Good Feelings.

Still, competing visions of America's route to prosperity endured. Under Chief Justice John Marshall, the Supreme Court supported the Federalist agenda, issuing rulings that stimulated commerce and industry. The Democratic-Republicans looked, instead, toward the vast and fertile Louisiana Territory. Fearful of European intentions to reassert influence in the Americas and emboldened by the nation's expanding boundaries, President Monroe proclaimed that the United States would not tolerate European intervention in American affairs. But even as its expanding boundaries strengthened the United States' international presence, territorial expansion threatened newfound political unity at home.

Tensions mounted in 1819, when the postwar economic boom came to a halt and congressmen sharply divided over whether to admit Missouri as a slave state. Henry Clay's compromise temporarily removed the issue of slavery's western expansion from political center stage.

Chapter Review

Political Visions

Was Jefferson's election and political vision truly "the revolution of 1800"?

Jefferson considered his election in 1800 a revolution, since it also gave his Democratic-Republican Party a majority in both houses of Congress. That made it easier to enact his vision of limited government, individual liberty (which required the separation of church and state), and an agrarian (versus commercial) republic. Since Democratic-Republicans viewed national debt as a sign of corruption, he authorized his treasury secretary to cut the federal budget and decrease the national debt (which Federalists saw as a tool to stimulate the economy). Jefferson also pardoned those convicted under the Alien and Sedition Acts, which he regarded as a violation of liberties, and attempted to remove from court appointments people opposed to his brand of politics. (He was ultimately unsuccessful, which maintained the Court's independence).

National Expansion Westward

Why was the Louisiana Purchase among Jefferson's most popular decisions as president?

The purchase of 827,000 square miles of land west of the Mississippi from France doubled the size of the United States, secured American interests from potential European incursion at its inland borders, and opened more land for American settlement (even though Native Americans were already living there). Moreover, by purchasing the land on the other side of the river, the United States controlled access to the Mississippi, which appealed to western settlers who relied on it to get their goods to market. Finally, it fed dreams of cheap, fertile lands for would-be settlers.

The Nation in the Orbit of Europe

What led to the War of 1812?

Freedom of the seas was the main cause. Ongoing hostilities between European nations spilled over onto American ships, as Great Britain often stopped and seized U.S. ships and forced those aboard into military service. Trade embargoes did little to stop the practice and ultimately hurt American merchants and the U.S. economy. Madison pointed to violation of neutral trading rights, British alliances with western Indians, and affronts to American independence as additional causes, while others saw war as an opportunity to annex British Canada. Although Britain reopened the seas and ordered its ships not to disturb American warships by June of 1812, news of the policy change did not reach America until long after Congress declared war.

The War of 1812

What were the consequences of the War of 1812?

Although the Treaty of Ghent ended the fighting and restored the prewar status quo, the United States did not get the results it wanted on impressments, blockades, and maritime rights for neutral parties. The war did, however, affirm American independence and guarantee no future battles with Britain over trade or territory. On the home front, the war shattered the U.S. economy and led some New England Federalists to threaten secession, which contributed to the party's demise when the war soon ended. Indians who had supported the British lost a major ally. And while Indians had their land and rights restored by the Treaty of Ghent, they had no power to enforce it. With the end of war, three trends emerged that were pivotal for the nation's future: westward expansion, the entrenchment of slavery, and industrial development.

The Nationalist Program

How did the American System mark the triumph of Federalist economic policy?

Long opposed to big government, Democratic-Republicans amended this philosophy to adopt the Federalist notion that the central government should aid economic growth. Their program was dubbed the American System, and included a national bank, development of transportation networks, and a protective tariff that would tax imported goods to protect American products from foreign competitors. Advocates of the American System, such as South Carolina leader John C. Calhoun, believed it could bridge sectional divides and expand the nation. Both parties embraced internal improvements for different reasons: Federalists saw them as spurring commercial development, while Jeffersonians (Democratic-Republicans) thought they would lead to western and agrarian expansion.

Sectionalism Exposed

How did the admission of new states after the War of 1812 ultimately divide the nation?

The question of slavery's westward expansion sparked controversy in 1819 when the Missouri Territory asked to be admitted as a slave state. Many feared it would give slaveholding states a two-vote Senate majority and would set a precedent for admitting other western states. And since Missouri was on the same latitude as free Illinois, Indiana, and Ohio, its admission as a slave state would move slavery northward. House Speaker Henry Clay suggested the winning compromise: to maintain the balance between free and slave states, Maine would enter as a free state, Missouri as a slave state, and all future new states north of Missouri's 36°30' border would prohibit slavery. As such, the Missouri Compromise divided the nation into two regions, north and south, according to the politics of slavery.

Suggestions for Further Reading

Stephen Aron, *American Confluence: The Missouri Frontier from Borderland to Border State* (2006)

David Edmunds, *Tecumseh and the Quest for Indian Leadership* (2006)

Joanne B. Freeman, *Affairs of Honor: National Politics in the New Republic* (2001)

Nancy Isenberg, *Fallen Founder: The Life of Aaron Burr* (2007)

John Lauritz Larson, *Internal Improvement: National Public Works and the Promise of Popular Government in the United States* (2001)

Jon Latimer, *1812: War with America* (2007)

Kent Newmyer, *John Marshall and the Heroic Age of the Supreme Court* (2001)

Jeffrey Ostler, *The Plains Sioux and U.S. Colonialism from Lewis and Clark to Wounded Knee* (2004)

Jeffrey Pasley, Andrew Robertson, and David Waldstreicher, eds., *Beyond the Founders: New Approaches to the Political History of the Early American Republic* (2004)

 CourseMate

Go to the CourseMate website for primary source links, study tools, and review materials for this chapter.
www.cengagebrain.com

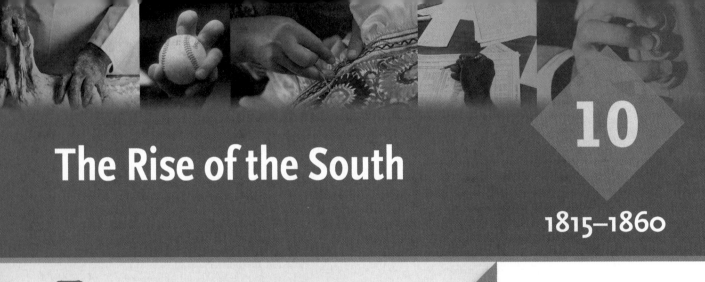

The Rise of the South

10

1815–1860

homas Jefferson died, as he had lived, in debt, on July 4, 1826, the same day his long-time rival John Adams died. At Monticello, Jefferson's home in Virginia, anxiety filled his white and black "families."

On January 15, 1827, a five-day estate sale took place at Monticello. Among the paintings, furniture, and mementoes were "130 valuable negroes." Monticello's blacksmith, Joseph Fossett, watched his wife Edith and eight children sold to four different bidders.

Jefferson was reportedly a caring slaveholder, who tried to keep families intact. After his wife, Martha (with whom he had two daughters), died in 1782, Jefferson had six children, four of whom lived beyond infancy, with his slave Sally Hemings. Sally was the half sister of Jefferson's wife and part of an extended family of light-skinned Hemingses.

Joe Fossett, as Jefferson promised, became free one year after his master's death. Jefferson had earlier freed his four children with Sally Hemings: William Beverly Hemings, Harriet Hemings II, James Madison Hemings, and Thomas Eston Hemings. Jefferson never freed Sally; Virginia law would have required him to attain, publicly, a dispensation from the state legislature to free her without removing her from the state. Jefferson wanted no more salacious publicity about his house servant and mistress. Sally died a slave in Charlottesville, Virginia, in 1835 at age sixty-two.

"Thank heaven the whole of this dreadful business is over," wrote Jefferson's granddaughter, Mary, after the auction. She consoled herself that most slaves were sold within the state. Monticello was sold in 1831. But across the South in the 1820s, the "business" of slavery's expansion and cotton production was not over.

In 1815, southern states and territories, with fertile soil and a growing slave labor force, were poised for prosperity and power. New lands were settled, new states were peopled, and the South emerged as the world's most extensive commercial agricultural economy. The Old South's wealth came from export crops, land, and slaves, and its population was almost wholly rural. Racial slavery also affected values, customs, laws, class structure, and the region's relationship to the nation and the world. As slaves were increasingly defined as chattel, they struggled to survive and resist, sometimes overtly, but typically in daily life and culture. By 1860, white Southerners asserted the moral and economic benefits of slavery and sought to advance their power over the national government.

As you read this chapter, keep the following questions in mind:

* How and why was the Old South a "slave society," with slavery permeating every class and group within it, free or unfree?

* How and why did white southerners come to see cotton as "king" of a global economy, and how did the cotton trade's international reach shape southern society from 1815 to 1860?

* How did African American slaves build and sustain a meaningful life and a sense of community amid the potential chaos and destruction of their circumstances?

* How would you weigh the comparative significance of the following central themes in the history of the Old South: class, race, migration, power, liberty, wealth?

VISUALIZING THE PAST *Imaging Nat Turner's Rebellion*

LEGACY FOR A PEOPLE AND A NATION *Reparations for Slavery*

SUMMARY

The "Distinctive" South

What made the antebellum South different from the North?

Not until the first half of the 1800s did slaveholding states from the Chesapeake and Virginia to Missouri, and from Florida to Texas, come to be designated as the South. Today, many consider it America's most distinctive region. Historians have long examined how the Old South was like and unlike the rest of the nation. Because of its unique history, has the South, in the words of poet Allen Tate, always been "Uncle Sam's other province"? Analyzing why the South seems more religious, conservative, or tragic than other regions of America has been an enduring practice.

American values, such as materialism, individualism, and faith in progress, have been associated with the North and values such as tradition, honor, and family loyalty, with the South. Stereotype has also labeled the South as static, even "backward," and the North as dynamic in the decades before the Civil War. In truth, there were many Souths: low-country rice and cotton regions with dense slave populations; mountainous regions of small farmers; semitropical wetlands in the Southeast; **plantation** culture in the Cotton Belt and Mississippi valley; tobacco- and wheat-growing regions in Virginia and North Carolina; bustling port cities; wilderness areas with rare hillfolk homesteads.

plantation: Large landholding devoted to a cash crop such as cotton or tobacco.

South-North Similarity The South shared much in common with the rest of the nation. The geographic sizes of the South and the North were roughly the same. In 1815, white southerners and free northerners shared heroes and ideology from the American Revolution and War of 1812. They worshiped the same Protestant God as northerners, lived under the same Constitution, and similarly combined nationalism and localism in their attitudes toward government.

Chronology

1810–20	137,000 slaves are forced to move from the Upper South to Alabama, Mississippi, and other western regions	1845	Florida and Texas gain admission to the Union as slave states
1822	Vesey's insurrection plot is discovered in South Carolina		Publication of Douglass's *Narrative of the Life of Frederick Douglass, an American Slave, Written by Himself*
1830s	Vast majority of African American slaves are native-born in America	1850	Planters' share of agricultural wealth in the South is 90 to 95 percent
1830s–40s	Cotton trade grows into largest source of commercial wealth and America's leading export	1850–60	Of some 300,000 slaves who migrate from the Upper to the Lower South, 60 to 70 percent go by outright sale
1831	Turner leads a violent slave rebellion in Virginia		
1832	Virginia holds the last debate in the South about the future of slavery; gradual abolition is voted down	1857	Publication of Hinton R. Helper's *The Impending Crisis,* denouncing the slave system
	Publication of Dew's proslavery tract *Abolition of Negro Slavery*		Publication of George Fitzhugh's *Southern Thought,* an aggressive defense of slavery
1836	Arkansas gains admission to the Union as a slave state	1860	405,751 mulattos in the United States, 12.5 percent of the African American population
1839	Mississippi's Married Women's Property Act gives married women some property rights		Three-quarters of all southern white families own no slaves
			South produces largest cotton crop ever

But as slavery and the plantation economy expanded, the South did not become a land of individual opportunity in the same manner as the North.

Research has shown that, despite enormous cruelties, slavery was a profitable labor system for planters. Southerners and northerners shared an expanding capitalist economy. As it grew, the slave-based economy of money-crop agriculture reflected planters' rational choices. More land and slaves generally converted into more wealth.

By the Civil War in 1860, the distribution of wealth and property in the two sections was almost identical: 50 percent of free adult males owned only 1 percent of real and personal property, and the richest 1 percent owned 27 percent of the wealth. North and South had ruling classes. Entrepreneurs in both sections sought their fortunes in an expanding market economy. The southern "master class" was more likely than propertied northerners to move west to make a profit.

South-North Dissimilarity

In terms of differences, the South's climate and longer growing season gave it a rural and agricultural destiny. Many great rivers provided rich soil and transportation routes. The South developed as a biracial society of brutal inequality, where the liberty and wealth of one race depended on the enslavement of another. Cotton growers spread out over large areas to maximize production and income. Consequently, population density in the South was low; by 1860, there were only 2.3 people per square mile in vast and largely unsettled Texas, 15.6 in Louisiana, and 18.0 in Georgia. The Northeast averaged 65.4 people per square mile. Massachusetts had 153.1 people per square mile, and New York City compressed 86,400 people into each square mile.

Where people were scarce, it was difficult to finance and operate schools, churches, libraries, and inns and restaurants. Similarly, the South's rural character and vision of the plantation as self-sufficient meant that the section spent little on public health. Southerners were strongly committed to their churches, and some embraced universities, but these institutions were far less developed than in the North. Factories were rare, because planters invested their capital primarily in slaves. The largest southern "industry" was lumbering, and the largest factories used slaves to make cigars. The South was slower than the North to develop a unified market economy and a regional transportation network and had only 35 percent of the nation's railroad mileage in 1860.

The Old South never developed its own banking and shipping capacity to any degree and relied heavily on the North for both. Most southern bank deposits were in the North, and as early as 1822, one-sixth of all southern cotton cleared for Liverpool or Le Havre from the port of New York and constituted two-fifths of all that city's exports. With cotton constituting two-fifths of New York's exports, merchants and bankers there became interested in the fate of slavery and cotton prices. In economic conventions from 1837 to 1839, southern delegates debated foreign trade, dependence on northern importers and financiers, and other alleged threats to their commercial independence. But nothing came of these conventions.

The South lagged far behind the North in industrial growth. Its urban centers were mostly ports like New Orleans and Charleston, which became crossroads of commerce and small-scale manufacturing. In the interior were small market towns dependent on agricultural trade. As a system of racial control, slavery did not work well in cities. Lacking manufacturing jobs, the South did not attract immigrants as readily the North. By 1860, only 13 percent of the nation's foreign-born population lived in the slave states.

Like most northerners, antebellum southerners embraced evangelical Christianity. Americans from all regions believed in a personal God and in conversion and piety as the means to salvation. But southern Baptists and Methodists concentrated on personal rather than social improvement. By the 1830s in the North, evangelicalism was a wellspring of reform movements (see Chapter 9); but in states where blacks were numerous and unfree, religion, as one scholar has written, preached "a hands-off policy concerning slavery." Moreover, distance and sparse population prevented reform-minded women from developing associations with each other. The reform movements that emerged in the South, such as temperance, focused on personal behavior, not social reform.

A Southern World-View and the Proslavery Argument

In the wake of the American Revolution, Enlightenment ideas of natural rights and equality stimulated antislavery sentiment in the Upper South, produced a brief flurry of manumissions and inspired hope for gradual emancipation. But that confidence waned in the new nation. As slavery spread, southerners vigorously defended it. In 1816, George Bourne, a Presbyterian minister exiled from Virginia for his antislavery sermons and for expulsion of slaveholders from his church, charged that, whenever southerners were challenged on slavery, "they were fast choked, for they had a Negro stuck fast in their throats."

By the 1820s, white southerners justified slavery as a "**positive good**," not merely a "necessary evil." They used the antiquity of slavery, as well as the Bible's

positive good: Southern justification for slavery as beneficial to the larger society, both to white owners and their black slaves.

many references to slaveholding, to foster a historical argument for bondage. But at the heart of the proslavery rationale was a deep and abiding racism. Whites were the more intellectual race, they claimed, and blacks more inherently physical and therefore destined for labor. In an 1851 proslavery tract, John Campbell declared that "there is as much difference between the lowest tribe of negroes and the white Frenchman, Englishman, or American, as there is between the monkey and the negro."

Some southerners defended slavery in practical terms; their bondsmen were economic necessities. In 1845, James Henry Hammond of South Carolina argued that slaveholding was a matter of property rights, protected by the Constitution because slaves were legal property. The deepest root of the proslavery argument was a hierarchical view of the social order with slavery prescribed by God. Southerners cherished tradition, believing social change should come slowly, if at all. As Nat Turner's slave rebellion compelled the Virginia legislature to debate the gradual abolition of slavery in 1831–1832, Thomas R. Dew, a slaveholder and professor at the College of William and Mary, contended that "that which is the growth of *ages* may require ages to remove." Dew's widely read work *Abolition of Negro Slavery* (1832) ushered an outpouring of proslavery writing that would intensify over the next thirty years. As slavery expanded westward and fueled national prosperity, Dew cautioned that gradual abolition threatened the South's "irremediable ruin." Dew declared black slavery the "order of nature," and the basis of the "well-ordered, well-established liberty" of white Americans.

Proslavery advocates invoked natural-law doctrine, arguing that the natural state of humankind was inequality of ability and condition, not equality. Proslavery writers believed that people were born to certain stations in life; they stressed dependence over autonomy and duty over rights as the human condition. As Virginia writer George Fitzhugh put it in 1854, "Men are not born entitled to equal rights. It would be far nearer the truth to say, that some were born with saddles on their backs, and others booted and spurred to ride them."

Many slaveholders saw themselves in a paternal role, as guardians of a familial relationship between masters and slaves. Although contradicted by countless examples of slave resistance and escape, and by slave sales, planters needed to believe in and exerted great energy in constructing the idea of the contented slave.

A Slave Society

In the Old South, whites and blacks grew up, were socialized, married, reared children, worked, conceived of property, and honed their most basic habits of behavior under the influence of slavery. This was true of slaveholding and nonslaveholding whites, as well as slave and free blacks. Slavery shaped the social structure of the South, fueled its economy, and dominated its politics.

The South was interdependent with the North, the West, and Europe in a growing capitalist market system. For its cotton trade, southerners relied on northern banks, northern steamship companies, and northern merchants. But there were elements of that system that southerners increasingly disliked, especially urbanism, the wage labor, a broadening right to vote, and threats to their racial and class order.

Americans have long struggled to define what one historian called the "Dixie difference." "The South is both American and something different," writes another historian, "at times a mirror or magnifier of national traits and at other times a counterculture." Distinctive and national, the South's story begins in what we have come to call the Old South, a term only conceivable after the eviction of native peoples from the region.

Southern Expansion, Indian Resistance and Removal

How did Native Americans living in western territories deal with increasing migration by southern whites?

When the trans-Appalachian frontier opened after the War of 1812, some 5 to 10 percent of the population moved annually, usually westward. In the first two decades of the century, they poured into the Ohio valley; by the 1820s, they were migrating into the Mississippi River valley and beyond. By 1850, two-thirds of Americans lived west of the Appalachians.

A Southern Westward Movement

After 1820, the heart of cotton cultivation and the slave-based plantation system shifted from the coastal states to Alabama and the newly settled Mississippi valley— Tennessee, Louisiana, Arkansas, and Mississippi. Southern slaveholders took slaves with them to the newer areas of the South, and **yeoman** farmers followed, also hoping for new wealth through cheap land and slaves.

yeoman: Independent small farmer, usually nonslaveholding.

A wave of migration was evident across the Southeast. As early as 1817, a Charleston, South Carolina, newspaper reported that migration out of that state had reached "unprecedented proportions." Almost half of the white people born in South Carolina after 1800 left the state, most for the Southwest. The way to wealth for southern seaboard planters was to go west to grow cotton for the booming world markets, by purchasing more land and slaves. The population of Mississippi soared from 73,000 in 1820 to 607,000 in 1850, with African American slaves in the majority. Across the Mississippi River, the population of Arkansas went from 14,000 in 1820 to 210,000 in 1850. By 1835, the American immigrant population in Texas reached 35,000, including 3,000 slaves, outnumbering Mexicans two to one. American settlers declared Texas's independence from Mexico in 1836, spurring further American immigration into the region. By 1845, "Texas fever" boosted the Anglo population to 125,000. Statehood that year opened the floodgates to more immigrants and to a confrontation with Mexico that would lead to war.

As the **cotton kingdom** grew to what southern political leaders dreamed would be national and world dominion, this westward migration, fueled initially by optimistic nationalism, ultimately made migrant planters more sectional and southern. In time, political dominance in the South migrated westward into the Cotton Belt. By the 1840s and 1850s, these capitalist planters, fearful that their slave-based economy was under attack, sought to protect and expand their system. Increasingly, they saw themselves, as one historian has written, less as "landowners who happened to own slaves" than as "slaveholders who happened to own land."

cotton kingdom: A broad swath of territory where cotton was a mainstay that stretched from South Carolina, Georgia, and northern Florida in the east through Alabama, Mississippi, central and western Tennessee, and Louisiana, and from there on to Arkansas and Texas.

But other Americans already occupied much of the desired land. Before 1830, large swaths of upper Georgia belonged to the Cherokees, and huge regions of Alabama and Mississippi were Creek, Choctaw, or Chickasaw land. Indians were also on the move, but in forced migrations. For most white Americans, Indians were in the way of their growing empire. Taking Indian land, so the reasoning went, reflected the natural course of history and progress: the "civilizers" had to displace

The Amistad Case

In April 1839 a Spanish slave ship, *Tecora*, sailed from Lomboko, the region of West Africa that became Sierre Leone. On board were Mende people, sold by their African enemies. In June they arrived in Havana, Cuba, a Spanish colony. Two Spaniards purchased 53 of the Mende and sailed aboard *La Amistad* for their plantations elsewhere in Cuba. After three days, the Africans revolted. Led by a man the Spaniards called Joseph Cinque, they killed the captain and seized control of the vessel. They ordered the two Spaniards to return them to Africa, but the slaveholders tried to reach the American South. Far off course, the Amistad was seized by the USS *Washington* in Long Island Sound and brought ashore in Connecticut.

New Haven Colony Historical Society

Joseph Cinque, by Nathaniel Jocelyn, 1840. Cinque led the rebellion aboard "The Amistad," a Spanish ship carrying captive Africans along the coast of Cuba in 1839. They commandeered the ship and sailed it north toward New England where they were rescued off the coast of Connecticut. Cinque, celebrated as a great leader, sat for the painting while he and his people awaited trial. They were freed by a decision of the U.S. Supreme Court in 1841 and returned to their homeland in Sierra Leone in West Africa.

The "Amistad Africans" soon became a cause for abolitionists and slaveholders, as well as in U.S.-Spanish relations. The Africans were imprisoned in New Haven, and a dispute ensued: Were they slaves and murderers and the property of their Cuban owners, or were they free people exercising their natural rights? Were they Spanish property, seized on the high seas in violation of a 1795 treaty? If a northern state could "free" captive Africans, what did it mean for enslaved African Americans in the South? Connecticut abolitionists went to court, where a U.S. circuit court judge dismissed the mutiny and murder charges but refused to release the Africans because their Spanish owners claimed them as property.

Meanwhile, a Yale professor of ancient languages, Josiah Gibbs, visited the captives and learned their words for numbers. In New York he walked along the docks repeating the Mende words until an African seaman, James Covey, responded. Covey journeyed to New Haven, conversed with the jubilant Africans, and soon their tale garnered sympathy throughout New England.

In a new trial, the judge ruled that the Africans were illegally enslaved and ordered them returned to their homeland. Slave trade between Africa and the Americas was outlawed in a treaty between Spain and Great Britain. Spain's lawyers demanded the return of their "merchandise." Needing southern votes to win reelection, President Martin Van Buren supported Spanish claims and advocated the Africans' return to a likely death in Cuba.

The administration appealed the case to the Supreme Court in February 1841. Arguing the abolitionists' case, former president John Quincy Adams pointed to a copy of the Declaration of Independence on the court wall, invoked the natural rights to life and liberty, and chastised Van Buren. In a 7-to-1 decision, the Court ruled that the Africans were "freeborn."

On November 27, 1841, thirty-five survivors and five American missionaries disembarked for Africa, arriving in Sierre Leone on January 15, 1842.

The Amistad case showed how intertwined slavery was with freedom, and the United States with the world. It poisoned diplomatic relations between America and Spain for a generation, and stimulated Christian mission work in Africa.

the "children of the forest." National leaders provided the rhetoric and justification needed. As president in 1830, Andrew Jackson spoke with certainty about why the Indians must go. "What good man would prefer a country," he asked, "covered with forests and ranged by a few thousand savages to our extensive Republic, studded with cities, towns, and prosperous farms?"

Indian Treaty Making   In theory, under the U.S. Constitution, the federal government recognized Indian sovereignty and treated Indian peoples as foreign nations. Agreements between Indian nations and the United States were signed and ratified like other international treaties. In practice, however, fraud dominated the government's approach to treaty making and Indian sovereignty. As the country expanded, new treaties would shrink Indian land holdings.

Although Indian resistance persisted against such pressure after the War of 1812, it only slowed the process. In the 1820s, native peoples in the Middle West, Ohio valley, Mississippi valley, and other parts of the cotton South ceded lands totaling 200 million acres for a pittance.

Indian Accommodation   Increasingly, Indian nations east of the Mississippi sought to survive through accommodation. In the first three decades of the century, the Choctaw, Creek, and Chickasaw peoples in the lower Mississippi became suppliers and traders. Under treaty provisions, trading posts and stores provided Indians with supplies and purchased or bartered for Indian-produced goods. The trading posts extended credit to chiefs, who increasingly fell into debt that they could pay off to the federal government only by selling their land.

By 1822, the Choctaw nation had sold 13 million acres but still carried a $13,000 debt. The Indians struggled, increasing agricultural production and hunting, working as farmhands and craftsmen, and selling produce at market stalls in Natchez and New Orleans. As the United States expanded westward, white Americans promoted their assimilation through education and conversion to Christianity. In 1819, in response to missionary lobbying, Congress appropriated $10,000 annually for "civilization of the tribes adjoining the frontier settlements."

Within five years, thirty-two boarding schools enrolled Indian students run by Protestant missionaries. They substituted English for American Indian languages and taught agriculture alongside the Christian gospel. But settlers continued to eye Indian land. Wherever native peoples lived, illegal settlers disrupted their lives. The federal government only halfheartedly enforced treaties, as legitimate Indian land rights gave way to the advance of white civilization.

With loss of land came dependency. The Choctaws relied on white Americans for manufactured goods and even food. Disease further facilitated removal of American Indian peoples to western lands. While other groups increased rapidly, the Indian population fell, some nations declining by 50 percent in three decades. The French traveler and author Alexis de Tocqueville concluded, after observing the tragedy of forced removal in 1831, "as they give way or perish, an immense and increasing people fill their place. There is no instance upon record of so prodigious a growth or so rapid a destruction." As many as 100,000 eastern and southern Indian peoples were removed between 1820 and 1850; about 30,000 died in the process.

Removal had a profound impact on all Shawnees, the people of the Prophet and Tecumseh. After giving up 17 million acres in Ohio in a 1795 treaty, the Shawnees scattered to Indiana and eastern Missouri. Many moved to Kansas territory in 1825. By 1854, Kansas was open to white settlement and the Shawnees had ceded seven-eighths of their land or 1.4 million acres. Men lost their traditional role as providers; their skills hunting woodland animals were useless on the prairies of Kansas. As grain became the tribe's dietary staple, Shawnee women played a greater role as providers, supplemented by government aid under treaty provisions. Remarkably, the Shawnees preserved their language and culture despite these devastating dislocations.

Indian Removal as Federal Policy

Cherokees, Creeks, Choctaws, Chickasaws, and Seminoles aggressively resisted white encroachment after the War of 1812. In his last annual message to Congress in late 1824, President James Monroe proposed that all Indians be moved beyond the Mississippi River. Monroe considered this an "honorable" proposal that would protect Indians from invasion and provide them with independence for "improvement and civilization." He believed force would be unnecessary.

But all four tribes unanimously rejected Monroe's proposition. Between 1789 and 1825, the four nations negotiated thirty treaties with the United States, and they reached their limit. Most wished to remain on what little was left of their ancestral land.

Pressure from Georgia had prompted Monroe's policy. In the 1820s, the state had accused the federal government of not fulfilling its 1802 promise to remove the Cherokees and Creeks from northwestern Georgia in return for the state's renunciation of its claim to western lands. In 1826, under federal pressure, the Creek nation ceded all but a small strip of its Georgia acreage, but for Georgians only their complete removal to the West would resolve the conflict.

In an unsuccessful attempt to hold on to the remainder of their traditional lands, which were in Alabama, the Creeks radically altered their political structure. In 1829, they centralized tribal authority and forbade any chief from ceding land.

In 1830, after extensive debate and a narrow vote, Congress passed the **Indian Removal Act**, authorizing the president to negotiate removal treaties with all tribes living east of the Mississippi. The bill, which provided federal funds for such relocations, would likely not have passed the House without the additional representation afforded slave states due to the Constitution's three-fifths clause.

Cherokees

No people met the challenge of assimilating to American standards more thoroughly than the Cherokees, whose traditional home centered on eastern Tennessee and northern Alabama and Georgia. Between 1819 and 1829, the tribe became economically self-sufficient and politically self-governing; during this Cherokee renaissance the nearly fifteen thousand adult Cherokees regarded themselves as a nation, not a collection of villages. In 1821 and 1822, Sequoyah, a self-educated Cherokee, devised an eighty-six-character phonetic alphabet that made possible a Cherokee-language Bible and a bilingual tribal newspaper, *Cherokee Phoenix* (1828). Between 1820 and 1823, the Cherokees created a formal government with a bicameral legislature, a court system, and in 1827 they adopted a written constitution modeled after that of the United States. They transformed their economy from hunting, gathering, and subsistence agriculture to commodity trade based on barter, cash, and credit. The Cherokee nation, however,

Link to the Indian Removal Act.

Indian Removal Act: Authorized Andrew Jackson to exchange public lands in the West for Indian territories in the East and appropriated federal funds to cover the expenses of removal.

Link to editorials by Elias Boudinot on Indian Removal.

collectively owned all tribal land and forbade land sales to outsiders. Nonetheless, many became individual farmers and slaveholders; by 1833, they held fifteen hundred black slaves. Over time, Cherokee racial identity became very complex.

But Cherokee transformations failed to win respect from white southerners. In the 1820s, Georgia pressed them to sell the 7,200 square miles of land they held in the state. Congress appropriated $30,000 in 1822 to buy the Georgia land, but the Cherokees resisted. Impatient, Georgia annulled the Cherokees' constitution, extended the state's sovereignty over them, prohibited the Cherokee National Council from meeting except to cede land, and ordered their lands seized. The discovery of gold on Cherokee land in 1829 further whetted Georgia's appetite for Cherokee territory.

Cherokee Nation v. Georgia

The Cherokees under Chief John Ross turned to the federal courts to defend their treaty with the United States. In *Cherokee Nation v. Georgia* (1831), Chief Justice John Marshall ruled that under the Constitution an Indian tribe was neither a foreign nation nor a state and therefore had no standing in federal courts. Indians were deemed "domestic, dependent nations." Legally, they were in but not of the United States. Nonetheless, said Marshall, the Indians had a right to their lands; they could lose title only by voluntarily giving it up.

A year later, in *Worcester v. Georgia,* Marshall declared that the Indian nation was a distinct political community in which "the laws of Georgia can have no force" and into which Georgians could not enter without permission or treaty. *Phoenix* editor Elias Boudinot called the decision "glorious news." Jackson, however, whose reputation was built as an Indian fighter, did his best to usurp the Court's action. Newspapers widely reported that Jackson had said, "John Marshall has made his decision: now let him enforce it." To open new lands for settlement, Jackson favored expelling the Cherokees.

Georgians, too, refused to comply, and they refused to hear Indians' pleas to share their American dream. A Cherokee census indicated that they owned 33 grist mills, 13 sawmills, 1 powder mill, 69 blacksmith shops, 2 tanneries, 762 looms, 2,486 spinning wheels, 172 wagons, 2,923 plows, 7,683 horses, 22,531 cattle, 46,732 pigs, and 2,566 sheep. "You asked us to form a republican government," declared the Cherokee leader, John Ridge, in 1832. "We did so—adopting your own as a model. You asked us to cultivate the earth, and learn the mechanic arts: We did so. You asked us to learn to read: We did so. You asked us to cast away our idols, and worship your God: We did so." But neither the plow nor the Bible earned the Cherokees respect in the face of the economic, imperial, and racial quests of their fellow southerners (see Map 10.1).

Trail of Tears

The Choctaws made the first forced journey from Mississippi and Alabama to the West in the winter of 1831 and 1832. Alexis de Tocqueville was visiting Memphis when they passed through: "The wounded, the sick, newborn babies, and the old men on the point of death.... I saw them embark to cross the great river," he wrote, "and the sight will never fade from my memory. Neither sob nor complaint rose from that silent assembly." The Creeks in Alabama resisted removal until 1836; a year later, the Chickasaws followed.

Some Cherokees believed that further resistance was hopeless and accepted removal, agreeing in 1835 to exchange their southern home for western land in the Treaty of New Echota. Most wanted to stand firm. John Ross, with petitions signed by fifteen thousand Cherokees, lobbied the Senate against ratification of the treaty. He lost. But when evacuation came in 1838, most Cherokees refused to move. President Martin Van Buren sent federal troops; about twenty thousand Cherokees were evicted, held in detention camps, and marched under military escort to Indian Territory in present-day Oklahoma. Nearly one-quarter died of disease and exhaustion on what came to be known as the **Trail of Tears**.

When the forced march ended, the Indians had traded about 100 million acres east of the Mississippi for 32 million acres west of the river plus $68 million. Forced removal had a disastrous impact on the Cherokees and other displaced Indian nations. In the West, they encountered an alien environment. Unable to live off the land, many became dependent on government payments. The Cherokees struggled over their tribal government. In 1839, followers of John Ross assassinated the leaders of the protreaty faction. Violence continued sporadically until a new treaty in 1846

Trail of Tears: Forced migration in 1838 of Cherokee Indians from their homelands in the southeast to what is now Oklahoma.

MAP 10.1

Removal of Native Americans from the South, 1820–1840

Over a twenty-year period, the federal government and southern states forced Native Americans to exchange their traditional homes for western land. Some tribal groups remained in the South, but most settled in the alien western environment.

Source: Copyright © Cengage Learning

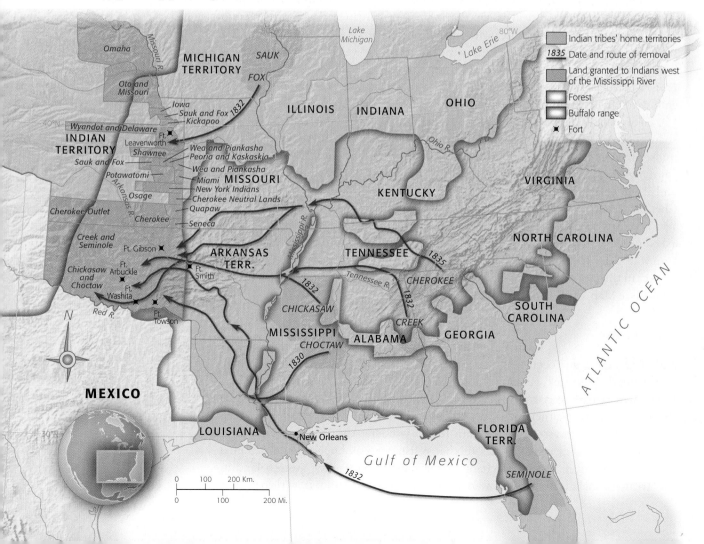

Thomas Gilcrease Institute of American History and Art

The Trail of Tears, by twentieth-century Pawnee artist Brummet Echohawk. About twenty thousand Cherokees were evicted in 1838–1839, and about one-quarter of them died on the forced march to present-day Oklahoma.

imposed a temporary truce. In time, the Cherokees reestablished their political institutions and a governing body in Tahlequah, in northeastern Oklahoma.

Seminole Wars In Florida, some Seminole leaders agreed in the 1832 Treaty of Payne's Landing to relocate to the West within three years, but others opposed the treaty. A minority under the charismatic leader Osceola refused to vacate and fought the protreaty group. When federal troops were sent to impose removal in 1835, Osceola waged a guerrilla war against them.

The Florida Indians were a varied group that included many Creeks and mixed Indian–African Americans (ex-slaves or descendants of runaway slaves). The U.S. Army, however, considered them all Seminoles. General Thomas Jesup believed that the runaway slave population was the key to the war. "And if it be not speedily put down," he wrote a friend in 1836, "the South will feel the effects of it on their slave population before the end of the next season."

Osceola was captured and died in an army prison in 1838, but Seminoles fought on under Chief Coacoochee (Wild Cat) and other leaders. In 1842, the United States abandoned removal. Most of Osceola's followers agreed to move west to Indian Territory after another war in 1858, but some remained in the Florida Everglades.

Social Pyramid in the Old South

What class tensions emerged in the antebellum South?

A large majority of white southerners (three-quarters in 1860) owned no slaves. Most were yeoman farmers who owned their own land and grew their own food. The social distance between poorer whites and the planter class could be great. Still greater was the distance between whites and blacks with free status. White yeomen, landless whites, and free blacks occupied the broad base of the social pyramid in the Old South.

Yeoman Farmers

After the War of 1812, white farmers—many with no slaves—moved in waves down the southern Appalachians into the Gulf lands or through the Cumberland Gap into Kentucky and Tennessee. In large sections of the South, especially inland from the coast and away from large rivers, small, self-sufficient farms were the norm. Lured by stories of good land, many men repeatedly uprooted their wives and children.

Their status as a numerical majority did not mean that they set the political or economic direction of the larger society. Self-reliant and often isolated, they operated both apart from and within the slave-based staple-crop economy.

On the southern frontier, men cleared fields, built log cabins, and established farms, while their wives labored in the household and patiently re-created the social ties—to relatives, neighbors, fellow churchgoers—that enriched everyone's experience. Women dreaded the isolation and loneliness of the frontier.

Some yeomen acquired large tracts of level land, purchased slaves, and became planters. They forged part of the new wealth of the cotton boom states of Mississippi and Louisiana, where mobility into the slaveowning class was possible. Others clung to familiar mountainous areas or sought self-sufficiency. As one historian has written, though they owned no slaves, yeomen were jealous of their independence, and "the household grounded their own claims to masterhood."

Yeoman Folk Culture

Yeomen enjoyed a folk culture based on family, church, and local region. Their speech patterns recalled their Scots-Irish and Irish backgrounds. They flocked to religious revivals called camp meetings and got together for house-raisings, logrollings, quilting bees, corn-shuckings, and hunting. Such occasions combined work with fun and fellowship, offering food and liquor in abundance.

Demanding rounds of work and family responsibilities shaped women's lives. They worked in the fields but the preparation of food consumed much of women's time. Household tasks continued during frequent pregnancies and childcare. Nursing and medical care also fell to mothers, who relied on folk wisdom. Women, too, wanted to be masters of their household, although it came at the price of their health.

Yeomen's Livelihoods

At age eighteen in 1841, North Carolinian John F. Flintoff went to Mississippi to seek his fortune. Like other aspiring yeomen, he worked as a slave overseer. Finding it impossible to please his employers, he returned to North Carolina, married, and lived in his parents' house. "Impatient to get along in the world," Flintoff tried Louisiana next and then Mississippi again.

In the Gulf region, routinely, "first rate employment" alternated with "very low wages." Moreover, as a young man on isolated plantations, Flintoff was lonely. His employers found fault with his work, and in 1846 Flintoff concluded that "managing negroes and large farms is soul destroying."

At twenty-six, even before he owned land, Flintoff bought his first slave, "a negro boy 7 years old." Soon he had purchased two more children, the cheapest slaves available. Conscious of his status as a slaveowner, Flintoff resented the low wages he was paid. In 1853, with nine young slaves and a growing family, Flintoff was fired. He returned to North Carolina, sold some of his slaves, and purchased 124 acres with

North Carolina Emigrants: Poor White Folks, oil on canvas, 1845, by James Henry Beard. This depicts a yeoman family, their belongings all on one hungry horse, as they migrate westward in search of new land and livelihood.

help from his in-laws. As he paid off his debts, he hoped to free his wife from labor and send his sons to college. Although Flintoff demonstrated that a farmer could move in and out of the slaveholding class, he never achieved cotton planter status (owning roughly twenty or more slaves).

Probably more typical of the southern yeoman was Ferdinand L. Steel, who as a young man moved from North Carolina to Tennessee to work as a river boatman but eventually took up farming in Mississippi. Steel rose every day at 5 a.m. and worked until sundown. He and his family raised corn and wheat, though cotton was his cash product: he sold five or six bales (about two thousand pounds) a year to obtain money for sugar, coffee, salt, calico, and gunpowder.

Steel's family in Mississippi in the 1840s survived on a household economy. He made the family's shoes; his wife and sister sewed dresses, shirts, and "pantaloons." As the nation fell deeper into crisis over slave labor, this independent southern farmer never came close to owning a slave.

The focus of Steel's life was family and religion. Family members prayed together, and he studied Scripture for an hour after lunch. Steel borrowed histories, Latin and Greek grammars, and religious books from his church. Eventually, he became a traveling Methodist minister.

Landless Whites

A sizable minority of white southerners—from 25 to 40 percent—were hired hands who owned no land and worked for others. Their property consisted of a few household items and some animals—usually pigs. The landless included some immigrants, especially Irish, who did heavy and dangerous work, such as building railroads and digging ditches.

In the countryside, white farm laborers struggled to purchase land in the face of low wages or, if they rented, unpredictable market prices for their crops. Scrimping, some climbed yeoman ranks. When James and Nancy Bennitt of North Carolina succeeded in their ten-year struggle to buy land, they avoided the unstable cotton market and raised extra corn and wheat for cash.

Herdsmen with pigs and other livestock had a desperate struggle. By 1860, as the South anticipated war to preserve its society, between 300,000 and 400,000 white people in Virginia, North and South Carolina, and Georgia—approximately one-fifth of the total white population—lived in poverty. Land and slaves determined wealth in the Old South, and many whites possessed neither.

Yeomen's Demands and White Class Relations

Class tensions emerged in the western, nonslaveholding parts of the seaboard states by the 1830s. There, yeoman farmers resented their underrepresentation in state legislatures and the corruption in local government. Voters in more recently settled states of the Old Southwest adopted white manhood suffrage and other electoral reforms, including popular election of governors, legislative apportionment based on white population only, and locally chosen county government. Slaveowners with new wealth, however, knew that a more open government could permit troubling class conflicts and were determined to hold the reins of power.

Historians have offered several explanations why these tensions did not fuel greater conflict between slaveholders and nonslaveholders. One of the most important factors was race. The South's racial ideology stressed the superiority of all whites to blacks. Thus, slavery became the basis of equality among whites, and white privilege inflated the status of poor whites, giving them a common interest with the rich. The dream of upward mobility blunted class conflict.

Most important, before the Civil War, yeomen worked their farms and avoided debt, largely unhindered by slaveholding planters. Likewise, slaveholders pursued their goals quite independently of yeomen. Suppression of dissent also played an increasing role. After 1830, white southerners who criticized the slave system were intimidated, attacked, or rendered politically powerless in a society held together partly by white racial solidarity.

Still, there were signs of class conflict in the late antebellum period. As cotton lands filled up, nonslaveholders faced narrower economic prospects; meanwhile, wealthy planters enjoyed expanding profits. The risks of entering cotton production were becoming too great and the cost of slaves too high for many yeomen to rise in society. From 1830 to 1860, the percentage of white southern families holding slaves declined steadily from 36 to 25 percent. Although slaveowners were a minority in the white population, planters' share of the South's agricultural wealth remained at 90 and 95 percent.

Anticipating secession, slaveowners stood secure. In the 1850s, they occupied from 50 to 85 percent of the seats in state legislatures and a similarly high percentage of the South's congressional seats. And planters' interests controlled all other major social institutions, such as churches and colleges.

Free Blacks

The nearly quarter-million free blacks in the South in 1860 often fared little better than slaves. Upper South free blacks were usually descendants people manumitted by their owners in the 1780s and 1790s. A remarkable number of slaveholders in Virginia and the Chesapeake had freed their slaves because of religious principles and revolutionary ideals in the wake of American independence (see Chapter 7). Many blacks also became free as runaways, especially by the 1830s.

Some free blacks worked in towns or cities, but most lived in rural areas and struggled to survive. They usually did not own land and labored in someone else's fields, often beside slaves. By law, free blacks could not own guns, buy liquor, violate curfew, assemble except in church, testify in court, or (throughout the South after 1835) vote. Despite obstacles, a minority bought land, and others found jobs as skilled craftsmen, especially in cities.

A few free blacks prospered and bought slaves. In 1830, there were 3,775 free black slaveholders in the South; 80 percent lived in Louisiana, South Carolina, Virginia, and Maryland, and approximately half of the total lived in New Orleans and Charleston. Most purchased their own wives and children, whom they could not free, because laws required newly emancipated blacks to leave their state. To free family members they had purchased, hundreds of black slaveholders petitioned for exemption from the antimanumission laws. At the same time, a few mulattos in New Orleans were active slave traders. Although rare in the United States, the greed and quest for power that lay at the root of slavery could cross any racial or ethnic barrier.

Free Black Communities

In the Cotton Belt and Gulf regions, a large proportion of free blacks were mulattos, the privileged offspring of wealthy white planters. Not all planters freed their mixed-race offspring, but those who did often gave their children a good education and financial backing. In cities like New Orleans, Charleston, and Mobile, extensive interracial sex, as well as migrations from the Caribbean, produced a mulatto population that was recognized as a distinct class.

Free black communities formed in many southern cities by the 1840s, especially around churches. By the late 1850s, Baltimore had fifteen churches, Louisville nine, and Nashville and St. Louis four each—most of them African Methodist Episcopal. Class and race distinctions were important to southern free blacks, but outside a few cities, most mulattos experienced hardship. In the United States, "one drop" of black "blood" made them black, and potentially enslavable.

The Planters' World

> How did paternalism function on southern plantations?

At the top of the southern social pyramid were slaveholding planters. Most lived in comfortable farmhouses, not in the opulence that legend suggests. The grand plantation mansions, with outlying slave quarters, are an enduring symbol of the Old South. But in 1850, 50 percent of southern slaveholders had fewer than five slaves; 72 percent had fewer than ten; 88 percent had fewer than twenty. Thus, the average slaveholder was not a wealthy aristocrat but an aspiring farmer.

Link to excerpts from
Bennet Barrow's diary.

The Newly Rich

The newly rich Louisiana cotton planter Bennet Barrow was preoccupied in the 1840s with moneymaking. He worried about his cotton crop, yet to overcome his worries, he hunted frequently and had a passion for racing horses and raising hounds. He could report the loss of a slave without feeling, but became emotional when illness afflicted his sporting animals. His strongest feelings surfaced when his horse Jos Bell—equal to "the best Horse in the South"—"broke down running a mile…ruined for Ever." The same day, Barrow gave his human property a "general Whipping." In 1841, diary entries he worried about a rumored slave insurrection. When a slave named Ginney Jerry "sherked" his cotton-picking duties and was rumored "about to run off," Barrow whipped him one day and the next.

The richest planters used their wealth to model genteel sophistication. Extended visits, parties, and balls to which women wore the latest fashions provided opportunities for friendship, courtship, and display. These entertainments were important diversions for plantation women, who relished social events to break the monotony of their domestic lives. Yet socializing also sustained a rigidly gendered society.

Most of the planters in the cotton-boom states of Alabama and Mississippi were newly rich by the 1840s. As one historian put it, "a number of men mounted from log cabin to plantation mansion on a stairway of cotton bales, accumulating slaves as they climbed." And many did not live like rich men. They put their new wealth into cotton acreage and slaves even as they sought refinement and high social status.

The cotton boom in the Mississippi valley created one-generation aristocrats. A case in point is Greenwood Leflore, a Chocktaw chieftain who owned a plantation in Mississippi with four hundred slaves. After selling his cotton on the world market, he spent $10,000 in France to furnish a single room of his mansion with handwoven carpets, furniture upholstered with gold leaf, tables and cabinets ornamented with tortoise-shell inlay, mirrors, paintings, and a clock and candelabra of brass and ebony.

Social Status and Planters' Values

Slave ownership was the main determinant of wealth in the South. Slaves were a commodity and an investment, much like gold; people bought them on speculation, hoping for a rise in their market value. Many slaveholders mortgaged their slaves and used them as collateral. People who could not pay cash for slaves would ask the sellers to purchase the mortgage, just as banks give mortgages on houses today. The slaveholder would repay the loan in installments with interest. The availability of slave labor tended to devalue free labor: where strenuous work under supervision was reserved for an enslaved race, few free people relished it. When Alexis de Tocqueville crossed from Ohio into Kentucky in his travels of 1831, he observed, "On the right bank of the Ohio [River] everything is activity, industry; labor is honoured; there are no slaves. Pass to the left bank and the scene changes so suddenly that you think yourself on the other side of the world; the enterprising spirit is gone. There, work is not only painful; it is shameful." Aristocratic values—lineage, privilege, pride, honor, and refinement of person and manner—commanded respect throughout the South. Many of those qualities were in short supply, however, in the recently settled portions of the cotton kingdom, where frontier values of courage and self-reliance ruled during the 1820s and 1830s. By the 1850s, a settled aristocratic group of planters did rule, however, in much of the Mississippi valley.

Instead of gradually disappearing, as it did in the North, the Code Duello, which required men to defend their honor through violence, endured in the South. In North Carolina in 1851, wealthy planter Samuel Fleming sought to settle disputes with lawyer William Waightstill Avery by "cowhiding" him in public. Under the code, Avery could redeem his honor violently or to brand himself a coward through inaction. Three weeks later, he shot Fleming dead at point-blank range. A jury took ten minutes to find Avery not guilty, and the spectators gave him a standing ovation.

Aristocratic planters expected to wield power and receive deference from poorer whites. But the independent yeoman class resented infringements of their rights, and many belonged to evangelical faiths that exalted simplicity and condemned the planters' wealth. Much of the planters' power and claims to leadership, after all, were built on their assumption of a monopoly on world cotton and a foundation of black slave labor.

King Cotton in a Global Economy

The American South so dominated the world's supply of cotton that southern planters gained enormous confidence that the cotton boom was permanent and that the industrializing nations of England and France would always bow to **King Cotton**. American cotton production doubled in yield each decade after 1800 and provided three-fourths of the world's supply by the 1840s. Southern staple crops were fully three-fifths of American exports by 1850, and one of every seven workers in England depended on American cotton for his job. Cotton production made slaves the most valuable financial asset in the United States—greater than banks, railroads, and manufacturing combined. In 1860 dollars, the slaves' total value as property equaled an estimated $3.5 billion. (Roughly $70 billion in early twenty-first century dollars.)

"Cotton is King," the *Southern Cultivator* declared in 1859, "and wields an astonishing influence over the world's commerce." Until 1840, the cotton trade furnished much of the export capital to finance northern economic growth. After that, the northern economy expanded without dependence on cotton profits. Nevertheless, southern planters and politicians continued to boast of King Cotton's supremacy. "No power on earth dares...to make war on cotton," James Hammond lectured the U.S. Senate in 1858. Although the South produced 4.5 million bales in 1861, its greatest crop ever, such world dominance was about to collapse. Thereafter, cotton became a shackle to the South.

King Cotton: Term expressing southern belief that U.S. and British economies depended on cotton making it 'king'.

Paternalism

Slaveholding men often embraced a paternalistic ideology that justified their dominance over black slaves and white women. They stressed their obligations, viewing themselves as custodians of society and of the black families they owned. The paternalistic planter saw himself not as an oppressor but as the benevolent guardian of an inferior race.

This comforting self-image let rich planters obscure the harsh dimensions of slave treatment. And slaves—accommodating to the realities of power—encouraged their masters to think their benevolence was appreciated. Paternalism also served as a defense against abolitionist criticism. In reality, paternalism grew as a give-and-take relationship between masters and slaves—owners took labor from the bondsmen, while slaves obligated masters to provide them a measure of autonomy and living space. Relations between men and women in the planter class were similarly defined by paternalism. The upper-class southern woman was raised and educated to be a wife, mother, and subordinate companion to men. South Carolina's Mary Boykin Chesnut wrote of her husband, "He is master of the house. … All the comfort of my life depends upon his being in a good humor." Women found it difficult to challenge society's rules on sexual or racial relations.

Planters' daughters usually attended one of the South's rapidly multiplying boarding schools. Typically, the young woman could entertain suitors whom her parents approved. But she quickly had to choose a husband and commit herself to a man whom she generally had known only briefly. Young women had to follow the wishes of their family, especially their father, even if it left them emotionally empty.

Upon marriage, a planter-class woman ceded to her husband most of her legal rights, becoming part of his family. She was isolated on a large plantation, where she supervised the cooking and preserving of food, managed the house, watched the children, and attended sick slaves. These realities were more confining on the frontier, where isolation was greater. Men on plantations could occasionally escape into the public realm—to town, business, or politics. Women could retreat from rural plantation culture only into kinship and associations with other women.

Marriage and Family Among Planters   A perceptive white woman sometimes approached marriage with anxiety. Lucy Breckinridge, a wealthy Virginia girl of twenty, lamented the autonomy she surrendered at the altar. In her diary, she recorded: "If [husbands] care for their wives at all it is only as a sort of servant, a being made to attend to their comforts and to keep the children out of the way."

Childbearing often involved grief, poor health, and death. In 1840, the birth rate for white southern women was almost 30 percent higher than the national average. The average southern white woman would bear eight children in 1800; by 1860, the figure had decreased to six. Childbirth complications were a major cause of death, occurring twice as often in the hot South as in the Northeast.

Sexual relations between planters and slaves were another problem that white women endured but were not supposed to notice. "Violations of the moral law… made mulattos as common as blackberries," protested a woman in Georgia, but wives had to play "the ostrich game." Such habits produced a large mixed race population by the 1850s.

In the 1840s and 1850s, as abolitionist attacks on slavery increased, southern men published a barrage of articles stressing that women should restrict their concerns to the home. The *Southern Quarterly Review* declared, "The proper place for a woman is at home. One of her highest privileges, to be politically merged in the existence of her husband."

But a study of women in Petersburg, Virginia, a large tobacco-manufacturing town, revealed behavior that valued financial autonomy. Over several decades before 1860, the proportion of women who never married, or did not remarry after the death of a spouse, grew to exceed 33 percent. Likewise, the number of women who worked for wages, controlled their own property, and ran dressmaking businesses increased.

Slave Life and Labor

Slaves knew a life of poverty, coercion, toil, and resentment. They provided the strength and know-how to build an agricultural empire. But they embodied a fundamental contradiction: in the world's model republic, slaves were on the wrong side of a brutally unequal power relationship.

> What was the true nature of the master-slave relationship?

Slaves' Everyday Conditions

Southern slaves enjoyed few material comforts beyond the bare necessities. Although they generally had enough to eat, their diet was monotonous and nonnutritious. Clothing was coarse and inexpensive. Few slaves received more than one or two changes of clothing for hot and cold seasons and one blanket each winter. Children of both sexes ran naked in hot weather and wore long cotton shirts in winter. Many slaves went without shoes until December. Conditions were generally better in cities, where slaves frequently lived in the same dwelling as their owners and were regularly hired out, enabling them to accumulate their own money.

The average slave lived in a crude, one-room cabin. Each dwelling housed one or two families. Crowding and lack of sanitation helped spread infection and such contagious diseases as typhoid fever, malaria, and dysentery. White plantation doctors were hired to care for sick slaves, but some "slave doctors" attained a degree of power in the quarters and with masters by healing through herbalism and spiritualism.

Slave Work Routines

Long hours and large work gangs characterized Gulf Coast cotton districts. Overseers rang the morning bell before dawn, and black people, tools in hand, walked toward the fields. Slaves who cultivated tobacco in the Upper South worked long hours picking the sticky, sometimes noxious, leaves under harsh discipline. As one woman recalled when interviewed in the 1930s, "it was way after sundown fore they could stop that field work. Then they had to hustle to finish their night work [such as watering livestock or cleaning cotton] in time for supper, or go to bed without it."

task system: Each slave had a daily or weekly quota of tasks to complete.

Working "from sun to sun" became a norm in much of the South. Profit took precedence over paternalism. Slave women did heavy fieldwork, as much as the men and even during pregnancy. Old people cared for children, doing light chores, or carding, ginning, and spinning cotton.

By the 1830s, planters in the South Carolina and Georgia low country used a **task system** whereby slaves were assigned measured amounts of work to be performed in a given time period. So much cotton per day was to be picked from a designated field, so many rows hoed or plowed in a specified section. Upon completion, slaves' time was their own for working garden plots, tending hogs, even hiring out their own labor. From this experience, many slaves developed a sense of property ownership.

Collection of the J. Paul Getty Museum, Malibu, CA

A portrait of a planter-slaveholder, his two daughters, and their household slave who probably was "nurse" (caretaker) for the children. The picture vividly depicts the attempt at domestic tranquility as well as the prescribed roles of patriarch and slave.

Of the 1860 population of 4 million slaves, half were under age sixteen. "A child raised every two years," wrote Thomas Jefferson, "is of more profit than the crop of the best laboring man." And in 1858, a slaveowner writing in an agricultural magazine calculated that a slave girl he purchased in 1827 for $400 had borne three sons now worth $3,000 as his field hands. Slave children gathered kindling, carried water to the fields, swept the yard, lifted cut sugar-cane stalks into carts, stacked wheat, chased birds away from sprouting rice plants, and labored in cotton and tobacco production.

As slave children matured, they faced psychological traumas, including powerlessness and an awareness that their parents could not protect them. They had to fight to keep from internalizing what whites labeled their inferiority. Many former slaves resented their denial of education. And for girls reaching maturity, the potential trauma of sexual abuse loomed.

Violence and Intimidation Against Slaves

Whites throughout the South believed that slaves "can't be governed except with the whip." One South Carolinian explained to a northern journalist that he whipped his slaves regularly, "the fear of the lash kept them in good order." Evidence suggests that whippings were less frequent on small farms than on large plantations. But beatings symbolized authority to the master and tyranny to the slaves, who used them to evaluate a master. Former slaves said a good owner was one who did not "whip too much," whereas a bad owner "whipped till he's bloodied you and blistered you."

The master wielded virtually absolute authority on his plantation. Slaveholders rarely had to answer to the law or the state. Pregnant women were whipped, and there were burnings, mutilation, torture, and murder. Yet physical cruelty may have been less prevalent in the United States than in other slaveholding parts of the New World, especially some of the sugar islands of the Caribbean, where death rates were so high that the heavily male slave population shrank in size. In the United States, the slave population experienced a steady natural increase, as births exceeded deaths.

The worst evil of American slavery was the nature of slavery itself: coercion, belonging to another person, virtually no hope for mobility or change. Recalling their time in bondage, some former slaves emphasized the physical abuse, memories focused on the tyranny of whipping as much as the pain. Delia Garlic made the essential point: "It's bad to belong to folks that own you soul an' body ... you couldn't guess the awfulness of it." To be a slave was to be the object of another person's will and material gain, as the saying went, "from the cradle to the grave."

Most American slaves retained their mental independence and self-respect despite their bondage. They had to be subservient to their masters, but they talked and behaved differently among themselves. In *Narrative of the Life of Frederick Douglass, an American Slave, Written by Himself* (1845), **Frederick Douglass** wrote that most slaves, when asked about "their condition and the character of their masters, almost universally say they are contented, and that their masters are kind." Slaves did this, said Douglass, because they were governed by the maxim that "a still tongue makes a wise head." Slaves often quarreled over who had the best master, Douglass remarked, when one had a bad master, he sought a better master; and when he had a better one, he wanted to "be his own master."

Frederick Douglass: A former slave who was the leading black abolitionist during the antebellum period.

Slave-Master Relationships

Some former slaves remembered warm feelings between masters and slaves, but the prevailing attitudes were distrust and antagonism. One woman said her mistress was "a mighty good somebody to belong to" but only "'cause she was raisin' us to work for her." Slaves also resented being used as beasts of burden. One man observed that his master "fed us reg'lar on good, 'stantial food, just like you'd tend to your horse, if you had a real good one."

Slaves were alert to the daily signs of their degraded status. One man recalled the general rule that slaves ate cornbread and owners ate biscuits. If blacks did get biscuits, "the flour that we made the biscuits out of was the third-grade sorts." If the owner took his slaves' garden produce to town to sell, slaves often suspected him of pocketing part of the profits.

Suspicion often grew into hatred. When a yellow fever epidemic struck in 1852, many slaves saw it as God's retribution. An elderly ex-slave named Minnie Fulkes cherished the conviction that God was going to punish white people for their cruelty to blacks. On the plantation, of course, slaves had to keep such thoughts to themselves and created ways to survive and to sustain their humanity in this world of repression.

Link to George and Lucy Skipworth's letters to their master.

Slave Culture and Resistance

The resource that enabled slaves to maintain defiance was their culture: beliefs, values, and practices born of their past and maintained in the present. As best they could, they built a community knitted together by stories, music, a religious world-view, leadership, the smells of their cooking, the sounds of their own voices, and the tapping of their feet. "The values expressed in folklore," wrote African American poet Sterling Brown, provided a "wellspring to which slaves…could return in times of doubt to be refreshed."

> How did slaves adapt Christianity to make it their own?

African Cultural Survival

Slave culture changed significantly after 1808, when Congress banned further importation of slaves and the generations born in Africa died out. For a few years, South Carolina illegally reopened the international slave trade, but by the 1830s, the majority of slaves in the South were native-born Americans.

Yet African influences remained strong. Some slave men plaited their hair into rows and designs; slave women often wore their hair tied in small bunches secured by string or piece of cloth. A few men and many women wrapped their heads in kerchiefs of the styles and colors of West Africa.

Music, religion, and folktales were parts of daily life for most slaves. Borrowing partly from their African background and forging new American folkways, they developed what scholars have called a sacred world-view, which affected work, leisure, and self-understanding. Slaves made musical instruments with carved motifs that resembled African stringed instruments. One visitor to Georgia in the 1860s described a ritual dance of African origin known as the ring shout: "A ring of singers is formed. … They then utter a kind of melodious chant, which gradually increases in strength, and in noise, until it fairly shakes the house, and it can be heard for a long distance."

Many slaves continued to believe in spirit possession. While whites believed in ghosts and charms, slaves' belief resembled the African concept of the living dead—deceased relatives visiting the earth for years until the process of dying is complete. Slaves also practiced conjuration and quasi-magical root medicine. By the 1850s, noted conjurers and root doctors were reputed to live in South Carolina, Georgia, Louisiana, and isolated coastal areas with high slave populations.

As they became African Americans, slaves increasingly developed a racial identity. In the colonial period, Africans arrived in America from many states and kingdoms, represented in distinctive languages and traditions. Africans arrived in the New World with virtually no concept of "race"; by the antebellum era, their descendants learned through bitter experience that race was now the defining feature of their lives.

Slaves' Religion and Music

Over time, more and more slaves adopted Christianity, fashioning it into an instrument of support and resistance. Theirs was a religion of justice and deliverance, quite unlike their masters' religious propaganda. "You ought to have heard that preachin,'" said one man. "'Obey your master and mistress, don't steal chickens and eggs and meat,' but nary a word about havin' a soul to save." Slaves believed that Jesus cared about their souls and their plight.

Devout slaves worshiped every day, "in the field or by the side of the road." Some slaves held secret prayer meetings that lasted into the night. Many nurtured an unshakable belief that God would end their bondage. This faith—and the emotional release that accompanied worship—sustained them.

Slaves also adapted Christianity to African practices. In West African belief, devotees are possessed by a god so thoroughly that the god's personality replaces the human personality. In the late antebellum era, Christian slaves experienced possession by the Protestant "Holy Spirit." The combination of shouting, singing, and dancing that seemed to overtake black worshipers formed the heart of their religious faith. "The old meeting house caught fire," recalled an ex-slave preacher. "The spirit was there....God saw our need and came to us." Out in brush arbors or in meetinghouses, slaves thrust their arms to heaven, made music with their feet, and sang away their woes.

Rhythm and physical movement were crucial to slaves' religious experience. In black preachers' chanted sermons, which pulled the sinner into a narrative of meanings and cadences en route to conversion, an American tradition was born. The chanted sermon was a scriptural and patterned form that required audience response punctuated by "yes sirs!" and "amens!" But it was in song that slaves left their most sublime gift to American culture.

Through spirituals, slaves tried to impose order on the chaos of their lives. Often referred to later as the "sorrow songs," lyrics covered many themes, especially imminent rebirth. Sadness could immediately give way to joy: "Oh, Oh, Freedom / Ojh, Oh, Freedom over me— / But before I'll be a slave, / I'll be buried in my grave, / And go home to my Lord, / And Be Free!"

Many songs also express intimacy and closeness with God. Some display rebelliousness, such as the enduring "He said, and if I had my way / If I had my way, if I had my way, / I'd tear this building down!" And some spirituals reached for a collective sense of hope in the black community as a whole.

O, gracious Lord! When shall it be,
That we poor souls shall all be free;
Lord, break them slavery powers—
Will you go along with me?
Lord break them slavery powers,
Go sound the jubilee!

In many ways, American slaves converted the Christian God to themselves. They sought an alternative world—a home other than the one fate had given them on earth. With variations on the Br'er Rabbit folktales—in which the weak survive by wit and power is reversed—and in songs, they fashioned survival from their cultural imagination.

The Black Family in Slavery

Although American law did not recognize slave families, slaveowners *expected* slaves to form families and have children. As a result, there was a normal ratio of men to women, young to old. On some of the largest cotton plantations of South Carolina, when masters allowed their slaves increased autonomy through the task system, the property accumulation in livestock, tools, and garden produce led to more stable and healthier families.

Following African kinship traditions, African Americans avoided marriage between cousins (commonplace among aristocratic slaveowners). By naming their children after relatives of past generations, African Americans emphasized family histories. Kinship networks and extended families held life together in many slave communities.

For slave women, sexual abuse and rape by white masters were ever-present threats. By 1860, there were 405,751 mulattos in the United States, comprising 12.5 percent of the African American population. White planters were sometimes open with their behavior toward slave women, but not in the way they talked about it. Buying slaves for sex was common at the New Orleans slave market. In what was called the "fancy trade" (a "fancy" was a young, attractive slave girl or woman), females were often sold for prices as much as 300 percent higher than the average. At such auctions, slaveholders exhibited some of the ugliest values at the heart of the slave system by paying $3,000 to $5,000 for female "companions."

Slave women like Harriet Jacobs spent years dodging their owners' sexual pursuit. In recollecting her desperate effort to protect her children, Jacobs asked a haunting question: "Why does the slave ever love? Why

This photograph of five generations of a slave family, taken in Beaufort, South Carolina, in 1862, is silent but powerful testimony to the importance that enslaved African Americans placed on their ever-threatened family ties.

Library of Congress

allow the tendrils of the heart to twine around objects which may at any moment be wrenched away by the hand of violence?"

Link to Harriet Jacobs's papers.

The Domestic Slave Trade

Slave families most feared and hated separation by violence from those they loved, sexual appropriation, and sale. Many struggled to keep their children together and, after emancipation, to reestablish contact with loved ones lost by forced migration and sale. Between 1820 and 1860, an estimated 2 million slaves were moved into the region from western Georgia to eastern Texas. When the Union Army registered thousands of black marriages in Mississippi and Louisiana in 1864 and 1865, 25 percent of the men over forty reported that they had been forcibly separated from a previous wife. Thousands of black families were disrupted annually to serve the needs of the expanding cotton economy.

Many antebellum white southerners made their living from the slave trade. In South Carolina by the 1850s, there were over one hundred slave-trading firms selling approximately 6,500 slaves to southwestern states. One estimate from 1858 indicated that slave sales in Richmond, Virginia, netted $4 million that year alone. A market guide to slave sales that same year in Richmond listed average prices for "likely ploughboys," ages twelve to fourteen, at $850 to $1,050; "extra number 1 fieldgirls" at $1,300 to $1,350; and "extra number 1 men" at $1,500.

At slave "pens" in cities like New Orleans, traders promoted "a large and commodious showroom…prepared to accommodate over 200 Negroes for sale." Traders made slaves appear young, healthy, and happy, cutting gray whiskers off men, using paddles as discipline to avoid scarring their merchandise, and forcing people to dance and sing as buyers arrived. When transported to the southwestern markets, slaves were often chained together, making journeys of 500 miles or more on foot.

The complacent mixture of racism and business among traders is evident in their own language. "I refused a girl 20 year[s] old at 700 yesterday," one trader wrote in 1853. "She is very badly whipped but good teeth." Some sales were transacted at owners' requests, often for tragically inhumane reasons. "Bought a cook yesterday that was to go out of state," wrote a trader; "she just made the people mad that was all."

Strategies of Resistance

Slaves brought to their resistance the common sense and determination that characterized their struggle to secure families. The scales weighed against overt revolution, but they seized opportunities to alter work conditions. They sometimes slacked off when they were not watched.

Daily discontent and desperation were also manifest in equipment sabotage; carelessness about work; theft of food, livestock, or crops; or getting drunk on stolen liquor. Some slaves who were hired out hoarded their earnings or became recalcitrant. A woman named Ellen, hired as a cook in Tennessee in 1856, quietly put mercury poison into a roasted apple for her unsuspecting mistress. And some slave women resisted by trying to control their own pregnancy, either by avoiding it or by seeking it to improve their conditions.

Many male, and some female, slaves violently attacked overseers or owners. Southern court records and newspapers contain accounts of resistant slaves who disproved the image of the docile bondsman. Rebels were customarily flogged, sold, or hanged.

Many slaves attempted to run away to the North, and some received assistance from the loose network known as the Underground Railroad (see pages 371–373). But it was more common for slaves to run off temporarily to hide in the woods. Approximately 80 percent of runaways were male; children prevented women from fleeing. Fear, disgruntlement over treatment, or family separation might motivate slaves to flee. Only a minority ever made it to freedom in the North, but these fugitives made slavery an insecure institution by the 1850s.

American slavery also produced some fearless revolutionaries. Gabriel's Rebellion involved about a thousand slaves when it was discovered in 1800, just before it would have exploded in Richmond, Virginia (see pages 213–214). According to controversial court testimony, a similar conspiracy existed in Charleston in 1822, led by a free black named Denmark Vesey. Born a slave in the Caribbean, Vesey won a lottery of $1,500 in 1799, bought his freedom, and became a religious leader. According to one long-argued interpretation, Vesey was a heroic revolutionary determined to free his people. But, in a recent challenge, historian Michael Johnson points out that court testimony is the only reliable source on the alleged insurrection. Might the testimony reveal less of reality than of white South Carolina's fears of slave rebellion? The court, says Johnson, built its case on rumors and intimidated witnesses, and "conjured into being" an insurrection that was not truly about to occur. Whatever the facts, thirty-seven "conspirators" were executed, and more than three dozen others were banished from the state.

Nat Turner's Insurrection

The most famous rebel, **Nat Turner**, struck for freedom in Southampton County, Virginia, in 1831. Turner was a precocious child who learned to read. Encouraged by his first owner to study the Bible, he enjoyed privileges but also endured hard work and changes of masters. His father successfully escaped to freedom.

Young Nat became a preacher known for eloquence and mysticism. After planning for years, Turner led rebels from farm to farm in the predawn darkness of August 22, 1831. The group severed limbs and crushed skulls with axes or killed their victims with guns. Before alarmed planters stopped them, Turner and his followers had in forty-eight hours slaughtered sixty whites. In retaliation, whites randomly killed slaves across the region. Turner was caught and hanged. As many as two hundred African Americans lost their lives as a result of the rebellion.

Nat Turner remains a haunting symbol in America's unresolved history with slavery and discrimination. While in jail, Turner was interviewed by a Virginia lawyer and slaveholder, Thomas R. Gray. Their intriguing creation, *The Confessions of Nat Turner*, became a bestseller within a month of Turner's hanging. Gray called the rebel a "gloomy fanatic," but in a manner that made him fascinating and produced one of the most remarkable documents of American slavery. After Turner's insurrection, many states passed stiffened legal codes against black education and religious practice.

Most importantly, in 1832 a shocked Virginia held a legislative and public debate over gradual emancipation. The plan debated would not have freed any slaves until 1858 and provided that eventually all blacks would be colonized outside Virginia. When the House of Delegates voted, gradual abolition lost, 73 to 58. Virginia merely reinforced its defense of slavery. It was the last time white southerners would debate emancipation.

Nat Turner: A slave who led a bloody rebellion in Southampton County, Virginia, in 1831.

Visualizing the Past

Imaging Nat Turner's Rebellion

Below is the title page from *The Confessions of Nat Turner*, by Thomas R. Gray, 1832. This document of nearly twenty pages was published by the lawyer, Gray, who recorded and likely refashioned Turner's lengthy statement during an interview in his jail cell before his execution. *The Confessions* became a widely sold and sensational documentation of Turner's identity and especially his motivations and methods during the rebellion. It portrayed Turner as a religious mystic

and fanatic and allowed the broad public to imagine the mind of a religiously motivated slave rebel. Below and to the right is "Horrid Massacre in Virginia," 1831, woodcut. This composite of scenes depicts the slaughter of innocent women and children, as well as white men as both victims and resistants. The fear, confusion, and fierce retribution that dominated the aftermath of the Turner rebellion are on display here. Why was Nat Turner's insurrection such a shock to the nation as well as to the South? What kind of impact did Nat Turner's rebellion have on the South's evolving defense of slavery in the coming decades?

William L. Clements Library, University of Michigan

Library of Congress

Summary

During the four decades before the Civil War, the South grew in land, wealth, and power along with the rest of the country. Although the southern states were enmeshed in the nation's heritage and political economy, they also developed as a distinctive region, ideologically and economically, because of slavery. More than the North, the antebellum South was a biracial society; whites grew up influenced by black folkways and culture; and blacks, the vast majority of whom were slaves, became cobuilders of a rural, agricultural society.

With the cotton boom, as well as state and federal Indian removal policies, the South grew into a slave society. The coercive influence of slavery affected southern life

Reparations for Slavery

How should the United States come to terms with 250 years of racial slavery? Is this period best forgotten as a terrible passage, or does the nation owe a long-overdue debt to black people for their oppression? After emancipation in 1865, and rooted in vague federal promises, many former slaves believed they were entitled to "forty acres and a mule," but these never materialized.

In 1897, Callie House—a poor mother of four born in 1865 in a contraband camp for ex-slaves—organized the National Ex-Slave Pension and Bounty Association, modeled after the soldiers' pension systems. House traveled throughout the South, recruiting 250,000 members at 10-cent dues. Her lobbying of the federal government for slave pensions failed; she was accused of mail fraud and imprisoned for one year in 1916.

More recently, a widespread debate over "reparations" for slavery has emerged. In the rewriting of slavery's history since the 1960s, Americans have learned how slave labor created American wealth: how insurance companies insured slaves, how complicit the U.S. government was in slavery's expansion, and how slaves built the U.S. Capitol while their owners received $5 a month for their labor.

The debate is fueled by analogies: reparations paid to Japanese Americans interned during World War II; reparations paid to Native American tribes for stolen land; reparations paid to Holocaust survivors and victims of forced labor; and a suit settled in 1999 that will pay an estimated $2 billion to some twenty thousand black farmers for discrimination practiced by the Agriculture Department in the early twentieth century.

Some argue that because there are no living former slaves or slaveholders, reparations can never take the form of money. But in 2002, a lawsuit was filed against three major corporations who allegedly profited from slavery, and the National Reparations Coordinating Committee promises a suit against the U.S. government. Some city councils passed resolutions forcing companies in their jurisdictions to investigate possible complicity with slave trading or owner-ship, prompting some firms to establish scholarship programs for African Americans.

Critics argue that resources would be better spent "making sure black kids have a credible education" and rebuilding inner cities. Advocates contend that, when "government participates in a crime against humanity," it is "obliged to make the victims whole." The movement for reparations has sparked broad public debate. The legacy of slavery for a people and a nation promises to become a test of how to reconcile its history with justice.

and politics and increasingly produced a leadership determined to preserve a hierar-chical social and racial order. Despite their shared white supremacy, the democratic values of yeomen often clashed with the profit motives of aristocratic planters. The benevolent self-image and paternalistic ideology of slaveholders was tested by the slaves' own judgments. African American slaves responded by fashioning a rich folk culture and a religion of deliverance. Their experiences could differ from one region and labor type to another. Some blacks were crushed by bondage; others transcended it through survival and resistance.

By 1850, through their own wits and on the backs of African labor, white southerners had aggressively built one of the last profitable, expanding slave societies on earth. North of them and deeply intertwined with them in the same nation, economy, constitutional system, and history, a different kind of society had grown even faster—driven by industrialism and free labor. The clash of these two deeply connected, yet mutually fearful and divided societies would soon explode in political storms over the nation's future.

Chapter Review

The "Distinctive" South

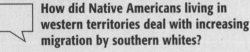

What made the antebellum South different from the North?

Both regions were capitalist and Christian (largely Protestant) and embraced the heroes and causes of the American Revolution. But they differed in their economic development: because of its climate and longer growing season, the South's development was agricultural and rural, whereas the North became increasingly urban and industrial. With a comparatively low population density and people spread out from each other, the South had little income for developing its commercial, educational, and health-related institutions. The South was also slower to develop a regional transportation network or market economy and relied on slaves for labor and the North for banking and other financial institutions. The South had fewer urban areas, and those that existed were primarily port cities such as Charleston that provided a link for commerce and small manufacturing. With few labor opportunities, the South also did not attract as many immigrants as the North.

Southern Expansion, Indian Resistance, and Removal

How did Native Americans living in western territories deal with increasing migration by southern whites?

Indians dealt with white encroachment on their land in several ways. Some embraced accommodation, establishing trading posts to exchange supplies with settlers, often ultimately falling into heavy debt that could only be repaid by selling their land. Others resisted, rejecting removal/relocation plans that whites offered, and holding fast to their land. The Creeks and Cherokees assimilated to American standards—even changed their political structure to more closely resemble that of whites—in an effort to keep their land. When Congress narrowly passed the Indian Removal Act in 1830, which provided funds to relocate Indians to territory further west, the Cherokees refused to leave and sued the state of Georgia in federal court. While the courts found them entitled to their land, President Jackson ignored the ruling and sent in troops to evacuate thousands of Cherokees and march them from Georgia to present-day Oklahoma.

Many refused to go and were imprisoned; others died of disease and exhaustion on the trek known as the Trail of Tears.

Social Pyramid in the Old South

What class tensions emerged in the antebellum South?

Although they were fewer in number, the slaveholding planter class occupied the highest rungs of southern society and dominated its political life (controlling up to 85 percent of legislative posts) as well as churches and colleges. Before the 1830s, the vast socioeconomic differences between rich planters and small, independent, nonslaveholding yeomen farmers were mediated by their shared racial status as white. However, tensions emerged as yeomen began to resent their underrepresentation in state government and the corruption of local governments. They sought universal manhood suffrage and other reforms, including popular election of governors and legislative apportionment based solely on the white population—all of which planters resisted. Moreover, as cotton farming made land less and less available, nonslaveholders faced fewer opportunities to improve their station, while planters enjoyed greater and greater profits.

The Planters' World

How did paternalism function on southern plantations?

Paternalism was a belief system that enabled slaveholders to justify slaveholding and their dominance over white women. In this view, slave owners portrayed themselves as benevolent guardians over their families, which included slaves. They stressed their obligations to those beneath them—wives, children, and the enslaved. Paternalism denied the truth of slavery's brutality and inhumanity, while providing a counter to abolitionism. As the system developed, it functioned as an exchange in which slaves labored and obligated their owners to provide them with necessities and some autonomy. Between husbands and wives, paternalism gave men control of women's legal rights in marriage—her property became his to manage—and she became his subordinate in every way.

Slave Life and Labor

What was the true nature of the master-slave relationship?

Generally speaking, distrust and antagonism were at the core of most master-slave relationships. For slaves, the vulnerability and frustration of being owned and at the mercy of another human being, along with being used for harsh physical labor, sparked much resentment. Slaves did not trust masters to deal fairly with them in their exchanges. There was also much cruelty and brutality—rather than paternalism—on the part of many owners, including whippings and beatings. Slave families were often separated, as one or more members were sold away to other plantations.

Slave Culture and Resistance

How did slaves adapt Christianity to make it their own?

While many slaves maintained and adapted aspects of the African heritage to their new circumstances, they also embraced and remade Christianity as a form of resistance. In secret prayer meetings, slaves focused on justice and deliverance, believing God would liberate them from their servitude and exact retribution from those who unjustly enslaved or abused them. They also merged their Christianity with African practices, adding shouting, singing, dancing, and other rituals to their religious meetings, along with chanted sermons, which were regarded as vital for the conversion experience. Their religious rituals not only attempted to restore order and meaning to their lives but also establish closeness with God and hope for the future. Finally, while prayer meetings were often held in secret, they helped forge relationships and community in slave quarters.

Suggestions for Further Reading

Ira Berlin, *Generations of Captivity: A History of African American Slaves* (2003)

David Brion Davis, *Inhuman Bondage: The Rise and Fall of Slavery in the New World* (2006)

Steven Deyle, *Carry Me Back: The Domestic Slave Trade in American Life* (2005)

Drew G. Faust, ed., *The Ideology of Slavery: Proslavery Thought in the Antebellum South, 1830–1860* (1981)

Walter Johnson, *Soul by Soul: Life Inside the Antebellum Slave Market* (1999)

Charles Joyner, *Down by the Riverside: A South Carolina Slave Community* (1984)

James D. Miller, *South by Southwest: Planter Emigration and Identity in the Slave South* (2002)

James Oakes, *Slavery and Freedom: An Interpretation of the Old South* (1991)

Michael O'Brien, *Conjectures of Order: Intellectual Life and the American South, 1810–1860*, 2 vols., (2004)

Daniel H. Usner Jr., *American Indians in the Lower Mississippi Valley* (1998)

Annette Gordon-Reed, *The Hemingses of Monticello: An American Family* (2008)

The Restless North

11

1815–1860

After 25 stormy days at sea, Mary Ann and James Archbald and their four children finally arrived in New York on April 17, 1807. The couple left their ancestral homeland in Scotland, envisioning a bright future in which their children would be beholden to no one—neither landlord nor employer. They were pursuing the Jeffersonian dream of republican independence.

The Archbalds bought a farm in central New York, along a Hudson River tributary, where they raised sheep, grew hay and vegetables, skinned rabbits for their meat and fur—and then sold whatever they did not need. From the wool shorn by her husband and sons, Mary Ann and her daughters spun thread and wove cloth for their own use and for sale. They used the cash to pay their mortgage. Twenty-one years after leaving Scotland, Mary Ann Archbald, in anticipation of their last payment, declared, "being out of debt is, in my estimation, being rich." By then, her sons were young adults with visions of wealth that centered on water, not land.

On April 17, 1817—a decade after the Archbalds reached American shores—the New York State legislature authorized construction of a canal connecting Lake Erie to the Hudson River, and surveyors mapped a route through the Archbalds' farm. The sons helped dig the canal, while Mary Ann and her daughters cooked and cleaned for the twenty Irish laborers whom the sons hired. The Archbald sons soon tried commercial speculation, borrowing money to buy wheat and lumber in western New York to resell it at substantial profits to merchants in Albany and New York City. As early as 1808, Mary Ann had reached an unpleasant conclusion about her new home: "We are a nation of traders in spite of all Mr. Jefferson can say or do."

After the War of 1812, the market economy took off in unanticipated ways. In the North, steamboats, canals, and then railroads remapped the young republic's geography and economy, setting off booms in westward migration, industry, commerce, and urban growth.

Even after the War of 1812, the United States' financial connections to Europe, particularly Britain, remained profound. When Europeans suffered hard times, so, did American merchants, manufacturers, farmers, and workers. For wage-earning Americans, economic downturns often meant unemployment and destitution.

The economy's rapid expansion following the War of 1812 inspired fears that, unless properly controlled, market growth could threaten the nation's moral fiber. It upset family patterns and relied on unskilled workers—often immigrants and free African Americans—who seemed unfit for republican citizenship. Commercially minded Americans saw cities as both exemplars of civilization and breeding grounds of depravity and conflict. Only through faith in progress and upward mobility could Americans remain hopeful that the nation's greatness lay with commercial expansion. They did so partly by articulating a free-labor ideology that rationalized the negative aspects of market expansion while promoting the northern labor system as superior to the South's.

As you read this chapter, keep the following questions in mind:

* **What factors contributed to the commercialization of northern society, and why did they have less of an influence on the South?**

* **How did the daily lives—work, family, leisure—of northerners change between 1815 and 1860?**

* **What factors contributed to rapid urbanization, and how did urban and rural life in the North compare with that in the South?**

Or Is It the North That Was Distinctive?

Historian James McPherson has proposed a new twist to the old question of southern distinctiveness: perhaps it was the *North*—New England, the Middle Atlantic, and the Old Northwest—that diverged from the norm. At the republic's birth, the two regions had much in common: slavery, ethnic homogeneity, a majority of the population engaged in agriculture, a small urban population. But that started to changed with economic development after the War of 1812. State and local governments and private entrepreneurs engaged in development, which happened faster and more extensively in the North. As the North embraced economic progress, it—rather than the South—diverged from the international norm. The North, writes McPherson, "hurtled forward toward a future that many Southerners found distasteful if not frightening." With its continual quest for improvement, the North—much more so than the South—embodied what Frenchman Alexis de Tocqueville, who toured the United States in 1831–1832, called the nation's "restless spirit."

While the South expanded as a slave society during and after the War of 1812, the North transformed, as one historian has put it, from a society with markets to a market society. In the colonial era, settlers lived in a society with markets, one in which they engaged in long-distance trade—selling their surpluses to merchants, who in turn sent raw materials to Europe, using the proceeds to purchase finished goods for resale—but in which most settlers remained self-sufficient. During and after the War of 1812, the North became more solidly a market society, one in which

> What happened to the North and South economically after the War of 1812?

Chronology

participation in long-distance commerce fundamentally altered individuals' aspirations and activities. With European trade largely halted during the war, entrepreneurs invested in domestic factories. More men, women, and children began working for wages—rather than on family farms—making the domestic demand for foodstuffs soar. Farming became commercialized, with farmers abandoning self-sufficiency and specializing in crops that would yield cash on the market. Farmers then used the cash to buy goods they once made for themselves, such as cloth and soap, along with some luxuries. Unlike the typical southern yeoman, they were not self-reliant, and isolation was rare. In the North, market expansion altered every aspect of life. Some historians see these rapid and pervasive changes as a market revolution.

Preindustrial Farms

As the nineteenth century dawned, few yeoman farmers, North or South, were entirely independent. Most practiced mixed agriculture, raising a variety of crops and livestock. Their goal was to procure what they called a "competence": everyday comforts and economic opportunities for their children. When they produced more than they needed, they traded the surplus with neighbors or sold it to local storekeepers. Such transactions often transpired without money; farmers might trade eggs for shoes, or they might labor in their neighbor's fields in exchange for hay. Farmers like the Archbalds engaged in long-distance market exchange, selling farm goods for cash to merchants, who sent the

National Gallery of Art, Washington, D.C. Gift of Edgar William and Bernice Chrysler Garbisch

Although separating flax fibers from their woody base could be arduous work, flax-scutching bees—much like corn-husking bees—brought together neighbors for frivolity as well as work.

goods to people far away. But for Mary Ann Archbald, the main reason to earn cash was not to accumulate wealth but to pay off the family's land debt. Although families like the Archbalds indulged in the occasional luxury, security and paying debts mattered more than profit.

Family members provided most farm labor, though some yeoman farmers, North and South, relied on slaves or indentured servants. Men and boys worked in the fields, herded livestock, chopped firewood, fished, and hunted. Women and girls tended gardens, milked cows, spun cloth, processed and preserved food, prepared meals, washed clothes, and watched infants and toddlers.

Farmers cooperated with one another, lending farm tools, harvesting each other's fields, bartering goods, raising their neighbors' barns, and husking their corn. Little cash exchanged hands, mostly because money was scarce. Still, New England farmers kept elaborate account books recording what they owed and were owed, whereas Southern farmers simply made mental notes of debts. In both regions, years might pass without debts being repaid. In the local economy—where farmers exchanged goods with people they knew—a system of "just price" prevailed, in which neighbors calculated value in terms of how much labor was involved. When the same farmers engaged in long-distance trade—selling goods through a network of merchants who eventually resold them as far away as Europe—they set prices based on what the market would bear.

Preindustrial Artisans

Farmers who lived near towns or villages often purchased crafted goods from local cobblers, saddlers, blacksmiths, gunsmiths, silversmiths, and tailors. Most artisans, though, lived in the nation's seaports, where master craftsmen (businessmen who owned shops and tools) employed apprentices and journeymen. Although the majority of craftsmen, North and South, were white, free blacks were well represented in some cities' trades, such as tailoring and carpentry in Charleston, South Carolina. Teenage apprentices lived with masters, who taught, lodged, and fed them in exchange for labor. The master's wife and daughters cooked, cleaned, and sewed for the workers. When their apprenticeship expired, apprentices became journeymen who earned wages, hoping to save money to open their own shops. The workplace had little division of labor or specialization. For example, a tailor measured, designed, and sewed an entire suit.

Men, women, and children worked long days on farms and in workshops, but the pace was uneven and unregimented. When busy, they worked dawn to dusk; work slowed after the harvest or after a large order had been completed. Husking bees and barn raisings brought people together to shuck corn and raise buildings and to eat, drink, and dance. Busy periods did not stop artisans from taking grog breaks or reading the newspaper aloud; they might even close their shops to attend a political meeting. Journeymen craftsmen often staggered in late on Monday mornings, if they showed up at all, after carousing on their day off. In this way, workers exerted a good deal of influence over the workplace.

Early Industrialization

Early industry in the United States reorganized daily work routines and market relationships. In the late eighteenth and early nineteenth centuries, a "putting-out" system developed in the Northeast, particularly in Massachusetts, New Jersey, and Pennsylvania. Women and children continued to produce goods but now a merchant supplied them with raw materials, paid them a wage (usually a price for each piece they produced), and sold their wares in distant markets, pocketing the profits himself. "Outwork," as it is sometimes called, appealed to women eager for cash, whether to secure economic independence or to save for additional land where their children might establish farms. Particularly in New England—where population density, small farms, and tired soil constricted farming opportunities—the putting-out system provided opportunities to earn money with which to buy more fertile western lands.

Drawing on technology from Europe, the earliest factories grew in tandem with the putting-out system. Samuel Slater helped set up the first American water-powered spinning mill in Rhode Island in 1790, using children to card and spin raw cotton into thread. He sent the spun thread to nearby farm families who were paid to weave it into cloth. Although the work remained familiar, women now operated their looms for wages and produced cloth primarily for the market.

The Transportation Revolution

How did the transportation revolution help lay the groundwork for a market economy?

In order to market goods at substantial distances from where they were produced, internal improvements were needed. Before the War of 1812, natural waterways provided the most readily available and cheapest transportation routes for people and goods, but they had limitations. Boatmen poled bateaux (cargo boats) down shallow rivers or floated flatboats down deep ones. Cargo generally moved in one direction—downstream—and most boats were destroyed for lumber at their destination. Upstream commerce was limited.

Roads

Overland transport was limited, too. Although some roads were built during the colonial and revolutionary eras, they often became obstructed by fallen trees, soaked by mud, or clouded in dust. To reduce mud and dust, some turnpike companies built "corduroy" roads, whose tightly lined-up logs resembled the ribbed cotton fabric. But passengers complained of nausea from being continually jolted, and merchants remained wary of transporting fragile wares by wagon. Land transportation was slow and expensive. In 1800, it cost as much to ship a ton of goods 30 miles into the interior as to ship the same goods from New York to England. The lack of cheap, quick transportation impeded westward expansion and industrial growth. With natural water routes unpredictable and roads predictably bad, an urgent need arose for better transportation.

Steamboats

The first major innovation was the steamboat. In 1807, Robert Fulton's Clermont traveled between New York and Albany on the Hudson River in thirty-two hours, demonstrating the feasibility of using steam engines to power boats. After the Supreme Court's ruling against steamboat monopolies in Gibbons v. Ogden (1824), steamboat companies flourished on eastern rivers and, to a lesser extent, on the Great Lakes. They transported settlers to the Midwest, where they would grow grain and raise pigs that fed northeastern factory workers. Along western rivers like the Mississippi and the Ohio, steamboats carried Midwestern timber and grain, and southern cotton to New Orleans, where they were transferred to oceangoing vessels destined for northern and international ports. To travel between Ohio and New Orleans by flatboat in 1815 took several months; in 1840, the same trip by steamboat took just ten days. Privately operated, steamboats became subject to federal regulations after frequent and deadly accidents in which boilers exploded, fires ignited, and boats collided.

Canals

In the late eighteenth and early nineteenth centuries, private companies (sometimes with state subsidies) built small canals to transport goods to and from interior locations. These projects rarely reaped substantial profits, making it difficult to court future investors. In 1815, only three canals measured more than 2 miles long; the longest was 27 miles. After Madison's veto of the Bonus Bill dashed commercially minded New Yorkers' hopes for a canal connecting Lake Erie to the port of New York, Governor DeWitt Clinton pushed successfully for a state-sponsored initiative. The **Erie Canal** was to run 363 miles between Buffalo and Albany and was to be 4 feet deep.

Construction began on July 4, 1817. The canal, its promoters emphasized, would demonstrate how American ingenuity and hard work could overcome any obstacle including the combined ascent and descent of 680 feet between Buffalo and Albany. By so doing, it would help unify the nation and secure its commercial independence from Europe.

Over the next eight years, nine thousand laborers felled forests, shoveled dirt, blasted rock, hauled boulders, rechanneled streams, and molded the canal bed. Stonemasons and carpenters built aqueducts and locks. The work was dangerous, often taking place in malaria- and rattlesnake-infested swamps. Gunpowder explosions blew up some workers along with the rock they blasted. Collapsing canal beds smothered others, while some fell to their death from aqueducts and locks.

The canal's promoters celebrated the waterway as the work of "republican free men," a tribute to the nation's republican heritage. But few of those involved in the canal's construction would have perceived their work as fulfilling Jefferson's notion of republican freedom. Although farmers and artisans provided important labor, unskilled laborers—including immigrants and convicts—outnumbered them. Once completed, the Erie Canal relied on child labor. Boys led the horses that pulled boats between the canal's eighty-three locks, while girls cooked and cleaned on the boats. When the canal froze shut in winter, many workers had neither employment nor shelter.

The Erie Canal's completion in November 1825 brought immediate commercial success. Horse-drawn boats, stacked with bushels of wheat, barrels of oats, and piles of logs, streamed eastward from western New York and Buffalo, where longshoreman transferred shipments to canal boats. Forty thousand passengers in 1825 alone traveled on the new waterway. The canal shortened the journey between Buffalo and New York City from twenty to six days and reduced freight charges by nearly 95 percent—thus securing New York City's position as the nation's preeminent port. Goods that were previously unavailable in the nation's interior now could be had easily and cheaply.

By 1840, canals crisscrossed the Northeast and Midwest, and total canal mileage reached 3,300. Because the South had easily navigable rivers, fewer canals were dug there. None of the new canals enjoyed the Erie's financial success. As the high cost of construction combined with economic contraction, investment in canals slumped in the 1830s. Several midwestern states could not repay their canal loans, leading them to bankruptcy or near-bankruptcy. By mid-century, the canal era had ended, though the Erie Canal (by then twice enlarged and rerouted) continued to prosper and operate until the late twentieth century.

Link to an illustration of Clinton promoting the Erie Canal.

Erie Canal: Major canal that linked Great Lakes to New York City, opening upper Midwest to wider development.

Railroads

The future belonged to railroads. Trains moved faster than canal boats and operated year-round. Railroads could connect the most remote locations to national and international markets. By 1860, the United States had 60,000 miles of track, mostly in the North, and railroads had dramatically reduced the cost and the time involved in shipping goods.

The United States railroad era began in 1830 when Peter Cooper's locomotive, Tom Thumb, steamed along 13 miles of Baltimore & Ohio Railroad track. Not until the 1850s did railroads offer long-distance service at reasonable rates. Even then, lack of a common standard for track width thwarted development of a national system. A journey from Philadelphia to Charleston involved eight different gauges, requiring passengers and freight to change trains seven times. Only at Bowling Green, Kentucky, did northern and southern railroads connect. Despite the race to construct internal improvements, the nation's canals and railroads did little to unite the regions and promote nationalism, as proponents of government-sponsored internal improvements had hoped.

Government Promotion of Internal Improvements

Northern state and local governments and private investors spent more on internal improvements than did southerners. Pennsylvania and New York together accounted for half of all state monies invested. Southern states invested in railroads, but—with smaller free populations—they collected fewer taxes and had less to spend.

For capitalists seeking dividends, southern railroads often seemed a poor bet. To be profitable for investors and affordable for shippers, trains could not ship only one way; if they took agricultural products to market, their cars had to be filled with manufactured or finished goods for the return trip. But slaves and cash-strapped farmers did not provide much of a consumer base. Although planters bought northern ready-made clothes and shoes for their slaves, such purchases—made annually—did not constitute a regular source of incoming freight. Because the wealthiest men lived along rivers and could send their cotton to market on steamboats, they sometimes saw little need for railroads.

The North and South laid roughly the same amount of railroad track per person before the Civil War, but when measured in mileage, the more populous North had tracks that stretched considerably farther, forming an integrated system of local lines branching off major trunk lines. In the South, railroads remained local. Neither people nor goods moved easily across the South, unless they traveled via steamboat or flatboat along the Mississippi River system—and even then, flooded banks often disrupted passage.

Regional Connections

The North's frenzy of canal and railroad building expanded transportation networks far into the hinterlands. In 1815, nearly all produce from the Old Northwest floated down the Mississippi to New Orleans, tying that region's fortunes to the South. By the 1850s, though, canals and railroads strengthened the economic, cultural, and political links between the Old Northwest—particularly the more densely populated northern regions—and the Northeast. (See Map 11.1.)

Internal improvements hastened westward migration, making western settlement more appealing by providing easy access to eastern markets. News, visitors,

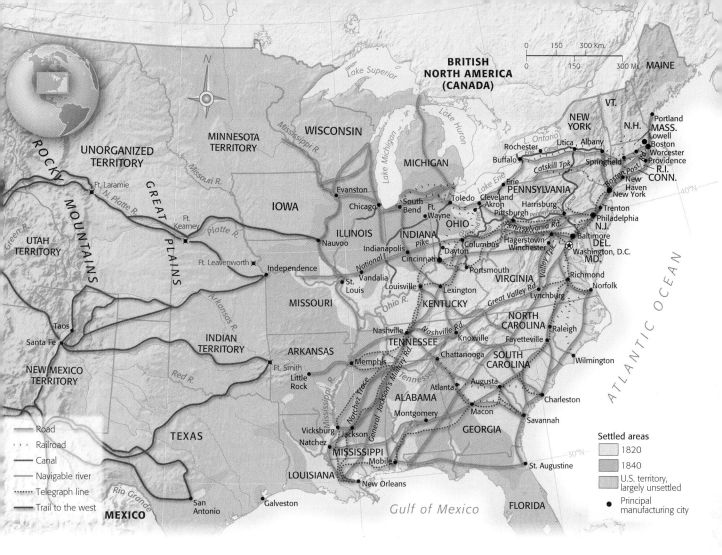

MAP 11.1

Major Roads, Canals, and Railroads, 1850

A transportation network linked the seaboard to the interior. Settlers followed those routes westward, and they sent back grain, grain products, and cotton to the port cities.

Source: Copyright © Cengage Learning

and luxuries now traveled regularly to previously remote areas of the Northeast and Midwest. Delighted that the Erie Canal brought fresh seafood to central New York, Mary Archbald explained that "distance ... is reduced to nothing here."

Samuel F. B. Morse's invention of the telegraph in 1844 allowed news to travel almost instantaneously along telegraph wires. By 1852, more than 23,000 miles of lines were strung nationwide. The telegraph enabled the birth of modern business practices involving the coordination of market conditions, production, and supply across great distances.

Ambivalence Toward Progress

Many northerners hailed internal improvements as symbols of progress. They proclaimed that, by building canals and railroads, they had completed God's design for the North American continent. Practically speaking, canals and railroads allowed them to seek opportunities in the West.

Links to the World

Internal Improvements

On July 4, 1827, ninety-one-year-old Charles Carroll, the only surviving signer of the Declaration of Independence, shoveled the first spadeful of earth on the Baltimore and Ohio Railroad, the nation's first westward railroad. Internal improvements, he and many others believed, would cement the United States' economic independence by supplying the nation's growing industrial centers with food and raw materials, while transporting manufactured goods back to its rural population.

Although boosters championed canals and railroads as the triumph of American republicanism, such projects depended on technology, funding, and labor from abroad. American engineers scrutinized canals and railroads in France, the Low Countries, and England. Railroad companies purchased locomotives from English manufacturers. Foreign investors financed significant portions of projects. Thousands of immigrants, mostly from Ireland, worked blasting boulders, draining malaria-filled swamps, picking at roots and rocks, and heaving dirt. After the Civil War, Chinese immigrants helped build the transcontinental railroad.

Internal improvements allowed people, raw materials, and goods to move inexpensively and quickly across the continent, spurring the nation's growth—but also strengthening its ties to Europe. Cotton and grain moved eastward, with much of it sold overseas. The cotton fed European textile mills; the grain fed their workers. Thus, whenever economic conditions constricted in Europe, American cotton and wheat farmers experienced similar downturns.

Canals and railroads, hailed as great symbols of American independence, linked American farmers to an increasingly complex and volatile international economy.

Workers repair a section of the Erie Canal, near Little Falls, in 1831. While hailed as a great achievement of human progress, the Canal required frequent repairs, frustrating travelers, merchants, boat workers, and people living along its banks.

But people who welcomed such opportunities could find much to lament. Mary Ann Archbald savored fresh seafood dinners but regretted that her sons turned to speculation. Others decried the enormous numbers of Irish canal diggers and railroad track layers, whom they deemed depraved and racially inferior. Still others worried that, by promoting urban growth, transportation innovations fostered social ills.

The degradation of the natural world proved worrisome, too. When streams were rerouted, swamps drained, and forests felled, natural habitats were disturbed, even destroyed. Deprived of water power, mills no longer ran. Without forests, wild animals—on which many rural people (Native American and European American) had relied for protein—sought homes elsewhere. Fishermen, too, found their sources of protein (and cash) dried up when natural waterways were dammed or rerouted to feed canals.

Factories and Industrialization

By dramatically lowering transportation costs, internal improvements facilitated the Northeast's rapid manufacturing and commercial expansion. Western farmers supplied raw materials and foodstuffs for northeastern factories and workers. They also expanded the domestic market for Northeastern manufactured goods. Focused on cultivating their lands, western settlers preferred to buy rather than make cloth, shoes, and other goods. They needed northeastern iron, too, for farm implements, nails, and railroad tracks.

> How was factory work different from the work life people previously knew?

Factory Work

With industrialization, daily life changed dramatically. Much early industrialization involved processing raw materials—milling flour, turning hogs into packaged meat, sawing lumber. The pork-packing industry illustrates how specialization turned skilled craftsmen into laborers. Traditionally, each butcher cut up an entire pig. Under the new industrial organization, each worker was assigned a particular task—such as cutting off the right front leg—as the pig moved down a "disassembly line."

The impersonal nature and formal rules of factory work contrasted with the informal atmosphere of artisan shops and farm households. In large factories, laborers never saw owners, working instead under paid supervisors, nor did they see the final product. Factory workers lost their sense of autonomy in the face of impersonal market forces, as the bell or steam whistle governed their day. Competition from cheaper, less-skilled workers—particularly after European immigration soared in the 1840s—created job insecurity, while opportunities for advancement were virtually nonexistent.

At first Americans imported or copied British machines that would make mass production possible in some industries. Soon, they built their own. The **American System of manufacturing** used precision machinery to produce interchangeable parts. Eli Whitney, the cotton gin's inventor, promoted interchangeable parts in 1798, when he contracted with the federal government to make ten thousand rifles in twenty-eight months. The American System quickly produced the machine-tool industry—the manufacture of machines for the purpose of mass production. The new system permitted large-scale production of inexpensive but high-quality household items.

American System of manufacturing: System of manufacturing that used interchangeable parts.

Textile Mills

Mechanization was most dramatic in textiles, with production centered in New England, near sources of water to power spinning machines and looms. After 1815, New England's rudimentary cotton mills developed into modern factories where machines mass-produced goods. Cotton cloth production rose from 4 million yards in 1817 to 323 million in 1840, and in the mid-1840s, the cotton mills employed approximately eighty thousand "operatives;" more than half were women.

Unable to find enough laborers near mills, managers recruited New England farm daughters, whom they housed in boarding houses in what became known as the **Waltham** or **Lowell** plan of industrialization. People who lived off the land were often suspicious of those who did not—particularly in the United States, where an agrarian lifestyle was associated with virtue. To ease concerns, mill owners offered paternalistic oversight to mill girls; they enforced curfews, prohibited alcohol, and required church attendance. Nonetheless, the Waltham system offered farm girls opportunities to socialize with other women and a sense of independence.

Working conditions in textile mills—the deafening roar of the power looms, the long hours, and regimentation—made young women cling to notions that their jobs were temporary. They used their wages to help their families buy land or send a brother to college, to save for their dowries or education, or to spend on personal items, such as clothing. The average girl arrived at sixteen and stayed five years, usually leaving to get married—often to men they met in town rather than farm boys at home. Although the Waltham plan drew international attention, more common was the Rhode Island (or Fall River) plan employed by **Samuel Slater**, among others. Mills hired entire families, lodging them in company boarding houses. Men often worked farm plots nearby while wives and children worked in the mills, though as the system developed, men worked in the factories, supervising wives and children in family-based work units.

Waltham, Lowell: Sites of early textile mills in New England which were precursors to modern factories. Nearly 80 percent of the workers in Waltham, Lowell, and similar mills were young, unmarried women who had been lured from farms by the promise of wages.

Samuel Slater: British mechanic who carried plans for textile mills to United States.

Labor Protests

Mill life got harder over time. To increase productivity, managers sped up machines and required each worker to operate more machines. Between 1836 and 1850, the number of spindles and looms in Lowell increased 150 and 140 percent, respectively, whereas the number of workers increased by only 50 percent. To boost profits, owners lengthened hours, cut wages, and packed boarding houses.

Workers organized, and in 1834, reacting to a 25 percent wage cut, they unsuccessfully "turned out" (struck) against the Lowell mills. As conditions worsened and strikes failed, workers resisted in new ways. In 1844, Massachusetts mill women formed the Lowell Female Reform Association and joined forces with other workers to press, unsuccessfully, for state legislation mandating a ten- instead of fourteen-hour day.

Women aired their complaints in worker-run newspapers: in 1842, the *Factory Girl* appeared in New Hampshire, the *Wampanoag and Operatives' Journal* in Massachusetts. Two years later, mill workers founded the *Factory Girl's Garland* and the *Voice of Industry*, nicknamed "the factory girl's voice." The owner-sponsored *Lowell Offering* faced controversy when workers charged its editors with suppressing articles criticizing working conditions.

Worker turnover weakened organizational efforts. Few militant native-born mill workers stayed to fight the managers and owners, and gradually, fewer New England daughters entered the mills. In the 1850s, Irish immigrant women replaced them. Technological improvements made the work less skilled and more routine, reducing

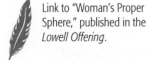

Link to "Woman's Proper Sphere," published in the *Lowell Offering*.

wages. Male workers, too, protested changes wrought by the **market economy**. As voters, they formed labor political parties first in Pennsylvania, New York, and Massachusetts in the 1820s, and then elsewhere. They advocated free public education and an end to imprisonment for debt, and opposed banks and monopolies. Aspiring to own land, some advocated for free homesteads.

market economy: Newly developing commercial economy that depended on goods and crops produced for sale rather than for personal consumption.

Labor Unions

The courts provided organized labor's greatest victory: protection from conspiracy laws. When journeyman shoemakers organized during the early 1800s, employers accused them of criminal conspiracy. The cordwainers' (shoemakers') cases between 1806 and 1815 left labor organizations in an uncertain position. Although the courts acknowledged journeymen's right to organize, judges viewed strikes as illegal until a Massachusetts case, **Commonwealth v. Hunt** (1842), ruled that Boston journeyman bootmakers could strike "to subserve their own interests."

Commonwealth v. Hunt: A court case in 1842 where the Massachusetts Supreme Judicial Court ruled that labor unions were not illegal monopolies that restrained trade.

The first unions arose among urban journeymen in printing, woodworking, shoemaking, and tailoring. Typically local, the strongest sought protection against competition from inferior workmen by regulating apprenticeships and establishing minimum wages. Umbrella organizations of individual craft unions, like the National Trade Union (1834), arose in several cities in the 1820s and 1830s. But the movement disintegrated amid wage reductions and unemployment in the hard times of 1839–1843.

Permanent labor organizations were difficult to sustain. Skilled craftsmen disdained less skilled workers. Moreover, workers divided along ethnic, religious, racial, and gender lines.

Consumption and Commercialization

Before the 1820s, women sewed most clothing at home, and some people purchased used clothing. Tailors and seamstresses made wealthy men's and women's clothing to order. By the 1820s and 1830s, much clothing was mass-produced for sale in retail clothing stores. Standard sizes replaced measuring, and a division of labor took hold: One worker cut patterns all day, another sewed hems, another affixed buttons. The sewing machine's invention in 1846 sped the process, especially with its wide availability in the 1850s. Many farm families still made their own clothing, yet bought clothes when they could afford to, creating more time for raising crops and children.

> How did farm women's work change as the commercial economy expanded?

The Garment Industry

Market expansion created demand for mass-produced clothing. Girls working in factories no longer had time to sew clothes. Young immigrant men, separated from mothers and sisters, bought the crudely made, loose-fitting clothing. But the biggest market for ready-made clothes initially was the cotton South. With the textile industry's success driving up the demand and price for raw cotton, planters bought ready-made shoes and clothes for slaves in whose hands they would rather place a hoe than a needle and thread.

Retailers often bought goods wholesale, though many manufactured shirts and trousers in their own factories. Lewis and Hanford of New York City boasted of cutting more than 100,000 garments in winter 1848–1849. The New York firm did business mostly in the South and owned a retail outlet in New Orleans. While southerners and westerners engaged in the clothing trade, its center remained in New York.

Images of Boom and Bust

The growth of the commercial economy, which saw the mass production of consumer items, also fostered economic boom and bust. Below we see an advertisement from the *Boston Directory* of 1848–1849 for readymade shirts, and we see how *Harper's Weekly* portrayed New York City, the heart of the garment industry, in the heat of the financial panic of 1857, less than a decade later. To what values does F.B. Locke appeal in his choice of imagery for his advertisement? Why does *Harper's Weekly* refer to the discounted goods, and the scramble to purchase them, as an "epidemic"? What is the significance, on the image's left side, of the police officer escorting two children out of the store? What does it indicate about how *Harper's* saw the consequences of the "epidemic"? What else does the picture imply about the social consequences of financial collapse? Do the two images suggest that American values shifted in the intervening decade? Why or why not?

Although F.B. Locke continued to make shirts to order, he adapted to the new market for readymade clothing by becoming a manufacturer, wholesaler, and retailer of men's shirts.

As the nation experienced a serious financial contraction in 1857, prices fell as business languished. But the availability of bargains did not compensate for widespread unemployment and falling wages.

Specialization of Commerce

Commercial specialization transformed some urban traders, especially in New York, into merchant princes. After the Erie Canal opened, New York City became a stop on every major trade route from Europe, southern ports, and the West. Traders sometimes invested in factories, further stimulating urban manufacturing. Some cities specialized: Rochester became a milling center ("The Flour City"), and Cincinnati ("Porkopolis") became the first meatpacking center.

Merchants who engaged in complex commercial transactions required large—mostly male—office staffs. At the bottom were messenger boys, often preteens, who delivered documents. Above them were copyists, who hand-copied documents. Clerks processed documents and did translations. Above them were the bookkeeper and confidential chief clerk. Those seeking employment in such counting houses took a course from a writing master. All hoped to rise to partner, although their chances grew increasingly slim.

Specialization lagged in small towns, where merchants continued to exchange goods with local farm women, and craftsmen continued to sell finished goods, such as shoes. In some rural areas, peddlers were general merchants. But as transportation improved and towns grew, small-town merchants increasingly specialized.

Commercial Farming

Even amid the manufacturing and commercial booms, agriculture remained the northern economy's backbone. But the **transportation revolution** and market expansion transformed semi-subsistence farms into commercial enterprises. Many families stopped practicing mixed agriculture and began to specialize in cash crops. Although most northerners continued to farm, on the eve of the Civil War, their daily lives and relationships often looked very different from those of their parents and grandparents.

transportation revolution: Rapid expansion of canals, steamships, and railroads.

By the 1820s, eastern farmers had cultivated nearly all available land, and their small farms, often with uneven terrains, were not suited for the labor-saving farm implements introduced in the 1830s, such as mechanical sowers, reapers, and threshers. Many northern farmers thus either moved west or quit farming for jobs in merchants' houses and factories. Those who remained, however, proved adaptable, their efforts encouraged by state governments that promoted agricultural innovation.

In 1820, about one-third of northern produce was intended for the market, but by 1850 it surpassed 50 percent. As farmers shifted toward market-oriented production, they invested in additional land (buying farms of neighbors who moved west), new equipment, and new labor sources (hired hands). Many New England and Middle Atlantic farm families faced steep competition from midwestern farmers after the Erie Canal opened. They began abandoning wheat and corn production, shifting to livestock and vegetable and fruit production. Much of what they produced fed the North's growing urban and manufacturing populations.

Farmers financed innovations through land sales and debts. Indeed, increasing land values promised the greatest profit. Farm families who owned land flourished, but by the 1840s it took more than ten years for a laborer in the Northeast to save enough to buy a farm. The number of tenant farmers and hired hands increased, and farmers who had previously employed unpaid family members and enslaved workers now leased portions of their farms or hired waged labor.

Farm Women's Changing Labor

As the commercial economy expanded, farm women added new responsibilities to their substantial duties. Some did outwork. Many increased production of eggs, dairy products, and garden produce for sale; others raised bees or silkworms.

With New England textile mills producing more finished cloth, farm women and children often abandoned time-consuming spinning and weaving, bought factory-produced cloth, and dedicated the saved time to producing additional products, such as butter and cheese, for the market rather than simply for their family's consumption. Some mixed-agriculture farms converted entirely to dairy production, with men taking over formerly female tasks. Canals and railroads carried cheese to eastern ports, where wholesalers sold it worldwide.

Rural Communities

Despite pressure to manage farms like time-efficient businesses, some farmers clung to old practices of gathering at market, general stores, taverns, and church. They continued barn raisings and husking bees, but by the 1830s with young women working in textile mills and young men laboring as clerks or factory hands, there were fewer young people at such events.

While farmers continued to swap labor and socialize with neighbors, they increasingly reckoned debts in dollars. They watched national and international markets more closely. When financial panics hit, cash shortages almost halted business activity, casting many farmers further into debt, sometimes bankruptcy. Faced with potentially losing their land, farmers called in neighbors' debts, sometimes rupturing long-established relationships.

Cycles of Boom and Bust

With market expansion came booms and busts. Prosperity stimulated demand for finished goods, such as clothing and furniture, which led to higher prices and still higher production and to land speculation. Investment money was plentiful as Americans saved and foreign, mostly British, investors bought U.S. bonds and securities. Then production surpassed demand. Prices and wages fell; land and stock values collapsed, and investment money left the United States. This boom-and-bust cycle touched the whole country, but particularly the Northeast.

Although the 1820s and 1830s were boom times, financial panic triggered a bust cycle in 1837, the year after the Second Bank of the United States closed. Economic contraction remained severe through 1843. Many banks could not repay depositors, and states, facing deficits, defaulted on bonds. Because of the **Panic of 1837**, European, especially British, investors became suspicious of U.S. loans and withdrew money from the United States.

Panic of 1837: A severe depression that struck the United States beginning in May 1837.

Hard times had come. "The streets seemed deserted," Sidney George Fisher observed of Philadelphia in 1842. "The largest [merchant] houses are shut up and to rent, there is no business…no money, no confidence." The hungry formed lines at soup societies, and beggars crowded the sidewalks. Laborers demanding their deposits gathered at closed banks. Sheriffs sold seized property at one-quarter of pre-hard-time prices. In smaller cities like Lynn, Massachusetts, shoemakers weathered hard times by fishing and gardening, while laborers scavenged for clams and dandelions. Congress passed the Federal Bankruptcy Law of 1841; by the time the law was repealed two years later, 41,000 bankrupts had sought protection under its provisions.

Families in Flux

What roles did families play in the new industrial era?

Anxieties about economic fluctuations reverberated into northern homes. Sweeping changes in the household economy led to new family ideals. In the preindustrial era, the families were primarily economic units; now they became a moral and cultural institution, though in reality few families could live up to this ideal.

The "Ideal" Family

In the North, the market economy increasingly separated the home from the workplace, leading to a new middle-class ideal in which men functioned in the public sphere, while women oversaw the private or domestic sphere. The home became, in theory, an emotional retreat from the competitive, selfish business world. Men provided and protected, while women nurtured and guarded the family's morality, ensuring that capitalism's excesses did not invade the home. Childhood expanded: children were to remain at home until their late teens or early twenties.

This ideal came to be known as separate-sphere ideology, the cult of domesticity or the cult of true womanhood. Although it rigidly separated the male and female spheres, this ideology elevated domestic responsibilities. In her widely read *Treatise on Domestic Economy* (1841), Catharine Beecher approached housekeeping as a science while trumpeting mothers' role as their family's moral guardian. Beecher maintained that women's natural superiority as moral, nurturing caregivers made them especially suited for teaching (when single) and parenting (once married). Beecher insisted that the private sphere be elevated to the same status as the public.

Shrinking Families

These new domestic ideals depended on smaller families enabling parents, particularly mothers, to give children better attention, education, and financial help. With the market economy, parents could afford to have fewer children because children no longer played a vital economic role. Urban families produced fewer household goods, and commercial farmers, unlike self-sufficient ones, relied on hired laborers. Although smaller families resulted partly from first marriages occurring at a later age, they also resulted from planning, made easier when cheap rubber condoms became available in the 1850s. Some women chose, too, to end accidental pregnancies with abortion.

As they strove to live according to new domestic ideals, middle-class families often relied on African American or immigrant servants, who sacrificed time with their own children in order to care for their employers' children.

St. Louis Art Museum, bequest of Edgar William and Bernice Chrysler Garbisch

In 1800, American women bore seven or eight children; by 1860, they had five or six. This decline occurred even though immigrants with large-family traditions were settling in the United States; thus, the birth rate among native-born women declined more sharply. Although rural families remained larger than urban ones, birth rates among both groups declined comparably.

Few northern women could fulfill the middle-class ideal of **separate spheres**. Most wage-earning women provided essential income for their families and could not stay home. They often saw domestic ideals as oppressive, as middle-class reformers mistook poverty for immorality, condemning working mothers for letting their children work or scavenge rather than attend school. Although most middle-class women could stay home, new standards of cleanliness drained their time. Women's contributions to their families were assessed in moral, not economic terms. Without servants, moreover, women could not devote themselves primarily to their children, making the ideals of the cult of domesticity impossible for many middle-class families.

separate spheres: Middle-class ideology that emerged with the market revolution and divided men's and women's roles into distinct and separate categories based on their perceived gender differences, abilities, and social functions. Men were assigned the public realm of business and politics, while women were assigned to the private world of home and family.

Women's Paid Labor   In working-class families, women left home as early as age twelve, earning wages most of their lives, with short respites for bearing and rearing children. Unmarried girls and women worked primarily as domestic servants or in factories; married and widowed women worked as laundresses, seamstresses, and cooks. Some hawked food and wares on city streets; other did piecework; and some became prostitutes. Few could support themselves or a family comfortably.

If middle-class girls left home to work in New England's textile mills, or in new urban stores as clerks, it was only briefly, before marriage. Otherwise, teaching was the only occupation consistent with genteel femininity. In 1823, Catharine and Mary Beecher established the Hartford Female Seminary, adding history and science to the traditional women's curriculum of domestic arts and religion. A decade later, Catharine Beecher successfully campaigned for teacher-training schools for women. Single, these women need not earn as much as their male counterparts, whom she presumed to be married. Unmarried women earned about half the salary of male teachers. By 1850, schoolteaching had become a woman's profession.

The proportion of single women in the population increased significantly in the nineteenth century. As more young men headed west, some eastern communities had a disproportionate number of young women. Other women chose to remain independent. Because women's work generally paid poorly, those who forswore marriage faced serious challenges, leaving many single women to rely on charitable or family assistance.

The Growth of Cities

How could cities be seen at once as symbols of progress and of moral decay?

No period in American history saw more rapid urbanization than between 1820 and 1860. The percentage of people living in urban areas (defined by a population of 2,500 or more) grew from 7 percent in 1820 to nearly 20 percent in 1860. The greatest growth occurred in the Northeast and Midwest. Although most northerners continued to live on farms or in small villages, cities boomed. Many urban residents were temporary, and many were immigrants.

Urban Boom   In 1820, the United States had 13 places with a population greater than 10,000; in 1860, it had 93. (see Map 11.2). New York City, already the nation's largest city in 1820, saw its population grow from 123,709 that year to 813,669 in 1860. Philadelphia, the nation's second-largest city, saw its population multiply ninefold during that forty-year period. In 1815, Rochester, New York, had just 300 residents. By 1830, the Erie Canal turned the sleepy agricultural town into the nation's twenty-fifth-largest city, with a population of just over 9,000.

Cities experienced geographic expansion too. Until 1830, New Yorkers could walk the entire length of the city in an hour. In 1825, Fourteenth Street was the city's northern boundary. By 1860, Forty-second Street was the city's northern limit. Public transit made city expansion possible. By the 1850s, all big cities had horse-drawn streetcars, allowing wealthier residents who could afford the fare to settle on the cities' outskirts.

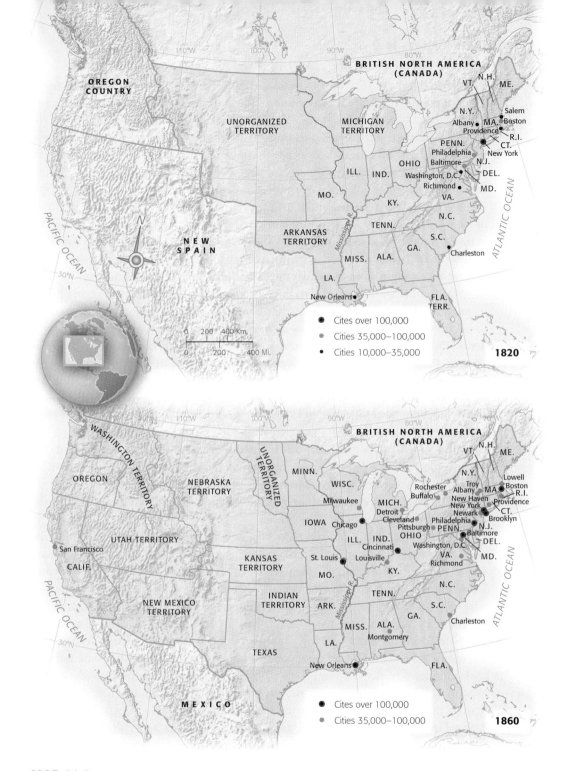

MAP 11.2

Major American Cities in 1820 and 1860

The number of Americans who lived in cities increased rapidly between 1820 and 1860, and the number of large cities grew as well. In 1820, only New York City had a population exceeding 100,000; forty years later, eight more cities had surpassed that level.

Source: Copyright © Cengage Learning

Market-Related Development

Cities sustained the North's market revolution by serving as transportation hubs, commercial centers, and manufacturing sites. Some cities grew up with manufacturing. The Boston Manufacturing Company selected the site for Lowell, Massachusetts, because of its proximity to the Merrimack River, which could power its textile mill. Incorporated in 1826, by the 1850s Lowell was the second-largest city in New England. Although most early manufacturing took place in rural areas, some cities, such as New York, experienced what historians call metropolitan industrialization, which relied on reorganization of labor similar to the earlier putting-out system. Most early ready-made clothing, for example, was produced as outwork by women in tenements throughout New York City. In 1860, 25,000 women worked in manufacturing jobs in New York City, constituting a quarter of the waged labor force; two-thirds worked in the garment industry.

Northern cities developed elaborate municipal services but lacked taxing power to provide services for all. At best, they could tax property adjoining new sewers, paved streets, and water mains. New services and basic sanitation depended on residents' ability to pay. Another solution was to charter private companies to sell basic services. Baltimore first chartered a private gas company in 1816. By mid-century, every major city had done so. Private firms lacked the capital to build adequate water systems, and they laid pipe only in commercial and well-to-do residential areas. Supplying water ultimately fell to city governments.

Extremes of Wealth

Wealth was increasingly concentrated in fewer hands. By 1860, the top 5 percent of American families owned more than half of the nation's wealth, and the top 10 percent owned nearly three-quarters. In the South, income extremes were most apparent on rural plantations, but in the North, cities revealed economic inequities.

A number of factors contributed to widespread poverty in America's industrial cities: poor wages, lack of full-time employment, and the increasingly widespread employment of women and children, which further drove down wages for everyone. Women and children, employers rationalized, did not need a living wage because they were dependent, meaning that they relied on men to support them. In reality, not all women or children had men to support them, nor were men's wages always adequate.

New York provides a striking example of the extremes of wealth accompanying industrialization. Houses built for two families often held four. Some families took in lodgers to pay the rent; such crowding encouraged poorer New Yorkers to head outdoors. But poor neighborhoods were filthy. Excess sewage from outhouses drained into ditches that carried urine and fecal matter into the streets. People piled garbage into gutters, backyards, or alleys. Pigs, geese, dogs, and vultures scavenged the streets, while rats roamed under wooden sidewalks and through large buildings. Typhoid, dysentery, malaria, and tuberculosis regularly visited the poorer sections of cities. Cholera struck in 1831, 1849, and 1866.

Just beyond poverty-stricken neighborhoods were lavish mansions, whose residents escaped to their country estates during summer's brutal heat or epidemics. Much of this wealth was inherited. Rich New Yorkers increased their fortunes by investing in commerce and manufacturing.

The middle class was larger than the wealthy elite but substantially smaller than the working classes. They were businessmen, traders, and professionals, and the rapid turn toward industrialization and commercial specialization made them a larger presence in northern cities than in southern ones. Middle-class families enjoyed new consumer items: wool carpeting, fine wallpaper, and rooms full of furniture. Houses were large, from four to six rooms. By the 1840s and 1850s, middle-class families used indoor toilets that were mechanical, though not yet flushing. These families formed the backbone of urban clubs and societies, filled the family pews in church, and sent their sons to college.

Immigration

Many of the urban poor were immigrants. The 5 million immigrants to the United States between 1830 and 1860 outnumbered the country's population in 1790 (see Figure 11.1). During peak pre-Civil War of immigration (1847–1857), 3.3 million immigrants entered the United States, including 1.3 million Irish and 1.1 million Germans. By 1860, 15 percent of the white population was foreign-born, with 90 percent of immigrants living in northern states.

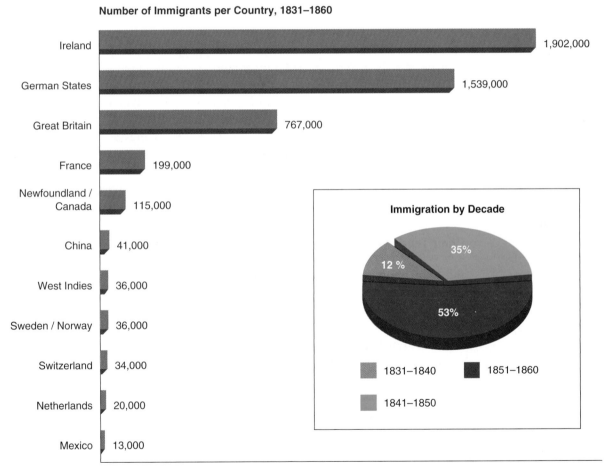

Number of Immigrants per Country, 1831–1860

Ireland	1,902,000
German States	1,539,000
Great Britain	767,000
France	199,000
Newfoundland / Canada	115,000
China	41,000
West Indies	36,000
Sweden / Norway	36,000
Switzerland	34,000
Netherlands	20,000
Mexico	13,000

Immigration by Decade

35% — 1831–1840
12% — 1841–1850
53% — 1851–1860

FIGURE 11.1
Major Sources of Immigration to the United States, 1831–1860

Most immigrants came from two areas: Great Britain, of which Ireland was a part, and the German states. These two areas sent more immigrants between 1830 and 1860 than the inhabitants of the United States enumerated at the first census in 1790. By 1860, 15 percent of the white population was of foreign birth.

Source: Data from Stephan Thernstrom, ed., *Harvard Encyclopedia of American Ethnic Groups* (Cambridge, Mass., and London: Harvard University Press, 1980), p. 1047.

Various factors "pushed" Europeans from their homes and "pulled" them to the northern United States. In Ireland, the potato famine (1845–1850)—a period of widespread starvation caused by a diseased potato crop—drove millions from their homeland. Although economic conditions pushed most Germans, some were political refugees—liberals, freethinkers, Socialists, communists, and anarchists—who fled after the abortive revolutions of 1848. Employers, states, and shipping companies promoted opportunities in America with this message: work and prosper in America or starve in Europe. Once in the United States, immigrants soon saw the fallacy of promoters' promises of riches and hundreds of thousands returned home.

Many early immigrants lived or worked in rural areas. Like the Archbalds, a few settled on farms and bought land. Others worked as hired farm hands, canal diggers, or railroad track layers—often hoping to buy land later. By the 1840s and 1850s—when the steady stream of immigration turned into a flood—the prospects of buying land became remote.

By 1860, most immigrants settled in cities, often the port at which they arrived. The most destitute could not afford the fare to places farther inland. Others had resources but fell victim to swindlers. Others liked the cities' ethnic flair. In 1855, 52 percent of New York's 623,000 inhabitants were immigrants, 28 percent from Ireland and 16 percent from the German states. Throughout the 1850s, about 35 percent of Boston was foreign-born; more than two-thirds were Irish.

Most of the new Irish immigrants were young, poor, Roman Catholics from rural districts. Women found work as domestic servants or mill hands, while men worked in construction or transportation. Most Germans came with enough resources to head to states such as Ohio, Illinois, Wisconsin, and Missouri. Although some southern cities like Charleston and Savannah had many Irish immigrants, most European immigrants disliked slavery and semitropical heat and preferred the Northeast or Midwest.

Ethnic Tensions

Tension—often over the era's economic changes—characterized the relationship between native-born Americans and immigrants, particularly Irish Catholics. Native-born workers blamed immigrants for scarce job opportunities and low wages. Middle-class whites blamed them for poverty and crime. They believed immigrants' moral depravity—not poor wages—led to poverty.

White northerners often portrayed Irish immigrants as nonwhite, as African in appearance. But Irish and African Americans did not develop a sense of solidarity. Instead, some of the era's most virulent riots erupted between Irish immigrants and African Americans.

Anti-Catholicism became strident in the 1830s. In Boston, anti-Catholic riots occurred frequently. Nearby Charlestown, Massachusetts, saw a mob burn a convent in 1834. In Philadelphia, a crowd attacked priests and nuns and vandalized churches in 1844, and in Lawrence, Massachusetts, a mob leveled the Irish neighborhood in 1854. Riots between native-born and Irish workers erupted along canals and railroads—but urban riots attracted more newspaper attention, fueling fears that cities were depraved places.

Protestant German immigrants fared better than the Irish. Because Germans generally arrived with resources and skills, Americans stereotyped them as hardworking. But non-Protestant Germans—Catholics and Jews (whom white Americans considered a separate race)—frequently encountered racial and religious prejudice.

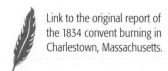

Link to the original report of the 1834 convent burning in Charlestown, Massachusetts.

Immigrants often lived in ethnic enclaves, setting up social clubs and mutual aid societies. Irish Catholics had their own neighborhoods, where they established Catholic churches and schools. In larger cities, immigrants from the same German states clustered together.

People of Color

African Americans also forged their own communities and culture. As late as the 1830s, many remained enslaved in New York and New Jersey, but the numbers of free African Americans grew steadily. By 1860, nearly 250,000 (many of them refugees from southern slavery) lived in the urban North. **African Methodist Episcopal churches** and preachers helped forge communities. Churches hosted schools, political reforms, and protest meetings.

White racism impinged on northern African Americans' lives. Streetcars, hotels, restaurants, and theaters could turn away African Americans without legal penalty. City laws barred African Americans from public buildings. Even where laws were liberal, whites' attitudes constrained African Americans' opportunities. In Massachusetts, for example, African Americans enjoyed more legal rights than anywhere else. Still, whites often refused to shop at black businesses. African Americans were excluded from factory and clerical jobs. Women worked as house servants, cooks, washerwomen, and child nurses. Most African American men worked as construction workers, porters, longshoremen, or day laborers—all jobs subject to frequent unemployment. Others took lower-paying but stable jobs as servants, waiters, cooks, barbers, and janitors. Many African American men became sailors and merchant seamen, jobs offering regular employment and advancement, though not protection from racial taunts.

In the growing cities, African Americans turned service occupations into businesses, opening restaurants, taverns, hotels, barber shops, and employment agencies for domestic servants. Some sold used clothing or were junk dealers. A few became wealthy, invested in real estate, and loaned money. With professionals—ministers, teachers, physicians, dentists, lawyers, and newspaper editors—they formed a small but growing African American middle class.

Still, African Americans became targets of urban violence. White rioters clubbed and stoned African Americans, destroying their houses, churches, and businesses—and sent many fleeing for their lives. Philadelphia experienced five major riots in the 1830s and 1840s. By 1860, hundreds of African Americans had died in urban riots.

Urban Culture

Living in cramped, squalid conditions, working-class families spent little time indoors. In the 1840s, a working-class youth culture developed

> **African Methodist Episcopal churches:** First American denomination established by and for African Americans.

North Carolina Museum of Art, purchased with funds from the State of North Carolina (52.9.2)

Immigrants often considered themselves superior to African Americans, fueling racial tensions. Here, a German immigrant demonstrates his sense of superiority even as he relies on an African American laborer for directions.

© Collection of the New York Historical Society

Thomas D. Rice playing "Jim Crow" in blackface at the Bowery Theater in New York City, 1833. The rowdy audience climbed onto the stage, leaving Rice little room to perform. In representing African Americans on stage, Rice and other minstrels contributed to establishing both black and white as racial categories.

on the Bowery, one of New York's entertainment strips. Lined with theaters, dance halls, and cafés, it became an urban midway. The Bowery boys' greased hair, distinctive clothing, and swagger frightened middle-class New Yorkers, as did the Bowery girls' colorful costumes. Equally scandalous were the middle-class clerks who succumbed to the city's temptations, notably prostitution.

Gangs of garishly dressed young men and women—flaunting their sexuality and drinking to excess—drove respectable citizenry to establish private clubs. Some men joined the Masonic order, which offered members an elaborate code of deference between ranks, while women organized literary clubs and benevolent societies.

Increasingly, urban recreation and sports became commodities. Horseracing, walking races, and, in the 1850s, baseball attracted urban men. Wall Street office workers formed the Knickerbocker Club in 1842 and in 1845 drew up rules for playing baseball. Large cities boasted two or more theaters catering to different classes. Some plays cut across class lines—Shakespeare was so widely performed that even illiterate theatergoers knew his plays.

In the 1840s, singing groups, theater troupes, and circuses traveled from city to city. Minstrel shows were particularly popular, featuring white men (often Irish) in makeup imitating African Americans in song, dance, and patter. In the early 1830s, Thomas D. Rice of New York became famous for portraying Jim Crow, an old southern slave. In ill-fitting patched clothing and torn shoes, the blackface Rice shuffled, danced, and sang. Minstrel performers told jokes mocking economic and political elites and evoked nostalgia for preindustrial work habits and morality. But blackface actors encouraged a racist stereotyping of African Americans as sensual and lazy.

The Penny Press

Accounts of urban culture peppered the penny press, which emerged in the 1830s and swept through northern cities. Made possible by technological advances—the advent of the steam-powered press, improved methods for producing paper, and transportation innovations—the penny press (each newspaper cost one cent) differed greatly from traditional (six-cent) newspapers. Where older papers covered mostly commercial news and identified with a political party, the penny press proclaimed political independence and hired reporters to cover local, national, and international stories. Where six-cent newspapers relied on subscriptions and political contributions for their revenue, penny newspapers were sold by newsboys on the street. They earned money from advertising, and drew an economically diverse readership. Working-class people could now afford to buy newspapers regularly.

Penny newspapers focused on daily life, giving one social class the opportunity to peer into the lives of other classes, ethnicities, and races. Working- and middle-class

P. T. Barnum's Publicity Stunts

Usually remembered for the Ringling Brothers and Barnum & Bailey Circus, P. T. Barnum (1810–1891) left another legacy: the publicity stunt. Using hoaxes and spectacles, Barnum's American Museum in New York City drew tens of millions of visitors between 1841 and 1868, making Barnum the era's second wealthiest American.

Barnum first gained widespread publicity in 1835 with his traveling exhibition of Joice Heth, whom he claimed was the 161-year-old former slave of George Washington. When interest waned, Barnum planted a rumor that she was a machine made of leather and bones. The penny press reveled in the ensuing controversy, swelling admissions and earning Barnum enough to purchase the American Museum, whose "500,000 natural and artificial curiosities" he promoted through similar stunts. Barnum also hosted the nation's first beauty pageant in 1854. Offensive to middle-class sensibilities, it flopped, but Barnum persevered with pageants featuring dogs, babies, and chickens. The baby show attracted 61,000 visitors. Selling more than a million copies, Barnum's autobiography inspired generations of entrepreneurs.

Many cultural icons began as promotional gimmicks, including the Miss America Pageant (1921), the Macy's Thanksgiving Day parade (1924), and the Goodyear blimp (1925). Since 1916, Nathan's has hosted a Fourth of July hotdog eating contest, now attracting forty thousand spectators and a television audience. The *Guinness Book of World Records* began as an Irish beer company's promotional brochure and inspires thousands each year to attempt to break records—and get publicity for it.

By staging stunts for media exposure, today's entrepreneurs reveal the enduring legacy of P. T. Barnum, the self-proclaimed greatest showman on earth.

readers, for example, could read about high society; wealthy readers learned about poorer neighborhoods. The penny press often sensationalized the news, thereby influencing urban dwellers' views of one another and of cities.

Cities as Symbols of Progress

To many northerners, cities symbolized both progress and decay. Cities nurtured churches, schools, civil governments, and museums—all signs of civilization and culture. As canals and railroads opened the West for mass settlement, many white northerners applauded the appearance of church steeples and public buildings in areas that had been "savage wilderness," that is, territory controlled by Native Americans. To many nineteenth-century white Americans, cities represented the moral triumph of civilization over savagery and heathenism.

Yet some middle-class Americans deplored the character of the nation's largest cities, which they saw as havens of disease, poverty, crime, and vice—all signs of moral decline. They considered epidemics to be divine scourges, striking the filthy, intemperate, and immoral. Theft and prostitution provided evidence of moral vice, and wealthy observers perceived these crimes not as by-products of poverty but as signs of individual failing. They pressed for laws against vagrancy and pushed city officials to establish police forces.

How did northerners reconcile urban vices and depravity of the city with their view of cities as symbols of progress? Middle-class reformers focused on purifying cities of disease and vice. If disease was a divine punishment—rather than an offshoot of cramped conditions—then it was within Americans' power to fix things. Middle-class reformers tried to convince the urban working classes that—unlike southern slaves—they could improve their lives by giving up alcohol, working harder, and praying frequently. This belief in upward mobility became central to many north-erners' ideas about progress.

The concept that, in a competitive marketplace, those who worked hard and lived virtuously could improve their status appealed especially to manufacturers and merchants eager to take credit for their own success. Likewise, they hoped factory hands and clerks would embrace the promise of upward mobility and remain opti-mistic despite hardships. Many laborers initially rejected this free-labor ideology as a veiled attempt to tout industrial work habits, rationalize poor wages, and quell worker protest. But by the 1850s, when the question of slavery's westward expansion returned to the political foreground, many northerners embraced free-labor ideol-ogy and regarded slavery as antithetical to it. This way of thinking, perhaps more than anything else, made the North distinctive.

Summary

During the first half of the nineteenth century, the North became enmeshed in commercial culture, as northern states and capitalists invested heavily in internal improvements. Most northerners shifted toward commercial farming or, in smaller numbers, industrial wage labor. Farmers now specialized in cash crops, while their children often worked in factories or countinghouses.

To many northerners, the market economy symbolized progress, bringing eas-ier access to cheap western lands, employment for surplus farm laborers, and the commercial availability of goods that had been time-consuming to produce. But the market economy also led to increased specialization, a depersonalized workplace, and a sharper divide between work and leisure. The market economy also tied north-erners more directly to fluctuating national and international markets, and during economic downturns, many northern families experienced destitution.

With less need for children's labor, northerners began producing smaller fami-lies. Even as working-class children worked, middle-class families created a model of childhood that had parents shielding children from the world's dangers. Mothers, in theory, became moral guardians, keeping the home safe from the new economy's competitiveness and selfishness. Few women, though, could devote themselves entirely to nurturing their families.

Immigrants and free African Americans performed the lowest paying work, and many native-born whites blamed them for problems spurred by rapid economic change. Anti-immigrant (especially anti-Catholic) and antiblack riots became com-monplace. Immigrants and African Americans responded by forming their own communities.

Cities came to symbolize the possibilities and limits of market expansion. Urban areas were marked by extremes of wealth, vibrant working-class cultures as well as poverty, crime, and mob violence. To reconcile the seeming contradictions, middle-class northerners articulated free-labor ideology, touting the possibility for upward mobility in a competitive marketplace. This ideology would become increasingly cen-tral to northern regional identity.

Chapter Review

Or Is It the North That Was Distinctive?

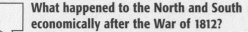

What happened to the North and South economically after the War of 1812?

The South continued as an agricultural region and expanded its slave system, while the North transformed quickly into a market economy. With the war cutting off European trade, northern entrepreneurs invested in domestic production and factories. Former artisans and farmers increasingly shifted from producers to wage workers. Early forms of market changes came from piecework or outwork, where manufacturers hired women and children in their homes to produce goods, often paying them for each piece produced. After the first mills were opened in the 1790s, women and children went to work there. People increasingly bought goods—clothes, shoes, and soap—that they once made for themselves. Commercial farming emerged in the North to meet the growing demand for foodstuffs that was created when people shifted from farming to factory jobs. Those farmers who remained in agriculture shifted increasingly to cash crops.

The Transportation Revolution

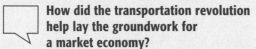

How did the transportation revolution help lay the groundwork for a market economy?

The lack of inexpensive, quick, and convenient transportation impeded westward expansion and industrial growth until the early nineteenth century. Beginning in the 1800s, however, several innovations—steamboats, canals, and railroads—dramatically reduced the cost and time to transport raw materials, goods, and people. Canals connected regions and shortened travel times, and steamboats reduced trips that previously took months to just days. Faster and less costly to build, railroads soon replaced canals, with transportation costs overall cut by as much as 95 percent. Goods that were previously unavailable in the nation's interior now could be had easily and cheaply. Westward migration expanded, creating new markets and cultural links between previously distant regions, as news, products, and people of various backgrounds fanned out from the Northeast to the Northwest.

Factories and Industrialization

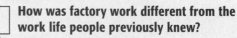

How was factory work different from the work life people previously knew?

The artisan shops and family farms that predated factories had fewer formal rules and less structure than the factories that arose in the late eighteenth and early nineteenth centuries. Artisans and farmers saw themselves as producers, in charge of their labor and its outcome and working side-by-side with hired helpers. In factories, workers infrequently saw owners and worked for wages under the watchful eye of supervisors with strict rules and a clock governing their day. Instead of learning how to make something from start to finish, workers now specialized in only one part of the process and never saw the finished item. There was no job security, and factory workers were often replaced by cheaper immigrant and women workers. Whereas artisan apprentices worked to learn a trade with the hope of setting up their own businesses, there was little or no opportunity for advancement in factories.

Consumption and Commercialization

How did farm women's work change as the commercial economy expanded?

Along with their regular farm and household duties, rural women took on new responsibilities to help pay for some of the items they now bought (such as textiles) instead of bartering for or making on their own. Some took in outwork; others increased production of eggs, milk, butter, and produce and other items for sale in the market. Daughters were often sent to work in textile mills, sending part of their wages home to aid their families.

Families in Flux

What roles did families play in the new industrial era?

Before the rise of the market economy, families were the center of production and economic activity. As industrialization took hold, however, new ideals transformed families into moral and cultural institutions. Men, particularly middle-class men, occupied the public sphere, providing for and protecting their families. In this new "separate spheres" ideology, women's roles were confined to the home, and they were charged with making it a retreat for husbands and children from the harshness of economic life. This ideology, which elevated women's domestic roles, was later dubbed *the cult of domesticity* or *the cult of true womanhood*. However, this ideology was rarely realized in practice.

The Growth of Cities

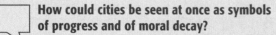

How could cities be seen at once as symbols of progress and of moral decay?

America experienced rapid urbanization between 1820 and 1860, particularly in the Northeast and Midwest, as some previously agricultural regions—such as Rochester near the Erie Canal—became cities and existing cities grew dramatically in population and size. People flocked to cities seeking opportunities. On the one hand, cities served as transportation and industrial hubs, and nurtured schools, churches, civil governments and museums—all signs of progress. On the other hand, some middle-class Americans regarded them as centers of disease, poverty, crowding, crime, and vice—symbols of moral decline. Prostitution, vagrancy, and theft led reformers to seek to purify cities. They targeted the working class—who many saw as contributing to urban decay—with the promise of upward mobility and free labor ideology—that those who worked hard, lived virtuous lives, and gave up alcohol—would become successful. Workers initially rejected such notions as an imposition on their lives, but with slavery's potential expansion westward in the 1850s, many embraced free-labor ideology.

Suggestions for Further Reading

Hal Barron, *Those Who Stayed Behind: Rural Society in Nineteenth-Century New England* (1984)

Jeanne Boydston, *Home and Work: Housework, Wages, and the Ideology of Labor in the Early Republic* (1990)

Nancy Cott, *The Bonds of Womanhood: "Women's Sphere" in New England, 1780–1835* (1977)

Daniel Walker Howe, *What Hath God Wrought: The Transformation of America, 1815–1848* (2007)

Bruce Laurie, *Artisans into Workers: Labor in Nineteenth-Century America* (1989)

Mary Ryan, *Cradle of the Middle Class: The Family in Oneida County, New York, 1790–1865* (1981)

Carol Sheriff, *The Artificial River: The Erie Canal and the Paradox of Progress, 1817–1862* (1996)

Christine Stansell, *City of Women: Sex and Class in New York, 1789–1860* (1986)

Melvyn Stokes and Stephen Conway, eds., *The Market Revolution in America: Social, Political, and Religious Expressions, 1800–1880* (1996)

George Rogers Taylor, *The Transportation Revolution, 1815–1860* (1951)

Reform and Politics

12

1824–1845

The twenty-eight-year-old mill hand steadied himself atop a cliff in Paterson, New Jersey, peered down the seventy-foot precipice to the river below, then leapt into the water. He resurfaced to cheers for his death-defying stunt—and what it symbolized. It was September 1827, and Sam Patch—who had worked in textile mills since he was eight years old—wanted to make a point.

Jumping from waterfalls had been a pastime among boys laboring in the mills. But Patch considered it an "art" imbued with political meaning. He timed his Paterson leap to steal the show from Timothy B. Crane, an entrepreneur who had dreamed up Forest Garden, a pleasure park offering "respectable" ladies and gentlemen a respite from the mill town. To reach the park, which was formerly open to everyone, visitors now had to cross a toll bridge. The toll would raise revenue to sustain the park, but it would, as Crane saw it, keep out the riffraff.

Patch and the mill hands understood that the riffraff meant *them*. Forest Garden symbolized a world in which manual labor was devalued, in which artisans became workers, in which industrialists and entrepreneurs increasingly held themselves as morally superior to wage earners. In previous months, town residents attacked (physically and verbally) the park, its workers, its buildings, and Crane. When Crane planned elaborate celebrations marking the toll bridge's completion, Patch determined to assert the pride of workers who made the industrial revolution possible.

In the two years following his Paterson leap—before his last, fatal, jump at the 125-foot Genesee Falls in Rochester, New York—Sam Patch became a professional waterfall jumper. He costumed himself in the symbolic clothing of the textile spinner and associated socially and politically with a raucous crowd of skilled operatives. His flaunting of middle-class values caught the attention of the political press, organs for the era's two main political parties—the Whigs and the Jacksonian Democrats. To Whigs, Patch exemplified what was, in one editor's words, "wrong with

Chapter Outline

The Whig Challenge and the Second Party System

Whigs and Reformers | Election of 1836 | Van Buren and Hard Times | Anglo-American Tensions | William Henry Harrison and the Election of 1840 | President Tyler

LEGACY FOR A PEOPLE AND A NATION *Moral Reformers' Abstinence Campaigns*

SUMMARY

democracy," whereas Jacksonians hailed Patch as a heroic artisan. In 1833, Philadelphia presented President Andrew Jackson with a horse, which the president named Sam Patch.

Like Patch, many Americans tried to reaffirm control over their lives in an era of rapid changes. The market economy, growing wealth and inequality, immigration, the westward thrust of settlement and slavery, and territorial expansion inspired Americans' hopes and fears. Many Americans embraced progress even as they hoped to limit what they saw as its unpleasant side effects. But Americans often divided over what defined progress, what constituted a social ill, and how such ills should be remedied.

To soothe anxieties, many Americans turned to evangelical religion, and, in the North, reform movements. Believing in human perfectibility, reformers worked to free individuals and society from sin. In the Northeast and Midwest in particular, people organized to end prostitution and alcohol abuse, improve prison and asylum conditions, and establish public schools. Other reformers created separate experimental—or utopian—communities. Opponents of slavery and proponents of women's rights, meanwhile, sought to radically alter the application of the revolutionary declaration that "all men are created equal."

Evangelical reformers generally aligned with the Whig Party, but Jacksonian Democrats, too, were concerned with social problems, mostly class inequities. They distrusted middle-class reformers who told working-class men and women how to live, and they opposed special privileges bestowed by government policies and institutions, such as the Second Bank of the United States. Yet when it came to slavery, the national parties often remained silent to keep sectional conflict submerged.

As political rivals, Democrats and Whigs held distinct positions on most other salient issues. Democrats emphasized that the best government is that which governs least, whereas the Whigs championed a strong federal government. Democrats focused on agricultural expansion west, whereas Whigs promoted industrial and commercial growth in the East. They hoped to stimulate growth through their American System of high protective tariffs, centralized banking, and federal funding for internal improvements. Together, Democrats and Whigs constituted what is often called the second party system, characterized by strong organizations, intense loyalty, and religious and ethnic voting patterns.

As you read this chapter, keep the following questions in mind:

* What were the "evils" in society that reformers hoped to eliminate, and what motivated them to do so?

* What was the relationship between reform and politics?

* What were the main issues dividing Democrats and Whigs?

Chronology

1790s–1840s	Second Great Awakening
1820s	Model penitentiaries established
1820s–1840s	Utopian communities founded
1824	No electoral-college majority in presidential election
1825	House of Representatives elects Adams president
1826	American Society for the Promotion of Temperance founded
1828	Tariff of Abominations passed
	Jackson elected president
1830	Joseph Smith organizes Mormon Church
1830s–40s	Democratic-Whig competition gels in second party system
1831	Garrison first publishes *The Liberator*
	Antimasons hold first national political convention
1832	Jackson vetoes rechartering Second Bank of the United States
	Jackson reelected president
1832–33	Nullification Crisis
1836	Specie Circular
	Van Buren elected president
1837	*Caroline* affair
	Financial panic ends boom of the 1830s
1837–1842	Croton Aqueduct constructed
1838–39	United States and Canada mobilize militias over border dispute
1839–43	Hard times spread unemployment and deflation
1840	Whigs win presidency under Harrison
1841	Tyler assumes presidency after Harrison's death
1846	Smithsonian Institution founded
1848	Seneca Falls Woman's Rights Convention
	American Association for the Advancement of Science established

From Revival to Reform

How did religious revival movements lead to social reform?

Religious revivals in the late eighteenth and early nineteenth centuries—sometimes called the **Second Great Awakening** for their resemblance to the eighteenth-century Great Awakening—raised people's hopes for the Second Coming of the Christian messiah and the establishment of God's kingdom on earth. Revivalists resolved to speed the millennium, or the thousand years of peace on earth that would accompany Christ's Second Coming, by combating sin. Some believed that the United States had a special mission in God's design and a special role in eliminating evil. Revivalists urged individuals to renounce sins, such as drinking, swearing, and licentiousness, and help combat social evils, including slavery. Not until all Americans were converted would Christ return.

Revivalists strove for large-scale conversions. Rural women, men, and children traveled long distances to camp meetings, where they heard fiery sermons delivered day and night from hastily constructed platforms and tents in forests or fields. In cities, women in particular attended daily services and prayer meetings. Converts vowed to live sanctified lives and help others see the light.

Second Great Awakening: Religious revival that swept the country and helped inspire reform movements.

Revivals

The most famous revival was at Cane Ridge, Kentucky, in August 1801. An estimated 25,000 people attended at a time when Kentucky's largest city, Lexington, had barely 2,000 inhabitants. The call to repentance and conversion invigorated southern Protestantism. Although laws often restricted or outlawed black churches and preachers, particularly after Nat Turner's 1831 revolt, black and mixed churches flourished locally. During the 1840s and 1850s, though, as slavery entered public debate, southern Presbyterian, Baptist, and Methodist churches seceded from their denominations' national conferences. For the white leaders of these secessionist churches, slavery did not impede human perfectibility but rather ensured it, as benevolent masters brought Africans to Christ.

Revivalists believed in individual self-improvement, but northern revivalists also emphasized communal improvement. Northern evangelists generated new religious groups and voluntary reform societies. Preachers like Lyman Beecher, who started in New England before moving to Cincinnati, and **Charles Finney**, who traveled the canals and roads linking the Northeast to the Midwest, argued that "God has made man a moral free agent," that Christians were not doomed by original sin, and that anyone could achieve salvation. Revivalism thrived among Methodists and Baptists, whose denominational structures maximized democratic participation and drew ministers from ordinary folk.

Charles G. Finney: A lawyer-turned-Presbyterian minister who conducted revivals in towns like Utica along the Erie Canal and who stressed individual responsibility.

Finney achieved his greatest successes in those areas of western New York experiencing rapid changes in transportation and industrialization—what he called the "Burned-Over District" because of the region's intense flames of evangelicalism. Rapid change raised fears of social disorder—family dissolution, drinking, swearing, and prostitution. Many individuals worried, too, about their economic fate during the era's booms and busts.

When northern revivalist preachers emphasized good works—good deeds—they helped ignite social reform movements, first in the Burned-Over District and then in New England, the Middle Atlantic, and the upper Midwest. Evangelically inspired reform associations together constituted what historians call the "benevolent empire." These associations shared a commitment to human perfectibility and often turned to the same wealthy men for financial resources and advice.

Moral Reform

Those resources enabled reformers to use the era's new technologies—steam presses and railroads. By mass-producing pamphlets and newspapers for distribution into the country's interior, reformers spread their message widely. With canals and railroads making travel easier, reformers could attend conventions and host speakers from distant places. Most reform organizations sponsored weekly newspapers, creating a virtual community of reformers.

While industrialists and merchants provided financial resources for evangelical reform, their wives and daughters solicited new members and circulated petitions. Reformers expanded the cult of domesticity's role for women as moral guardians beyond the home into the public realm. Women helped run reformatories for wayward youth or establish asylums for orphans. Participation in reform movements thus allowed women to exercise moral authority outside the household, giving them new influence. Although some elite women in Upper South cities formed and joined reform societies, moral reform was primarily a northeastern and midwestern phenomenon.

Many female reformers had attended a female academy or seminary. These schools' curriculum included arts of "refinement"—music, dance, penmanship—but focused on science and literature and was modeled on men's colleges. By 1820, roughly equal numbers of men and women attended institutions of higher education. Educated women prepared to influence public opinion even as many maintained domestic responsibilities. A few women became prominent editors and writers, but most influenced society as educators and reformers.

For women and some men, reform represented political influence at a time when only property-owning men could vote. In 1830, as female reformers in New York City organized a shelter for prostitutes, they publicized the names of brothel clients to shame men contributing to women's waywardness. They then organized the Female Moral Reform Society, and by 1840 it had 555 affiliated chapters nationwide. It soon lobbied successfully for criminal sanctions in New York State against men who seduced women into prostitution.

Link to the Female Moral Reform Society of the City of New York's first annual report.

Penitentiaries and Asylums

A similar belief in perfectibility led reformers to establish penitentiaries that aimed to move beyond punishment into transforming criminals into productive members of society through disciplined regimens. Other reformers sought to improve treatment of the mentally ill, who were frequently imprisoned, often alongside criminals, and put in cages or dark dungeons, chained to walls, and brutalized. **Dorothea Dix**, the movement's leader, exemplifies the reformer who started with a religious belief in human perfectibility and moved into social action. Investigating asylums, petitioning the Massachusetts legislature, and lobbying other states and Congress, Dix encouraged twenty-eight states to build institutions for the mentally ill by 1860.

Dorothea Dix: Leader of movement to improve conditions for the insane.

Temperance

Temperance advocates, who railed against alcoholic beverages, likewise crossed from the personal into the political sphere. Drinking was widespread in the early nineteenth century, when men like Sam Patch gathered in public houses and inns to drink. Politics were discussed, contracts were sealed, celebrations commemorated, and harvests toasted with liquor. "Respectable" women did not drink in public, but many tippled alcohol-based patent medicines promoted as cure-alls.

temperance: Abstinence from alcohol; name of the movement against alcohol.

Evangelicals considered drinking sinful, and forsaking alcohol was often part of conversion. Preachers condemned alcohol for violating the Sabbath—workers' one day off, which some spent at the public house. Factory owners claimed alcohol made workers unreliable. Civic leaders connected alcohol with crime. Middle-class reformers, often women, condemned it for diverting men from family responsibilities and fostering abusive behavior. In the early 1840s, thousands of women formed Martha Washington societies to reform alcoholics, raise children as teetotalers, and spread the temperance message.

Link to an illustration of the Tree of Temperance.

As the temperance movement grew, its goal shifted from moderation to abstinence to prohibition. By the mid-1830s, five thousand state and local temperance societies touted teetotalism, and more than a million people had pledged abstinence. Per capita consumption of alcohol fell from five gallons per year in 1800 to below two gallons in the 1840s. The American Society for the Promotion of Temperance, organized in 1826, pushed for legislation ending alcohol manufacture and sale. In 1851, Maine became the first state to ban alcohol except for medicinal purposes, and by 1855 similar laws were passed throughout New England and in New York, Pennsylvania, and the Midwest.

The temperance campaign had an anti-immigrant and anti-Catholic strain to it. Along the nation's canals, reformers lamented taverns catering to Irish workers, and

Engaging Children

Hundreds of thousands of children joined the temperance movement, often by enlisting in the so-called Cold Water Army. Like adult temperance societies, the Cold Water Army advocated for complete abstinence from alcoholic beverages. On holidays such as George Washington's birthday and the Fourth of July, they marched at public gatherings, singing temperance songs and carrying banners and fans such as the one pictured to the right. Reverend Thomas P. Hunt, a Presbyterian minister, founded the Cold Water Army because he believed that by recruiting children, he stood a much greater chance of eradicating alcohol consumption than if he aimed his temperance efforts directly at adults. What might have been his logic? Why might children have wanted to join a Cold Water Army? Do the images on the certificate and fan offer any clues? What were the benefits of participating in the movement? What were the implied consequences of failing to do so? Why might Hunt have chosen the term "army," and what about that choice might have proved appealing to his young recruits?

Collection of the New York Historical Society

Children who participated in a Cold Water Army often received a certificate that acknowledged their commitment to the cause while reiterating the pledge they had taken.

Museum of American Political Life

Children in Cold Water Army parades sometimes carried decorative fans, which they may have displayed in their homes as well, as reminders to themselves and their parents of temperance's virtues.

in the cities, they expressed outrage at the Sunday tradition of German families' gathering at beer gardens. Some Catholics heeded the message, pledging abstinence and forming organizations such as the St. Mary's Mutual Benevolence Total Abstinence Society in Boston.

But many workers—Protestants and Catholics—rejected middle-class temperance campaigns. Workers agreed that poverty and crime were problems but blamed poor wages, not drinking habits. Even some who abstained from alcohol opposed prohibition, believing that drinking should be a matter of self-control, not state coercion.

Public Schools

Protestants and Catholics often quarreled over education. Public education usually included religious education, but when teachers taught Protestant beliefs and used the King James Bible, Catholics established their own schools. Some Protestants feared that Catholics would never assimilate into American culture and charged Catholics with plotting to impose papal control. Still, public education touched more Americans than did any other reform movement.

Horace Mann, a Massachusetts lawyer and reformer from humble beginnings, advocated free, tax-supported education to replace church and private schools. Universal education, Mann proposed, would end crime and help Americanize immigrants.

During Mann's tenure as secretary of the Massachusetts Board of Education from 1837 to 1848, Massachusetts led the "common school" movement, establishing teacher training, lengthening the school year, and raising teachers' salaries to make the profession more attractive. Adhering to notions that women had special claims to morality and could be paid less than men, Mann envisioned a system in which women educated future clerks, farmers, and workers with a practical curriculum that emphasized geography, arithmetic, and science. Educational reformers believed that individuals could educate themselves out of their circumstances. Thanks partly to expanding public education, by 1850 the majority of native-born white Americans were literate.

Horace Mann: First secretary of the newly created Massachusetts Board of Education who presided over sweeping reforms to transform schools into institutions that occupied most of a child's time and energy.

Engineering and Science

Public education's emphasis on science reflected a broader belief that engineering and science could help remedy the nation's problems. Scientists and doctors blamed not immorality, but rather unclean, stagnant water for epidemics. After the devastating cholera epidemic of 1832, New York City planned a massive waterworks and, between 1837 and 1842, built the forty-one-mile Croton Aqueduct that brought water from upstate New York to Manhattan.

Several scientific institutions were also founded in this era. After James Smithson, a wealthy British scientist, left his estate to the United States government, Congress established the Smithsonian Institution (1846), which promoted scientific knowledge. Joseph Henry, the Smithsonian's director, was a nationally renowned scientist; his experiments in electromagnetism helped make possible the telegraph and, later in the century, telephone. Like Henry, many nineteenth-century Americans considered religious devotion and scientific inquiry compatible. They saw scientific discoveries as signs of progress, symbolizing that the millennium was approaching. God had created the natural world, they believed, and it was their Christian duty to perfect it in preparation for God's return.

Utopian Experiments

What were the goals of utopian communities?

Some idealists dreamed of an entirely new social order. They established dozens of utopian communities based on religious principles, a resistance to the market economy's excessive individualism, or both. Some groups, like the **Mormons**, arose during the Second Great Awakening. Utopian communities attempted to recapture what they perceived as the past's more communal nature, even while offering radical departures from marriage and child rearing.

Mormons: Members of the Church of Jesus Christ of Latter-Day Saints, the first major denomination founded in 1830 in the United States; members were persecuted for many years.

Joseph Smith: Founder of the Mormon Church.

Mormons

No utopian experiment was more enduring than the Church of Jesus Christ of Latter-day Saints, whose members were known as Mormons. During the 1820s religious ferment in western New York, **Joseph Smith**, a young farmer, reported that an angel called Moroni gave him divinely engraved gold plates. Smith published his revelations as the *Book of Mormon* and organized a church in 1830. The next year, the community moved to Ohio to build a "New Jerusalem" and await the Second Coming of Jesus.

After angry mobs drove the Mormons from Ohio, they settled in Missouri. Anti-Mormons charged that Mormonism was a scam by Joseph Smith and feared Mormon economic and political power. In 1838, Missouri's governor charged Smith with fomenting insurrection and worked to indict him and other leaders for treason. Smith and his followers left for Nauvoo, Illinois. The state legislature gave them a city charter making them self-governing. But again the Mormons met antagonism, especially after Smith introduced polygamy in 1841, allowing men several wives at once. In 1844, after Smith and his brother were charged with treason and jailed, and then murdered, the Mormons left Illinois to seek security in the western wilderness. Under Brigham Young's leadership, they established a cooperative community in the Great Salt Lake valley. There, the Mormons distributed agricultural land according to family size. An extensive irrigation system transformed the arid valley into a rich oasis. As the colony developed, church elders gained control of water, trade, industry, and eventually the territorial government of Utah.

Shakers: Utopian sect that stressed celibacy and emphasized agriculture and handicrafts; became known for furniture designs long after the community itself ceased to exist.

Shakers

The **Shakers**, the largest communal utopian experiment, reached their peak between 1820 and 1860, with six thousand members in twenty settlements in eight states. Shaker communities emphasized agriculture and handcrafts, contrasting with the new factory regime. Founded in England in 1772 by Mother Ann Lee, their name derived from their worship service, which included shaking their bodies. Ann Lee's children died in infancy, and she saw their deaths as retribution for her sin of intercourse; thus she advocated celibacy. After imprisonment in England in 1773–1774, she settled in America.

Shakers lived communally, with men and women in separate quarters; individual families were abolished. Men and women shared leadership equally. Many Shaker settlements became temporary refuges for orphans, widows, runaways, abused wives, and laid-off workers. Their settlements depended on new recruits, partly because celibacy meant no reproduction, but also because some members left, unsuited to communal living or the Shakers' spiritual message.

Oneidans, Owenites, and Fourierists

Other utopian communities joined in resisting social change. John Humphrey Noyes, a lawyer converted by Finney's revivals, established two perfectionist communities: in Putney, Vermont, in 1835, and—after being indicted for adultery—in Oneida, New York, in 1848. Noyes advocated communal property, communal child rearing, and "complex marriage," in which all the community's men were married to all its women, but women could reject a sexual proposition. The Oneida Colony required pregnancies to be planned; couples applied to Noyes for permission to have a child, or Noyes assigned two people to reproduce. Robert Dale Owen's community in **New Harmony**, Indiana (1825–1828), abolished private property and advocated communal child rearing. The Fourierists, named after French philosopher Charles Fourier, established more than two dozen communities in the Northeast and Midwest that resisted individualism and promoted sexual equality.

The most famous Fourier community was Brook Farm, in West Roxbury, Massachusetts. Inspired by **transcendentalism**—the belief that the physical world is secondary to the spiritual realm, which humans can reach only by intuition—Brook Farm's rural communalism combined spirituality, manual labor, intellectual life, and play. Founded in 1841 by Unitarian minister George Ripley, Brook Farm attracted farmers, craftsmen, and writers, among them Nathaniel Hawthorne. The Brook Farm school drew students from outside the community, and Brook Farm residents contributed regularly to the *Dial,* the leading transcendentalist journal. In 1845, Brook Farm's hundred members organized into phalanxes (working-living units), following Fourier's model. As regimentation replaced individualism, membership dropped. A year after a disastrous fire in 1846, the experiment collapsed.

American Renaissance

Ralph Waldo Emerson, a pillar of transcendentalism, was the prime inspiration for a literary outpouring now known as the American Renaissance. He quit his Boston Unitarian ministry in 1831 and spent two years in Europe, before he returned to lecture and write, preaching self-reliance. Widely admired, he influenced Hawthorne, *Dial* editor Margaret Fuller, Herman Melville, and Thoreau. The American Renaissance was distinctively

New Harmony: An important and well-known utopian community, founded in Indiana by Robert Owen.

transcendentalism: The belief that the physical world is secondary to the spiritual realm, which humans can reach only by intuition.

Joslyn Art Museum, Omaha, Nebraska, Gift of Enron Art Foundation

This bucolic image of New Harmony, painted several years after the experiment's collapse, belies the rancorous history of the short-lived community, which attracted many settlers who proved unwilling or unable to commit themselves fully to communitarian life. Pictured here on the far left is the "Hive," which housed the kitchen, office, and meeting rooms; along the hilltop are buildings that housed residents, a laundry, and printing presses.

American and an outgrowth of the European romantic movement. It addressed universal themes using American settings and characters. Hawthorne, for instance, used Puritan New England as a backdrop.

Henry David Thoreau championed individualism. In his 1849 essay on "Resistance to Civil Government" (known after his death as "Civil Disobedience"), Thoreau advocated resistance to a government engaged in immoral acts. During the War with Mexico (see Chapter 14), Thoreau refused to pay taxes, believing they would aid an immoral war to expand slavery, and was briefly jailed. "I cannot for an instant recognize that political organization as my government which is the *slave's* government also," Thoreau wrote.

Abolitionism

How did the Second Great Awakening transform the antislavery movement?

Thoreau joined evangelical abolitionists in trying to eradicate slavery, which they deemed a sin. Inspired by the Second Great Awakening, their efforts built on those of an earlier generation of antislavery activists.

Early Abolitionism and Colonization

From the nation's earliest days—in Philadelphia, New York, Albany, Boston, and Nantucket—free blacks formed societies to petition legislatures, seek judicial redress, stage marches, and publish tracts chronicling slavery's horrors. African American abolitionists wrote about slavery's devastating impact on black and white families, advocated slavery's immediate termination, assisted escaped slaves, and promoted legal equality for free blacks. By 1830, there were fifty African American abolitionist societies. But David Walker, a southern-born free African American, captured white Americans' attention like none other with his *Appeal...to the Colored Citizens* (1829). Walker advocated slavery's violent overthrow, igniting fear throughout the white South and the North.

Violence was not a strategy for early white abolitionists. After the American Revolution, antislavery advocates united in places like Boston and Philadelphia, with its large population of Quakers, whose religious beliefs emphasized human equality. These reformers pressed gradual abolition and an end to the international slave trade. Although they aided African Americans seeking freedom through judicial decisions, their assumptions about blacks' racial inferiority kept them from advocating for equal rights. Early white abolitionists were typically wealthy men whose societies excluded women, African Americans, and non-elites.

Elites were more likely to support colonization, which crystallized in 1816 with the organization of the American Colonization Society. Its members planned to purchase and relocate American slaves and free blacks to Africa or the Caribbean. Supporters included Thomas Jefferson, James Madison, James Monroe, and Henry Clay. In 1824, the society founded Liberia, on Africa's west coast, and began a settlement for African Americans who were willing to go. The society had resettled nearly twelve thousand by 1860. Some colonizationists aimed to strengthen slavery by ridding the South of troublesome slaves or to purge the North of African Americans. Others hoped colonization would improve African Americans' conditions. Although some African Americans supported the movement, black abolitionists generally denounced it.

The International Antislavery Movement

The heart of the international antislavery movement had been in Great Britain, but in the 1830s many of Britain's antislavery societies considered their work finished and disbanded. The international slave trade greatly diminished, and in 1833 Parliament ended slavery in the British Empire.

American abolitionists revived the international antislavery movement. American abolitionism in the 1830s was invigorated by the militancy of black abolitionists and by William Lloyd Garrison's conversion to immediatism. To raise money and pressure the United States to abolish slavery, African American abolitionists in the 1840s toured Britain regularly. Ex-slaves recounted their experiences of slavery and bared their scarred bodies. After fugitive slave Moses Gandy toured England, he published his autobiography, the first of dozens of slave narratives published in London. The next year, 1845, Frederick Douglass began a nineteen-month tour, giving three hundred lectures in Britain.

In 1849, black abolitionists William Wells Brown, Alexander Crummell, and J. W. C. Pennington were among twenty American delegates at the international Paris Peace Conference. Brown's lecture tour in Britain became a five-year exile because, after passage of the 1850 Fugitive Slave Law, he feared being seized and re-enslaved if he returned to the United States. In 1854, British abolitionists purchased his freedom.

By the early 1850s, abolitionists helped abolish slavery in Colombia, Argentina, Venezuela, and Peru. In the United States, black abolitionists were instrumental in reviving the worldwide antislavery movement, and, as advocates of women's rights, international peace, temperance, and other reforms, in linking Americans to other worldwide reform movements.

William Wells Brown's autobiography stirred abolitionists in the United States and England. In 1849, Brown was among the American delegates to the Paris Peace Conference, then spent the next five years as an exile in Britain, fearing being sent back to slavery under the 1850 Fugitive Slave Act. He returned to the United States only after British abolitionists purchased his freedom from his former master.

Used with Permission of Documenting the American South, The University of North Carolina at Chapel Hill Libraries.

297

William Lloyd Garrison:
Founder of *The Liberator* and a controversial white abolitionist, he demanded an immediate end to slavery and embraced civil rights for blacks on par with whites.

In the early 1830s, a new group of more radical white abolitionists—most prominently, **William Lloyd Garrison**—demanded immediate, complete, and uncompensated emancipation. Garrison began publishing his abolitionist newspaper, *The Liberator,* in 1831, two years before founding the American Antislavery Society, the era's largest abolitionist organization.

Immediatism

Immediatists believed slavery was a sin needing eradication. They were influenced by African American abolitionist societies and evangelicals' notion that humans, not God, determined their spiritual fate by choosing good or evil. In that sense, all were equal before God's eyes. When all humans had chosen good over evil, the millennium would come. Slavery, however, denied enslaved men and women the ability to make such choices, the ability to act as what Finney called "moral free agents." For every day that slavery continued, the millennium was postponed.

Because the millennium depended on *all* hearts being won over to Christ, Garrison advocated "moral suasion." He and his followers hoped to bring emancipation by winning over slaveowners and others who supported or tolerated slavery. Evangelical abolitionism depended, then, on large numbers of ministers and laypeople spreading the word nationwide.

The Lane Debates

In 1829, Congregationalists and Presbyterians founded the Lane Seminary in Cincinnati to train ministers. With Lyman Beecher as president, it drew northern and southern students and encouraged "people of color" to apply. After Theodore Weld, one of Charles Finney's converts, arrived at Lane in 1833, he organized the Lane Debates, eighteen days of discussion among students and faculty about colonization versus immediatism. Immediatism won.

Led by Weld, the Lane students and faculty founded an antislavery society and tried to reach Cincinnati's growing African American population, which in 1829 had been brutally attacked by white people. Fearful of renewed disorder, white business leaders protested the antislavery society. Lane's trustees, with Beecher's sanction, barred further antislavery activities. The "Lane Rebels" left and enrolled in a new seminary at Oberlin, a northern Ohio town founded as a Christian perfectionist settlement. This seminary became the first college to admit women and one of the first to admit African Americans.

The American Antislavery Society

By 1838, at its peak, the society had 2,000 local affiliates and over 300,000 members. Unlike earlier white abolitionists, the immediatists welcomed men and women of all races and classes. Lydia Maria Child, Maria Chapman, and Lucretia Mott served on its executive committee; Child edited its official paper, the *National Anti-Slavery Standard,* from 1841 to 1843, and Chapman coedited it from 1844 until 1848.

With the "great postal campaign" in 1835, the society flooded the mails with antislavery tracts. Women went door to door collecting signatures on antislavery petitions; by 1838, more than 400,000 petitions were sent to Congress. Abolitionist-minded women met in "sewing circles," making clothes for escaped slaves while organizing activities, such as antislavery fairs at which they sold goods—often handmade items—donating the proceeds to antislavery causes.

African American Abolitionists

Even as white abolitionist societies included African Americans and sponsored speaking tours by former slaves, African Americans continued independent efforts to end slavery and improve free African Americans' status into the 1840s and 1850s. Former slaves—famously, Frederick Douglass, Henry Bibb, Harriet Tubman, and Sojourner Truth—fought slavery through speeches, publications, and participation in a secret network known as the Underground Railroad, which spirited enslaved men, women, and children to freedom. By the thousands, African Americans established churches, founded moral reform societies, published newspapers, created schools and orphanages, and held conventions.

Opposition to Abolitionism

But abolitionists' gains inspired virulent opposition. In the South, mobs blocked the distribution of antislavery tracts. In South Carolina, officials intercepted and burned abolitionist literature, and in 1835 proslavery assailants killed four abolitionists in South Carolina and Louisiana, as well as forty people allegedly plotting a slave rebellion in Mississippi and Louisiana.

White northerners who opposed abolition recognized cotton's vital economic role and feared emancipation would prompt an influx of freed slaves into their region. They believed blacks to be inherently inferior and incapable of the virtue and diligence required of freedom and citizenship.

The North, too, experienced anti-abolitionist violence. In Boston, David Walker died under mysterious circumstances in 1830. Among northerners who despised abolitionists, most were commercial and political elites with strong connections to the southern cotton economy and political connections to leading southerners. Northern gentlemen incited anti-abolitionist riots. Mob violence peaked in 1835, with more than fifty riots aimed at abolitionists or African Americans. In 1837 in Alton, Illinois, a mob murdered white abolitionist editor Elijah P. Lovejoy, and rioters sacked his printing office. In 1838, Philadelphia rioters hurled stones at three thousand black and white women attending the Anti-Slavery Convention of American Women in the new Pennsylvania Hall, constructed to house abolitionist meetings and an abolitionist bookstore, before burning down the building.

Moral Suasion Versus Political Action

Violence made some immediatists question moral suasion as a tactic. James G. Birney, the son of a Kentucky slaveowner, embraced immediatism but believed abolition could be effected only through political action. Involving women violated the natural order of things and detracted from the ultimate goal: freedom for slaves. Thus, when William Lloyd Garrison, an ardent women's rights supporter, endorsed Abby Kelly's appointment to the American Antislavery Society's business committee in 1840, he provoked an irreparable split in the abolitionist movement. Arthur Tappan and Theodore Weld led a dissident group that established the American and Foreign Anti-Slavery Society. That society formed a new political party: the Liberty Party, which nominated Birney for president in 1840 and 1844.

Although committed to immediate abolition, the Liberty Party doubted the federal government's authority to abolish slavery. Only states, they thought, had the jurisdiction to determine slavery's legality. They believed the federal government could act only in western territories, and the party demanded that new territories prohibit slavery. Prominent black abolitionists, including Frederick Douglass, endorsed the party, whose leaders also emphasized combating northern prejudice.

Women's Rights

What inspired the rise of the women's movement in the mid-nineteenth century?

At the first World Anti-Slavery Convention in London in 1840, abolitionists Lucretia Mott and Elizabeth Cady Stanton were dismayed when female abolitionists were denied seats in the convention's main hall; eight years later, these women helped organize the first American women's rights convention. Born to a South Carolina slaveholding family, **Angelina and Sarah Grimké** moved north and became active abolitionists. After critics attacked them for speaking to audiences that included men, they became advocates for women's legal and social equality.

Angelina and Sarah Grimké: Southern-born sisters who were powerful antislavery speakers; later leaders of women's rights movement

The political consciousness of lesser-known women similarly developed from abolitionist activities, particularly petitioning campaigns. After Congress voted to automatically table antislavery petitions in 1836, women defended their right to have their petitions considered. Female petitioners increasingly saw themselves as citizens rather than political subjects.

Religious revivalism helped women see themselves as equal to men, and reform movements brought middle-class women into the public sphere. Female reformers' lobbying helped to effect legal change, making some think the next step was citizenship rights for women.

Legal Rights

After independence, American states carried over traditional English marriage law, giving husbands absolute control over the family. Men owned their wives' property, were their children's legal guardians, and owned whatever family members produced or earned. A father could legally oppose his daughter's choice of husband, though by 1800 most American women chose their spouses.

Married women made modest gains in property and spousal rights after 1830. Arkansas in 1835 passed the first married women's property law, and by 1860 sixteen more states allowed women to own and convey property and write wills. When a wife inherited property, it was hers, though money earned still belonged to her husband. Such laws were popular among wealthy Americans, hoping to protect family fortunes during economic downturns; property in a woman's name was safe from her husband's creditors. In the 1830s, states also added cruelty and desertion as grounds for divorce, but divorce remained rare.

Radical reformers argued that marriage constituted a form of bondage. Lucy Stone, an outspoken critic of marriage, consented to marry fellow abolitionist Henry Blackwell only if she could eschew a vow of obedience and keep her own surname.

Political Rights

The women's movement was launched in July 1848, when Elizabeth Cady Stanton, Lucretia Mott, Mary Ann McClintock, Martha Wright, and Jane Hunt—all abolitionists—organized the first Woman's Rights Convention at **Seneca Falls**, New York.

Seneca Falls: The location of a women's rights convention in 1848.

Three hundred women and men demanded women's social and economic equality. Their Declaration of Sentiments, modeled on the Declaration of Independence, broadcast the injustices suffered by women and proclaimed "All men and women are created equal." The similarities between abolitionism and women's rights led reformers, including former slaves like Sojourner Truth, to work for both movements in the 1850s. The question of female suffrage became divisive. William Lloyd Garrison and Frederick Douglass supported women's right to vote, but most men opposed it. The Seneca Falls' suffrage resolution passed only after Douglass passionately endorsed it. In 1851, **Elizabeth Cady Stanton** joined with temperance advocate **Susan B. Anthony** to become the most vocal suffrage activists.

Elizabeth Cady Stanton, Susan B. Anthony: Vocal advocates of women's suffrage.

Jacksonianism and Party Politics

Like reformers, politicians sought to control the direction of the expanding nation. They reached out to an increasingly broad-based electorate. Hotly contested elections drew the interest of voters and nonvoters alike and fueled bitter rivalries.

How did changing demographics influence the outcome of the 1824 presidential election and the future of political parties?

Expanding Political Participation

Property restrictions for voters, which states began abandoning during the 1810s, remained in only seven of twenty-six states by 1840. Some states even allowed foreign nationals who officially declared their intention of becoming American citizens to vote. The net effect was that between 1824 and 1828 the number of votes cast in presidential elections tripled, from 360,000 to over 1.1 million. The proportion of eligible voters who cast ballots also grew, from about 27 percent in 1824 to more than 80 percent in 1840.

The selection of presidential electors also became more democratic. Previously, a caucus of party leaders picked them in most states, but by 1824 eighteen out of twenty-four states chose electors by popular vote. Consequently, politicians augmented their appeals to voters, and the 1824 election saw the end of the congressional caucus, when House and Senate members of the same political party united to select their candidate.

Election of 1824

As a result, five Democratic-Republican candidates ran for president in 1824. The poorly attended Republican caucus chose William H. Crawford of Georgia, secretary of the treasury, as its candidate. Instead of Congress, state legislatures now nominated candidates, offering the expanded electorate a slate of sectional candidates. John Quincy Adams drew support from New England, while westerners backed House Speaker Henry Clay of Kentucky. Some southerners initially supported Secretary of War John C. Calhoun, who later ran for the vice presidency instead. The Tennessee legislature nominated military hero Andrew Jackson.

Jackson led in electoral and popular votes, but no candidate received an electoral-college majority. Adams finished second. Under the Constitution, the House of Representatives, voting by state delegation, one vote to a state, would select the next president from among the three electoral vote leaders. Clay, with the fewest votes, was dropped. Crawford, disabled from a stroke, never received consideration. Clay backed Adams, who won with thirteen of the twenty-four state delegations and became president (Map 12.1). Adams named Clay as secretary of state, the traditional steppingstone to the presidency.

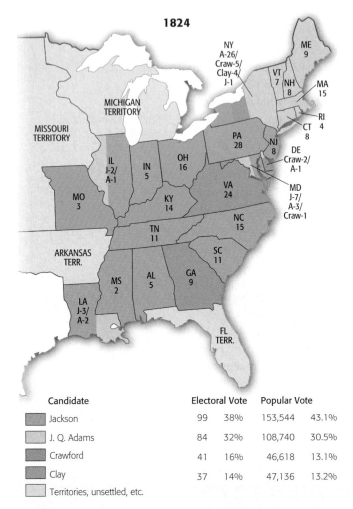

1824

Candidate	Electoral Vote		Popular Vote	
Jackson	99	38%	153,544	43.1%
J. Q. Adams	84	32%	108,740	30.5%
Crawford	41	16%	46,618	13.1%
Clay	37	14%	47,136	13.2%
Territories, unsettled, etc.				

MAP 12.1

Presidential Election, 1824

Andrew Jackson led in both electoral and popular votes but failed to win a majority of electoral college votes. The House elected John Quincy Adams president.

Source: Copyright © Cengage Learning

Democrats: Members of the party that emerged from Jefferson's Republican party as one of the two dominant parties in the second party system.

Angry Jacksonians denounced the election as a "corrupt bargain," claiming Adams had stolen the election by offering Clay a cabinet position for his votes. The Republican Party split. The Adams wing emerged as the National Republicans, and the Jacksonians became the **Democrats**.

As president, Adams proposed a strong nationalist policy incorporating Clay's American System of protective tariffs, a national bank, and internal improvements. Adams believed the federal government's active role should extend to education, science, and the arts. He proposed a national university in Washington, D.C. Brilliant as a diplomat and secretary of state, Adams fared less well as chief executive.

Election of 1828

The 1828 election pitted Adams against Jackson. Nicknamed "Old Hickory," Andrew Jackson was a tough, ambitious man. Born in South Carolina in 1767, he rose from humble beginnings to become a wealthy Tennessee planter and slaveholder. After leading the Tennessee militia campaign to remove Creeks from the Alabama and Georgia frontier, Jackson gained national acclaim in 1815 as the hero of the Battle of New Orleans. In 1818, his fame increased with his expedition against Seminoles in Spanish Florida. Jackson served as a congressman and senator from Tennessee and the first territorial governor of Florida (1821).

Jackson's supporters accused Adams of stealing the 1824 election and, when he was envoy to Russia, of securing prostitutes for the czar. Anti-Jacksonians countered with reports that Jackson's wife, Rachel, married Jackson before her divorce from her first husband was final. In 1806, while attempting to defend Rachel's integrity, Jackson killed a man during a duel, and the cry of "murderer!" reappeared in the election.

Although Adams kept the states he won in 1824, Jackson swamped him, polling 56 percent of the popular vote and winning in the electoral college by 178 to 83 votes (Map 12.2). Through a lavishly financed coalition of state parties, political leaders, and newspaper editors, a popular movement had elected the president. The Democratic Party became the first well-organized national party.

Democrats

Democrats shared a commitment to the Jeffersonian concept of an agrarian society. They viewed a strong central government as antithetical to individual liberty, and they condemned government intervention in the economy as favoring the rich over the artisan and farmer. When it came to westward expansion, though, Jacksonians called for federal intervention, with Jackson initiating Indian removal despite northeastern reformers' protests.

Like Jefferson, Jackson strengthened the government's executive branch even while advocating limited government. Combining the roles of party leader and chief of state, he centralized power in the White House. He relied on political friends, his "Kitchen Cabinet," for advice, rarely consulting his official cabinet. Rotating officeholders, Jackson claimed, made government more responsive to the public, and he appointed loyal Democrats, a practice his critics called the **spoils system**, in which the victor gives the spoils of victory to his supporters. The spoils system, opponents charged, corrupted the government because it based appointments on loyalty, not competency.

King Andrew Opponents mocked Jackson as "King Andrew I," charging him with abuse of power by ignoring the Supreme Court's ruling on Cherokee rights, sidestepping his cabinet, and replacing officeholders with his cronies.

Jackson's critics especially disliked his frequent use of the veto to promote limited government. In 1830, he vetoed the Maysville Road bill, which would have funded construction of a 60-mile turnpike from Maysville to Lexington, Kentucky. Constitutionally, he insisted, states bore responsibility for internal improvements within a single state. The veto undermined Clay's American System and embarrassed Clay because the project was in his home district.

The first six presidents vetoed nine bills; Jackson vetoed twelve. Previous presidents believed vetoes were justified only on constitutional grounds; Jackson considered policy disagreements legitimate grounds. He made the veto an effective weapon for controlling Congress, which had to weigh the possibility of a veto as it deliberated.

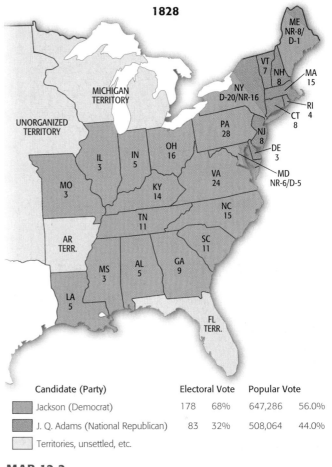

1828

Candidate (Party)	Electoral Vote		Popular Vote	
Jackson (Democrat)	178	68%	647,286	56.0%
J. Q. Adams (National Republican)	83	32%	508,064	44.0%
Territories, unsettled, etc.				

MAP 12.2

Presidential Election, 1828

Andrew Jackson avenged his 1824 loss of the presidency, sweeping the election in 1828.

Source: Copyright © Cengage Learning

spoils system: Practice of rewarding political supporters with public office.

Federalism at Issue: The Nullification and Bank Controversies

What was at issue in the Nullification Controversy?

The slave South feared federal power. That was especially true for South Carolina, where the planter class was strongest and slavery most concentrated. Southerners resented protectionist tariffs, which in 1824 and 1828 protected manufactures by imposing import duties on manufactured cloth and iron. In protecting northern factories, the tariff raised the costs of manufactured goods to southerners, who labeled the high 1828 tariff the **Tariff of Abominations**.

Tariff of Abominations: Protective tariff of 1828 that infuriated southerners; spawned nullification crisis.

The Hermitage: Home of President Andrew Jackson, Nashville, TN

Even as his critics portrayed him as monarchical, Jackson presented himself as the president of the common man. Here he sits atop his prized horse, Sam Patch, named after the disgruntled factory worker and daring waterfall jumper.

Nullification

South Carolina's political leaders rejected the 1828 tariff, invoking the doctrine of nullification, which held that a state had the right to overrule, or nullify, federal legislation. Nullification borrowed from the Virginia and Kentucky Resolutions the idea that the states, representing the people, have a right to judge the constitutionality of federal actions. Jackson's vice president, John C. Calhoun of South Carolina, argued in his unsigned *Exposition and Protest* that, in disagreements between the federal government and a state, a special state convention should decide the conflict by either nullifying or affirming the federal law. As Jackson's running mate in 1828, Calhoun avoided endorsing nullification and embarrassing the Democratic ticket; he also hoped to win Jackson's support as the Democratic presidential heir apparent. Thus, in early 1830, Calhoun presided silently over the Senate when Massachusetts Senator Daniel Webster and South Carolina Senator Robert Y. Hayne debated states' rights. The debate over the tariff soon focused on the nature of the Union, with nullification a subtext. Hayne charged the North with threatening to bring disunity. Webster defended New England and the republic, keeping nullification supporters on the defensive.

Though sympathetic to states' rights and distrustful of the federal government, Jackson rejected state sovereignty. Believing in the Union, he shared Webster's dread of nullification. The president articulated his position at a Jefferson Day dinner with the toast "Our Federal Union, it must and shall be preserved." Vice President Calhoun toasted "The Federal Union—next to our liberty the most dear," revealing his adherence to states' rights. Calhoun and Jackson grew apart, and Jackson looked to Secretary of State Martin Van Buren as his successor.

Tension resumed when Congress passed a new tariff in 1832, reducing some duties but retaining high taxes on imported iron, cottons, and woolens. Although a majority of southern representatives supported the new tariff, South Carolinians did not. They feared the act could set a precedent for congressional legislation on slavery. In November 1832, a South Carolina state convention nullified the 1828 and the 1832 tariffs, declaring it unlawful for federal officials to collect duties in the state.

Link to Jackson's proclamation against South Carolina's nullification.

The Force Act

In December, Jackson issued a proclamation opposing nullification. He moved troops to federal forts in South Carolina and prepared U.S. marshals to collect the duties. At Jackson's request, Congress passed the Force Act, authorizing the president to call up troops but offering a way to avoid force by collecting duties before foreign ships reached Charleston's harbor. Jackson also extended an olive branch by recommending tariff reductions.

Calhoun, disturbed by South Carolina's drift toward separatism, resigned as vice president and soon won election to the U.S. Senate, where he worked with Henry Clay on the compromise Tariff of 1833. Quickly passed by Congress and signed by the president, the new tariff lengthened the list of duty-free items and reduced duties over nine years. Satisfied, South Carolina repealed its nullification law. Nullification offered a genuine debate on the nature of the republic. Each side believed it was upholding the Constitution. South Carolina opposed the tyranny of the federal government and manufacturing interests. Jackson fought the tyranny of South Carolina, whose actions threatened to split the republic. It took another crisis, over a central bank, to define the federal powers more clearly.

Second Bank of the United States

At stake was the Second Bank of the United States, whose twenty-year charter would expire in 1836. The bank served as a depository for federal funds and provided business credit. Its bank notes circulated as currency nationwide; they could be readily exchanged for gold. Through its twenty-five branch offices, the Second Bank acted as a clearing-house for state banks, refusing bank notes from state banks lacking sufficient gold reserves. Most state banks saw the central bank's police role as potentially ruinous. Moreover, state banks could not compete equally with the Second Bank, which had more money in reserve.

Many states regarded the national bank as unresponsive to local needs. Westerner settlers and urban workers bitterly remembered the bank's conservative credit policies during the Panic of 1819. As a private, profit-making institution, its policies reflected its owners' interests, especially its president, Nicholas Biddle. An eastern patrician, Biddle symbolized all that westerners resented about the bank, and all that eastern workers disliked about the commercial elite.

Political Violence

Controversy over the Second Bank inflamed longstanding political animosities, bringing violence to the streets. Elections often involved fraud, and with no secret ballot, political parties employed operatives to intimidate voters. New York City had the most powerful political machine, the Democrats' Tammany Hall, and thus in the midst of the Bank controversy, New York's mayoral election of 1834 sparked mayhem.

Three days of rioting began when Democratic operatives stormed Whig headquarters. After beating some **Whigs** unconscious, the Democrats attacked police; eight of them suffered severe wounds, and the mayor was also injured. Vowing revenge, more than five hundred Whigs stole weapons from the armory, but the state militia arrived to restore order.

Whigs: Formerly called the National Republicans; a major political party in the 1830s.

Months later, an election-day riot in Philadelphia left two dead and five buildings burned to the ground. These riots are remarkable for their intensity, but voter intimidation and fraud characterized the second party system.

Antimasonry

Violence was a catalyst for the formation of the Antimason Party, which started in upstate New York in the mid-1820s as a grassroots movement against Freemasonry, a secret male fraternity of middle- and upper-class men prominent in commerce and civic affairs. Opponents claimed Masons colluded to bestow business and political favors on each other, and—in the incident that sparked the organized Antimasonry movement—Masons had obstructed justice in the investigation of the 1826 disappearance and presumed murder of a disgruntled former member who had written an exposé of the society. Evangelicals denounced Masonry, claiming its members neglected their families for alcohol and ribald entertainment. In the 1828 presidential election, the Antimasons opposed Jackson, a Mason. They held their first national political convention in Baltimore in 1831, nominating William Wirt of Maryland for president and Amos Ellmaker of Pennsylvania for vice president.

Election of 1832

Following the Antimasons' lead, the Democrats and National Republicans also held conventions. Democrats reaffirmed Jackson for president and nominated Martin Van Buren of New York for vice president. The National Republican convention selected Clay and John Sergeant of Pennsylvania. The Independent Democrats ran John Floyd and Henry Lee of Virginia.

The Bank of the United States became the election's main issue. Jacksonians denounced it as a vehicle for special privilege, while the Republicans supported it within their plan for economic nationalism. The bank's charter was valid until 1836, but Clay persuaded Biddle to ask Congress for an early rechartering. If Jackson signed the rechartering bill, then Clay could attack the president's inconsistency. If he vetoed it, Clay hoped voters would favor him. The plan backfired. The president vetoed the bill with a message appealing to voters who feared that rapid economic development spread advantages undemocratically. Jackson took a strong stand against special interests that tried to use the government to their own unfair advantage and won 54 percent of the popular vote to Clay's 37 percent. He captured 76 percent of the electoral college. The Antimasons won only Vermont but nonetheless galvanized anti-Jackson opposition.

Jackson's Second Term

Jackson moved in 1833 to dismantle the Second Bank. He deposited federal funds in state-chartered banks. Without federal money, the Second Bank shriveled, becoming a Pennsylvania-chartered private bank in 1836. Five years later, it closed.

Congress passed the Deposit Act of 1836, authorizing the secretary of the treasury to designate one bank per state and territory to provide services formerly performed by the Bank of the United States. The act also provided that federal surplus over $5 million—income derived from the sale of public lands to speculators, who gobbled up land to resell at a profit—be distributed to the states as interest-free loans beginning in 1837.

Eager to use the money for state-funded internal improvements, Democrats joined Whigs in supporting the measure. Fearing that the Act would fuel speculation, promote inflation, and thus undermine farmers' interests, Jackson opposed it. Because support was strong enough to override a veto, Jackson signed the bill but first insisted on a provision prohibiting state banks from issuing or accepting small-denomination paper money. Jackson hoped that by encouraging the use of coins, the provision would prevent unscrupulous businessmen from paying workers in devalued paper bills.

Specie Circular

The president then ordered Treasury Secretary Levi Woodbury to issue the Specie Circular, which provided that after August 1836 only settlers could use paper money to buy land; speculators had to use specie (gold or silver). The policy proved disastrous, significantly reducing public-land sales, which in turn reduced the federal government's surplus and its loans to the states.

Meanwhile, a banking crisis emerged. Fearful that their banknotes would lose value, people redeemed them for specie, creating a shortage that forced banks to suspend payment, further reducing confidence.

Jackson's opponents were irate. Jackson had used his presidential powers to defeat a bill passed by the Senate months earlier that was similar to the Specie Circular. In the waning days of Jackson's administration, Congress repealed the circular, but the president pocket-vetoed the bill by holding it unsigned until Congress adjourned. In May 1838, after Jackson left office, a joint resolution of Congress overturned the circular.

The Whig Challenge and the Second Party System

> How did the Whigs and Democrats differ ideologically?

In the 1830s, the Democrats' opponents, including remnants of the National Republican and Antimason parties, united as the Whig Party. Resentful of Jackson's domination of Congress, the Whigs borrowed the name of the eighteenth-century British party that opposed the Hanoverian monarchs' tyranny. From 1834 through the 1840s, the Whigs and the Democrats competed on nearly equal footing, and each drew supporters from all regions. The era's political competition—the second party system—was more intense and better organized than what scholars have labeled as the first party system of Democratic-Republicans versus Federalists.

Whigs and Reformers Whigs favored economic expansion through an activist government. They supported corporate charters, a national bank, and paper currency; Democrats opposed all three. Whigs professed a belief in progress and perfectibility, and they favored social reforms, prison and asylum reform, and temperance. Jacksonians criticized reform associations for undermining the people's will by giving undue influence to political minorities; Whigs countered they served the common good. Nor did Whigs object to helping special interests if doing so promoted the general welfare. The chartering of corporations, they argued, expanded economic opportunity for everyone. Democrats, distrustful of concentrated economic power, held to the Jeffersonian principle of limited government.

Whigs stressed a "harmony of interests" among all classes along with equal opportunity. Democrats saw society as divided into the "haves" and the "have nots," and embraced "equal rights." They championed "heroic artisans" like Sam Patch, whereas Whigs preferred to see society ruled from the top down. Whigs believed in free-labor ideology and thought that society's wealthy had risen by their own merits. Democrats alleged that, instead, their political opponents had benefited from special favors.

But religion and ethnicity, as much as class, influenced party affiliation. The Whigs' support for moral reform won over evangelical Protestants. Methodists and Baptists were overwhelmingly Whigs, as were the small number of free black voters. In many locales, the membership rolls of reform societies overlapped those of the party. Whigs' rallies resembled camp meetings; their speeches employed pulpit rhetoric; their programs embodied perfectionist beliefs.

By appealing to evangelicals, Whigs alienated other faiths. The evangelicals' ideal Christian state had no room for nonevangelical Protestants, Catholics, Mormons, or religious freethinkers. Those groups opposed Sabbath laws and temperance legislation and preferred to keep religion and politics separate. Consequently, more than 95 percent of Irish Catholics, 90 percent of Reformed Dutch, and 80 percent of German Catholics voted Democratic.

The parties' platforms thus attracted a seemingly odd coalition of voters. Favoring government-sponsored commercial development and fearful of social disorder, the Whigs wanted slower, more controlled settlement of western lands; later, they opposed slavery's westward expansion. Groups as diverse as black New Englanders and slave owners, in the Upper South, liked these ideas; the former, to undercut slavery, and the latter to protect their investments from cheap western competition. Democrats' promises to open additional lands for settlement attracted yeoman farmers, wage earners, frontier slaveowners, and immigrants. With broad voter coalitions, there was room within each party for a spectrum of beliefs, particularly about slavery.

Some politicians went to extremes to keep the potentially divisive issue of slavery out of national political debate. In response to the American Antislavery Society's petitioning campaign, the House of Representatives in 1836 adopted what abolitionists labeled the "gag rule," which automatically tabled abolitionist petitions. Former president John Quincy Adams, now a representative from Massachusetts, defended the right to petition and spoke against the gag rule, which was repealed in 1844.

Election of 1836

Vice President Martin Van Buren headed the Democratic ticket in the 1836 presidential election. A career politician, Van Buren built a political machine—the Albany Regency—in New York and then joined Jackson's cabinet in 1829, first as secretary of state and then as U.S. minister to Great Britain.

Not yet a national party in 1836, Whigs entered three sectional candidates: Daniel Webster (New England), Hugh White (the South), and William Henry Harrison (the West). Van Buren captured the electoral college even though he had only a 25,000-vote lead. No vice-presidential candidate received a majority of electoral votes, and for the only time in American history, the Senate decided a vice-presidential race, selecting Democratic candidate Richard M. Johnson of Kentucky.

Van Buren and Hard Times

Van Buren took office weeks before the American credit system collapsed. With banks refusing to redeem paper currency with gold in response to the Specie Circular, a downward economic spiral began, curtailing bank loans. Credit contraction made things worse. After a brief recovery, hard times persisted from 1839 until 1843.

Van Buren cut federal spending, causing prices to drop further, and opposed a national bank, which would have expanded credit. The president proposed a new regional treasury system for government deposits that became law in 1840. Treasury branches would accept and disperse only gold and silver coin. Increasing the demand for hard coin, it deprived banks of gold and accelerated price deflation. Whigs favored new banks, more paper currency, and readily available corporate and bank charters. As the party of hard money, Democrats favored eliminating paper currency; by the mid-1840s, most favored eliminating bank corporations.

Anglo-American Tensions

Amid hard times came renewed Anglo-American tensions. After the privately owned steamer *Caroline* carried supplies to aid an unsuccessful Canadian uprising against Great Britain, British loyalists burned the ship, killing an American. Britain refused to apologize, and American newspapers called for revenge. Fearing war, President Van Buren posted troops at the border to discourage vigilante retaliation. Tensions subsided in late 1840 when New York arrested a Canadian deemed responsible for the American's death. The alleged murderer was acquitted. Had the verdict gone otherwise, Lord Palmerston, the British foreign minister, might have sought war.

An old border dispute between Maine and New Brunswick also disrupted Anglo-American relations. When Canadian lumbermen cut trees in the disputed region in winter 1838–1839, a Maine posse assembled to expel them. The lumbermen captured the posse, both sides mobilized militias, and Congress authorized a call-up of fifty thousand men. General Winfield Scott was dispatched to Aroostook, Maine, where he arranged a truce. The Webster-Ashburton Treaty (1842) settled the boundaries between Maine and New Brunswick and along the Great Lakes.

Franklin D. Roosevelt Library

Even as the Whigs opposed the Democrats, they adopted many of the Democrats' campaign techniques, appealing to the common man with their "log cabin and cider" campaign of 1840. The band in this street scene is riding a wagon decorated with a log-cabin painting. The campaign's excitement appealed to nonvoters as well as voters, and eighty percent of eligible voters cast ballots.

William Henry Harrison and the Election of 1840

With the nation facing hard times, Whigs confidently approached the 1840 election. Their strategy was simple: maintain supporters and court independents by blaming hardship on Democrats. Whigs rallied behind military hero General William Henry Harrison, conqueror of the Shawnees at Tippecanoe Creek in 1811. Democrats renominated President Van Buren, and the newly formed Liberty Party ran James Birney.

Harrison and his running mate, John Tyler of Virginia, ran a people's crusade against the aristocratic president in "the Palace." Although from a Virginia plantation family, Harrison presented himself as an ordinary farmer. Whigs wooed voters with huge rallies, parades, songs, posters, campaign mementos, and a party newspaper, *The Log Cabin*. Roughly 80 percent of eligible voters cast ballots. Winning the popular vote by a narrow margin, Harrison swept the electoral college, 234 to 60.

Immediately after taking office in 1841, President Harrison convened Congress in special session to pass the Whig program: repeal of the independent treasury system, a new national bank, and a higher protective tariff. But the sixty-eight-year-old

Link to Ellen Kay Bond's speech in support of William Henry Harrison.

Moral Reformers' Abstinence Campaigns

For female moral reformers in the 1830s and 1840s, safeguarding the nation against social ills often meant enforcing a new sexual propriety: premarital celibacy for men and women. Their calls are echoed in today's "purity" movements, which advocate sexual abstinence until marriage.

Moral reformers worried that devastating social byproducts accompanied economic expansion. As young people left home for jobs or schooling, they also moved beyond parental controls that kept them from licentiousness and sin, which could damage the nation's spiritual health. Northern women formed nearly six hundred local reform associations to ward off such threats. They lobbied against prostitution, assisted "fallen" women, preached chastity, and publicly shamed men seeking sexual gratification outside of marriage by visiting brothels or "seducing" virtuous young women. Some men openly criticized reformers' tactics, but few publicly questioned their goals.

Similarly emerging from secular and religious concerns, modern purity campaigns began in the early 1990s, amid escalating AIDS awareness and public outcries over teen pregnancies. Purity activists encourage youth to pledge abstinence to honor "God with your body." Pledging purity, notes one organization's web site, means avoiding pregnancy and sexually transmitted diseases while maintaining "every opportunity to fulfill your dreams." Nineteenth-century reformers, too, reminded youth that their dreams—business ownership, middle-class respectability—depended on sexual propriety. And just as moral reformers offered redemption, today's purity advocates talk about "second virginity."

To foster fellowship and win new pledges, today's purity organizations sponsor concert-like events, modern adaptations of revival-inspired reform meetings. At highly publicized purity balls, daughters and fathers exchange vows: Fathers promise to protect daughters' purity; daughters, to remain chaste until marriage. Young men and women wear purity rings, and pop stars highlight their purity pledges in publicity campaigns. But now as then, purity advocates face criticism for their tactics.

By advocating premarital celibacy as a weapon against society's ills, moral reformers left to a people and a nation an enduring, if controversial, legacy.

Harrison caught pneumonia and died within a month of his inauguration. The Constitution did not stipulate what should happen, but Tyler took full possession of executive powers, setting a precedent that would not be codified in the Constitution until 1967 with the Twenty-fifth Amendment.

TABLE 12.1   United States Presidents, 1824–1845

President	Party	Years in Office
James Monroe	Democratic-Republican	1817–1825
John Quincy Adams	Democratic-Republican	1825–1829
Andrew Jackson	Democratic	1829–1837
Martin Van Buren	Democratic	1837–1841
William Henry Harrison	Whig	1841
John Tyler	elected as Whig, but broke with party	1841–1845

President Tyler Tyler became more Democrat than Whig. He repeatedly vetoed Clay's protective tariffs, internal improvements, and bills to revive the Bank of the United States. Two days after Tyler's second veto of a bank bill, the cabinet except Secretary of State Daniel Webster resigned; Webster, after negotiating the Webster-Ashburton treaty, followed. Disgusted Whigs referred to Tyler as "His Accidency."

Like Jackson, Tyler expanded presidential powers and emphasized westward expansion. During his presidency, the United States negotiated its first treaties with China, and Tyler expanded the Monroe Doctrine to include Hawaii. But Tyler's vision for national greatness fixed on Texas and the westward expansion of slavery.

Summary

Religion and reform shaped politics from 1824 through the 1840s. Driven by a belief in human perfectibility, many evangelicals, especially women, worked to right the wrongs of American society. They hoped to trigger the millennium, the thousand years of earthly peace accompanying Christ's return. Some utopians joined experimental communities that modeled radical alternatives to existing society. Abolitionists worked to perfect American society by ending slavery. As women entered the public sphere as reformers and abolitionists, some embraced women's rights.

Struggles between the National Republicans and the Democrats, then between the Democrats and the Whigs, stimulated interest in politics. Democrats and Whigs competed for voters by building strong organizations that faced off in national and local elections often characterized by fraud and sometimes violence. Both parties favored economic development, but Whigs advocated centralized government, whereas Democrats advocated limited government and agricultural expansion. Controversies over the Second Bank of the United States and nullification exposed different interpretations of the nation's founding principles.

The late 1830s and early 1840s brought uncertainty: The economy experienced a period of bust, tensions with the British resurfaced, and a president died in office. John Tyler's vision of American greatness depended on westward expansion.

Chapter Review

From Revival to Reform

How did religious revival movements lead to social reform?

Ministers and preachers in the Second Great Awakening raised hope for their audiences that the second coming of Jesus Christ was at hand—as long as listeners were able to renounce sin and purge society of sinful behaviors such as drinking, swearing, and even slavery. Revivalists stressed human perfectibility and promoted self-improvement. They preached that there was a direct link between how people lived and whether they would enter God's Kingdom, and in so doing, inspired social and moral reform. Women were often a major force in reform movements, expanding their domestic roles in the home into efforts to counteract the evils of the market economy. Reform goals included reformatories for wayward youth, orphan asylums, rehabilitation for criminals, temperance, and improvements in education.

Utopian Experiments

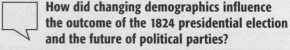

What were the goals of utopian communities?

Often inspired by religious revivalism, the utopian movement sought to hold the line on the rapid social change that members found disturbing, in particular, the rising market economy's excessive individualism. Some dreamed of creating a new social order; others wanted to recapture the supposed communal nature of the past and at the same time reshape marriage, child rearing, and other social arrangements. The Shakers, for example, built a profitable community around agriculture and handcrafts, but also abolished individual families in favor of men and women living in separate quarters and sharing leadership. The Oneida community centered on communal property ownership, communal child-rearing, and "complex marriage" in which all men were married to all women. The Fourierists included writers and intellectuals who inspired an American renaissance in literature and the arts, with Brook Farm in West Roxbury, Massachusetts, its most famous community. During its brief existence, the community embraced transcendentalism, the notion that the physical world is secondary to the spiritual realm.

Abolitionism

How did the Second Great Awakening transform the antislavery movement?

Abolitionism dates back to the nation's earliest days, when efforts to end slavery were initiated by both free blacks and elite whites. After 1830, however, evangelical abolitionists seeking to eradicate America's sins focused on slavery with renewed vigor. The activist and newspaper editor William Lloyd Garrison led a new, more radical strain of abolitionism known as "immediatism," which called for the immediate and complete end of slavery without compensating slave owners. Immediatists shared the evangelical belief that people determined their spiritual fate through good or evil acts and that by ending slavery, they could bring about the millennium, or Christ's return to earth. Unlike earlier movements, these abolitionists relied on participation of ministers and many others, and as such encouraged women to not only join but serve on executive committees, a controversial move that ultimately led to the split of the abolitionist movement in 1840.

Women's Rights

What inspired the rise of the women's movement in the mid-nineteenth century?

The religious revivals of the Second Great Awakening provided the first impetus for a later women's movement by encouraging women to see themselves as equal spiritually to men and urging them to take part in reforming society. Women's growing participation in the antislavery movement had many seeing parallels between slave bondage and marriage as a form of bondage as well as women's lack of citizenship rights. Traditional marriage law, borrowed from the English, gave husbands control over the family, including wives' property and earnings. Eight years after being denied a seat at the World Anti-Slavery Convention because of their sex, Elizabeth Cady Stanton and Lucretia Mott joined others in holding the first Woman's Rights Convention in 1848 at Seneca Falls, N.Y. There, three hundred participants outlined their demands for political and social equality, including the right to vote (a controversial issue that was not unanimously approved), in their Declaration of Sentiments, a document that paralleled the Declaration of Independence.

Jacksonianism and Party Politics

How did changing demographics influence the outcome of the 1824 presidential election and the future of political parties?

As suffrage laws changed to eliminate property requirements and allow immigrants to vote, the number of eligible voters tripled from 1824 to 1828. Politicians broadened their outreach to these new voters and successfully urged states to shift from appointing presidential electors to electing them by popular vote. That, combined with the end of candidate selection by congressional caucus, meant that five Democratic-Republican candidates ran for president in 1824. Although Andrew Jackson led in both electoral and popular vote, no one had a clear majority, leaving the House of Representatives to choose the president. Its members chose second-place John Quincy Adams, which led to charges of election-stealing and divided the party into the National Republicans (behind Adams) and the Democrats (behind Jackson). With two parties and only two candidates in the 1828 election, Jackson handily won the presidency, and the Democratic Party became the first well-organized national political party in the United States.

Federalism at Issue: The Nullification and Bank Controversies

What was at issue in the Nullification Controversy?

At the core of the Nullification Controversy were differing interpretations of the Constitution regarding federal power and states' rights. The doctrine of nullification—that states could overrule federal legislation—was based on the Virginia and Kentucky Resolutions of 1798, which argued that states could judge whether federal actions were constitutional, and ultimately nullify federal laws that did not pass the test. President Jackson rejected state sovereignty and saw nullification as leading to disunion. When South Carolina nullified a federal tariff, Jackson threatened force to collect the duties. As a compromise, the tariff was reduced and South Carolina withdrew its nullification. But the debate on the nature of the republic and of federal power continued.

The Whig Challenge and the Second Party System

How did the Whigs and Democrats differ ideologically?

Unlike the Democrats, Whigs advocated for economic growth via an activist government. They were for corporate charters, a national bank and paper currency, and promoted public schools and prison reform. Nor did Whigs worry about government aiding special interests; to them, as long as the public benefited, they saw no problem in it. Democrats believed in the Jefferson model of limited government and worried about government intrusion. Whigs thought government should be ruled from the top down, and they embraced the notion of a meritocracy—that the wealthy obtained their status and power through their own hard work. Democrats saw the world divided into "haves" and "have nots" and sought equal rights for all to restore some form of balance.

Suggestions for Further Reading

Philip F. Gura, *American Transcendentalism: A History* (2007)

Daniel Walker Howe, *What Hath God Wrought: The Transformation of America, 1815–1848* (2007)

Paul E. Johnson, *Sam Patch, the Famous Jumper* (2003)

Mary Kelley: *Learning to Stand and Speak: Women, Education, and Public Life in America's Republic* (2006)

Steven Mintz, *Moralists and Modernizers: America's Pre-Civil War Reformers* (1995)

Richard S. Newman, *The Transformation of American Abolitionism: Fighting Slavery in the Early Republic* (2002)

Susan Zaeske, *Signatures of Citizenship: Petitioning, Antislavery, and Women's Political Identity* (2003)

Harry L. Watson, *Liberty and Power: The Politics of Jacksonian America* (2006)

 **CourseMate** Go to the CourseMate website for primary source links, study tools, and review materials for this chapter. www.cengagebrain.com

The Contested West

13

1815–1860

To eight-year-old Henry Clay Bruce, moving west was an adventure. In April 1844, the Virginia boy began a 1,500-mile, two-month trip to his new home in Missouri. Henry marveled at the beautiful terrain, impressive towns, and the steamboat ride from Louisville to St. Louis. Once in Missouri, Henry noticed how much the West differed from the East. Farms were farther apart, and the countryside abounded with wild fruits, game, and fish. Yet rattlesnakes, wolves, and vicious hogs kept Henry and his playmates close to home.

A slave, Henry made the trip with his mother and siblings after his owner, Pettis Perkinson, decided to seek a fresh start in the West. Perkinson and three other white Virginians crammed their families, their slaves, and whatever belongings they could fit into three wagons. In Missouri, Pettis resided with his brother Jack Perkinson, who—according to Henry—yelled at and whipped his slaves. Henry's first year in Missouri was as carefree as a slave child's life could be. The boy fished, hunted (with dogs, not guns), and gathered prairie chickens' eggs. But by age nine, Henry was hired out, first to a brickmaker, then to a tobacco factory. He worked sunup to sundown, and when he failed to satisfy his bosses, he was whipped.

Meanwhile, Pettis Perkinson, unenamored with Missouri, returned to Virginia, later summoning some of his slaves, including Henry. Slaves' work was less rigorous in Virginia, but that did not compensate for leaving loved ones behind in Missouri.

Soon Pettis Perkinson again grew weary of Virginia, and renewed his quest for opportunity in the West, this time, in Mississippi. But cotton plantation life suited neither Henry nor his master, who now decided—to his slaves' joy—to give Missouri another chance.

Two years later, the restless Perkinson decided to head for Texas. Henry, now in his late teens, and his brothers refused to go. Although livid, Pettis Perkinson abandoned his plans rather than deal with recalcitrant slaves. Henry became the foreman on Perkinson's Missouri farm, where he remained until escaping during the Civil War to the free state of Kansas. Finally, Henry Clay Bruce found the opportunity and freedom that led so many to the West.

In 1820, about 20 percent of the nation's population lived west of the Appalachian Mountains. By 1860, nearly 50 percent did. Most whites and free blacks moved west seeking better opportunities. Easterners generally envisioned in the West enormous tracts of fertile, uncultivated land or, beginning in the late 1840s, gold and silver mines that promised quick riches. Some saw opportunities for lumbering or ranching, or selling goods or services to farmers, miners, lumbermen, and cattlemen.

Men often decided to head west without consulting their wives and children, and slaves' wishes received even less consideration. Nor did western settlers consider the impact of their migration on Indian peoples living there. The federal government had displaced many of those Indians from their Eastern homes. It also sponsored westward exploration, made laws regulating settlement and the establishment of territorial governments, surveyed and fixed prices on public lands, and sold land. It invested in transportation routes and established a military presence. In the 1820s, the Mexican government, too, encouraged Anglo-American settlement in the West along its northern borderlands—which it would later regret. U.S. settlers vied with the region's other inhabitants—Indians, Hispanics, and people of mixed heritage— for land and natural resources. A decade later, Mexico's northern province of Texas declared its independence and sought annexation by the United States. Thus began heightened tensions between the United States and Mexico, and within the United States, as Texas's future became entangled with slavery.

For some white Americans, mostly southerners, the ability to own slaves in the West signaled freedom. For others, from the North and the South, slavery's westward expansion frustrated dreams for a new beginning in a region free from slavery's degrading influence on white labor.

Even as Democrats and Whigs skirted the slavery issue, they took distinct stands on westward expansion's role in national economic development. But once the spotlight focused on Texas, political leaders would find it increasingly difficult to disentangle westward expansion from slavery.

With each passing decade, conflict—between expectations and reality, between people with different aspirations and world-views—increasingly defined life in the West. By the mid-1840s, western events would aggravate long-simmering discord between southern and northern political interests.

As you read this chapter, keep the following questions in mind:

* How did tensions in the East influence western migration and settlement?

* How did public, private, and individual initiatives converge to shape the West's development?

* What motivated cooperation in the West, and what spurred conflict?

The West in the American Imagination

What were the myths that helped shape white Americans' perceptions of the West?

For historian Frederick Jackson Turner, writing in the late nineteenth century, the western frontier, with its abundance of free land, was the "meeting point between savagery and civilization." It bred American democracy, shaped the American character, and made the United States exceptional. Modern

Chronology

1812	General Land Office established		U.S. Army Corps of Topographical Engineers established
1820	Price lowered on public lands		
1821	Santa Fe Trail charted	1840–1860	250,000 to 500,000 migrants travel overland
	Mexico's independence	1841	Log Cabin Bill
1823	Mexico allows Stephen Austin to settle U.S. citizens	1844	Presidential campaign features Texas annexation
1824	Congressional General Survey Act	1845	"Manifest destiny" coined
	Jedediah Smith's South Pass publicized		Texas annexed (March 1) and becomes twenty-eighth state (December 29)
	Indian Office established	1846–1848	War with Mexico (see Chapter 14)
1825–1832	*Empresario* contracts signed	1847	Mormons settle Great Salt Lake valley
1826	Fredonia rebellion fails	1848	California gold discovered
1830	Indian Removal Act (see Chapter 10)	1849–50s	Migrants stream into Great Plains and Far West
1832	Black Hawk War	1855	Ash Hollow Massacre
1834	McCormick reaper patented	1857–1858	Mormons and U.S. Army in armed conflict
1836	Lone Star Republic founded	1862	Homestead Act

historians generally eschew the notion of American exceptionalism, stressing instead the complex connections between the United States and the world. Although today's scholars reject the racialist assumptions of Turner's definition of *frontier,* some see value in the term when signifying a meeting place of different cultures. Others see the West as a place, not a process, though they disagree over what delineates it.

Defining the West

For early-nineteenth-century Americans of European descent, the West included anything west of the Appalachian Mountains. It represented the future—a place offering economic and social betterment, typically through land ownership. The West's seeming abundance of land meant that anyone could hope to become an independent farmer. Men who already owned land, like Pettis Perkinson, looked westward for cheaper, bigger, and more fertile landholdings. With the discovery of gold in California in 1848, the West became a place to strike it rich. Others went west by force, including slaves and Indians removed from their eastern homelands by the U.S. military under the Indian Removal Act of 1830.

To others, the notion of the West would have been baffling. Emigrants from Mexico and Central or South America traveled north to get to what European-Americans called the West. Chinese nationals traveled eastward to California. Many Indians considered the West home. Other Indians and French Canadians journeyed southward to the West. All arrived in the western portion of the North American continent because of factors that pushed and pulled them.

Frontier Literature

For European-Americans, Daniel Boone became the archetypical frontiersman, whose daring individualism opened the Eden-like West for hard-working freedom lovers. Through biographies, Boone became a familiar figure in American and European households. The mythical Boone lived in the wilderness and shrank from society. He overpowered bears and

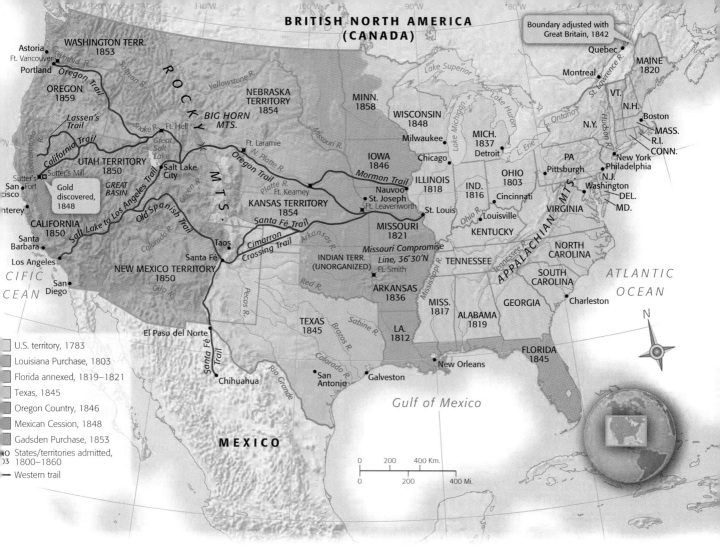

MAP 13.1

Westward Expansion, 1800–1860

Through exploration, purchase, war, and treaty, the United States became a continental nation, stretching from the Atlantic to the Pacific.

Source: Copyright © Cengage Learning

Indians but also became the pathfinder for civilization. As a friend wrote, Boone "has been the instrument of opening the road to millions of the human family… to a Land flowing with milk and honey." By borrowing biblical language—the land of milk and honey denoting the Promised Land—Boone's friend suggested that Boone was Moses-like, leading his people to a land of abundance.

With the invention of the steam press in the early 1830s, western adventure stories became cheap and widely read. Davy Crockett, another real-life figure turned into mythical hero, was featured in many of them. Crockett first fought the Creeks under Andrew Jackson but later championed Indian rights. After losing his life defending the Alamo mission during Texas's fight for independence (1836), Crockett appeared in stories portraying the West as violent, a place where one escaped civilized society and fought Indians and Mexicans. But even in this myth, the American West symbolized what white Americans saw as their nation's core value: freedom.

Western Art

In artists' renderings, the West was sometimes an untamed wilderness inhabited by savages (noble or otherwise), and sometimes a cultivated garden, a land of milk and honey where the Jeffersonian agrarian dream was realized. Such artwork revealed more about white Americans' ideals than about the West itself.

Smithsonian American Art Museum, Washington, DC

In one of his most famous portraits, George Catlin painted Wi-Jun-Jon, an Assiniboine Indian, both before and after he had mingled with white men. In the "before" stance, the Indian is a dignified, peace-pipe-bearing warrior; in the "after" portrait, the "corrupted" Indian has abandoned dignity for vanity and his peace pipe for a cigar.

George Catlin: American painter who traveled throughout the West and produced numerous portraits of Native Americans that reflected his fascination and beliefs about them.

The first Anglo-American artists to travel west were Samuel Seymour and Titian Ramsay Peale, whom the federal government hired to accompany explorer Stephen H. Long to the Rocky Mountains in 1820. They pioneered an influential genre: facsimiles in government reports. Between 1840 and 1860, Congress published nearly sixty works on western exploration, featuring hundreds of lithographs and engravings of plants, animals, and people. Some reports became bestsellers. The government distributed more than fifty-three thousand copies of its popular twelve-volume Pacific Railway Survey (1855–1860), which helped easterners visualize the continent's western reaches.

Sometimes government reports made telling alterations to the paintings they included. When Richard Kern accompanied explorer James H. Simpson in 1849 to the Southwest, he painted a Navajo man in a submissive pose. The reproduction transformed the man's pose into a rebellious one. In other cases, the government reports changed artists' depictions of Indian-occupied landscapes into empty terrain free for the taking.

Artists' cultural assumptions colored their portrayals of the West, too, and commercial artists produced what they thought the public craved. When **George Catlin** traveled west immediately following the Indian Removal Act of 1830, he painted the West with a moral in mind. Indians came in two varieties—those who preserved their original, almost noble qualities of freedom and moderation, and those who, after coming in contact with whites, had become "dissolute." Indians, he implied, benefited from removal from white Americans' corrupting influence.

Countering the Myths

But western realities often clashed with promoters' promises, and disappointed settlers sometimes tried to clarify matters for future migrants. Rebecca Burlend and her son were lured to Illinois by a fellow Englishman's letters extolling "a land flowing with milk and honey." Later, Burlend and her son wrote *A True Picture of Emigration* (1831), which described Illinois' hardships—intemperate weather, difficult working conditions, and swindlers. Her account sought not to discourage emigration, but to substitute a realistic for a rosy description.

Expansion and Resistance in the Trans-Appalachian West

What made the Midwest appealing to white settlers?

In the 1820s and 1830s, settlers streamed into the Old Northwest and the Old Southwest by foot, horseback, wagon, canal boat, steamboat, or a combination of means. Many people, like Pettis Perkinson and his slaves, moved several times, and when opportunities failed to materialize, some returned home.

Both the Old Northwest and the Old Southwest saw population explosions during the early nineteenth century. In 1790, the Northwest region's white population numbered just a few hundred people. By 1860, nearly 7 million people called it home. Between 1810 and 1830, Ohio's population more than quadrupled, while Indiana and Illinois grew fourteenfold and thirteenfold, respectively. Michigan's population multiplied fiftyfold between 1820 and 1850. Migration accounted for most of this growth. Once in the Old Northwest, people did not stay put. Geographic mobility, the search for better opportunities, and connections to the market economy defined the region that became known as the Midwest.

MAP 13.2

Settlement in the Old Southwest and Old Northwest, 1820 and 1840

Removal of Indians and a growing transportation network opened up land to white and black settlers in the regions known as the Old Southwest and the Old Northwest, as the U.S. population grew from 9.6 million in 1820 to 17.1 million in 1840.

Source: Copyright © Cengage Learning

Deciding Where to Move

Moving west meant leaving behind worn-out soil and areas with little land available for purchase, but it also meant leaving family, friends, and communities. The journey promised to be arduous, as did the backbreaking labor of clearing new lands. The West was a land of opportunity but also of uncertainty. What if the soil proved less fertile than anticipated? What if neighbors proved unfriendly, or worse? Settlers tried to control every possible variable. Like Pettis Perkinson, people often relocated where they had relatives or friends and traveled with acquaintances. They chose areas with familiar climates. Migrants also settled in ethnic communities or with people of similar religious affiliations.

The legal status of slavery also influenced where people settled. Some white southerners, tired of the planter elite's power, sought areas free from slavery—or at least where there were few plantations. Many others went west to improve their chances of owning slaves, or of purchasing additional slaves. White northerners also hoped to distance themselves from slavery as well as from free blacks. In the 1850s, many midwestern states passed "black laws" prohibiting African Americans, free or enslaved, from living within their boundaries. Ironically, many free blacks migrated west to free themselves from eastern prejudice.

Between 1815 and 1860, few western migrants settled on the Great Plains, a region reserved for Indians until the 1850s, and few easterners risked the journey to California and Oregon before the transcontinental railroad's completion in 1869. At first, the Southwest appealed most to settlers. But starting in the 1820s, the Midwest drew more settlers with its better-developed transportation routes, democratic access to economic markets, smaller African American population, cheaper average landholding, and climatic similarity to New England and northern Europe. The Old Northwest's thriving transportation hubs also made good first stops for western migrants lacking cash to purchase land. They found work unloading canal boats, planting and harvesting wheat, grinding wheat into flour, sawing trees into lumber or, more often, they cobbled together a combination of these seasonal jobs. With the Old Northwest's population growing quickly, white southerners worried increasingly about congressional representation and laws regarding slavery.

Indian Removal and Resistance

In the Midwest and the Southwest, white settlement depended on Indian removal. Even as the U.S. Army escorted Indians from the Old Southwest (see Chapter 10), the federal government arranged eighty-six treaties between 1829 and 1851 in which northeastern Indian nations relinquished land titles in exchange for lands west of the Mississippi River. Some northern Indians evaded removal, including the Miamis in Indiana, the Ottawas and Chippewas in the upper Midwest, and the Winnebagos in southern Wisconsin. In 1840, Miami chiefs acceded to pressure to exchange 500,000 acres in Indiana for equivalent acreage in Indian Country. Under the treaty, their people had five years to move or be escorted out by federal troops. But about half of the Miami nation dodged the soldiers—and many of those who trekked to Indian Country later returned. In Wisconsin, some Winnebagos eluded removal or returned to Wisconsin after being escorted west by soldiers.

Black Hawk War

In a series of treaties between 1804 and 1830, Sauks (or "Sacs") and Fox leaders exchanged lands in northwestern Illinois and southwestern Wisconsin for lands across the Mississippi River in Iowa

Territory. The Sauk warrior Black Hawk disputed the treaties' validity and in 1832 he led Sauk and Fox families to Illinois, panicking white settlers. The state's governor activated the militia, who were joined by militia from surrounding states and territories and U.S. Army regular soldiers. Over several months, hundreds of Indians and dozens of whites died under gruesome circumstances in the Black Hawk War. As the Sauks and Fox tried to flee across the Mississippi River, American soldiers fired indiscriminately. Those who survived the river crossing met gunfire from Lakota (Sioux), now allied with the Americans.

Black Hawk surrendered, and U.S. officials undertook to impress upon him and other leaders the futility of resistance. After being imprisoned, then sent to Washington, D.C., along a route meant to underscore the United States' immense size and population, and imprisoned again, the Indians were returned to their homes. The Black Hawk War ended militant Indian uprisings in the Old Northwest.

Selling the West

Land speculators, developers of "paper towns" (ones existing on paper only), steamboat companies, and manufacturers of farming implements promoted the Midwest as a tranquil place of unbounded opportunity. Land proprietors emphasized the region's connections to eastern customs and markets. They knew that, when families moved west, they did not seek to escape civilization. Western settlement generally followed connections to national and international markets. Eastern farmers, looking to escape tired soil or tenancy, sought fertile lands for growing commercial crops. Labor-saving devices, such as Cyrus McCormick's reaper (1834) and John Deere's steel plow (1837), made the West more alluring. McCormick, a Virginia inventor, patented a horse-drawn reaper that allowed two men to harvest the same number of acres of wheat that previously required between four and sixteen men. The reaper's efficiency achieved its greatest payoffs on the large, flat prairie lands, so McCormick relocated his factory to Chicago

Wisconsin Historical Society

In his advertisements, Cyrus McCormick portrayed his reapers as making the West into a place of prosperity and leisure.

in 1847. Without John Deere's steel plow, which could break through tough grass and roots without constant cleaning, "breaking the plains" might not have been possible.

Clearing the Land

After locating a suitable land claim, settlers constructed a rudimentary cabin if none already existed. Time did not permit more elaborate structures; settlers first had to clear the land. At the rate of five to ten acres a year, depending on a family's size, the average family needed ten years to clear a farm. Prairie land took less time.

Whereas farming attracted families, lumbering and mining appealed to single young men. By the 1840s, as eastern forests became depleted, northeastern lumber companies and laborers migrated to Wisconsin, Michigan, and Minnesota. Recently arrived Scandinavians and French Canadians also worked in the lumber industry. As the Great Lakes forests thinned, lumbermen moved again—some to the Gulf States' pine forests, some to Canada, and some to the Far West, where Mexicans in California and British in Canada had already established flourishing lumber industries. With the rapid growth of California's cities following the 1849 **Gold Rush**, timber's demand soared, drawing midwestern lumbermen farther west.

Gold Rush: After an American carpenter discovered gold in the foothills of California's Sierra Nevada range in 1848, Americans and people from around the world moved to California to look for gold.

Midwestern cities nurtured the surrounding countryside's settlement. Steamboats turned river settlements like Louisville and Cincinnati into commercial centers, while Chicago, Detroit, and Cleveland grew up on the Great Lakes' banks. By the mid-nineteenth century, Chicago, with its railroads, stockyards, and grain elevators, dominated the region's economy; western farmers transported livestock and grain by rail to that city, where pigs became packed meat and grain became flour before being shipped east. The promise of future flour and pigs gave rise to commodities markets. Some of the world's most sophisticated and speculative economic practices began in Chicago.

The Federal Government and Westward Expansion

How did the federal government sponsor and speed up westward expansion?

Few white Americans considered settling in the West before the region had been explored, surveyed, secured, and "civilized," which meant Indian removal and the establishment of churches, businesses, and American legal structures. Wide-scale settlement depended on the federal government's sponsorship.

The Fur Trade

Fur trappers were among the first white Americans in the trans-Appalachian West, but their lives bore faint resemblance to their mythical representation as mountain men who dared to go where whites never trod. Fur trappers lived among Indians, became multilingual, and often married Indian women. Indian women transformed animal carcasses into finished pelts, and they smoothed trade relations between their husbands and their native communities. The offspring of such marriages—métis or mestizos (people of mixed Indian and European heritage)—added to the West's cultural complexity.

The fur trade was an international business, with pelts from the American interior reaching Europe and Asia. Until the 1820s, British companies dominated the trade, but American ventures prospered in the 1820s and 1830s. Beginning in the 1820s, trappers and traders met annually for a "rendezvous"—a multiday gathering

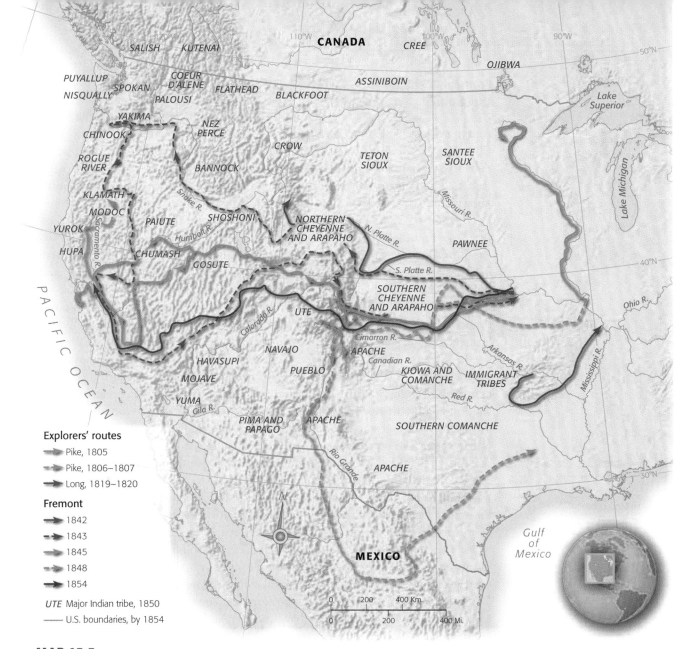

MAP 13.3

Western Indians and Routes of Exploration

Although western explorers believed they were discovering new routes and places, Indians had long lived in most of the areas through which explorers traveled.

Source: Robert Utley, *The Indian Frontier of the American West, 1846–1890,* University of New Mexico Press, 1984. p. 5. Reprinted by permission of the University of New Mexico Press.

where they traded fur for guns, tobacco, and beads that they could later exchange with Indians. Modeled on Indian gatherings that had occurred for generations, the rendezvous united Americans, Indians, Mexicans, and people of mixed heritage from throughout the West to trade and socialize.

By the 1840s, the American fur trade was declining. Beavers had been over-hunted, and fashions shifted toward silk and away from fur for hats. The traders' legacy includes resource depletion, introducing native peoples to devastating diseases, and developing trails across the trans-Mississippi West.

Santa Fe Trail: Trading route from St. Louis, Missouri, to Santa Fe, New Mexico, that enabled commerce to expand its reach farther west.

Transcontinental Exploration

A desire for quicker and safer routes for transporting goods to trading posts drove much early exploration. In 1821, merchant William Becknell helped chart the **Santa Fe Trail** running between Missouri and Santa Fe, New Mexico, where it connected to the Chihuahua Trail running into Mexico, allowing American and Mexican merchants to develop a vibrant trade. In 1824, fur trader Jedediah Smith rediscovered the South Pass, a 20-mile break in the Rocky Mountains in present-day Wyoming previously known only to Native Americans and some Pacific Fur Company trappers. The South Pass became the route followed by most overland travelers to California and Oregon.

Lewis and Clark's Corps of Discovery was the first of many federally sponsored expeditions to chart the trans-Mississippi West. Some expeditions sought to establish cordial relations with Indian groups with whom Americans might trade or enter military alliances. Others were scientific, exploring native inhabitants, flora, and fauna. But they were also commercial. Like Lewis and Clark, later explorers hoped to locate land, water, and rail routes that would allow American businessmen and farmers to trade nationally and internationally.

In 1805, the U.S. Army dispatched Zebulon Pike to find the Mississippi River's source and a navigable route west. He was instructed to research natural resources and native peoples and foster diplomatic relationships with Indian leaders. Before the Supreme Court ruled in *Johnson v. M'Intosh* (1823) that Indians did not own land but merely had a "right of occupancy," government officials instructed Pike and other explorers to purchase lands for military garrisons.

Although Pike failed to identify the Mississippi's source and had limited success in purchasing land, he gathered important information. When Pike and his men wandered into Spanish territory to the south, military officials held Pike captive for months in Mexico, inadvertently showing him areas he might not have otherwise explored. After his release, Pike wrote about a potential market in southwestern cities. The province of Tejas (Texas), with its fertile soil, enchanted him. But Pike dismissed the other northern provinces of Mexico, whose boundaries stretched to present-day Nevada and Utah, as unsuitable for human habitation.

Although nomadic Indians might sustain themselves there, he explained, the region was unfit for cultivation by civilized people. In 1820, army explorer Stephen Long, similarly deemed modern-day Oklahoma, Kansas, and Nebraska as "the Great American Desert," incapable of cultivation. Until the 1850s, when a transcontinental railroad was planned, this "desert" was reserved for Indian settlement. In 1838, Congress established the U.S. Army Corps of Topographical Engineers to systematically explore the West. As a second lieutenant in that corps, **John C. Frémont** undertook three expeditions to the region between the upper Mississippi and Missouri rivers, the Rockies, the Great Basin, Oregon, and California. He helped survey the Oregon Trail. Aided by his wife, Jessie Benton Frémont, he published bestselling accounts of his explorations. The Corps of Topographical Engineers' most significant contributions came in the 1850s with its surveying of possible routes for a transcontinental railroad.

John C. Frémont: Explorer who played a role in a California rebellion against Mexico; later a senator and presidential candidate and force in national politics.

A Military Presence

The army also helped ready the West for settlement. With the General Survey Act of 1824, Congress empowered the military to chart transportation improvements vital to military protection or commercial growth. Army engineers helped design state- and privately sponsored roads,

Gold in California

When James Marshall discovered gold in Sutter's Mill, California, in January 1848, word spread quickly worldwide. Within a year, tens of thousands of adventurers from other countries rushed to California, making it the most cosmopolitan place in North America.

In an era before the telegraph crossed the oceans, the news traveled surprisingly fast. Mexicans heard first. Next, word spread to Chile, Peru, and throughout South America; then across the Pacific to Hawai'i, China, and Australia; and then to Europe—Ireland, France, and the German states. Overland travelers brought the news south to Baja California and Sonora in Mexico. By spring 1849, some six thousand Mexicans were panning for gold; many came seasonally, spreading news of California on every trip home.

The newspaper *Honolulu Polynesian* announced California gold in the kingdom on June 24, 1848. Regular steamship service between Hawai'i and California transported gold seekers as early as 1853.

A ship brought news of California gold discoveries to Valparaiso, Chile, in August 1848. People in Chile's cities talked feverishly about gold, and rumors of California's overnight riches. Before year's end, two thousand Chileans left for California.

Word of gold reached Australia in December 1848, and by 1850 every ship in Sydney Harbour was California-bound. News reached China in mid-1848. Widespread poverty and gold's allure prompted many Chinese to migrate. By the mid-1850s, one in five gold miners was Chinese.

In 1850, the new state of California had nearly 40 percent foreign-born inhabitants, the majority non-European. Through word of mouth, rumor, letters home, and newspaper reports, the 1848 gold discovery linked California to millions of people around the globe.

Collection of the New York Historical Society

This 1855 Frank Marryat drawing of a San Francisco saloon dramatizes the international nature of the California gold rush. Like theater performers, the patrons of the saloon dress their parts as Yankees, Mexicans, Asians, and South Americans.

canals, and railroads, and its soldiers cleared forests and lay roadbeds. A related bill, also in 1824, authorized the army to improve the Ohio and Mississippi rivers; a later amendment did the same for the Missouri.

By the 1850s, 90 percent of the U.S. military was stationed west of the Mississippi River. When Indians refused to relinquish their lands, the army escorted them westward; when they harmed whites, the army waged war. The army sometimes destroyed the crops and buildings of white squatters refusing to vacate lands settled illegally. But, primarily, the army assisted overland migration. Army forts intimidated Indians, defended settlers from Indian attacks, and supplied information and provisions. In theory, the army was also supposed to protect Indians by driving settlers off Indian lands and enforcing laws prohibiting alcohol sales to Indians. Yet the army's small size relative to the territory it regulated made it impossible to do so, even when officers were so disposed.

The Office of Indian Affairs handled the government's other Indian interactions, including treaty negotiations, school management, and trade oversight. Created in 1824 as part of the War Department, the Indian Office cooperated with the military in removing Indians from lands necessary for American expansion and in protecting citizens who relocated west. In 1849, the Indian Office became part of the newly established Department of the Interior and soon shifted from removal to civilization through a reservation system. Whereas some Indians accepted reservations as protection from white incursion, others rejected them, sometimes sparking deadly intratribal disagreements.

Public Lands

The federal government controlled vast tracts of land, procured either from the states' cessions of their western claims after the Revolution or through treaties with foreign powers, including Indian nations. The General Land Office, established in 1812 as part of the Treasury Department, handled those lands' distribution. Its earliest policies divided western lands into 640-acre tracts to be auctioned at a minimum $2 an acre. These policies favored speculators—who bought up millions of acres—over individual, cash-poor farmers. Many settlers became squatters, prompting Congress in 1820 to lower land prices to $1.25 per acre and to sell tracts as small as 80 acres. Twelve years later, it sold 40-acre tracts. Yet it demanded that the land be bought outright; few would-be settlers (particularly after the Panic of 1819) had enough cash to purchase government land. Because speculators sold land on credit, many small-time farmers bought from them at inflated prices.

Farmers pressed for a federal policy of preemption—that is, the right to settle on land without obtaining title, improve it, and buy it later at the legal minimum price ($1.25 an acre). Some states offered lands through preemption, and Congress sometimes authorized preemption of federal lands in the 1820s and 1830s. But the first general preemption law, the so-called Log Cabin Bill, came in 1841, and it applied only to surveyed land. Preemption extended to unsurveyed lands with the **Homestead Act** of 1862, which provided that land would be given free to any U.S. citizen (or foreigner who had declared the intention of becoming a citizen), after residing on it for five years and improving it. Alternatively, settlers could buy land outright at $1.25 an acre after six months of residency, which allowed them to use the land as collateral for loans for additional land, farming supplies, or machinery.

Homestead Act: Passed in 1862, it embodied the Republican party's ideal of "free soil, free labor, free men" by granting 160 acres of public land to settlers who resided on it for five years and improved it.

The Southwestern Borderlands

Along the Louisiana Territory's southwestern border lay vast provinces controlled mostly by the Comanches and other Indians but claimed first by Spain and then—after 1821—by the newly independent nation of Mexico. **New Mexico**, with commercial centers in Albuquerque and Santa Fe, remained under Mexican control until the United States conquered the territory during its War with Mexico. Texas became an autonomous state in 1824, giving it greater independence from federal authorities than New Mexico enjoyed. This situation fostered Texas's struggle for national independence and then annexation to the United States, which returned slavery to the forefront of American political debate.

What factors led white Americans to settle in Texas?

New Mexico: Former Spanish colony in the upper Rio Grande Valley that became part of Mexico after 1821.

Southwestern Slavery Slavery in the Southwest was centuries-old. Yet as practiced by indigenous peoples—Comanches, Apaches, Kiowas, Navajos, Utes, and Pueblos—and by Spaniards, slavery centered on capturing women and children, who were then assimilated into their captors' communities, where they provided labor and status while fostering economic and diplomatic exchanges with their former communities.

This system was built on racial mixing—a practice anathema to most white Americans. As white slaveholders from the Southeast pushed into Mexican territory during the 1820s and 1830s, they often justified their conquest in racial terms. The region's Hispanic settlers, they reasoned, had been rendered lazy and barbarous by racial intermixing and were thus destined to be supplanted.

The New Mexican Frontier When Mexico gained independence from Spain in 1821, New Mexico's Hispanic population outnumbered the indigenous Pueblo peoples by three to one. There were twenty-eight thousand Hispanics, including people born in Spain and criollos—people born in New Spain to parents of Spanish descent. Most New Mexicans engaged in irrigated agriculture. To the north of Santa Fe, they farmed small plots, but to the south, larger farms and ranches predominated. Rancheros became wealthy selling wool and corn in distant markets, and from using unpaid laborers: often relatives, bound by debt. Threatened by the province's raiding Indian tribes— Apaches, Utes, Navajos, and Comanches—Hispanics, Pueblos, and mestizos sometimes united in defense. But their numerical superiority allowed Hispanics to seize many Pueblos' villages and lands in the rich northern river valleys.

The Santa Fe Trail caused a commercial explosion in New Mexico, doubling the value of imports in two years. Whereas the Spanish tried to keep foreigners out, the Mexican government offered enormous land grants to Anglo-American and French entrepreneurs, hoping they would develop the region's industry and agriculture and strengthen commercial ties with the United States.

Although commercial relationships grew, few Americans settled in New Mexico during the 1820s and 1830s. The best lands were occupied by Indians and Hispanics. And Americans seeking cheap, fertile land could find it in Texas.

The Texas Frontier In 1821, indigenous Indians remained the dominant group in Texas, though there were also Hispanics, Anglos, mestizos, and immigrant Indians. Of the thirty thousand indigenous people, most

MAP 13.4

Mexico's Far North

What is now considered the American Southwest was made up of the northern provinces of Mexico until the United States conquered the territory during the Mexican War (1846–1848).

Source: Copyright © Cengage Learning.

were Comanches. Texas was part of what one historian has called the Comanche Empire, an enormous territory from northern Mexico to Louisiana that the Comanches dominated through kinship, trade, diplomacy, and violence. People of European heritage were a small presence in Texas in 1821. Hispanic peoples had been there since the 1500s, establishing missions and presidios, but by 1820 they numbered only five thousand. Most raised livestock on ranches, while others traded (and intermarried) with Indians. They formed a distinctive identity as **Tejanos** (or Texans) rather than as Spaniards.

After the War of 1812, Anglo-Americans started entering Texas, where they sought furs, silver, or adventure. They traded manufactured goods—guns, ammunition, and kettles—for animal hides, horses, and mules, quickly supplanting the Tejanos as the Indians' trading partners. Although some Anglos settled in Texas, most traveled the Santa Fe and Chihuahua trails without settling.

Tejano: A native Texan of Mexican descent.

Visualizing the Past

Paintings and Cultural Impressions

Although few people of Spanish descent settled in Texas, those who did developed a distinctive and proud cultural identity. Calling themselves Tejanos, they adapted their inherited culture—music, dances, and cuisine—to their new surroundings. In the painting below of an 1844 celebration in San Antonio, French-born painter Theodore Gentilz captures the mixture of cultural carryovers and frontier adaptations. Which elements of the scene seem reminiscent of life in Spain or in the colonial capital of Mexico City? Which elements seem to be adaptations to life along a cultural frontier and political borderland? Which elements of the painting seem to celebrate Tejanos' culture, and which, if any, seem critical of it? If you were using this painting as a source of information about Tejano culture and its influence on contemporary music and dance, what else would you want to know about the artist and the scene he has captured?

Photo by Robert Corwin

Although the musician in Gentilz's painting is playing the fiddle, other artistic depictions record the widespread use of the guitar, which helped give rise to the corrido, *a folk ballad whose legacy is still apparent in today's country and western music.*

Daughters of the Republic of Texas Library

Theodore Gentilz arrived in Texas in the 1840s and soon began portraying the region's culture with his paintbrush. Here, Tejano settlers perform the fandango, a Spanish dance.

329

The Comanche Empire   As Indians competed for resources, the southwestern borderlands experienced intermittent but brutal violence. Mounted on horses, the Comanches hunted bison, took captives, and stole horses, livestock, and crops from their enemies. Smaller groups, such as the Wichitas and Caddos, grew corn, beans, squash, and pumpkins. When crops failed, farmers often turned to bison hunting as well, sometimes causing conflict with the Comanches.

Tensions increased around the time of Mexican independence, when another ten thousand Indians migrated into the region. From the Old Northwest came Shawnees and Kickapoos—former members of Tecumseh's confederacy. From the Old Southwest came Cherokees, Creeks, Choctaws, Chickasaws, and Seminoles, some with African American slaves. Indian newcomers vied for land and animals, often clashing with established groups. Some immigrant Indians, having adopted Anglo clothing and racial ideologies, dismissed as "savage" the indigenous Indians who hunted buffalo, wore skins, and did not regard land as a commodity.

Because violence threatened Indian removal and disrupted trade, the U.S. government brokered a treaty in 1835: The Comanches would allow immigrants onto their lands in exchange for trade opportunities. Trade quickly boomed. Immigrant Indians swapped agricultural products and manufactured goods, such as rifles and ammunition, for the Comanches' meats, robes, horses, and captives. That same year, the Comanches ended their longstanding war with the Osages. With peace came American traders. Meanwhile, the U.S. government's Indian removal continued, fueling Americans' commitment to cotton cultivation and expansionism.

American *Empresarios*   A decade earlier, before Mexican independence, the Spanish worried about the security of Texas, which they considered a buffer between hostile Indians and the United States. Their solution was to populate it. Thus, when Missouri miner and trader Moses Austin approached Spanish authorities in January 1821 about settling Americans in Texas, they agreed as long as Austin brought Americans willing to assimilate into Texas society. In exchange for promising to bring three hundred Catholic families—and no slaves—Austin would receive 200,000 acres along the Brazos River. Before Austin could act, though, he died, and Mexico won its independence from Spain in September 1821.

Austin's son, Stephen, pursued his father's scheme, pressing the new Mexican government to honor the grant, which it did in 1823, provided that Austin renounce his American citizenship and become a Mexican national. By 1825, Stephen Austin had settled two thousand white people and four hundred "contract laborers" of African descent. With ninety-year contracts, these African Americans were essentially slaves. Austin later brought nine hundred additional families in exchange for more land.

Satisfied with the Austin experiment, in 1824 Mexico passed a Colonization Law providing land and tax incentives to future foreign settlers. Coahuila y Texas specified that the head of a family could obtain up to 4,428 acres of grazing land or 177 acres of farming land. The land was cheap and could be paid for in installments over six years, with nothing due until the fourth year. Foreigners had to be upstanding Christians and permanent residents. To encourage settlers to assimilate into Mexican society, the Coahuila y Texas government provided additional land to those who married Mexican women.

Most U.S. citizens who settled in Mexico did so under an *empresario,* or immigration agent, who selected "moral" colonists, distributed lands, and enforced regulations. In exchange, he received nearly 25,000 acres of grazing land and 1,000 acres of farming land for every hundred families he settled. Between 1825 and 1832, approximately twenty-four *empresario* contracts (seventeen of which went to Anglo-Americans) were signed covering eight thousand families. The land grants covered almost all of present-day Texas.

During the 1820s, some Anglo-Americans who emigrated to Texas felt pushed by the Panic of 1819 and pulled by cheap land and generous credit terms. Despite Mexican efforts to encourage assimilation, these Americans tended to settle in separate communities. Anglo-Americans outnumbered Tejanos two to one. Authorities worried that the transplanted Americans would try to make Texas part of the United States.

Texas Politics
In 1826, an *empresario* named Haden Edwards called for an independent Texas, the "Fredonia Republic." Other *empresarios,* seeing advantages in peaceful relations with the Mexican government, resisted Edwards's secessionist movement. Although the Fredonia revolt failed, Mexican authorities dreaded what it might foreshadow.

Consequently, in 1830 Mexican authorities terminated legal immigration from the United States while encouraging immigration from Europe and other parts of Mexico. They prohibited American slaves from entering Texas, which brought Texas in line with the rest of Mexico—where slavery had been outlawed the previous year. Yet these laws did not discourage Americans and their slaves from coming; soon they controlled most of the Texas coastline and its U.S. border. Mexican authorities repealed the anti-immigration law in 1833, reasoning that it discouraged upstanding settlers without deterring undesirables. By 1835, the non-Indian population of Texas was nearly thirty thousand, with Americans outnumbering Tejanos seven to one.

Among white Texans, some, like Stephen Austin, favored staying in Mexico but demanded more autonomy, the legalization of slavery, and free trade with the United States. Others pushed for Texas secession from Mexico and wanted annexation to the United States. In 1835, the secessionists overtook a Mexican military installation charged with collecting taxes at Galveston Bay. Austin advocated a peaceful resolution, but, suspicious, Mexican authorities jailed him for eighteen months, which converted him to the independence cause.

The Lone Star Republic
With discontent over Texas increasing throughout Mexico, Mexican president **General Santa Anna** declared himself dictator and marched his army toward Texas. Fearing Santa Anna would free their slaves, Texans rebelled. After initial defeats at the Alamo mission in San Antonio and at Goliad in March 1836, the Texans easily triumphed by year's end. They declared themselves the Lone Star Republic and elected Sam Houston as president. Their constitution legalized slavery and banned free blacks.

Texas then faced the challenge of nation building, which to its leaders involved Indian removal. When the Indians refused to leave, Mirabeau Lamar, the nation's second president, mobilized the Texas Rangers—mounted nonuniformed militia—to drive them out through terror. The Rangers raided Indian villages, where they robbed, raped, and murdered. This "ethnic cleansing," as one historian has labeled it, ultimately cleared the land of native settlers to make room for white Americans and their African American slaves.

General Santa Anna: Mexican president and dictator whose actions led Texans to revolt.

Wartime Losses and Profits

After annexing Texas in 1845, the United States, seeking further territorial expansion, waged war against Mexico from 1846 to 1848 (see Chapter 14). In the borderlands, as in Mexico, some civilians—Indians, Tejanos, californios, and Mexicans—lost their lives, and many more suffered wartime depredations. If they aided the Mexicans, the U.S. Army destroyed their homes; if they refused aid to the Mexicans, the Mexicans destroyed their homes. An 1847 U.S. army report acknowledged that its "wild volunteers…committed…all sorts of atrocities on the persons and property of Mexicans." After the war ended in the borderlands, violence continued, with Texas Rangers slaughtering Indians from 1847–1848.

Some civilians profited from the war. Farmers sold provisions and mules to the armies; peddlers sold alcohol and food to soldiers; and others set up gambling and prostitution businesses near army camps.

Cultural Frontiers in the Far West

How did the gold rush influence the development of the Far West?

Even before the United States seized expansive territory during the War with Mexico, some Americans moved to the Far West, often to California, Utah, and other places Mexico controlled. Some sought religious freedom or to convert others to Christianity, but most wanted fertile farmland.

Western Missionaries

Catholic missionaries maintained a strong presence in the Far West. In Spanish missions, priests introduced Indians to Catholic sacraments; enforced rigid rules about prayer, sexual conduct, and work; and treated them as legal minors. Indians who did not measure up were subject to corporeal punishment. When they ran away, they were forcibly returned. With few options, Indians often responded to abusive practices with armed uprisings, ultimately weakening the mission system.

A Mexican law secularized the California missions in 1833, using them to organize Indian labor. Some Indians stayed at the missions, others left to farm their own land or to find employment, but for almost all, secularization brought enhanced personal freedom despite limited legal rights.

Still, Catholic missionaries—Americans, Europeans, and converted Indians—continued ministering to immigrants, working to convert Indians. Missionaries founded schools, introduced medical services, and even aided in railroad explorations.

In the Pacific Northwest, Catholics vied directly with Protestants for Indian souls. Under the auspices of the American Board of Commissioners for Foreign Missions, two missionary couples—credited as being the first white migrants along the Oregon Trail—traveled to the Pacific Northwest in 1836. Narcissa and Marcus Whitman built a meetinghouse for Cayuse Indians in Waiilatpu, near present-day Walla Walla, Washington, while Eliza and Henry Spalding worked to convert the Nez Percé at Lapwai, in what is now Idaho. With their superior attitude, the Whitmans could not convert the Cayuses. The Whitmans turned their attention to white migrants flowing into Oregon in the 1840s.

Tensions escalated when a devastating measles epidemic struck in 1847, and the Cayuses saw it as a calculated assault. They retaliated by murdering the Whitmans and twelve other missionaries. The Spaldings abandoned their successful mission, blamed Catholics for inciting the massacre, and became farmers in Oregon.

Mormons

Persecuted in Missouri and Illinois, the Mormons in 1847 followed Brigham Young to their "Promised Land" in the Great Salt Lake valley, still under Mexican control but soon to become part of the U.S. territory of Utah. As non-Mormons settled in Utah, Young diluted their influence by attracting new Mormon settlers to what he called the state of Deseret.

The Mormon's arrival in the Great Basin complicated relations among Indians. The Utes, for example, had long traded in stolen goods and captured people, particularly Paiutes. After Mormons tried to curtail the slave trade, Ute slavers tortured Paiute captives, particularly children, calculating that Mormons would buy them. When they did not, Ute slavers sometimes killed the children. The purchased children often worked as servants in Mormon homes. Although the Mormons tried to convert the Paiutes, their condescending treatment caused friction, even violence. Sharing the Utes as a common enemy, the Mormons and Paiutes formed an uneasy alliance in the early 1850s.

With their slave trade threatened and their economy in shambles, the Utes attacked Mormon and Paiute settlements. War erupted in 1853, and although an uneasy truce was reached in 1854, tensions continued between Mormons and Indians.

Mormons also tussled with their white neighbors. Although Mormons prospered from providing services and supplies to California-bound settlers, Young discouraged "gentiles" (his term for non-Mormons) from settling in Deseret and advocated boycotts of gentile businesses. When in 1852 the Mormons openly sanctioned polygamy, anti-Mormon sentiment increased nationwide. In June 1857, President James Buchanan dispatched 2,500 federal troops to suppress an alleged Mormon rebellion.

Anxious over their safety, some Mormons joined Paiutes in attacking a passing wagon train of non-Mormon migrants. Approximately 120 men, women, and children died in the so-called Mountain Meadows Massacre in August 1857. In the next two years, the U.S. Army and the Mormons engaged in armed conflict, with property destruction but no fatalities.

Oregon and California Trails

From 1840 until 1860, between 250,000 and 500,000 people, including children, walked across much of the continent, usually taking seven months. Although they traveled armed, most of their encounters with Indians were peaceful, if tense.

The overland journeys began at one of the so-called jumping-off points—towns such as Independence, St. Joseph, and Westport Landing—along the Missouri River, where migrants bought supplies for the 2,000-mile trip. While miners frequently traveled alone or with fortune-seeking young men, farmers traveled with relatives, neighbors, church members, and other acquaintances.

They timed their departures to be late enough to forage grass for their oxen and livestock, but not so late that they would encounter the treacherous snows of the Rockies and the Sierra Nevada. Not all were successful. From 1846–1847, the Donner Party took a wrong turn, got caught in a blizzard, and resorted to cannibalism. More fortunate overland migrants trudged alongside their wagons roughly 15 miles a day, in weather from freezing cold to blistering heat. Men generally tended livestock, while women set up camp, prepared meals, and tended small children.

Indians were usually peaceful, if cautious. During the trails' early days, Indians provided food and information, or ferried migrants across rivers. In exchange, migrants offered wool blankets, knives, metal pots, tobacco, ornamental beads, and other items. When exchanges went bad—due to misunderstandings or conscious attempts to swindle—tensions escalated.

Link to the overland trail diary of Lucia Eugenia Lamb Everett.

Livestock thefts continuously aggravated migrants, who usually blamed Indians even though whites stole livestock, too. Indians often took livestock when whites failed to offer gifts in exchange for grazing rights. One such incident, the so-called Mormon Cow Incident (or the Grattan Massacre), forever altered relationships along the Oregon Trail.

In August 1854, a Lakota in present-day Wyoming slaughtered a cow that strayed from a nearby Mormon camp. When Lakota leaders offered compensation, U.S. Army Lieutenant John Grattan, intent on making a point, refused. Grattan ordered his men to shoot, and after a Lakota chief fell dead, Indians returned fire, killing Grattan and twenty-nine men. The following year, General William Harney led six hundred soldiers to a village near Ash Hollow, where migrants and Indians had traded for years. When Indian leaders refused to surrender, Harney ordered his men to fire. Thirty minutes later, eighty-seven Indians lay dead, and seventy women and children were taken prisoner. The event disrupted peace along the trail and ignited nearly two decades of warfare between the Lakotas and the U.S. Army.

Indian Treaties

Fort Laramie Treaty: A treaty between the United States and eight northern Plains tribes in which the Indians agreed to maintain intertribal peace, accepted the U.S.-defined territorial regions for each tribe, and allowed the United States to construct roads. In exchange, they received annual payouts of provisions and agricultural necessities.

Still, the Indian Office negotiated treaties to keep Indians—and their intertribal conflicts—from interfering with western migration and commerce. The **Fort Laramie Treaty** of 1851 (or the Horse Creek Council Treaty) was signed by the United States and eight northern Plains tribes—the Lakotas, Cheyennes, Arapahos, Crows, Assiniboines, Gros-Ventres, Mandans, and Arrickaras—who occupied the Platte River valley through which the three great overland routes westward—the Oregon, California, and Mormon Trails—all passed. Two years later, in 1853, the United States signed a treaty with three southwestern nations, the Comanches, Kiowas, and Apaches, who lived near the Sante Fe Trail. Under both treaties, Indians agreed to maintain intertribal peace, recognize government-delineated tribal boundaries, allow the United States to construct roads and forts within those boundaries, refrain from depredations against western migrants, and issue restitution for any depredations nonetheless committed. In return, they would receive annual allotments from the U.S. government for ten years, paid with provisions, domestic animals, and agricultural implements.

Contrary to U.S. expectations, Indian chiefs did not see such treaties as perpetually binding. Government officials, meanwhile, promised allotments but did little to ensure their timely arrival, often leaving Indians starving. Treaties did not end intratribal warfare, nor did they fully secure overlanders' safety. But they represented the U.S. government's efforts to promote expansion and protect its westward-bound citizens.

Ecological Consequences of Cultural Contact

Armed conflict took relatively few lives compared to cholera, smallpox, and other maladies. The trails' jumping-off points bred disease, which migrants inadvertently carried to their Indian trading partners. Fearful of infection, Indians and migrants increasingly shied away from trading.

The disappearance of the buffalo (American bison) from the region further inflamed tensions. The buffalo provided protein to Plains Indians and held spiritual significance. Many Native Americans blamed the migrants for the buffalo's disappearance, even though most overlanders never saw a buffalo. By the time the overland migration peaked in the late 1840s and 1850s, the herds were long overhunted, partly by Native Americans eager to trade their hides. The surviving buffalo scattered to where the grass was safe from the overlanders' livestock. On rare occasions when wagon trains stumbled upon bison herds, men rushed to fulfill their frontier fantasies and shot the animals. For sport, overlanders also hunted antelopes, wolves, bears, and birds—animals that held spiritual significance for many Native Americans.

Gold Rush

Migrants especially intruded on Indian life near the California gold strikes. In January 1848, John Wilson Marshall discovered gold on John Sutter's property along a shallow tributary to the American River near present-day Sacramento, California. During the next year, tens of thousands of "forty-niners" rushed to California, where they practiced placer mining, panning, and dredging for gold in the hope of instant riches.

Some made fortunes. Peter Brown, a black man from Ste. Genevieve, Missouri, wrote his wife in 1851 that "California is the best country in the world to make money. It is also the best place for black folks on the globe." Most forty-niners, however, never found enough gold to pay their expenses. With their dreams dashed, many forty-niners took wage-paying jobs with large mining companies that used dangerous machinery to cut deep into the earth's surface.

As a remote Mexican province, California had small settlements surrounded by military forts (presidios) and missions. It was inhabited mostly by Indians, along with some Mexican rancheros, who raised cattle and sheep on enormous landholdings worked by coerced Indian laborers. With gold strikes, new migrants—from South America, Asia, Australia, and Europe—rushed to California. Although a California Supreme Court ruling—*People v. Hall* (1854)—made it impossible to prevent violence against Chinese immigrants, Chinese citizens continued to seek fortune in California; by 1859, approximately thirty-five thousand Chinese worked in the goldfields.

With hungry gold miners to feed, California experienced an agricultural boom. Wheat became the preferred crop: it required minimal investment, was easily planted, and had a short growing season. California's large-scale wheat farming depended on bonded Indian laborers.

Mining Settlements

Mining brought commercial and industrial booms, too, as enterprising merchants rushed to supply new settlers. Among them was Levi Strauss, a German Jewish immigrant, whose tough mining pants found a ready market with prospectors. Because men greatly outnumbered women, women's skills (and company) were in demand. As men set up all-male households and performed traditionally female tasks, women received high fees for cooking, laundering, and sewing. Women also ran boarding houses, hotels, and brothels.

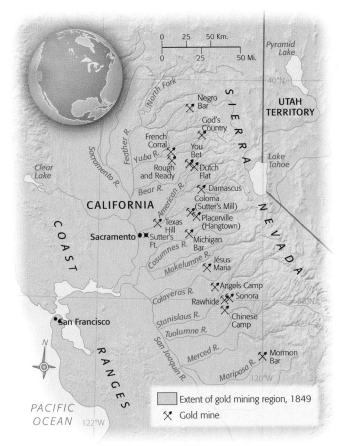

MAP 13.5
The California Gold Rush

Gold was discovered at Sutter's Mill in 1848, sparking the California gold rush that took place mostly along the western foothills of the Sierra Nevada mountains.
Source: Copyright © Cengage Learning

Link to John Sutter's account of discovering gold in California and its consequences.

Link to the original text of "Ahine, Chinaman."

Cities sprang up. In 1848, San Francisco was a small mission settlement of about a thousand Mexicans, Anglos, soldiers, friars, and Indians. With the gold rush, it became a city, ballooning to thirty-five thousand people in 1850. It was the West Coast gateway to the interior, and ships bringing people and supplies jammed the harbor.

Although California was admitted into the Union as a free state in 1850, its legislature soon passed "An Act for the Government and Protection of Indians" that legalized Indians' enslavement. Using enslaved Indians in the mines between 1849 and 1851 ended when newly arrived miners brutally attacked Indian workers, believing they degraded white labor and gave an unfair advantage to established miners. Those slaves who survived the violence became field workers and house servants. Between 1821 and 1860, the Indian population of California fell from 200,000 to 30,000, as Indians died from disease, starvation, and violence. Because masters separated male and female workers, Indians failed to reproduce in large numbers.

The Politics of Territorial Expansion

How did territorial expansion expose political fissures?

The population's westward movement shifted the locus of political power, and Democratic and Whig politicians tried to keep slavery out of the politics of territorial expansion. Westward expansion was central to Democratic ideology, which saw the West's fertile and abundant lands as essential for creating a society of independent white men, freed from the influence of established slaveholders or urban elites. Whigs were more suspicious of rapid westward expansion, though they welcomed the commercial opportunities it might bring. Instead, they pushed for industrial and commercial development within the nation's current boundaries.

Sam Houston: Military and political leader of Texas during and after the Texas Revolution.

The Texas issue, however, made it impossible to disentangle westward expansion and slavery. Soon after establishing the Lone Star Republic, **Sam Houston** approached American authorities to propose annexation as a state. But a new slave state would upset the balance of slave and free states in the Senate. Neither Whigs nor Democrats, wary of causing sectional divisions, were inclined to confront the issue. In the 1830s, Democratic presidents Andrew Jackson and Martin Van Buren—one a strong slavery proponent, the other a mild opponent—sidestepped the issue. But by the mid-1840s—with cotton cultivation expanding rapidly—some Democratic politicians equated Texas annexation with **manifest destiny**.

manifest destiny: Coined by editor John L. O'Sullivan, it was the belief that the United States was endowed by God with a mission to spread its republican government and brand of freedom and Christianity to less fortunate and uncivilized peoples; it also justified U.S. territorial expansion.

Manifest Destiny   The belief that American expansion westward and southward was inevitable, just, and divinely ordained dated to the nation's founding but was first labeled "manifest destiny" in 1845, by John L. O'Sullivan, editor of the *United States Magazine and Democratic Review*. O'Sullivan claimed that Texas annexation would be "the fulfillment of our manifest destiny to overspread the continent allotted by Providence for the free development of our yearly multiplying millions." Manifest destiny implied that Americans had a God-given right, perhaps an obligation, to expand their republican and Christian institutions to less fortunate and less civilized peoples. Implicit in manifest destiny was the belief that American Indians and Hispanics, much like people of African descent, were inferior peoples best controlled or conquered. Manifest destiny provided a political rationale for territorial expansion.

Some, however, felt that an expanding American empire defied God's will. During debates over Texas annexation, Transcendentalist William Ellery Channing argued that the United States should expand its empire by example not conquest: It should be a "sublime moral empire, with a mission to diffuse freedom by manifesting its fruits, not to plunder, crush, and destroy."

In June 1846, impatient expansionists, including John C. Frémont, staged an armed rebellion against Mexican authorities and declared California an independent republic. Because the U.S. military soon conquered California in its War with Mexico, the "Bear Flag Rebellion"—so named for the symbol on the revolutionaries' flag—was short-lived but inflamed racial tensions in California.

Fifty-Four Forty or Fight

To the north, Britain and the United States had jointly occupied the disputed Oregon Territory since 1818. Beginning with John Quincy Adams's administration, the United States tried to fix the boundary at the 49th parallel, but Britain wanted access to Puget Sound and the Columbia River. In the early 1840s, expansionists demanded the entire Oregon Country for the United States, up to its northernmost border at latitude 54° 40'. Soon "fifty-four forty or fight" became their rallying cry.

President Tyler wanted both Oregon and Texas, but was obsessed with Texas. He argued that slavery's expansion would spread the nation's black population more thinly, causing the institution's gradual demise. But when word leaked out that Secretary of State John Calhoun had written to the British minister in Washington justifying Texas annexation to protect slavery, the Senate rejected annexation in 1844 by a vote of 35 to 16.

Polk and the Election of 1844

Worried southern Democrats persuaded their party's 1844 convention to require that the presidential nominee receive two-thirds of the convention votes, effectively giving the southern states a veto and allowing them to block the nomination of Martin Van Buren, who opposed annexation. Instead, the party ran "Young Hickory," House Speaker James K. Polk, an avid expansionist and Tennessee slaveholding cotton planter. The Democratic platform, designed to appeal to voters across regional lines, called for occupation of the entire Oregon Territory and annexation of Texas. The Whigs, who ran Henry Clay, argued that the Democrats' belligerent nationalism would lead to war with Great Britain, Mexico, or both. Clay favored expansion through negotiation, whereas many northern Whigs opposed annexation altogether, fearful it would lead to additional slave states and strain relations with trading partners. Polk won the election by 170 electoral votes to 105, though with a margin of just 38,000 out of 2.7 million votes cast.

Annexation of Texas

Interpreting Polk's victory as a mandate for annexation, President Tyler proposed that Texas be admitted by joint resolution of Congress. The usual method of annexation, by treaty negotiation, required a two-thirds vote in the Senate, which expansionists did not have. Joint

Library of Congress

This 1845 portrayal of Oregon City, the western terminus of the Oregon Trail, was provided by a British army officer sent to investigate the influence of large-scale American immigration into a territory jointly occupied by Great Britain and the United States. After the Oregon Treaty (1846) drew the boundary between British and American territory at the forty-ninth parallel, Oregon City became the capital of the Oregon Territory from 1848 to 1851.

resolution required a simple majority in each house. On March 1, 1845, the resolution passed the House by 120 to 98 and the Senate by 27 to 25. Three days before leaving office, Tyler signed the measure. Mexico, which had never recognized Texas independence, broke relations with the United States. In October, Texas citizens ratified annexation, and Texas joined the Union, with a constitution permitting slavery, in December 1845. The nation was on the brink of war with Mexico. That conflict would lay bare the inextricable relationships among westward expansion, slavery, and sectional discord.

Summary

Encouraged by literary and artistic images of the frontier as a place of natural abundance and opportunity, millions poured into the Old Southwest and Old Northwest in the early nineteenth century. The federal government promoted westward expansion through support for transportation improvements, surveying, cheap land, and protection from Indians. Still, western migrants did not always find what they were seeking. Some returned home, some moved to new locations, and some stayed in the West, abandoning their dreams of economic independence.

Large numbers of African American slaves were moved westward by their owners between 1820 and 1860. Native Americans saw their lands and livelihoods constrict, and their environments drastically altered, threatening their economic and spiritual lives. Some Indians responded to white incursion through accommodation and peaceful overtures; others resisted. For Indians in Texas and California, white incursions brought devastation.

Descendants of Early Latino Settlers

Today, American news media frequently report about Latinos in the United States, for current census figures identify them as the largest racial or ethnic minority. Stories focus on the growing number of documented and undocumented Latino immigrants, their increasing social impact, and their occasionally difficult relationships with African Americans. Yet all the attention to recent arrivals overlooks the sizable number of Latinos who are descended from people whose residency in North America predated the existence of the United States.

When the region stretching from eastern Texas to California was acquired by the United States in the 1840s, its population included indigenous Indian nations and thousands of people with at least partial European ancestry, primarily Spanish or Portuguese. Their descendants have included such U.S. congressmen as Manuel Luján (1969–1988) and such senators as Kenneth Salazar (who served from 2004 to 2009, when he resigned to become Secretary of the Interior). Their families have resided in what is now U.S. territory for twelve or fourteen generations.

Persuasive evidence suggests that many of the early Iberian settlers in New Mexico were *conversos*, or of New Christian descent—that is, people whose Jewish ancestors converted to Catholicism in the fifteenth century to avoid religious persecution. After Jews were expelled from Spain and Portugal in 1492, many fled to the Spanish empire's far corners. Some participated in Juan de Oñate's 1598 expedition to New Mexico. There, some secretly maintained such Jewish customs as Sabbath observances and food restrictions. Today, some Latino residents of New Mexico have acknowledged their *converso* roots and reclaimed a Jewish identity.

These long-standing Latino citizens of the United States, not just those of *converso* descent, have given the nation and its people an important multicultural legacy.

White beliefs about Native Americans' supposed inferiority allowed many to rationalize the Indians' fate; white attitudes toward black people and slavery drove where they settled in the West. Those who believed that slavery degraded white labor headed along a northern trajectory, whereas those who dreamed of slave ownership headed southward, where they clashed with yet another group they deemed racially inferior: Mexicans. When American settlers in Texas achieved independence from Mexico and applied for annexation by the United States, they brought the divisive issue of slavery's westward expansion to the surface. Although Democratic politicians initially tried to maintain a geographic equilibrium by proposing an ambitious territorial agenda in Oregon as well, Texas annexation set the stage for military conflict, the addition of vast territories in the Southwest, and reinvigorated sectional conflict.

Chapter Review

The West in the American Imagination

What were the myths that helped shape white Americans' perceptions of the West?

In dime store novels, artists' paintings, and materials recruiting settlers, the West was depicted as a place of cheap or free, abundant and unoccupied land where anyone could seek to better him- or herself. They often neglected to include that many of these lands were home to native peoples. Artists often depicted Indians as savages (sometimes noble savages) or as docile and easily conquered. Frontiersmen like Daniel Boone were portrayed as having the courage and independent spirit needed to tame the so-called uncivilized wilderness and open the West to freedom-loving white settlers. The West effectively symbolized core American values of freedom, independence, and opportunity.

Expansion and Resistance in the Trans-Appalachian West

What made the Midwest appealing to white settlers?

Migrants who headed west in search of a better life often chose the Midwest because they wanted a region with the same features and conveniences they had come to know. The Midwest, compared to the Old Southwest, had better-developed transportation routes, easier access to markets, a smaller African American population, cheaper landholdings, and a climate similar to New England's. The region proved a good first stop for those who did not yet have enough cash to purchase land; in the Midwest, they could obtain jobs unloading canal boats or working in farms or mills, before moving on.

The Federal Government and Westward Expansion

How did the federal government sponsor and speed up westward expansion?

Federal Indian and land policies, particularly Indian removal from desirable lands, did much to encourage white movement into the West. Many whites, in fact, awaited government efforts to clear lands before moving there. The federal government funded expeditions to chart the trans-Mississippi West, including efforts to find the best location for a transcontinental railroad. Army engineers helped design roads, canals, and railroads, while soldiers cleared forests and did other work. The military also removed Indians from lands that whites desired, defended settlers from Indian attacks, or pushed squatters from land they did not own. Sales of government-controlled land also encouraged settlement.

The Southwestern Borderlands

What factors led white Americans to settle in Texas?

First, the Panic of 1819 pushed some Anglo-Americans to seek cheap land and a fresh start in the Texas territory controlled by Mexico. Beginning in 1824, officials in Mexico also encouraged settlement by offering tax incentives and land grants to foreigners. American Stephen Austin initially settled over two thousand whites, who, contrary to their agreement, brought four hundred slaves. He later brought another nine hundred families. Mexico required settlers be Christians willing to establish permanent residences and to assimilate. But early on, Mexican officials rightly feared that the transplanted Americans would seek to annex Texas to the United States. Beginning in 1826, there were calls for an independent Texas under the name "Fredonia Republic"; and as the proportion of Americans to Tejanos reached seven to one in 1835, calls for secession heightened, culminating in battles and the eventual declaration of Texas as the Lone Star Republic in 1836.

Cultural Frontiers in the Far West

How did the gold rush influence the development of the Far West?

As miners flooded into California seeking gold, an agricultural boom emerged, with wheat becoming the main crop, often farmed by Indian slaves. Wherever mining areas sprung up, a commercial and industrial boom usually followed, as merchants provided necessities and other goods to new settlers. Cities also grew up fast; San Francisco went from one thousand people in 1848 to thirty-five thousand two years later. While California was admitted as a free state that year, it quickly legalized the enslavement of Indians, using them to work in the mines and later in fields or homes.

The Politics of Territorial Expansion

How did territorial expansion expose political fissures?

Efforts to expand the territorial holdings of the United States ultimately magnified sharp regional and political divisions and ended the second party system's cross-sectional alliances. While Democrats embraced westward expansion as part of their vision of a society of independent white farmers, Whigs preferred to focus on commercial development within the nation's existing boundaries. Still, both parties were able to reach compromises with factions in the North and South, until the divisive issue of slavery's role in westward expansion became unavoidable. Those who embraced widening America's territory to the Pacific as its manifest destiny sought to annex Texas—formerly Mexico's holding—and Oregon, which the U.S. jointly occupied with Great Britain. Whigs feared annexation of Texas would widen slavery's reach, tip the balance of free-and-slave states, lead to war with Mexico and strain trade relations. Southern Democrats, including President James Polk, wanted to extend slavery as part of westward expansion,

taking the first step by annexing Texas in 1845 as a slave state. The move made regional divisions unavoidable and moved the nation toward a war with Mexico and its own sectional crisis.

Suggestions for Further Reading

Gary Clayton Anderson, *The Conquest of Texas: Ethnic Cleansing in the Promised Land, 1820–1875* (2005)

Stuart Banner, *How the Indians Lost Their Land: Law and Power on the Frontier* (2005)

Ned Blackhawk, *Violence over the Land: Indians and Empires in the Early American West* (2006)

Andrew R. L. Cayton and Peter S. Onuf, *The Midwest and the Nation: Rethinking the History of an American Region* (1990)

Pekka Hämäläinen, *The Comanche Empire* (2008)

Robert V. Hine and John Mack Faragher, *The American West: A New Interpretive History* (2000)

Albert L. Hurtado, *Indian Survival on the California Frontier* (1998)

Susan L. Johnson, *Roaring Camp: The Social World of the California Gold Rush* (2000)

Andrés Reséndez, *Changing National Identities at the Frontier: Texas and New Mexico, 1800–1850* (2005)

Michael L. Tate, *Indians and Emigrants: Encounters on the Overland Trails* (2006)

Go to the CourseMate website for primary source links, study tools, and review materials for this chapter. www.cengagebrain.com

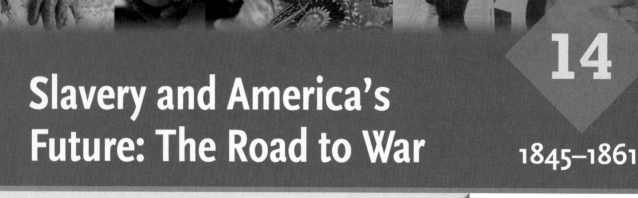

Slavery and America's Future: The Road to War

14

1845–1861

On a stiflingly hot evening, June 16, 1858, former one-term congressman Abraham Lincoln stepped onto the platform of the legislative chamber in the Springfield, Illinois, state house to accept the Republican Party's nomination for the U.S. Senate against America's leading Democrat—the incumbent, Stephen A. Douglas. At six feet, four inches, Lincoln towered over the packed hall. The nation was at a historic crossroads, and he had worked on this speech for weeks, delivering his poetic prose with intellectual power. "Slavery agitation" had convulsed American politics and exploded in guerrilla war in Kansas. "It will not cease," ventured Lincoln, "until a crisis shall have been reached, and passed." Then, in familiar biblical imagery, he gave the crisis its unforgettable metaphor:

> A house divided against itself cannot stand. I believe this government cannot endure permanently half slave and half free.... It will become *all* one thing, or *all* the other. Either the *opponents* of slavery will arrest the further spread of it, and place it where the public mind shall rest in the belief that it is in the course of ultimate extinction; or its *advocates* will push it forward, till it shall become alike lawful in *all* the States, *old* as well as *new*—North as well as South.

Lincoln contended that a conspiracy—a "design" led by the Democratic Party's "chief bosses"—sought to make slavery a *national* institution. He charged Douglas with not caring "whether slavery be voted down or voted up."

In the ensuing campaign, Lincoln and Douglas squared off over the issues dividing the country: westward expansion of slavery, the character of federal authority over property in slaves, whether the Declaration of Independence had signaled racial equality, and ultimately the moral integrity and future of the American republic. Reluctantly, Douglas agreed to seven debates, one in each congressional district of Illinois, except Chicago and Springfield, where the candidates had already appeared.

The Lincoln-Douglas debates were three-hour marathons of confrontation, political analysis, and theater, with the candidates speaking in long addresses and rebuttals. Tens of thousands of people attended these outdoor events, arriving by foot, wagon, or trains. Perhaps never before or since have Americans demonstrated such an appetite for democratic engagement.

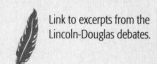

Link to excerpts from the Lincoln-Douglas debates.

As Douglas accused his opponent and Republicans of radicalism—of being "abolitionists" and favoring racial equality—Lincoln was forced to admit that he opposed social equality between whites and blacks. He embraced, however, the natural-rights doctrine of the Declaration of Independence and condemned slavery as an "evil" that must be constrained. Lincoln insisted on stopping slavery's expansion, while maintaining that the federal government could not legally end it in the South. A foot shorter than Lincoln, better dressed, and resplendent in oratorical manner, Douglas appealed to racial prejudice and to a vague unionism. Lincoln cast the election as a moral choice between free-labor—Free-Soil doctrine—and a republic ultimately dominated by slaveholders and their abettors, determined to erase ordinary citizens' liberties.

Of the quarter-million votes cast, Lincoln received four thousand more than Douglas. But senators were elected by state legislatures in the nineteenth century; due to an outdated apportionment, Democrats maintained a 54-to-46 margin and returned Douglas to the U.S. Senate. Lincoln would be heard from again, however.

Well before 1858, conflict and violence were enveloping the nation. In Kansas Territory, warfare exploded between proslavery and antislavery settlers. In the U.S. Senate, a southern representative had beaten a northern senator senseless. A new fugitive slave law sent thousands of free and fugitive blacks fleeing into Canada in fear for their lives. The Supreme Court issued a dramatic decision about slavery's constitutionality in westward expansion as well as the status of African American citizenship—to the delight of most southerners and the dread of many northerners. And abolitionist John Brown was planning a raid into Virginia to start a slave rebellion.

As the 1850s advanced, divergent economic and political aims, North and South, which had long been held in check, now flew apart over slavery. Political parties fractured, replaced by a realignment that reinforced sectional interests. Each time the nation expanded, it confronted a thorny issue: Should new territories and states be slave or free?

North and South, a feeling grew that America's future was at stake—the character of its economy, its labor system, its definition of constitutional liberty, and its racial self-definition. Blacks could take heart that political strife over slavery might lead to their liberation. In 1855, Frederick Douglass spoke for the enslaved when he wrote, "the thought of only being a creature of the present and the past, troubled me, and I longed to have a future—a future with hope in it."

As you read this chapter, keep the following questions in mind:

* **After 1845, how and why did westward expansion become so intertwined with the future of slavery and freedom?**

* **During the 1850s, why did Americans (white males, virtually all of whom could vote, and blacks, few of whom had the franchise) seem to care so deeply about electoral politics?**

* **What were the long-term and immediate causes of the Civil War?**

Chronology

1846 War with Mexico begins Oregon Treaty negotiated Wilmot Proviso inflames sectional divisions	Buchanan elected president, but Republican Frémont wins most northern states
1847 Cass proposes idea of popular sovereignty	**1857** *Dred Scott v. Sanford* endorses southern views on black citizenship and slavery in territories Economic panic and widespread unemployment begin
1848 Treaty of Guadalupe Hidalgo gives United States new territory in the Southwest Free-Soil Party formed Taylor elected president Gold discovered in California, which later applies for admission to Union as free state	**1858** Kansas voters reject Lecompton Constitution Lincoln-Douglas debates attract attention Douglas contends popular sovereignty prevails over *Dred Scott* decision in territories
1850 Compromise of 1850 passes, containing controversial Fugitive Slave Act	**1859** Brown raids Harpers Ferry
1852 Stowe publishes *Uncle Tom's Cabin* Pierce elected president	**1860** Democratic Party splits in two; southern Democrats demand constitutional guarantee for the territories Lincoln elected president in divided, sectional election Crittenden Compromise fails South Carolina secedes from Union
1854 Publication of "Appeal of the Independent Democrats" Kansas-Nebraska Act wins approval and ignites controversy Republican Party formed Return of fugitive Burns to slavery in Virginia	**1861** Six more Deep South states secede Confederacy established at Montgomery, Alabama Attack on Fort Sumter begins Civil War Four states in the Upper South join the Confederacy
1856 Bleeding Kansas troubles nation Brooks attacks Sumner in Senate chamber	

The War with Mexico and Its Consequences

Which of Polk's decisions pushed the United States toward war with Mexico?

In the 1840s, territorial expansion surged forward under President **James K. Polk** of North Carolina. The annexation of Texas just before his inauguration did not make war with Mexico inevitable, but several of Polk's decisions did. Mexico broke off relations with the United States, and during the annexation process, Polk urged Texans to seize all land to the Rio Grande and claim the river as their southern and western border. Mexico held that the Nueces River was the border; hence, the stage was set for conflict. In Polk's determination to fulfill the nation's manifest destiny to rule the continent, he wanted Mexico's territory to the Pacific and Oregon Country as well. He and his expansionist cabinet achieved their goals but were unaware of expansionism's price in domestic harmony.

James K. Polk: President from 1845–1849; supporter of immediate annexation of Texas and wanted to gain California and Oregon for the United States as well.

Oregon

During the 1844 campaign, Polk's supporters threatened war with Great Britain to gain Oregon. Not wanting to fight Mexico and Great Britain simultaneously, Polk sought diplomacy in the Northwest, where America and Britain had since 1819 jointly occupied disputed territory. Dropping the demand for a boundary at latitude 54°40', he pressured the British to accept the forty-ninth parallel. In 1846, the Oregon Treaty gave the United

States present-day Oregon, Washington, and Idaho, and parts of Wyoming and Montana. Thus, a new era of land acquisition and conquest began under the eleventh president of the United States, the sixth to be a slaveholder and one who, through an agent, secretly bought and sold slaves from the White House.

"Mr. Polk's War"

Toward Mexico, Polk was more aggressive. In early 1846, he ordered American troops under "Old Rough and Ready," General Zachary Taylor, to defend the contested border of the Rio Grande across from the town of Matamoros, Mexico. Polk saw California as the prize, and he attempted to buy from Mexico a huge tract of land extending to the Pacific. When that failed, Polk waited for war. After a three-week standoff, on April 24, 1846, Mexican cavalry ambushed a U.S. cavalry unit on the north side of the river; eleven Americans were killed, and sixty-three were taken captive. On April 26, Taylor sent a dispatch to Washington, D.C., announcing, "Hostilities may now be considered as commenced."

Polk then drafted a message to Congress: Mexico had "passed the boundary of the United States, had invaded our territory, and shed American blood on American soil." Polk deceptively declared that "war exists by the act of Mexico itself." Two days later, on May 13, the House recognized a state of war with Mexico by a vote of 174 to 14, and the Senate, by 40 to 2. Because Polk withheld key facts, the full reality of what had happened on the distant Rio Grande was not known. Manifest destiny launched the United States into its first major war on foreign territory.

Foreign War and the Popular Imagination

The idea of war unleashed public celebrations in southern and northern cities. After news came of General Taylor's first victories at Palo Alto and Resaca de la Palma, volunteers swarmed recruiting stations. New York, writer Herman Melville remarked that "Nothing is talked of but the Halls of the Montezumas." Publishers rushed books about Mexican geography into print. And new daily newspapers boosted sales by giving the war a romantic appeal.

Here was an adventurous war of conquest, the fulfillment of an Anglo-Saxon—Christian destiny to possess the North American continent, and to civilize the "semi-Indian" Mexicans. Racism fueled the expansionist spirit. In 1846, an Illinois newspaper justified the war by calling Mexicans "reptiles in the path of progressive democracy." Because of newspapers, the War with Mexico became the first national event experienced with immediacy. War correspondents reported on battles, and ships from Vera Cruz on the Gulf Coast of Mexico carried news dispatches to New Orleans. Near war's end, news traveled by telegraph in only three days from New Orleans to Washington, D.C.

The war spawned poetry, song, drama, travel, literature, and lithographs that glorified the conflict. But not everyone cheered. Abolitionist James Russell Lowell considered the war a "national crime committed in behoof of slavery, our common sin." Even proslavery spokesman John C. Calhoun saw the perils of expansionism.

Link to John C. Calhoun's 1850 speech on preserving the Union.

Conquest

Early in the war, U.S. forces made significant gains. In May 1846, Polk ordered Colonel Stephen Kearny and a small detachment to invade the remote provinces of New Mexico and California. Taking Santa Fe, Kearny pushed into California, where he joined forces with two

The Mexican War in Popular Imagination

The War with Mexico was the first American foreign conflict to be covered by the press with actual correspondents and the first to stimulate the creation of widespread promotional popular art and commemorative objects. General Zachary Taylor, the American commander in Mexico, became the hero of the war, and in its wake, was elected president in 1848 in a campaign that featured countless forms of this art. Why was the War with Mexico the first American foreign war to be covered by journalists and so widely depicted in political and military art? Do you think the artistic depictions of the War with Mexico increased or decreased the popularity of the war?

Presentation pitcher: ca. 1848–1850 (porcelain), French School, (19th century) Portrait of Zachary Taylor (1784–1850) on one side, 12th president of the United States (1849–1850); landscape with battle on the other side, hero of the Mexican war (1846–1848); commemorates Taylor's triumph in the 1847 battle of Buena Vista.

Painting, General Zachary Taylor in command at the Battle of Buena Vista, in Mexico, 1847, oil on canvas, by William Henry Powell (1823–79).

U.S. naval units and American settlers led by Captain John C. Frémont. General Zachary Taylor's forces attacked Monterrey, which surrendered in September, securing northeastern Mexico.

New Mexico did not prove easy for U.S. forces. In January 1847, in Taos, northwest of Santa Fe, Hispanics and Indians led by Pablo Montoya and Tomas Romero rebelled against the Americans and killed government officials. In what became known as the Taos Revolt, some 500 Mexican and Indian insurgents laid siege to a mill in Arroyo Hondo, outside Taos. The U.S. command swiftly suppressed the revolt, and the insurgents retreated to a thick-walled church in Taos Pueblo. With cannon, the U.S. Army killed 150 and captured 400 rebels. After many arrests, approximately 28 insurgent leaders were hanged in the Taos plaza, ending bloody resistance to U.S. occupation.

Before the end of 1846, American forces also established dominion over California. Because losses on the periphery had not broken Mexican resistance, General Winfield Scott carried the war to the enemy's heartland. He led 14,000 men toward Mexico City in what proved to be the war's decisive campaign. Outnumbered and threatened by yellow fever, Scott's men repeatedly discovered flanking routes around their foes. After several hard-fought battles, U.S. troops captured the Mexican capital.

Treaty of Guadalupe Hidalgo

Representatives of both countries signed the **Treaty of Guadalupe Hidalgo** in February 1848. The United States gained California and New Mexico (including present-day Nevada, Utah, and Arizona, and parts of Colorado and Wyoming), and recognition of the Rio Grande as Texas's southern boundary. The American government agreed to settle the claims of its citizens (mostly Texans) against Mexico ($3.2 million) and to pay Mexico a mere $15 million.

Treaty of Guadalupe Hidalgo: Agreement that ended the U.S. War with Mexico in which Mexico ceded vast amounts of its territory and was forced to recognize the Rio Grande as Texas's southern boundary.

The costs of the war included the deaths of thirteen thousand Americans (mostly from disease) and fifty thousand Mexicans. Enmity between Mexico and the United States endured into the twentieth century. Domestically, southwesterners and southern planters were enthusiastic about the war; New Englanders opposed it. Whigs in Congress charged that Polk, a Democrat, had "provoked" an unnecessary war and "usurped the power of Congress." Abolitionists and a minority of antislavery Whigs charged that the war was a plot to extend slavery.

"Slave Power Conspiracy"

These charges fed northern fear of the "Slave Power." Abolitionists had long warned of a slaveholding oligarchy that would dominate the nation through its hold on federal power. Slaveholders gained control of the South by suppressing dissent. They forced the gag rule on Congress in 1836. To many white northerners, even those who saw nothing wrong with slavery, this battle over free speech made the idea of a Slave Power credible. The War with Mexico deepened such fears, as antislavery northerners wondered if it had been launched to acquire vast, new slave territory.

The war's impact on southern opinion was dramatic. Initially, some southern Whigs attacked the Democratic president for causing the war, and few southern congressmen saw slavery as the paramount issue. Many whites, North and South, feared that large land seizures would bring nonwhite Mexicans into the United States and upset the racial order. An Indiana politician did not want "any mixed races in our Union, nor men of any color except white, unless they be slaves." Despite their racism and exaggerations, many statesmen soon saw other potential outcomes of a war of conquest in the Southwest.

Wilmot Proviso

In August 1846, David Wilmot, a Pennsylvania Democrat, proposed an amendment, or proviso, to a military appropriations bill: that "neither slavery nor involuntary servitude shall ever exist" in any territory gained from Mexico. Although the proviso never passed, its repeated introduction by northerners transformed the debate over slavery's expansion. Southerners intensified efforts to protect slavery's future. Alexander H. Stephens declared that slavery was based on the Bible, and John C. Calhoun insisted that slaveholders had a constitutional right to take their slaves (as property) anywhere in the territories.

This position, often called "state sovereignty," was a radical reversal of history. In 1787, the Confederation Congress discouraged if not fully excluded slavery from the Northwest Territory. Article IV of the U.S. Constitution authorized Congress to make "all needful rules and regulations" for the territories, and the Missouri Compromise barred slavery from most of the Louisiana Purchase. Now, southern leaders demanded future guarantees for slavery.

Wilmot Proviso: A proposed amendment that would have prohibited slavery in territories acquired from Mexico; though it never passed, it transformed the national debate over slavery.

In the North, the **Wilmot Proviso** became a rallying cry for abolitionists. While fourteen northern states endorsed it, not all of its supporters were abolitionists. David Wilmot was neither an abolitionist nor an antislavery Whig. Instead, his goal was to defend "the rights of white freemen" and to obtain California "for free white labor."

As Wilmot demonstrated, it was possible, however, to be a racist and an opponent of slavery. The vast majority of white northerners were not active abolitionists, and their desire to keep the West slavery-free was often matched by their desire to keep blacks from settling there. At stake was the free individual's access to social mobility by acquiring land in the West. Slave labor, thousands of northerners believed, would degrade the toil of free men and render them unemployable. The West therefore must not include slavery.

The Election of 1848 and Popular Sovereignty

The divisive slavery question infested national politics. After Polk renounced a second term as president, the Democrats nominated Senator Lewis Cass of Michigan for president and General William Butler of Kentucky for vice president. Cass, a party loyalist who had served in Jackson's cabinet, devised in 1847 the idea of "popular sovereignty"—letting residents in the western territories decide the slavery question for themselves. His party's platform declared that Congress lacked the power to interfere with slavery's expansion. The Whigs nominated General Zachary Taylor, a southern slaveholder and war hero; New York Congressman Millard Fillmore was his running mate. The Whig convention similarly denied that Congress had power over slavery in the territories.

Free-Soil Party: A political party that sprung from and represented the movement to prevent slavery in the western territories.

Many southern Democrats distrusted Cass and voted for Taylor because he was a slaveholder. New York Democrats committed to the Wilmot Proviso nominated former president Martin Van Buren. Antislavery Whigs and former Liberty Party supporters joined them to organize the **Free-Soil Party**, with Van Buren as its candidate (see Table 14.1). This party, which sought to restrict slavery expansion to western territories and whose slogan was "Free Soil, Free Speech, Free Labor, and Free Men," won almost 300,000 northern votes. Taylor polled 1.4 million votes to Cass's 1.2 million and won the White House, but the results were ominous.

TABLE 14.1 New Political Parties

Party	Period of Influence	Area of Influence	Outcome
Liberty Party	1839–1848	North	Merged with other antislavery groups to form Free-Soil Party
Free-Soil Party	1848–1854	North	Merged with Republican Party
Know-Nothings (American Party)	1853–1856	Nationwide	Disappeared, freeing most to join Republican Party
Republican Party	1854–present	North (later nationwide)	Became rival of Democratic Party and won presidency in 1860

Religious denominations, too, severed into northern and southern wings. As the 1850s dawned, the legacies of the War with Mexico and the conflicts of 1848 threatened the nature of the Union.

1850: Compromise or Armistice?

More than eighty thousand Americans flooded into California during the 1849 gold rush. With Congress unable to agree on a governing formula for the territories, President Taylor urged settlers to apply for admission to the Union. They did, proposing a state constitution that banned slavery. Because California's admission as a free state would upset the sectional balance in the Senate (the ratio of slave to free states was fifteen to fifteen), southern politicians wanted to postpone admission and make California a slave territory, or at least extend the Missouri Compromise to the Pacific.

> What were the two troubling issues inherent in the Compromise of 1850?

Debate over Slavery in the Territories Twice before—in 1820 and 1833—Henry Clay, the Whig leader and "Great Pacificator," had shaped sectional compromise; now he struggled one last time to preserve the nation. In the winter of 1850, Clay and Senator Stephen A. Douglas of Illinois steered their compromise package through debate and amendment.

The problems were numerous. Would California become a free state? How should the territory acquired from Mexico be organized? Texas, which allowed slavery, claimed areas extending as far west as Santa Fe. Southerners complained that fugitive slaves were not returned as the Constitution required, and northerners objected to slave auctions in the nation's capital. Eight years earlier, in *Prigg v. Pennsylvania* (1842), the Supreme Court ruled that enforcement of the Constitution's fugitive slave clause was a federal obligation. Most troublesome, however, was the status of slavery in the territories.

Clay and Douglas discovered in the idea of popular sovereignty what one historian called a "charm of ambiguity." Ultimately, Congress would have to approve statehood for a territory, but "in the meantime," said Lewis Cass, it should allow the people living there "to regulate their own concerns in their own way."

To avoid dissension within their party, northern and southern Democrats explained Cass's statement to constituents in incompatible ways. Southerners claimed that neither Congress nor a territorial legislature could bar slavery. Northerners, however, insisted that Americans living in a territory were entitled to local self-government and thus could outlaw slavery.

Link to the full text of Daniel Webster's March 7, 1850, speech.

The cause of compromise gained a powerful supporter when Senator Daniel Webster committed his prestige and eloquence to Clay's bill. Abandoning his earlier support for the Wilmot Proviso, Webster urged northerners not to "taunt or reproach" the South with antislavery measures. He warned southern firebrands that disunion inevitably would cause violence and destruction. Many of Webster's former abolitionist friends in New England condemned his compromise efforts and accused him of going over to the "devil."

Only three days earlier, Calhoun was carried from his sickbed to oppose the compromise. With Calhoun unable to speak, Senator James Mason of Virginia read his address, which predicted disunion if southern demands went unanswered, frightening some into supporting compromise.

With Clay sick, Douglas reintroduced the compromise measures one at a time. Douglas realized that because southerners favored some bills and northerners the rest, a small majority for compromise could be achieved on each distinct issue. The strategy worked, and the Compromise of 1850 became law.

Compromise of 1850   The compromise had five essential measures:

1. California became a free state.
2. The Texas boundary was set at its present limits (see Map 14.1), and the United States paid Texas $10 million for the loss of New Mexico Territory.
3. The territories of New Mexico and Utah were organized on a basis of popular sovereignty.
4. The fugitive slave law was strengthened.
5. The slave trade was abolished in the District of Columbia.

At best, the Compromise of 1850 was an artful evasion. Douglas found a way to pass the five proposals without convincing northerners and southerners to agree on fundamentals. The compromise bought time, but it did not resolve territorial questions.

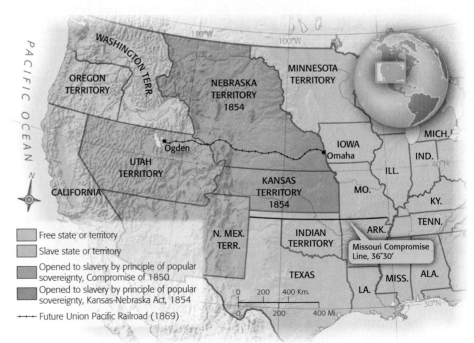

MAP 14.1

The Kansas-Nebraska Act and Slavery Expansion, 1854

The vote on the Kansas-Nebraska Act in the House of Representatives (see also Table 14.2 on page 354) demonstrates the sectionalization of American politics due to the slavery question.

Source: Copyright © Cengage Learning

Furthermore, the compromise had two flaws. The first concerned the ambiguity of popular sovereignty. Southerners insisted on no prohibition of slavery during the territorial stage, and northerners declared that settlers could bar slavery whenever they wished. The compromise allowed for the appeal of a territorial legislature's action to the Supreme Court.

Fugitive Slave Act

The second flaw lay in the **Fugitive Slave Act**, which gave new—and controversial—protection to slavery. The law empowered slaveowners to go into state court to present evidence that a slave had escaped. The resulting transcript and a description of the fugitive would serve as legal proof of slave status, even in free states and territories. Court officials adjudicated the identity of the person described, not whether he or she was indeed a slave. The law made it a felony to harbor fugitives and stated that northerners could be summoned to hunt fugitives. The fees paid favored slaveholders: $10 if the alleged fugitive was returned; $5 if not returned.

Abolitionist newspapers attacked the Fugitive Slave Act as a violation of American rights. Why were alleged fugitives denied a trial by jury? Why would northerners be arrested if they harbored runaways? These questions convinced some northerners that free blacks were vulnerable to kidnapping and enslavement. An estimated twenty thousand blacks fled to Canada after the Fugitive Slave Act.

Between 1850 and 1854, protests and violent resistance to slave catchers occurred in northern towns. Sometimes a captured fugitive was broken out of jail by abolitionists, as in the 1851 Boston case of Shadrach Minkins, who was spirited by wagons and trains to Montreal, Canada. That same year, the small black community in Lancaster County, Pennsylvania, defended four escaped slaves from a federal posse charged with reenslaving them. At this "Christiana riot," fugitives killed Edward Gorsuch, the Maryland slaveowner who sought the return of his

Fugitive Slave Act: Part of the Compromise of 1850; controversial measure that gave additional powers to slaveowners in recapturing slaves and angered northerners by requiring them to hunt so-called fugitives.

Link to Frederick Douglass's "What to the Slave is the Fourth of July" speech given at the Rochester Ladies' Anti-Slavery Society in 1852.

Courtesy Amherst College Archives and Special Collections

Eliza crossing the Ohio River, leaping on icebergs, is perhaps the most famous and oft-repeated image from *Uncle Tom's Cabin*. The drawing is from a series by twentieth century Mexican artist Miguel Covarrubias.

"property." A headline reporting the Christiana affair screamed, "Civil War, The First Blow Struck!"

Many abolitionists became convinced that violence was a legitimate means of opposing slavery. In an 1854 column, Frederick Douglass said that the only way to make the fugitive slave law "dead letter" was to make a "few dead slave catchers."

Uncle Tom's Cabin

Uncle Tom's Cabin: Harriet Beecher Stowe's best-selling 1852 novel that aroused widespread northern sympathy for slaves (especially fugitives) and widespread southern anger.

Meanwhile, Harriet Beecher Stowe, whose New England family produced prominent ministers, wrote a novel portraying the humanity and suffering of slaves. Her story, **Uncle Tom's Cabin**, was serialized in 1851 and published as a book in 1852. It touched millions of northerners with its tale of a mother's dash to freedom with her child across the frozen Ohio River. Stowe also portrayed slavery's evil effects on slaveholders, indicting the institution more harshly than southerners caught in its web. Moreover, Stowe exposed northern racism and complicity with slavery by making the worst slaveholder a man of New England birth.

By mid-1853, the book sold over 1 million copies. Its popularity alarmed southern whites, who saw their way of life threatened. Behind southern claims about territorial rights lay the fear that, if nearby areas outlawed slavery, they would become bases from which abolitionism would spread into slave states.

Fifteen to twenty proslavery novels were published in the 1850s as responses to *Uncle Tom's Cabin*. Most paled in comparison to Stowe's masterpiece, but southern writers defended their system as more humane than wage labor. In awkward stories, such as J. W. Page's *Uncle Robin in His Cabin and Tom Without One in Boston,* slaves were induced to run away by visiting abolitionists, and then starved in northern cities.

The Underground Railroad

Underground Railroad: A loosely organized process by which fugitive slaves, often of their own volition, escaped to freedom in the northern United States and Canada.

By the 1850s, slaveholders were especially disturbed by the **Underground Railroad**, a loose, illegal network, spiriting runaways to freedom. Thousands of slaves escaped by these often disorganized routes, but largely through their own wits and courage with assistance from blacks in northern cities. Lewis Hayden in Boston, David Ruggles in New York, William Still in Philadelphia, and Jacob Gibbs in Washington, D.C., were among the many black abolitionists who managed fugitive slave escapes.

Harriet Tubman, herself an escapee in 1848, returned to her native Maryland and to Virginia at least a dozen times, and secretly helped as many as three hundred slaves, some her family members, to freedom. Outraged Maryland planters offered a $40,000 reward for her capture.

In Ohio, white abolitionists, often Quakers, joined with blacks to help slaves cross the river to freedom. The Underground Railroad also had numerous maritime routes, as coastal slaves escaped aboard ships from Virginia, the Carolinas, or New Orleans, and ended up in northern port cities, the Caribbean, or England. Many fugitives from the Lower South and Texas escaped to Mexico, which abolished slavery in 1829. Some joined Seminole communities in Florida, where they fought with them against the U.S. Army in the Seminole Wars of 1835–1842 and 1855–1858.

Slave escapes were a testament to human courage and the will for freedom. They never reached the scale believed by angry slaveholders or claimed by northern towns and local historical societies today. But, in reality and legend, the Underground Railroad applied pressure to the institution of slavery and gave slaves hope.

Election of 1852 and the Collapse of Compromise

The 1852 election gave southern leaders hope that slavery would be secure under a new president. Franklin Pierce, a New Hampshire Democrat, won easily over the Whig presidential nominee, General Winfield Scott. Pierce firmly supported the Compromise of 1850, where Scott's views on the compromise were unknown.

President Pierce's embrace of the compromise appalled many northerners. His enforcement of the Fugitive Slave Act provoked fear especially in the case of the fugitive slave Anthony Burns, who fled Virginia in 1852. In Boston, thinking he was safe, Burns began a new life. But in 1854, federal marshals placed him under guard in Boston's courthouse. An interracial crowd of abolitionists attacked the courthouse, killing a jailer while attempting to free Burns.

Pierce telegraphed local officials to "incur any expense to insure the execution of the law" and sent troops to Boston. Soldiers marched Burns to Boston harbor, while Burns's supporters draped the streets in black and hung American flags at half-mast. At a cost of $100,000, a single black man was returned to slavery.

This demonstration of federal support for slavery radicalized opinion, even among many conservatives. Juries refused to convict the abolitionists who stormed the Boston courthouse. New England states passed personal liberty laws that blocked federal enforcement and absolved local judges from enforcing the Fugitive Slave Act, effectively nullifying federal authority. What northerners now saw as evidence of a dominating Slave Power, slaveholders saw as legal defense of their rights.

Pierce confronted sectional conflict at every turn. His proposal for a transcontinental railroad derailed when congressmen fought over its location, North or South. An annexation treaty with Hawai'i failed because southern senators would not vote for another free state, and efforts to acquire slaveholding Cuba angered northerners.

Events in the Pacific also triggered debate over how far American expansion should extend. With two orchestrated landings in the Bay of Tokyo, in 1853 and 1854, Commodore Matthew Perry established U.S. intentions to trade with Japan. Offended and intrigued, the Japanese were impressed with Perry's steam-powered warships, the first they had seen. Perry's Treaty of Kanagawa in March 1854 negotiated two ports as coaling stations for American ships, but sought-after trading arrangements were slow in coming.

Back home, another territorial bill threw Congress and the nation into greater turmoil, and the Compromise of 1850 collapsed.

Slavery Expansion and Collapse of the Party System

The new controversy began in a surprising way. Stephen A. Douglas introduced a bill to establish the Kansas and Nebraska Territories. Ambitious for the presidency, Douglas did not view slavery as a fundamental problem and was willing to risk controversy to economically aid his home state of Illinois. A transcontinental railroad would encourage Great Plains settlement and stimulate the Illinois economy, but no company would build a railroad before Congress organized the territories it would cross. Thus, interest in promoting a railroad drove Douglas to introduce a bill that inflamed sectional passions.

> How did the Kansas-Nebraska Act lead to the collapse of existing political parties?

Kansas-Nebraska Act: Effectively repealed the Missouri Compromise and inflamed sectional disputes around the expansion of slavery in the territories. The act left the decision of whether to allow slavery in the new territories of Kansas and Nebraska up to the people residing there (popular sovereignty).

The Kansas-Nebraska Act

The **Kansas-Nebraska Act** exposed conflicting interpretations of popular sovereignty. Douglas's bill left "all questions pertaining to slavery in the Territories...to the people residing therein." Northerners and southerners, however, still disagreed over what territorial settlers could constitutionally do. Moreover, the Kansas and Nebraska Territories lay within the Louisiana Purchase, and the Missouri Compromise prohibited slavery there from latitude 36°30' north to the Canadian border. If popular sovereignty were applied in Kansas and Nebraska, it would mean that the Missouri Compromise was no longer in effect.

Southern congressmen, anxious to establish slaveholders' right to take slaves into any territory, pressed Douglas for an explicit repeal of the 36°30' limitation in exchange for their support. During a carriage ride with Kentucky Senator Archibald Dixon, Douglas conceded: "I will incorporate it in my bill, though I know it will raise a hell of a storm."

Douglas believed that climate and soil conditions would keep slavery out of Kansas and Nebraska. Nevertheless, his bill allowed slavery on land from which it had been prohibited for thirty-four years. Many Free-Soilers and antislavery forces considered this turn of events a betrayal of trust. The bill became law in May 1854 by a vote that demonstrated the dangerous sectionalization of American politics (see Map 14.1 and Table 14.2).

Opposition to the Fugitive Slave Act grew dramatically; between 1855 and 1859, Connecticut, Rhode Island, Massachusetts, Michigan, Maine, Ohio, and Wisconsin passed personal-liberty laws. These laws enraged southerners by providing counsel for alleged fugitives and requiring trial by jury. The Kansas-Nebraska Act had a devastating impact on political parties. The weakened Whig Party broke into northern and southern wings. The Democrats survived, but their support in the North plummeted in the 1854 elections. Northern Democrats lost sixty-six of their ninety-one congressional seats and lost control of all but two free-state legislatures.

Birth of the Republican Party

The beneficiary of northern voters' wrath was a new political party. During debate on the Kansas-Nebraska Act, six congressmen—most prominently, Joshua Giddings, Salmon Chase, and Charles Sumner—published an "Appeal of the Independent Democrats." In it, they attacked Douglas's legislation as a violation of the Missouri Compromise and a "criminal betrayal of precious rights" that would make free

TABLE 14.2   The Vote on the Kansas-Nebraska Act

The vote was 113 to 100 in favor.

	Aye	Nay
Northern Democrats	44	42
Southern Democrats	57	2
Northern Whigs	0	45
Southern Whigs	12	7
Northern Free-Soilers		4

territory a "dreary region of despotism." Their appeal tapped a reservoir of northern concern, cogently expressed by Illinois's Abraham Lincoln.

Although Lincoln did not condemn southerners, he exposed the meaning of the Kansas-Nebraska Act. Lincoln argued that the founders, from love of liberty, banned slavery from the Northwest Territory, kept the word *slavery* out of the Constitution, and treated it as a "cancer" on the republic. Rather than encouraging liberty, the Kansas-Nebraska Act promised to extend slavery. America's future, Lincoln warned, was being mortgaged to slavery.

Thousands of white northerners agreed. During summer and fall 1854, antislavery Whigs and Democrats, Free-Soilers, and reformers throughout the Old Northwest formed the new Republican Party, dedicated to keeping slavery from the territories. Republicans' influence rapidly spread to the East. They won a stunning victory in the 1854 elections, capturing a majority of northern House seats and inspiring roughly a quarter of northern Democrats to desert their party.

For the first time, too, a sectional party gained significant power. The Whigs were gone, and Democrats struggled to maintain national membership. The emergence of the Republican coalition of antislavery interests is the most rapid transformation in party allegiance in American history.

Know-Nothings

Republicans also drew into their coalition a fast-growing nativist movement that called itself the American Party, or **Know-Nothings** (because initial members kept their purposes secret, answering, "I know nothing" to questions). This group exploited fear of foreigners and Catholics. Between 1848 and 1860, nearly 3.5 million immigrants entered the United States—proportionally the heaviest inflow of foreigners in American history. Democrats courted these new citizens, but many native-born Anglo-Saxon Protestants believed that Irish and German Catholics would owe primary allegiance to the pope in Rome.

Know-Nothings: Anti-Catholic and anti-immigrant party that enjoyed brief surge of popularity in the early 1850s.

In 1854, anti-immigrant fears made the Know-Nothings successful in some northern states, particularly Massachusetts, where they elected 11 congressmen, a governor, all state officers, all state senators, and all but 2 of 378 state representatives. The temperance movement also gained ground early in the 1850s with its promises to stamp out the evils associated with liquor and immigrants (a decidedly anti-Irish campaign). The Know-Nothings strove to reinforce Protestant morality and restrict voting and office holding to the native-born. As the Whig Party vanished, the Know-Nothings filled the void. But, like the Whigs, the Know-Nothings could not keep their northern and southern wings together due to the slavery expansion issue. They dissolved after 1856. Instead, Republicans wooed nativists with temperance ordinances and laws postponing suffrage for naturalized citizens (see Table 14.1).

Party Realignment and the Republicans' Appeal

The Whig Party's demise ensured a major realignment of the political system. Immigration, temperance, homestead bills, the tariff, internal improvements were crucial issues for voters during the 1850s. Commercial agriculture was booming in the Ohio–Mississippi–Great Lakes area, but residents desired more canals, roads, and river and harbor improvements. Because credit was scarce, a homestead program—the idea that western land should be free to individuals who would farm and make a home on it—attracted voters. Republicans appealed to those interested in the economic development of the West.

Links to the World

William Walker and Filibustering

Between 1848 and 1861, the United States was at peace with foreign nations. But that did not stop private citizens, sometimes supported by politicians and businessmen, from launching adventurous attempts to take over foreign lands, especially in Mexico, Central America, and the Caribbean. The 1850s was the heyday of "filibustering," defined in this era as private military expeditions to destabilize or conquer foreign lands in the name of Manifest Destiny, commerce, the spread of slavery and white supremacy, or masculine daring.

At least a dozen filibustering schemes emerged in this era of expansion and sectional crises, all violations of a Neutrality Act of 1818. Such laws did not stop some senators, railroad and shipping entrepreneurs, or the self-styled soldier of fortune, William Walker, from seeking the "Southern dream" of a Latin American empire.

They also did not stop several American presidents from attempting to annex Cuba.

Born in Tennessee, Walker studied in Europe in 1848 before returning to New Orleans for a short stint editing a newspaper. He moved to California, practiced law, and courted conflict by fighting at least three duels. After an ill-fated attempt in 1853 to forcibly create an American "colony" in Sonora and the Baja peninsula in Mexico, Walker turned to Nicaragua, where its isthmus was the fastest route to the California gold fields.

With a small army of mercenaries Walker invaded Nicaragua in 1856, seized its government, declared himself president, and reintroduced slavery, which Nicaragua had banned. Defeated by a coalition of Nicaraguans and British in 1857, Walker returned to the United States and launched a fund-raising and speaking campaign on which he was often treated as a romantic hero. Upon his return to Nicaragua, he was arrested by a U.S. Navy squadron, returned to American soil, tried, and acquitted.

In 1860, Walker published an account of his exploits, *War in Nicaragua*. Famous for his swashbuckling character; Walker was regarded by some as a pirate serving the "Slave Power Conspiracy," and by others as the "grey-eyed man of destiny" advancing slavery and American hegemony. On Walker's third return to Central America in 1860, he was arrested and Honduran authorities executed him by firing squad. These filibustering adventures fired the imagination of Manifest Destiny and were small precursors of a larger United States exploitation and conquest of Latin American in the century to follow. Walker's legend, heroic and notorious, lives on today in Central America and in two American movies, *Burn* (1969), starring Marlon Brando, and *Walker* (1987), starring Ed Harris. Filibusters were links to the world that gave the United States a difficult legacy to overcome with its neighbors from Cuba to Hawaii.

Portrait of William Walker, Tennessee-born filibusterer, a self-styled soldier of fortune who attempted to create his own empire in Nicaragua, where he reinstituted slavery. To some, especially Southerners, he was a romantic hero, but to others, especially Northerners and the U.S. government, he was a notorious villain and arch proponent of the worst aspects of Manifest Destiny.

Library of Congress

Partisan ideological appeals became the currency of the realigned political system. As Republicans preached, "Free Soil, Free Labor, Free Men," they conveyed many northerners' self-image. These phrases resonated with traditional ideals of equality, liberty, and opportunity under self-government—the heritage of republicanism. Invoking that heritage also undercut charges that the Republican Party was radical and abolitionist.

The northern economy was booming, and thousands of migrants moved west to establish farms and communities. Midwesterners multiplied their yields using new machines, such as mechanical reapers. Railroads were carrying their crops to urban markets. And industry was making available goods that had recently been unaffordable for most people.

Republican Ideology   The key to progress appeared, to many people, to be free labor—the dignity of work and the incentive of opportunity. Any hard-working virtuous man, it was thought, could improve his condition and achieve economic independence. Republicans argued that the South, with little industry and slave labor, was backward by comparison.

Traditional republicanism hailed the virtuous common man as the nation's backbone. In Abraham Lincoln, a man of humble origins who became a successful lawyer and political leader, Republicans had a symbol of that tradition. They portrayed their party as the guardian of economic opportunity, giving individuals a chance to work, acquire land, and attain success.

At stake in the crises of the 1850s were two competing definitions of "liberty": southern planters' claims of their liberty to own and transport their slaves nationwide, and northern workers' and farmers' claims of their liberty to seek a new start on free land, unimpeded by a system that defined labor as slave and black.

Opposition to the extension of slavery helped create the Republican Party, but members broadened their appeal by adopting other causes. Their coalition ideology consisted of many elements: resentment of southern political power, devotion to unionism, antislavery based on free-labor arguments, moral revulsion to slavery, and racial prejudice. As *New York Tribune* editor Horace Greeley wrote in 1860, "an Anti-Slavery man per se cannot be elected." But, "a Tariff, River-and-Harbor, Pacific Railroad, Free Homestead man, may succeed although he is Anti-Slavery."

Southern Democrats   In the South, the disintegration of the Whig Party had left many southerners at loose ends politically, including wealthy planters, smaller slaveholders, and urban businessmen. In the tense atmosphere of sectional crisis, southerners were susceptible to strong states' rights positions and the defense of slavery. Hence, most formerly Whig slaveholders became Democrats.

Since Andrew Jackson's day, however, nonslaveholding yeomen had been the heart of the Democratic Party. Democratic politicians, though often slaveowners, lauded the common man and claimed to advance his interests. According to the southern version of republicanism, white citizens in a slave society enjoyed liberty and equality because black people were enslaved. As Jefferson Davis explained in 1851, in the South, slavery elevated every white person to "stand upon the broad level of equality with the rich man." To retain support from ordinary whites, southern Democrats appealed to racism, asking, "Shall negroes govern white men, or white men govern negroes?"

Racial fears and traditional political loyalties kept the political alliance between yeoman farmers and planters intact through the 1850s. Across class lines, white southerners united against what they perceived as the Republican Party's capacity to cause slave unrest. In the South, no viable party emerged to replace the Whigs, and political realignment sharpened sectional identity.

Northern and southern political leaders used race in their arguments about opportunity. The *Montgomery* (Alabama) *Mail* warned southern whites in 1860 that the Republicans intended "to free the negroes" and force amalgamation between them and the children of the poor men of the South. Republicans warned northern workers that, if slavery entered the territories, the great reservoir of opportunity for ordinary citizens would be poisoned.

Bleeding Kansas

The Kansas-Nebraska Act spawned violence as land-hungry partisans clashed in Kansas Territory. Abolitionists and religious groups sent armed Free-Soil settlers; southerners sent reinforcements to establish slavery and prevent "northern hordes" from stealing Kansas. Conflicts led to bloodshed, and soon the nation was talking about "Bleeding Kansas."

Politics in the territory resembled war more than democracy. During 1855 elections for a territorial legislature, thousands of proslavery Missourians—known as Border Ruffians—invaded the polls and ran up a fraudulent majority for pro-slavery candidates. They murdered and intimidated free state settlers. The resulting legislature legalized slavery. Free-Soilers responded with an unauthorized convention at which they created their own government and constitution.

In May, a proslavery posse sent to arrest the Free-Soil leaders sacked the town of Lawrence, Kansas, killing several people and destroying a hotel. In revenge, the radical abolitionist John Brown and his followers murdered five proslavery settlers along Pottawatomie Creek. The victims' heads and limbs were hacked by heavy broadswords. Brown did not wield a sword, but he fired a fatal shot into the head of one foe. Soon, armed bands of guerrillas battled over land claims and slavery.

Violence reached the U.S. Senate in May 1856, when Charles Sumner of Massachusetts denounced "the Crime against Kansas." Radically opposed to slavery, Sumner assailed the president, the South, and Senator Andrew P. Butler of South Carolina. Butler's cousin, Representative Preston Brooks, approached Sumner, raised his cane in defense of his kin's honor, and beat Sumner on the head. The senator collapsed.

Shocked northerners recoiled from another seeming case of wanton southern violence and assault on free speech. William Cullen Bryant, editor of the *New York Evening Post,* asked, "Has it come to this, that we must speak with bated breath in the presence of our southern masters?" Popular opinion in Massachusetts supported Sumner; South Carolina voters reelected Brooks.

Election of 1856

The election of 1856 showed extreme polarization. For their nominee, Democrats chose James Buchanan of Pennsylvania, who as ambassador to Britain for four years, was uninvolved in territorial controversies. Superior party organization helped Buchanan win 1.8 million votes and the election, but he owed his victory to southern support. Hence, he was dubbed "a northern man with southern principles."

Eleven of sixteen free states voted against Buchanan, and Democrats did not regain those states for decades. The Republican candidate, John C. Frémont, won those eleven free states and 1.3 million votes; Republicans became the dominant party in the North after only two years of existence. The coming battle would pit a sectional Republican Party against an increasingly divided Democratic Party, with voter turnouts as high as 75 to 80 percent in many states.

Slavery and the Nation's Future

For years, Congress tried to settle the issue. In 1857, the Supreme Court attempted to definitively silence controversy.

> How did the issue of slavery—and the *Dred Scott* decision—further divide the nation?

Dred Scott Case

A Missouri slave named Dred Scott and his wife, Harriet Robinson Scott, sued for their freedom. Scott argued that his former owner, an army surgeon, had taken him into and kept him for years in Illinois, a free state, and to Fort Snelling in the Minnesota Territory, from which slavery was barred by the Missouri Compromise. Scott first won and then lost his case on appeal in the Supreme Court.

Harriet and Dred Scott were legally married at Fort Snelling in 1836 when Dred was forty and Harriet seventeen. She had lived as a slave on free soil for about five years and had four children, also born on free soil: two sons who died in infancy and two daughters, Eliza and Lizzie, who lived. The quest for "freedom papers" through a lawsuit—begun in 1846 as two separate cases, one in his name and one in hers—possibly came partly from Harriet's desire to protect her teenage daughters from potential sale and sexual abuse. Indeed, her legal case for freedom may have been stronger than Dred's, but lawyers subsumed her case into his during the long appeal process.

Link to excerpts from Chief Justice Roger B. Taney's ruling in the *Dred Scott* case.

After hesitation, the Supreme Court agreed to hear *Dred Scott v. Sanford*. Two northern justices indicated that they would dissent from the assigned opinion and argue for Scott's freedom and the constitutionality of the Missouri Compromise. Their decision emboldened southerners on the Court, who were eager to declare the 1820 geographical restriction on slavery unconstitutional. Several justices felt they should resolve sectional strife once and for all.

In March 1857, Chief Justice Roger B. Taney of Maryland delivered the majority opinion of a divided Court (the vote was 7 to 2). Taney declared that Scott was not a citizen of the United States or Missouri; that residence in free territory did not make Scott free; and that Congress had no power to bar slavery from any territory. The decision not only overturned a thirty-seven year-old sectional compromise, it also invalidated the Wilmot Proviso and popular sovereignty.

The Slave Power seemed to have won a major constitutional victory. African Americans were especially dismayed, for Taney's decision asserted that the founders had never intended for blacks to be citizens. Taney was mistaken, however. African Americans had been citizens in several original states and had voted.

Nevertheless, the ruling seemed to shut the door permanently on black hopes for justice. In northern

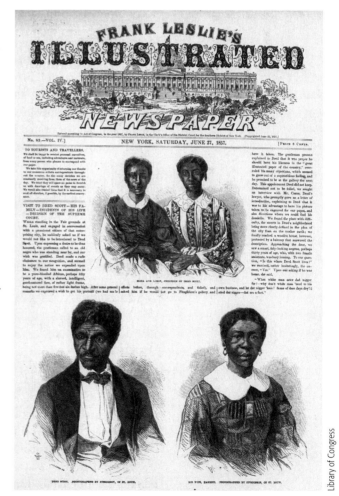

Frank Leslie's *Illustrated Newspaper*, June 27, 1857. Dred Scott and his wife, Harriet, below, and their two children, Eliza and Lizzie, above. Such dignified pictures and informative articles provided Americans broadly with images of the otherwise mysterious Dred Scott and his family in the landmark Supreme Court case.

Library of Congress

black communities, rage and despair prevailed. Many fugitive slaves sought refuge in Canada; others considered the Caribbean or Africa. One black abolitionist said that the **Dred Scott decision** made slavery "the supreme law of the land." In this state of social dislocation and fear, blacks contemplated whether they had any future in the United States.

Northern whites who rejected the decision were suspicious of the circumstances that produced it. Five of the nine justices were southerners; three northern justices dissented or refused to concur in parts of the decision. The only northerner who supported Taney's opinion, Justice Robert Grier of Pennsylvania, was close to President Buchanan. In fact, Buchanan secretly applied improper but effective influence on him.

The decision seemed to confirm every charge against the aggressive Slave Power. The *Cincinnati Freeman* asked, "What security have the Germans and the Irish that their children will not, within a hundred years, be reduced to slavery in this land of their adoption?"

Dred Scott decision: Controversial 1857 Supreme Court decision that stated that slaves were not U.S. citizens and had no legal right to sue in federal court. It also deemed the Missouri Compromise unconstitutional because Congress lacked the authority to ban slavery in the territories.

Abraham Lincoln and the Slave Power

Republican politicians used these fears to strengthen their antislavery coalition. Abraham Lincoln declared as early as 1854 that the nation wanted the territories reserved as "homes of free white people. This they cannot be, to any considerable extent, if slavery shall be planted within them."

More important, Lincoln warned of slavery's increasing control over the nation. While the founders recognized slavery's existence, the public, Lincoln argued in the "House Divided" speech of 1858, believed that slavery would die naturally or by legislation. The next step in the unfolding Slave Power conspiracy, Lincoln alleged, would be a Supreme Court decision "declaring that the Constitution does not permit a State to exclude slavery from its limits." Indeed, lawsuits soon challenged state laws that freed slaves brought within their borders.

By endorsing the South's doctrine of state sovereignty, the Court had effectively declared that the Republican Party's central position—no extension of slavery—was unconstitutional. Republicans could only repudiate the decision, appealing to a "higher law," or hope to change the personnel of the Court. They did both and gained politically as fear of the Slave Power grew.

The Lecompton Constitution and Disharmony Among Democrats

Northern voters were alarmed by the prospect that the territories would be opened to slavery. To retain their support, northern Democrats like Stephen Douglas had to reassure these voters. Yet, given his presidential ambitions, Douglas could not alienate southern Democrats.

Douglas chose to stand by popular sovereignty, even if the result angered southerners. In 1857, Kansans voted on a proslavery constitution drafted at Lecompton. It was defeated by more than ten thousand votes in a referendum boycotted by proslavery voters. Kansans did not want slavery, yet President Buchanan tried to force the Lecompton Constitution through Congress to hastily organize the territory.

Never had the Slave Power's influence over the government seemed more blatant; the Buchanan administration and southerners demanded a proslavery outcome, contrary to majority will in Kansas. Douglas threw his weight against the Lecompton Constitution, infuriating southern Democrats like Senator Albert G. Brown of Mississippi. Increasingly, many southerners believed that their sectional rights and slavery would be safe only in a separate nation. And northern Democrats, led by Douglas, found it harder to support the territorial protection for slavery that southern Democrats insisted was a constitutional right.

Disunion

What were the issues leading to secession and the dissolution of the Union?

But in the late 1850s, most Americans were not entirely caught up in the slavery crisis. They were preoccupied with personal affairs, especially the economic panic that began in spring 1857. In the Midwest, clerks, mechanics, domestics, railroad hands, and lumber camp workers lost jobs by the thousands. Bankers did not know what to do about a weak credit system caused by frenzied western land speculation earlier in the decade. In parts of the South, such as Georgia, the panic intensified class divisions between upcountry yeomen and coastal slaveholding planters. Farmers blamed the tight money policies of Georgia's budding commercial banking system on wealthy planters who controlled the state's Democratic Party.

The panic was caused by several shortcomings of the unregulated American banking system, by speculation in western lands and railroads, and by a weak and overburdened credit system. By 1858, Philadelphia had 40,000 unemployed workers and New York City, nearly 100,000. Fear of bread riots and class warfare gripped many northern cities. Blame for the crisis became sectionalized, as southerners saw their system justified by the temporary collapse of industrial prosperity and northerners feared further incursions of the Slave Power on an insecure future.

John Brown's Raid on Harpers Ferry

Born in Connecticut in 1800, John Brown was raised by staunchly religious antislavery parents. Between 1820 and 1855, he engaged in some twenty business ventures, nearly all of them failures. In his abolitionism, Brown relied on an Old Testament conception of justice—"an eye for an eye"—and he believed that slavery was an "unjustifiable" state of war conducted by one group against another. He also believed that violence in a righteous cause was a holy act. To Brown, the destruction of slavery in America required revolutionary ideology and revolutionary acts.

On October 16, 1859, Brown led a small band of eighteen whites and blacks in an attack on the federal arsenal at Harpers Ferry, Virginia. Hoping to trigger a slave rebellion, Brown failed and was quickly captured. In a celebrated trial in November and a widely publicized execution in December in Charles Town, Virginia, Brown became one of the most enduring martyrs, as well as villains, of American history.

White southerners outrage intensified when they learned that Brown received financial backing from several prominent abolitionists and that such northern intellectuals as Ralph Waldo Emerson and Henry David Thoreau praised Brown as a holy warrior. The South interpreted Brown's attack at Harpers Ferry as an act of terrorism and the fulfillment of their dread of "abolition emissaries" who would infiltrate the region to incite slave rebellion.

When Brown went to the gallows, he handed a note to his jailer with the famous prediction "I John Brown am now quite certain that the crimes of this guilty land will never be purged away, but with blood."

Election of 1860

Many Americans believed that the election of 1860 would decide the Union's fate. Until then, the Democratic Party was the only party that was truly national in scope. But, fatefully, at its 1860 convention in Charleston, South Carolina, the Democratic Party split.

Stephen Douglas wanted his party's presidential nomination, but he feared alienating northern voters by accepting the southern position on the territories. Southern Democrats, however, insisted on recognition of their rights as defined by the *Dred Scott* decision. When Douglas obtained a majority for his version of the

TABLE 14.3   Presidential Votes in 1860 (by State)

Lincoln (Republican)*	Carried all northern states and all electoral votes except three in New Jersey
Breckinridge (Southern Democrat)	Carried all slave states except Virginia, Kentucky, Tennessee, Missouri
Bell (Constitutional Union)	Carried Virginia, Kentucky, Tennessee
Douglas (Northern Democrat)	Carried only Missouri

*Lincoln received only twenty-six thousand votes in the entire South and was not even on the ballot in ten slave states. Breckinridge was not on the ballot in three northern states.

platform, delegates from the Deep South walked out. Compromise efforts failed, and the Democrats presented two nominees: Douglas for the northern wing, and Vice President John C. Breckinridge of Kentucky for the southern.

Republicans nominated Abraham Lincoln, a reflection of the Midwest's growing power. Lincoln was perceived as more moderate on slavery than the early front runner, Senator William H. Seward of New York. A Constitutional Union Party nominated John Bell of Tennessee.

Bell's only issue in the ensuing campaign was preserving the Union. Douglas sought to unite his northern and southern supporters, while Breckinridge backed away from the appearance of extremism, and his supporters in several states stressed his unionism. Although Lincoln and the Republicans denied any intent to interfere with slavery where it existed, they stood firm against its extension into the territories.

The 1860 election was sectional in character, and the only one in American history in which the losers refused to accept the result. Lincoln won, but Douglas, Breckinridge, and Bell together received a majority of the votes. Douglas had broad-based support but won few states. Breckinridge carried nine southern states in the Deep South. Bell won pluralities in Virginia, Kentucky, and Tennessee. Lincoln prevailed in the North, but in the four slave states that remained loyal to the Union (Missouri, Kentucky, Maryland, and Delaware—the border states) he gained only a plurality (see Table 14.3. Lincoln's victory was won in the electoral college. He polled only 40 percent of the total vote and was not on the ballot in ten slave states.

Opposition to slavery's extension was the core issue for Lincoln and the Republican Party. Moreover, northern abolitionists and Free-Soil supporters held them to it. Meanwhile, in the South, proslavery advocates and secessionists whipped up public opinion and demanded that state conventions assemble to consider secession.

Lincoln did not soften his party's position on the territories. Although many conservative Republicans—eastern businessmen and former Whigs who did not feel strongly about slavery—hoped for a compromise, the original and most committed Republicans—old Free-Soilers and antislavery Whigs—held firm on slavery expansion.

In winter 1860–1861, Senator John J. Crittenden of Kentucky offered a late-hour compromise. Hoping to avert disunion, Crittenden proposed that the two sections divide the territories between them at the Missouri Compromise line, 36°30'. When Lincoln ruled out concessions on the territorial issue, Crittenden's peacemaking effort collapsed.

Secession and the Confederate States of America

Meanwhile, on December 20, 1860, South Carolina passed an ordinance of secession. Strategists concentrated on the most extreme proslavery state, hoping that South Carolina's move would induce other states to follow toward disunion.

No longer was secession unthinkable. Secessionists now argued that other states should follow suit and that those favoring compromise could make a better deal outside the Union than in it.

Southern extremists called separate state conventions and passed secession ordinances in Mississippi, Florida, Alabama, Georgia, Louisiana, and Texas. By February 1861, these states joined South Carolina to form a new government in Montgomery, Alabama: the Confederate States of America. The delegates at Montgomery chose Jefferson Davis of Mississippi as their president, and the Confederacy began to function independently of the United States.

This apparent unanimity of action was deceiving. Many southerners—perhaps as much as 40 percent even in the deep South—opposed immediate secession. In some state conventions the secession vote was close, decided by overrepresentation of plantation districts. Four Upper South states—Virginia, North Carolina, Tennessee, and Arkansas—rejected secession and did not join the Confederacy until after fighting began. In border states, popular sentiment was divided; minorities in Kentucky and Missouri tried to secede, but these slave states ultimately came under Union control, along with Maryland and Delaware (see Map 14.2).

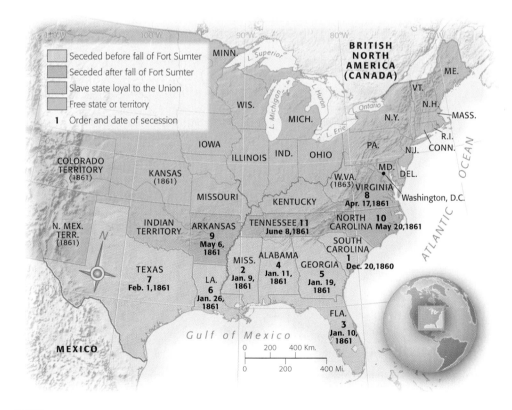

MAP 14.2

The Divided Nation—Slave and Free Areas, 1861

After fighting began, the Upper South joined the Deep South in the Confederacy. How does the nation's pattern of division correspond to the distribution of slavery and the percentage of blacks in the population?

Source: Copyright © Cengage Learning

Secession posed new and troubling issues for southerners. Analysis of election returns from 1860 and 1861 indicates that slaveholders and nonslaveholders were beginning to part company politically. Slaveholding counties strongly supported secession. But nonslaveholding areas proved less willing to support secession" (see Figure 14.1). With war looming, yeomen were beginning to ask themselves how far they would go to support slavery and slaveowners.

In speeches and writings, secession commissioners from the seven seceded states revealed why the Deep South broke away. Repeatedly they stressed independence as the only way to preserve white racial security and the slave system. Upon "slavery," said the Alabama commissioner, Stephen Hale, to the Kentucky legislature, rested "not only the wealth and prosperity of the southern people." Only secession, Hale contended, could sustain the "heaven-ordained superiority of the white over the black race."

Fort Sumter and Outbreak of War

The dilemma facing President Lincoln on inauguration day in March 1861 was how to maintain the authority of the federal government without provoking war. By holding onto forts in the states that had left the Union, he could assert federal sovereignty while waiting for a restoration. But Jefferson Davis could not claim to lead a sovereign nation if the Confederate ports were under foreign (that is, U.S.) control. The two sides collided in the early morning of April 12, 1861, at **Fort Sumter** in Charleston harbor. A federal garrison there ran low on food, and Lincoln notified the South

Fort Sumter: Federal fort in Charleston, South Carolina, harbor, where first shots of Civil War were fired when the Union attempted to resupply troops.

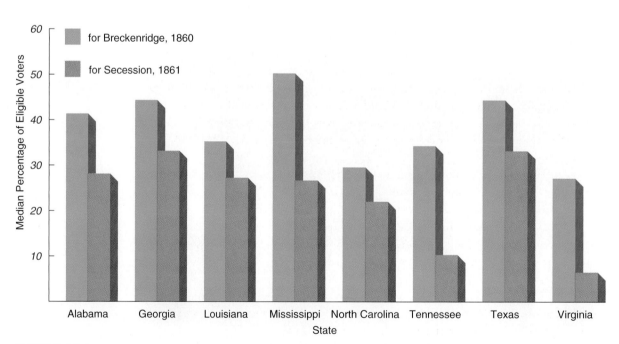

FIGURE 14.1
Voting Returns of Counties with Few Slaveholders, Eight Southern States, 1860 and 1861
This graph depicts voting in counties whose percentage of slaveholders ranked them among the lower half of the counties in their state. How does voters' support for secession in 1861 compare with support for John Breckinridge, the southern Democratic candidate in 1860? Why was their support for secession so weak? At this time, counties with many slaveholders were giving increased support to secession.

Terrorist or Freedom Fighter?

The greatest significance of John Brown's 1859 raid on Harpers Ferry rests in its hold on American memory. Brown has been at once one of the most beloved and loathed figures in American history. In the song that bears his name, "John Brown's Body," a popular marching tune during the Civil War, his "soul goes marching on."

In the wake of his execution, in painting, song, and poetry people constructed a John Brown mythology. Was he a Christ-like figure who died for the nation's sins, who had to commit crimes to expose the nation's larger crime? Or was he a terrorist, who murdered according to his vision of God's will? Brown can be inspiring and disturbing, a warrior saint and a monster. He represents the highest ideals and the most ruthless deeds. He killed for justice and was hanged as a traitor. Over the years, many organizations have adopted John Brown as their justifying symbol, from left-wing students opposing American foreign policy to current anti-abortion groups who target clinics and doctors.

In today's world, terrorism and revolutionary violence are often in the news. Suicide bombers attack buses in Israel; a federal building explodes in Oklahoma City; Al Qaeda operatives blow up trains in Madrid; American embassies are attacked in Africa and Europe; on September 11, 2001, four hijacked passenger airplanes become weapons of death that bring terrorism to American soil as never before; and in Iraq an insurgency resists the American occupation, as a country falls into sectarian civil war between Shi'ites and Sunnis. The story of John Brown's 1859 raid forces us to ask when and how revolutionary violence—for political or spiritual end—is justified. That is his legacy for a people and a nation.

Carolinians that he was sending a supply ship. For the Montgomery government, the alternatives were to attack the fort or acquiesce to Lincoln's authority. The secretary of war ordered local commanders to obtain a surrender or attack the fort. After two days of heavy bombardment, the federal garrison surrendered. Confederates permitted U.S. troops to sail away on unarmed vessels while Charlestonians celebrated. The Civil War—the bloodiest war in America's history—had begun.

Causation

Historians have long debated the causes of the Civil War. Some have interpreted it as a clash of two civilizations on divergent historical trajectories. But the issues dividing Americans in 1861 were fundamental to the republic's future. Republican ideology tended toward abolishing slavery, even though Republicans denied such intention. Southern ideology led to establishing slavery everywhere, though southern leaders, too, denied such motives.

Lincoln put these facts succinctly. In a postelection letter to his colleague, Alexander Stephens of Georgia, soon to be vice president of the Confederacy, Lincoln stated, "You think slavery is right and ought to be expanded; while we think it is wrong and ought to be restricted. That I suppose is the rub."

Without slavery, there would have been no war. Many Americans still believe that the war was about states' rights. But the significance of states' rights is always in the cause in which it is employed. To borrow from Frederick Douglass, it is the meaning within the fight that we must understand.

Summary

The War with Mexico fostered massive land acquisition, which forced an open debate about slavery in the West. The Compromise of 1850 attempted to settle the dispute but only exacerbated sectional tensions, leading to the fateful Kansas-Nebraska Act of 1854, which tore asunder the political party system and gave birth to an antislavery coalition. With Bleeding Kansas and the *Dred Scott* decision by 1857, Americans faced clear and dangerous choices about the future of labor and the meaning of liberty in an expanding society. Finally, by 1859, when radical abolitionist John Brown attacked Harpers Ferry to foment a slave insurrection, southerners and northerners regarded each other in conspiratorial terms. Meanwhile, African Americans, slave and free, feared slave catchers and expected violent resolutions to their dreams of freedom in America.

Throughout the 1840s and 1850s, many leaders worked to avert disunion. Secession dismayed northern editors and voters, and it also plunged some planters into depression. Paul Cameron, the largest slaveowner in North Carolina, confessed to being "very unhappy. I love the Union." Many blacks, however, shared Frederick Douglass's outlook. "The contest must now be decided," he wrote in March 1861, "and decided forever, which of the two, Freedom or Slavery, shall give law to this Republic."

Why had all efforts to prevent war failed? The emotions bound up in attacking and defending slavery's future were too powerful, and the interests it affected too vital for a compromise. Advocates of compromise anticipated it would yet again save the Union in 1860, but their hopes were dashed.

During the 1850s, every southern victory in territorial expansion increased fear of the Slave Power, and each new expression of Free-Soil sentiment prompted slaveholders to harden their demands. In the profoundest sense, slavery was the root of the war. As a people and a nation, Americans reached the most fateful turning point in their history. Resolution would now come from the battlefield.

Chapter Review

The War with Mexico and Its Consequences

Which of Polk's decisions pushed the United States toward war with Mexico?

President Polk wanted to expand America's borders to the Pacific during the 1840s and was not going to take "no" for an answer. He supported annexation of Texas and contested the U.S. border with Mexico, urging Texans to claim territory to the Rio Grande. Mexico had considered the Nueces River its border with Texas. While unsuccessfully attempting to buy California from Mexico, Polk also sent troops to defend the Rio Grande dividing line. There, they were met by Mexican cavalry. After a three week stand-off, the Mexican cavalry ambushed a U.S. unit, killing eleven Americans and taking sixty-three captive. Polk informed Congress that Mexico had crossed what he considered the U.S. boundary (the disputed area), and thereby deceptively claimed that Mexico had incited the conflict that would become the war with Mexico.

1850: Compromise or Armistice?

What were the two troubling issues inherent in the Compromise of 1850?

The Compromise of 1850 attempted to resolve the debate between the North and South over slavery in the territories. In the end, it only furthered controversy. First, it left the definition of popular sovereignty unclear so that southerners could interpret it to mean that a region could not ban slavery during the territorial stage, whereas northerners believed it was up to the people to decide. Second, the Fugitive Slave Act enabled slave owners to present evidence in state courts that a slave had escaped, which would then serve as proof of slave status even in free states and territories—and without investigation into its truth. Abolitionists feared that free blacks would be vulnerable to kidnapping and enslavement. Moreover, the law made it a felony to harbor fugitives and said northerners could be compelled to hunt runaway slaves, which further angered northerners and aggravated regional tensions.

Slavery Expansion and Collapse of the Party System

How did the Kansas-Nebraska Act lead to the collapse of existing political parties?

The Kansas-Nebraska Act, which ultimately eroded the 1850 Compromise, prompted sectional divisions within the political parties that led to each party's breakdown. The act established the Kansas and Nebraska territories, but it applied popular sovereignty to let the territories decide what to do about slavery. Northerners argued that since the territories were within the Louisiana Purchase, they were subject to the Missouri Compromise (which prohibited slavery from latitude 36°30 north to the Canadian border). When the Act was passed in 1854, sectional divisions intensified. The weakened Whig Party split into northern and southern wings. Democrats' support in the North plummeted, costing them most of their congressional seats and control of all but two state legislatures. In late 1854, antislavery Whigs and Democrats, Free-Soilers, and reformers throughout the Old Northwest formed the new Republican Party to keep slavery from the territories.

Slavery and the Nation's Future

How did the issue of slavery—and the *Dred Scott* decision—further divide the nation?

The *Dred Scott* decision validated northern fears of a southern slave power, and inspired new fears about the territories being open to slavery. The Supreme Court was ultimately stacked in favor of the southern position on slavery and its extension into the new territories. Five of the nine justices were southerners. The court's decision in the *Dred Scott* case—that Scott was a slave despite the fact that he lived in the free territory of Missouri and that Congress could not make any laws that barred slavery—invalidated popular sovereignty, the Wilmot Proviso, and the Missouri Compromise. African Americans were devastated by the court's opinion that the nation's founders had never intended them to be citizens, while white northerners saw the decision as proof of the Slave Power's growing reach.

Disunion

What were the issues leading to secession and the dissolution of the Union?

Abraham Lincoln's contested election by his Democratic rivals, along with the inability to reach a compromise on the extension of slavery in the territories, ultimately fueled the movement to secede. Lincoln, the Republican candidate, won by carrying the North and winning in the Electoral College, but the losing side (with its large southern base) refused to accept the result. Southern Democrats distrusted his claims that he would not interfere with slavery where it existed, and disliked his firm rejection of slavery's expansion into the territories. When President Lincoln rejected a compromise that would divide the territories into slave and free at the Missouri Compromise line (36°30'), hopes for preventing secession collapsed. South Carolina passed the first secession ordinance in December 1860; Mississippi, Florida, Alabama, Georgia, Louisiana, and Texas followed. A month after Lincoln's inauguration, these states established their own national capitol in Montgomery, Alabama, dubbing themselves the Confederate States of America.

Suggestions for Further Reading

Edward L. Ayers, *What Caused the Civil War: Reflections on the South and Southern History* (2005)

Richard J. Carwardine, *Lincoln* (2003)

Charles Dew, *Apostles of Disunion: Southern Secession Commissioners and the Causes of the Civil War* (2001)

Nicole Etcheson, *Bleeding Kansas: Contested Liberty in the Civil War Era* (2004)

Don E. Fehrenbacher, *The Slaveholding Republic: An Account of the United States Government's Relations to Slavery* (2001)

Eric Foner, *Free Soil, Free Labor, Free Men: The Ideology of the Republican Party* (1970)

Robert W. Johannsen, *To the Halls of the Montezumas: The Mexican War and the American Imagination* (1985)

Marc Egnal, *Clash of Extremes: The Economic Origins of the Civil War* (2009)

David S. Reynolds, *John Brown, Abolitionist: The Man Who Killed Slavery, Sparked the Civil War, and Seeded Civil Rights* (2005)

Elizabeth R. Varon, *Disunion! The Coming of the American Civil War, 1789–1859* (2008)

Go to the CourseMate website for primary source links, study tools, and review materials for this chapter.
www.cengagebrain.com

Transforming Fire: The Civil War

15

1861–1865

Slave pens were the ugly crossroads of American history. Wallace Turnage, a seventeen-year-old slave from a cotton plantation in Pickens County, Alabama, entered wartime Mobile in December 1862 through the slave traders' yard; he would leave Mobile from that same yard twenty months later.

Turnage was born on a tobacco farm near Snow Hill, North Carolina, in 1846. In mid-1860, as the nation teetered toward disunion, he was sold to a Richmond, Virginia, slave trader named Hector Davis. Turnage worked in Davis's three-story slave jail, organizing daily auctions until he was sold for $1,000 in early 1861 to a cotton planter from Pickens County, Alabama. Frequently whipped, the desperate teenager tried four times over the next two years to escape to Union army lines in Mississippi. He was captured each time and returned to his owner.

Frustrated, his owner sold Turnage for $2,000 at the Mobile slave traders' yard to a wealthy merchant in the port city. During 1864, as Mobile came under siege, its slaves were enlisted to build trenchworks. Turnage did many urban tasks for his new owner's family, including driving their carriage on errands.

In early August, Turnage crashed the carriage on a Mobile street. Furious, his owner took him to the slave pen, hiring the jailer to administer thirty lashes in the "whipping house." Stripped naked, his hands tied, Turnage was hoisted up on a hook. When it was over, his owner instructed Wallace to walk home. Instead, Turnage "took courage," as he wrote in his postwar narrative, and walked southwest through the Confederate encampment. The soldiers mistook the bloodied and tattered black teenager for one among hundreds of slaves who did camp labor.

For the next three weeks, Turnage crawled and waded for twenty-five miles through the snake-infested swamps of the Foul River estuary, down the west edge of Mobile Bay. Nearly starved and narrowly escaping Confederate patrols, Turnage made it to Cedar Point, where he could see Dauphin Island, now occupied by Union forces. Alligators swam nearby, as Turnage hid from

Confederates in a swampy den. He remembered: "It was death to go back and it was death to stay there and freedom was before me."

Then, Turnage noticed an old rowboat that rolled in with the tide. The veteran runaway began to row out into the bay. He suddenly "heard the crash of oars and behold there was eight Yankees in a boat." Turnage jumped into the Union gunboat. For a few moments, he remembered, the oarsmen in blue "were struck with silence" by the frail young black man crouched before them. Turnage looked back at Confederate soldiers on the shore. Then he took his first breaths of freedom.

The Civil War brought astonishing changes to individuals and daily life, North and South. Millions of men were swept into training camps and regiments. Armies numbering in the hundreds of thousands marched over the South, devastating the countryside. Families struggled to survive without men; businesses tried to cope with fewer workers. Women took on extra responsibilities and moved into new work force jobs, with many becoming nurses and hospital workers. But southerners also experienced utter defeat. For most, wealth changed to poverty as countless farms were ruined. Late in the war, many southerners yearned only for an end to inflation, shortages, slave escapes, and the death that visited most families. Southern slaves did not always encounter sympathetic liberators such as those who aided Turnage, fed and clothed him, and took him before a Union general, where the freedman could either join a black regiment or become a white officer's camp servant. Until war's end, Turnage cooked for a Maryland captain.

In the North, farm boys and mechanics would be asked for heretofore unimagined sacrifices. The conflict ensured vast government expenditures and lucrative federal contracts. Businessmen, however, found war profitable. "The battle of Bull Run," predicted an eminent financier in *Harper's Monthly,* "makes the fortune of every man in Wall Street who is not a natural idiot."

Change was most drastic in the South, where secessionists had launched a conservative revolution for their section's independence. Born of states' rights doctrine, the Confederacy had to be transformed into a centralized nation to fight a vast war. Southern whites feared that a peacetime government of Republicans would interfere with slavery and ruin plantation life. Instead, their actions led to a war that turned southern society upside down and imperiled the existence of slavery.

The war created social strains in both North and South. To the alarm of many, the powers of the federal government and of the president increased during the war. Disaffection was strongest, though, in the Confederacy, where poverty and class resentment threatened the South from within. In the North, dissent also flourished, and antiwar sentiment occasionally erupted into violence.

The Civil War forced a social and political revolution regarding race. It compelled leaders and citizens to finally face the question of slavery. And blacks embraced the most fundamental turning point in their experience as Americans.

As you read this chapter, keep the following questions in mind:

* How and why did the Civil War bring social transformations to both South and North?

* How did the war to preserve the Union or for southern independence become the war to free the slaves?

* By 1865, when Americans on all sides searched for the *meaning* of the war they had just fought, what might some of their answers have been?

America Goes to War, 1861–1862

The onset of hostilities sparked patriotic sentiments, speeches, and ceremonies in both North and South. Northern communities raised companies of volunteers eager to save the Union. Southern recruits boasted of whipping the Yankees and returning home before Christmas. Southern women sewed dashing uniforms for men who would soon be lucky to wear drab gray or butternut homespun. Americans went to war in 1861 filled with romantic notions.

What was the impact of the North's naval victories along the southern coast?

First Battle of Bull Run   Through spring 1861, both sides scrambled to organize and train their undisciplined armies. On July 21, 1861, the first battle took place outside Manassas Junction, Virginia, near a stream called **Bull Run**. General Irvin McDowell and thirty thousand Union troops attacked General P. G. T. Beauregard's twenty-two thousand southerners. Federal forces gained ground until they ran into a line of Virginia troops under General Thomas Jackson. Jackson's line held, and the arrival of nine thousand Confederate reinforcements won the day for the South. Union troops fled to Washington.

Bull Run: The location of the first major land battle in the Civil War.

The unexpected rout at Bull Run proved that although the United States enjoyed an advantage in resources, victory would not be easy. Pro-Union feeling was growing in western Virginia, and loyalties were divided in the four border slave states—Missouri, Kentucky, Maryland, and Delaware. But the rest of the Upper South—North Carolina, Virginia, Tennessee, and Arkansas—joined the Confederacy after Fort Sumter. Half a million southerners volunteered to fight—so many that the Confederate government could hardly arm them all. The United States therefore undertook a massive mobilization of troops around Washington, D.C.

Lincoln gave command of the army to General **George B. McClellan**, who proved better at organization and training than fighting. McClellan devoted fall and winter of 1861 to readying a force of a quarter-million men take Richmond, the Confederate capital.

George B. McClellan: Union general very popular with troops who proved better at organization and training than at fighting.

Grand Strategy   While McClellan prepared, the Union began to implement other parts of its strategy, which called for a blockade of southern ports and capture of the Mississippi River. Like a constricting snake, this **"Anaconda plan"** would strangle the Confederacy. The Union Navy had too few ships to patrol 3,550 miles of the southern coastline. Gradually, the navy increased the blockade's effectiveness, though it never stopped southern commerce completely.

Anaconda plan: Called for the Union to blockade southern ports, capture the Mississippi River, and, like a snake, strangle the Confederacy.

Chronology

1861	Battle of Bull Run
	McClellan organizes Union Army
	Union blockade begins
	U.S. Congress passes first confiscation act
	Trent affair
1862	Union captures Fort Henry and Fort Donelson
	U.S. Navy captures New Orleans
	Battle of Shiloh shows the war's destructiveness
	Confederacy enacts conscription
	McClellan's peninsula campaign fails to take Richmond
	U.S. Congress passes second confiscation act, initiating emancipation
	Confederacy mounts offensive in Maryland and Kentucky
	Battle of Antietam ends Lee's drive into Maryland in September
	British intervention in the war on Confederate side is averted
1863	Emancipation Proclamation takes effect
	U.S. Congress passes National Banking Act
	Union enacts conscription

	African American soldiers join Union Army
	Food riots occur in southern cities
	Battle of Chancellorsville ends in Confederate victory but Jackson's death
	Union wins key victories at Vicksburg and Gettysburg
	Draft riots take place in New York City
1864	Battles of the Wilderness and Spotsylvania produce heavy casualties on both sides
	Battle of Cold Harbor continues carnage in Virginia
	Sherman captures Atlanta
	Confederacy begins to collapse on home front
	Lincoln wins reelection, eliminating any Confederate hopes for negotiated end to war
	Jefferson Davis proposes arming slaves
	Sherman marches through Georgia to the sea
1865	Sherman marches through Carolinas
	U.S. Congress approves Thirteenth Amendment
	Lee abandons Richmond and Petersburg
	Lee surrenders at Appomattox Court House
	Lincoln assassinated
	Death toll in war reaches 620,000

The Confederate strategy was essentially defensive, given the South's claim of independence and the North's resource advantage (see Figure 15.1). But Jefferson Davis called the southern strategy an "offensive defensive," taking advantage of opportunities to attack and using its interior transportation lines to concentrate troops at crucial points. The Confederacy did not need to conquer the North; the Union effort, however, required conquest of the South.

Both sides slighted the importance of the West, that vast expanse between Virginia and the Mississippi River and beyond. Guerrilla warfare broke out in 1861 in the politically divided Missouri, and key locations along the Mississippi and other western rivers would prove crucial prizes in the North's eventual victory. Beyond the Mississippi, the Confederacy hoped to gain an advantage by negotiating treaties with the Creeks, Choctaws, Chickasaws, Cherokees, Seminoles, and smaller groups of Plains Indians. Meanwhile, the Republican U.S. Congress carved the West into territories in anticipation of state making. For most Indians west of the Mississippi, the Civil War was nearly three decades of an enveloping strategy of conquest, relocation, and slaughter.

Union Naval Campaign   The last half of 1861 brought no major land battles, but in late summer, Union naval forces captured Cape Hatteras and Hilton Head, one of the Sea Islands off Port Royal, South Carolina. A few months later, federal naval operations established significant beachheads along the Confederate coastline, including vital points in North Carolina, as well as Fort Pulaski, which defended Savannah.

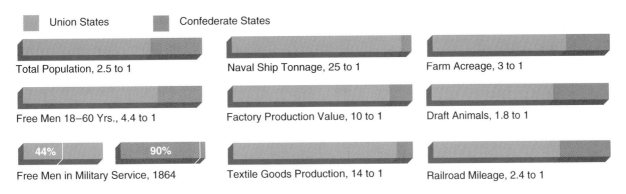

FIGURE 15.1
Comparative Resources, Union and Confederate States, 1861
The North had vastly superior resources. Although the North's advantages in manpower and industrial capacity proved very important, the South still had to be conquered, its society and its will crushed.
Source: The Times Atlas of World History. Used with permission.

The coastal victories off South Carolina foreshadowed a revolution in slave society. As federal gunboats approached, planters abandoned their land and fled. The Confederate cavalry tried to round up slaves and move them to the interior. But thousands of slaves greeted what they hoped to be freedom with rejoicing and broke the hated cotton gins. Some entered their masters' homes and took clothing and furniture. Many runaways poured into Union lines. Unwilling at first to wage a war against slavery, the federal government did not acknowledge the slaves' freedom—though it used their labor. These emancipated slaves, defined by Union officers as war "contraband" (confiscated enemy property), forced first a debate within the Union Army and government over how to treat the freedmen, and then a forthright attempt to harness their labor and military power.

Spring 1862 brought southerners stronger evidence of the war's gravity. In March, two ironclad ships—the *Monitor* (a Union warship) and the *Merrimack* (a Union ship seized by the Confederacy)—fought off the coast of Virginia. Their battle, though indecisive, ushered in a new era in naval design. In April, Union ships commanded by Admiral David Farragut smashed through log booms blocking the Mississippi River and moved upstream to capture New Orleans. The South's greatest seaport and slave-trading center was now in federal hands.

War in the Far West   Farther west, three full Confederate regiments were organized, mostly of Cherokees, but a Union victory at Elkhorn Tavern, Arkansas, shattered southern control of the region. Thereafter, dissension within Native American groups and a Union victory the following year at Honey Springs, Arkansas, reduced Confederate operations in Indian Territory to guerrilla raids.

In the westernmost campaign of the war, from February to May 1862, some three thousand Confederate and four thousand Union forces fought to control New Mexico Territory. The Confederate invasion had aimed to seize the trade riches of the Santa Fe Trail and take possession of gold mines in Colorado and California. But Colorado and New Mexico Unionists fought back, and in a series of battles at Glorieta Pass, 20 miles east of Santa Fe, on March 26 through 28, they blocked the Confederates. By May 1, Confederate forces straggled down the Rio Grande River into Texas, abandoning efforts to take New Mexico.

Grant's Tennessee Campaign and the Battle of Shiloh

Ulysses S. Grant: Commander of the Union army.

Meanwhile, in February 1862, forces in northern Tennessee won significant victories for the Union. A Union commander named **Ulysses S. Grant** saw the strategic importance of Fort Henry and Fort Donelson, the Confederate outposts guarding the Tennessee and Cumberland Rivers. In just ten days, he seized the forts—completely cutting off the Confederates and demanding "unconditional surrender" of Fort Donelson. A path into Tennessee, Alabama, and Mississippi now lay open before the Union Army.

Grant moved into southern Tennessee and the first of the war's shockingly bloody encounters, the **Battle of Shiloh**. On April 6, Confederate general Albert Sidney Johnston caught federal troops with their backs to the Tennessee River awaiting reinforcements. The Confederates attacked and inflicted heavy damage all day. Close to victory, General Johnston was killed. Union reinforcements arrived that night. The next day the battle turned, and after ten hours of combat, the Confederates withdrew.

Battle of Shiloh: The bloodiest battle in American history to that date (April 6–7, 1862).

Neither side won a decisive victory at Shiloh, yet losses were staggering, and the Confederates were forced to retreat into northern Mississippi. Northern troops lost thirteen thousand men (killed, wounded, or captured) out of sixty-three thousand; southerners sacrificed eleven thousand out of forty thousand. Total casualties in this battle exceeded those in all three of America's previous wars combined. Before Shiloh, Grant hoped that southerners would soon tire of the conflict. After Shiloh, he recalled, "I gave up all idea of saving the Union except by complete conquest." Memories of the Shiloh battlefield would haunt the surviving soldiers for the rest of their lives.

McClellan and the Peninsula Campaign

On the Virginia front, President Lincoln had problems with General McClellan. Only thirty-six, McClellan had achieved success as an army officer and railroad president. Habitually overestimating the size of enemy forces, he called repeatedly for reinforcements and ignored Lincoln's directions to advance. McClellan advocated war of limited aims that would lead to a quick reunion. He intended neither disruption of slavery nor war on noncombatants. McClellan finally sailed his troops down the Chesapeake, landing them on the peninsula between the York and James Rivers, and advanced on Richmond.

After a bloody battle at Fair Oaks on May 31 through June 1, the federal armies moved to within seven miles of the Confederate capital. The Confederate commanding general, Joseph E. Johnston, was wounded at Fair Oaks, and President **Jefferson Davis** placed his chief military adviser, **Robert E. Lee**, in command. The fifty-five-year-old Lee was an aristocratic Virginian, a lifelong military officer, and a veteran of distinction from the War with Mexico. Although he initially opposed secession, Lee gave his allegiance to his state and became a staunch Confederate. He soon foiled McClellan's legions.

Jefferson Davis: President of the Confederacy.

Robert E. Lee: Commander of the Confederate army.

First, Lee sent Stonewall Jackson's corps of seventeen thousand northwest into the Shenandoah valley behind Union forces, where they threatened Washington, D.C., and drew some federal troops away from Richmond to protect their own capital. Further, in mid-June, in an extraordinary four-day ride around the entire Union Army, Confederate cavalry under J. E. B. Stuart confirmed the exposed position of McClellan's army north of the Chickahominy River. Then, in the Seven Days Battles, from June 26 through July 1, Lee struck at McClellan's army. Lee's daring move of taking the majority of his army northeast and attacking the Union right flank, while leaving only a small force to defend Richmond, forced McClellan to retreat toward the James River.

During the sustained fighting of the Seven Days, the Union forces suffered 20,614 casualties and the Confederates, 15,849. By August 3, McClellan withdrew his army to the environs of Washington. Richmond remained safe for almost two more years.

Confederate Offensive in Maryland and Kentucky

Buoyed by these results, Jefferson Davis conceived an ambitious plan to gain wartime advantage and recognition of the Confederacy by European nations. He ordered a general offensive, sending Lee into Maryland and Generals Kirby Smith and Braxton Bragg into Kentucky. Calling on residents of Maryland and Kentucky, still slave states, to make a peace with his government, Davis also invited northwestern states like Indiana, which sent much of their trade down the Mississippi to New Orleans, to leave the Union. This was a coordinated effort to take the war to the North and force both a military and a political turning point.

The plan was promising, but the offensive ultimately failed. Lee's forces achieved a striking success at the battle of Second Bull Run, August 29 through 30. The entire Union army retreated to the federal capital. Thousands of wounded occupied schools and churches, and two thousand suffered on cots in the U.S. Capitol rotunda.

But in the bloodiest day of the war, September 17, 1862, McClellan turned Lee back from Sharpsburg, Maryland. In the **Battle of Antietam**, five thousand men died, and another eighteen thousand were wounded. McClellan intercepted a battle order, wrapped around cigars for each Confederate corps commander and lost by a courier. But McClellan moved slowly, failed to use his larger forces in simultaneous attacks,

Battle of Antietam: First major battle on Northern soil.

Library of Congress

In October 1862 in New York City, photographer Mathew Brady opened an exhibition of photographs from the Battle of Antietam. Although few knew it, Brady's vision was very poor, and this photograph of Confederate dead was actually made by his assistants, Alexander Gardner and James F. Gibson.

and allowed Lee's stricken army to retreat to across the Potomac. Lincoln removed McClellan from command.

In Kentucky, Generals Smith and Bragg secured Lexington and Frankfort, but their effort to force the Yankees back to the Ohio River was stopped at the Battle of Perryville on October 8. Bragg's army retreated back into Tennessee, where on December 31, 1862 to January 2, 1863, they fought an indecisive but bloody battle at Murfreesboro. Casualties exceeded even those of Shiloh.

Outnumbered and disadvantaged, the South could not continue the offensive. Davis admitted to Confederate representatives that southerners were entering "the darkest and most dangerous period we have yet had."

Link to reports in *Harper's Weekly* of the Battle of Fredericksburg.

But 1862 also brought painful lessons to the North. On December 13, Union general Ambrose Burnside, now in command of the Army of the Potomac, unwisely ordered his soldiers to attack Lee's army, which held fortified positions at Fredericksburg, Virginia. Lee's men performed efficiently in killing northerners, and Burnside's repeated assaults up Marye's Heights shocked his opponents, killing thirteen hundred and wounding ninety-six hundred Union soldiers. The scale of carnage now challenged people on both sides to question the meaning of such a war.

War Transforms the South

What happened to the South's embrace of state sovereignty during the war?

War disrupted civilian life; one of the first traditions to fall was the southern preference for local and limited government. States' rights had been a formative ideology for the Confederacy, but state governments were weak. To withstand the North's massive power, the South needed to centralize; like the colonial revolutionaries, southerners could unite or die separately.

The Confederacy and Centralization

Jefferson Davis brought arms, supplies, and troops under centralized control. But by early 1862, the scope and duration of the conflict required more recruits. Tens of thousands of Confederate soldiers volunteered for just one year planning to return home in the spring to plant their crops. Faced with a critical manpower shortage, in April 1862 the Confederate government enacted the first national conscription (draft) law in American history.

Davis adopted a firm leadership role toward the Confederate Congress, which raised taxes and later passed a tax-in-kind—paid in farm products. Nearly forty-five hundred agents dispersed to collect the tax. Where opposition arose, the government suspended the writ of habeas corpus (which prevented individuals from being held without trial) and imposed martial law. Still, this tax system proved inadequate for the South's war effort.

To replace the food that men in uniform would have grown, Davis exhorted state governments to require farmers to switch from cash crops to food crops. But army food and labor shortages continued. The War Department impressed slaves to work on fortifications, and after 1861 officers raided farms and carted away grain, meat, wagons, and draft animals to feed the troops. Such raids caused increased hardship and resentment for women managing farms without husbands and sons.

Soon, the Confederate administration in Richmond gained control over the southern economy. The Confederate Congress also gave the central government almost complete control of the railroads. A large bureaucracy of over seventy thousand civilians administered Confederate operations. By the war's end, the southern bureaucracy was larger in proportion to population than its northern counterpart.

Confederate Nationalism

Historians have long argued over whether the Confederacy itself was a "rebellion," a "revolution," or the creation of a genuine "nation." Whatever the label, Confederates created a culture and ideology of nationalism. In flags, songs, language, seals, school readers, and other national characteristics, Confederates created their own story.

Southerners believed the Confederacy was the true legacy of the American Revolution—a bulwark against centralized power that was in keeping with the war. To southerners, theirs was a continuing revolution against the excesses of Yankee democracy, and George Washington (a Virginian) on horseback formed the center of the Confederacy's official seal.

Also central to Confederate nationalism was a refurbished defense of slavery as a benign, protective institution, complete with the image of the "faithful slave." In wartime schoolbooks, children were instructed in the divinely inspired, paternalistic character of slavery. A poem popular among whites captured an old slave's rejection of the Emancipation Proclamation.

> Now, Massa, dis is berry fine, dese words
> You've spoke to me,
> No doubt you mean it kindly, but ole Dinah
> Won't be free…
> Ole Massa's berry good to me—and though I am
> His slave,
> He treats me like I'se kin to him—and I would
> Rather have
> A home in Massa's cabin, and eat his black
> Bread too,
> Dan leave ole Massa's children and go and
> Lib wid you.

This and other forms of Confederate nationalism collapsed in the war's final years. But it would revive in the postwar period in a new ideology of the Lost Cause.

Southern Cities and Industry

Clerks and subordinate officials crowded towns and cities where Confederate departments established offices. "Government girls" staffed the formerly all-male Confederate bureaucracy. The sudden urban migration overwhelmed the housing supply and stimulated new construction. Richmond's population increased 250 percent. Mobile's population jumped from twenty-nine thousand to forty-one thousand; and ten thousand people poured into war-related industries in little Selma, Alabama.

As the Union blockade disrupted imports, the traditionally agricultural South forged new industries. Many planters shared Davis's hope that industrialization would bring "deliverance… from all commercial dependence" on the North or the world. Indeed, the Confederacy achieved tremendous industrial development. Chief of Ordnance Josiah Gorgas increased the capacity of Richmond's Tredegar Iron Works and other factories so that by 1865 his Ordnance Bureau was supplying all Confederate small arms and ammunition. The government constructed new railroad lines and ironworks, using slaves relocated from farms and plantations.

The Panhandle-Plains Historical Society, Canyon, Texas

Five Texans in the Confederate cavalry sitting for a formal photograph. Four have the "lone star" on their hats. Like thousands of others, these men posed to send their image to the folks back home, but also perhaps as an act of comradeship at the war front.

Changing Roles of Women

White women, restricted to narrow roles in antebellum society, gained new responsibilities in wartime. The wives and mothers of soldiers now headed households and performed men's work, including raising crops and tending animals. Women in nonslaveowning families cultivated fields, while wealthier women acted as overseers and managed field work. In the cities, white women—previously all but excluded from the labor force—found respectable paying jobs, often in the Confederate bureaucracy. Female schoolteachers appeared in the South for the first time.

Patriotic sacrifice appealed to some women; others resented their new burdens. A Texas woman who had struggled to discipline slaves pronounced herself "sick of trying to do a man's business." Others grew angry over shortages and resented contact with lower-class women. Some scorned the war and demanded that their men return to provide for their families.

Human Suffering, Hoarding, and Inflation

For millions of southerners, the war brought privation and suffering. Mass poverty descended on a large minority of the white population. Many yeoman families lost their breadwinners to the army. Women sought help from relatives, neighbors, friends, anyone. Sometimes they pleaded with the Confederate government to discharge their husbands.

The South was in many places so sparsely populated that the conscription of one craftsman could wreak hardship on an entire county. Often people begged together for the exemption or discharge of the local miller, neighborhood tanner, or wheelwright. Most serious, however, was the loss of a blacksmith, who could repair farming tools.

The blockade of Confederate shipping created shortages of important supplies—salt, sugar, coffee, nails—and speculation and hoarding made shortages worse. Greedy businessmen cornered the supply of some commodities; prosperous citizens stocked up on food. The *Richmond Enquirer* criticized a planter who purchased so many wagonloads of supplies that his "lawn and paths looked like a wharf covered with a ship's loads."

Inflation raged out of control, fueled by the Confederate government's heavy borrowing and inadequate taxes, until prices increased almost 7,000 percent. Inflation particularly imperiled urban dwellers without their own food sources. As early as 1861 and 1862, officials predicted that "women and children are bound to come to suffering if not starvation." Hoarding continued, and a rudimentary relief program organized by the Confederacy failed to meet the need.

Inequities of the Confederate Draft

Not all classes sacrificed equally. The Confederate government's policies decidedly favored the upper class. Until the war's last year, for example, prosperous southerners could avoid military service by hiring substitutes. Well over fifty thousand upper-class southerners purchased such substitutes, despite skyrocketing prices that reached $5,000 or $6,000 per man. Mary Boykin Chesnut knew of one aristocrat who "spent a fortune in substitutes....He is at the end of his row now, for all able-bodied men are ordered to the front."

Anger at such discrimination exploded in October 1862, when the Confederate Congress exempted from military duty anyone who was supervising at least twenty slaves. Protests poured in from across the Confederacy, and North Carolina's legislators condemned the law. Its defenders argued, however, that exemption preserved order and aided food production, and the statute remained on the books.

This "twenty Negro" law is indicative of the racial fears many Confederates felt as the war threatened to overturn southern society. But it also fueled desertion and stimulated Unionism in nonslaveholding regions of the South. In Jones County, Mississippi, a wooded area with few slaves or plantations, Newt Knight, a Confederate soldier, led renegades who took over the county, declared their allegiance to the Union, and called their district the "Free State of Jones." They held out for the remainder of the war as an enclave of Union sympathizers.

The bitterness of letters to Confederate officials suggests the depth of the dissension and class anger. One woman swore to the secretary of war that, unless help was provided to poverty-stricken wives and mothers, "an allwise god...will send down his fury...[on] those that are in power."

Wartime Northern Economy and Society

How did the war affect workers in the North?

War dramatically altered northern society as well. Factories and citizens' associations geared up to support the war, and the federal government and its executive branch gained new powers. Idealism and greed flourished together, and the northern economy proved its awesome productivity.

Northern Business, Industry, and Agriculture

At first, the war was a shock to business. Northern firms lost their southern markets, and many companies changed their products and found new customers. Southern debts became uncollectible, jeopardizing northern merchants and western banks. Farm families struggled with a labor shortage caused by army enlistments. Cotton mills lacked cotton; construction declined; shoe manufacturers sold few of the cheap shoes that planters bought for slaves.

Certain entrepreneurs, such as wool producers, benefited from shortages of competing products, and soaring demand for war-related goods swept some businesses to new success. The Treasury issued $3.2 billion in bonds and paper money called "greenbacks," and the War Department spent over $360 million in revenues from new taxes, including the nation's first income tax.

War-related spending revived business in many northern states. The northern economy also grew because of a complementary relationship between agriculture and industry. Mechanization of agriculture had begun before the war. Wartime recruitment and conscription gave western farmers an added incentive to purchase labor-saving machinery. The shift from human labor to machines created new markets for industry and expanded the food supply. Cyrus and William McCormick built an industrial empire in Chicago from the sale of their reapers. Between 1862 and 1864, the manufacture of mowers and reapers doubled to 70,000 yearly; by war's end, 375,000 reapers were in use, triple the number in 1861. Thus, northern farm families whose breadwinners went to war did not suffer as much as their counterparts in the South.

The Quartermaster and Military-Government Mobilization

This government-business marriage emerged from a greatly empowered Quartermaster Department, which became the single largest employer in the United States, issuing thousands of manufacturing contracts to hundreds of firms.

Secretary of War Edwin M. Stanton's list of the supplies needed by the Ordnance Department indicates the scope of the demand for government and business cooperation: "7,892 cannon, 11,787 artillery carriages, 4,022,130 small-arms… 1,022,176,474 cartridges for small-arms, 1,220,555,435 percussion caps,… 26,440,054 pounds of gunpowder,… and 90,416,295 pounds of lead." The government also purchased huge quantities of uniforms, boots, food, camp equipment, saddles, horses, ships, and other necessities. By 1865, the government had purchased some 640,000 horses and 300,000 mules at a cost well over $100 million.

Two-thirds of all U.S. war spending went to supply troops, and President Lincoln appointed West Point–trained engineer, Montgomery Meigs, to command that process. Meigs spent $1.8 billion to wage the war, more than all previous U.S. government expenditures combined since independence. His efforts, argued one historian, made the Union army "the best fed, most lavishly supplied army that had ever existed." The success of such military mobilization left an indelible mark on American political-economic history and provided perhaps the oldest root of the modern American "military-industrial state."

The story of Jay Cooke, a wealthy New York financier, best illustrates the wartime partnership between business and government. Cooke earned hefty commissions marketing government bonds to finance the war. But the financier's profit served the Union cause, as the interests of capitalism and government merged in American history's first era of "big government."

Northern Workers' Militancy

Northern industrial and urban workers did not fare as well as. After the initial slump, jobs became plentiful, but inflation ate up much of a worker's paycheck. The price of coffee tripled; rice and sugar doubled; and between 1860 and 1864, consumer prices rose at least 76 percent, while daily wages rose only 42 percent. Workers' families consequently suffered a substantial decline in their standard of living.

Industrial workers also lost job security. To increase production, some employers replaced workers with labor-saving machines. Others urged the government to promote immigration to secure cheap labor. Workers responded by forming unions and sometimes striking. Indeed, thirteen occupational groups—including tailors, coal miners, and railway engineers—formed national unions during the Civil War, and the number of strikes climbed.

Manufacturers viewed labor activism as a threat and formed statewide or craft-based associations to pool information. They shared blacklists of union members and required new workers to sign "yellow dog" contracts (promises not to join a union). To put down strikes, they hired strikebreakers from among blacks, immigrants, and women, and sometimes used federal troops.

Labor militancy, however, did not keep employers from profiting or profiteering on government contracts. With immense demand for army supplies, unscrupulous businessmen sold clothing and blankets made of "shoddy"—wool fibers reclaimed from rags or worn cloth. Shoddy goods often came apart in the rain; most of the shoes purchased early in the war were worthless. Contractors sold inferior guns for double the usual price and passed off tainted meat as good. Rampant corruption led to a year-long investigation by the House of Representatives.

Economic Nationalism and Government-Business Partnership

Legitimate enterprises also made healthy profits. The output of woolen mills increased so dramatically that industry dividends nearly tripled. Some cotton mills made record profits, even while reducing output. Brokerage houses earned unheard-of commissions. Railroads increased their business so much that railroad stocks skyrocketed.

Railroads were a leading beneficiary of government largesse. With southern representatives absent from Congress, the northern route of the transcontinental railroad prevailed. In 1862 and 1864, Congress chartered two corporations, the Union Pacific Railroad and the Central Pacific Railroad, and assisted them financially in connecting Omaha, Nebraska, with Sacramento, California. For each mile of track laid, railroads received a loan of from $16,000 to $48,000 in government bonds plus 20 square miles of land along a free 400-foot-wide right of way. Overall, the two corporations gained approximately 20 million acres and nearly $60 million in loans.

Other businessmen benefited handsomely from the **Morrill Land Grant Act** (1862). To promote public education in agriculture, engineering, and military science, Congress granted each state 30,000 acres of federal land for each of its congressional districts. The law eventually fostered sixty-nine colleges and universities, and enriched a few prominent speculators. Similarly, the Homestead Act of 1862 offered cheap, and sometimes free, land to people who would settle the West and improve their property.

Before the war, banks operating under state charters issued seven thousand different kinds of currency notes. During the war, Congress and the Treasury Department established a national banking system to issue national bank notes, and by 1865 most state banks were forced by a prohibitive tax to join the national system. This created sounder currency but also inflexibility in the money supply and an eastern-oriented financial structure.

Morrill Land Grant Act: Law in which Congress granted land to states to establish colleges focusing on agriculture, engineering, and military science.

In the excitement of wartime moneymaking, an eagerness to display one's wealth flourished in the largest cities. *Harper's Monthly* reported that "the men button their waistcoats with diamonds…and the women powder their hair with gold and silver dust." The *New York Herald* noted: "This war has entirely changed the American character….The individual who makes the most money—no matter how—and spends the most—no matter for what—is considered the greatest man."

The Union Cause

In the first two years of the war, northern morale remained remarkably high for a cause that today may seem abstract—the Union—but at the time meant the preservation of a social and political order that people cherished.

Secular and church leaders supported the cause, and even ministers who preferred to separate politics and pulpit denounced "the iniquity of causeless rebellion. Abolitionists campaigned to turn the war into a crusade against slavery." Free black communities and churches—both black and white—sent clothing, ministers, and teachers to aid the freedpeople. Indeed, thousands of northern blacks volunteered to join the war effort in spite of the initial rejection they received from the Lincoln administration. Thus, in wartime northern society, materialism and greed flourished alongside idealism, religious conviction, and self-sacrifice.

Northern Women on Home Front and Battlefront

Northern women, like their southern counterparts, took on new roles. They organized over ten thousand soldiers' aid societies, rolled bandages, and raised $3 million for injured troops. Women pressed for the first trained ambulance corps in the Union Army, and they formed the backbone of the **U.S. Sanitary Commission**, a civilian agency recognized by the War Department in 1861, which provided nutritional and medical aid to soldiers. Although most of its officers were men, the bulk of the volunteers who ran its seven thousand auxiliaries were women. Women organized elaborate "Sanitary Fairs" to raise money and awareness for soldiers' health and hygiene.

U.S. Sanitary Commission: Civilian organization in the North staffed by large numbers of women that was a major source of medical and nutritional aid for soldiers.

Approximately thirty-two hundred women also served as nurses in frontline hospitals. Yet women had to fight to serve; the professionalization of medicine since the Revolution created a medical system dominated by men, who often did not want women's aid. Even **Clara Barton**, famous for working in the worst hospitals at the front, was ousted from her post in 1863. But women such as Dorothea Dix, who sought to reform asylums for the insane, and Illinois widow Mary Ann Bickerdyke, who served in Sherman's army in the West, established a heroic tradition for Civil War nurses. They also advanced the professionalization of nursing, as several schools of nursing were established in northern cities during or after the war.

Clara Barton: Nurse who worked for the Sanitary Commission and later founded the Red Cross.

Women also wrote sentimental war poetry, short stories, and novels, and songs that reached thousands of readers in illustrated weeklies, monthly periodicals, and special "story papers." In many stories, female characters seek recognition for their loyalty and Union service, while others probe the suffering and death of loved ones. Louisa May Alcott arrived at her nursing job in Washington, D.C. after the horrific Union defeat at Fredericksburg, in December 1862, and later immortalized her experience in *Hospital Sketches* (1863), providing northern readers a view of the hospitals where loved ones agonized and perished.

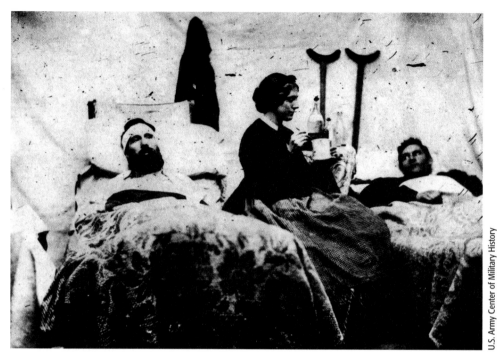

U.S. Army Center of Military History

Nurse Anne Bell tending to wounded soldiers in a federal hospital, Nashville, Tennessee, ca. 1863. The distant gaze of the man on the left and the grateful gaze of the one on the right realistically represent agonies of military hospitals.

By 1863, many women found the liberation of slaves an inspiring subject, as Julia Ward Howe did in her immortal "Battle Hymn of the Republic": "As He died to make men holy / Let us die to make men free."

Walt Whitman's War   The poet **Walt Whitman** recorded his experiences as a volunteer nurse in Washington, D.C. As he dressed wounds and comforted suffering men, Whitman found "the marrow of the tragedy concentrated in those Army Hospitals." But he also found inspiration and a deepening faith in American democracy.

In "The Wound Dresser," Whitman meditated unforgettably on the deaths he witnessed:

> On, on I go, (open doors of time! open hospital doors!)
> The crush'd head I dress, (poor crazed hand tear not the bandage away,)
> The neck of the cavalry-man with the bullet through and through I examine,
> Hard the breathing rattles, quite glazed already the eye, yet life struggles hard, (Come sweet death! be persuaded O beautiful death!
> In mercy come quickly.)

Indeed, the scale of death in this war shocked many Americans into believing that the conflict had to be for purposes larger than themselves.

The Advent of Emancipation

Despite the loyalty of soldiers and civilians on both sides, the governments of the United States and the Confederacy lacked clarity about the war's purpose. Throughout the war's early months, Davis and Lincoln avoided

Walt Whitman: Well-known poet and author of *Leaves of Grass*; Whitman wrote about his experiences as a nurse and his renewed faith in democracy.

Why did Lincoln and Davis both avoid the slavery issue in the early days of the war?

references to slavery. Davis realized that emphasis on the issue could increase class conflict in the South. Instead, he told southerners that they were fighting for constitutional liberty: northerners betrayed the founders' legacy, and southerners seceded to preserve it.

Lincoln had his reasons for avoiding slavery. It was crucial at first not to antagonize the Union's border slave states, whose loyalty was tenuous. Lincoln also hoped that a pro-Union majority would assert itself in the South and help coax the South back into the Union. And there were powerful political considerations. Some Republicans burned with moral outrage over slavery; others were frankly racist, dedicated to protecting free whites from the Slave Power and the competition of cheap slave labor. No Republican or northern consensus on slavery existed early in the war.

Lincoln and Emancipation

Lincoln's compassion, humility, and moral anguish during the war were evident in his speeches and writings. But as a politician, Lincoln distinguished between his convictions and his official acts. The latter were calculated for maximum advantage.

Many blacks attacked Lincoln furiously during the war's first year for his refusal to convert the struggle into an "abolition war." When Lincoln countermanded General John C. Frémont's order of liberation for slaves owned by disloyal masters in Missouri in September 1861, the *Anglo-African* declared that the president "hurls back into the hell of slavery thousands…rightfully set free." As late as July 1862, Frederick Douglass characterized administration policy as reconstruction of "the old union on the old and corrupting basis of compromise, by which slavery shall retain all the power that it ever had." Douglass wanted slavery destroyed and the Constitution rewritten in the name of human equality. Within a year, just such a profound result began to take place.

Lincoln first substantively broached the subject of slavery in March 1862, when he proposed that states consider emancipation. He asked Congress to promise aid to any state that emancipated, appealing especially to border state representatives. What Lincoln proposed was gradual emancipation, with compensation for slaveholders and colonization of the freed slaves outside the United States.

Until well into 1864, Lincoln's administration promoted an impractical scheme to colonize 4.2 million freed slaves in Central America or the Caribbean. He was as yet unconvinced that America could become a biracial society, and he feared that white northerners might not support a war for black freedom. Black abolitionists vehemently opposed the Lincoln administration's machinations.

Radical Republicans: A group of Republicans who assailed the U.S. President early in the war for failing to make emancipation a war goal and later making it too easy for defeated rebel states to return to the Union.

A group of Republicans in Congress, known as the **Radical Republicans**—led by George Julian, Charles Sumner, and Thaddeus Stevens—dedicated themselves to a war for emancipation. They were instrumental in creating a special House-Senate committee on the conduct of the war, which investigated Union reverses, sought to improve wartime efficiency, and prodded the president to take stronger measures against slavery.

Confiscation Acts

In August 1861, at the Radicals' instigation, Congress passed its first confiscation act. Designed to punish Confederates, the law confiscated all property used for "insurrectionary purposes." A second confiscation act (July 1862) confiscated the property of anyone who supported the rebellion, even those who merely resided in the South and paid Confederate taxes. Their slaves were declared "forever free of their servitude."

In the summer 1862, Lincoln stood by his proposal of voluntary gradual emancipation and made no effort to enforce the second confiscation act. In protest, Horace Greeley, editor of the powerful *New York Tribune,* published an open letter to the president entitled "The Prayer of Twenty Millions," Greeley declared, "Mr. President, there is not one...intelligent champion of the Union cause who does not feel that all attempts to put down the Rebellion and at the same time uphold its inciting cause are preposterous and futile." Lincoln offered a calculated reply. He disagreed with those who would make slavery the paramount issue of the war and said, "If I could save the Union without freeing any slave I would do it, and if I could save it by freeing all the slaves I would do it; and if I could save it by freeing some and leaving others alone I would also do that. What I do about slavery, and the colored race, I do because I believe it helps to save the Union."

But Lincoln had already decided to issue a presidential **Emancipation Proclamation**. He was waiting for a Union victory so that it would not appear an act of desperation. The letter to Greeley represents Lincoln's concern with conditioning public opinion for the coming social revolution.

Emancipation Proclamation: Lincoln's decree freeing all slaves in Confederate-held territories. It exempted border slave states that remained within the Union.

Emancipation Proclamations

On September 22, 1862, shortly after Union success at the Battle of Antietam, Lincoln issued the first part of his two-part proclamation. Invoking his powers as commander-in-chief, he announced that on January 1, 1863, he would emancipate the slaves in the states "in rebellion" (those lacking legitimate representatives in the U.S. Congress by January). Thus, his September 1862 proclamation was less a declaration of the right of slaves to be free than a threat to southerners: unless they put down their arms and returned to Congress, they would lose their slaves. Lincoln had little expectation that southerners would give up, but he wanted a response.

In the fateful January 1, 1863, proclamation, Lincoln declared that "all persons held as slaves" in areas in rebellion "shall be then, thenceforward, and forever free." But he excepted every Confederate county or city that had fallen under Union control. Those areas, he declared, "are, for the present, left precisely as if this proclamation were not issued." Nor did Lincoln liberate slaves in the border slave states that remained in the Union. "The President has... proclaimed emancipation only where he has notoriously no power to execute it," charged the anti-administration *New York World.*

But Lincoln was worried about the constitutionality of his acts, and he anticipated that after the war southerners might sue for restoration of their "property." Making the liberation of the slaves "a fit and necessary war measure" raised a variety of legal questions: Would it expire with the suppression of a rebellion? The proclamation did little to clarify the status of freed slaves, but did it open the possibility of military service for blacks?

If the Emancipation Proclamation was legally ambiguous, as a moral and political document it had great meaning. Because the proclamation defined the war as a war against slavery, congressional Radicals could applaud it. Yet it also protected Lincoln's position with conservatives, enabling him to retreat and forcing no immediate changes on the border slave states.

Most important, though, thousands of slaves had already reached Union lines across the South. They "voted with their feet" for emancipation well before the proclamation. And now, every advance of federal forces into slave society was a liberating step.

Across the North and in Union-occupied sections of the South, blacks and their white allies celebrated the Emancipation Proclamation. At a large "contraband camp" in Washington, D.C., some six hundred black men, women, and children gathered at the superintendent's headquarters on New Year's Eve and sang through the night. In chorus after chorus of "Go Down, Moses" they announced the magnitude of their painful but beautiful exodus.

African American Recruits

The need for men soon convinced the administration to recruit northern and southern blacks for the Union Army. By the spring of 1863, African American troops were answering the call of a dozen or more black recruiters in northern cities and towns. Lincoln came to see black soldiers as "the great available and yet unavailed of force for restoring the Union."

African American leaders hoped that military service would secure equal rights for their people. Once the black soldier had fought for the Union, wrote Frederick Douglass, "there is no power on earth which can deny that he has earned the right of citizenship in the United States."

In June 1864, with thousands of former slaves in blue uniforms, Lincoln gave his support to a constitutional ban on slavery. On the eve of the Republican national convention, Lincoln called on the party to "put into the platform as the keystone, the amendment of the Constitution abolishing and prohibiting slavery forever." The party promptly called for the **Thirteenth Amendment**., which passed in early 1865 and was sent to the states for ratification. The war to save the Union had become the war to free the slaves.

Thirteenth Amendment: Ended slavery in all U.S. territory.

Who Freed the Slaves?

It has long been debated whether Abraham Lincoln deserved the label (one he never claimed for himself) of "Great Emancipator." Was Lincoln ultimately a reluctant emancipator, following rather than leading Congress and public opinion? Or did Lincoln give essential presidential leadership by going slow but, once moving, never backpedaling on black freedom? Once he focused on the unconditional surrender of the Confederates, Lincoln made slavery's destruction central to the war's purpose.

Others have argued, however, that slaves were central in achieving their own freedom. When they were in proximity to war zones, slaves fled by the thousands. Some worked as camp laborers for the Union armies, and eventually more than 180,000 black men served in the Union Army and Navy. Some found freedom as individuals in 1861, and some not until 1865, as refugees trekking to contraband camps.

Nevertheless, emancipation was a historical confluence of a policy directed by and dependent on the military authority of the president and the will and courage for self-emancipation. Wallace Turnage's escape in Mobile Bay in 1864 demonstrates that emancipation could result from both a slave's own heroism and Union forces. Most blacks comprehended their freedom as given and taken, but also as their human right. "I now dreaded the gun and handcuffs…no more," remembered Turnage. "I could now speak my opinion," Turnage concluded, "to men of all grades and colors."

A Confederate Plan of Emancipation

Before the war was over, the Confederacy, too, addressed emancipation. Late in the war, Jefferson Davis was willing to sacrifice slavery to achieve independence. He proposed that the Confederate government purchase 40,000 slaves to work as army laborers, with a promise of freedom at the end of their service. He then called for the recruitment and arming of slaves as soldiers, who likewise would gain their freedom at war's end, as would their wives and children. Bitter debate over Davis's plan resounded through the Confederacy. When the Confederate Congress finally approved slave enlistments in March 1865, owners had to comply only on a "voluntary" basis. With manpower shortages, General Lee supported the idea of slave soldiers, while most Confederate slaveholders and editors vehemently opposed the enlistment plan. Supporters hoped to fight to a stalemate, achieve independence, and control the postwar racial order through their limited wartime emancipation schemes, but it was too late. By contrast, Lincoln's Emancipation Proclamation stimulated a vital infusion of forces into the Union armies: 134,000 former slaves (and 52,000 free blacks) fought for freedom and the Union. Their participation was pivotal in northern victory.

The Soldiers' War

Military service altered their lives. Enlistment submerged young men in large organizations whose military discipline ignored their individuality. Army life meant tedium, physical hardship, and separation from loved ones, yet it held powerful attractions as well.

> What led previously reluctant white military leaders to accept black soldiers?

Hospitals and Camp Life

Soldiers benefited from certain new products, such as canned condensed milk, but blankets, clothing, and arms were often of poor quality. Hospitals were badly managed at first. Rules of hygiene in large camps were scarcely enforced. Water supplies were unsafe and typhoid common. About 57,000 men died from dysentery and diarrhea; 224,000 Union troops died from disease or accidents, double the 110,100 who died from battle. Confederate troops were less well supplied, and they had no sanitary commission. Still, an extensive hospital network, aided by white female volunteers and black woman slaves, sprang up.

On both sides, troops quickly learned that soldiering was far from glorious. Fighting, wrote a North Carolina volunteer in 1862, taught him "the realities of a soldier's life.... Without time to wash our clothes or our persons...the whole army became lousy more or less with body lice." Union troops "skirmished" against lice by boiling their clothes, but to little avail.

War soon exposed them to the blasted bodies of friends and comrades. "It is a sad sight to see the dead and if possible more sad to see the wounded—shot in every possible way you can imagine," wrote one Confederate.

Still, as campaigns dragged on, most soldiers who did not desert grew determined to see the struggle through. "We now, like true Soldiers go determined not to yield one inch," wrote a New York corporal. When at last the war was over, "it seemed like breaking up a family to separate," one man observed.

The Rifled Musket

Advances in technology made the Civil War particularly deadly. The most important were the rifle and the "minie ball." Bullets fired from a smoothbore musket were not accurate at distances over eighty yards. Cutting spiraled grooves inside the barrel gave the projectile greater accuracy, but rifles remained difficult to load and use until the Frenchman Claude Minie and the American James Burton developed a new kind of bullet that expanded on firing and flew accurately. With these bullets, rifles were deadly at four hundred yards.

This meant that soldiers assaulting a position defended by riflemen were in greater peril. While artillery now fired from a safe distance, there was no substitute for the infantry assault or the popular turning movements aimed at an enemy's flank. Thus, advancing soldiers exposed themselves repeatedly to accurate rifle fire. Because medical knowledge was rudimentary, even minor wounds often led to amputation and death through infection. Never before in Europe or America had such massive forces pummeled each other with weapons of such destructive power.

The Black Soldier's Fight for Manhood

At the outset of the war, racism in the Union Army was strong. Most white soldiers wanted nothing to do with black people and regarded them as inferior. For many, acceptance of black troops grew only because they could do heavy labor and "stop Bullets as well as white people." A popular song celebrated "Sambo's Right to Be Kilt" as the only justification for black enlistments.

But white officers who volunteered to lead segregated black units to gain promotion found that experience altered their opinions. After one month with black troops, a white captain informed his wife, "I have a more elevated opinion of their abilities than I ever had before. I know that many of them are vastly the superiors of those…who would condemn them all to a life of brutal degradation."

Link to Hannah Johnson's letter to President Lincoln asking the government to protect black soldiers.

Black troops had a mission to destroy slavery and demonstrate their equality. "When Rebellion is crushed," wrote a black volunteer from Connecticut, "who will be more proud than I to say, I was one of the first of the despised race to leave the free North with a rifle on my shoulder." Corporal James Henry Gooding of Massachusetts's black Fifty-fourth Regiment explained that his unit intended "to live down all prejudice against its color, by a determination to do well in any position it is put."

Indeed, blacks and whites of the Fifty-fourth Massachusetts forged deep bonds. Just before the regiment launched its costly assault on Fort Wagner in Charleston harbor, in July 1863, a black soldier called out to abolitionist Colonel Robert Gould Shaw, who would perish that day, "Colonel, I will stay by you till I die." The Fort Wagner assault was celebrated for demonstrating the valor of black men, but this bloody chapter in the history of American racism also proved that black men had to die in battle to be acknowledged as men.

Such valor emerged despite persistent discrimination. The Union government paid white privates $13 per month plus a clothing allowance of $3.50, whereas black privates earned only $10 per month less $3 for clothing. Outraged, several regiments refused to accept any pay, and Congress eventually remedied the inequity.

Black Soldiers in the Civil War

The image below is of the storming of Fort Wagner, July 1863, by the Fifty-fourth Massachusetts regiment, in Charleston, South Carolina, by Chicago printmakers, Kurtz and Allison. Kurtz and Allison issued vivid and colorful chromolithographs in the 1880s, celebrating the military valor of African Americans. This scene depicts the most famous combat action of black troops in the Civil War; the Fifty-fourth was the first northern-recruited black unit, and their bravery and sacrifice served as a measure of African American devotion to the Union cause. At right is a medal for valor won by a member of the 54th Massachusetts Regiment. Why was the 54th Massachusetts regiment such a symbolic test case for the military ability and political meaning of black soldiers in the Civil War? Why did black men have to die on battlefields for many Americans in the Civil War era to consider them fully men and citizens?

Private Collection/Picture Research Consultants & Archives

THE GALLANT CHARGE OF THE FIFTY FOURTH MASSACHUSETTS (COLORED REGIMENT.
On the Rebel works at Fort Wagner, Morris Island, near Charleston, July 18th 1863, and death of Colonel Robt. G. Shaw.

The Granger Collection, New York

1863: The Tide of Battle Turns

What turned the tide of war toward Union victory?

The fighting in spring and summer of 1863 did not settle the war, but it suggested the outcome. The campaigns began in a deceptively positive way for Confederates, as Lee's army performed brilliantly in battles in central Virginia.

Vicksburg: Union victory that gave the North complete control of Mississippi River.

Battle of Chancellorsville

On May 2 and 3, west of Fredericksburg, Virginia, some 130,000 members of the Union Army of the Potomac bore down on fewer than 60,000 Confederates. Boldly, Lee and Stonewall Jackson divided their forces, ordering 30,000 men under Jackson on a day-long march westward to prepare a flank attack.

Arriving at their position in late afternoon, Jackson's seasoned "foot cavalry" found unprepared Union troops laughing, smoking, and playing cards. The Confederate attack drove the entire right side of the Union Army back. Eager to press his advantage, Jackson rode forward with a few officers to study the ground. Returning at night, southern troops mistook them for federals and fired, fatally wounding their commander. The next day, Union forces left in defeat. Southern forces won at Chancellorsville, but it cost them Stonewall Jackson, who would remain a legend in Confederate memory.

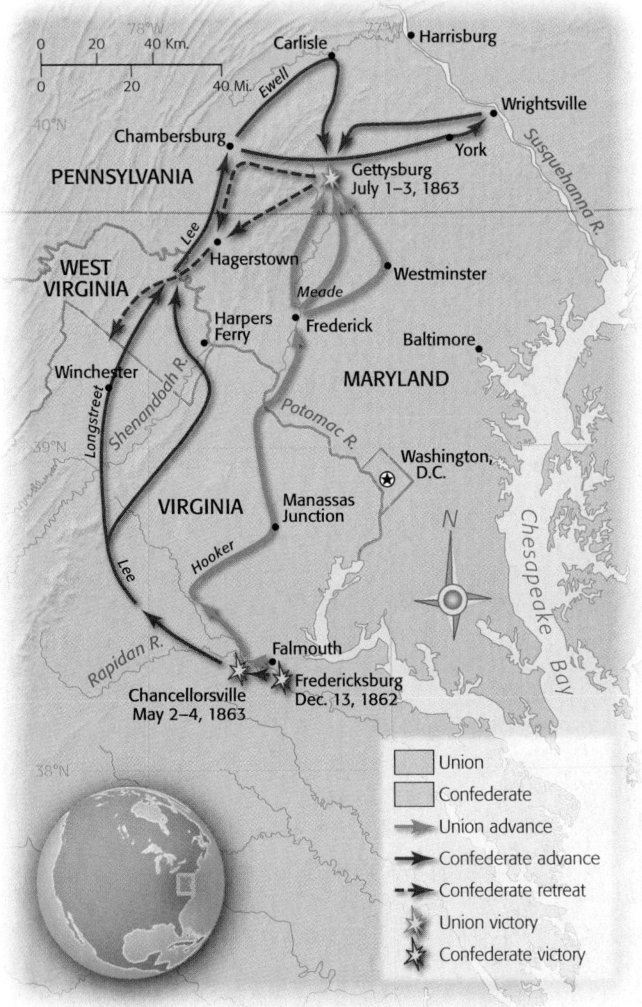

Siege of Vicksburg

July brought crushing defeats for the Confederacy in two critical battles—**Vicksburg** and **Gettysburg**—that damaged Confederate hopes for independence. Vicksburg was the last major fortification on the Mississippi River in southern hands. General Ulysses S. Grant laid siege to Vicksburg in May, bottling up the defending army of General John Pemberton. If Vicksburg fell, Union forces would control the river, cutting the Confederacy in two and gaining an open path into its interior. To stave off such results, Jefferson Davis put General Joseph E. Johnston in charge and beseeched him to aid Pemberton. Meanwhile, General Robert E. Lee proposed a Confederate invasion of the North, which, though it would not relieve Vicksburg directly, could stun the North and possibly lead to peace. By invading the North a second time, Lee hoped to move away from war-weary Virginia, garner civilian support in Maryland, win a crucial victory on northern soil, threaten major cities, and thereby force a Union capitulation.

MAP 15.1

Battle of Gettysburg

In the war's greatest battle, fought around a small market town in southern Pennsylvania, Lee's invasion of the North was repulsed. Union forces had the advantage of high ground, shorter lines, and superior numbers. The casulties for the two armies—dead, wounded, and missing—exceeded fifty thousand men.

Source: Copyright © Cengage Learning

As Lee's emboldened army advanced through western Maryland and into Pennsylvania, Confederate prospects along the Mississippi darkened. Davis repeatedly wired General Johnston, urging him to attack Grant's army. Johnston, however, considered "saving Vicksburg hopeless." Grant's men, meanwhile, were supplying themselves from the abundant crops of the Mississippi River valley and could continue their siege indefinitely.

Battle of Gettysburg

Gettysburg: Union victory that halted Confederate invasion of Pennsylvania; turning point in the war in the East.

On July 4, 1863, Vicksburg's commander surrendered. The same day, a battle that had been raging for three days concluded at Gettysburg, Pennsylvania (see Map 15.1). On July 1, Confederate forces hunting for a supply of shoes collided with the Union Army. Heavy fighting on the second day left federal forces in possession of high ground along Cemetery Ridge, where they were shielded by a stone wall and had a clear view of their foe across almost a mile of open field.

Undaunted, Lee believed his reinforced troops could break the Union line, and on July 3 he ordered an assault. Virginians under General George E. Pickett and North Carolinians under General James Pettigrew marched up the slope in a doomed assault known as Pickett's Charge. They breached the enemy's line, but most fell in heavy slaughter. On July 4, Lee had to withdraw, having suffered almost four thousand dead and about twenty-four thousand missing and wounded. The Confederate general blamed himself and offered to resign, but President Davis refused. The Confederacy had reached what many consider its "high water mark" at Gettysburg.

After Gettysburg and Vicksburg, the Confederacy was split; west of the Mississippi, General E. Kirby Smith had to operate on his own, virtually independent of Richmond. Moreover, the heartland of Louisiana, Tennessee, and Mississippi lay exposed to invasion. Lee's northern defeat spelled the end of major southern offensive actions. Severely weakened, the Confederacy henceforth relied on a prolonged defense. By wearing down northern morale, the South might yet win, but its prospects were darker than before.

Disunity: South, North, and West

What were the causes of wartime dissent in the South?

Northern and southern governments waged the final two years of the war with increasing opposition at home. The gigantic costs of a civil war fed the unrest. But protest also arose from stresses in the regions' various social structures.

Union Occupation Zones

Wherever Union forces invaded, they imposed a military occupation consisting of three zones: garrisoned towns, with many troops in control of civilian and economic life; the Confederate frontier, areas still under southern control but with some federal military penetration; and "no man's land," regions between the two armies, beyond Confederate authority and under frequent Union patrols.

About one hundred southern towns were garrisoned, causing severe social disruption. Large regions of Tennessee, Virginia, Louisiana, Mississippi, and Georgia were occupied and suffered food shortages, crop and property destruction, disease, roadway banditry, guerrilla warfare, summary executions, and the random flow of escaped slaves. After two years of occupation, a southern white woman wrote to a kinsman about their native Clarksville, Tennessee: "it is nothing but a dirty hole filled…with niggers and Yankees."

Disintegration of Confederate Unity

Vastly disadvantaged in industrial capacity, natural resources, and labor, southerners felt the cost of the war more painfully than northerners. Worse, internally, the southern class system threatened the Confederate cause.

Planters were increasingly opposed to their own government. Along with new taxation, Confederate military authorities impressed slaves to build fortifications. And when Union forces advanced, Confederate commanders burned cotton stores that lay in the enemy's path, enraging planters about such interference with their agricultural production and finances.

Nor were the centralizing policies of the Davis administration popular. The Confederate constitution granted substantial powers to the central government, especially in war time. But many planters took the position articulated by R. B. Rhett, editor of the *Charleston Mercury,* that the Confederate constitution "leaves the States untouched in their Sovereignty, and commits to the Confederate Government only a few simple objects, and a few simple powers to enforce them."

Confused and embittered planters struck out at Jefferson Davis. Conscription, thundered Governor James E. Brown, was "subversive of [Georgia's] sovereignty, and at war with all the principles for the support of which Georgia entered into this revolution." To frustrate the law, Brown ordered local enrollment officials not to cooperate with the Confederacy.

Southern courts ultimately upheld Davis's power to conscript. Though Davis was devoted to southern independence, some of Davis's actions earned him the hatred of influential citizens.

Food Riots in Southern Cities

Widespread hunger and suffering sparked food riots in spring 1863 in Atlanta, Macon, Columbus, and Augusta, Georgia, and in Salisbury and High Point, North Carolina. On April 2, a crowd assembled in Richmond to demand relief. Responding to a passerby's questions about the group, a young girl replied, "We are starving. We are going to the bakeries and each of us will take a loaf of bread." That action fueled a riot that Davis ordered quelled at gunpoint.

Throughout the rural South, ordinary people resisted more quietly—by refusing to cooperate with conscription, tax collection, and impressments of food. Farmers who did provide food for the army refused to accept payment in certificates of credit or government bonds, as required by law. Conscription officers increasingly found no one to draft. In some areas, tax agents were killed.

Austere and private by nature, Jefferson Davis was ill-equipped to deal with such discontent. His class perspective also distanced him from common people's suffering. While his social circle in Richmond dined on duck and oysters, ordinary southerners went hungry.

Desertions from the Confederate Army

Such discontent affected the Confederate armies. Worried about their loved ones and resentful of what they saw as a rich man's war, large numbers of men abandoned the army, supported by friends and neighbors. Mary Chesnut observed a man being dragged back to the army as his wife looked on. "Desert agin, Jake!" she cried.

Desertion did not become a serious problem for the Confederacy until mid-1862, and stiffer policing solved the problem that year. But from 1863 on, the number of men on duty fell rapidly. By mid-1863, John A. Campbell, the South's assistant secretary of war, estimated that 40,000 to 50,000 troops were absent without leave and that 100,000 were evading duty. By November 1863, one-third of the army could not be accounted for.

The defeats at Gettysburg and Vicksburg dealt a heavy blow to Confederate morale. Desperate, President Davis and several state governors resorted to racial scare tactics to drive southern whites to further sacrifice. Defeat, Davis warned, would mean "extermination of yourselves, your wives, and children." Mississippi Governor Charles Clark predicted "elevation of the black race to a position of equality—aye, of superiority, that will make them your masters and rulers."

Internal disintegration of the Confederacy quickened. A few newspapers began to call for peace. "There has been enough of blood and carnage, enough of widows and orphans," admitted the *Raleigh* (North Carolina) *Daily Progress*. Confederate leaders realized they were losing the people's support. It is remarkable how long and how effectively the Confederacy sustained a military effort facing such internal division.

Antiwar Sentiment, South and North

In North Carolina, William W. Holden, a popular Democratic politician and editor, led a growing peace movement. Over one hundred public meetings supporting peace negotiations took place during summer 1863. In Georgia early in 1864, Governor Brown and Alexander H. Stephens, vice president of the Confederacy, led a similar effort. Ultimately, the lack of a two-party system made questionable the legitimacy of any government criticism.

In the 1863 congressional elections, secessionists and supporters of the administration lost seats to men not identified with the government. In the war's last years, Davis's support in the Confederate Congress dwindled. Some newspaper editors and soldiers, especially in Lee's Army of Northern Virginia, kept the Confederacy alive despite disintegrating popular support.

Link to Alexander H. Stephens's "Slavery is the Cornerstone of the Confederacy" speech.

By 1864, southerners were giving up the struggle. Deserters dominated whole towns and counties. Active dissent was particularly common in upland and mountain regions, where Union support always held fast. Opposition to the war, though less severe, existed in the North as well. Alarm intensified over the growing centralization of government. The draft sparked protest, especially among poor citizens, and the Union Army struggled with a troubling desertion rate. But with vast human resources, the Union government's effectiveness was never threatened.

Moreover, unlike Davis, Lincoln knew how to connect with ordinary citizen. Through public letters to newspapers and private ones to soldiers' families, he reached the common people. The battlefield carnage, political problems, and criticism weighed on him, but his administration never lost control of the war effort.

Peace Democrats

Much of the wartime protest in the North was political. The Democratic Party fought to regain power by blaming Lincoln for the war's death toll, the expansion of federal powers, inflation and the high tariff, and the emancipation of blacks. Its leaders called for an end to the war and reunion on the basis of "the Constitution as it is and the Union as it was." Democrats denounced conscription and martial law, and defended states' rights. They charged repeatedly that Republican policies were designed to flood the North with blacks, threatening white men's privileges. In the 1862 congressional elections, Democrats made a strong comeback, with peace Democrats wielding influence in New York State and majorities in the legislatures of Illinois and Indiana.

Led by outspoken men like Representative Clement L. Vallandigham of Ohio, the peace Democrats became highly visible. Vallandigham criticized Lincoln as a "dictator" who suspended the writ of habeas corpus without congressional authority arrested thousands of innocent citizens, and shut down opposition newspapers (which were true). He urged voters to depose "King Abraham." Vallandigham's attacks seemed so damaging that military authorities arrested him for treason. Lincoln wisely decided against punishment—and martyr's status—for the Ohioan and exiled him to the Confederacy. (Eventually, Vallandigham returned to the North through Canada.)

Some antiwar Democrats did encourage draft resistance, sabotage communications, and plot to aid the Confederacy. Republicans sometimes branded them—and by extension the peace Democrats—as **"Copperheads"** after the poisonous snake. Although some Confederate agents were active in the North and Canada, they never genuinely threatened the Union war effort.

Copperheads: A dangerous snake; Republican nickname for antiwar northern Democrats, some of whom were pacifists, others were activists who encouraged draft resistance, sabotage, and efforts to aid the Confederacy.

New York City Draft Riots

Although many soldiers risked their lives willingly, others sought to avoid service. Under the 1863 draft law, a draftee could stay at home by providing a substitute or paying a $300 commutation fee. Many wealthy men chose these options, and with high demand, clubs, cities, and states provided the money for others to escape conscription. In all, 118,000 substitutes were provided and 87,000 commutations paid before Congress ended the commutation system in 1864.

Urban poor and immigrants in strongly Democratic areas were especially hostile to conscription. The North's poor viewed the system as discriminatory, and many immigrants suspected (wrongly, on the whole) that they were disproportionately called. (Approximately 200,000 men born in Germany and 150,000 born in Ireland served in the Union Army.)

As a result, enrolling officers received rough treatment in many northern areas, and riots occurred in New Jersey, Ohio, Indiana, Pennsylvania, Illinois, and Wisconsin. The most serious violence occurred in New York City in July 1863. The war was unpopular there, and racial, ethnic, and class tensions ran high. Shippers had recently broken a longshoremen's strike by hiring black strikebreakers. Working-class New Yorkers feared an inflow of black labor from the South and regarded blacks as the cause of the war. Poor Irish workers resented being forced to serve in the place of others who could afford to avoid the draft.

Military police officers were attacked first, and then mobs crying, "Down with the rich" looted wealthy homes and stores. But blacks became the special target. Mobs rampaged through African American neighborhoods, beating and murdering people in the streets, and burning an orphan asylum. At least seventy-four people died during three days of violence. Army units dispatched from Gettysburg ended this tragic episode.

War Against Indians in the Far West

A civil war of another kind raged on the Great Plains and in the Southwest. By 1864, U.S. troops under the command of Colonel John Chivington waged full-scale war against the Sioux, Arapahos, and Cheyennes to eradicate Indian title to eastern Colorado. Indian chiefs sought peace, but American commanders had orders to "burn villages and kill Cheyennes." A Cheyenne chief, Lean Bear, was shot as he rode toward U.S. troops, holding papers given him by President Lincoln during a visit to Washington, D.C. Another chief, Black Kettle, was told by the U.S. command that his people would find safe haven in Sand Creek, Colorado. Instead on November 29, 1864, 700 cavalrymen, many drunk, attacked the Cheyenne village. With most men away hunting, the slaughter at the Sand Creek Massacre included 105 Cheyenne women and children and 28 men. American soldiers scalped and mutilated victims, carrying women's body parts on their saddles or hats back to Denver.

In New Mexico and Arizona Territories, an authoritarian and brutal commander, General James Carleton, waged war on the Apaches and Navajos. For generations, both tribes raided the region's Pueblo and Hispanic peoples to maintain their security and economy. During the Civil War years, Anglo-American farms also became Indian targets. In 1863, the New Mexico Volunteers, commanded by former mountain man Kit Carson, defeated the Mescalero Apaches and forced them onto a reservation at Bosque Redondo in the Pecos River valley.

But the Navajos resisted. Carson destroyed their livestock, orchards, and crops, causing the starving Navajos to surrender for food in January 1864. Three-quarters of the 12,000 Navajos were forced to march 400 miles (the "Long Walk") to the Bosque Redondo Reservation, suffering malnutrition and death en route. Permitted to return to a fraction of their homelands later that year, the Navajos never forgot the federal government's ruthless policies of removal and eradication of Indian peoples.

Election of 1864 Back east, war-weariness reached a peak in summer of 1864, when the Democratic Party nominated popular general George B. McClellan for president and inserted a peace plank into its platform. Written by Vallandigham, it called for an armistice and spoke vaguely about preserving the Union. Democrats made racist appeals to white insecurity, calling Lincoln "Abe the nigger-lover." No incumbent president had been reelected since 1832, and some Republicans worked to dump Lincoln from their ticket for Salmon P. Chase or John C. Frémont, although little came of either effort.

With the fall of Atlanta and Union victories in the Shenandoah Valley by early September, Lincoln's prospects rose. A decisive factor: eighteen states allowed troops to vote at the front. Lincoln won 78 percent of the soldier vote. With 55 percent of the popular vote, Lincoln's reelection—a referendum on the war and emancipation—devastated southern morale. Without this political outcome, a Union military victory and a redefined nation might never have happened.

1864–1865: The Final Test of Wills

The Confederates could still have won their version of victory in the war's final year if military stalemate and northern antiwar sentiment had forced a negotiated settlement. But the North prevailed.

Why was it so crucial to northern military strategy that Europe remain neutral during the Civil War?

Northern Diplomatic Strategy From the outset, the North had pursued one paramount goal: to prevent recognition of the Confederacy by European nations. Foreign recognition would belie Lincoln's claim that the United States was fighting an illegal rebellion and might lead to the financial and military aid that could ensure Confederate independence. Both England and France stood to benefit from a divided and weakened America. Thus, Lincoln and Secretary of State Seward needed to avoid serious military defeats and controversies with European powers.

Since the textile industry employed one-fifth of the British population, southerners banked on British recognition of the Confederacy. But at the war's start, British mills had a 50 percent surplus of cotton, and they later found new supplies in India, Egypt, and Brazil. The British government flirted with recognition of the Confederacy but awaited southern battlefield successes. France was unwilling to act without Britain. Confederate agents purchased arms and supplies in Europe and obtained loans from European financiers, but they never achieved a diplomatic breakthrough.

An acute crisis occurred in 1861 when the overzealous commander of an American frigate stopped the British steamer *Trent* and removed two Confederate ambassadors, James Mason and John Slidell, to a Boston prison. The British interpreted the capture as a violation of freedom of the seas and demanded the prisoners' release. Lincoln and Seward waited until northern public opinion cooled before releasing them. The incident strained U.S.-British relations.

Then the sale to the Confederacy of warships constructed in England sparked protest from U.S. ambassador Charles Francis Adams. Over twenty-two months, the English-built ship, the *Alabama,* destroyed or captured more than sixty U.S. ships.

Battlefield Stalemate and a Union Strategy for Victory

On the battlefield, northern victory was far from won in 1864. General Nathaniel Banks's Red River campaign to capture more of Louisiana and Texas fell apart, and the capture of Mobile Bay in August did not cause the fall of Mobile. Union general William Tecumseh Sherman soon brought total war to the southern heartland. On the eastern front during winter of 1863–1864, the two armies in Virginia settled into a stalemate awaiting another northern spring offensive.

Military authorities have historically agreed that deep invasion is risky: the farther an army penetrates enemy territory, the more vulnerable its communications and supply lines become. Moreover, observed the Prussian expert Karl von Clausewitz, if the invader encounters a "truly national" resistance, his troops will be "everywhere exposed to attacks by an insurgent population."

General Grant, by now in command of the entire federal army, tested southern will with massive raids. Grant proposed to use armies to destroy Confederate railroads, thus ruining the enemy's transportation and economy. Union troops would live off the land while destroying resources useful to the Confederate military and to the civilian population. After General George H. Thomas's troops won the Battle of Chattanooga in November 1863, Georgia's heartland lay open. Grant entrusted General Sherman with 100,000 men for an invasion toward Atlanta's rail center.

Fall of Atlanta

Jefferson Davis positioned General Joseph E. Johnston's army in Sherman's path. Davis's political strategy for 1864 was to demonstrate Confederate military strength and defend Atlanta. Davis anxiously sought assurances that Atlanta would be held. From a military viewpoint, Johnston maneuvered skillfully. But when Johnston fell silent and continued to retreat, Davis replaced him with the one-legged General John Hood, who knew his job was to fight.

Hood attacked but was beaten, and Sherman's army occupied Atlanta on September 2, 1864. The victory buoyed northern spirits and ensured Lincoln's reelection. Davis exhorted southerners to fight on. Hood's army marched north to

The Civil War in Britain

Because of the direct reliance of the British textile industry on southern cotton (cut off by the war), the American conflict was significant in Britain's economy and domestic politics. The British aristocracy and most cotton mill owners were pro-Confederate and proslavery, whereas clergymen, shopkeepers, artisans, and radical politicians worked for the causes of Union and emancipation. Most British workers saw their future at stake in a war for slave emancipation. "Freedom" to the huge British working class (who could not vote) meant basic political and civil rights, as well as secure jobs in an industrializing economy.

English aristocrats saw Americans as untutored and took satisfaction in America's troubles. Conservatives believed in the superiority of the British system of government and looked askance at America's leveling tendencies. And some aristocratic British Liberals sympathized with the Confederacy's demand for independence. English racism also intensified, exemplified by the popularity of minstrelsy and the employment of science in racial theory.

The British propaganda war over the American conflict was widespread: public meetings organized by both sides were huge affairs, with competing banners, carts and floats, orators and resolutions. In a press war, the British argued over when rebellion is justified, whether secession was right or legal, whether slavery was at the heart of the conflict, and especially over the democratic image of America. This bitter debate became a test of reform in Britain: those eager for a broadened franchise and increased democracy were pro-Union, and those who preferred Britain's class-ridden political system favored the Confederacy.

The nature of the internal British debate was symbolized by the dozens of African Americans who served as pro-Union agents in England. The most popular was William Andrew Jackson, Confederate president Jefferson Davis's former coachman, who escaped from Richmond in September 1862. At British public meetings, Jackson countered pro-Confederate arguments that the war was not about slavery.

In the end, the British government did not recognize the Confederacy, and by 1864 English cotton lords found new sources in Egypt and India. But in this link between America and its English roots at its time of greatest travail, we can see the Civil War's international significance.

Some southern leaders pronounced that cotton was king and would bring Britain to their cause. This British cartoon shows King Cotton brought down in chains by the American eagle, anticipating the cotton famine to follow and the intense debate in Great Britain over the nature and meaning of the American Civil War.

Granger Collection

cut Sherman's supply lines and force him to withdraw, but Sherman marched sixty thousand of his marauding men to the sea (see Map 15.2).

Sherman's March to the Sea

Sherman's army was formidable, composed almost entirely of battle-tested veterans and officers who rose through the ranks from the Midwestern states. Before the march, army doctors weeded out men who were weak or sick. Although many harbored racist attitudes, most now supported emancipation because, as one said, "Slavery stands in the way of putting down the rebellion."

As Sherman's men moved across Georgia, they cut a path 50 to 60 miles wide and more than 200 miles long. The destruction they caused was awesome; indeed, it was Sherman's campaign that later prompted historians to deem this the first modern "total war." A Georgia woman described the "Burnt Country" this way: "The fields were trampled down and the road was lined with carcasses of horses, hogs, and cattle that the invaders, unable either to consume or to carry with them, had wantonly shot down to starve our people." After reaching Savannah in December, Sherman marched his armies into the Carolinas. To his soldiers, South Carolina was "the root of secession." They burned and destroyed as they marched, encountering little resistance. The opposing army of General Johnston was small, but Sherman's men should have faced guerrilla raids and attacks by local defense units. The absence of both led South Carolina's James Chesnut Jr. (a politician and the husband of Mary Chesnut) to write that his state "was shamefully and unnecessarily lost." Southerners lost the will to continue.

MAP 15.2

Sherman's March to the Sea

The deep South proved a decisive theater at the end of the war. From Chattanooga, Union forces drove into Georgia, capturing Atlanta. Following the fall of Atlanta, General Sherman embarked on his march of destruction through Georgia to the coast and then northward through the Carolinas.

Source: Copyright © Cengage Learning

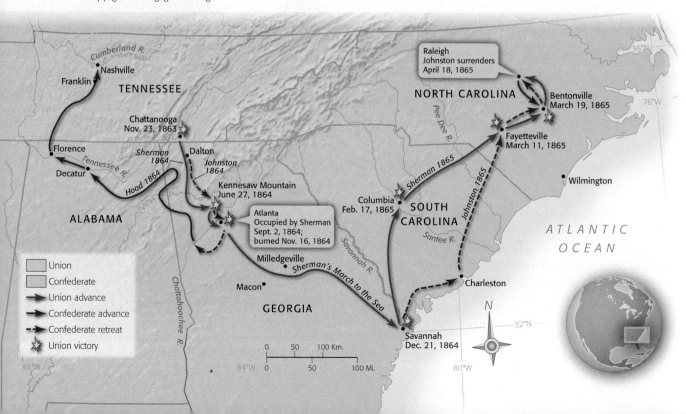

In Georgia alone, as many as nineteen thousand slaves followed the marauding Union troops. Others remained on the plantations to await the war's end, because of either wariness of whites or negative experiences with federal soldiers. The destruction of food harmed slaves as along with white rebels, and many blacks lost livestock, clothing, crops, and other valuables to their liberators.

Virginia's Bloody Soil

Throughout spring and summer 1864, intent on capturing Richmond, Grant hurled his troops at Lee's army and suffered appalling losses: almost eighteen thousand casualties in the Battle of the Wilderness; more than eight thousand at Spotsylvania; and twelve thousand in just hours at Cold Harbor.

Before the assault at Cold Harbor, Union troops pinned scraps of paper bearing their names to their backs, certain they would be mowed down as they rushed Lee's trenches. In four weeks in May and June, Grant lost as many men as were enrolled in Lee's entire army. From early May until July, when Union forces fought from forests west of Fredericksburg to Petersburg, south of Richmond, the two armies engaged each other nearly every day. Wagon trains carrying thousands of Union wounded crawled back toward Washington.

Undaunted, Grant kept up the pressure. Although costly, these battles enabled eventual victory: Lee's army shrank until offensive action was no longer possible, while Grant's army kept replenishing itself with new recruits. The siege of Petersburg, with the armies facing each other in miles of trenches, lasted throughout winter 1864–1865.

Surrender at Appomattox

With the numerical superiority of Grant's army now greater than two to one, Confederate defeat was inevitable. On April 2, Lee abandoned Richmond and Petersburg. On April 9, he surrendered at **Appomattox Court House**. Grant treated his rival respectfully and paroled the defeated troops, allowing cavalrymen to keep their horses. Within weeks, Johnston surrendered to Sherman in North Carolina, and Davis, who had fled Richmond, was captured in Georgia. The war was over; the North rejoiced, and most southerners fell into despair.

Appomattox Court House: Site of Lee's surrender to Grant marking the end of the Civil War.

Lincoln lived to see but a few days of the war's aftermath. On the evening of April 14, he accompanied his wife to Ford's Theatre in Washington. There John Wilkes Booth, an embittered southern sympathizer, shot the president in the head at point-blank range. Lincoln died the next day. Twelve days later, troops tracked and killed Booth. Relief at the war's end mingled with a renewed sense of loss and anxiety about the future.

Financial Tally

U.S. loans and taxes during the conflict totaled almost $3 billion, and interest on the war debt was $2.8 billion. The Confederacy borrowed over $2 billion but lost far more in the destruction of homes, crops, livestock, and other property. Union troops looted factories and put two-thirds of the South's railroad system out of service.

Estimates of the total cost of the war exceed $20 billion—five times the total expenditures of the federal government from its creation until 1861. By 1865, the federal government's spending soared to twenty times the prewar level and accounted for over 26 percent of the gross national product. Many changes were more or less

Link to the text of Lincoln's Second Inaugural Address.

Abraham Lincoln's "Second Inaugural Address"

Historian Don Fehrenbacher wrote that "some of Lincoln's words have acquired transcendent meaning as contributions to the permanent literary treasure of the nation." How is this so with the short oration Lincoln delivered at the Capitol on March 4, 1865? In a 701-word prose poem at his second inauguration, Lincoln probed the tragedy of the Civil War and interpreted its meanings. The first paragraph acknowledges the "progress of our arms" over four years of war. In the second paragraph, Lincoln entwines North and South in a mutual fate, but suggests responsibility for which side "would *make* war," and which side "would *accept* war," and leaves it to posterity: "And the war came."

Then Lincoln offers a theological-historical explanation of the war that still resonates today in how Americans interpret this turning point in their history. Lincoln declares that "all knew…somehow" slavery was the "*cause*" of the conflict. Both sides appealed to the "same God." But Lincoln called it "strange that any men should dare to ask a just God's assistance in ringing their bread from the sweat of other men's faces." Lincoln imagined slavery as an "offence" that came "in the providence of God," and brought "this mighty scourge of war" as its awful price.

Suddenly, in rhetoric unusual for presidential inaugurals, Lincoln assumed the prophet's mantle: "Yet if God wills that it [the war] continue, until all the wealth piled by the bond-man's two hundred and fifty years of unrequited toil shall be sunk, and until every drop of blood drawn by the lash, shall be paid by another drawn with the sword, as was said three thousand years ago, so still it must be said 'the judgments of the Lord are true and righteous altogether."

Famously, Lincoln ended with a single sentence, where he declared "malice toward none… charity for all" the healing balm for the "nation's wounds." Whether Lincoln was the nation's healer or its war-maker who would demand any sacrifice to restore the Union and destroy slavery has always animated the study of his personal story. The legacy of the Civil War, and Lincoln's own place in it, are forever enmeshed in interpretations of this oratorical masterpiece.

permanent, as wartime measures left the government more deeply involved in manufacturing, banking, and transportation.

Death Toll and its Impact

More men died in the Civil War than in all other American wars combined until Vietnam. The total number of casualties exceeded 1 million—frightfully high for a nation of 31 million people. Approximately 360,000 Union soldiers died, most from disease. Another 275,175 Union soldiers were wounded but survived. On the Confederate side, an estimated 260,000 lost their lives, and almost as many suffered wounds. Not all died on the battlefield: Roughly 30,218 northerners died in southern prisons and 25,976 Confederates died in Union prisons.

The scale and the anonymous nature of death (approximately 620,000 total dead) overwhelmed American culture and led to the establishment of national cemeteries, where the large majority of the fallen were buried without identification. The desperate urge to memorialize individual soldiers in this war, writes historian

Drew Faust, stemmed from "the anguish of wives, parents, siblings, and children who found undocumented, unconfirmed, and unrecognizable loss intolerable."

Summary

The Civil War altered American society forever. Although precise figures on enlistments are unavailable, it appears that 700,000 to 800,000 men served in the Confederate armies. Far more, possibly 2.3 million, served in the Union armies. All were taken from home and family; their lives, if they survived, were permanently altered. During the war, northern and southern women took on new roles to manage the hardships of the home front and to support the war effort.

Industrialization and economic enterprises grew exponentially with the war. Ordinary citizens' futures were increasingly tied to huge organizations. Under Republican leadership, the federal government expanded its power to preserve the Union and extend freedom. A social revolution and government authority emancipated the slaves. It was unclear at war's end how or whether the nation would use its power to protect former slaves' rights. The war left many unanswered questions: How would white southerners, embittered and impoverished, respond to efforts to reconstruct the nation? How would the country care for the maimed, the orphans, the farm widows? What would be the place of black men and women in American life?

In the West, a second civil war resulted in conquest of southwestern Indians by U.S. troops and land-hungry settlers. On the diplomatic front, the Union government managed to keep Great Britain and other foreign powers out of the war. Dissent played a crucial role in the Confederacy's collapse.

In the Civil War, Americans experienced a dramatic transformation. White southerners experienced defeat that few other Americans ever faced. Blacks were moving proudly but anxiously from slavery to freedom. White northerners were self-conscious victors in a massive war for the nation's existence and for new definitions of freedom. The war would leave a compelling memory in American hearts and minds for generations.

Chapter Review

America Goes to War, 1861–1862

What was the impact of the North's naval victories along the southern coast?

In essence, it triggered a revolution in slave society. As federal gunboats drew near the South Carolina coast, planters fled their land. Confederate soldiers were unable to round up slaves, who saw the arrival of the Union navy as a possible door to their freedom. As such, slaves broke cotton gins, stole clothing and furniture from masters' homes, and ran away to join the Union army. While the Union initially did not acknowledge the slaves as free—and instead labeled them war "contraband"—it did put them to work for the Union army.

War Transforms the South

What happened to the South's embrace of state sovereignty during the war?

The state power that had been so sacred to the South before the war was forced—by the need to mobilize—to yield to a central authority. To maintain the war effort, the Confederacy centralized its operations, troops, and supplies, seeing the efforts of individual states as likely to fragment the greater cause. President Jefferson Davis took a firm leadership role toward the Confederate Congress and urged state governments to require farmers to switch from cash crops to food production. The central government assumed control of the southern economy and nearly complete control of the railroads. Much to the dismay of many secessionists, the Southern bureaucracy ironically became larger than its northern counterpart and provided new opportunities for women to work in government jobs.

Wartime Northern Economy and Society

> **How did the war affect workers in the North?**

Northern urban and industrial workers did not fare as well as business owners and merchants during the war. While they enjoyed more job opportunities and higher wages as the wartime economy grew, inflation devoured much of their earnings. Consumer price hikes were nearly twice the rate of workers' salary increases, and workers' families saw their standard of living decline. They also lost job security as employers replaced workers with new labor-saving machines or cheap immigrant workers. Workers in several industries responded by starting unions or going out on strike, but manufacturers fought back with black-lists or by requiring workers to sign "yellow dog" contracts promising not to join a union.

The Advent of Emancipation

> **Why did Lincoln and Davis both avoid the slavery issue in the early days of the war?**

Davis feared the issue would increase class conflict between slaveless yeoman farmers and slave-owning plantation owners in the South. Instead, he preferred to say that southerners were fighting to preserve their constitutional liberties against northerners. Lincoln avoided the topic of slavery to keep from antagonizing the Union's border states, whose loyalty he sought to preserve. He also hoped to inspire a pro-Union majority in the South that might push the region back to the national fold. Avoiding the topic was also politically expedient, since no Republican or northern consensus on slavery existed early in the war—some were strident abolitionists, others were racists who wanted to protect whites from both the Southern Slave Power and the competition of slave labor.

The Soldiers' War

> **What led previously reluctant white military leaders to accept black soldiers?**

At the beginning of the war, the Union army was racist, and many soldiers did not want to fight with blacks, whom they considered inferior. They tolerated them because black recruits would do the jobs white soldiers disliked. White officers' opinions changed when they witnessed the bravery and determination of the segregated black units they led. Black soldiers, too, felt they were fighting prejudice through their military successes, thereby proving their manhood and legitimate claim to freedom. Black soldiers' willingness to die in battle also earned the respect of white men. Many black and white soldiers who fought together did forge deep ties, especially those of the ill-fated fifty-fourth Massachusetts regiment.

1863: The Tide of Battle Turns

> **What turned the tide of war toward Union victory?**

Battles at Vicksburg and Gettysburg changed the course of war from a possible Confederate victory to one assured for the Union. Vicksburg was the last major fortification on the Mississippi River in southern hands, while Gettysburg marked Lee's attempts to break the Union line and invade the North. Both battles produced heavy losses, but also left the Confederate army divided, so that west of the Mississippi General E. Kirby Smith operated alone, while Louisiana, Tennessee, and Mississippi were vulnerable to invasions. After Gettysburg, there were no more Confederate offensive moves; severely weakened, the Confederate army could only act defensively.

Disunity: South, North, and West

> **What were the causes of wartime dissent in the South?**

People across class lines increasingly disliked the actions taken by their government. Planters opposed new taxation and the impressments of their slaves to build fortifications. They also resented that Confederate commanders burned planters' cotton stores as Union soldiers advanced. People universally rejected the increasing size and power of the central government in Richmond and conscription for military service. Many people faced hunger shortages and refused to comply with conscription, taxation, or the demand to provide food for soldiers. The ability of wealthy people to buy their way out of military service by hiring substitutes fueled resentment among soldiers, some of whom abandoned the army.

1864–1865: The Final Test of Wills

 Why was it so crucial to northern military strategy that Europe remain neutral during the Civil War?

Lincoln felt that if foreign countries recognized the Confederacy, it would legitimize what Lincoln considered an illegal rebellion. He also feared it could lead to military and financial aid that would facilitate a Confederate victory and its ultimate independence. The president knew that both England and France would gain by a divided America, but France would not act without Britain, and Britain wasn't making a move until there were major southern battlefield successes. While England's relationship with southern textile mills made the confederacy hopeful for an alliance, Britain's large cotton surplus and new supplies in India, Egypt, and Brazil kept it from doing more than selling arms and supplies or offering loans.

Suggestions for Further Reading

Stephen V. Ash, *When the Yankees Came: Conflict and Chaos in the Occupied South* (1995)

Edward L. Ayers, *In the Presence of Mine Enemies: War in the Heart of America, 1859–1863* (2002)

Ira Berlin et al., eds., *Freedom: A Documentary History of Emancipation, 1861–1867*, 3 vols. (1979–1982)

David W. Blight, *Frederick Douglass' Civil War: Keeping Faith in Jubilee* (1989)

Alice Fahs, *The Imagined Civil War: Popular Literature of the North and South* (2001)

Drew G. Faust, *This Republic of Suffering: Death and the American Civil War* (2008)

Chandra Manning, *What This Cruel War Is Over: Soldiers, Slavery, and the Civil War* (2007)

Gary W. Gallagher, *The Confederate War* (1997)

Bruce Levine, *Confederate Emancipation: Southern Plans to Free and Arm Slaves During the Civil War* (2006)

James M. McPherson, *Battle Cry of Freedom: The Civil War Era* (1987)

Philip S. Paludan, *"A People's Contest": The Union and the Civil War* (1989)

Mark R. Wilson, *The Business of Civil War: Military Mobilization and the State, 1861–1865* (2006)

 Go to the CourseMate website for primary source links, study tools, and review materials for this chapter. www.cengagebrain.com

Reconstruction: An Unfinished Revolution

16

1865–1877

The lower half of secession's seedbed, Charleston, South Carolina, lay in ruin when most of the white population evacuated on February 18, 1865. A bombardment by Union forces around Charleston harbor destroyed many of the low-country planters' homes. Fires broke out everywhere, ignited in bales of cotton stockpiled in public squares. To many observers, the flames were the funeral pyres of a dying civilization.

Among the first Union troops to enter Charleston, the Twenty-first U.S. Colored Regiment received the city's surrender from its mayor. For black Charlestonians, who were mostly former slaves, this was a time to celebrate their freedom. Charleston's freedpeople converted Confederate ruin into a vision of Reconstruction based on Union victory and black liberation.

During the war's last year, the Confederates transformed the planters' Race Course, a horseracing track, and its famed Jockey Club, into a prison. Kept outdoors in the middle of the track, 257 Union soldiers died there of exposure and disease and were buried in a mass grave behind the judges' stand. After the city fell, more than twenty black workmen reinterred the dead in marked graves. On the archway over the cemetery's entrance, they painted the inscription "Martyrs of the Race Course."

On the morning of May 1, 1865, a thousand people marched around the planters' Race Course, led by three thousand children carrying roses and singing "John Brown's Body." Black women with flowers and wreaths came next, followed by black men. The parade concluded with black and white Union regiments and white missionaries and teachers. At the gravesite, five black ministers read from Scripture, and a black children's choir sang "America," "The Star-Spangled Banner," and Negro spirituals. After the ceremony, the crowd retired to the Race Course for speeches, picnics, and military festivities.

African Americans founded this "Decoration Day"—now Memorial Day, to remember those lost in battle. In their vision, they were creating the Independence Day of a Second American Revolution.

The Civil War and its aftermath wrought unprecedented changes in American society, law, and politics, but economic power, racism, and judicial conservatism limited Reconstruction's revolutionary potential. The nation had to determine the nature of federal-state relations, whether confiscated land could be redistributed, and how to bring justice to freedpeople and aggrieved white southerners. Americans also had to heal psychologically from a bloody and fratricidal war. How they negotiated the relationship between healing and justice would determine the extent of change during Reconstruction.

The turmoil wrought by Reconstruction was most evident in national politics. Lincoln's successor, Andrew Johnson, fought with Congress over Reconstruction policies. Although a southerner, Johnson disliked the South's wealthy planters, and his initial actions suggested that he would be tough on "traitors." By late 1865, however, Johnson became the protector of southern interests.

Johnson imagined a lenient and rapid "restoration" of the South to the Union rather than the fundamental "reconstruction" that Republican congressmen favored. Between 1866 and 1868, the president and Republican leadership in Congress disagreed. Before it ended, Congress impeached the president, enfranchised freedmen, and gave them a role in reconstructing the South. The nation also adopted the Fourteenth and Fifteenth Amendments, ensuring equal protection of the law, citizenship, and universal manhood suffrage. But the cause of equal rights for African Americans fell almost as fast as it had risen.

By 1869, the Ku Klux Klan employed violence to thwart Reconstruction and undermine black freedom. As white Democrats in the South took over state governments, they encountered little opposition. Moreover, the wartime industrial boom created new opportunities and priorities. The West drew American resources like never before. Political corruption became a nationwide scandal, and bribery a part of business.

The white South's desire to reclaim control of its states and of race relations overwhelmed the national interest in stopping it. Thus, Reconstruction became a revolution eclipsed, leaving legacies with which the nation has struggled ever since.

As you read this chapter, keep the following questions in mind:

* **Should the Reconstruction era be considered the Second American Revolution? By what criteria should we make such a judgment?**

* **What were the origins and meanings of the Fourteenth Amendment in the 1860s? What is its significance today?**

* **Reconstruction is judged to have "ended" in 1877. Over the course of the 1870s, what caused its end?**

Chronology

1865	Johnson begins rapid and lenient Reconstruction
	White southern governments pass restrictive black codes
	Congress refuses to seat southern representatives
	Thirteenth Amendment ratified, abolishing slavery
1866	Congress passes Civil Rights Act and renewal of Freedmen's Bureau over Johnson's veto
	Congress approves Fourteenth Amendment
	In *Ex parte Milligan,* the Supreme Court reasserts its influence
1867	Congress passes First Reconstruction Act and Tenure of Office Act
	Constitutional conventions called in southern states
1868	House impeaches and Senate acquits Johnson
	Most southern states readmitted to Union under Radical plan
	Fourteenth Amendment ratified
	Grant elected president
1869	Congress approves Fifteenth Amendment (ratified in 1870)
1871	Congress passes second Enforcement Act and Ku Klux Klan Act
	Treaty with England settles Alabama claims
1872	Amnesty Act frees almost all remaining Confederates from restrictions on holding office
	Grant reelected
1873	*Slaughter-House* cases limit power of Fourteenth Amendment
	Panic of 1873 leads to widespread unemployment and labor strife
1874	Democrats win majority in House of Representatives
1875	Several Grant appointees indicted for corruption
	Congress passes weak Civil Rights Act
	Democratic Party increases control of southern states with white supremacy campaigns
1876	*U.S. v. Cruikshank* further weakens Fourteenth Amendment
	Presidential election disputed
1877	Congress elects Hayes president

Wartime Reconstruction

> Which two political acts recognized the centrality of slavery to the war?

How to best reconstruct the Union was an issue as early as 1863, well before the war ended. Specifically, four vexing problems compelled early thinking and would haunt the Reconstruction era. One, who would rule in the South once it was defeated? Two, who would rule in the federal government—Congress or the president? Three, what were the dimensions of black freedom, and what rights under law would the freedmen enjoy? And four, would Reconstruction be a preservation of the old republic or a second Revolution, inventing a new republic?

Lincoln's 10 Percent Plan

Abraham Lincoln had never been anti-southern. His fear was that the war would collapse into guerrilla warfare by surviving Confederates. Lincoln insisted on leniency for southern soldiers once they surrendered. In his Second Inaugural Address, delivered a month before his assassination, Lincoln promised "malice toward none; with charity for all."

Lincoln planned early for a swift and moderate Reconstruction. In his 1863 "Proclamation of Amnesty and Reconstruction," he proposed replacing majority rule with "loyal rule" to reconstruct southern state governments and pardoning ex-Confederates except the highest-ranking military and civilian officers. Once

10 percent of a given state's voting population in the 1860 general election had taken an oath to the United States and established a government, the new state would be recognized. Lincoln did not consult Congress in these plans, and "loyal" assemblies (known as "Lincoln governments") were created in Louisiana, Tennessee, and Arkansas in 1864, states largely occupied by Union troops on which they depended for survival.

Congress and the Wade-Davis Bill

Congress was hostile toward Lincoln's moves to readmit southern states prematurely. Radical Republicans, proponents of emancipation and of aggressively defeating the South, regarded the 10 percent plan a "mere mockery" of democracy. Led by Pennsylvania Congressman Thaddeus Stevens and Massachusetts Senator Charles Sumner, congressional Republicans proposed a harsher approach. Stevens advocated a "conquered provinces" theory, arguing that southerners organized as a foreign nation to war on the United States and, by secession, destroyed their statehood status. They therefore must be treated as "conquered foreign lands" and returned to the status of "unorganized territories" before applying for readmission.

In July 1864, the Wade-Davis bill, sponsored by Ohio Senator Benjamin Wade and Maryland Congressman Henry W. Davis, emerged from Congress with three specific conditions for southern readmission.

Link to the Wade-Davis bill.

1. It demanded a "majority" of white male citizens participating in the creation of a new government.
2. To vote or be a delegate to constitutional conventions, men had to take an "iron-clad" oath (declaring that they never aided the Confederate war effort).
3. All officers above the rank of lieutenant, and all civil officials in the Confederacy, would be disfranchised and deemed "not a citizen of the United States."

Lincoln pocket-vetoed the bill and issued a conciliatory proclamation that he would not commit to any "one plan" of Reconstruction.

This exchange occurred when the war's outcome and Lincoln's reelection were still in doubt. On August 5, Radical Republicans issued the "Wade-Davis Manifesto" to newspapers, accusing Lincoln of usurpation of presidential powers and disgraceful leniency toward an eventually conquered South. Lincoln saw Reconstruction as a means of weakening the Confederacy and winning the war; the Radicals saw it as a transformation of the nation's political and racial order.

Thirteenth Amendment

In early 1865, Congress and Lincoln joined in two important measures that recognized slavery's centrality to the war. On January 31, Congress passed the **Thirteenth Amendment**, which abolished involuntary servitude and declared that Congress shall have the power to enforce this outcome by "appropriate legislation." When the measure passed by 119 to 56, just 2 votes more than the necessary two-thirds, Congress rejoiced.

Thirteenth Amendment: The Constitutional amendment that abolished slavery; passed by Congress in 1865.

But the Thirteenth Amendment had emerged from a congressional debate and considerable petitioning and public advocacy. One of the first and most remarkable petitions for a constitutional amendment abolishing slavery was submitted early in 1864 by Elizabeth Cady Stanton, Susan B. Anthony, and the Women's Loyal National League. Union women accumulated thousands of signatures. It was a long road from the Emancipation Proclamation to the Thirteenth Amendment—through treacherous constitutional theory about individual "property rights," beliefs that the sacred document (the Constitution) ought never to be altered, and partisan politics.

Freedmen's Bureau

On March 3, 1865, Congress created the Bureau of Refugees, Freedmen, and Abandoned Lands—the **Freedmen's Bureau**, an unprecedented agency of social uplift. With thousands of refugees in the South, the government continued what private freedmen's aid societies started in 1862. In its four-year existence, the Freedmen's Bureau supplied food and medical services, built several thousand schools and some colleges, negotiated several hundred thousand employment contracts between freedmen and their former masters, and managed confiscated land.

Freedmen's Bureau: Created by Congress in March 1865, this agency had responsibility for the relief, education, and employment of former slaves as well as white refugees

The Bureau was a controversial aspect of Reconstruction. Southern whites hated it, and politicians divided over its constitutionality. Some bureau agents were devoted to freedmen's rights; others exploited the chaos of the postwar South. The war prompted an eternal question of republics: what are the social welfare obligations of the state toward its people, and what do people owe their governments in return? Apart from their conquest and displacement of the eastern Indians, Americans were inexperienced at the Freedmen's Bureau's task—social reform through military occupation.

Ruins and Enmity

In 1865, with the war's devastation, America was a land with ruins. Some cities lay in rubble, large stretches of the countryside were depopulated and defoliated, and thousands of people, white and black, were refugees. Many white refugees faced genuine starvation. Of the approximately 18,300,000 rations distributed across the South in the Freedmen's Bureau's first three years, 5,230,000 went to whites.

In October 1865, after a five-month imprisonment in Boston, former Confederate Vice President Alexander H. Stephens rode a train southward. When he reached northern Georgia, his native state, his expressed shock: "War has left a terrible impression.... Fences gone, fields all a-waste, houses burnt." Every northern traveler encountered hatred from white southerners. A North Carolina innkeeper told a journalist that Yankees killed his sons, burned his house, stole his slaves and left him "one inestimable privilege ... to hate 'em."

The Meanings of Freedom

How did blacks exert their newfound freedom?

Black southerners entered life after slavery with hope and circumspection. A Texas man recalled his father's telling him, "Our forever was going to be spent living among the Southerners, after they got licked." Often the changes freed people valued most were personal—alterations in employer or living arrangements.

The Feel of Freedom

For former slaves, Reconstruction meant a chance to explore freedom. Former slaves remembered singing into the night after federal troops, who confirmed rumors of their emancipation, reached their plantations. A few people gave in to the desire to do what was formerly impossible. One angry grandmother dropped her hoe and confronted her mistress with, "I'm free! Ain't got to work for you no more!" Another man recalled that he and others "started on the move," either to search for family members or just to move on.

As slaves, they had learned to expect hostility from white people; they did not presume it would instantly disappear. Many freedpeople evaluated potential employers cautiously. After searching for better circumstances, a majority of blacks eventually settled as agricultural workers back on their former farms or plantations. But they relocated their houses and tried to control the conditions of their labor.

Reunion of African American Families

Throughout the South, former slaves focused on reuniting their families, separated during slavery by sale or hardship, and during the war by dislocation. By relying on the black community for help and by placing ads in black newspapers into the 1880s, some succeeded, while others searched in vain.

Husbands and wives who belonged to different masters established homes together to raise their children. When her old master claimed a right to whip her children, a mother replied, "he warn't goin' to brush none of her chilluns no more."

Blacks' Search for Independence

Many black people wanted to minimize contact with whites because, as Reverend Garrison Frazier told General Sherman in January 1865, "There is a prejudice against us ... that will take years to get over." As such, blacks abandoned slave quarters and fanned out to distant corners of the land they worked. Some described moving "across the creek" or building a "saplin house ... back in the woods." Other rural dwellers established small, all-black settlements that still exist along the South's back roads.

Link to Jourdan Anderson's letter to his former master.

Freedpeople's Desire for Land

In addition to a fair employer, freedpeople wanted to own land, which represented self-sufficiency and compensation for generations of bondage. General Sherman's special Field Order Number 15, issued in February 1865, set aside 400,000 acres of land in the Sea Islands for settlement of freedpeople. Hope swelled among ex-slaves as forty-acre plots and mules were promised to them. But President Johnson ordered them removed in October and the land returned to its original owners under army enforcement.

Most members of both political parties opposed land redistribution to the freedmen. Even northern reformers who administered the Sea Islands during the war showed little sympathy for black aspirations. The former Sea Island slaves wanted small, self-sufficient farms. Northern soldiers, officials, and missionaries brought education and aid to the freedmen but insisted that they grow cotton for competitive market. Ultimately, the U.S. government eventually sold thousands of acres in the Sea Islands, 90 percent of which went to wealthy northern investors.

Black Embrace of Education

Blacks hungered for education that previously belonged only to whites. With freedom, they started schools and filled dirt-floor classrooms, studying day and night. Children brought infants to school, and adults attended at night or after "the crops were laid by." Despite their poverty, many blacks paid tuition, typically $1 or $1.50

Smithsonian Institution, photo by Rudolf Eickemeyer

African Americans of all ages eagerly pursued the opportunity to gain an education in freedom. This young woman in Mt. Meigs, Alabama, is helping her mother learn to read.

a month, which constituted major portions of a person's agricultural wages and totaled more than $1 million by 1870.

In its brief life, the Freedmen's Bureau founded over four thousand schools, and northern reformers established others through private philanthropy. The Yankee schoolmarm—dedicated, selfless, and religious—became an agent of progress in many southern communities. By 1877, more than 600,000 African Americans were enrolled in elementary school.

Blacks and their white allies also established colleges and universities. The American Missionary Association founded seven colleges, including Fisk and Atlanta Universities, between 1866 and 1869. The Freedmen's Bureau helped establish Howard University in Washington, D.C., and northern religious groups, such as the Methodists, Baptists, and Congregationalists, supported seminaries and teachers' colleges.

During Reconstruction, African American leaders often were highly educated members of the prewar elite of free people of color. Francis Cardozo, who held various offices in South Carolina, attended universities in Scotland and England. P. B. S. Pinchback, who became lieutenant governor of Louisiana, was the son of a planter who sent him to school in Cincinnati.

Growth of Black Churches

Freed from slavery's restrictions, blacks could build their own institutions. The secret churches of slavery became public; in communities throughout the South, ex-slaves "started a brush arbor…shelter with leaves for a roof," where freed men and women worshiped.

Within a few years, branches of the Methodist and Baptist denominations attracted most southern black Christians. By 1877 in South Carolina, the African Methodist Episcopal (A.M.E.) Church had a thousand ministers, forty-four thousand members, and a school of theology, while the A.M.E. Zion Church had forty-five thousand members. In these churches, some of which became the wealthiest and most autonomous institutions in black life, freedpeople created enduring communities.

sharecropping: A system where landowners and former slaves managed a new arrangement, with laborers paying with a portion of their crops for the right to work their own land, thereby usually ending up in permanent debt.

Rise of the Sharecropping System

Since most former slaves lacked money to buy land, they preferred the next best thing: renting it. But the South had few sources of credit, and few whites would rent to blacks. Consequently, black farmers and white landowners turned to **sharecropping**, a system in which a landlord or a merchant "furnished" food and supplies, such as draft animals and seed, to farmers who worked the land and received payment from

Sharecropping: Enslaved to Debt

Sharecropping became an oppressive system in the postwar South. A new labor structure that began as a compromise between freedmen who wanted independence and landowners who wanted a stable work force, evolved into a method of working on "halves" and where tenants owed endless debts to the furnishing merchants, who owned plantation stores like this one, photographed in Mississippi in 1868. Merchants recorded in ledger books, like the one at right, the debts that few sharecroppers were able to repay. Why did both former slaves and former slaveowners initially find sharecropping an agreeable, if difficult, new labor arrangement? What were the short- and long-term consequences of the sharecropping system for the freedpeople and for the Southern economy?

Amistad Center for Art & Culture, Hartford, CT. Simpson Collection/Art Resource, New York

This Mississippi plantation store, shown in 1868, is a typical example of the new institution of the furnishing merchant and its power over post-slavery agriculture in the South.

Smithsonian Institution, Division of Community Life

Furnishing merchants kept such ledger books for decades; they became the record of how sharecroppers fell deeper in debt from year to year, and "owed their soul" to the country store.

the crop. White landowners and black farmers bargained with one another; sharecroppers would hold out, or move from year to year. As the system matured during the 1870s and 1880s, most sharecroppers worked "on halves"—half for the owner and half for themselves.

The sharecropping system, which materialized as early as 1868, originated as a compromise between former slaves and landowners. It eased landowners' problems with cash and credit, and provided a permanent, dependent labor force; blacks accepted it because freed them from daily supervision. But sharecropping proved disastrous. Owners and merchants developed a monopoly of control over the agricultural economy, as sharecroppers faced ever-increasing debt (see page 411).

The fundamental problem was that southern farmers still concentrated on cotton. In freedom, black women often stayed away from cotton picking, favoring domestic chores, given the diminishing incentives of the cotton system. Even as the South recovered its prewar share of British cotton purchases, the rewards diminished. Cotton prices began a long decline, as world demand fell off.

Thus, southern agriculture slipped into depression. Black sharecroppers struggled under growing debt that bound them to landowners and to furnishing merchants almost as oppressively as slavery. Many white farmers gradually lost their land and became sharecroppers. By the end of Reconstruction, over one-third of southern farms were worked by sharecropping tenants, white and black.

Link to a sample sharecropping contract.

Johnson's Reconstruction Plan

What was Johnson's vision for Reconstruction?

Many people expected Reconstruction under President Andrew Johnson to be harsh. Throughout his career in Tennessee, he criticized wealthy planters and championed small farmers. When an assassin's bullet thrust Johnson into the presidency, former slaveowners feared Johnson would deal sternly with them. When northern Radicals suggested the exile or execution of ten or twelve leading rebels, Johnson replied, "How are you going to pick out so small a number?"

Andrew Johnson of Tennessee

Like Lincoln, Johnson moved from obscurity to power. With no education, he became a tailor's apprentice. But from 1829, while in his early twenties, he held nearly every office in Tennessee politics: alderman, state representative, congressman, two terms as governor, and U.S. senator by 1857. Although elected as a Democrat, Johnson was the only senator from a seceded state who refused to leave the Union. Lincoln appointed him war governor of Tennessee in 1862; hence his symbolic place on the ticket in the president's 1864 bid for reelection.

Although a Unionist, Johnson's political beliefs made him an old Jacksonian Democrat. Before the war, he supported tax-funded public schools and homestead legislation, fashioning himself as a champion of the common man. Still, Johnson advocated limited government. His philosophy toward Reconstruction: "The Constitution as it is, and the Union as it was."

Through 1865, Johnson alone controlled Reconstruction policy; Congress recessed before he became president and did not reconvene until December. Johnson formed new state governments in the South by using his power to grant pardons and offered easy terms to former Confederates.

Johnson's Racial Views

Johnson had owned house slaves, although he was never a planter. He accepted emancipation but did not believe that black suffrage could be imposed on a southern state by the federal government. This set him on a collision course with the Radicals. On race, Johnson was a white supremacist. He declared in his annual message of 1867 that blacks possessed less "capacity for government than any other race of people ... wherever they have been left to their own devices they have shown a constant tendency to relapse into barbarism."

Such racial views affected Johnson's policies. Where whites were concerned, however, Johnson proposed rules that would keep the wealthy planter class at least temporarily out of power.

Johnson's Pardon Policy

White southerners were required to swear an oath of loyalty to gain amnesty, but Johnson barred from the oath former federal officials, high-ranking Confederate officers, and political leaders or graduates of West Point or Annapolis who joined the Confederacy. He also added ex-Confederates whose taxable property was worth more than $20,000. These individuals had to apply to the president for pardon. The president, it seemed, sought revenge on the old planter elite and to promote a new yeoman leadership.

Johnson appointed provisional governors, who began Reconstruction by calling state constitutional conventions. The delegates had to draft new constitutions that eliminated slavery and invalidated secession. After ratification, new governments could be elected, and the states restored to the Union. But only southerners who had taken the oath of amnesty and were eligible voters when the state seceded could participate. Thus, unpardoned whites and former slaves were ineligible.

Presidential Reconstruction

The old white leadership proved resilient; prominent Confederates won elections and turned up in appointive offices. Then Johnson started pardoning planters and leading rebels. By September 1865, hundreds of pardons were issued in one day. These pardons, plus the return of planters' abandoned lands, restored the old elite to power and made Johnson seem the South's champion.

Why did Johnson allow the planters to regain power? He may have enjoyed turning proud planters into pardon seekers. He also sought rapid Reconstruction to deny the Radicals any opportunity for thorough racial and political changes in the South. And Johnson needed southern support in the 1866 elections; hence, he declared Reconstruction complete only eight months after Appomattox. In December 1865, many Confederate congressmen claimed seats in the U.S. Congress, including former Confederate vice president Alexander Stephens, who was now Georgia's senator-elect.

Black Codes

Furthermore, to define the status of freed people and control their labor, some legislatures revised the slave codes by substituting the word *freedmen* for *slaves*. The new black codes compelled former slaves to carry passes, observe a curfew, and live in housing provided by a landowner. Vagrancy laws and restrictive labor contracts bound freedpeople to plantations, and "anti-enticement" laws punished anyone luring these workers to other employment. State-supported schools and orphanages excluded blacks.

It seemed to northerners that the South was intent on returning African Americans to servility and that Johnson's Reconstruction policy held no one responsible for the war. Thus, the Republican majority in Congress halted Johnson's plan. The House and Senate refused to admit newly elected southern representatives. Instead, they bluntly challenged the president's authority and established a joint committee to study a new direction for Reconstruction.

The Congressional Reconstruction Plan

What made Radical Reconstruction different from Johnson's plan?

The Constitution mentioned neither secession nor reunion, but it gave Congress the primary role in admitting states. Moreover, the Constitution declared that the United States shall guarantee to each state a "republican form of government." This provision, legislators believed, gave them the authority to devise Reconstruction policies.

The key question: What had rebellion done to the relationship between southern states and the Union? Congressmen who favored vigorous Reconstruction measures argued that the war had broken the Union and that the South was subject to the victor's will. Moderate congressmen held that the states forfeited their rights through rebellion and thus came under congressional supervision.

The Radicals

Northern Democrats, weakened by their opposition to the war in its final year, denounced racial equality and supported Johnson's policies. Conservative Republicans, despite their party loyalty, favored a limited federal role in Reconstruction. Although a minority, Radical Republicans, led by Thaddeus Stevens, Charles Sumner, and George Julian, wanted to democratize the South, establish public education, and ensure freedpeople's rights. They favored black suffrage, supported some land confiscation and redistribution, and were willing to exclude the South from the Union to achieve their goals.

Link to Thaddeus Stevens's reconstruction speech.

The Radicals brought a new civic vision; they wanted to create an activist federal government and the beginnings of racial equality. Many moderate Republicans, led by Lyman Trumbull, opposed Johnson's leniency but wanted to restrain the Radicals. They were, however, committed to federalizing the enforcement of civil, if not political, rights for the freedmen.

With the 1866 elections looming, Johnson and the Democrats sabotaged the possibility of a conservative coalition by refusing to cooperate with conservative or moderate Republicans. They insisted that Reconstruction was over, that the new state governments were legitimate, and that southern representatives should be admitted to Congress. The Radicals' influence grew with Johnson's intransigence.

Congress Versus Johnson

Republicans believed they reached a compromise with Johnson in spring 1866. Under its terms, Johnson would modify his program by extending the Freedmen's Bureau for another year and passing of a civil rights bill to counteract the black codes. This would force southern courts to practice equality under the scrutiny of the federal judiciary. Its provisions applied to public, not private, acts of discrimination. The Civil Rights Bill of 1866 was the first statutory definition of the rights of American citizens.

Link to the text of President Johnson's veto of the 1866 Civil Rights bill.

Fourteenth Amendment: Defined U.S. citizens as anyone born or naturalized in the United States, barred states from interfering with citizens' constitutional rights, and stated for first time that voters would be male.

Johnson, however, vetoed both bills; they became law when Congress overrode his veto. Because the civil rights bill defined U.S. citizens as native-born persons who were taxed, Johnson claimed that it discriminated against "large numbers of intelligent, worthy, and patriotic foreigners...in favor of the negro." Hope of presidential-congressional cooperation was dead. In 1866, newspapers reported daily violations of blacks' rights in the South and carried alarming accounts of anti-Black violence. In Memphis, forty blacks were killed and twelve schools burned by white mobs, and in New Orleans, the toll was thirty-four African Americans dead and two hundred wounded. Violence convinced Republicans, and the northern public, that more needed to be done. A new Republican plan focused on the **Fourteenth Amendment** to the Constitution.

Fourteenth Amendment

Of the five sections of the Fourteenth Amendment, the first would have the greatest legal significance. It conferred citizenship on "all persons born or naturalized in the United States" and prohibited states from abridging their constitutional "privileges and immunities" (see the Appendix for the Constitution and all amendments). It also barred states from taking a person's life, liberty, or property "without due process of law" and from denying "equal protection of the laws." These phrases have become powerful guarantees of African Americans' civil rights and the rights of all citizens, except for Indians, who were not granted citizenship rights until 1924.

Republicans almost universally agreed on the amendment's second and third sections. The fourth declared the Confederate debt null and void, and guaranteed the United States' war debt. Northerners rejected paying taxes to reimburse those who financed a rebellion, and business groups agreed on the necessity of upholding the U.S. government's credit. The second and third sections barred Confederate leaders from holding state and federal office. Only Congress, by a two-thirds vote of each house, could remove the penalty, thereby guaranteeing some punishment for Confederate leaders.

The second section of the amendment also dealt with representation and embodied the compromises that produced it. Northerners disagreed about whether blacks should have the right to vote. In truth, public will, North and South, lagged behind the egalitarianism of enactments that became constitutional cornerstones. Many northern states still maintained black disfranchisement laws during Reconstruction.

Emancipation ended the three-fifths clause for the purpose of counting blacks, which would increase southern representation. Thus, the postwar South stood to gain power in Congress, and if white southerners did not allow blacks to vote, former secessionists would derive the political benefit from emancipation. Consequently, Republicans determined that, if a southern state did not grant black men the vote, their representation would be reduced proportionally. The Fourteenth Amendment specified for the first time that voters were "male." As such, it provoked frustration in the women's rights movement. Advocates of women's equality worked with abolitionists for decades, often subordinating their cause to the slaves'. During the drafting of the Fourteenth Amendment, however, some leaders, such as Elizabeth Cady Stanton and Susan B. Anthony, ended their alliance with abolitionists and fought for women, infusing new life into the women's rights movement. Other female activists, however, argued that it was "the Negro's hour," causing strife among old allies. Many former male abolitionists, white and black, were willing to delay woman suffrage to secure freedmen the vote.

The South's and Johnson's Defiance

Johnson tried to block the Fourteenth Amendment. He urged state legislatures in the South to vote against ratification, and all but Tennessee rejected the amendment by a wide margin.

To present his case to northerners, Johnson organized a National Union Convention. He boarded a special train for a "swing around the circle" that carried his message into the Northeast, the Midwest, and back to Washington. Increasingly, audiences rejected his views, jeering at him. Johnson handed out American flags with thirty-six rather than twenty-five stars, declaring the Union already restored. And he labeled the Radicals "traitors" for attempting to take over Reconstruction.

MAP 16.1

The Reconstruction

This map shows the five military districts established when Congress passed the Reconstruction Act of 1867. As the dates within each state indicate, conservative Democratic forces quickly regained control of government in four southern states. So-called Radical Reconstruction was curtailed in most of the others, as factions within the weakened Republican Party began to cooperate with conservative Democrats.

Source: Copyright © Cengage Learning

In the 1866 elections, radicals and moderates whom Johnson denounced won reelection by large margins, and the Republican majority grew to two-thirds of both congressional houses. The North was clear: Johnson's policies of states' rights and white supremacy were giving the advantage to rebels and traitors. Thus Republican congressional leaders won a mandate to pursue their Reconstruction plan.

But nothing could be accomplished as long as the "Johnson governments" existed and the southern electorate remained exclusively white. Republicans resolved to form new state governments in the South and enfranchise the freedmen.

Reconstruction Acts of 1867–1868

After embittered debate, the First Reconstruction Act passed in March 1867. This plan, under which the southern states were readmitted to the Union, incorporated only a part of the Radical program. Union generals, commanding small garrisons and charged with supervising elections, assumed control in five military districts in the South (see Map 16.1). Confederate leaders designated in the Fourteenth Amendment were barred from voting until new state constitutions were ratified. The act guaranteed freedmen the right to vote and serve in state constitutional conventions. In addition, each southern state was required to ratify the Fourteenth Amendment and its new constitution by majority vote, then submit it to Congress for approval (see Table 16.1).

TABLE 16.1   Plans for Reconstruction Compared

	Johnson's Plan	Radicals' Plan	Fourteenth Amendment	Reconstruction Act of 1867
Voting	Whites only; high-ranking Confederate leaders must seek pardons	Give vote to black males	Southern whites may decide but can lose representation if they deny black suffrage	Black men gain vote; whites barred from office by Fourteenth Amendment cannot vote while new state governments are formed
Officeholding	Many prominent Confederates regain power	Only loyal white and black males eligible	Confederate leaders barred until Congress votes amnesty	Fourteenth Amendment in effect
Time out of Union	Brief	Several years; until South is thoroughly democratized	Brief	3–5 years after war
Other change in southern society	Little; gain of power by yeomen not realized; emancipation grudgingly accepted, but no black civil or political rights	Expand public education; confiscate land and provide farms for freedmen; expansion of activist federal government	Probably slight, depending on enforcement	Considerable, depending on action of new state governments

The Second, Third, and Fourth Reconstruction Acts, passed between March 1867 and March 1868, provided the details for voter registration boards, the adoption of constitutions, and the administration of "good faith" oaths by white southerners.

Failure of Land Redistribution

The Radicals blocked Johnson, but they had hoped Congress could do much more. Thaddeus Stevens, for example, argued that economic opportunity was essential to the freedmen. "He drew up a plan for extensive confiscation and redistribution of land, but it was never realized."

Racial fears and an American obsession with the sanctity of private property made land redistribution unpopular. Thus, black farmers were forced to seek work in a hostile environment in which landowners opposed their acquisition of land.

Constitutional Crisis

To restrict Johnson's influence and safeguard its plan, Congress passed several controversial laws. First, it limited Johnson's power over the army by requiring the president to issue military orders through the General of the Army, Ulysses S. Grant. Then Congress passed the Tenure of Office Act, which gave the Senate power to approve changes in the president's cabinet. Designed to protect Secretary of War Stanton, a Radical sympathizer, this law violated the tradition of presidents controlling cabinet appointments. These measures, along with the Reconstruction Acts, were passed by a two-thirds override of presidential vetoes. In response, Johnson limited the military's power in the South, increasing the powers of the civil governments he created in 1865. Then he removed military officers who were enforcing Congress's new law, preferring commanders who allowed disqualified Confederates to vote. Finally, he tried to remove Secretary of War Stanton, pushing the confrontation to its climax.

Impeachment of President Johnson

Impeachment: Process to remove a president from office; attempted but failed in case of Andrew Johnson.

Impeachment is a political procedure provided for in the Constitution as a remedy for crimes or serious abuses of power by presidents, federal judges, and other high government officials. Those who are impeached (judged or politically indicted) in the House are then tried in the Senate. Historically, this power was not used to investigate and judge the private lives of presidents, although more recently it was used this way against President Bill Clinton.

Twice in 1867, the House Judiciary Committee considered impeachment of Johnson, first rejecting it and then recommending it by a 5-to-4 vote, which was defeated by the House. After Johnson tried to remove Stanton, however, a third attempt to impeach him carried in early 1868. The indictment concentrated on his violation of the Tenure of Office Act, though modern scholars regard his efforts to obstruct enforcement of the Reconstruction Act of 1867 as a more serious offense.

Johnson's trial in the Senate lasted more than three months. The prosecution, led by Radicals, attempted to prove that Johnson was guilty of "high crimes and misdemeanors." But they also argued that the trial was a means to judge Johnson's performance. The Senate rejected such reasoning, which could have made removal from office a political weapon against any chief executive who disagreed with Congress. The prosecution fell one vote short of the necessary two-thirds majority. Johnson remained in office, politically weakened.

Election of 1868

congressional Reconstruction: The process by which the Republican-controlled Congress sought to make the Reconstruction of the ex-Confederate states longer, harsher, and under congressional control.

In the 1868 presidential election, Ulysses S. Grant, running as a Republican, defeated Horatio Seymour, a New York Democrat. Grant was not a Radical, but his platform supported **congressional Reconstruction** and endorsed black suffrage in the South. (Significantly, Republicans stopped short of endorsing black suffrage in the North.) Democrats, meanwhile, denounced Reconstruction and preached white supremacy, conducting the most openly racist campaign to that point in American history. Both sides waved the "bloody shirt," blaming each other for the war's sacrifices. By associating with rebellion and Johnson's repudiated program, Democrats were defeated in all but eight states, though the popular vote was close. Blacks voted en masse for General Grant.

In office, Grant vacillated in dealing with southern states, sometimes defending Republican regimes and sometimes currying favor with Democrats. Occasionally, Grant called out federal troops to stop violence or enforce congressional acts. But he never imposed a military occupation on the South. Rapid demobilization reduced a federal army of more than 1 million to 57,000 within a year of the Appomattox surrender. Thereafter, the number of troops in the South declined, until in 1874 there were only 4,000 in southern states outside Texas. The legend of "military rule," so important to southern claims of victimization during Reconstruction, was steeped in myth.

Fifteenth Amendment

Fifteenth Amendment: Prohibited states from denying the vote to any citizen on account of "race, color, or previous condition of servitude."

In 1869, the Radicals pushed through the **Fifteenth Amendment**, the final major measure in Reconstruction's constitutional revolution. It forbade states to deny the vote "on account of race, color, or previous condition of servitude." Such wording did not guarantee the right to vote. It left states free to restrict suffrage on other grounds so that northern states could continue to deny suffrage to women and certain men—Chinese immigrants, illiterates, and those too poor to pay poll taxes.

The Fifteenth Amendment became law in 1870. Although African Americans rejoiced, it left open the possibility for states to create countless qualification tests to obstruct voting.

Politics and Reconstruction in the South

How did black voters in the early days of Reconstruction transform the South?

From the start, white southerners resisted Reconstruction and opposed emancipation, as evident in the black codes. The former planter class proved especially unbending because of their tremendous financial loss in slaves. For many poor whites who never owned slaves and yet sacrificed in the war, destitution, plummeting agricultural prices, disease, and the uncertainties of a growing urban industrialization drove them off land toward cities and into hatred of black equality.

White Resistance   Some planters attempted to postpone freeing slaves by denying or misrepresenting events. Former slaves reported that their owners "didn't tell them it was freedom" or "wouldn't let [them] go." To retain workers, some landowners claimed control over black children and used guardianship and apprentice laws to bind black families to the plantation.

Adamant resistance by whites soon manifested itself in other ways, including violence. A local North Carolina magistrate clubbed a black man on a public street, and in several states bands of "Regulators" terrorized blacks who displayed independence. And after President Johnson encouraged the South to resist congressional Reconstruction, many white conservatives captured the new state governments, while others boycotted the polls to defeat Congress's plans.

Black Voters and the Southern Republican Party   Enthusiastically, blacks went to the polls, voting Republican, as one man said, to "stick to the end with the party that freed me." Illiteracy did not prohibit blacks (or uneducated whites) from making intelligent choices. Mississippi's William Henry could read only "a little," but he said, "We saw D. Sledge vote; he owned half the county. We knowed he voted Democratic so we voted the other ticket so it would be Republican." Women, who could not vote, encouraged their husbands and sons, and preachers exhorted their congregations to use the franchise.

Thomas Waterman Wood, who had painted portraits of society figures in Nashville before the war, sensed the importance of Congress's decision in 1867 to enfranchise the freedmen. This oil painting, one in a series on suffrage, emphasizes the significance of the ballot for the black voter.

Cheekwood Museum of Art, Nashville, Tennessee

Thanks to a large black turnout and the restrictions on prominent Confederates, a new southern Republican Party came to power in the 1868–1870 constitutional conventions. Republican delegates consisted of a sizable black contingent (265 out of the more than 1,000 delegates throughout the South), northerners who had moved to the South, and native southern whites seeking change. The new constitutions they drafted were more democratic than anything previously adopted in the South. They eliminated property qualifications for voting and holding office, turned many appointed offices into elective posts, and provided for public schools and institutions to care for the mentally ill, the blind, the deaf, the destitute, and the orphaned.

The conventions broadened women's rights in property holding and divorce. Usually the goal was not equality but providing relief to thousands of suffering debtors. Since husbands typically contracted the debts, giving women legal control over their own property provided some protection for families.

Triumph of Republican Governments

Under these new constitutions, southern states elected Republican-controlled governments. For the first time, state legislators in 1868 included black southerners. Contrary to what white southerners later claimed, Republican state governments did not disfranchise ex-Confederates as a group. James Lynch, a leading black politician from Mississippi, saw disfranchising whites as foolish. Landless former slaves "must be in friendly relations with the great body of the whites in the state," he explained. "Otherwise…peace can be maintained only by a standing army." Despised and lacking power, southern Republicans strove for safe ways to gain a foothold in a depressed economy.

Far from vindictive toward the race that enslaved them, most southern blacks appealed to white southerners to be fair. Hence, the South's Republican Party condemned itself to defeat if white voters would not cooperate. Within a few years, most fledgling Republican parties in southern states would be struggling for survival against violent white hostility.

Industrialization and Mill Towns

Reconstruction governments promoted industry via loans, subsidies, and short-term exemptions from taxation. The southern railroad system was rebuilt and expanded, and coal and iron mining made possible Birmingham's steel plants. Between 1860 and 1880, the number of manufacturing establishments in the South nearly doubled.

This emphasis on big business, however, produced higher state debts and taxes, drew money from schools and other programs, and multiplied possibilities for corruption. The alliance between business and government often operated at the expense of farmers and laborers. It also doomed Republicans to failure in building support among poorer whites.

Poverty remained the lot of many southern whites. The war caused a massive loss of income-producing wealth, such as livestock, and a steep decline in land values. From 1860 to 1880, the South's share of per capita income fell to 51 percent of the national average. In many regions, the old planter class still ruled the best land and access to credit or markets.

As poor whites and blacks found farming less tenable, they moved to cities and mill towns. Industrialization did not sweep the South as it did the North, but it laid deep roots. Attracting textile mills to southern towns became a competitive crusade.

In 1860, the South counted some 10,000 mill workers; by 1880, the number grew to 16,741 and by century's end to 97,559. Many poor southerners moved from farmer to mill worker and other low-income wage work.

Republicans and Racial Equality

Whites who controlled the southern Republican Party were reluctant to allow blacks a share of offices proportionate to their electoral strength. Aware of their weakness, black leaders did not push hard for revolutionary change. Instead, they led efforts to establish public schools, although without pressing for integrated facilities. In 1870, South Carolina passed the first comprehensive school law in the South. By 1875, 50 percent of that state's black school-age children were enrolled in school, and approximately one-third of the three thousand teachers were black.

Those African American politicians who did fight for civil rights and integration were typically from cities such as New Orleans or Mobile, where large populations of light-skinned free blacks existed before the war. Their experience made them sensitive to issues of status. Laws requiring equal accommodations won passage but often went unenforced.

Economic progress, particularly land ownership, was a major concern for most freedpeople. Land reform failed because in most states whites were the majority, and former slaveowners controlled the best land and financial resources. Much land did fall into state hands for nonpayment of taxes. Such land was sold in small lots. But most freedmen had too little cash to bid against investors or speculators. Any widespread land redistribution had to arise from Congress, which never supported such action.

Myth of "Negro Rule"

Within a few years, white hostility to congressional Reconstruction increasingly prevailed. Conservatives had always wanted to fight Reconstruction through pressure and racist propaganda began to do so. Charging that the South had been turned over to ignorant blacks, conservatives used "black domination," as a rallying cry for a return to white supremacy.

Such attacks were part of the growing myth of "Negro rule," which would become a central theme in battles over the memory of Reconstruction. African Americans participated in politics but hardly dominated. They were a majority in only two of ten state constitutional conventions. In state legislatures, only in South Carolina's lower house did blacks constitute a majority. Sixteen blacks won seats in Congress before Reconstruction was over. Only eighteen served in a high state office, such as lieutenant governor, treasurer, superintendent of education, or secretary of state.

Some four hundred blacks served in political office during Reconstruction, an enormous achievement. Elected officials, such as Robert Smalls in South Carolina, labored for cheaper land prices, better healthcare, access to schools, and the enforcement of civil rights. For too long, the black politicians of Reconstruction were forgotten heroes of this seedtime of America's long civil rights movement.

Carpetbaggers and Scalawags

Conservative propaganda denounced northern whites as "**carpetbaggers**," greedy crooks planning to pour stolen tax revenues into their luggage made of carpet material. In fact, most northerners who settled in the South came seeking business opportunities, as schoolteachers, or to find a warmer climate; most never entered politics. Those who entered politics generally wanted to democratize the South and to introduce northern ways such as industry and public education.

carpetbaggers: Derogatory nickname southerners gave to northerners who moved south after the Civil War, perceiving them as greedy opportunists who hoped to cash in on the South's plight.

scalawags: Term used by conservative southerners to describe other white southerners who were perceived as aiding or benefiting from Reconstruction.

Conservatives also invented the term **scalawag** to discredit white southerners cooperating with Republicans, as many wealthy men did. Most scalawags were yeoman farmers from mountain areas and nonslaveholding districts who were Unionists under the Confederacy. They hoped to benefit from the education and opportunities Republicans promoted. Sometimes banding with freedmen, they pursued common class interests to make headway against long-dominant planters. Over time, however, most black-white coalitions floundered due to racism.

Tax Policy and Corruption as Political Wedges

Republicans wanted to repair the war's destruction, stimulate industry, and support such new ventures as public schools—all of which required tax money. But the Civil War damaged the South's tax base. One category of valuable property—slaves—had disappeared entirely. Hundreds of thousands of citizens lost much their property—money, livestock, and buildings—to the war. Tax increases (sales, excise, and property) was necessary for even traditional services. Inevitably, Republican tax policies aroused strong opposition, especially among yeomen.

Corruption charges also plagued Republicans. Many carpetbaggers and black politicians engaged in fraudulent schemes or sold their votes, participating in what scholars recognize was a nationwide surge of corruption in an age ruled by "spoilsmen" (see pages 516). Corruption crossed party lines, but Democrats pinned the blame on unqualified blacks and greedy carpetbaggers among southern Republicans.

Ku Klux Klan: A terrorist organization established by six Confederate war veterans that sought to reestablish white supremacy in the South, suppress black voting, and topple Reconstruction governments.

Ku Klux Klan

Republican leaders also allowed factionalism along racial and class lines to undermine party unity. At the same time, the **Ku Klux Klan**, a secret veterans' club that began in Tennessee in 1866, spread through the South, rapidly becoming a terrorist organization. Klansmen sought to frustrate Reconstruction and keep the freedmen in subjection with nighttime harassment, whippings, rapes, and murders.

Although the Klan tormented blacks, its main purpose was political. Lawless nightriders targeted active Republicans, killing leading whites and blacks in several states. After freedmen who worked for a South Carolina scalawag started voting, terrorists visited the plantation and, as one victim noted, "whipped every … [black] man they could lay their hands on." Klansmen also attacked Union League clubs—Republican organizations that mobilized the black vote—and schoolteachers who aided freedmen.

Specific social forces shaped and directed Klan violence, with Alamance and Caswell Counties in North Carolina receiving the worst Klan violence. Slim Republican majorities there rested on cooperation between black voters and white yeomen. Together, these black and white Republicans ousted long-entrenched officials. The wealthy and powerful men who lost their accustomed political control were the Klan's county officers and local chieftains. By intimidation and murder, the Klan weakened the Republican coalition and restored a Democratic majority.

The Granger Collection, New York

Cartoon, depicting a freedman, John Campbell, vainly begging for mercy in Moore County, North Carolina, August 10, 1871. The image evokes the power, fear, and mystery of the Klan without actually showing its bloody deeds.

Klan violence injured Republicans across the South. One of every ten black delegates to the 1867–1868 state constitutional conventions was attacked, seven fatally. In one judicial district of North Carolina, the Ku Klux Klan was responsible for twelve murders, over seven hundred beatings, along with many cases of rape and arson. A single attack on Republicans in Eutaw, Alabama, left four blacks dead and fifty-four wounded. According to historian Eric Foner, the Klan "made it virtually impossible for Republicans to campaign or vote in large parts of Georgia."

Thus Republican mistakes, racial hostility, and terror brought down the Republican regimes. In most states, Radical Reconstruction lasted only a few years (see Map 16.1). The most enduring failure of Reconstruction, however, was that it failed to alter the South's social structure or its distribution of wealth and power.

Retreat from Reconstruction

During the 1870s, northerners lost the will to sustain Reconstruction, as they confronted economic and social transformations in their regions and the West. Radical Republicans like Albion Tourgée, a former Union soldier who moved to North Carolina and was elected a judge, condemned Congress's timidity. He and many African Americans believed that, during Reconstruction, the North "threw all the Negroes on the world without any way of getting along." As the North lost interest in the South, Reconstruction collapsed.

> What led the North to lose interest in reconstructing the South?

Political Implications of Klan Terrorism

Whites in the old Confederacy referred to this decline of Reconstruction as "southern redemption." During the 1870s, "redeemer" Democrats claimed to be the South's saviors from alleged "black domination" and "carpetbag rule." Violence and terror emerged as a tactic in politics.

In 1870 and 1871, the Ku Klux Klan's violent campaigns forced Congress to pass two **Enforcement Acts** and an anti-Klan law. These laws made actions by individuals against the civil and political rights of others a federal criminal offense. They also provided for election supervisors and permitted martial law and suspension of the writ of habeas corpus to combat murders, beatings, and Klan threats. In 1872 and 1873, Mississippi and the Carolinas saw many prosecutions; but in other states, the laws were ignored. Southern juries sometimes refused to convict Klansmen; less than half of the 3,310 cases ended in convictions. Although many Klansmen fled their state to avoid prosecution, and the Klan officially disbanded, paramilitary organizations known as Rifle Clubs and Red Shirts often took the Klan's place.

Enforcement Acts: Laws that sought to protect black voters and made violations of civil and political rights a federal offense and sought to end Ku Klux Klan violence.

Still, there were ominous signs that the North's commitment to racial justice was fading, as some influential Republicans opposed the anti-Klan laws. Rejecting other Republicans' arguments that the Thirteenth, Fourteenth, and Fifteenth Amendments made the federal government the protector of citizens' rights, dissenters charged that Congress was infringing on states' rights. This foreshadowed a general revolt within Republican ranks in 1872.

Industrial Expansion and Reconstruction in the North

Immigration and industrialization surged in the North. Between 1865 and 1873, 3 million immigrants entered the country, most settling in the industrial cities of the North and West. Within only eight years, industrial production increased by 75 percent. For the first time, nonagricultural workers outnumbered farmers, and wage earners outnumbered independent craftsmen. Government policies encouraged this rapid growth. Low taxes on investment and high tariffs on manufactured goods helped create a new class of powerful industrialists, especially railroad entrepreneurs.

From 1865 to 1873, 35,000 miles of new track were laid, this fueled the banking industry and made Wall Street the center of American capitalism. Eastern railroad magnates, such as Thomas Scott of the Pennsylvania Railroad, created economic empires with the assistance of huge government subsidies of cash and land. Railroad corporations also bought up mining operations, granaries, and lumber companies. Big business now employed lobbyists to curry favor with government. Corruption ran rampant, with some congressmen and legislators paid retainers by major companies.

As captains of industry amassed unprecedented fortunes, gross economic inequality polarized American society. The work force, worried a Massachusetts business leader, was in a "transition state … living in boarding houses" and becoming a "permanent factory population." In New York or Philadelphia, workers increasingly lived in unhealthy tenement housing. Thousands would list themselves on the census as "common laborer" or "general jobber." Concerned, in 1868 Republicans passed an eight-hour workday bill that applied to federal workers. The "labor question" (see Chapter 18) now preoccupied northerners far more than the "southern" or "freedmen" question.

Then the Panic of 1873 ushered in more than five years of economic contraction. Three million people lost their jobs, especially in large cities. Debtors and the unemployed sought easy-money policies to spur expansion (workers and farmers desperately needed cash). Businessmen, disturbed by the strikes and industrial violence that accompanied the panic, defended property rights and demanded "sound money" policies. The chasm between farmers and workers and wealthy industrialists widened.

Liberal Republican Revolt

Disenchanted with Reconstruction, a largely northern group calling itself the Liberal Republicans bolted the party in 1872 and nominated Horace Greeley, editor of the *New York Tribune,* for president. A varied group, Liberal Republicans included foes of corruption and advocates of a lower tariff. Two popular attitudes united them: distaste for federal intervention in the South and an elitist desire to let market forces and the "best men" determine policy.

Democrats also nominated Greeley in 1872, but it was not enough to keep Grant from reelection. Greeley's campaign for North-South reunion was a harbinger of the future in American politics. Organized Blue-Gray fraternalism (gatherings of Union and Confederate veterans) began as early as 1874. Grant continued to use military force sparingly and in 1875 refused a desperate request from Mississippi's governor for troops to quell racial and political terrorism there.

Grant made a series of poor appointments that fueled public dissatisfaction with his administration. His secretary of war, his private secretary, and officials in the Treasury and Navy Departments were involved in bribery or tax-cheating scandals. Instead of exposing the corruption, Grant defended the culprits. In 1874,

Democrats recaptured the House of Representatives, signaling the end of the Radical Republican vision of Reconstruction.

General Amnesty

Democratic gains in Congress weakened legislative resolve on southern issues. Congress already lifted the political disabilities of the Fourteenth Amendment from many former Confederates. In 1872, it adopted an Amnesty Act, which pardoned most of the remaining rebels. In 1875, Congress passed a **Civil Rights Act**, partly in tribute to the recently deceased Charles Sumner, purporting to guarantee black people equal accommodations in public places, such as inns and theaters, but the bill was watered down and contained no enforcement provisions. (The Supreme Court later struck down this law; see page 523.)

Civil Rights Act of 1875: Designed to desegregate public places but lacked enforcement provisions.

Democrats regained control of four state governments before 1872 and eight by the late January 1876 (see Map 16.1). In the North, Democrats successfully stressed the failure and scandals of Reconstruction governments. Sectional reconciliation now seemed crucial for commerce. The nation was expanding westward, and the South was a new investment frontier.

The West, Race, and Reconstruction

As the Fourteenth Amendment and other enactments granted blacks the beginnings of citizenship, other nonwhites faced continued persecution. Across the West, the federal government pursued a containment policy against Native Americans. In California, where white farmers and ranchers often forced Indians into captive labor, some civilians practiced "Indian hunting." By 1880, thirty years of violence left an estimated forty-five hundred California Indians dead at the hands of white settlers.

In Texas and the Southwest, expansionists still deemed Mexicans and other mixed-race Hispanics to be "lazy" and incapable of self-government. In California and the Far West, initially few whites objected to the Chinese who did the dangerous work of building railroads through the Rocky Mountains. But when the Chinese competed for urban, industrial jobs, conflict emerged. Anti-coolie clubs appeared in California in the 1870s, seeking laws against Chinese labor, inciting racism, and organizing vigilante attacks on Chinese workers and the factories that employed them. Western politicians sought white votes by pandering to prejudice, and in 1879 the new California constitution denied Chinese the vote.

Viewing America from coast to coast, the Civil War and Reconstruction years dismantled racial slavery and fostered a volatile new racial complexity, especially in the West. Some African Americans asserted that they were more like whites than "uncivilized" Indians, while others, like the Creek freedmen of Indian Territory, sought an Indian identity. In Texas, whites, Indians, blacks, and Hispanics had mixed for decades, and by the 1870s forced reconsideration in law and custom of exactly who was white.

America was undergoing what one historian has called a reconstruction of the concept of race itself. The turbulence of the expanding West reinforced the new nationalism and the reconciliation of North and South based on a resurgent white supremacy.

Foreign Expansion

In 1867, new expansion pressures led Secretary of State William H. Seward to purchase Alaska from Russia (see Chapter 22). Opponents ridiculed Seward's $7.2 million venture, but Seward convinced congressmen of Alaska's economic potential, and other lawmakers favored the dawning of friendship with Russia.

The "Back to Africa" Movement

In the wake of the Civil War, and especially after the despairing end of Reconstruction, some African Americans sought to leave the South for the American West or North, but also to relocate to Africa. Liberia had been founded in the 1820s by the white-led American Colonization Society (ACS), an organization dedicated to relocating blacks "back" in Africa. Some eleven thousand African Americans had emigrated voluntarily to Liberia by 1860, with largely disastrous results. Many died of disease, and others felt disoriented in the strange new land and ultimately returned to the United States.

Reconstruction reinvigorated the emigration impulse, especially in cotton-growing districts where blacks had achieved political power before 1870 but were crushed by violence and intimidation in the following decade. When blacks felt confident in their future, the idea of leaving America fell quiet; but when threatened or under assault, whole black communities dreamed of a place where they could become an independent "race," a "people," or a "nation" as their appeals often announced. Often that dream, more imagined than realized, lay in West Africa.

Before the Civil War, most blacks had denounced the ACS for its racism and its hostility to their sense of American birthright. But letters of inquiry flooded into the organization's headquarters after 1875. Wherever blacks felt the reversal of the promise of emancipation the keenest, they formed local groups such as the Liberia Exodus Association of Pinesville, Florida, or the Liberian Exodus Arkansas Colony, and many others.

At emigration conventions, and especially in churches, blacks penned letters to the ACS asking for maps or any information about a new African homeland. Some local organizers would announce 80 or 100 recruits "widawake for Liberia," although such enthusiasm rarely converted into an Atlantic voyage. The impulse was genuine, however. "We wants to be a People," wrote the leader of a Mississippi emigration committee; "we can't be it heare and find that we ar compel to leve this Cuntry." Henry Adams, a former Louisiana slave, Union soldier, and itinerant emigration organizer, advocated Liberia, but also supported "Kansas fever" with both Biblical and natural rights arguments. "God ... has a place and a land for all his people," he wrote in 1879. "It is not that we think the soil climate or temperature" elsewhere is "more congenial to us—but it is the idea that pervades our breast 'that at last we will be free,' free from oppression, free from tyranny, free from bulldozing, murderous southern whites."

By the 1890s, Henry McNeal Turner, a freeborn former Georgia Reconstruction politician, and now Bishop of the African Methodist Episcopal Church, made three trips to Africa and vigorously campaigned through press and pulpit for blacks to "Christianize" and "civilize" Africa. Two shiploads of African Americans did sail to Liberia, although most returned disillusioned or ill. Turner's plan of "Africa for the Africans" was as much a religious vision as an emigration system, but like all such efforts then and since, it reflected the despair of racial conditions in America more than realities in Africa. The numbers do not tell the tale of the depth of the impulse in this link to the world: in 1879–1880, approximately twenty-five thousand southern blacks moved to Kansas, whereas from 1865 to 1900, just under four thousand emigrated to West Africa.

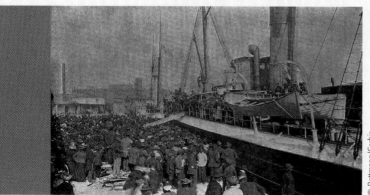

© Bettmann/Corbis

Departure of African American emigrants to Liberia aboard the Laurada, *Savannah, Georgia, March 1896. The large crowd bidding farewell to the much smaller group aboard the ship may indicate both the fascination and the ambivalence for this issue among blacks in the South. (*Illustrated American Magazine, *March 21, 1896).*

Also in 1867 the United States took control of the Midway Islands, a thousand miles northwest of Hawai'i. Through diplomacy, Seward and his successor, Hamilton Fish, resolved wartime grievances with Great Britain by arranging a financial settlement for damage done by the *Alabama* and other cruisers built in England and sold to the Confederacy. Sectional reconciliation in Reconstruction America would serve new ambitions for world commerce and expansion.

Judicial Retreat from Reconstruction   Meanwhile, the Supreme Court played its part in the northern retreat from Reconstruction. During the Civil War, the Court was cautious and inactive. Reaction to the *Dred Scott* decision (1857) was so vehement, and the Union's wartime emergency so great, that the Court had avoided interference with government actions. But that changed in 1866 when *Ex parte Milligan* reached the Court.

Lambdin P. Milligan of Indiana had plotted to free Confederate prisoners of war and overthrow state governments. Consequently, a military court sentenced Milligan, a civilian, to death. Milligan challenged the military tribunal's authority, claiming he was entitled to a civil trial. The Supreme Court declared that military trials were illegal when civil courts were open and functioning.

In the 1870s, the Court renewed its challenge to Congress's actions when it narrowed the meaning of the Fourteenth Amendment. The *Slaughter-House* cases (1873) began in 1869, when the Louisiana legislature granted one company a monopoly on livestock slaughtering in New Orleans. Rival butchers sued, and their attorney, former Supreme Court justice John A. Campbell, argued that Louisiana had violated the rights of some citizens in favor of others. The Fourteenth Amendment, Campbell contended, had brought individual rights under federal protection.

But in the *Slaughter-House* decision, the Supreme Court dealt a blow to the scope of the Fourteenth Amendment. It declared state citizenship and national citizenship separate. National citizenship involved only matters such as the right to travel freely from state to state, and only such narrow rights, held the Court, were protected by the Fourteenth Amendment.

Shrinking from a role as "perpetual censor" for civil rights, the Court's majority declared that the framers of the recent amendments had not intended to "destroy" the federal system, in which the states exercised "powers for domestic and local government, including the regulation of civil rights." Thus, the justices severely limited the amendment's potential for protecting the rights of black citizens—its original intent.

The next day, the Court decided *Bradwell v. Illinois,* a case in which Myra Bradwell, a female attorney, was denied the right to practice law in Illinois because she was a married woman, and hence not a free agent. Using the Fourteenth Amendment, Bradwell's attorneys contended that the state had unconstitutionally abridged her "privileges and immunities" as a citizen. The Supreme Court disagreed, declaring a woman's "paramount destiny ... to fulfill the noble and benign offices of wife and mother."

In 1876, the Court further weakened the Reconstruction era amendments. In *U.S. v. Cruikshank,* the Court overruled the conviction under the 1870 Enforcement Act of Louisiana whites who had attacked a meeting of blacks and conspired to deprive them of their rights. The justices ruled that the Fourteenth Amendment did not give the federal government power to act against these whites. The duty of protecting citizens' equal rights, the Court said, "rests alone with the States." Such judicial conservatism blunted the revolutionary potential of the Civil War amendments.

1876

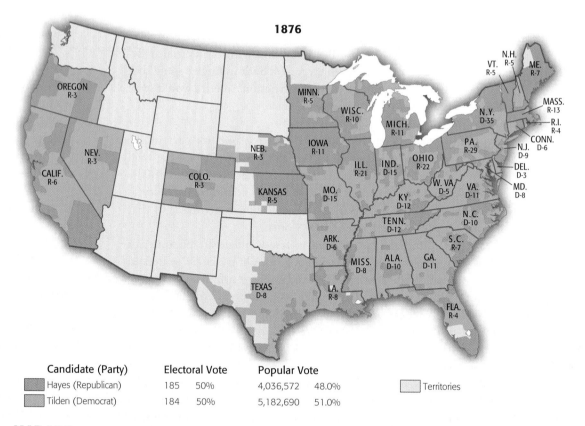

Candidate (Party)	Electoral Vote		Popular Vote	
Hayes (Republican)	185	50%	4,036,572	48.0%
Tilden (Democrat)	184	50%	5,182,690	51.0%

Territories

MAP 16.2

Presidential Election of 1876 and the Compromise of 1877

In 1876, a combination of solid southern support and Democratic gains in the North gave Samuel Tilden the majority of popular votes, but Rutherford B. Hayes won the disputed election in the electoral college, after a deal satisfied Democratic wishes for an end to Reconstruction.

Source: Copyright © Cengage Learning

Disputed Election of 1876 and Compromise of 1877

As the 1876 presidential election approached, the nation was focused on economic issues, and the North lost interest in Reconstruction. Samuel J. Tilden, the Democratic governor of New York, ran strongly in the South and needed one electoral vote to beat Rutherford B. Hayes, the Republican nominee. Nineteen electoral votes from Louisiana, South Carolina, and Florida (the only southern states not yet under Democratic rule) were disputed; both Democrats and Republicans claimed to have won those states despite fraud committed by their opponents (see Map 16.2).

To resolve this unprecedented situation, Congress established a fifteen-member electoral commission, balanced between Democrats and Republicans. Because the Republicans held the majority in Congress, they prevailed, 8 to 7, on every attempt to count the returns, with commission members voting along strict party lines. Hayes would become president if Congress accepted the commission's findings.

But Democrats controlled the House and could filibuster to block action on the vote. Many citizens feared another civil war, as some southerners vowed, "Tilden or Fight!" The crisis ended when Democrats acquiesced in the election of Hayes

The Lost Cause

All major wars compel a struggle over their histori-cal memory. After the Civil War, white southerners and their northern allies constructed a "Lost Cause" tradition, a racially exclusive version of the war and Reconstruction which persists today.

For ex-Confederates, the Lost Cause served as a psy-chological response to the trauma of defeat. Over time, it also included reinterpretations of the war's causes, southern resistance to Reconstruction, doctrines of white supremacy, and a mythic popular culture in the North and South. Lost Cause advocates—from officers to soldiers to women leading memorial associations—argued that the war was never about slavery, that the Confederates lost due to Yankee numbers and resources, and that southern and northern sacrifice should be equally honored. In the industrial, multiethnic America of the emerging twentieth century, an Old South of benevolent masters and faithful slaves, of Robert E. Lee as America's truest Christian soldier, provided a sentimentalized road to reunion.

By the 1890s, elite southern white women—among them the United Daughters of the Confederacy—built monuments, lobbied congressmen, delivered lectures, ran contests for schoolchildren, and strove to control the content of history textbooks, to exalt the South. Above all, Lost Causers advocated what one historian has called a "victory narrative" of the nation's triumph over Reconstruction's racial revolution and constitutional transformations. In his 1881 memoir, Jefferson Davis declared: "Well may we rejoice in the regained possession of self-government. . . . This is the great victory . . . a total non-interference by the Federal government in the domestic affairs of the States."

These stories endure in Civil War memorabilia, such as the epic *Gone with the Wind*, the 2003 film *Gods and Generals*, and uses of the Confederate flag to oppose civil rights. And the Confederate state rights tradition is employed today by states and advocacy groups to resist federal stimulus money and national healthcare reform.

based on a "deal" between Hayes's supporters and southerners who wanted fed-eral aid to railroads, internal improvements, and removal of troops from southern states. Northern and southern Democrats decided not to contest the election of a Republican who would not continue Reconstruction.

Southern Democrats rejoiced, but African Americans grieved over the betrayal of their hopes for equality. In a Fourth of July speech in Washington, D.C., in 1875, Frederick Douglass reflected on fifteen years of unparalleled change for his people and worried about the hold of white supremacy on America's historical memory: "If war among the whites brought peace and liberty to the blacks, what will peace among the whites bring?"

Summary

Reconstruction left a contradictory record. It was an era of tragic aspirations and failures but also of unprecedented legal, political, and social change. The Union victory brought increased federal power, stronger nationalism, sweeping federal intervention in the southern states, and landmark Constitutional amendments. But northern commitment to make lasting changes eroded, leaving the revolution unfin-ished. The promise for new lives and liberties among the freedpeople had eroded if not died.

The North embraced emancipation, black suffrage, and constitutional alterations strengthening the central government primarily to defeat the rebellion. As wartime pressures declined, Americans, especially northerners, retreated from Reconstruction. The people and the courts maintained a preference for state authority and distrusted federal power. Free labor ideology stressed respect for property and individual self-reliance. Racism transformed into Klan terror and theories of black degeneration.

New challenges gradually overwhelmed the aims of Reconstruction. Industrialization promised prosperity but also wrought increased exploitation of labor. Moreover, industry increased the nation's power and laid the foundation for an enlarged American role in international affairs. In the wake of the Civil War, Americans faced two profound tasks—healing and dispensing justice. Making sectional reunion compatible with black freedom and equality overwhelmed American politics, and the nation faced this ongoing dilemma more than a century later.

Chapter Review

Wartime Reconstruction

Which two political acts recognized the centrality of slavery to the war?

Passage of the Thirteenth Amendment and establishment of the Freedmen's Bureau in early 1865 sent a clear signal that slavery was a major cause for the Civil War. The Thirteenth Amendment first abolished slavery ("involuntary servitude") and second gave Congress the power to enforce it. Then, a few months later in March, Congress established the Bureau of Refugees, Freedmen and Abandoned Lands, known as the Freedmen's Bureau, to help former slaves. During its four years as a federal agency, it supplied food and medical services, built thousands of schools and colleges, negotiated job contracts between former slaves and masters, and managed confiscated lands.

The Meanings of Freedom

How did blacks exert their newfound freedom?

With emancipation, former slaves sought to reunite families broken apart through slave sales. Community also became important, as they built their own churches that ultimately served to unify racial ties. Seeking greater control over their work lives, African Americans wanted fairer employers and hoped to own land; when that was not possible, they rented land from former masters under the sharecropping system, in which they paid for supplies and rent by giving owners' half their crops on average. Former slaves also embraced the education that had been denied them under slavery and started schools, colleges, and universities throughout the South or attended those launched by the Freedmen's Bureau.

Johnson's Reconstruction Plan

What was Johnson's vision for Reconstruction?

Johnson's approach to Reconstruction could be summed up in a single quote: "The Constitution as it is, and the Union as it was." As president, he controlled Reconstruction policy through 1865, pardoning former Confederates and reestablishing state governments in the South. Despising the planter class, he initially insisted that ex-Confederates with property worth more than $20,000 apply directly to him for pardons. Gradually, Johnson pardoned planters, too, which restored the former elite to power, possibly because he wanted to block Radical Republicans from implementing extensive and racial political changes in the South. Deeply racist, Johnson remained silent when southern states implemented black codes to restrict former slaves' freedom by requiring them to carry passes, obey curfew laws, and live in housing provided by a landowner. Nonetheless, after just eight months, Johnson declared Reconstruction was completed.

The Congressional Reconstruction Plan

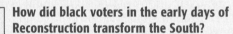 **What made Radical Reconstruction different from Johnson's plan?**

Radical Republicans in Congress were upset at Johnson's moderate approach, which seemed to hold no one responsible for the war and reestablished racial hierarchies and the southern elite. Initially a minority, the Radicals' popularity grew as Johnson increasingly dug in his heels. Radicals wanted to democratize the South through black suffrage, civil rights, and land confiscation and redistribution. They secured passage of the Fourteenth Amendment, which conferred citizenship on "all persons born or naturalized in the United States," and granted voting rights to males. They also passed four strident Reconstruction acts with strict and detailed plans for readmitting southern states to the Union. They barred ex-Confederates from voting until freedmen could and outlined the rules for voter registration boards and the adoption of state constitutions. Unpopular, land redistribution never materialized, but in 1869, Radicals pushed through their final measure, the Fifteenth Amendment, which prohibited states from denying the vote based on "race, color, or previous condition of servitude."

Reconstruction Politics and Economy in the South

How did black voters in the early days of Reconstruction transform the South?

With a large black voter turnout and prominent confederates barred from the polls and political positions, a new southern variant on the Republican Party came to power during the 1868 to 1870 state constitutional conventions. Their constitutions were highly democratic, eliminating property qualifications for voting and political office, shifting some appointed offices to elected ones, and establishing public schools. They also gave women greater rights in terms of property-holding and divorce. Blacks became state legislators for the first time in 1868. Angry whites charged they were being ruled by Negroes, and some resorted to violent resistance. In truth, while blacks did play a greater role in government, they remained a minority.

Retreat from Reconstruction

What led the North to lose interest in reconstructing the South?

During the 1870s, northerners faced economic and social transformations at home and became increasingly disillusioned with Reconstruction. Some northerners thought federal expansion had cut too far into states' rights. Second, while immigration and industrialization made northern economies boom from 1865 to 1873, it also widened the gap between the richest and the poorest and created a powerful new class of industrialists. When the Panic of 1873 brought hard times and job losses, interest in Reconstruction faded beside regional economic concerns. The Supreme Court also played a role, challenging congressional Reconstruction in several decisions. The Court ultimately narrowed the meaning of the Fourteenth Amendment by declaring state and national citizenship as separate issues and limited the amendment's ability to safeguard black citizens, as it was intended to do.

Suggestions for Further Reading

David W. Blight, *Race and Reunion: The Civil War in American Memory* (2001)

W. E. B. Du Bois, *Black Reconstruction in America* (1935)

Eric Foner, *Reconstruction: America's Unfinished Revolution, 1863–1877* (1988)

William Gillette, *Retreat from Reconstruction, 1869–1879* (1980)

Moon-Ho Jung, *Coolies and Cane: Race, Labor, and Sugar in the Age of Emancipation* (2006)

Gerald Jaynes, *Branches Without Roots: The Genesis of the Black Working Class in the American South, 1862–1882* (1986)

Michael Perman, *The Road to Redemption* (1984)

George Rable, *But There Was No Peace* (1984)

Heather Richardson, *West from Appomattox: The Reconstruction of America after the Civil War* (2007)

Elliot West, "Reconstructing Race," *Western Historical Quarterly* (Spring 2003)

 Go to the CourseMate website for primary source links, study tools, and review materials for this chapter.
www.cengagebrain.com

Appendix

Declaration of Independence in Congress, July 4, 1776

When, in the course of human events, it becomes necessary for one people to dissolve the political bonds which have connected them with another, and to assume, among the powers of the earth, the separate and equal station to which the laws of nature and of nature's God entitle them, a decent respect to the opinions of mankind requires that they should declare the causes which impel them to the separation.

We hold these truths to be self-evident: That all men are created equal; that they are endowed by their Creator with certain unalienable rights; that among these are life, liberty, and the pursuit of happiness; that, to secure these rights, governments are instituted among men, deriving their just powers from the consent of the governed; that whenever any form of government becomes destructive of these ends, it is the right of the people to alter or to abolish it, and to institute new government, laying its foundation on such principles, and organizing its powers in such form, as to them shall seem most likely to effect their safety and happiness. Prudence, indeed, will dictate that governments long established should not be changed for light and transient causes; and accordingly all experience hath shown that mankind are more disposed to suffer, while evils are sufferable, than to right themselves by abolishing the forms to which they are accustomed. But when a long train of abuses and usurpations, pursuing invariably the same object, evinces a design to reduce them under absolute despotism, it is their right, it is their duty, to throw off such government, and to provide new guards for their future security. Such has been the patient sufferance of these colonies; and such is now the necessity which constrains them to alter their former systems of government. The history of the present King of Great Britain is a history of repeated injuries and usurpations, all having in direct object the establishment of an absolute tyranny over these states. To prove this, let facts be submitted to a candid world.

He has refused his assent to laws, the most wholesome and necessary for the public good.

He has forbidden his governors to pass laws of immediate and pressing importance, unless suspended in their operation till his assent should be obtained; and, when so suspended, he has utterly neglected to attend to them.

He has refused to pass other laws for the accommodation of large districts of people, unless those people would relinquish the right of representation in the legislature, a right inestimable to them, and formidable to tyrants only.

He has called together legislative bodies at places unusual, uncomfortable, and distant from the depository of their public records, for the sole purpose of fatiguing them into compliance with his measures.

He has dissolved representative houses repeatedly, for opposing, with manly firmness, his invasions on the rights of the people.

He has refused for a long time, after such dissolutions, to cause others to be elected; whereby the legislative powers, incapable of annihilation, have returned to the people at large for their exercise; the state remaining, in the mean time, exposed to all the dangers of invasions from without and convulsions within.

He has endeavored to prevent the population of these states; for that purpose obstructing the laws for naturalization of foreigners; refusing to pass others to encourage their migration hither, and raising the conditions of new appropriations of lands.

He has obstructed the administration of justice, by refusing his assent to laws for establishing judiciary powers.

He has made judges dependent on his will alone, for the tenure of their offices, and the amount and payment of their salaries.

He has erected a multitude of new offices, and sent hither swarms of officers to harass our people and eat out their substance.

He has kept among us, in times of peace, standing armies, without the consent of our legislatures.

He has affected to render the military independent of, and superior to, the civil power.

He has combined with others to subject us to a jurisdiction foreign to our constitution, and unacknowledged by our laws, giving his assent to their acts of pretended legislation:

For quartering large bodies of armed troops among us;

For protecting them, by a mock trial, from punishment for any murders which they should commit on the inhabitants of these states;

For cutting off our trade with all parts of the world;

For imposing taxes on us without our consent;

For depriving us, in many cases, of the benefits of trial by jury;

For transporting us beyond seas, to be tried for pretended offenses;

For abolishing the free system of English laws in a neighboring province, establishing therein an arbitrary government, and enlarging its boundaries, so as to render it at once an example and fit instrument for introducing the same absolute rule into these colonies;

For taking away our charters, abolishing our most valuable laws, and altering fundamentally the forms of our governments;

For suspending our own legislatures, and declaring themselves invested with power to legislate for us in all cases whatsoever.

He has abdicated government here, by declaring us out of his protection and waging war against us.

He has plundered our seas, ravaged our coasts, burned our towns, and destroyed the lives of our people.

He is at this time transporting large armies of foreign mercenaries to complete the works of death, desolation, and tyranny already begun with circumstances of cruelty and perfidy scarcely paralleled in the most barbarous ages, and totally unworthy the head of a civilized nation.

He has constrained our fellow-citizens, taken captive on the high seas, to bear arms against their country, to become the executioners of their friends and brethren, or to fall themselves by their hands.

He has excited domestic insurrection among us, and has endeavored to bring on the inhabitants of our frontiers the merciless Indian savages, whose known rule of warfare is an undistinguished destruction of all ages, sexes, and conditions.

In every stage of these oppressions we have petitioned for redress in the most humble terms; our repeated petitions have been answered only by repeated injury. A prince, whose character is thus marked by every act which may define a tyrant, is unfit to be the ruler of a free people.

Nor have we been wanting in our attentions to our British brethren. We have warned them, from time to time, of attempts by their legislature to extend an unwarrantable jurisdiction over us. We have reminded them of the circumstances of our emigration and settlement here. We have appealed to their native justice and magnanimity; and we have conjured them, by the ties of our common kindred, to disavow these usurpations, which would inevitably interrupt our connections and correspondence. They, too, have been deaf to the voice of justice and of consanguinity. We must, therefore, acquiesce in the necessity which denounces our separation, and hold them, as we hold the rest of mankind, enemies in war, in peace friends.

We, therefore, the representatives of the United States of America, in General Congress assembled, appealing to the Supreme Judge of the world for the rectitude of our intentions, do, in the name and by the authority of the good people of these colonies, solemnly publish and declare, that these United Colonies are, and of right ought to be, FREE AND INDEPENDENT STATES; that they are absolved from all allegiance to the British crown, and that all political connection between them and the state of Great Britain is, and ought to be, totally dissolved; and that, as free and independent states, they have full power to levy war, conclude peace, contract alliances, establish commerce, and do all other acts and things which independent states may of right do. And for the support of this declaration, with a firm reliance on the protection of Divine Providence, we mutually pledge to each other our lives, our fortunes, and our sacred honor.

Articles of Confederation

Whereas the Delegates of the United States of America in Congress assembled did on the fifteenth day of November in the Year of our Lord One Thousand Seven Hundred and Seventy seven, and in the Second Year of the Independence of America agree to certain articles of Confederation and perpetual Union between the States of Newhampshire, Massachusetts Bay, Rhode Island and Providence Plantations, Connecticut, New York, New Jersey, Pennsylvania, Delaware, Maryland, Virginia, North Carolina, South Carolina and Georgia in the Words following, viz. "Articles of Confederation and perpetual Union between the states of Newhampshire, Massachusetts Bay, Rhode Island and Providence Plantations, Connecticut, New York, New Jersey, Pennsylvania, Delaware, Maryland, Virginia, North Carolina, South Carolina and Georgia.

Article I

The Stile of this confederacy shall be "The United States of America."

Article II

Each state retains its sovereignty, freedom and independence, and every Power, Jurisdiction and right, which is not by this confederation expressly delegated to the United States, in Congress assembled.

Article III

The said states hereby severally enter into a firm league of friendship with each other, for their common defence, the security of their Liberties, and their mutual and general welfare, binding themselves to assist each other, against all force offered to, or attacks made upon them, or any of them, on account of religion, sovereignty, trade, or any other pretence whatever.

Article IV

The better to secure and perpetuate mutual friendship and intercourse among the people of the different states in this union, the free inhabitants of each of these states, paupers, vagabonds and fugitives from Justice excepted, shall be entitled to all privileges and immunities of free citizens in the several states; and the people of each state shall have free ingress and regress to and from any other state, and shall enjoy therein all the privileges of trade and commerce, subject to the same duties, impositions and restrictions as the inhabitants thereof respectively, provided that such restriction shall not extend so far as to prevent the removal of property imported into any state, to any other state of which the Owner is an inhabitant; provided also that no imposition, duties or restriction shall be laid by any state, on the property of the united states, or either of them.

If any Person guilty of, or charged with treason, felony, or other high misdemeanor in any state, shall flee from Justice, and be found in any of the united states, he shall upon demand of the Governor or executive power, of the state from which he fled, be delivered up and removed to the state having jurisdiction of his offence.

Full faith and credit shall be given in each of these states to the records, acts and judicial proceedings of the courts and magistrates of every other state.

Article V

For the more convenient management of the general interests of the united states, delegates shall be annually appointed in such manner as the legislature of each state shall direct, to meet in Congress on the first Monday in November, in every year, with a power reserved to each state, to recall its delegates, or any of them, at any time within the year, and to send others in their stead, for the remainder of the Year.

No state shall be represented in Congress by less than two, nor by more than seven Members; and no person shall be capable of being a delegate for more than three years in any term of six years; nor shall any person, being a delegate, be capable of holding any office under the united states, for which he, or another for his benefit receives any salary, fees or emolument of any kind.

Each state shall maintain its own delegates in a meeting of the states, and while they act as members of the committee of the states.

In determining questions in the united states, in Congress assembled, each state shall have one vote.

Freedom of speech and debate in Congress shall not be impeached or questioned in any Court, or place out of Congress, and the members of congress shall be protected in their persons from arrests and imprisonments, during the time of their going to and from, and attendance on congress, except for treason, felony, or breach of the peace.

Article VI

No state without the Consent of the united states in congress assembled, shall send any embassy to, or receive any embassy from, or enter into any conference, agreement, or alliance or treaty with any King, prince or state; nor shall any person holding any office of profit or trust under the united states, or any of them, accept of any present, emolument, office or title of any kind whatever from any king, prince or foreign state; nor shall the united states in congress assembled, or any of them, grant any title of nobility.

No two or more states shall enter into any treaty, confederation or alliance whatever between them, without the consent of the united states in congress assembled, specifying accurately the purposes for which the same is to be entered into, and how long it shall continue.

No state shall lay any imposts or duties, which may interfere with any stipulations in treaties, entered into by the united states in congress assembled, with any king, prince or state, in pursuance of any treaties already proposed by congress, to the courts of France and Spain.

No vessels of war shall be kept up in time of peace by any state, except such number only, as shall be deemed necessary by the united states in congress assembled, for the defence of such state, or its trade; nor shall any body of forces be kept up by any state, in time of peace, except such number only, as in the judgment of the united states, in congress assembled, shall be deemed requisite to garrison the forts necessary for the defence of such state; but every state shall always keep up a well regulated and disciplined militia, sufficiently armed and accoutred, and shall provide and constantly have ready for use, in public stores, a due number of field pieces and tents, and a proper quantity of arms, ammunition and camp equipage.

No state shall engage in any war without the consent of the united states in congress assembled, unless such state be actually invaded by enemies, or shall have received certain advice of a resolution being formed by some nation of Indians to invade such state, and the danger is so imminent as not to admit of a delay, till the united states in congress assembled can be consulted: nor shall any state grant commissions to any ships or vessels of war, nor letters of marque or reprisal, except it be after a declaration of war by the united states in congress assembled, and then only against the kingdom or state and the subjects thereof, against which war has been so declared, and under such regulations as shall be established by the united states in congress assembled, unless such state be infested by pirates, in which case vessels of war may be fitted out for that occasion, and kept so long as the danger shall continue, or until the united states in congress assembled shall determine otherwise.

Article VII

When land-forces are raised by any state for the common defence, all officers of or under the rank of colonel, shall be appointed by the legislature of each state respectively by whom such forces shall be raised, or in such manner as such state shall direct, and all vacancies shall be filled up by the state which first made the appointment.

Article VIII

All charges of war, and all other expences that shall be incurred for the common defence or general welfare, and allowed by the united states in congress assembled, shall be defrayed out of a common treasury, which shall be supplied by the several states, in proportion to the value of all land within each state, granted to or surveyed for any Person, as such land and the buildings and improvements thereon shall be estimated according to such mode as the united states in congress assembled, shall from time to time direct and appoint. The taxes for paying that proportion shall be laid and levied by the authority and direction of the legislatures of the several states within the time agreed upon by the united states in congress assembled.

Article IX

The united states in congress assembled, shall have the sole and exclusive right and power of determining on peace and war, except in the cases mentioned in the sixth article—of sending and receiving ambassadors—entering into treaties and alliances, provided that no treaty of commerce shall be made whereby the legislative power of the respective states shall be restrained from imposing such imposts and duties on foreigners, as their own people are subjected to, or from prohibiting the exportation or importation of any species of goods or commodities whatsoever—of establishing rules for deciding in all cases, what captures on land or water shall be legal, and in what manner prizes taken by land or naval forces in the service of the united states shall be divided or appropriated—of

granting letters of marque and reprisal in times of peace—appointing courts for the trial of piracies and felonies committed on the high seas and establishing courts for receiving and determining final appeals in all cases of captures, provided that no member of congress shall be appointed a judge of any of the said courts.

The united states in congress assembled shall also be the last resort on appeal in all disputes and differences now subsisting or that hereafter may arise between two or more states concerning boundary, jurisdiction or any other cause whatever; which authority shall always be exercised in the manner following. Whenever the legislative or executive authority or lawful agent of any state in controversy with another shall present a petition to congress, stating the matter in question and praying for a hearing, notice thereof shall be given by order of congress to the legislative or executive authority of the other state in controversy, and a day assigned for the appearance of the parties by their lawful agents, who shall then be directed to appoint by joint consent, commissioners or judges to constitute a court for hearing and determining the matter in question: but if they cannot agree, congress shall name three persons out of each of the united states, and from the list of such persons each party shall alternately strike out one, the petitioners beginning, until the number shall be reduced to thirteen; and from that number not less than seven, nor more than nine names as congress shall direct, shall in the presence of congress be drawn out by lot, and the persons whose names shall be so drawn or any five of them, shall be commissioners or judges, to hear and finally determine the controversy, so always as a major part of the judges who shall hear the cause shall agree in the determination: and if either party shall neglect to attend at the day appointed, without showing reasons, which congress shall judge sufficient, or being present shall refuse to strike, the congress shall proceed to nominate three persons out of each state, and the secretary of congress shall strike in behalf of such party absent or refusing; and the judgment and sentence of the court to be appointed, in the manner before prescribed, shall be final and conclusive; and if any of the parties shall refuse to submit to the authority of such court, or to appear to defend their claim or cause, the court shall nevertheless proceed to pronounce sentence, or judgment, which shall in like manner be final and decisive, the judgment or sentence and other proceedings being in either case transmitted to congress, and lodged among the acts of congress for the security of the parties concerned: provided that every commissioner, before he sits in judgment, shall take an oath to be administered by one of the judges of the supreme or superior court of the state, where the cause shall be tried, "well and truly to hear and determine the matter in question, according to the best of his judgment, without favour, affection or hope of reward:" provided also that no state shall be deprived of territory for the benefit of the united states.

All controversies concerning the private right of soil claimed under different grants of two or more states, whose jurisdictions as they may respect such lands, and the states which passed such grants are adjusted, the said grants or either of them being at the same time claimed to have originated antecedent to such settlement of jurisdiction, shall on the petition of either party to the congress of the united states, be finally determined as near as may be in the same manner as is before prescribed for deciding disputes respecting territorial jurisdiction between different states.

The united states in congress assembled shall also have the sole and exclusive right and power of regulating the alloy and value of coin struck by their own authority, or by that of the respective states—fixing the standard of weights and measures throughout the united states—regulating the trade and managing all affairs with the Indians, not members of any of the states, provided that the legislative right of any state within its own limits be not infringed or violated—establishing and regulating post-offices from one state to another, throughout all the united states, and exacting such postage on the papers passing thro' the same as may be requisite to defray the expences of the said office—appointing all officers of the land forces, in the service of the united states, excepting regimental officers—appointing all the officers of the naval forces, and commissioning all officers whatever in the service of the united states—making rules for the government and regulation of the said land and naval forces, and directing their operations.

The united states in congress assembled shall have authority to appoint a committee, to sit in the recess of congress, to be denominated "A Committee of the States," and to consist of one delegate from each state; and to appoint such other committees and civil officers as may be necessary for managing the general affairs of the united states under their direction—to appoint one of their number to preside, provided that no person be allowed to serve in the office of president more than one year in any term of three years; to ascertain the necessary sums of Money to be raised for the service of the united states, and to appropriate and apply the same for defraying the public expences—to borrow money, or emit bills on the credit of the united states, transmitting every half year to the respective states an account of the sums of money so borrowed or emitted—to build and equip a navy—to agree upon the number of land forces, and to

make requisitions from each state for its quota, in proportion to the number of white inhabitants in such state; which requisition shall be binding, and thereupon the legislature of each state shall appoint the regimental officers, raise the men and cloath, arm and equip them in a soldier like manner, at the expence of the united states, and the officers and men so cloathed, armed and equipped shall march to the place appointed, and within the time agreed on by the united states in congress assembled: But if the united states in congress assembled shall, on consideration of circumstances judge proper that any state should not raise men, or should raise a smaller number than its quota, and that any other state should raise a greater number of men than the quota thereof, such extra number shall be raised, officered, cloathed, armed and equipped in the same manner as the quota of such state, unless the legislature of such state shall judge that such extra number cannot be safely spared out of the same, in which case they shall raise, officer, cloath, arm and equip as many of such extra number as they judge can be safely spared. And the officers and men so cloathed, armed and equipped, shall march to the place appointed, and within the time agreed on by the united states in congress assembled.

The united states in congress assembled shall never engage in a war, nor grant letters of marque and reprisal in time of peace, nor enter into any treaties or alliances, nor coin money, nor regulate the value thereof, nor ascertain the sums and expences necessary for the defence and welfare of the united states, or any of them, nor emit bills, nor borrow money on the credit of the united states, nor appropriate money, nor agree upon the number of vessels of war, to be built or purchased, or the number of land or sea forces to be raised, nor appoint a commander in chief of the army or navy, unless nine states assent to the same: nor shall a question on any other point, except for adjourning from day to day be determined, unless by the votes of a majority of the united states in congress assembled.

The congress of the united states shall have power to adjourn to any time within the year, and to any place within the united states, so that no period of adjournment be for a longer duration than the space of six Months, and shall publish the Journal of their proceedings monthly, except such parts thereof relating to treaties, alliances or military operations as in their judgment require secresy; and the yeas and nays of the delegates of each state on any question shall be entered on the Journal, when it is desired by any delegate; and the delegates of a state, or any of them, at his or their request shall be furnished with a transcript of the said Journal, except such parts as are above excepted, to lay before the legislatures of the several states.

Article X

The committee of the states, or any nine of them, shall be authorised to execute, in the recess of congress, such of the powers of congress as the united states in congress assembled, by the consent of nine states, shall from time to time think expedient to vest them with; provided that no power be delegated to the said committee, for the exercise of which, by the articles of confederation, the voice of nine states in the congress of the united states assembled is requisite.

Article XI

Canada acceding to this confederation, and joining in the measures of the united states, shall be admitted into, and entitled to all the advantages of this union: but no other colony shall be admitted into the same, unless such admission be agreed to by nine states.

Article XII

All bills of credit emitted, monies borrowed and debts contracted by, or under the authority of congress, before the assembling of the united states, in pursuance of the present confederation, shall be deemed and considered as a charge against the united states, for payment and satisfaction whereof the said united states, and the public faith are hereby solemnly pledged.

Article XIII

Every state shall abide by the determinations of the united states in congress assembled, on all questions which by this confederation are submitted to them. And the Articles of this confederation shall be inviolably observed by every state, and the union shall be perpetual; nor shall any alteration at any time hereafter be made in any of them; unless such alteration be agreed to in a congress of the united states, and be afterwards confirmed by the legislatures of every state.

AND WHEREAS it hath pleased the Great Governor of the World to incline the hearts of the legislatures we respectively represent in congress, to approve of, and to authorize us to ratify the said articles of confederation and perpetual union. Know Ye that we the under-signed delegates, by virtue of the power and authority to us given for that purpose, do by these presents, in the name and in behalf of our respective constituents, fully and entirely ratify and confirm each and every of the said articles of confederation and perpetual union, and all and singular the matters and things therein contained: And we do further solemnly plight and engage the faith of our respective constituents, that they shall abide by the determinations of the united states in congress assembled, on all questions, which by the said confederation are submitted to them. And that the articles thereof shall be inviolably observed by the states we respectively represent, and that the union shall be perpetual. In Witness whereof we have hereunto set our hands in Congress. Done at Philadelphia in the state of Pennsylvania the ninth Day of July in the Year of our Lord one Thousand seven Hundred and Seventy-eight, and in the third year of the independence of America.

Constitution of the United States of America and Amendments*

Preamble

We the people of the United States, in order to form a more perfect union, establish justice, insure domestic tranquillity, provide for the common defense, promote the general welfare, and secure the blessings of liberty to ourselves and our posterity, do ordain and establish this Constitution for the United States of America.

Article I

Section 1 All legislative powers herein granted shall be vested in a Congress of the United States, which shall consist of a Senate and a House of Representatives.

Section 2 The House of Representatives shall be composed of members chosen every second year by the people of the several States, and the electors in each State shall have the qualifications requisite for electors of the most numerous branch of the State Legislature.

No person shall be a Representative who shall not have attained to the age of twenty-five years, and been seven years a citizen of the United States, and who shall not, when elected, be an inhabitant of that State in which he shall be chosen.

Representatives and direct taxes shall be apportioned among the several States which may be included within this Union, according to their respective numbers, *which shall be determined by adding to the whole number of free persons, including those bound to service for a term of years and excluding Indians not taxed, three-fifths of all other persons.*

---

*Passages no longer in effect are printed in italic type.

The actual enumeration shall be made within three years after the first meeting of the Congress of the United States, and within every subsequent term of ten years, in such manner as they shall by law direct. The number of Representatives shall not exceed one for every thirty thousand, but each State shall have at least one Representative; *and until such enumeration shall be made, the State of New Hampshire shall be entitled to choose three, Massachusetts eight, Rhode Island and Providence Plantations one, Connecticut five, New York six, New Jersey four, Pennsylvania eight, Delaware one, Maryland six, Virginia ten, North Carolina five, South Carolina five, and Georgia three.*

When vacancies happen in the representation from any State, the Executive authority thereof shall issue writs of election to fill such vacancies.

The House of Representatives shall choose their Speaker and other officers; and shall have the sole power of impeachment.

Section 3 The Senate of the United States shall be composed of two Senators from each State, chosen by the legislature thereof, for six years; and each Senator shall have one vote.

Immediately after they shall be assembled in consequence of the first election, they shall be divided as equally as may be into three classes. The seats of the Senators of the first class shall be vacated at the expiration of the second year, of the second class at the expiration of the fourth year, and of the third class at the expiration of the sixth year, so that one-third may be chosen every second year; and if vacancies happen by resignation or otherwise, during the recess of the legislature of any State, the Executive thereof may make temporary appointments until the next meeting of the legislature, which shall then fill such vacancies.

No person shall be a Senator who shall not have attained to the age of thirty years, and been nine years a citizen of the United States, and who shall not, when elected, be an inhabitant of that State for which he shall be chosen.

The Vice-President of the United States shall be President of the Senate, but shall have no vote, unless they be equally divided.

The Senate shall choose their other officers, and also a President *pro tempore,* in the absence of the Vice-President, or when he shall exercise the office of President of the United States.

The Senate shall have the sole power to try all impeachments. When sitting for that purpose, they shall be on oath or affirmation. When the President of the United States is tried, the Chief Justice shall preside: and no person shall be convicted without the concurrence of two-thirds of the members present.

Judgment in cases of impeachment shall not extend further than to removal from the office, and disqualification to hold and enjoy any office of honor, trust or profit under the United States: but the party convicted shall nevertheless be liable and subject to indictment, trial, judgment and punishment, according to law.

Section 4 The times, places and manner of holding elections for Senators and Representatives shall be prescribed in each State by the legislature thereof; but the Congress may at any time by law make or alter such regulations, except as to the places of choosing Senators.

The Congress shall assemble at least once in every year, and such meeting shall be on the first Monday in December, unless they shall by law appoint a different day.

Section 5 Each house shall be the judge of the elections, returns and qualifications of its own members, and a majority of each shall constitute a quorum to do business; but a smaller number may adjourn from day to day, and may be authorized to compel the attendance of absent members, in such manner, and under such penalties, as each house may provide.

Each house may determine the rules of its proceedings, punish its members for disorderly behavior, and with the concurrence of two-thirds, expel a member.

Each house shall keep a journal of its proceedings, and from time to time publish the same, excepting such parts as may in their judgment require secrecy; and the yeas and nays of the members of either house on any question shall, at the desire of one-fifth of those present, be entered on the journal.

Neither house, during the session of Congress, shall, without the consent of the other, adjourn for more than three days, nor to any other place than that in which the two houses shall be sitting.

Section 6 The Senators and Representatives shall receive a compensation for their services, to be ascertained by law and paid out of the treasury of the United States. They shall in all cases except treason, felony and breach of the peace, be privileged from arrest during their attendance at the session of their respective houses, and in going to and returning from the same; and for any speech or debate in either house, they shall not be questioned in any other place.

No Senator or Representative shall, during the time for which he was elected, be appointed to any civil office under the authority of the United States, which shall have been created, or the emoluments whereof shall have been increased, during such time; and no person holding any office under the United States shall be a member of either house during his continuance in office.

Section 7 All bills for raising revenue shall originate in the House of Representatives; but the Senate may propose or concur with amendments as on other bills.

Every bill which shall have passed the House of Representatives and the Senate, shall, before it become a law, be presented to the President of the United States;

if he approve he shall sign it, but if not he shall return it with objections to that house in which it originated, who shall enter the objections at large on their journal, and proceed to reconsider it. If after such reconsideration two-thirds of that house shall agree to pass the bill, it shall be sent, together with the objections, to the other house, by which it shall likewise be reconsidered, and, if approved by two-thirds of that house, it shall become a law. But in all such cases the votes of both houses shall be determined by yeas and nays, and the names of the persons voting for and against the bill shall be entered on the journal of each house respectively. If any bill shall not be returned by the President within ten days (Sundays excepted) after it shall have been presented to him, the same shall be a law, in like manner as if he had signed it, unless the Congress by their adjournment prevent its return, in which case it shall not be a law.

Every order, resolution, or vote to which the concurrence of the Senate and House of Representatives may be necessary (except on a question of adjournment) shall be presented to the President of the United States; and before the same shall take effect, shall be approved by him, or being disapproved by him, shall be repassed by two-thirds of the Senate and House of Representatives, according to the rules and limitations prescribed in the case of a bill.

Section 8 The Congress shall have power

To lay and collect taxes, duties, imposts, and excises, to pay the debts and provide for the common defense and general welfare of the United States; but all duties, imposts and excises shall be uniform throughout the United States;

To borrow money on the credit of the United States;

To regulate commerce with foreign nations, and among the several States, and with the Indian tribes;

To establish an uniform rule of naturalization, and uniform laws on the subject of bankruptcies throughout the United States;

To coin money, regulate the value thereof, and of foreign coin, and fix the standard of weights and measures;

To provide for the punishment of counterfeiting the securities and current coin of the United States;

To establish post offices and post roads;

To promote the progress of science and useful arts by securing for limited times to authors and inventors the exclusive right to their respective writings and discoveries;

To constitute tribunals inferior to the Supreme Court;

To define and punish piracies and felonies committed on the high seas and offenses against the law of nations;

To declare war, grant letters of marque and reprisal, and make rules concerning captures on land and water;

To raise and support armies, but no appropriation of money to that use shall be for a longer term than two years;

To provide and maintain a navy;

To make rules for the government and regulation of the land and naval forces;

To provide for calling forth the militia to execute the laws of the Union, suppress insurrections, and repel invasions;

To provide for organizing, arming, and disciplining the militia, and for governing such part of them as may be employed in the service of the United States, reserving to the States respectively the appointment of the officers, and the authority of training the militia according to the discipline prescribed by Congress;

To exercise exclusive legislation in all cases whatsoever, over such district (not exceeding ten miles square) as may, by cession of particular States, and the acceptance of Congress, become the seat of government of the United States, and to exercise like authority over all places purchased by the consent of the legislature of the State, in which the same shall be, for erection of forts, magazines, arsenals, dockyards, and other needful buildings;—and

To make all laws which shall be necessary and proper for carrying into execution the foregoing powers, and all other powers vested by this Constitution in the government of the United States, or in any department or officer thereof.

Section 9 *The migration or importation of such persons as any of the States now existing shall think proper to admit shall not be prohibited by the Congress prior to the year 1808; but a tax or duty may be imposed on such importation, not exceeding $10 for each person.*

The privilege of the writ of habeas corpus shall not be suspended, unless when in cases of rebellion or invasion the public safety may require it.

No bill of attainder or ex post facto law shall be passed.

No capitation, or other direct, tax shall be laid, unless in proportion to the census or enumeration herein before directed to be taken.

No tax or duty shall be laid on articles exported from any State.

No preference shall be given by any regulation of commerce or revenue to the ports of one State over those of another; nor shall vessels bound to, or from, one State, be obliged to enter, clear, or pay duties in another.

No money shall be drawn from the treasury, but in consequence of appropriations made by law; and a regular statement and account of the receipts and expenditures of all public money shall be published from time to time.

No title of nobility shall be granted by the United States: and no person holding any office of profit or trust under them, shall, without the consent of the Congress, accept of any present, emolument, office, or title, of any kind whatever, from any king, prince, or foreign state.

Section 10 No State shall enter into any treaty, alliance, or confederation; grant letters of marque and reprisal; coin money; emit bills of credit; make anything but gold and silver coin a tender in payment of debts; pass any bill of attainder, ex post facto law, or law impairing the obligation of contracts, or grant any title of nobility.

No State shall, without the consent of Congress, lay any imposts or duties on imports or exports, except what may be absolutely necessary for executing its inspection laws: and the net produce of all duties and imposts, laid by any State on imports or exports, shall be for the use of the treasury of the United States; and all such laws shall be subject to the revision and control of the Congress.

No State shall, without the consent of Congress, lay any duty of tonnage, keep troops or ships of war in time of peace, enter into any agreement or compact with another State, or with a foreign power, or engage in war, unless actually invaded, or in such imminent danger as will not admit of delay.

Article II

Section 1 The executive power shall be vested in a President of the United States of America. He shall hold his office during the term of four years, and, together with the Vice-President, chosen for the same term, be elected as follows:

Each State shall appoint, in such manner as the legislature thereof may direct, a number of electors, equal to the whole number of Senators and Representatives to which the State may be entitled in the Congress; but no Senator or Representative, or person holding an office of trust or profit under the United States, shall be appointed an elector.

The electors shall meet in their respective States, and vote by ballot for two persons, of whom one at least shall not be an inhabitant of the same State with themselves. And they shall make a list of all the persons voted for, and of the number of votes for each; which list they shall sign and certify, and transmit sealed to the seat of government of the United States, directed to the President of the Senate. The President of the Senate shall, in the presence of the Senate and House of Representatives, open all the certificates, and the votes shall then be counted. The person having the greatest number of votes shall be the President, if such number be a majority of the whole number of electors appointed; and if there be more than one who have such majority, and have an equal number of votes, then the House of Representatives shall immediately choose by ballot one of them for President; and if no person have a majority, then from the five highest on the list said house shall in like manner choose the President. But in choosing the President the votes shall be taken by States, the representation from each State having one vote; a quorum for this purpose shall consist of a member or members from two-thirds of the States, and a majority of all the States shall be necessary to a choice. In every case, after the choice of the President, the person having the greatest number of votes of the electors shall be the Vice-President. But if there should remain two or more who have equal votes, the Senate shall choose from them by ballot the Vice-President.

The Congress may determine the time of choosing the electors and the day on which they shall give their votes; which day shall be the same throughout the United States.

No person except a natural-born citizen, *or a citizen of the United States at the time of the adoption of this Constitution,* shall be eligible to the office of President; neither shall any person be eligible to that office who shall not have attained to the age of thirty-five years, and been fourteen years a resident within the United States.

In cases of the removal of the President from office or of his death, resignation, or inability to discharge the powers and duties of the said office, the same shall devolve on the Vice-President, and the Congress may by law provide for the case of removal, death, resignation, or inability, both of the President and Vice-President, declaring what officer shall then act as President, and such officer shall act accordingly, until the disability be removed, or a President shall be elected.

The President shall, at stated times, receive for his services a compensation, which shall neither be increased nor diminished during the period for which he shall have been elected, and he shall not receive within that period any other emolument from the United States, or any of them.

Before he enter on the execution of his office, he shall take the following oath or affirmation:—"I do solemnly swear (or affirm) that I will faithfully execute the office of the President of the United States, and will to the best of my ability preserve, protect and defend the Constitution of the United States."

Section 2 The President shall be commander in chief of the army and navy of the United States, and of the militia of the several States, when called into the actual service of the United States; he may require the opinion, in writing, of the principal officer in each of the executive departments, upon any subject relating to the duties of their respective offices, and he shall have power to grant reprieves and pardons for offenses against the United States, except in cases of impeachment.

He shall have power, by and with the advice and consent of the Senate, to make treaties, provided two-thirds of the Senators present concur; and he shall nominate, and by and with the advice and consent of the Senate, shall appoint ambassadors, other public ministers and consuls, judges of the Supreme Court, and all other officers of the United States, whose appointments are not herein otherwise provided for, and which shall be established by law: but Congress may by law vest the appointment of such inferior officers, as they think proper, in the President alone, in the courts of law, or in the heads of departments.

The President shall have power to fill up all vacancies that may happen during the recess of the Senate, by granting commissions which shall expire at the end of their next session.

Section 3 He shall from time to time give to the Congress information of the state of the Union, and recommend to their consideration such measures as he shall judge necessary and expedient; he may, on extraordinary occasions, convene both houses, or either of them, and in case of disagreement between them, with respect to the time of adjournment, he may adjourn them to such time as he shall think proper; he shall receive ambassadors and other public ministers; he shall take care that the laws be faithfully executed, and shall commission all the officers of the United States.

Section 4 The President, Vice-President and all civil officers of the United States shall be removed from office on impeachment for, and on conviction of, treason, bribery, or other high crimes and misdemeanors.

Article III

Section 1 The judicial power of the United States shall be vested in one Supreme Court, and in such inferior courts as the Congress may from time to time ordain and establish. The judges, both of the Supreme and inferior courts, shall hold their offices during good behavior, and shall, at stated times, receive for their services a compensation which shall not be diminished during their continuance in office.

Section 2 The judicial power shall extend to all cases, in law and equity, arising under this Constitution, the laws of the United States, and treaties made, or which shall be made, under their authority;—to all cases affecting ambassadors, other public ministers and consuls;—to all cases of admiralty and maritime jurisdiction;—to controversies to which the United States shall be a party;—to controversies between two or more States;—*between a State and citizens of another State;*—between citizens of different States;—between citizens of the same State claiming lands under grants of different States, and between a State, or the citizens thereof, and foreign states, citizens or subjects.

In all cases affecting ambassadors, other public ministers and consuls, and those in which a State shall be party, the Supreme Court shall have original jurisdiction. In all the other cases before mentioned, the Supreme Court shall have appellate jurisdiction, both as to law and fact, with such exceptions, and under such regulations, as the Congress shall make.

The trial of all crimes, except in cases of impeachment, shall be by jury; and such trial shall be held in the State where said crimes shall have been committed; but when not committed within any State, the trial shall be at such place or places as the Congress may by law have directed.

Section 3 Treason against the United States shall consist only in levying war against them, or in adhering to their enemies, giving them aid and comfort. No person shall be convicted of treason unless on the testimony of two witnesses to the same overt act, or on confession in open court.

The Congress shall have power to declare the punishment of treason, but no attainder of treason shall work corruption of blood, or forfeiture except during the life of the person attainted.

Article IV

Section 1 Full faith and credit shall be given in each State to the public acts, records, and judicial proceedings of every other State. And the Congress may by general laws prescribe the manner in which such acts, records, and proceedings shall be proved, and the effect thereof.

Section 2 The citizens of each State shall be entitled to all privileges and immunities of citizens in the several States.

A person charged in any State with treason, felony, or other crime, who shall flee from justice, and be found in another State, shall on demand of the executive authority of the State from which he fled, be delivered up, to be removed to the State having jurisdiction of the crime.

No person held to service or labor in one State, under the laws thereof, escaping into another, shall, in consequence of any law or regulation therein, be discharged from such service or labor, but shall be delivered up on claim of the party to whom such service or labor may be due.

Section 3 New States may be admitted by the Congress into this Union; but no new State shall be formed or erected within the jurisdiction of any other State; nor any State be formed by the junction of two or more States, or parts of States, without the consent of the legislatures of the States concerned as well as of the Congress.

The Congress shall have power to dispose of and make all needful rules and regulations respecting the territory or other property belonging to the United States; and nothing in this Constitution shall be so construed as to prejudice any claims of the United States, or of any particular State.

Section 4 The United States shall guarantee to every State in this Union a republican form of government, and shall protect each of them against invasion; and on application of the legislature, or of the executive (when the legislature cannot be convened), against domestic violence.

Article V

The Congress, whenever two-thirds of both houses shall deem it necessary, shall propose amendments to this Constitution, or, on the application of the legislatures of two-thirds of the several States, shall call a convention for proposing amendments, which, in either case, shall be valid to all intents and purposes, as part of this Constitution, when ratified by the legislatures of three-fourths of the several States, or by conventions in three-fourths thereof, as the one or the other mode of ratification may be proposed by the Congress; provided *that no amendments which may be made prior to the year one thousand eight hundred and eight shall in any manner affect the first and fourth clauses in the ninth section of the first article;* and that no State, without its consent, shall be deprived of its equal suffrage in the Senate.

Article VI

All debts contracted and engagements entered into, before the adoption of this Constitution, shall be as valid against the United States under this Constitution, as under the Confederation.

This Constitution, and the laws of the United States which shall be made in pursuance thereof; and all treaties made, or which shall be made, under the authority of the United States, shall be the supreme law of the land; and the judges in every State shall be bound thereby, anything in the Constitution or laws of any State to the contrary notwithstanding.

The Senators and Representatives before mentioned, and the members of the several State legislatures, and all executive and judicial officers, both of the United States and of the several States, shall be bound by oath or affirmation to support this Constitution; but no religious test shall ever be required as a qualification to any office or public trust under the United States.

Article VII

The ratification of the conventions of nine States shall be sufficient for the establishment of this Constitution between the States so ratifying the same.

Done in Convention by the unanimous consent of the States present, the seventeenth day of September in the year of our Lord one thousand seven hundred and eighty-seven and of the Independence of the United States of America the twelfth. In witness whereof we have hereunto subscribed our names.

Amendments to the Constitution*

Amendment I

Congress shall make no law respecting an establishment of religion, or prohibiting the free exercise thereof; or abridging the freedom of speech, or of the press; or the right of the people peaceably to assemble, and to petition the government for a redress of grievances.

Amendment II

A well-regulated militia being necessary to the security of a free State, the right of the people to keep and bear arms shall not be infringed.

Amendment III

No soldier shall, in time of peace, be quartered in any house without the consent of the owner, nor in time of war, but in a manner to be prescribed by law.

Amendment IV

The right of the people to be secure in their persons, houses, papers, and effects, against unreasonable searches and seizures, shall not be violated, and no warrants shall issue but upon probable cause, supported by oath or affirmation, and particularly describing the place to be searched, and the persons or things to be seized.

Amendment V

No person shall be held to answer for a capital, or otherwise infamous crime, unless on a presentment or indictment of a grand jury, except in cases arising in the land or naval forces, or in the militia, when in actual service in time of war or public danger; nor shall any person be subject for the same offense to be twice put in jeopardy of life or limb; nor shall be compelled in any criminal case to be a witness against himself, nor be deprived of life, liberty, or property, without due process of law; nor shall private property be taken for public use without just compensation.

Amendment VI

In all criminal prosecutions, the accused shall enjoy the right to a speedy and public trial, by an impartial jury of the State and district wherein the crime shall have been committed, which district shall have been previously ascertained by law, and to be informed of the nature and cause of the accusation; to be confronted with the witnesses against him; to have compulsory process for obtaining witnesses in his favor, and to have the assistance of counsel for his defense.

*The first ten Amendments (the Bill of Rights) were adopted in 1791.

Amendment VII

In suits at common law, where the value in controversy shall exceed twenty dollars, the right of trial by jury shall be preserved, and no fact tried by a jury shall be otherwise reexamined in any court of the United States, than according to the rules of the common law.

Amendment VIII

Excessive bail shall not be required, nor excessive fines imposed, nor cruel and unusual punishments inflicted.

Amendment IX

The enumeration in the Constitution, of certain rights, shall not be construed to deny or disparage others retained by the people.

Amendment X

The powers not delegated to the United States by the Constitution, nor prohibited by it to the States, are reserved to the States respectively, or to the people.

Amendment XI

[Adopted 1798]

The judicial power of the United States shall not be construed to extend to any suit in law or equity, commenced or prosecuted against one of the United States by citizens of another State, or by citizens or subjects of any foreign state.

Amendment XII

[Adopted 1804]

The electors shall meet in their respective States, and vote by ballot for President and Vice-President, one of whom, at least, shall not be an inhabitant of the same State with themselves; they shall name in their ballots the person voted for as President, and in distinct ballots the person voted for as Vice-President, and they shall make distinct lists of all persons voted for as President, and of all persons voted for as Vice-President, and of the number of votes for each, which lists they shall sign and certify, and transmit sealed to the seat of government of the United States, directed to the President of the Senate;—the President of the Senate shall, in the presence of the Senate and House of Representatives, open all the certificates and the votes shall then be counted;—the person having the greatest number of votes for President shall be the President, if such number be a majority of the whole number of electors appointed; and if no person have such majority, then from the persons having the highest numbers not exceeding three on the list of those voted for as President, the House of Representatives shall choose immediately, by ballot, the President. But in choosing the President, the votes shall be taken by States, the representation from each State having one vote; a quorum for this purpose shall consist of a member or members from two-thirds of the States, and a majority of all the States shall be necessary to a choice. And if the House of Representatives shall not choose a President whenever the right of choice shall devolve upon them, before *the fourth day of March* next following, then the Vice-President shall act as President, as in the case of the death or other constitutional disability of the President.

The person having the greatest number of votes as Vice-President shall be the Vice-President, if such number be a majority of the whole number of electors appointed; and if no person have a majority, then from the two highest numbers on the list the Senate shall choose the Vice-President; a quorum for the purpose shall consist of two-thirds of the whole number of Senators, and a majority of the whole number shall be necessary to a choice. But no person constitutionally ineligible to the office of President shall be eligible to that of Vice-President of the United States.

Amendment XIII

[Adopted 1865]

Section 1 Neither slavery nor involuntary servitude, except as a punishment for crime whereof the party shall have been duly convicted, shall exist within the United States, or any place subject to their jurisdiction.

Section 2 Congress shall have power to enforce this article by appropriate legislation.

Amendment XIV

[Adopted 1868]

Section 1 All persons born or naturalized in the United States, and subject to the jurisdiction thereof, are citizens of the United States and of the State wherein they reside. No State shall make or enforce any law which shall abridge the privileges or immunities of citizens of the United States; nor shall any State deprive any person of life, liberty, or property, without due process of law; nor deny to any person within its jurisdiction the equal protection of the laws.

Section 2 Representatives shall be apportioned among the several States according to their respective numbers, counting the whole number of persons in each State, excluding Indians not taxed. But when the right to vote at any election for the choice of Electors for President and Vice-President of the United States, Representatives in Congress, the executive and judicial officers of a State, or the members of the legislature thereof, is denied to any of the male inhabitants of such State, being twenty-one years of age and citizens of the United States, or in any way abridged, except for participation in rebellion, or other crime, the basis of representation therein shall be reduced in the proportion which the number of such male citizens shall bear to the whole number of male citizens twenty-one years of age in such State.

Section 3 No person shall be a Senator or Representative in Congress, or Elector of President and Vice-President, or hold any office, civil or military, under the United States, or under any State, who, having previously taken an oath, as a member of Congress, or as an officer of the United States, or as a member of any State legislature, or as an executive or judicial officer of any State, to support the Constitution of the United States, shall have engaged in insurrection or rebellion against the same, or given aid or comfort to the enemies thereof. Congress may, by a vote of two-thirds of each house, remove such disability.

Section 4 The validity of the public debt of the United States, authorized by law, including debts incurred for payment of pensions and bounties for services in suppressing insurrection or rebellion, shall not be questioned. But neither the United States nor any State shall assume or pay any debt or obligation incurred in aid of insurrection or rebellion against the United States, or any claim for the loss of emancipation of any slave; but all such debts, obligations, and claims shall be held illegal and void.

Section 5 The Congress shall have power to enforce, by appropriate legislation, the provisions of this article.

Amendment XV

[Adopted 1870]

Section 1 The right of citizens of the United States to vote shall not be denied or abridged by the United States or by any State on account of race, color, or previous condition of servitude.

Section 2 The Congress shall have power to enforce this article by appropriate legislation.

Amendment XVI

[Adopted 1913]

The Congress shall have power to lay and collect taxes on incomes, from whatever source derived, without apportionment among the several States, and without regard to any census or enumeration.

Amendment XVII

[Adopted 1913]

Section 1 The Senate of the United States shall be composed of two Senators from each State, elected by the people thereof, for six years; and each Senator shall have one vote. The electors in each State shall have the qualifications requisite for electors of [voters for] the most numerous branch of the State legislatures.

Section 2 When vacancies happen in the representation of any State in the Senate, the executive authority of such State shall issue writs of election to fill such vacancies: Provided, that the Legislature of any State may empower the executive thereof to make temporary appointments until the people fill the vacancies by election as the Legislature may direct.

Section 3 This amendment shall not be so construed as to affect the election or term of any Senator chosen before it becomes valid as part of the Constitution.

Amendment XVIII

[Adopted 1919; Repealed 1933]

Section 1 After one year from the ratification of this article the manufacture, sale, or transportation of intoxicating liquors within, the importation thereof into, or the exportation thereof from the United States and all territory subject to the jurisdiction thereof, for beverage purposes, is hereby prohibited.

Section 2 The Congress and the several States shall have concurrent power to enforce this article by appropriate legislation.

Section 3 This article shall be inoperative unless it shall have been ratified as an amendment to the Constitution by the legislatures of the several States, as provided by the Constitution, within seven years from the date of the submission thereof to the States by the Congress.

Amendment XIX

[Adopted 1920]

Section 1 The right of citizens of the United States to vote shall not be denied or abridged by the United States or by any State on account of sex.

Section 2 The Congress shall have power to enforce this article by appropriate legislation.

Amendment XX

[Adopted 1933]

Section 1 The terms of the President and Vice-President shall end at noon on the 20th day of January, and the terms of Senators and Representatives at noon on the 3rd day of January, of the years in which such terms would have ended if this article had not been ratified; and the terms of their successors shall then begin.

Section 2 The Congress shall assemble at least once in every year, and such meeting shall begin at noon on the 3d day of January, unless they shall by law appoint a different day.

Section 3 If, at the time fixed for the beginning of the term of the President, the President-elect shall have died, the Vice-President–elect shall become President. If a President shall not have been chosen before the time fixed for the beginning of his term, or if the President-elect shall have failed to qualify, then the Vice-President–elect shall act as President until a President shall have qualified; and the Congress may by law provide for the case wherein neither a President-elect nor a Vice-President–elect shall have qualified, declaring who shall then act as President, or the manner in which one who is to act shall be selected, and such persons shall act accordingly until a President or Vice-President shall have qualified.

Section 4 The Congress may by law provide for the case of the death of any of the persons from whom the House of Representatives may choose a President whenever the right of choice shall have devolved upon them, and for the case of the death of any of the persons from whom the Senate may choose a Vice-President whenever the right of choice shall have devolved upon them.

Section 5 Sections 1 and 2 shall take effect on the 15th day of October following the ratification of this article.

Section 6 This article shall be inoperative unless it shall have been ratified as an amendment to the Constitution by the Legislatures of three-fourths of the several States within seven years from the date of its submission.

Amendment XXI

[Adopted 1933]

Section 1 The eighteenth article of amendment to the Constitution of the United States is hereby repealed.

Section 2 The transportation or importation into any State, Territory, or Possession of the United States for delivery or use therein of intoxicating liquors, in violation of the laws thereof, is hereby prohibited.

Section 3 This article shall be inoperative unless it shall have been ratified as an amendment to the Constitution by conventions in the several States, as provided in the Constitution, within seven years from the date of submission thereof to the States by the Congress.

Amendment XXII

[Adopted 1951]

Section 1 No person shall be elected to the office of President more than twice, and no person who has held the office of President, or acted as President, for more than two years of a term to which some other person was elected President shall be elected to the office of President more than once. But this article shall not apply to any person holding the office of President when this article was proposed by the Congress, and shall not prevent any person who may be holding the office of President, or acting as President, during the term within which this article becomes operative from holding the office of President or acting as President during the remainder of such term.

Section 2 This article shall be inoperative unless it shall have been ratified as an amendment to the Constitution by the legislatures of three-fourths of the several States within seven years from the date of its submission to the States by the Congress.

Amendment XXIII

[Adopted 1961]

Section 1 The District constituting the seat of Government of the United States shall appoint in such manner as the Congress may direct:

A number of electors of President and Vice-President equal to the whole number of Senators and Representatives in Congress to which the District would be entitled if it were a State, but in no event more than the least populous State; they shall be in addition to those appointed by the States, but they shall be considered for the purposes of the election of President and Vice-President, to be electors appointed by a State; and they shall meet in the District and perform such duties as provided by the twelfth article of amendment.

Section 2 The Congress shall have the power to enforce this article by appropriate legislation.

Amendment XXIV

[Adopted 1964]

Section 1 The right of citizens of the United States to vote in any primary or other election for President or Vice-President, for electors for President or Vice-President, or for Senator or Representative in Congress, shall not be denied or abridged by the United States or any State by reason of failure to pay any poll tax or other tax.

Section 2 The Congress shall have the power to enforce this article by appropriate legislation.

Amendment XXV

[Adopted 1967]

Section 1 In case of the removal of the President from office or of his death or resignation, the Vice-President shall become President.

Section 2 Whenever there is a vacancy in the office of the Vice-President, the President shall nominate a Vice-President who shall take office upon confirmation by a majority vote of both Houses of Congress.

Section 3 Whenever the President transmits to the President pro tempore of the Senate and the Speaker of the House of Representatives his written declaration that he is unable to discharge the powers and duties of his office, and until he transmits to them a written declaration to the contrary, such powers and duties shall be discharged by the Vice-President as Acting President.

Section 4 Whenever the Vice-President and a majority of either the principal officers of the executive departments or of such other body as Congress may by law provide, transmit to the President pro tempore of the Senate and the Speaker of the House of Representatives their written declaration that the President is unable to discharge the powers and duties of his office, the Vice-President shall immediately assume the powers and duties of the office as Acting President.

Thereafter, when the President transmits to the President pro tempore of the Senate and the Speaker of the House of Representatives his written declaration that no inability exists, he shall resume the powers and duties of his office unless the Vice-President and a majority of either the principal officers of the executive department[s] or of such other body as Congress may by law provide, transmit within four days to the President pro tempore of the Senate and the Speaker of the House of Representatives their written declaration that the President is unable to discharge the powers and duties of his office. Thereupon Congress shall decide the issue, assembling within forty-eight hours for that purpose if not in session. If the Congress, within twenty-one days after receipt of the latter written declaration, or, if Congress is not in session, within twenty-one days after Congress is required to assemble, determines by two-thirds vote of both Houses that the President is unable to discharge the powers and duties of his office, the Vice-President shall continue to discharge the same as Acting President; otherwise, the President shall resume the powers and duties of his office.

Amendment XXVI

[Adopted 1971]

Section 1 The right of citizens of the United States, who are eighteen years of age or older, to vote shall not be denied or abridged by the United States or by any State on account of age.

Section 2 The Congress shall have power to enforce this article by appropriate legislation.

Amendment XXVII

[Adopted 1992]

No law, varying the compensation for the services of the Senators and Representatives, shall take effect, until an election of Representatives shall have intervened.

Presidential Elections

Year	Number of States	Candidates	Parties	Popular Vote	% of Popular Vote	Electoral Vote	% Voter Participation[a]
1789	10	**George Washington**	No party			69	
		John Adams	designations			34	
		Other candidates				35	
1792	15	**George Washington**	No party			132	
		John Adams	designations			77	
		George Clinton				50	
		Other candidates				5	
1796	16	**John Adams**	Federalist			71	
		Thomas Jefferson	Democratic-Republican			68	
		Thomas Pinckney	Federalist			59	
		Aaron Burr	Democratic-Republican			30	
		Other candidates				48	
1800	16	**Thomas Jefferson**	Democratic-Republican			73	
		Aaron Burr	Democratic-Republican			73	
		John Adams	Federalist			65	
		Charles C. Pinckney	Federalist			64	
		John Jay	Federalist			1	
1804	17	**Thomas Jefferson**	Democratic-Republican			162	
		Charles C. Pinckney	Federalist			14	
1808	17	**James Madison**	Democratic-Republican			122	
		Charles C. Pinckney	Federalist			47	
		George Clinton	Democratic-Republican			6	
1812	18	**James Madison**	Democratic-Republican			128	
		DeWitt Clinton	Federalist			89	
1816	19	**James Monroe**	Democratic-Republican			183	
		Rufus King	Federalist			34	
1820	24	**James Monroe**	Democratic-Republican			231	
		John Quincy Adams	Independent Republican			1	
1824	24	**John Quincy Adams**	Democratic-Republican	108,740	30.5	84	26.9
		Andrew Jackson	Democratic-Republican	153,544	43.1	99	
		Henry Clay	Democratic-Republican	47,136	13.2	37	
		William H. Crawford	Democratic-Republican	46,618	13.1	41	
1828	24	**Andrew Jackson**	Democratic	647,286	56.0	178	57.6
		John Quincy Adams	National Republican	508,064	44.0	83	
1832	24	**Andrew Jackson**	Democratic	701,780	54.2	219	55.4
		Henry Clay	National Republican	484,205	37.4	49	
		Other candidates		107,988	8.0	18	

Presidential Elections (continued)

Year	Number of States	Candidates	Parties	Popular Vote	% of Popular Vote	Electoral Vote	% Voter Participation[a]
1836	26	**Martin Van Buren**	Democratic	764,176	50.8	170	57.8
		William H. Harrison	Whig	550,816	36.6	73	
		Hugh L. White	Whig	146,107	9.7	26	
1840	26	**William H. Harrison**	Whig	1,274,624	53.1	234	80.2
		Martin Van Buren	Democratic	1,127,781	46.9	60	
1844	26	**James K. Polk**	Democratic	1,338,464	49.6	170	78.9
		Henry Clay	Whig	1,300,097	48.1	105	
		James G. Birney	Liberty	62,300	2.3		
1848	30	**Zachary Taylor**	Whig	1,360,967	47.4	163	72.7
		Lewis Cass	Democratic	1,222,342	42.5	127	
		Martin Van Buren	Free Soil	291,263	10.1		
1852	31	**Franklin Pierce**	Democratic	1,601,117	50.9	254	69.6
		Winfield Scott	Whig	1,385,453	44.1	42	
		John P. Hale	Free Soil	155,825	5.0		
1856	31	**James Buchanan**	Democratic	1,832,955	45.3	174	78.9
		John C. Frémont	Republican	1,339,932	33.1	114	
		Millard Fillmore	American	871,731	21.6		
1860	33	**Abraham Lincoln**	Republican	1,865,593	39.8	180	81.2
		Stephen A. Douglas	Democratic	1,382,713	29.5	12	
		John C. Breckinridge	Democratic	848,356	18.1	72	
		John Bell	Constitutional Union	592,906	12.6	39	
1864	36	**Abraham Lincoln**	Republican	2,206,938	55.0	212	73.8
		George B. McClellan	Democratic	1,803,787	45.0	21	
1868	37	**Ulysses S. Grant**	Republican	3,013,421	52.7	214	78.1
		Horatio Seymour	Democratic	2,706,829	47.3	80	
1872	37	**Ulysses S. Grant**	Republican	3,596,745	55.6	286	71.3
		Horace Greeley	Democratic	2,843,446	43.9	b	
1876	38	**Rutherford B. Hayes**	Republican	4,036,572	48.0	185	81.8
		Samuel J. Tilden	Democratic	4,284,020	51.0	184	
1880	38	**James A. Garfield**	Republican	4,453,295	48.5	214	79.4
		Winfield S. Hancock	Democratic	4,414,082	48.1	155	
		James B. Weaver	Greenback-Labor	308,578	3.4		
1884	38	**Grover Cleveland**	Democratic	4,879,507	48.5	219	77.5
		James G. Blaine	Republican	4,850,293	48.2	182	
		Benjamin F. Butler	Greenback-Labor	175,370	1.8		
		John P. St. John	Prohibition	150,369	1.5		
1888	38	**Benjamin Harrison**	Republican	5,447,129	47.9	233	79.3
		Grover Cleveland	Democratic	5,537,857	48.6	168	
		Clinton B. Fisk	Prohibition	249,506	2.2		

Presidents and Vice Presidents (continued)

Year	Number of States	Candidates	Parties	Popular Vote	% of Popular Vote	Electoral Vote	% Voter Participation[a]
		Anson J. Streeter	Union Labor	146,935	1.3		
1892	44	**Grover Cleveland**	Democratic	5,555,426	46.1	277	74.7
		Benjamin Harrison	Republican	5,182,690	43.0	145	
		James B. Weaver	People's	1,029,846	8.5	22	
		John Bidwell	Prohibition	264,133	2.2		
1896	45	**William McKinley**	Republican	7,102,246	51.1	271	79.3
		William J. Bryan	Democratic	6,492,559	47.7	176	
1900	45	**William McKinley**	Republican	7,218,491	51.7	292	73.2
		William J. Bryan	Democratic; Populist	6,356,734	45.5	155	
		John C. Wooley	Prohibition	208,914	1.5		
1904	45	**Theodore Roosevelt**	Republican	7,628,461	57.4	336	65.2
		Alton B. Parker	Democratic	5,084,223	37.6	140	
		Eugene V. Debs	Socialist	402,283	3.0		
		Silas C. Swallow	Prohibition	258,536	1.9		
1908	46	**William H. Taft**	Republican	7,675,320	51.6	321	65.4
		William J. Bryan	Democratic	6,412,294	43.1	162	
		Eugene V. Debs	Socialist	420,793	2.8		
		Eugene W. Chafin	Prohibition	253,840	1.7		
1912	48	**Woodrow Wilson**	Democratic	6,296,547	41.9	435	58.8
		Theodore Roosevelt	Progressive	4,118,571	27.4	88	
		William H. Taft	Republican	3,486,720	23.2	8	
		Eugene V. Debs	Socialist	900,672	6.0		
		Eugene W. Chafin	Prohibition	206,275	1.4		
1916	48	**Woodrow Wilson**	Democratic	9,127,695	49.4	277	61.6
		Charles E. Hughes	Republican	8,533,507	46.2	254	
		A. L. Benson	Socialist	585,113	3.2		
		J. Frank Hanly	Prohibition	220,506	1.2		
1920	48	**Warren G. Harding**	Republican	16,143,407	60.4	404	49.2
		James M. Cox	Democratic	9,130,328	34.2	127	
		Eugene V. Debs	Socialist	919,799	3.4		
		P. P. Christensen	Farmer-Labor	265,411	1.0		
1924	48	**Calvin Coolidge**	Republican	15,718,211	54.0	382	48.9
		John W. Davis	Democratic	8,385,283	28.8	136	
		Robert M. La Follette	Progressive	4,831,289	16.6	13	
1928	48	**Herbert C. Hoover**	Republican	21,391,993	58.2	444	56.9
		Alfred E. Smith	Democratic	15,016,169	40.9	87	
1932	48	**Franklin D. Roosevelt**	Democratic	22,809,638	57.4	472	56.9
		Herbert C. Hoover	Republican	15,758,901	39.7	59	
		Norman Thomas	Socialist	881,951	2.2		

Presidential Elections (continued)

Year	Number of States	Candidates	Parties	Popular Vote	% of Popular Vote	Electoral Vote	% Voter Participation[a]
1936	48	**Franklin D. Roosevelt**	Democratic	27,752,869	60.8	523	61.0
		Alfred M. Landon	Republican	16,674,665	36.5	8	
		William Lemke	Union	882,479	1.9		
1940	48	**Franklin D. Roosevelt**	Democratic	27,307,819	54.8	449	62.5
		Wendell L. Willkie	Republican	22,321,018	44.8	82	
1944	48	**Franklin D. Roosevelt**	Democratic	25,606,585	53.5	432	55.9
		Thomas E. Dewey	Republican	22,014,745	46.0	99	
1948	48	**Harry S Truman**	Democratic	24,179,345	49.6	303	53.0
		Thomas E. Dewey	Republican	21,991,291	45.1	189	
		J. Strom Thurmond	States' Rights	1,176,125	2.4	39	
		Henry A. Wallace	Progressive	1,157,326	2.4		
1952	48	**Dwight D. Eisenhower**	Republican	33,936,234	55.1	442	63.3
		Adlai E. Stevenson	Democratic	27,314,992	44.4	89	
1956	48	**Dwight D. Eisenhower**	Republican	35,590,472	57.6	457	60.6
		Adlai E. Stevenson	Democratic	26,022,752	42.1	73	
1960	50	**John F. Kennedy**	Democratic	34,226,731	49.7	303	62.8
		Richard M. Nixon	Republican	34,108,157	49.5	219	
1964	50	**Lyndon B. Johnson**	Democratic	43,129,566	61.1	486	61.7
		Barry M. Goldwater	Republican	27,178,188	38.5	52	
1968	50	**Richard M. Nixon**	Republican	31,785,480	43.4	301	60.6
		Hubert H. Humphrey	Democratic	31,275,166	42.7	191	
		George C. Wallace	American Independent	9,906,473	13.5	46	
1972	50	**Richard M. Nixon**	Republican	47,169,911	60.7	520	55.2
		George S. McGovern	Democratic	29,170,383	37.5	17	
		John G. Schmitz	American	1,099,482	1.4		
1976	50	**James E. Carter**	Democratic	40,830,763	50.1	297	53.5
		Gerald R. Ford	Republican	39,147,793	48.0	240	
1980	50	**Ronald W. Reagan**	Republican	43,904,153	50.7	489	52.6
		James E. Carter	Democratic	35,483,883	41.0	49	
		John B. Anderson	Independent	5,720,060	6.6		
		Ed Clark	Libertarian	921,299	1.1		
1984	50	**Ronald W. Reagan**	Republican	54,455,075	58.8	525	53.3
		Walter F. Mondale	Democratic	37,577,185	40.6	13	
1988	50	**George H. W. Bush**	Republican	48,886,097	53.4	426	50.1
		Michael S. Dukakis	Democratic	41,809,074	45.6	111c	
1992	50	**William J. Clinton**	Democratic	44,909,326	43.0	370	55.2
		George H. W. Bush	Republican	39,103,882	37.4	168	
		H. Ross Perot	Independent	19,741,048	18.9		

Justices of the Supreme Court (continued)

Year	Number of States	Candidates	Parties	Popular Vote	% of Popular Vote	Electoral Vote	% Voter Participation[a]
1996	50	**William J. Clinton**	Democratic	47,402,357	49.2	379	49.1
		Robert J. Dole	Republican	39,196,755	40.7	159	
		H. Ross Perot	Reform	8,085,402	8.4		
		Ralph Nader	Green	684,902	0.7		
2000	50	**George W. Bush**	Republican	50,455,156	47.9	271	51.2
		Albert Gore	Democratic	50,992,335	48.4	266	
		Ralph Nader	Green	2,882,955	2.7		
2004	50	**George W. Bush**	Republican	62,039,073	50.7	286	55.3
		John F. Kerry	Democratic	59,027,478	48.2	251	
		Ralph Nader	Independent	240,896	0.2		
2008	50	**Barack Obama**	Democratic	69,498,459	53.0	365	61.7
		John McCain	Republican	59,948,283	46.0	173	
		Ralph Nader	Independent	739,165	0.55		

Candidates receiving less than 1 percent of the popular vote have been omitted. Thus the percentage of popular vote given for any election year may not total 100 percent.

Before the passage of the Twelfth Amendment in 1804, the electoral college voted for two presidential candidates; the runner-up became vice president.

Before 1824, most presidential electors were chosen by state legislatures, not by popular vote.

[a]Percent of voting-age population casting ballots.

[b]Greeley died shortly after the election; the electors supporting him then divided their votes among minor candidates.

[c]One elector from West Virginia cast her electoral college presidential ballot for Lloyd Bentsen, the Democratic Party's vice-presidential candidate.

Presidents and Vice Presidents

1. President	**George Washington**	1789–1797	
Vice President	John Adams	1789–1797	
2. President	**John Adams**	1797–1801	
Vice President	Thomas Jefferson	1797–1801	
3. President	**Thomas Jefferson**	1801–1809	
Vice President	Aaron Burr	1801–1805	
Vice President	George Clinton	1805–1809	
4. President	**James Madison**	1809–1817	
Vice President	George Clinton	1809–1813	
Vice President	Elbridge Gerry	1813–1817	
5. President	**James Monroe**	1817–1825	
Vice President	Daniel Tompkins	1817–1825	
6. President	**John Quincy Adams**	1825–1829	
Vice President	John C. Calhoun	1825–1829	
7. President	**Andrew Jackson**	1829–1837	
Vice President	John C. Calhoun	1829–1833	
Vice President	Martin Van Buren	1833–1837	
8. President	**Martin Van Buren**	1837–1841	
Vice President	Richard M. Johnson	1837–1841	
9. President	**William H. Harrison**	1841	
Vice President	John Tyler	1841	
10. President	**John Tyler**	1841–1845	
Vice President	None		
11. President	**James K. Polk**	1845–1849	
Vice President	George M. Dallas	1845–1849	
12. President	**Zachary Taylor**	1849–1850	
Vice President	Millard Fillmore	1849–1850	
13. President	**Millard Fillmore**	1850–1853	
Vice President	None		
14. President	**Franklin Pierce**	1853–1857	
Vice President	William R. King	1853–1857	
15. President	**James Buchanan**	1857–1861	
Vice President	John C. Breckinridge	1857–1861	
16. President	**Abraham Lincoln**	1861–1865	
Vice President	Hannibal Hamlin	1861–1865	
Vice President	Andrew Johnson	1865	
17. President	**Andrew Johnson**	1865–1869	
Vice President	None		

18. President	**Ulysses S. Grant**	1869–1877	
Vice President	Schuyler Colfax	1869–1873	
Vice President	Henry Wilson	1873–1877	
19. President	**Rutherford B. Hayes**	1877–1881	
Vice President	William A. Wheeler	1877–1881	
20. President	**James A. Garfield**	1881	
Vice President	Chester A. Arthur	1881	
21. President	**Chester A. Arthur**	1881–1885	
Vice President	None		
22. President	**Grover Cleveland**	1885–1889	
Vice President	Thomas A. Hendricks	1885–1889	
23. President	**Benjamin Harrison**	1889–1893	
Vice President	Levi P. Morton	1889–1893	
24. President	**Grover Cleveland**	1893–1897	
Vice President	Adlai E. Stevenson	1893–1897	
25. President	**William McKinley**	1897–1901	
Vice President	Garret A. Hobart	1897–1901	
Vice President	Theodore Roosevelt	1901	
26. President	**Theodore Roosevelt**	1901–1909	
Vice President	Charles Fairbanks	1905–1909	
27. President	**William H. Taft**	1909–1913	
Vice President	James S. Sherman	1909–1913	
28. President	**Woodrow Wilson**	1913–1921	
Vice President	Thomas R. Marshall	1913–1921	
29. President	**Warren G. Harding**	1921–1923	
Vice President	Calvin Coolidge	1921–1923	
30. President	**Calvin Coolidge**	1923–1929	
Vice President	Charles G. Dawes	1925–1929	
31. President	**Herbert C. Hoover**	1929–1933	
Vice President	Charles Curtis	1929–1933	
32. President	**Franklin D. Roosevelt**	1933–1945	
Vice President	John N. Garner	1933–1941	
Vice President	Henry A. Wallace	1941–1945	
Vice President	Harry S Truman	1945	
33. President	**Harry S Truman**	1945–1953	
Vice President	Alben W. Barkley	1949–1953	
34. President	**Dwight D. Eisenhower**	1953–1961	
Vice President	Richard M. Nixon	1953–1961	

Presidents and Vice Presidents (continued)

35. President	**John F. Kennedy**	1961–1963	
Vice President	Lyndon B. Johnson	1961–1963	
36. President	**Lyndon B. Johnson**	1963–1969	
Vice President	Hubert H. Humphrey	1965–1969	
37. President	**Richard M. Nixon**	1969–1974	
Vice President	Spiro T. Agnew	1969–1973	
Vice President	Gerald R. Ford	1973–1974	
38. President	**Gerald R. Ford**	1974–1977	
Vice President	Nelson A. Rockefeller	1974–1977	
39. President	**James E. Carter**	1977–1981	
Vice President	Walter F. Mondale	1977–1981	
40. President	**Ronald W. Reagan**	1981–1989	
Vice President	George H. W. Bush	1981–1989	
41. President	**George H. W. Bush**	1989–1993	
Vice President	J. Danforth Quayle	1989–1993	
42. President	**William J. Clinton**	1993–2001	
Vice President	Albert Gore	1993–2001	
43. President	**George W. Bush**	2001–2009	
Vice President	Richard Cheney	2001–2009	
44. President	**Barack Obama**	2009–	
Vice President	Joseph Biden	2009–	

Justices of the Supreme Court

	Term of Service	Years of Service	Life Span
John Jay	1789–1795	5	1745–1829
John Rutledge	1789–1791	1	1739–1800
William Cushing	1789–1810	20	1732–1810
James Wilson	1789–1798	8	1742–1798
John Blair	1789–1796	6	1732–1800
Robert H. Harrison	1789–1790	—	1745–1790
James Iredell	1790–1799	9	1751–1799
Thomas Johnson	1791–1793	1	1732–1819
William Paterson	1793–1806	13	1745–1806
*John Rutledge**	1795	—	1739–1800
Samuel Chase	1796–1811	15	1741–1811
Oliver Ellsworth	1796–1800	4	1745–1807
Bushrod Washington	1798–1829	31	1762–1829
Alfred Moore	1799–1804	4	1755–1810
John Marshall	1801–1835	34	1755–1835
William Johnson	1804–1834	30	1771–1834
H. Brockholst Livingston	1806–1823	16	1757–1823
Thomas Todd	1807–1826	18	1765–1826
Joseph Story	1811–1845	33	1779–1845
Gabriel Duval	1811–1835	24	1752–1844
Smith Thompson	1823–1843	20	1768–1843
Robert Trimble	1826–1828	2	1777–1828
John McLean	1829–1861	32	1785–1861
Henry Baldwin	1830–1844	14	1780–1844
James M. Wayne	1835–1867	32	1790–1867
Roger B. Taney	1836–1864	28	1777–1864
Philip P. Barbour	1836–1841	4	1783–1841
John Catron	1837–1865	28	1786–1865
John McKinley	1837–1852	15	1780–1852
Peter V. Daniel	1841–1860	19	1784–1860
Samuel Nelson	1845–1872	27	1792–1873
Levi Woodbury	1845–1851	5	1789–1851
Robert C. Grier	1846–1870	23	1794–1870
Benjamin R. Curtis	1851–1857	6	1809–1874
John A. Campbell	1853–1861	8	1811–1889
Nathan Clifford	1858–1881	23	1803–1881
Noah H. Swayne	1862–1881	18	1804–1884
Samuel F. Miller	1862–1890	28	1816–1890
David Davis	1862–1877	14	1815–1886
Stephen J. Field	1863–1897	34	1816–1899
Salmon P. Chase	1864–1873	8	1808–1873
William Strong	1870–1880	10	1808–1895
Joseph P. Bradley	1870–1892	22	1813–1892
Ward Hunt	1873–1882	9	1810–1886
Morrison R. Waite	1874–1888	14	1816–1888
John M. Harlan	1877–1911	34	1833–1911
William B. Woods	1880–1887	7	1824–1887
Stanley Mathews	1881–1889	7	1824–1889
Horace Gray	1882–1902	20	1828–1902
Samuel Blatchford	1882–1893	11	1820–1893
Lucius Q. C. Lamar	1888–1893	5	1825–1893
Melville W. Fuller	1888–1910	21	1833–1910
David J. Brewer	1890–1910	20	1837–1910
Henry B. Brown	1890–1906	16	1836–1913
George Shiras Jr.	1892–1903	10	1832–1924
Howell E. Jackson	1893–1895	2	1832–1895
Edward D. White	1894–1910	16	1845–1921
Rufus W. Peckham	1895–1909	14	1838–1909
Joseph McKenna	1898–1925	26	1843–1926
Oliver W. Holmes	1902–1932	30	1841–1935
William D. Day	1903–1922	19	1849–1923
William H. Moody	1906–1910	3	1853–1917
Horace H. Lurton	1910–1914	4	1844–1914
Charles E. Hughes	1910–1916	5	1862–1948
Willis Van Devanter	1911–1937	26	1859–1941
Joseph R. Lamar	1911–1916	5	1857–1916
Edward D. White	1910–1921	11	1845–1921
Mahlon Pitney	1912–1922	10	1858–1924
James C. McReynolds	1914–1941	26	1862–1946
Louis D. Brandeis	1916–1939	22	1856–1941
John H. Clarke	1916–1922	6	1857–1945
William H. Taft	1921–1930	8	1857–1930
George Sutherland	1922–1938	15	1862–1942
Pierce Butler	1922–1939	16	1866–1939
Edward T. Sanford	1923–1930	7	1865–1930
Harlan F. Stone	1925–1941	16	1872–1946
Charles E. Hughes	1930–1941	11	1862–1948
Owen J. Roberts	1930–1945	15	1875–1955
Benjamin N. Cardozo	1932–1938	6	1870–1938

Justices of the Supreme Court (continued)

	Term of Service	Years of Service	Life Span
Hugo L. Black	1937–1971	34	1886–1971
Stanley F. Reed	1938–1957	19	1884–1980
Felix Frankfurter	1939–1962	23	1882–1965
William O. Douglas	1939–1975	36	1898–1980
Frank Murphy	1940–1949	9	1890–1949
Harlan F. Stone	1941–1946	5	1872–1946
James F. Byrnes	1941–1942	1	1879–1972
Robert H. Jackson	1941–1954	13	1892–1954
Wiley B. Rutledge	1943–1949	6	1894–1949
Harold H. Burton	1945–1958	13	1888–1964
Fred M. Vinson	1946–1953	7	1890–1953
Tom C. Clark	1949–1967	18	1899–1977
Sherman Minton	1949–1956	7	1890–1965
Earl Warren	1953–1969	16	1891–1974
John Marshall Harlan	1955–1971	16	1899–1971
William J. Brennan Jr.	1956–1990	34	1906–1997
Charles E. Whittaker	1957–1962	5	1901–1973
Potter Stewart	1958–1981	23	1915–1985
Byron R. White	1962–1993	31	1917–

	Term of Service	Years of Service	Life Span
Arthur J. Goldberg	1962–1965	3	1908–1990
Abe Fortas	1965–1969	4	1910–1982
Thurgood Marshall	1967–1991	24	1908–1993
Warren C. Burger	1969–1986	17	1907–1995
Harry A. Blackmun	1970–1994	24	1908–1998
Lewis F. Powell Jr.	1972–1987	15	1907–1998
William H. Rehnquist	1972–2005	33	1924–2005
John P. Stevens III	1975–	—	1920–
Sandra Day O'Connor	1981–	—	1930–
Antonin Scalia	1986–	—	1936–
Anthony M. Kennedy	1988–	—	1936–
David H. Souter	1990–	—	1939–
Clarence Thomas	1991–	—	1948–
Ruth Bader Ginsburg	1993–	—	1933–
Stephen Breyer	1994–	—	1938–
John G. Roberts	2005–	—	1955–
Samuel A. Alito, Jr.	2006–	—	1950–
Sonia Sotomayor	2009–	—	1954–
Elena Kagan	2010–	—	1960–

Note: Chief justices are in italics.

*Appointed and served one term, but not confirmed by the Senate.

Index